Volume equivalents

METRIC	IMPERIAL	METRIC	IMPERIAL
30ml	1fl oz	450ml	15fl oz
60ml	2fl oz	500ml	16fl oz
75ml	2½fl oz	600ml	1 pint
100ml	3½fl oz	750ml	1¼ pints
120ml	4fl oz	900ml	1½ pints
150ml	5fl oz (¼ pint)	1 litre	1¾ pints
175ml	6fl oz	1.2 litres	2 pints
200ml	7fl oz (⅓ pint)	1.4 litres	2½ pints
240ml	8fl oz	1.5 litres	2¾ pints
300ml	10fl oz (½ pint)	1.7 litres	3 pints
350ml	12fl oz	2 litres	3½ pints
400ml	14fl oz	3 litres	5¼ pints

Weight equivalents

METRIC	IMPERIAL	METRIC	IMPERIAL
15g	½oz	150g	5½oz
20g	¾oz	175g	6oz
25g	scant 1oz	200g	7oz
30g	1oz	225g	8oz
45g	1½oz	250g	9oz
50g	1¾oz	300g	10oz
60g	2oz	450g	1lb
75g	2½oz	500g	1lb 2oz
85g	3oz	675g	1½lb
100g	3½oz	900g	2lb
115g	4oz	1kg	2¼lb
125g	4½oz	1.5kg	3lb 3oz
140g	5oz	1.8kg	4lb

cook
STEP BY STEP

cook
STEP BY STEP

DK

LONDON, NEW YORK, MELBOURNE, MUNICH, AND DELHI

Editor Lucy Bannell
Project Editor Sarah Ruddick
Managing Editor Dawn Henderson
Managing Art Editors Christine Keilty, Marianne Markham
Senior Jacket Creative Nicola Powling
Senior Presentations Creative Caroline de Souza
Category Publisher Mary-Clare Jerram
Art Director Peter Luff
Production Editor Maria Elia
Production Controller Alice Holloway
Creative Technical Support Sonia Charbonnier

DK INDIA
Designer Devika Dwarkadas
Senior Editors Rukmini Kumar Chawla, Saloni Talwar
Design Manager Romi Chakraborty
DTP Designers Dheeraj Arora, Manish Chandra,
Nand Kishore, Arjinder Singh, Jagtar Singh, Pushpak Tyagi
DTP Manager Sunil Sharma
Production Manager Pankaj Sharma

First published in Great Britain in 2010
by Dorling Kindersley Limited
80 Strand, London WC2R 0RL
Penguin Group (UK)

A CIP catalogue record for this book is available
from the British Library

ISBN 978-1-4053-5718-0

Colour reproduction by Media Development Printing, UK
Printed and bound in China by Toppan

Discover more at www.dk.com

Contents

Introduction 6

Recipe choosers 8

Starters and light bites 30

Salads 80

Meat-free 120

One-pot dishes 172

Home from work 226

Food to share 272

Comfort food 326

Bread 378

Pies, tarts, and cakes 416

Spectacular desserts 474

Index 538

Acknowledgments 544

Introduction

We used to learn to cook by peering over our mother's shoulder as she chopped and sautéed onions, browned meat, added her favourite seasonings, and fried, simmered, or roasted her way to a delicious family meal. We marvelled at her impressive "special occasion" cakes and puddings, and vowed to make them just as well when we grew up.

These days, this time-honoured way of learning how to feed ourselves good food is disappearing. Many of our mothers were not taught to cook themselves, so could not pass on their knowledge to us. This book will bridge that gap. The step-by-step images will lead you through every aspect of making a meal, from something as basic as how to chop an onion, to showing you when a custard is thick enough, to what a caramel should look like in the saucepan.

Whether you have never picked up a wooden spoon before or are already an experienced cook, these recipes will work for you and your family and will enable you to improve your skills. Reassuringly, they give you exact timings for every stage of making a dish, making it almost impossible for you to go wrong.

In this book, you'll find more than 300 delicious recipes, from time-honoured classics such as roast beef and Yorkshire pudding or lemon meringue pie, to the mouthwatering modern treats of sushi, crisp salmon with coriander pesto, or homemade pasta. Before you know it you'll be producing baguettes to beat any you can buy, or turning out irresistible chocolate-orange truffle cake.

There is something for everyone in this book, whether you prefer not to eat meat, have only minutes each day to cook, love to entertain with flair, or simply need to feed a growing family. Many of the recipes suggest simple ways to vary a dish, serving as starting points for your own imagination as your cooking confidence grows.

You'll find a recipe for every occasion here, too. A summer party will be a huge hit when you serve a whole poached salmon with watercress sauce, while friends will clamour for an invite to supper when they know you'll serve an exotic and delicious Moroccan chicken tagine followed by a cinnamon-orange crème brûlée.

Your cooking education starts here. Enjoy the journey!

Crostini p32
PREP 15-20 MINS   COOK 5-10 MINS

Tapenade p33
PREP 30-35 MINS   COOK 10-15 MINS

Cheddar and courgette soufflés p60
PREP 30-35 MINS   COOK 25-30 MINS

Leeks vinaigrette p50
PREP 15-20 MINS   COOK 15-25 MINS

Herb and flower garden salad p82
PREP 15-20 MINS   COOK NONE

Basque hot pepper omelette p54
PREP 20-25 MINS   COOK 15-25 MINS

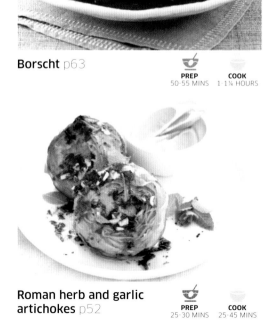

Borscht p63
PREP 50-55 MINS   COOK 1-1¼ HOURS

Roman herb and garlic artichokes p52
PREP 25-30 MINS   COOK 25-45 MINS

Pear, fennel, and walnut salad p109

 PREP 30-35 MINS   **COOK** NONE

Stuffed vine leaves p68

 PREP 40-45 MINS   **COOK** 45-60 MINS

MORE VEGETARIAN STARTERS:

Stuffed mushrooms with herbs p36

Genoese minestrone with red pesto p46

Marinated goat's cheese salad p83

Roast pepper and artichoke salad p88

Greek salad p90

Tortilla bean salad p106

Spinach gnocchi in tomato cream p356

Tabbouleh with cacik p108

 PREP 35-40 MINS **COOK** NONE

Gado gado p98

 PREP 35-45 MINS **COOK** 20-25 MINS

Warm salad of wild mushrooms p91

 PREP 25-30 MINS   **COOK** 8-10 MINS

Herbed salmon cakes p70

PREP 35-40 MINS COOK 15-20 MINS

Cod and mussel chowder p44

PREP 45-50 MINS COOK 55-60 MINS

Asian noodle salad p112

PREP 30-35 MINS COOK 6-9 MINS

Grilled pepper-stuffed mussels p229

PREP 25-30 MINS COOK 1-2 MINS

Tuna Niçoise salad p84

PREP 25-30 MINS COOK 20-25 MINS

Saltimbocca of salmon p260

PREP 20-25 MINS COOK 1-2 MINS

Clear soup with sea bass p34

PREP 30-35 MINS COOK 25 MINS

Scallops with lemon-herb potatoes p370

PREP 45-50 MINS COOK 20 MINS

Blini with smoked salmon p66

PREP
25-30 MINS
COOK
8-16 MINS

Tuna and bacon kebabs p265

PREP
20-25 MINS
COOK
10-12 MINS

Nori-maki sushi p78

PREP
50-60 MINS
COOK
12 MINS

Mussels with saffron cream sauce p41

PREP
25-30 MINS
COOK
10-12 MINS

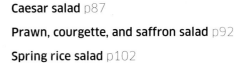

Spiced seafood salad p94

PREP
30-40 MINS
COOK
12-15 MINS

MORE FISH STARTERS:

Cheese gougères with salmon p64

Caesar salad p87

Prawn, courgette, and saffron salad p92

Spring rice salad p102

Pasta and mussel salad p116

Warm salmon and orange salad p118

Scallop and sweetcorn chowder p174

Sole fillets in wine vinegar p228

Sole turbans with wild mushrooms p306

Tropical prawn kebabs p58

PREP
20-25 MINS
COOK
4-6 MINS

Smoked trout mousse p37

PREP
20-25 MINS
COOK
NONE

Chicken liver and apple pâté p51

 PREP 30-35 MINS **COOK** 12-15 MINS

Chicken and cheese quesadillas p72

PREP 35-40 MINS **COOK** 3-6 MINS

Chicken Pojarski p300

 PREP 35-40 MINS **COOK** 40-50 MINS

Tex-Mex chicken p259

  PREP 20-25 MINS **COOK** NONE

Sauté of chicken with mussels p286

 PREP 30-35 MINS **COOK** 40-50 MINS

Thai skewered chicken p62

 PREP 20-30 MINS **COOK** 6-8 MINS

Devilled drumsticks p241

 PREP 20-25 MINS **COOK** 35-40 MINS

Chicken mousse with Madeira sauce p42

PREP 25-35 MINS | COOK 20-30 MINS

Cobb salad p119

PREP 20-25 MINS | COOK 5 MINS

Japanese one-pot yosenabe p218

PREP 40-50 MINS | COOK 5-7 MINS

MORE POULTRY STARTERS:

Festive wild rice salad p104

Indonesian chicken satay p247

Grilled chicken thighs in yoghurt p270

Cold chicken and ham pie p340

Pinwheel chicken with goat's cheese p230

PREP 30-40 MINS | COOK 15-20 MINS

Lacquered chicken salad p105

PREP 25-30 MINS | COOK 10-15 MINS

Lemongrass chicken p76

PREP 45-55 MINS | COOK 10 MINS

Waldorf chicken salad p111

PREP 25-30 MINS | COOK 25-35 MINS

Gratin of chicory and ham p48

PREP
15-20 MINS
COOK
1-1¼ HOURS

Steak salad with red onions p114

PREP
20-30 MINS
COOK
6-12 MINS

Vietnamese spring rolls p56

PREP
50-60 MINS
COOK
25 MINS

Spinach-stuffed veal p362

PREP
45-50 MINS
COOK
30-40 MINS

Home-made straw and hay pasta p374

PREP
55-60 MINS
COOK
10 MINS

Country terrine p366

PREP
35-40 MINS
COOK
1¼-1½ HOURS

Beef carpaccio p77

PREP
20-25 MINS
COOK
NONE

Szechuan sweet and sour spare ribs p40

PREP
15-20 MINS
COOK
1½ HOURS

Spiced lamb pies p360

PREP
40-45 MINS
COOK
20-25 MINS

Cabbage with chestnut and pork p350

PREP 35-40 MINS   COOK 50-60 MINS

Turkish lamb kebabs p234

PREP 30-35 MINS   COOK 10-15 MINS

Avocado, grapefruit, and Parma ham p97

PREP 25-30 MINS   COOK NONE

Quiche Lorraine p372

PREP 45-50 MINS   COOK 30-35 MINS

MORE MEAT STARTERS:

Parma ham pizzas p74

Red cabbage and bacon salad p100

Salade Lyonnaise p110

Ham with prunes in a wine sauce p364

Beef noodle soup p38

PREP 1½ HOURS   COOK 4-5 HOURS

Stir-fried Thai vegetables p140

PREP 30-35 MINS   COOK 15-20 MINS

Tempura p128

PREP 45-50 MINS   COOK 3-5 MINS

Vegetable couscous p154

PREP 35-40 MINS   COOK 30-35 MINS

Aubergine cannelloni p144

PREP 40-45 MINS   COOK 50-60 MINS

Potato and blue cheese filo pie p162

PREP 35-40 MINS   COOK 45-55 MINS

Herbed aioli platter p126

PREP 50-60 MINS   COOK 65-70 MINS

Summer frittata with ratatouille p133

PREP 20-25 MINS   COOK 20-25 MINS

Buddha's delight p134

PREP 40-50 MINS　COOK 15-20 MINS

Roast pepper lasagne p143

PREP 1½ HOURS　COOK 35-45 MINS

Mixed vegetable curry p148

PREP 45-50 MINS　COOK 25-35 MINS

Three-cheese Swiss chard crêpes p130

PREP 1 HOUR　COOK 20-25 MINS

Stuffed veggies with walnut sauce p156

PREP 40-45 MINS　COOK 15-20 MINS

Mexican cheese-stuffed peppers p138

PREP 30-35 MINS　COOK 45-50 MINS

MORE VEGETARIAN MAINS:

Tomato tagliatelle with artichokes p124

Fusilli with pesto p132

Artichokes stuffed with olives p136

Courgette tian p146

Pumpkin stew p150

Perfect pasta and cheese p153

Broccoli and mushroom quiche p158

Polenta with vegetable stew p160

Spaghetti primavera p163

Onion and Roquefort quiche p164

Aubergine Parmigiana p166

Flemish vegetable tart p168

Baked polenta with wild mushrooms p152

PREP 40-45 MINS　COOK 20-25 MINS

Fisherman's pie p348

PREP 35-45 MINS COOK 20-30 MINS

Oriental halibut en papillote p236

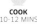

PREP 15-20 MINS COOK 10-12 MINS

Perfect fish and chips p336

PREP 45-50 MINS COOK 20-25 MINS

Five-spice fillet of salmon p254

PREP 30-35 MINS COOK 20-25 MINS

Sole bonne femme p376

PREP 30-35 MINS COOK 25-30 MINS

Roast monkfish with two sauces p294

PREP 25-30 MINS COOK 12-15 MINS

Monkfish Americaine p302

PREP 45-50 MINS COOK 35-40 MINS

Spicy, saucy fish p266

PREP 30-35 MINS COOK 30-35 MINS

Crisp salmon with
coriander pesto p235

 PREP
5-10 MINS

 COOK
10-15 MINS

Seafood and tomato
cioppino p180

 PREP
45-50 MINS

 COOK
20-25 MINS

MORE FISH MAINS:

Monkfish and white wine stew p176

Fish plaits with warm vinaigrette p244

Pan-fried mackerel in rolled oats p258

Roast sea bass with herb butter p276

Poached salmon, watercress sauce p310

Bouillabaisse p318

Trout with orange-mustard glaze p322

Sautéed trout with hazelnuts p271

 PREP
20-25 MINS

 COOK
10-15 MINS

Prawn risotto p363

 PREP
15-20 MINS

COOK
25-30 MINS

Griddled tuna steaks
with salsa p250

PREP
25-30 MINS

COOK
5-7 MINS

Duck with turnips and apricots p196

PREP
35-40 MINS

COOK
1½-2 HOURS

Chinese roast duck p296

PREP
45 MINS

COOK
1¾-2 HOURS

Chicken pot pies with herb crust p214

PREP
25-35 MINS

COOK
22-25 MINS

Coq au vin p278

PREP
30 MINS

COOK
1½-1¾ HOURS

Chicken en cocotte with parmesan p344

PREP
15-20 MINS

COOK
45-55 MINS

Southern fried chicken p248

PREP
10-15 MINS

COOK
20-30 MINS

Szechuan pepper chicken p282

PREP 20-25 MINS   COOK 40-50 MINS

Turkey mole p190

PREP 45-50 MINS   COOK 1¼-1¾ HOURS

Indonesian fried rice p334

PREP 40-45 MINS   COOK 10-15 MINS

Very garlicky sautéed chicken p324

PREP 15-20 MINS   COOK 1-1¼ HOURS

Sweet-sour duck with cherries p284

PREP 30-35 MINS   COOK 1¼-1½ HOURS

MORE POULTRY MAINS:

Hunter's chicken p175

Chicken paprika with dumplings p182

Chicken and beer stew p184

Poule au pot p188

Poussins with plums and cabbage p192

Chicken and prawn laksa p194

Brunswick stew p204

Moroccan chicken tagine p275

Sauté of chicken with prawns p287

Poussins in vine leaves p292

Hindle Wakes chicken with prunes p298

Herbed roast chicken p331

Oriental stir-fried chicken p242

PREP 15-20 MINS   COOK 10-12 MINS

Poussins with mushroom sauce p320

PREP 30-40 MINS   COOK 35-40 MINS

Rack of lamb coated with parsley p280

PREP 35-40 MINS COOK 25-30 MINS

Malaysian fried rice noodles p256

PREP 30-40 MINS COOK 8-12 MINS

Hungarian beef goulash p187

PREP 25-30 MINS COOK 2½-3 HOURS

Lamb shanks in red wine p222

PREP 45-50 MINS COOK 2½-2¾ HOURS

Provençal daube of beef p210

PREP 45-50 MINS COOK 3½-4 HOURS

Lamb dhansak p202

PREP 40-45 MINS COOK 1½-1¾ HOURS

Minute steak marchand du vin p268

PREP 15-20 MINS COOK 40-50 MINS

Milanese veal escalopes p232

PREP 20-25 MINS COOK 4-12 MINS

Pork and ginger sukiyaki p252

PREP 15-20 MINS COOK 15-20 MINS

Leg of lamb with roasted garlic p308

PREP 15-20 MINS COOK 1¼-2 HOURS

Steak and wild mushroom pie p368

PREP 50-55 MINS COOK 2½-3 HOURS

Beef rendang p312

PREP 40-50 MINS COOK 3½-4 HOURS

Steak au poivre p238

PREP 25-30 MINS COOK 10-15 MINS

Mexican barbecued pork with salsa p240

PREP 35-40 MINS COOK 40-50 MINS

Roast leg of pork with orange p301

PREP 20-25 MINS COOK 3½-4 HOURS

MORE MEAT MAINS:

Cassoulet p198

Lamb chops champvallon p201

Russian beef sauté p246

Veal saltimbocca p253

Butterflied leg of lamb p288

Fillet of beef with mushrooms p290

Osso bucco p313

Korean grilled beef p314

Pork loin with garlic and rosemary p316

Rib of beef with Yorkshire pudding p328

Lamb chops in paper with fennel p332

Spicy tomato-bacon pasta p346

Pork chops with mustard sauce p347

Baked rigatoni with meatballs p352

Raspberry soufflés, kirsch custard p504

PREP 20-25 MINS   COOK 10-12 MINS

Baked peaches with Amaretti p498

PREP 15-20 MINS   COOK 1-1¼ HOURS

Chocolate soufflés p523

PREP 20-25 MINS   COOK 15-18 MINS

Caramelized mango tartlets p488

PREP 40-45 MINS   COOK 20-25 MINS

Cherry clafoutis p458

PREP 20-25 MINS   COOK 30-35 MINS

Crêpes Suzette p508

PREP 40-50 MINS   COOK 45-60 MINS

Chocolate and pear tartlets p526

PREP 30-35 MINS   COOK 25-30 MINS

Mincemeat tart with whisky butter p448

PREP 40-45 MINS   COOK 40-45 MINS

Grand Marnier soufflé p518

 PREP 30-35 MINS COOK 20-25 MINS

Flaky pear tartlets p449

  PREP 35-40 MINS COOK 30-40 MINS

Blackberry and apple pie p418

 PREP 35-40 MINS COOK 50-60 MINS

Baked Alaska p536

PREP 45-50 MINS COOK 30-40 MINS

Filo apricot turnovers p440

PREP 35-40 MINS COOK 12-15 MINS

MORE HOT DESSERTS:

Pear pie with walnut pastry p424

Bavarian plum tart p428

Peach pie p434

Cherry strudel p444

Gratin of fresh berries with sabayon p505

Tarte tatin p442

PREP 45-50 MINS COOK 20-25 MINS

Apple and almond galettes p510

PREP 25-30 MINS COOK 20-30 MINS

Tiramisu p481

PREP
35-40 MINS
COOK
30-40 MINS

Chocolate decadence p506

PREP
30-40 MINS
COOK
20 MINS

Chocolate ice cream p486

PREP
15-20 MINS
COOK
10-15 MINS

Tri-chocolate terrine
p520

PREP
35-40 MINS
COOK
20-25 MINS

Creamy rice pudding with peaches p492

PREP
15-20 MINS
COOK
3 HRS

**Apricot and hazelnut
ice cream** p500

PREP
35-40 MINS
COOK
25-30 MINS

Pavlova with tropical fruit p482

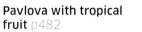
PREP 25-30 MINS   COOK 2-2½ HOURS

Poires belle Hélène p517

PREP 30-35 MINS   COOK 25-35 MINS

Mango sorbet p522

PREP 25-30 MINS   COOK 2-3 MINS

Profiteroles with ice cream p499

PREP 25-30 MINS   COOK 25-30 MINS

MORE COLD DESSERTS:

Lemon meringue pie p420

Chocolate orange truffle cake p476

Cold lemon soufflé p484

Blackberry fool p487

Creamy rice pudding with peaches p492

Chocolate walnut torte p494

Oeufs à la neige p496

Grapefruit granita, almond biscuits p511

Hazelnut meringue gâteau p512

Trio of sorbets p514

Chocolate mousse with hazelnuts p516

Amaretti and chocolate bombe p524

Chocolate mocha sorbet p529

Ginger cheesecake p493

PREP 40-45 MINS   COOK 50-60 MINS

Orange and cinnamon crème brulée p480

PREP 15-20 MINS   COOK 30-35 MINS

Multi-grain breakfast bread p388

PREP
45-50 MINS
COOK
40-45 MINS

Dinner rolls p396

PREP
45-55 MINS
COOK
15-18 MINS

Onion and walnut crown p398

PREP
40-45 MINS
COOK
45-50 MINS

Sourdough bread p384

PREP
45-50 MINS
COOK
40-45 MINS

Sesame grissini p387

PREP
40-45 MINS
COOK
15-18 MINS

Split-top white bread p380

PREP
40-50 MINS
COOK
35-40 MINS

Cornbread p386

PREP
15-20 MINS
COOK
20-25 MINS

Seeded rye bread p394

PREP
35-40 MINS
COOK
50-55 MINS

Focaccia with rosemary p392

PREP
30-35 MINS
COOK
15-20 MINS

Lemon-blueberry muffins p466

PREP 20-25 MINS   COOK 15-20 MINS

Marbled chocolate cheesecake p472

PREP 35-40 MINS   COOK 50-60 MINS

Apple cake p464

PREP 20-25 MINS   COOK 1¼-1½ HRS

Chocolate bread p414

PREP 35-40 MINS   COOK 45-50 MINS

Buttermilk scones p403

PREP 15-20 MINS   COOK 12-15 MINS

MORE BAKING:

Wholemeal bread p382

Baguette p390

Pesto garland bread p400

Irish soda bread p402

Pitta bread p404

Potato-chive monkey bread p406

Walnut, bacon, and herb kugelhopf p408

Yule bread p412

Walnut cake with caramel topping p465

Chocolate orange pound cake p470

Small brioches p410

PREP 45-50 MINS   COOK 15-20 MINS

Rich chocolate cake p468

PREP 15 MINS   COOK 30-35 MINS

Starters and light bites

Tempting small plates for appetizers and snacks

Crostini

AN UNLIMITED VARIETY OF TOPPINGS can be invented for these. Authentic crostini call for Italian peasant-style bread, but use any crusty loaf with a chewy crumb. An assertive, fragrant, preferably unrefined olive oil is the best choice, to stand up to the strong flavours of the topping.

SERVES	PREP	COOK
SERVES 8	15–20 MINS	5–10 MINS

Ingredients

750g (1lb 10oz) ripe tomatoes

small bunch of basil

4 garlic cloves, finely chopped

salt and pepper

4 tbsp extra virgin olive oil

150g (5½oz) Italian or Greek black olives, stoned and chopped

4 canned anchovy fillets, chopped

1 small loaf Italian peasant-style bread

PREPARE THE TOPPING

1 **Cut the cores** from the tomatoes and score an "x" on their bases with a small knife. Immerse in a pan of boiling water until the skin starts to split, 8–15 seconds, depending on ripeness. Plunge into a bowl of cold water, then peel off the skins. Halve, squeeze out the seeds, then coarsely chop.

2 **Strip the basil leaves** from the stalks, reserving 8 sprigs for garnish, and coarsely chop. Mix the tomatoes, garlic, and basil in a bowl. Stir in a little salt and pepper with the olive oil. Cover and let stand at room temperature for 30–60 minutes.

3 **Stir in the olives** and anchovies and taste for seasoning. You probably won't need any salt, as the anchovies and olives are salty enough, but the topping should have a strong flavour, so season well with pepper.

MAKE THE CROSTINI

4 **Preheat the oven** to 200°C (400°F/ Gas 6). Cut the bread into 8 x 1cm (½in) thick slices. Spread out the slices on a baking sheet and toast in the oven for 5–10 minutes, until lightly browned, turning once.

5 **Spoon the topping** on to the toasted bread, spreading it roughly. Garnish each with a basil sprig. Arrange the crostini on a platter and serve warm or at room temperature.

Tapenade

THIS PROVENÇAL SAUCE combines all the flavours of the Mediterranean: black olives, anchovies, garlic, capers and olive oil. It can be made up to 1 week ahead. Pour a thin layer of olive oil over the top so all the surface is protected from the air and keep it, tightly covered, in the refrigerator.

SERVES SERVES 6-8 | **PREP** 30-35 MINS | **COOK** 10-15 MINS

Ingredients

FOR THE TAPENADE

6 slices of white bread, crusts cut off

4 garlic cloves, peeled

200g (7oz) oil-cured black olives, stoned

30g (1 oz) capers, drained

6 canned anchovy fillets

125ml (4fl oz) olive oil

lemon juice, to taste

black pepper, to taste

FOR THE CRUDITÉS

1 red pepper

1 green pepper

1 bunch of spring onions, trimmed

1 cucumber

1 baguette

1 bunch of radishes, trimmed

250g (9oz) cherry tomatoes

MAKE THE TAPENADE

1 Tear the bread into pieces, place in a bowl and cover with cold water. Leave to soak for 5 minutes, then squeeze dry and put into a food processor.

2 Add the garlic, olives, capers, and anchovies and chop coarsely. With the blades turning, gradually add the oil. Add lemon juice and pepper to taste and work until the texture is as you prefer; it can be either a coarse or rough paste. Transfer to a bowl, cover, and set aside.

PREPARE THE CRUDITÉS AND TOASTS

3 With a small knife, cut around the core of the peppers, twist them and pull them out. Halve each pepper lengthways, scrape out the seeds and the white ribs. Slice each half lengthways into strips.

4 Cut the spring onions into 5cm (2in) pieces, including some green tops. Trim the ends from the cucumber, peel, cut in half lengthways, and scoop out the seeds with a teaspoon. Cut each half into 2-3 strips lengthways, then across into 5cm (2in) pieces.

5 Preheat the oven to 190°C (375°F/Gas 5). Cut the baguette into 5mm (¼in) slices on the diagonal. Set the slices on a baking sheet and bake for 10-15 minutes, until crisp.

6 Set the tapenade in the centre of a platter, or serve smaller bowls to each guest. Arrange the crudités, with the radishes and cherry tomatoes, around the tapenade and serve the toasted bread separately.

Clear soup with sea bass

THIS HEARTY SOUP is served in the winter in Japan. White radish, or daikon, gives a crisp bite and a pleasantly hot flavour to the broth. Almost every Japanese meal includes a soup, ranging from a classic, light miso to a thick broth that is a satisfying meal in itself. This clear soup, which is based on the fish- and seaweed-flavoured stock, dashi, should be served piping hot.

SERVES	PREP	COOK
SERVES 4	30-35 MINS	25 MINS

Ingredients

FOR THE STOCK

10cm (4in) piece of dried kelp

5g (¼oz) dried bonito flakes

1 tsp Japanese soy sauce, or to taste

FOR THE SOUP

½ small carrot, cut into 8 slices

salt

2.5cm (1in) piece daikon, cut into 8 wedges

1 sea bass (about 375g/13oz), cleaned

1 tbsp Japanese rice wine

1 tbsp cornflour

zest of 1 lemon

125g (4½oz) spinach, or 1 small bunch watercress

PREPARE THE SOUP STOCK

1 Put **1 litre (1¾ pints) cold water** in a large saucepan and add the dried kelp. Bring to a boil over high heat, then immediately remove and discard the kelp. Remove the pan from the heat. If the kelp is allowed to boil, the stock will be bitter and cloudy.

2 **Sprinkle the dried bonito flakes** evenly over the surface of the kelp-infused water.

3 **Let the stock stand** until the flakes settle to the bottom. It should take 3-5 minutes, depending on how thick and dry the flakes are. Line a sieve with damp muslin (the damp cloth will not shed fibres). Strain the stock through the muslin.

PREPARE THE VEGETABLES

4 Half-fill a saucepan with water and bring to the boil. Add the carrot slices and a pinch of salt and simmer for 3–5 minutes, until tender. Drain and set aside. Repeat with the daikon wedges, simmering for 8–10 minutes until just tender. Drain and set aside.

PREPARE THE FISH AND LEMON ZEST

5 Cut the sea bass across into 4 steaks, discarding both the head and tail (unfortunately, bass is no good for making fish stock, so there's nothing you can do with these trimmings). Toss the fish with the rice wine. Put the cornflour on a plate and press both sides of each sea bass steak into it, shaking off any excess. Make sure all the cut surfaces of the fish are finely and evenly covered with the flour.

6 Bring a wide saucepan of water to the boil. Drop in the sea bass steaks and bring back to a gentle simmer. Do not allow the water to heat any further than a very slow bubble, or the fish steaks may break up, or overcook and turn to mush. Cook for 2–3 minutes, until just firm, then drain the fish and set aside.

7 With a vegetable peeler, pare 2–3 strips of zest from the lemon, being sure to leave behind any bitter white pith. (If you pick up any pith by mistake, put the strip of zest on a flat work surface and remove it with a very sharp knife.) Cut the zest into 12 very thin strips. These are known as julienne. Meanwhile, trim and discard any tough stalks from the spinach and wash the leaves thoroughly. Bring a pan of water to the boil, add the spinach and simmer for 3 minutes, or until tender. Drain, rinse with cold water to cool the spinach rapidly, then gently squeeze with your fist to remove the excess water. Chop, divide into 4 small, neat piles and keep warm until serving.

FINISH THE SOUP

8 Bring the soup stock to a very gentle boil with the soy sauce. Taste, adding more soy sauce if you like. Arrange the fish, carrots, and daikon in 4 warmed soup bowls. Carefully ladle in the boiling soup and sprinkle each bowl with 3 strips of lemon zest. Decorate each with a bundle of spinach, or with a sprig of watercress, if you prefer.

Stuffed mushrooms with herbs

LIFE ISN'T TOO SHORT to stuff a mushroom! In fact these are hard to beat when they are filled with wild mushrooms and walnuts, then perfumed with garlic and plenty of herbs. They can be made up to 4 hours ahead and kept in the refrigerator.

SERVES	PREP	COOK
SERVES 4	25-30 MINS	15-20 MINS

Ingredients

12 large cap mushrooms, total weight about 500g (1lb 2oz)

90g (3oz) fresh wild mushrooms, or 20g (¾oz) dried wild mushrooms

12-14 tarragon sprigs, leaves chopped, plus a few sprigs for garnish

10-12 chervil sprigs, leaves chopped, plus a few sprigs for garnish

7-10 thyme sprigs, leaves chopped, plus a few sprigs for garnish

3-4 tbsp grated Parmesan cheese

4 tbsp olive oil

3 garlic cloves, finely chopped

juice of ½ lemon

salt and pepper

90ml (3fl oz) double cream

100g (3½oz) walnuts, coarsely chopped

PREPARE THE MUSHROOMS AND STUFFING

1 **Pull out the stalks** from the large mushrooms, leaving the caps whole for stuffing. Wipe the caps with damp kitchen paper and trim the separated stalks. Wipe the fresh wild mushrooms and trim the stalks. If using dried mushrooms, soak them in hot water until plump, about 30 minutes. Drain them and cut into pieces.

2 **Finely chop the wild mushrooms** and the large mushroom stalks with a sharp knife, or chop in a food processor, taking care to retain their texture and not to overwork them to a purée. Combine a quarter of the chopped herbs with the Parmesan and set aside.

3 **Heat half the oil** in a frying pan. Add the chopped mushrooms and garlic with the lemon juice and salt and pepper. Cook, stirring, for 3-5 minutes, or until all the liquid has evaporated. Stir in the cream and cook for 1-2 minutes, until slightly thickened. Add the walnuts and herbs and stir to mix. Remove from the heat and taste for seasoning.

STUFF AND BAKE THE MUSHROOMS

4 **Preheat the oven** to 180°C (350°F/Gas 4). Lightly oil a baking dish. Season the mushroom caps and spoon 1-2 spoonfuls stuffing into each, mounding it well. Set in the baking dish.

5 **Sprinkle about 1 tsp Parmesan** and herb topping on each mushroom along with the remaining oil. Bake for 15-20 minutes, or until the mushrooms are tender when pierced with a knife and the filling is very hot. Serve garnished with the reserved herbs.

Smoked trout mousse

A REFRESHING START to any meal, lifted with pungent horseradish and fragrant dill and lightened with yogurt. If you use a mould made from aluminium or tin, do not store in the refrigerator for more than 4 hours, or it will taint the flavour.

SERVES	**PREP**	**COOK**
SERVES 8-10	20-25 MINS PLUS CHILLING	NONE

Ingredients

2 eggs, hard-boiled

small bunch of dill

2 smoked trout, total weight about 750g (1lb 10oz)

1 tbsp powdered gelatine

3 small spring onions, finely sliced

125ml (4fl oz) mayonnaise

125ml (4fl oz) plain yogurt

60g (2oz) grated fresh horseradish, or to taste

juice of 1 lemon

salt and pepper

175ml (6fl oz) double cream

bunch of watercress, to serve

PREPARE THE INGREDIENTS

1 **Coarsely chop the eggs.** Strip the dill fronds from the stalks and finely chop them. Peel the skin from the smoked trout with a sharp knife, then carefully lift the fish from the bones. Discard the heads, bones, and skin and gently flake the flesh, removing any remaining small bones.

2 **Sprinkle the gelatine** evenly over 4 tbsp cold water in a small bowl and let it stand for about 5 minutes, until the granules become spongy. Brush a 1.2 litre (2 pint) terrine mould with oil.

MAKE THE MOUSSE

3 **Put the eggs,** trout, dill, spring onions, mayonnaise, and yogurt in a bowl. Add the horseradish, lemon juice, salt, and pepper and stir. Taste; it should be well seasoned.

4 **Whip the cream** for 3-5 minutes, until soft peaks form. Melt the gelatine in a small saucepan placed over low heat. Add it to the trout mixture and mix thoroughly. At once, fold in the cream, working quickly. Spoon into the mould and smooth the top. Cover with a lid, or with clingfilm, and chill in the refrigerator for 3-4 hours, until set.

UNMOULD THE MOUSSE

5 **Run a small knife** around the edges of the mould. Dip the base in a bowl of warm water for a few seconds to loosen the mousse, then wipe the base dry.

6 **Set a platter** on top of the mould and invert to unmould the mousse. Cut the mousse into 2cm (¾in) slices and set a slice on each plate. Decorate each serving with 1-2 sprigs of watercress.

Beef noodle soup (pho)

FRAGRANT WITH SPICES, this Vietnamese soup takes time to simmer, but gives a rich, meat-laden broth that is a meal in itself. It should be quite hot with chillies, so use as many as you dare here, and deseed them or not, depending on the strength of heat you prefer (if you leave in the seeds, the dish will be much hotter).

SERVES	PREP	COOK
SERVES 4	1½ HRS	4-5 HRS

Ingredients

FOR THE SOUP STOCK

1.4kg (3lb) oxtail, cut into pieces

1kg (2¼lb) beef bones, cut into pieces

1 large onion, halved

5cm (2in) piece of fresh root ginger, thickly sliced

3 shallots

4 star anise

10cm (4in) cinnamon stick

3 whole cloves

FOR THE RICE STICKS AND TOPPINGS

250g (9oz) 5mm (¼in) dried rice sticks

2 spring onions, trimmed

250g (9oz) beef fillet

4 tbsp fish sauce

125g (4½oz) beansprouts

4 coriander sprigs

1 hot red chilli, deseeded and thinly sliced, or to taste

1 lime, cut into wedges

MAKE THE SOUP STOCK

1 **Put the oxtail and beef bones** in a large saucepan. Add water to cover, bring to a boil and simmer for 10 minutes. Drain in a colander and rinse with cold water. Rinse the pan then return the oxtail and bones. Add 3 litres (5¼ pints) of water, cover, and bring slowly to a boil.

2 **Meanwhile,** heat the grill. Put the onion halves and ginger pieces on the grill rack. Add the unpeeled shallots. Grill 7.5cm (3in) from the heat for 3-5 minutes, until well browned, then turn and brown the other sides for another 3-5 minutes. Add them to the saucepan with the star anise, cinnamon stick, and cloves.

3 **Cover and simmer** over low heat for 3-4 hours, until the oxtail pieces are tender. While it cooks, add more water, if needed, to keep the bones covered, and occasionally skim the fat from the surface. Remove the oxtail pieces from the stock and set aside. When cool enough to handle, remove the meat from the oxtail bones with your fingers and reserve.

4 **Return the oxtail bones to the stock,** and continue simmering for another hour. Line a colander with a piece of dampened muslin large enough to hang generously over the side. Strain the stock through this into a large, clean saucepan. Discard the bones, spices, and vegetables. Skim off all the fat and taste for seasoning. You should have 2 litres (3½ pints).

PREPARE THE RICE STICKS AND TOPPINGS

5 Put the rice sticks in a bowl and cover with warm water. Let soak for 20 minutes, until soft, or according to packet directions. Cut the spring onions into diagonal slices. Cut the beef across the grain into very thin slices. Arrange the slices on a tray, cover them tightly and refrigerate.

ASSEMBLE THE SOUP

6 Add the oxtail meat and fish sauce to the soup stock and bring to a boil. Remove the beef from the refrigerator.

7 Half-fill a large pan with water and bring to a boil. Drain the rice sticks, add them to the boiling water and stir to help prevent them sticking together. Return the water to a boil, then drain thoroughly in a colander, shaking to remove as much water as possible. Divide the rice sticks equally between 4 large, warmed soup bowls and top with the beansprouts, raw beef slices, and spring onions.

8 Carefully ladle some of the boiling soup stock and shredded oxtail meat evenly into each bowl. Serve at once, while still very hot, decorated with a few coriander sprigs. Allow each guest to add slices of chilli and squeeze over lime juice to taste. Urge them not to be too timid: this soup is supposed to be devilishly hot.

Szechuan sweet and sour spare ribs

SERVE WITH BOILED OR FRIED RICE to make this recipe into a main course for 4. These ribs are first browned in chilli-flavoured oil, then very slowly simmered until completely tender, and finally coated in a delectable sauce.

SERVES SERVES 6	**PREP** 15–20 MINS	**COOK** 1½ HRS

Ingredients

4 tbsp dark soy sauce

4 tbsp cider vinegar

3 tbsp honey

1 tbsp sesame oil

1 tsp chilli paste

4 tbsp dry sherry

4 tbsp vegetable oil

1 dried red chilli

1.4kg (3lb) spare ribs

PREPARE THE SAUCE AND BROWN THE RIBS

1 **In a small bowl,** whisk together the soy sauce, cider vinegar, honey, sesame oil, chilli paste, and sherry. Cover tightly with cling film and set this sweet and sour sauce aside.

2 **Heat the vegetable oil** in a wok, add the chilli and cook for 1 minute until dark brown. Add 3–4 ribs and stir over high heat for 2–3 minutes, until browned on all sides. Transfer to a plate. Working in batches, brown the remaining ribs in the same way. Pour off all but 2 tbsp oil from the wok.

SIMMER THE SPARE RIBS

3 **Return the ribs** to the wok, pour in enough water to completely cover and bring to a boil. Reduce the heat and cover the wok. Simmer, for about 1 hour, stirring occasionally. The ribs are cooked when the meat shrinks slightly on the bone and feels tender to the tip of a knife.

4 **Remove the chilli** and discard. Pour the sauce into the wok and stir thoroughly to mix. Simmer, stirring occasionally, for 25–30 minutes, until the liquid is reduced to a thick brown sauce and the ribs are glazed. If necessary, remove the ribs and reduce the sauce further by boiling fast. Serve the ribs on a warmed plate, coated with the sauce.

Mussels with saffron-cream sauce

FROM THE SHORES OF BRITTANY comes this interesting dish. The mussel juices add rich flavour to the cooking liquid. Make sure you steam the mussels briefly, just until the shells pop open, so they remain juicy and sumptuous.

SERVES	PREP	COOK
SERVES 4–6	25–30 MINS	10–12 MINS

Ingredients

3kg (6½lb) mussels

3 shallots, very finely chopped

250ml (9fl oz) dry white wine

1 bouquet garni, made with 5–6 parsley stalks, 2–3 thyme sprigs, and 1 bay leaf

large pinch of saffron

salt and pepper

125ml (4fl oz) double cream

leaves from 5–7 parsley sprigs, finely chopped

PREPARE THE MUSSELS

1 **Clean the mussels**: scrub each thoroughly under cold running water with a small stiff brush, then scrape with a knife to remove any barnacles.

2 **Discard any damaged mussels** that have cracked or broken shells and any that do not close when tapped lightly on the work surface. Detach and discard any weeds or 'beards' from each mussel.

COOK THE MUSSELS

3 **Put the shallots,** wine, bouquet garni, saffron, and plenty of pepper in a casserole which has a lid. Bring to a boil and simmer for 2 minutes. Add the mussels, cover and cook over high heat, stirring occasionally, for 5–7 minutes. Discard any mussels that have not opened. With a slotted spoon, transfer the mussels to a large, warmed bowl.

4 **Cover tightly with foil** and keep in a warm place while making the sauce. You must work quickly now, so the mussels remain as plump and moist as possible and lose none of their fresh-cooked savour.

MAKE THE SAUCE

5 **Discard the bouquet garni** and bring the cooking liquid to a boil. Simmer until reduced by half. Pour in the cream, stirring, and bring back to the boil. Simmer until slightly thickened, stirring; it should take 2–3 minutes. Lift out the spoon and run your finger across; it should leave a clear trail. Stir in the parsley and season to taste. Remove the foil and spoon the saffron-cream sauce over the mussels.

Chicken mousse with Madeira sauce

THIS SMOOTH, CREAMY MOUSSE wrapped in fine slices of courgette makes an excellent hot first course. If you would like to serve it as a light main dish instead, add some delicious saffron rice (p262) as an accompaniment.

SERVES	PREP	COOK
SERVES 4	25-35 MINS	20-30 MINS

Ingredients

500g (1lb 2oz) skinless, boneless chicken breasts

2 egg whites

salt and pepper

pinch of ground nutmeg

175ml (6fl oz) double cream

2 courgettes, trimmed

butter, for the ramekins

FOR THE BUTTER SAUCE

125g (4½oz) butter

2 garlic cloves, finely chopped

2 shallots, finely chopped

4 tbsp Madeira

1 tbsp double cream

MAKE THE CHICKEN MOUSSE

1 **Cut the chicken** into chunks and work it through the fine blade of a food mincer, or process in a food processor until not too fine. It should remain a coarsely minced mixture.

2 **Whisk the egg whites** until frothy. With a wooden spoon, gradually add them to the chicken, beating until smooth and firm after each addition. Season with salt, pepper, and nutmeg.

3 **Beat in the cream**, a little at a time. Chill the mixture for about 15 minutes, or until firm. It should hold its shape. To test for seasoning, fry a little piece in a frying pan and taste. Adjust the seasoning if necessary.

PREPARE THE COURGETTES

4 **Cut the courgettes** into very thin slices. Bring a saucepan of salted water to the boil. Add the courgettes and simmer for 1-2 minutes, until softened. Drain in a colander, rinse under cold water to stop the cooking, then drain thoroughly on kitchen paper.

PREPARE THE RAMEKINS

5 **Using a ramekin as a guide**, cut out 6 circles of baking parchment. Butter 6 ramekins. Lay a parchment paper circle in the base of each and brush it, too, with butter. Be sure to cover all the paper, to prevent the courgette slices from sticking. Meanwhile, preheat the oven to 180°C (350°F/Gas 4).

ASSEMBLE AND COOK THE MOUSSE

6 **Line the bottoms and sides** of the ramekins with overlapping slices of courgettes.

7 **Spoon the chicken mousse** mixture in, smoothing the top, then put in a baking dish. Pour in boiling water to come more than halfway up the sides.

8 **Cover the dish** with baking parchment and bake for 20-30 minutes, or until a skewer inserted in the centre is hot to the touch. During baking, do not let the water boil or the mousse will separate.

MAKE THE SAUCE AND FINISH THE DISH

9 Heat about 30g (1oz) of the butter in a small saucepan, add the garlic and shallots and cook, stirring, for 2-3 minutes. Make sure the garlic does not brown too much, or the sauce will taste bitter. Add the Madeira and bring to a boil, stirring to dissolve the pan juices, for 2-3 minutes, or until it has reduced to a syrupy glaze. Add the cream and boil again until reduced to a glaze. Remove from the heat and add the remaining butter, a few pieces at a time, whisking constantly and moving the pan on and off the heat. The butter should thicken the sauce creamily without melting to oil. Make sure the sauce does not become too hot, or it will separate.

10 Run a fine, sharp knife around the edge of each ramekin. Unmould the chicken mousses on to warm plates, carefully rearranging any slices of courgette which have become displaced. Spoon the warm Madeira sauce around each mousse.

VARIATION: Cold chicken mousse with tomato and mint coulis

Served at room temperature with a vibrant red sauce.

1 Prepare and cook the mousse as directed in the main recipe. Leave it to cool to room temperature.

2 Omit the butter sauce and make a tomato coulis instead: skin, seed and roughly chop 250g (8oz) fresh tomatoes; purée in a food processor until very smooth. With the motor running, gradually add 1 tbsp olive oil to make an emulsion. Season to taste.

3 Run a fine-bladed knife around the edge of each ramekin, then unmould the mousses on to individual plates. Spoon around the tomato coulis and sprinkle evenly with chopped fresh mint.

Cod and mussel chowder

A HEARTY DISH laden with chunks of cod and potatoes, with mussels to add colour and flavour. The recipe can be made up to and including step 7 and kept, tightly covered, in the refrigerator. Finish the chowder just before serving.

SERVES	PREP	COOK
SERVES 8	45-50 MINS	55-60 MINS

Ingredients

3 potatoes, total weight about 500g (1lb 2oz)

1kg (2¼lb) skinned cod fillets

1kg (2¼lb) mussels

1.5 litres (2¾ pints) fish stock

2 bay leaves

125ml (4fl oz) white wine

175g (6oz) streaky bacon rashers, diced

2 onions, finely chopped

2 celery sticks, peeled and finely chopped

1 carrot, finely chopped

2 tsp dried thyme

60g (2oz) plain flour

250ml (9fl oz) double cream

salt and pepper

leaves from 5-7 dill sprigs, finely chopped

PREPARE THE INGREDIENTS

1 **Peel and dice** the potatoes into 1cm (½in) cubes and put in a bowl of cold water so they do not discolour. Rinse the cod fillets and pat dry with kitchen paper. Cut into 2.5cm (1in) cubes. Prepare the mussels (see p41).

2 **Put the fish stock** and bay leaves into a large saucepan and pour in the wine. Bring to the boil and simmer for 10 minutes, until very hot and all the flavours have combined.

3 **Put the bacon** in a casserole dish and cook, stirring occasionally, for 3-5 minutes, until crisp and the fat is rendered. Add the onions, celery, carrot, and thyme. Cook, stirring, for 5-7 minutes, until soft but not brown.

MAKE THE CHOWDER

4 **Sprinkle the flour** over the casserole and cook, stirring, for a minute.

5 **Add the hot stock** mixture and bring to a boil, stirring until the liquid thickens slightly.

6 **Drain the potatoes** and add them to the casserole. Simmer, stirring occasionally, until the potatoes are very tender, about 40 minutes.

7 **Remove the casserole** from the heat. With a fork, crush about a third of the potatoes against the side of the casserole, then stir to combine.

FINISH THE CHOWDER

8 Return the casserole to the heat and tip in the mussels. Simmer for 1–2 minutes until the shells start to open. Stir in the cod and simmer until the fish just flakes easily, 2–3 minutes more. Do not continue to cook, or the fish will start to break apart. Pour in the cream and bring just to a boil. Taste for seasoning, adding salt and pepper to taste.

9 Discard the bay leaves and any mussels that have not opened, and warn your guests to do the same, should they come across any firmly shut shellfish. Ladle the chowder into warmed soup bowls and sprinkle each with dill. Serve very hot. The traditional New England accompaniment to this chowder is oyster crackers, crumbled into the bowls by each diner, to taste.

 VARIATION: Manhattan chowder

This adds tomatoes for a colourful finish.

1 Peel, seed, and coarsely chop 1.2kg (2¾lb) tomatoes, or use 2 x 400g (14oz) cans tomatoes. If tomatoes are not ripe and in season, canned are usually the better choice. Finely chop 4 garlic cloves.

2 Make the chowder as directed, using double the amount of wine, 1 tbsp dried thyme, and half the plain flour. Add the garlic and 1–2 tbsp tomato puree with the onion, celery, and carrots.

3 Add the tomatoes with the potatoes; do not crush any of the potatoes. Omit the double cream. Sprinkle with chopped thyme and serve with crusty wholewheat bread.

Genoese minestrone with red pesto

A PURÉE OF TOMATO, GARLIC, AND BASIL is stirred in at the finish here to give a burst of fresh flavour. A hearty soup full of beans and pasta, this recipe makes a perfect starter for the colder months; follow it with a lighter main course. Both the soup and the pesto can be made 1 day ahead and refrigerated separately; reheat the soup before adding the sauce.

SERVES	PREP	COOK
SERVES 6	45–50 MINS	2½ HRS

Ingredients

FOR THE MINESTRONE

175g (6oz) dried red kidney beans

175g (6oz) dried cannellini beans

salt and pepper

125g (4½oz) elbow macaroni

175g (6oz) French beans

3 carrots, total weight about 250g (9oz)

3 potatoes, total weight about 375g (13oz)

1 courgette

175g (6oz) shelled fresh peas or defrosted frozen peas

125g (4½oz) Parmesan cheese, grated

FOR THE TOMATO PESTO

large bunch of basil

2 tomatoes, peeled, deseeded, and chopped

4 garlic cloves, peeled

1 tsp salt

pepper

175ml (6fl oz) olive oil

PREPARE THE DRIED BEANS AND MACARONI

1 Put the kidney and cannellini beans in separate bowls. Add water to cover generously and leave to soak overnight. Drain, rinse with cold water, and drain again. Put the beans in separate saucepans, and add water to cover generously.

2 Bring to a boil and boil for 10 minutes. Reduce the heat to a simmer. Cook for about 1½ hours, seasoning with salt and pepper halfway through cooking, until tender but still slightly firm when gently squeezed. Drain thoroughly.

3 Fill a medium saucepan with water, bring to a boil and add salt. Add the macaroni and cook, stirring occasionally, for 5–7 minutes, until just tender. Drain and rinse with hot water, then set aside.

MAKE THE SOUP

4 Break the ends from the French beans and cut them into 1cm (½in) pieces. Peel the carrots and potatoes; trim the ends from the courgette. Dice the carrots, potatoes, and courgette.

5 Put the cooked, dried beans in a large saucepan and add the French beans, carrots, potatoes, courgette, peas, and a little salt and pepper. Add 2 litres (3½ pints) of water and bring to a boil, then reduce the heat and simmer for 1 hour, until the vegetables are very tender.

6 Strip the leaves from the basil stalks, reserving 6 sprigs. Put the basil, tomatoes, garlic, salt, and a little pepper in a food processor or blender and purée until smooth.

7 With the blades turning, gradually add the oil. Scrape down the sides of the processor bowl from time to time during the process with a rubber spatula. Taste the sauce for seasoning.

8 Add the macaroni to the soup and taste again for seasoning. Gently reheat to boiling, but do not cook further or the pasta and vegetables will overcook, rather than staying firm and vibrant. Remove from the heat, and stir in the tomato pesto. Ladle the soup into warmed bowls, top each serving with basil leaves, and serve the Parmesan separately.

 VARIATION: Soupe au pistou, croûtes gratinées

With a few changes, Genoese minestrone becomes the famous French soup, pistou. It's hardly surprising, as the Italian town that gives its name to the main minestrone recipe here is very close to the French border.

1 Cook the dried beans and macaroni, and make the vegetable soup as directed, omitting the fresh or frozen peas. Make the tomato pesto sauce as directed, then set aside.

2 Preheat the oven to 180°C (350°F/Gas 4). Make toasted cheese croûtes: cut 1 small loaf of French bread (weighing about 175g/6oz) into 24 slices, each 2cm (¾inch) thick.

3 Spread the slices on a baking sheet. Brush each lightly with olive oil and sprinkle evenly with 60g (2oz) finely grated Parmesan cheese. Bake for about 5 minutes.

4 Stir the pesto sauce into the hot soup, ladle into warmed bowls, and float a croûte on each serving. Pass the remaining croûtes separately. Omit the grated Parmesan for sprinkling.

Gratin of chicory and ham

A SIMPLE DISH from Belgium, home of chicory. Make sure you remove the bitter core at the bottom of each head of chicory as you trim it, to allow it to cook more evenly. This is a great starter or side dish for a party, as it can be assembled up to the end of step 6 the day before, then covered tightly and refrigerated. Bring the gratin to room temperature before sprinkling it with Gruyère cheese and baking.

SERVES	PREP	COOK
SERVES 4	15–20 MINS	1–1¼ HRS

Ingredients

8 heads of chicory, trimmed

1 tsp granulated sugar

salt and pepper

500ml (16fl oz) milk

1 slice of onion

1 bay leaf

6 peppercorns

30g (1oz) plain flour

60g (2oz) butter

ground nutmeg

45g (1½oz) Gruyère cheese

8 thin slices of cooked ham

BRAISE THE CHICORY

1 **Preheat the oven** to 180°C (350°F/Gas 4). Brush a flan dish with butter. Arrange the chicory evenly spaced apart in the dish and sprinkle with the sugar, salt, and pepper. Butter a piece of foil and press it, butter-side down, on top. Bake, turning once or twice, for 45–55 minutes, until brown and slightly caramelized. The chicory should be tender right to the centre when pierced with a knife. Transfer the chicory to a plate and let cool slightly. Wipe the flan dish.

MAKE THE BÉCHAMEL SAUCE

2 **Scald the milk** in a saucepan with the onion slice, bay leaf, and peppercorns (you should be able to hear the milk begin to sizzle at the sides of the pan, but it should not come to the boil). Cover the pan and set it aside in a warm place off the heat for 10 minutes, for the milk to infuse with all the other flavours. Melt the butter in another saucepan over medium heat. Whisk in the flour and cook for 30-60 seconds, whisking all the time, until foaming.

3 **Remove the pan from the heat,** then strain in the hot milk and whisk. Return to the heat, whisking constantly to avoid lumps, until the sauce boils and begins to thicken. Season with salt, pepper, and a pinch of nutmeg (or to taste), and simmer the sauce for 2 minutes more, to cook out the raw taste of the flour, stirring to spread the heat and ensure the sauce does not catch on the bottom of the saucepan.

ASSEMBLE AND BAKE THE GRATIN

4 **Increase the oven temperature** to 200°C (400°F/Gas 6). Butter the flan dish again. Grate the Gruyère cheese and set aside.

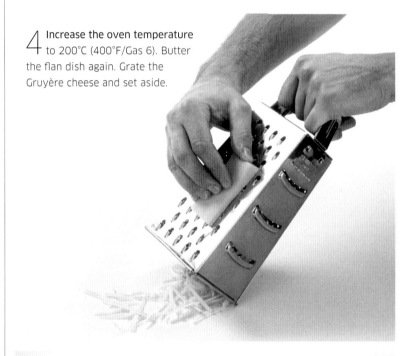

5 **Lay a slice of ham** on a work surface. Set a head of chicory on top and roll the ham slice round to form a neat cylinder. Repeat with the remaining ham and chicory, arranging the cylinders neatly in the dish, seam-side down, to keep them intact.

6 **Ladle the béchamel sauce** evenly over the chicory and ham cylinders.

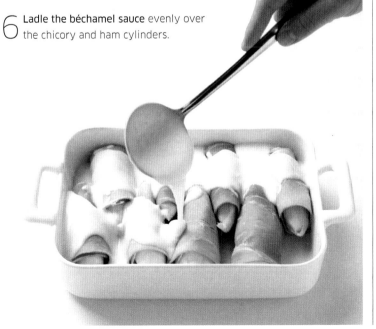

7 **Sprinkle with the cheese.** Bake for 20-25 minutes, until bubbling and browned. Serve hot from the dish.

Leeks vinaigrette

COMPLETELY DELICIOUS; so much more than the sum of its parts. This simple, elegant dish should be prepared with the freshest leeks you can find. They can be left to marinate in the vinaigrette, covered and refrigerated, for up to 1 day. Let them come to room temperature before sprinkling with the egg and parsley. Substitute baby leeks if you prefer; use the same weight, but do not tie them together in step 2 of the recipe, and simmer them for only 5 minutes, or until just tender to the tip of a knife.

SERVES	PREP	COOK
SERVES 4-6	15-20 MINS PLUS MARINATING	15-25 MINS

Ingredients

6 leeks, total weight about 1kg (2¼lb)

salt and pepper

3 tbsp white wine vinegar

1 tsp Dijon mustard

175ml (6fl oz) flavourless vegetable oil

2 shallots, finely chopped

1 egg

leaves from 5-7 parsley sprigs, finely chopped

COOK THE LEEKS

1 Trim the leeks, discarding the roots and tough green tops. Slit lengthways, leaving the leeks attached at the root end. Wash thoroughly, fanning the leeks out under cold, running water.

2 Divide the leeks into 2 bundles, then tie them together at each end with kitchen string. Fill a wide shallow pan with salted water, and bring to a boil. Add the leeks, and simmer for about 10 minutes, or until just tender.

MAKE THE VINAIGRETTE

3 Whisk together the vinegar, mustard, salt, and pepper. Gradually whisk in the oil, so the vinaigrette emulsifies and thickens slightly. Whisk in the shallots; taste for seasoning.

DRESS THE LEEKS

4 Test whether the leeks are tender by piercing with the tip of a small knife. Drain in a colander, remove the strings, pat dry with kitchen paper, and cut on the diagonal into 7.5cm (3in) lengths.

5 Lay the leeks in a dish and pour over the vinaigrette. Cover and refrigerate for 1 hour, then bring to room temperature. Meanwhile, hard-boil and shell the egg.

FINISH THE SALAD

6 Divide the leeks between plates. Cut the egg in half, and separate yolk from white. Chop the white. Work the yolk through a sieve with a spoon. Sprinkle the leeks with parsley, egg whites, and yolks.

Chicken liver and apple pâté

TOPPED WITH GOLDEN SLICES of caramelized apple, these individual pâtés make an elegant first course. The smooth richness of the chicken livers is pleasantly contrasted with the sweet apples. A touch of Calvados is added and then flamed for a greater depth of flavour.

SERVES	PREP	COOK
SERVES 6	30–35 MINS	12–15 MINS

Ingredients

3 dessert apples

250g (9oz) butter

salt and pepper

500g (1lb 2oz) chicken livers, trimmed

4 shallots, finely diced

2 garlic cloves, finely chopped

4 tbsp Calvados or cognac

2 tbsp caster sugar

6 slices wholemeal bread

6 mint sprigs, to serve (optional)

PREPARE THE APPLES

1 **Core, peel, and dice** 2 of the apples. Melt 2 tbsp butter in a frying pan. Add the diced apples, salt and pepper. Sauté, stirring frequently, for 5–7 minutes, until tender. Transfer to a bowl with a slotted spoon.

PREPARE THE LIVERS

2 **Melt another 2 tbsp butter** in the frying pan. Add the chicken livers and season. Fry, stirring, for 2–3 minutes, until brown on the outside. Tip in the shallots and garlic. Cooking, stirring, for 1–2 minutes, until the shallots are slightly softened. Remove a liver from the frying pan, then slice into it. It should still be pink in the centre.

3 **Increase the heat** to medium-high. Pour the Calvados into the pan and bring to a boil. Stand back and hold a lighted match to the pan's side to set the alcohol alight. Baste the chicken livers for 20–30 seconds, until the flames subside. Let the livers cool.

MAKE THE PÂTÉ

4 **Purée the chicken liver mixture** in a food processor until almost smooth. Wipe out the frying pan. With an electric mixer, cream 150g (5oz) butter until soft. Add the livers with the diced and sautéed apples. Mix and season.

5 **Spoon into six ramekins**, filling them at least three-quarters full. Smooth the tops with the back of a spoon dipped in hot water so it does not stick to the pâté. Cover and chill for 2–3 hours, until firm.

PREPARE THE GARNISH AND SERVE

6 **Core the remaining apple** and slice into 6. Melt the remaining butter in the frying pan. Add the apple and sprinkle with half the sugar. Turn and sprinkle with the remaining sugar. Fry for 2–3 minutes each side, until caramelized. Meanwhile, toast the slices of bread. Set a caramelized apple slice and a mint sprig, if liked, on top of each pâté and serve with the toast.

Roman herb and garlic artichokes

YOUNG GLOBE ARTICHOKES with tender stalks are best for this delicious appetizer. Serve warm or at room temperature. If you can only find the older vegetables, you will have to trim away the more fibrous green parts. When choosing artichokes, check the cut stalks: buy only those that are moist, not dry, as they will be the freshest.

SERVES
SERVES 6

PREP
25–30 MINS

COOK
25–45 MINS

Ingredients

6 young globe artichokes

2 lemons, halved, plus 1 for garnish

6 garlic cloves, finely chopped

leaves from 1 small bunch of flat-leaf parsley, finely chopped

leaves from 8–10 mint sprigs, finely chopped, plus more for decoration

salt and pepper

125ml (4fl oz) olive oil

PREPARE THE ARTICHOKES

1 **Trim** the tough end of an artichoke stalk, leaving about 4cm (1½in) of stalk. Snap off the large bottom leaves with your fingers. Continue to remove the leaves, tearing off about three-quarters of each leaf so the edible white part remains attached to the artichoke heart.

3 **Peel the stalk** of the artichoke, cutting away the tough, fibrous exterior. Trim the green parts of the base to remove any tough, fibrous leaves.

2 **Continue** until you reach the cone of soft, small leaves in the centre. Trim the cone of leaves with a sharp knife. Rub the cut edges of the artichoke with a lemon half to prevent discolouration.

4 **Scoop out** the hairy choke with a teaspoon and squeeze lemon juice into the hollowed-out centre. Rub the juice thoroughly around the inside with your finger. Prepare the remaining artichokes in the same way.

STUFF AND COOK THE ARTICHOKES

5 **Combine the garlic,** parsley, mint, and a little salt in a bowl. Put 2–3 spoonfuls of the garlic-herb stuffing in the centre of an artichoke and press it down well against the bottom and sides so that they are as full as possible and the stuffing will not fall out when the artichokes are cooked upside-down. Stuff the remaining artichokes, keeping back 2–3 tbsp of the stuffing to sprinkle on top.

6 **Set the artichokes,** tops down and stalks up, in a single, tight layer in a large pan. They should be packed tightly enough so they do not topple over during cooking. Sprinkle the remaining stuffing over and pour on the oil. Sprinkle with salt and pepper and add enough water to come halfway up the sides, not including the stalks.

7 **Bring to a boil,** then cover the pan and simmer for 25–45 minutes, until tender. Add more water if necessary, so the artichokes are always half covered. To test if the artichokes are cooked, pierce them with the point of a knife; they should be tender.

8 **Transfer the artichokes** to a large, warmed serving dish with a slotted spoon, arranging them in a single layer, still with their stalks upwards. Try to make sure you take as little as possible of the cooking liquid from the pan. Boil the cooking liquid until it is strongly flavoured and reduced to about 250ml (8fl oz).

9 **Squeeze the juice** from the remaining lemon half, discarding any seeds, then add this to the cooking liquid to lift all the flavours. Taste for seasoning, adding more salt, pepper, or lemon if you think it needs it. Pour the cooking liquid over the artichokes and let cool to room temperature. Slice the lemon for garnish.

10 **Serve the artichokes warm** or at room temperature, decorated with lemon wedges and mint sprigs. They are delicious at either temperature, which makes them a very forgiving dish. If necessary, you can prepare the artichokes up to 1 day ahead, cover, and refrigerate. Let them come to room temperature before serving.

Basque hot pepper omelette

LIKE A SPANISH TORTILLA, this omelette is browned on both sides. Use this recipe as a template for whatever varieties of sweet peppers and chillies you prefer, or can find. It's even better if you can use a good selection of shapes, colours, and levels of heat.

SERVES	**PREP**	**COOK**
SERVES 2	20-25 MINS	15-25 MINS

Ingredients

250g (9oz) tomatoes

60g (2oz) butter

1 onion, thinly sliced

1 red pepper, thinly sliced

1-2 small hot red chillies, deseeded and finely chopped

2 garlic cloves, finely chopped

salt and pepper

leaves from small bunch of parsley, finely chopped

5 eggs

PREPARE THE FILLING

1 **Cut the cores** from the tomatoes, and score an "x" on their bases. Immerse in boiling water for 8-15 seconds, or until the skin starts to split. Plunge into cold water, peel, halve, squeeze out the seeds, and coarsely chop.

2 **Melt half the butter** in a frying pan, add the onion, pepper, and chillies, and cook for 5-8 minutes, or until softened. Add the tomatoes, garlic, salt, and pepper, and cook for 5-10 minutes, until thick. Stir in the parsley.

COOK THE OMELETTE

3 **Crack the eggs** into a bowl, season, and beat until thoroughly mixed. Melt the remaining butter in an omelette or frying pan. When it stops foaming and starts to brown, pour in the eggs. Stir briskly with the flat of a fork for 8-10 seconds, until the eggs start to thicken.

4 **Quickly but carefully,** use a fork to pull the cooked egg mixture from the sides of the pan to the centre, so the uncooked egg flows to the sides. Continue until the eggs are partly set, about 30 seconds.

5 **Stir the filling** into the eggs until well mixed. Reduce the heat and cook undisturbed for 2-3 minutes, until the omelette is set on top and browned underneath.

6 **Remove the pan** from the heat. Working quickly, place a large plate, that is bigger in diameter than the pan, over the omelette, and, holding both plate and pan firmly, invert to turn out the omelette on to the plate. Carefully slide it back into the pan, and brown the other side for only 30–60 seconds, or until the egg is cooked (lift an edge carefully with a palette knife to check). Alternatively, make the omelette entirely in a flameproof frying pan and don't invert the omelette to cook the other side; instead, preheat the grill and, at the end of step 5, slide the frying pan under the grill until the top is browned and the egg just cooked.

7 **Slide the omelette** on to a warmed serving plate. Cut it into wedges and serve hot, or at room temperature, with a crisp green salad, if you like. Once you have mastered making a Spanish-type omelette such as this, you can ring the changes as you please. There are one or two basic rules, however: if adding a watery vegetable, or a mushroom, these should be first sautéed until all their moisture has been drawn out and has evaporated from the pan, otherwise the omelette will be sloppy and the flavour diluted. When adding cheese, sprinkle it over at the last minute and flash the frying pan under the grill so it melts on top of the omelette (be sure to use a flameproof frying pan in this instance).

 VARIATION: Country omelette

With potatoes, onion, and bacon, this is typical fare in French cafés.

1 Omit the garlic, red pepper, chillies, and tomatoes. Slice the onion and chop the parsley as directed in the main recipe, reserving a few small parsley sprigs for decoration.

2 Take 250g (9oz) of streaky bacon rashers. Cut them across into strips. Peel 500g (1lb 2oz) potatoes and square off the sides. Cut them into 1cm (½in) cubes, stacking them up first for ease. Heat the bacon in a large frying pan and cook over medium heat, stirring occasionally, for 5 minutes, or until the fat has rendered. Remove all but 2 tbsp of the bacon fat.

3 Stir the onions and potatoes into the remaining fat in the frying pan. Cook, stirring occasionally, for 20 minutes, or until the onion and potatoes are tender and golden. Season to taste with salt and pepper. Cook the omelette as directed in the main recipe, adding the potato mixture in place of the tomato and pepper filling. Serve hot or at room temperature, cut into wedges, and decorate with the reserved parsley sprigs.

Vietnamese spring rolls

THESE ARE WRAPPED IN SOFT RICE PAPER, unlike the crisp, fried version, and are served with a sweet and spicy dipping sauce. The rolls are light and very adaptable; you can use almost any meat or fish you wish in place of the prawns and pork.

SERVES	**PREP**	**COOK**
SERVES 4	50-60 MINS	25 MINS

Ingredients

FOR THE DIPPING SAUCE

2 garlic cloves, finely chopped

1 small hot red chilli, finely chopped

2 tbsp sugar

4 tbsp rice vinegar

4 tbsp fish sauce

2 tbsp lime juice

FOR THE SPRING ROLLS

250g (9oz) boneless loin of pork

8 raw, unpeeled prawns, total weight 125g (4½oz)

1 large carrot, in julienne strips

1 tsp sugar

60g (2oz) dried thin rice noodles

8 small lettuce leaves, plus more to serve

75g (2½oz) beansprouts

12-15 mint sprigs

15-20 coriander sprigs

8 round sheets of rice paper, 21cm (8½in) in diameter

MAKE THE DIPPING SAUCE

1 In a small bowl, combine the garlic, chilli, sugar, rice vinegar, fish sauce, and 4 tbsp water. Pour in the lime juice and whisk well until thoroughly mixed. Set aside for the flavours to meld together.

PREPARE THE FILLING

2 Half-fill 2 pans with water and bring to a boil. Add the pork to 1 pan and simmer for 15-20 minutes, just until tender. Drain the pork, rinse with cold water and drain again. Cut it across the grain into 3 mm (⅛in) slices.

3 Add the prawns to the other pan and simmer for 1-2 minutes, until pink. Drain, rinse with cold water and drain again. Peel off the shells. Cut each lengthways in half. Using the tip of a knife, remove the dark intestinal vein.

4 In a bowl, toss the carrot with the sugar and set aside. Bring a large pan of water to a boil. Add the noodles and cook for 1-2 minutes, until tender but still slightly chewy. Drain and cut into 7.5cm (3in) lengths.

5 Wash the lettuce leaves. Dry, then tear large leaves into 2-3 pieces. Pick over the beansprouts, discarding any that are discoloured. Strip the mint and coriander leaves from the stalks, reserving a few sprigs for garnish.

ASSEMBLE THE SPRING ROLLS

6 Pour about 1cm (½in) of hot water into a shallow dish. Work with 1 sheet of rice paper at a time and keep the remaining sheets wrapped. Dip 1 sheet of rice paper into the water for 20-25 seconds, to soften. Remove and spread it out on a dry tea towel.

7 Place a lettuce leaf on the rice paper. Top with one-eighth of the noodles, carrot, pork, beansprouts, and mint and coriander leaves. Roll up the paper, halfway, into a cylinder. Fold both ends over the filling.

8 Place a few more coriander leaves on top, then 2 prawn halves. Continue rolling the paper into a cylinder and press the end lightly to seal. Place the roll, prawn-side up, on a tray or plate and cover with a dampened tea towel to keep the roll moist. Repeat with the remaining rice papers and filling. Serve with small bowls of dipping sauce, and sprinkled with the reserved herbs.

 VARIATION: Vegetarian spring rolls

Mushrooms and onions replace the meat in this version.

1 Omit the pork, prawns, and dipping sauce. Soak 8 Chinese black mushrooms in about 175ml (6fl oz) boiling water for 15 minutes, until plump and soft. Prepare the noodles and carrots as directed. Drain the mushrooms, reserving 120ml (4fl oz) liquid. Cut off the mushroom stalks and slice the caps. Thinly slice 1 onion.

2 Heat a wok over medium-high heat and drizzle in 1 tbsp oil. When hot, add the onion and cook, stirring, for 2 minutes, until softened. Add the mushrooms and reserved liquid. Cover and cook for 4 minutes, until the mushrooms are tender. Uncover and cook until the liquid is evaporated. Stir in 1 tsp soy sauce, 1 tsp sugar, and salt to taste. Leave to cool. Assemble the spring rolls as directed, using all the carrots and replacing the prawns with the mushrooms.

3 Make a hoisin dipping sauce: finely chop 1 garlic clove. In a small pan, heat 2 tsp oil, add the garlic and cook until fragrant. Stir in 120ml (4fl oz) hoisin sauce, 3 tbsp water, 1 tbsp light soy sauce and a pinch of crushed dried chilli. Let cool. Pour into 4 bowls and sprinkle with 2 tbsp chopped peanuts. Serve the rolls and sauce with a salad of carrot julienne, lettuce and herbs.

Tropical prawn kebabs

SERVED WITH A PEANUT SAUCE, these make a great starter for a summer meal. They can be cooked on a barbecue or grilled indoors if the weather is bad; either method will give a fabulous result. Try serving them with Chilli-Cucumber Salad (see p95) and boiled rice to turn them into a more substantial main course dish.

SERVES SERVES 8   **PREP** 20–25 MINS   **COOK** 4–6 MINS

Ingredients

For the kebabs

125ml (4fl oz) vegetable oil, more for grill rack

6 tbsp lime juice (about 2 limes)

1cm (½in) piece of fresh root ginger, peeled and finely chopped

2 large garlic cloves, finely chopped

½ tsp granulated sugar, or to taste

½ tsp chilli powder

leaves from a small bunch of coriander, chopped

1 tbsp soy sauce

salt and pepper

32 large raw prawns, total weight about 750g (1lb 10oz)

For the peanut sauce

60ml (2fl oz) vegetable oil

1 small onion, finely chopped

2 large garlic cloves, finely chopped

½ tsp crushed chillies

juice of ½ lime

2 tsp soy sauce

5 tbsp crunchy peanut butter

1 tsp soft brown sugar

250ml (9fl oz) coconut milk

2 Soak 8 bamboo skewers in water for 30 minutes, then thread 4 prawns on to each skewer and lay them in a shallow dish. (If using metal skewers, marinate the prawns before putting them on the skewers.)

MARINATE THE PRAWNS

1 Whisk together the oil, lime juice, ginger, and garlic. Add the sugar, chilli powder, chopped coriander, soy sauce, and salt and pepper to taste; stir well to mix.

3 Pour the marinade over the prawns. Cover and refrigerate for 1–2 hours, turning occasionally.

MAKE THE PEANUT SAUCE

4 Heat the oil in a small saucepan. Add the onion and cook, stirring, for 2–3 minutes, until lightly browned. Add the garlic and chillies and cook until the onion is golden, but do not let the garlic brown or it will be bitter.

5 Add the lime juice and soy sauce to the onion mixture; stir to combine. Remove from the heat and stir in the peanut butter and brown sugar. Let cool to room temperature.

6 Whisk the coconut milk in its tin until smooth, then measure the amount needed and pour it into the peanut sauce. Stir until the sauce is evenly mixed. Season to taste and let stand.

7 Heat the grill and brush the grill rack with oil. Transfer the kebabs from the dish to the rack. Brush the kebabs with marinade. Grill them 5–7.5 cm (2–3in) from the heat for 2–3 minutes, until they turn pink. Brush with marinade once or twice during grilling. Turn and brush again with marinade. Continue grilling until the prawns are pink on the other side, 2–3 minutes longer.

8 Set the kebabs on warmed plates, adding a small bowl of peanut sauce. Lime wedges are a great addition – a squeeze of lime juice really lifts the flavours of this dish.

Cheddar and courgette soufflés

USE MATURE OR MILD CHEDDAR according to your taste. The courgette mixture can be prepared up to 3 hours ahead to the end of step 6. Whisk the egg whites and finish the recipe just before baking. If you would prefer to make a large soufflé instead of individual dishes, use a 2 litre (3½ pint) dish and cook the whole mixture for 25–30 minutes.

SERVES	PREP	COOK
SERVES 6	30–35 MINS	25–30 MINS

Ingredients

60g (2oz) unsalted butter, plus more for the dishes

2 shallots, finely chopped

500g (1lb 2oz) courgettes, trimmed and coarsely grated

salt and pepper

175ml (6fl oz) milk

20g (¾oz) plain flour

125ml (4fl oz) double cream

pinch of ground nutmeg

4 eggs, separated, plus 2 egg whites

90g (3oz) Cheddar cheese, coarsely grated

PREPARE THE COURGETTES

1 **Melt half the butter** in the frying pan. Stir in the shallots and cook over a medium heat for about 2 minutes, until soft. Add the courgettes, season, and cook, stirring, for 3–5 minutes, until just tender. Transfer to a sieve set over a bowl and allow the liquid to drain thoroughly.

MAKE THE SAUCE

2 **Scald the milk** in a small saucepan. Melt the remaining butter in a medium saucepan. Over the heat add the flour all at once and cook, whisking briskly, until the mixture starts to foam, 30–60 seconds.

3 **Remove the pan** from the heat then slowly pour in the hot milk, whisking all the time, and continue to whisk until well mixed. Return to the heat, whisking constantly to prevent lumps.

4 **When the sauce boils** and thickens, pour in the cream and whisk until thoroughly combined. Season to taste with salt, pepper, and nutmeg. Simmer for 2 minutes longer.

MAKE THE SOUFFLÉ

5 Whisk the egg yolks into the hot sauce, one at a time, whisking well after each addition. Return the pan to the heat. Bring the mixture back to a boil, whisking constantly, and simmer for 1 minute longer to ensure the egg yolks are fully cooked.

6 Remove the pan from the heat and stir in the Cheddar and courgettes. Taste for seasoning; it should be highly seasoned. Preheat the oven to 190°C (375°F/Gas 5). Melt a little butter and use it to grease 6 x 350ml (12fl oz) capacity ramekins. Reheat the courgette mixture until hot.

FINISH THE SOUFFLÉ

7 Beat all the egg whites with a pinch of salt in a metal bowl for 3-5 minutes, until stiff peaks form. Do not overbeat or they will become grainy. Add about a quarter to the warm sauce and gently stir.

8 Add the lightened sauce to the remaining egg whites in the bowl. Fold the mixture together until the egg whites are thoroughly incorporated. Spoon into the prepared dishes. Bake until puffed and brown, 10-15 minutes. The centre should remain quite soft.

9 Serve immediately: the soufflés will lose much of their volume within minutes as they cool. Instruct your diners to plunge small spoons straight into the centre of the dish.

 ## VARIATION: Onion and sage soufflé

A classic combination; try this for a satisfying and unusual vegetarian Sunday lunch, alongside the more conventional pairing of roast pork or chicken for the meat eaters.

1 Omit the courgettes, shallots, and Cheddar. Thinly slice 8 onions. Melt 45g (1½oz) butter in a saucepan. Add the onions with salt and pepper, press a piece of buttered foil on top, and cover. Cook very gently for 15-20 minutes, until the onions are very soft but not brown. Stir occasionally so the onions cook evenly and do not catch on the base of the pan. Uncover and cook, stirring, until any liquid has evaporated.

2 Meanwhile, strip the leaves from 5-7 sprigs of fresh sage and chop them as finely as possible. Don't be tempted to add more herbs here, though it may not look like very much, as sage has a very strong taste and even a little bit too much could easily overpower the subtle balance of the flavourings in this dish.

3 Make the white cream sauce as directed. Add the onions and sage to the sauce and stir well to mix evenly. Finish and bake the soufflé as directed, using a 2 litre (3½ pint) dish and allowing 25-30 minutes for this larger soufflé to bake through fully. Make sure the centre remains quite soft; soufflés should not be solid in the middle: rather unctuous and melting is the ideal texture here.

Thai skewered chicken

COCONUT MILK AND FISH SAUCE flavour this popular street food snack threaded on to bamboo skewers. The sauce can be prepared 1 day ahead and the chicken can be marinated up to 12 hours in advance. Keep both, covered, in the refrigerator and grill the chicken just before serving.

SERVES	PREP	COOK
SERVES 4	20-30 MINS PLUS MARINATING	6-8 MINS

Ingredients

6 large boneless chicken thighs, total weight about 1kg (2¼lb)

FOR THE MARINADE

2 garlic cloves, chopped

150ml (5fl oz) canned coconut milk

2 tsp ground coriander

1 tsp ground cumin

1 tsp ground turmeric

FOR THE SAUCE

leaves from 8-10 coriander sprigs, chopped, plus a few more for garnish

juice of 1 lemon

3 tbsp light brown sugar

2 tbsp fish sauce

3 tbsp light soy sauce

½ tsp crushed chillies

PREPARE AND MARINATE THE CHICKEN

1 **Cut each thigh** into 6 even chunks, discarding any sinew. Combine all the marinade ingredients in a large bowl and mix. Add the chicken and toss to coat. Cover and refrigerate for at least 2 and up to 12 hours.

MAKE THE SAUCE

2 **In a small bowl,** combine all the sauce ingredients and stir until mixed. Cover the bowl and refrigerate for the flavours to combine, but remember to bring it to room temperature before serving.

SKEWER AND COOK THE CHICKEN

3 **Put 12 bamboo skewers** in water to soak for 30 minutes, so they do not burn during grilling. Heat the grill and lightly oil the grill rack. Thread the chicken chunks on to the skewers, dividing them equally.

4 **Arrange the skewers,** skin-side up, on the oiled rack. Grill about 7.5 cm (3in) from the heat for 4-5 minutes, until speckled with brown. Turn the skewers and continue grilling for 2-3 minutes longer, until the chicken is no longer pink in the centre. (Grill in batches if necessary to avoid crowding.)

5 **Arrange the chicken skewers** on a warmed serving platter, decorate with the reserved coriander leaves and serve with the sauce. Serve with Cucumber-chilli salad (see p95) for a burst of refreshing heat.

Borscht

THE CLASSIC SOUP of Eastern Europe. During a spell of cold weather, there is little that can be more cheering on the dinner table than a bowl of this startlingly bright, deep pink broth with its hearty and warming flavours.

SERVES	**PREP**	**COOK**
SERVES 8-10	50-55 MINS	1-1¼ HRS

Ingredients

6 raw beetroot

60g (2oz) butter

2 small carrots, chopped

2 small onions, chopped

1 small white cabbage, cored and shredded

2 x 400g (14oz) cans chopped tomatoes

2 litres (3½ pints) chicken stock or water, plus more if needed

salt and pepper

1 tsp sugar, or to taste

leaves from 3-4 dill sprigs, finely chopped

leaves from 3-4 parsley sprigs, finely chopped

juice of 1 lemon

2-3 tbsp red wine vinegar

125ml (4fl oz) soured cream

PREPARE THE BEETROOT

1 Trim and wash the beetroot. Never peel beetroot before cooking because they 'bleed'. Bring to a boil in a pan of salted water. Cook for about 30 minutes, until tender when tested with the tip of a knife.

2 **Drain the beetroot.** When cool enough to handle, peel off the skin and grate the flesh on to a plate, using the coarse side of a box grater. (You may want to wear kitchen gloves for this, to avoid staining your fingers with beetroot juice.)

MAKE THE BORSCHT

3 **Melt the butter** in a large saucepan. Add the carrots and onions and cook, stirring, for 3-5 minutes, until soft but not brown. Add the cabbage, beetroot, tomatoes, stock, salt, pepper, and sugar to taste, and bring to a boil. Simmer for 45-60 minutes. Taste for seasoning and add more stock if the soup is too thick.

4 **Just before serving,** stir in the herbs, lemon juice, and red wine vinegar, and taste for seasoning. Pour the soup into warmed bowls and top each with a spoonful of the soured cream.

Cheese gougères with salmon

TRADITIONAL IN BURGUNDY, so a glass of white Burgundy is the perfect accompaniment! Here, smoked salmon and spinach gives the puffs a luxurious edge. You will need to make a choux pastry, which is a useful skill. Don't be put off; it's easy as long as you follow the steps carefully. You'll find that, once mastered, you will make choux pastry often for both sweet and savoury dishes.

SERVES	PREP	COOK
SERVES 8	40–45 MINS	30–35 MINS

Ingredients

FOR THE CHOUX PASTRY

75g (2½oz) unsalted butter cut into small pieces, plus more for the baking sheets

1¼ tsp salt

150g (5½oz) plain flour, sifted

5–6 eggs

125g (4½oz) Gruyère cheese, grated

FOR THE FILLING

1kg (2¼lb) fresh spinach

30g (1oz) butter

1 onion, finely chopped

4 garlic cloves, finely chopped

1 pinch of ground nutmeg

salt and pepper

250g (9oz) cream cheese

175g (6oz) smoked salmon, sliced into strips

4 tbsp milk

MAKE THE CHOUX PASTRY

1 **Butter 2 baking sheets** and preheat the oven to 190°C (375°F/Gas 5). Melt the butter in a saucepan with 250ml (8fl oz) water and ¾ tsp salt. Bring just to a boil. Remove from the heat and vigorously beat in the flour all at once, until the mixture is smooth and pulls away from the pan.

2 **Return the pan to the stove** and beat over a very low heat to dry out the dough, about 30 seconds. Remove from the heat. Add 4 of the eggs, one at a time, beating well after each. Beat the fifth egg; add it gradually until the choux is shiny and soft. Lift some of the mixture on a wooden spoon held over the saucepan; it should fall off by a count of three.

3 **Add half the Gruyère** to the mixture and stir it into the choux until thoroughly mixed.

4 **Using 2 spoons,** drop eight 6cm (2½in) mounds of dough on to the baking sheets, leaving room for the dough to puff as it bakes.

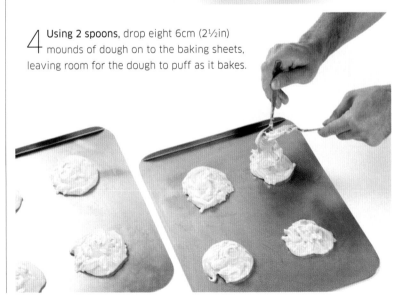

GLAZE AND BAKE THE CHOUX PASTRY

5 Lightly beat the remaining egg with the remaining ½ tsp salt. Brush some glaze over each of the choux puffs. Sprinkle the remaining cheese over the puffs. Bake in the oven for 30-35 minutes, until firm and brown.

6 With a palette knife, carefully remove the cheese puffs from the baking sheets and transfer them to a wire rack. Using a serrated knife, slice the top off each puff and leave them to cool for 5-10 minutes.

MAKE THE FILLING AND FILL THE PUFFS

7 Discard the tough ribs and stalks from the spinach, then wash the leaves thoroughly. Bring a large saucepan of salted water to a boil. Add the spinach and simmer for 1-2 minutes, until tender. Drain the spinach, rinse with cold water and drain again. Squeeze the cooked spinach in your fists to remove excess water, then finely chop.

8 Melt the butter in a frying pan. Add the onion and cook for 3-5 minutes, until soft but not brown. Add the garlic and nutmeg, salt and pepper to taste, and the spinach. Continue cooking, stirring occasionally, for about 5 minutes longer, until any remaining liquid has evaporated. Make sure that the garlic is not browning; if it does, its slightly bitter taste will then spoil the flavour of the dish.

9 Add the cream cheese to the spinach and stir until it has melted and the mixture is thoroughly and evenly combined. Remove the frying pan from the heat. Add the smoked salmon and pour in the milk. Stir thoroughly, heat for 1-2 minutes until piping hot, then taste the sauce for seasoning.

10 Mound 2-3 spoonfuls of the filling in each cheese puff, making sure to distribute it evenly between the portions. Rest the lid against the side of each filled puff and serve at once, before the choux pastry absorbs the liquid and becomes soft.

Blini with smoked salmon

BLINI ARE RUSSIAN PANCAKES, with a lightness and nutty flavour from buckwheat flour. Soured cream is the mandatory and delicious traditional accompaniment, but you can add melted butter, too, if you like, for an even richer version.

SERVES	PREP	COOK
SERVES 8	25-30 MINS	8-16 MINS

Ingredients

FOR THE BLINI

250ml (8fl oz) milk, plus more if needed

1½ tsp dried yeast or 9g (⅓oz) fresh yeast

60g (2oz) plain flour

100g (3½oz) buckwheat flour

½ tsp salt

2 eggs

60g (2oz) butter, plus more if needed

2 tbsp soured cream

FOR THE CONDIMENTS

2-3 tbsp capers, drained

1 small red onion, very finely diced

8 radishes, thinly sliced

175g (6oz) sliced smoked salmon

175ml (6fl oz) soured cream, to serve

125g (4½oz) butter, to serve (optional)

MAKE THE BLINI BATTER

1 Pour three-quarters of the milk into a saucepan and bring just to a boil over a medium heat. Let the milk cool to lukewarm. Meanwhile, sprinkle or crumble the yeast over 4 tbsp lukewarm water in a small bowl and let stand until dissolved, about 5 minutes.

2 Sift the flours and salt into a large bowl. Using your fingers, make a well in the centre. Add the yeast mixture and the lukewarm milk to the well. Stir the mixture with a wooden spoon, gradually drawing the flour into the centre, then beat to make a smooth batter, about 2 minutes.

3 Dampen a tea towel and cover the bowl. Transfer to a warm place and let the batter rise for 2-3 hours, until it is light and full of bubbles.

PREPARE THE CONDIMENTS

4 Coarsely chop the drained capers if they are large. Transfer them to a small serving bowl. Put the onion and radish in separate serving bowls. Cover all the bowls. Arrange the slices of smoked salmon on a serving plate and cover. Keep everything in the refrigerator until ready to serve.

COOK THE BLINI

5 Preheat the oven to low for keeping the blini warm. Separate the eggs. Melt half the butter in a small saucepan and cool slightly. Pour the remaining milk into the risen batter and stir until mixed. Stir in the egg yolks, melted butter, and soured cream. Add more milk if necessary so the consistency is that of double cream.

6 **Put the egg whites** into a metal bowl and beat until stiff peaks form. Add about one-quarter to the blini batter and gently stir until thoroughly mixed together. Pour the batter and egg-white mixture into the metal bowl with the remaining beaten egg whites. Fold together gently until everything is thoroughly blended.

7 **Heat half the remaining butter** in a frying pan. Ladle in the batter to make 7.5cm (3in) rounds, being sure not to overcrowd the pan. Cook for 1–2 minutes, until the undersides are lightly browned and the tops are bubbling. Turn them over and brown the other side. Transfer to a heatproof plate, overlapping them so they remain moist, and keep warm in the oven while you make the rest, adding more butter to the pan as needed.

8 **Melt the butter for serving,** if using. Arrange the blini on a serving plate with the capers, onions, radishes, and smoked salmon. Serve a bowl of soured cream separately and a bowl of melted butter if you like.

VARIATION: Blini with red and black caviar

Choose lumpfish or beluga caviar, depending on your budget.

1 Make the blini batter as directed in the main recipe. Omit the capers, red onion, radishes, and smoked salmon accompaniments for this version of the dish.

2 Hard-boil 2 eggs and leave to cool. Peel the eggs then separate the yolks and whites; finely chop them both. Trim 2 spring onions and cut the green tops into thin diagonal slices.

3 Finish the batter and cook the blini as directed. Serve them with 30g (1oz) each red and black caviar (or more to taste), egg yolks and whites, spring onion slices, and a spoonful of soured cream.

Stuffed vine leaves (dolmades)

FROM GREECE, this is one of the great first courses. If you find fresh vine leaves, they must be steamed or blanched before use. More likely you will find them, year round, either canned, vacuum-packed, or bottled in brine. All work well here.

SERVES
SERVES 8

PREP
40–45 MINS
PLUS MARINATING

COOK
45–60 MINS

Ingredients

60g (2oz) pine nuts

200g (7oz) long-grain rice

175ml (6fl oz) olive oil

2 onions, diced

45g (1½oz) sultanas

1 bunch of dill, leaves coarsely chopped, plus a few sprigs to serve

1 small bunch of mint, leaves coarsely chopped, plus a few sprigs to serve

juice of 2 lemons

salt and pepper

40 vine leaves packed in brine, plus more if needed

750ml (1¼ pints) chicken stock or water, plus more if needed

MAKE THE STUFFING

1 **Preheat the oven** to 190°C (375°F/Gas 5). Toast the pine nuts on a baking sheet for 5–8 minutes, until lightly browned, stirring occasionally. Take care not to let them burn.

2 **Bring a saucepan** of salted water to a boil. Add the rice and bring back to a boil. Simmer for 10–12 minutes, until just tender. Stir occasionally to prevent the rice from sticking. Drain the rice in a sieve, rinse with cold water to wash away the starch and drain again thoroughly.

3 **Heat one-third of the oil** in a large saucepan. Add the onions and cook for 3–5 minutes, until soft but not brown. Stir in the rice, toasted pine nuts, sultanas, herbs, and a quarter of the lemon juice. Season and taste; it should be highly seasoned at this stage as the flavours will mellow during cooking.

STUFF THE VINE LEAVES

4 **Bring a saucepan** of water to a boil. Put the vine leaves in a large bowl and cover them generously with the boiling water. Separate them with a wooden spoon, so they do not stick together. Let the leaves stand for about 15 minutes, or according to the package directions, to rinse off most of the brine in which they were packed. Stir occasionally, to make sure they are not sticking together. Drain in a colander, rinse under cold running water, then drain again thoroughly.

5 **Gently place the vine leaves** in layers between sheets of kitchen paper and pat gently to dry. Spread about 8 over the bottom of a sauté pan.

6 **Spread 1 vine leaf** flat on a work surface, vein-side up, stem end towards you. Put 1–2 spoonfuls of the rice stuffing in the centre.

7 **Fold the sides** and stem end over the stuffing. Starting at the stem end, roll up the leaf away from you into a neat cylinder. Repeat with the remaining leaves and stuffing.

8 **Pack the stuffed leaves** tightly, in a single layer, in the sauté pan and pour over the stock. Add half the remaining oil and half the remaining lemon juice. Cover with a heatproof plate to weigh the leaves down for even cooking. Bring to a boil on top of the stove, then cover the pan with its lid and simmer over low heat, 45–60 minutes. Check every now and then to make sure the pan does not dry out, adding a splash of water if it looks as though it might.

9 **Pierce the leaves** with a skewer or sharp knife; they should be very tender and offer no resistance. Let them cool in the pan, then transfer to a non-metallic dish with a slotted spoon. Spoon over any remaining cooking liquid, cover and marinate in the refrigerator for at least 12 hours so the flavours can mellow.

10 **Set the stuffed vine leaves** on a serving platter, bring to room temperature, and spoon over the remaining olive oil and lemon juice cooking liquid. Garnish with the reserved dill and mint sprigs. Let your guests help themselves.

 VARIATION: Lamb and rice stuffed vine leaves

Minced lamb adds substance and a simple yogurt and mint sauce piquancy to this recipe.

1 Omit the pine nuts, fresh dill, and sultanas from the stuffing. Cook 150g (5½oz) rice as directed. Sauté the chopped onions in 4 tbsp olive oil. Add 375g (13oz) minced lamb to the softened onions and cook, stirring, for 5–7 minutes, until it loses its pink colour.

2 Chop the leaves from a large bunch of mint. Stir the rice, mint, juice of ½ lemon, ½ tsp ground cinnamon, a pinch of ground nutmeg, salt, and pepper into the lamb mixture.

3 Stuff the vine leaves as directed. Cook, using water instead of chicken stock. Serve warm, with a plain yogurt and chopped mint sauce. Garnish with fresh mint, if you like.

Herbed salmon cakes

THIS IS AN EXCELLENT WAY to use up leftover cooked fish. A tangy sweetcorn relish is the perfect foil to the richness of the salmon. This recipe does not include mashed potato; instead, breadcrumbs bring the mixture together and make the cakes a light and airy start to any meal. Vary the herbs, to taste.

SERVES	PREP	COOK
SERVES 8	35-40 MINS	15-20 MINS

Ingredients

FOR THE RELISH

500g (1lb 2oz) canned or frozen sweetcorn, drained

1 onion, finely chopped

1 celery stick, peeled and thinly sliced

1 green pepper, diced

125ml (4fl oz) olive oil

1 tbsp caster sugar

1 tsp mustard powder

salt and pepper

75ml (2½fl oz) red wine vinegar

FOR THE SALMON CAKES

butter, for the baking dish and foil

2 lemons

1kg (2¼lb) salmon fillet

175ml (6fl oz) fish stock or water, plus more if needed

4 slices of white bread

leaves from a small bunch of parsley, chopped

leaves from a small bunch of dill, chopped

4 tbsp mayonnaise

salt and pepper

2 eggs

4 tbsp vegetable oil

MAKE THE RELISH AND SALMON CAKE MIXTURE

1 **Put the sweetcorn,** onion, celery, and pepper in a large bowl and mix thoroughly. Take a look at the mixture and decide whether you would like more of any of the vegetables, to taste.

2 **Put the oil,** sugar, and mustard powder in a medium bowl with salt and pepper. Pour in the vinegar. Whisk together and pour this over the vegetables. Toss to mix thoroughly and season to taste. Cover and let stand at room temperature for 2-4 hours, to let the flavours combine and mellow and the dressing infuse the vegetables.

3 **Preheat the oven** to 180°C (350°F/Gas 4) and butter a baking dish. Squeeze the juice from 1 lemon. Remove the skin from the salmon, then rinse in cold water and pat dry. Arrange in a single layer in the dish. Sprinkle with the lemon juice, salt, and pepper. Add enough stock or water to half cover. Brush a little butter over a piece of foil and use to cover the salmon. Seal the foil to the sides of the baking dish. Poach in the heated oven for 15-20 minutes.

4 **Meanwhile,** trim and discard the crusts from the bread. Put the slices in a food processor and pulse-blend until they form even-sized crumbs.

5 **Test if the salmon is cooked:** it should just flake easily when pierced with a fork. Remove from the oven; reduce the oven temperature to its lowest setting. Drain the salmon and flake with 2 forks. Pick over with your fingers, making sure there are no small bones. Transfer the flaked salmon to a large bowl.

6 **Add the breadcrumbs,** herbs, and mayonnaise, and season. Stir gently but thoroughly. Lightly beat the eggs. Add them to the salmon mixture and stir to combine. To test for seasoning, heat 1 tbsp oil in a frying pan and fry a little piece of the mixture until brown on both sides. Taste, then adjust the seasoning of the remaining mixture if necessary.

SHAPE AND COOK THE SALMON CAKES

7 **Divide the salmon cake mixture** into 16 portions. Roll each into a ball, wetting your hands if the mixture is sticky, and flatten into a cake, about 1cm (½in) thick. Work gently, so the cakes will be light.

8 **Heat the remaining oil** in a frying pan. Add a batch of salmon cakes to fill the pan without overcrowding. Fry over medium-high heat for 3-4 minutes, until golden. Carefully turn over each cake with a palette knife and brown the other side.

9 **Line a heatproof plate** with kitchen paper and transfer the cooked salmon cakes to the plate to drain off any excess oil. Pat the tops of the cakes with kitchen paper, too, so each remains as light and grease-free as possible. Keep warm in the oven while cooking the remaining cakes. Work as quickly as possible as you finish frying the cakes, so the delicate insides of the cooked cakes do not dry out, or the cakes become tough on the outside, before you're ready to eat. Make sure your oven is on its lowest possible setting, as fierce heat at this stage will spoil the cakes. Cut the second lemon into wedges for serving.

10 **Stir the sweetcorn relish** to evenly amalgamate all the flavours and distribute the dressing, then divide it between 8 warmed plates and serve 2 salmon cakes on each, with a lemon wedge. Alternatively, serve all the salmon cakes together on a warmed platter, and the sweetcorn relish and lemon wedges in bowls on the side, and allow your diners to help themselves to everything.

 VARIATION:
Maryland crab cakes

Fresh or canned crab work equally well in this recipe.

1 Prepare the sweetcorn relish as directed, replacing the green pepper with a red pepper.

2 Omit the salmon fillets. Pick over 1kg (2¼lb) crab meat with your fingers, discarding any cartilage or shell. Work carefully, as any hard matter in the crab mixture will spoil the dish. Prepare the crab mixture as for the salmon cakes. Divide into 16 portions. Shape the crab cakes about 1cm (½inch) thick. Fry them as directed.

3 Serve 2 crab cakes per person with the sweetcorn relish. Decorate with dill sprigs, if you like.

Chicken and cheese quesadillas

A GREAT WAY to use up cooked chicken. Mild Cheddar would make a good substitute for the traditional American Monterey Jack cheese. Don't use a strongly flavoured mature cheese, as it will upset the delicate balance of this dish.

SERVES	PREP	COOK
SERVES 8	35–40 MINS	3–6 MINS

Ingredients

FOR THE QUESADILLAS

500g (1lb 2oz) tomatoes, peeled, deseeded and chopped

2 onions, diced

salt and pepper

3 hot green chillies

4 tbsp vegetable oil, plus more if needed

4 garlic cloves, finely chopped

125ml (4fl oz) chicken stock or water

375g (13oz) cooked boneless chicken, shredded

12 flour tortillas, each about 15cm (6in) in diameter

250g (9oz) Monterey Jack cheese, grated

FOR THE GUACAMOLE

leaves from 5–7 coriander sprigs, finely chopped

1 small ripe tomato, peeled, deseeded and finely chopped

1 small onion, chopped

1 garlic clove, chopped

1 ripe avocado

2–3 drops Tabasco sauce

juice of ½ lime

MAKE THE GUACAMOLE AND FILLING

1 **Combine the tomatoes** with one-quarter of the chopped onion. Season to taste and set aside. Slice the stalks from 2 of the chillies; remove the cores and seeds with a teaspoon or by tapping against the work surface. Cut into thin rings and set aside. Core, seed, and dice the remaining chilli.

2 **Heat 3 tbsp of the oil** in a frying pan. Add the remaining chopped onion, garlic, and diced chilli and cook for 2–3 minutes, until the onions are soft but not brown. Add the stock and simmer for 5–7 minutes, until almost all the liquid has evaporated. Stir in the chicken and cook for 1–2 minutes. Season to taste. Transfer to a bowl and wipe the frying pan.

3 **Place the coriander,** tomato, onion, and garlic for the guacamole in a bowl and toss to combine all the flavours. It's fine to do this ahead of time, as the ingredients will only enhance each other.

4 **Cut lengthwise around the avocado.** Twist to separate each half, remove the stone and scrape the flesh into the bowl. Mash with the other ingredients. Add a pinch of salt and a few drops of Tabasco.

5 **Add the lime juice** and stir well to mix. Taste for seasoning. Cover and refrigerate until serving to allow the flavours to combine and the seasonings to infuse throughout.

COOK THE QUESADILLAS

6 **Heat the oven** to its lowest setting. Heat the remaining oil in a frying pan and add 1 tortilla. Sprinkle with about 2 tbsp grated cheese, leaving a 1cm (½in) border. Put about 2 spoonfuls of the chicken mixture on top and cook until the cheese begins to melt.

7 **Using a palette knife,** fold the quesadilla over in half to enclose the filling. Cook for 1–2 minutes, until the tortilla is crispy and golden brown.

8 **Turn the quesadilla** over and cook until crispy. Transfer to a heatproof plate and keep warm in the oven while cooking the remaining quesadillas, adding oil to the pan as necessary. Halve the quesadillas and serve 3 halves on each plate with the guacamole, tomato-onion garnish, and chilli rings.

VARIATION: Pork quesadillas

Cubes of pork add body to the filling and again, this is an excellent way to use up cooked pork.

1 Prepare the filling ingredients, but omit the chicken and instead cut 500g (1lb 2oz) cooked, boneless pork into 2.5cm (1in) cubes. Use only 2 hot chillies and dice both of them. Use 60g (2oz) mild Cheddar cheese instead of Monterey Jack. Chop the leaves from 5-7 coriander sprigs quite finely and set aside.

2 Sauté all the chopped onion with the garlic and diced chillies, then add the pork and cook until browned, 3-5 minutes longer. Omit the chicken stock or water and stir in the chopped tomatoes. Continue cooking until the filling is slightly thickened, 5-7 minutes. Taste for seasoning and add salt and pepper and necessary; let cool slightly.

3 Omit the guacamole. Cook the quesadillas as directed, sprinkling each with 1-2 tsp Cheddar cheese and a pinch of chopped coriander before adding the pork filling and folding over the quesadillas. Cut into halves and serve decorated with finely sliced red onion rings and more coriander sprigs.

Parma ham pizzas

A WELCOME OPENING to any meal and enjoyed by children and adults alike. Vary the toppings as you prefer, adding sliced salami, grated Parmesan cheese, anchovies, olives, artichokes, chillies, or peppers, to taste. The dough and tomato sauce can be made up to 12 hours ahead, covered and kept refrigerated until needed.

SERVES	PREP	COOK
SERVES 8	15–20 MINS	5–10 MINS

Ingredients

FOR THE DOUGH

1½ tsp dried yeast or 9g (⅓oz) fresh yeast

375g (13oz) strong flour, plus more if needed

salt and pepper

2 tbsp olive oil, plus more for the bowl

FOR THE TOPPING

1–2 tbsp olive oil

1 small onion, diced

1 garlic clove, finely chopped

625g (1lb 6oz) tomatoes, peeled, deseeded, and chopped

1½ tbsp tomato purée

pinch of sugar

90g (3oz) Parma ham slices, cut into strips

small bunch of basil

375g (13oz) mozzarella cheese, thinly sliced

MAKE THE DOUGH

1 **Sprinkle or crumble the yeast** over 2–3 tbsp of lukewarm water in a small bowl; let stand for 5 minutes until completely dissolved and well blended. Make sure no crumbs of yeast remains on the side of the bowl, it should all be well mixed into the water. Sift the flour into a large bowl with 1 tsp salt, lifting the sieve high in the air to aerate the flour as it floats down, then add ½ tsp pepper.

2 **Make a well in the centre** of the flour and add the yeast mixture, making sure you leave none behind, 250ml (9fl oz) lukewarm water, and the oil. Work the ingredients together well with your hands, drawing in the dry ingredients from the centre until you reach the outside and all the flour is mixed into the wet ingredients.

3 **When the ingredients are combined,** continue to mix well with your hands, ensuring that there are no lumps in the mixture and that the crumbs of dough start to come together to form a ball. Empty the dough out of the bowl on to a lightly floured work surface, for kneading.

KNEAD THE DOUGH

4 **Draw in the flour** with a pastry scraper, if liked, or your hands, and work it into the other ingredients with your fingertips to form a smooth ball of dough.

5 **Peel back the dough** in one piece, then shape it into a loose ball and turn it 90 degrees. Continue kneading the dough by pushing it away from you and gathering it up into a ball, for 5–8 minutes, until it is smooth and very elastic.

6 **Lightly oil a large bowl.** Transfer the dough to the bowl, cover with cling film and let rise in a warm place for about 1 hour, until doubled in bulk. Alternatively, leave the dough to rise overnight in the refrigerator.

PREPARE THE TOPPING

7 Heat the olive oil in a small saucepan and sauté the onion and garlic for 1–2 minutes, until soft but not brown. Stir in the tomatoes, tomato purée, salt, pepper, and a pinch of sugar. Cook, stirring occasionally, for 7–10 minutes, until thick.

ASSEMBLE AND BAKE THE PIZZAS

8 Preheat the oven to 230°C (450°F/Gas 8) and place a baking sheet near the bottom. Generously sprinkle another baking sheet with flour. Knead the dough lightly to knock out the air and cut into 8 equal pieces. Lightly flour a work surface and shape 4 pieces of dough into balls.

9 Roll each ball into a 15cm (6in) round with a rolling pin, then transfer to the floured baking sheet. Fold over about 1cm (½inch) of the edge of each round with your fingertips to form a shallow rim, if you would like a deeper filling. Leave it flat if you prefer a thinner pizza.

10 Spoon half the tomato sauce on to the pizzas and arrange half the Parma ham on top. Place 2 basil leaves on each pizza and cover with half the slices of mozzarella cheese. Let stand in a warm place for 10–15 minutes, until the dough has puffed up.

11 Carefully transfer the pizzas on to the heated baking sheet and bake until the topping is lightly browned and the dough is crisp, 10–12 minutes. Shape, top, and bake the remaining 4 pizzas. Garnish with basil sprigs and serve at once.

Lemongrass chicken

A DELICIOUS WARM Southeast Asian salad. Chillies can vary wildly in strength, so choose ones as mild or as fiery as you dare! You may wish to wear kitchen gloves when slicing them, to protect your fingers from picking up their hot juices.

SERVES	PREP	COOK
SERVES 4	45–55 MINS PLUS MARINATING	10 MINS

Ingredients

FOR THE STIR-FRY

8 large skinless boneless chicken thighs, total weight about 1.15kg (2½lb)

2 stalks lemongrass, peeled and finely chopped

2 garlic cloves, finely chopped

3 tbsp fish sauce, more if needed

¼ tsp freshly ground black pepper

2 tbsp oil

2 red chillies, thinly sliced

1 tsp sugar

3 spring onions, thinly sliced

30g (1oz) roasted unsalted peanuts

FOR THE SALAD

1 small cucumber

leaves from ½ head of round lettuce

125g (4½oz) beansprouts

leaves from 1 small bunch basil, preferably Asian

PREPARE AND MARINADE THE CHICKEN

1 **Cut the chicken** into 2.5cm (1in) cubes. For the marinade, combine the lemongrass, garlic, 2 tbsp of the fish sauce, and the pepper in a large bowl and stir until well mixed. Add the chicken and toss until well coated. Cover the bowl tightly and refrigerate for at least 1 or up to 24 hours.

MAKE THE SALAD

2 **Trim the cucumber.** With a vegetable peeler, remove strips of its skin to create a striped effect. Slice in half lengthways, then slice each half finely. Arrange the lettuce, beansprouts, half the basil and the cucumber in piles on a plate. Cover tightly and chill.

MAKE THE STIR-FRY

3 **Heat a wok** over high heat until hot. Drizzle in the oil to coat the bottom and sides. Continue heating until the oil is hot. Add the chicken and marinade; stir-fry, stirring and tossing frequently, for 8–10 minutes, until the chicken is no longer pink.

4 **Add the remaining fish sauce,** the chillies, sugar, and spring onions. Stir-fry for about 1 minute. Add the remaining basil and toss quickly to mix. Taste for seasoning, adding more fish sauce, if necessary.

5 **Serve the chicken** with the salad. Invite each guest to make a bed of salad and top with chicken and a few peanuts.

Beef carpaccio

HERE, LEAN BEEF FILLET is semi-frozen so it is easy to cut into paper-thin slices, so thin, it's said, that light will shine through them. The success of the dish will depend on using the very best quality lean beef, so make friends with a butcher you can trust and don't rely on supermarket pre-wrapped meat for this recipe.

SERVES	PREP	COOK
SERVES 4	20-25 MINS PLUS FREEZING	NONE

Ingredients

500g (1lb 2oz) beef fillet

8 canned anchovy fillets

45g (1½oz) drained capers

125g (4½oz) rocket .

125g (4½oz) Parmesan cheese

1 small onion, very finely diced

2 lemons

125ml (4fl oz) extra virgin olive oil, or to taste

freshly ground black pepper

PREPARE THE BEEF AND GARNISHES

1 **Wrap the beef fillet** tightly in aluminium foil. Twist the ends of the foil to seal well and form a cracker shape, then freeze for 2½ –3 hours, until firm but not frozen solid.

2 **Meanwhile,** drain the anchovies and spread them out on kitchen paper. If the capers are large, coarsely chop them. Wash the rocket then dry the leaves very well with a tea towel and strip out and discard any tough stalks. Set aside.

ASSEMBLE THE CARPACCIO

3 **Take the beef** from the freezer and unwrap it. If the meat is too hard to cut, let it thaw slightly at room temperature. Using a very sharp knife, cut paper-thin slices from the fillet. Slice as much of the meat as you can; there will be a little left at the end.

4 **As you slice** the beef, arrange it, overlapping, on 4 plates. Shave over the Parmesan, using a vegetable peeler. Divide the anchovies, chopped onion, and capers between the plates. Squeeze the juice from the lemons and spoon over the beef. Sprinkle with the olive oil. Arrange the rocket on top. Serve at room temperature. Pass the pepper mill separately.

Nori-maki sushi

THE JAPANESE TERM 'SUSHI' covers a wide assortment of vinegared rice dishes. In *nori-maki*, a bamboo mat is used to roll sheets of roasted seaweed (*nori*), around a filling. Needless to say, the fish must be absolutely fresh.

SERVES	PREP	COOK
SERVES 12	50–60 MINS	12 MINS

Ingredients

FOR THE RICE

500g (1lb 2oz) short-grain white rice

75ml (2½fl oz) rice vinegar

2 tbsp caster sugar, more if needed

1 tsp salt, more if needed

FOR THE ROLLS

4 tsp wasabi powder

20cm (8in) piece of cucumber

125g (4½oz) fresh raw tuna, well chilled

6 sheets of *nori* (roasted seaweed)

TO SERVE

pink pickled ginger

Japanese soy sauce

PREPARE THE RICE

1 **Put the rice** in a bowl, cover with water, and stir until the water turns milky. Drain. Repeat until the water is fairly clear. Drain in a sieve, then put it in a saucepan. Add 600ml (1 pint) water, cover, and bring to a boil.

2 **Reduce the heat** to low and simmer until the water is absorbed and the rice is tender, about 12 minutes. Remove from the heat and let the rice stand, without lifting the lid, for about 30 minutes.

3 **Meanwhile**, in a small saucepan, combine the rice vinegar, sugar, and salt. Bring to a boil, stirring until the sugar dissolves. Let cool. Turn the hot rice into a bowl. Dampen a spatula with water. Drizzle the vinegar and sugar mixture evenly over the rice and mix together gently but thoroughly.

4 **Quickly cool the rice** to room temperature by fanning it while tossing with the spatula. Taste and add more vinegar, sugar, or salt if needed, then cover the bowl with a dampened tea towel.

PREPARE THE FILLING

5 **Put the wasabi powder** in a small bowl. Mix in 1 tbsp water to make a thick paste. Halve the cucumber lengthways and scoop out the seeds. Set one half cut-side down; cut it lengthways into 6 strips, then trim to the width of the roasted seaweed sheets. Reserve the other cucumber half for the decoration, if you like. Rinse the tuna and pat dry with kitchen paper. Cut it into 1cm (½in) slices, then into 1cm (½in) strips.

ASSEMBLE THE ROLLS

6 **Cut each sheet of seaweed** across in half with scissors. Lay one piece, smooth-side down, on a bamboo mat. Moisten your fingers, then spread about 90g (3oz) of the cooked rice in an even 5mm (¼in) layer on the seaweed, leaving a 1cm (½in) strip uncovered at the end furthest from you. Spread a thin line of wasabi lengthways along the centre of the rice. Arrange one of the cucumber strips lengthways over the wasabi paste.

7 **Make 6 cucumber rolls:** Starting from the edge closest to you, lift the mat and seaweed securely together and roll away from you over the filling. Press down firmly and roll up the seaweed, lifting the mat at the same time.

8 **Once you have reached** the exposed end of the seaweed, moisten it lightly with wet fingertips to seal the roll. Wrap and press the mat around the roll to shape a smooth, tight cylinder. Unroll the mat and transfer the cucumber roll to the chopping board. Repeat to make 5 more cucumber rolls.

9 **Make 6 tuna sushi rolls** in the same way as the cucumber rolls, piecing the tuna strips together as necessary to cover the full length of the seaweed and rice.

CUT AND SERVE

10 **Moisten a sharp knife** with a damp tea towel. Cut 1 cucumber roll into 3 equal pieces, wiping the knife clean between cuts with the damp towel. Cut each small piece of cucumber roll crosswise in half. Repeat with the remaining rolls.

11 **Cut each tuna roll** crosswise into 8 equal pieces, again wiping the knife with the damp cloth between cuts. This will help each cut be sharp and clean, to keep each roll looking pristine on its cut edges.

12 **Divide the pieces of tuna** and cucumber *nori-maki* among 12 individual serving plates, or on a large platter for the whole table of diners, setting them neatest side up.

13 **Decorate each plate** with pickled ginger, if you like, or leave it in a big pile on the table for your guests to serve themselves. Serve with Japanese soy sauce, decanted into small bowls, for dipping, and make sure you have supplied chopsticks on the table.

Salads

Fresh and light, or hearty
and filling; on the side,
or a meal in itself

Herb and flower garden salad

FEEL FREE TO TRY A NUT OIL, or a favourite vinegar, until you achieve your perfect vinaigrette. A sprinkling of edible flowers, or just their petals (make sure they are unsprayed), makes a beautiful finishing touch. Serve this during high summer.

SERVES	PREP	COOK
SERVES 8	15–30 MINS	NONE

Ingredients

FOR THE SALAD

2 heads of chicory

leaves from 1 small head of frisée

leaves from 1 head of radicchio

125g (4½oz) lamb's lettuce

125g (4½oz) rocket

1 small bunch of chives, with flowers if possible

leaves from 5–7 basil sprigs

leaves from 5–7 tarragon sprigs

1 package of edible flowers (optional)

FOR THE VINAIGRETTE

4 tbsp red wine vinegar

salt and pepper

2 tsp Dijon mustard (optional)

175ml (6fl oz) extra-virgin olive oil

PREPARE THE GREENS

1 **Using a small knife,** cut out and discard the core from the base of each head of chicory. Discard any withered leaves, and cut into 1cm (½in) diagonal slices. Put in a large bowl with the frisée, radicchio, lamb's lettuce, and rocket.

PREPARE THE HERBS AND DRESSING

2 **If the chives have flowers,** cut them 5cm (2in) below the flowers, and set aside. Snip the remaining chives into 2.5cm (1in) lengths. Add the chives, basil, and tarragon to the salad leaves.

3 **In a small bowl,** whisk the vinegar with the salt, pepper, and mustard, if using. Gradually whisk in the oil in a steady steam, until it emulsifies and thickens slightly. Taste for seasoning.

FINISH THE SALAD

4 **Briskly whisk the vinaigrette,** and pour it over the salad. Gently toss, until the greens are evenly coated. Taste the leaves, to be sure the seasoning is well-balanced.

5 **Carefully arrange any chive flowers** and other edible flowers or petals on top of the salad. Serve immediately, while the leaves and flowers are still fresh and vibrant.

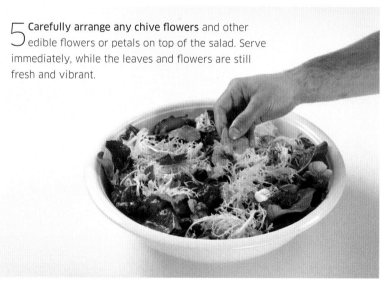

Marinated goat's cheese salad

A GLASS JAR of little goat's cheeses, herbs, and chillies in golden oil is an eye-catcher in any kitchen. The goat's cheese should be firm but not dry. You'll need to begin marinading it 1 week in advance of serving, for the best flavour.

SERVES	PREP	COOK
SERVES 8	20–25 MINS PLUS MARINATING	5–8 MINS

Ingredients

8 slices of wholemeal bread

FOR THE MARINATED GOAT'S CHEESES

4 small round goat's cheeses, each weighing about 60–90g (2–3oz) each, or 1 goat cheese log, weighing about 320g (11oz)

2 bay leaves

2–3 thyme sprigs

2–3 rosemary sprigs

2–3 oregano sprigs

2 tsp black peppercorns

2 small dried red chillies

500ml (16fl oz) olive oil, plus more if needed

FOR THE VINAIGRETTE

2 tbsp red wine vinegar

1 tsp Dijon mustard

salt and pepper

leaves from 5–7 thyme sprigs

FOR THE SALAD

2 heads chicory, leaves separated

1 oak leaf lettuce, leaves separated

MARINATE THE CHEESES

1 **Put the cheeses** in a large glass jar with the bay leaves, thyme, rosemary, oregano, peppercorns, and chillies. Add enough oil to cover generously. Cover and leave at least 1 week before using. Alternatively, if using a goat's cheese log, put it in a non-metallic bowl with the other ingredients, cover with clingfilm and marinate for 1–3 days.

MAKE THE VINAIGRETTE

2 **Remove the cheeses** from the marinade with a slotted spoon, draining off excess oil. Strain the oil. You will need 90ml (3fl oz) for the vinaigrette and a little more for the bread.

3 **Whisk the vinegar in the bowl** with the mustard, salt, and pepper. Gradually whisk in the reserved oil so the vinaigrette emulsifies and thickens slightly. Stir in half the thyme and taste for seasoning.

MAKE THE GOAT'S CHEESE TOASTS

4 **Preheat the oven** to 200°C (400°F/Gas 6). Cut each goat cheese in half horizontally. If using a goat cheese log, cut it into 8 equal slices. With a pastry cutter, cut out a round from each slice of bread.

5 **Set the bread rounds** on a baking sheet and brush with a little of the strained olive oil. Bake for 3–5 minutes, until lightly toasted. Heat the grill. Put a piece of cheese on top of each toasted bread round. Grill for 2–3 minutes, until bubbling and golden.

6 **Arrange the salad leaves** on individual plates and drizzle with the vinaigrette. Place the cheese toasts on top and sprinkle with thyme.

Tuna Niçoise salad

MADE WITH CANNED TUNA ORIGINALLY, these days using the fresh fish is far more popular. This salad is from Nice in southern France, home town of the great French chef, Escoffier, who wrote various recipes for it. The dressing can be made up to 1 week ahead and stored in a sealed jar in the refrigerator; do not add the garlic and herbs until just before using.

SERVES	PREP	COOK
SERVES 6	25-30 MINS PLUS MARINATING	20-25 MINS

Ingredients

FOR THE SALAD

1kg (2¼lb) potatoes

1kg (2¼lb) fresh tuna steaks

salt and pepper

375g (13oz) French beans

6 eggs

500g (1lb 2oz) tomatoes

10 anchovy fillets

125g (4½oz) black olives

FOR THE HERB VINAIGRETTE

125ml (4fl oz) red wine vinegar

2 tsp Dijon mustard

3 garlic cloves, finely chopped

375ml (12fl oz) olive oil

leaves from 7-10 thyme sprigs

leaves from 1 bunch of chervil, chopped

COOK THE POTATOES AND MAKE THE DRESSING

1 **Peel the potatoes** and, if large, cut each into 2-4 pieces. Put them in a large saucepan of cold, salted water, cover, and bring to a boil. Simmer just until tender when pierced with the tip of a knife, 15-20 minutes.

2 **Meanwhile,** make the vinaigrette. In a bowl, whisk the vinegar with the mustard, garlic, salt, and pepper. Slowly whisk in the olive oil so the dressing emulsifies and thickens slightly. Add the herbs, whisk well, and taste for seasoning.

3 **Drain the potatoes,** rinse with warm water and drain again thoroughly. Cut into chunks and put them in a large bowl. Briskly whisk the vinaigrette then spoon 75ml (2½fl oz) of it over the warm potatoes, stir, and allow to cool.

PREPARE THE TUNA

4 **Cut the tuna** into 2.5cm (1in) cubes and transfer to a shallow, non-metallic dish. Briskly whisk the herb vinaigrette dressing and pour over 75ml (2½fl oz) . Cover and refrigerate, turning occasionally, for 1 hour.

PREPARE THE SALAD

5 **Top and tail the beans.** Bring a saucepan of salted water to a boil, add the beans and cook for 5-7 minutes, until tender but still firm, then drain. Put the beans in a bowl. Whisk the remaining vinaigrette and add 3 tbsp of it to the beans. Toss them to coat.

6 **Put the eggs** in a saucepan of cold water, bring to a boil, and simmer for 10 minutes. Plunge into a bowl of cold water to cool, then shell and cut each into quarters.

PREPARE THE TOMATOES

7 **Bring a small saucepan** of water to a boil. Cut the cores from the tomatoes and score an 'X' on the base of each with a small knife.

8 **Immerse the tomatoes** in the boiling water until the skins start to split, 8-15 seconds, depending on their ripeness. Transfer them at once to a bowl of cold water.

9 When the tomatoes are cool, peel off the skins. Cut each tomato in half, then slice each half into 4 wedges.

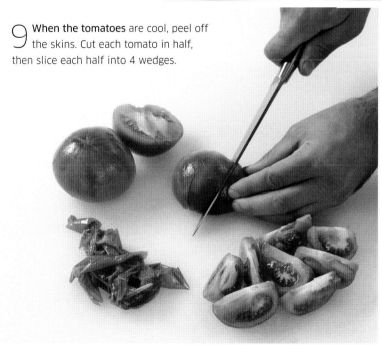

ASSEMBLE THE SALAD AND COOK THE TUNA

10 Drain the anchovies. Arrange the potatoes, beans, egg, and tomato attractively on a large platter, or on individual plates if you prefer. Briskly whisk the remaining dressing and spoon most of it evenly over everything, making sure all the elements on the plate are well moistened. Do not dress the salad too far in advance or the vinegar will start to break down the tomatoes and make them mushy in texture.

11 Heat the grill and oil the grill rack. Put the tuna on the rack, reserving the marinade, and season the fish well. Grill the tuna about 7.5cm (3in) from the heat for about 2 minutes. Turn, baste with some of the reserved marinade and grill until lightly brown on the outside but still slightly rare in the centre, about 2 minutes longer. It is very important to retain a juicy pink centre to each tuna piece, so do not overcook or the fish will be dry and mealy in texture.

12 Arrange the grilled tuna, olives, and anchovy fillets attractively on top of the salad platter or the individual plates. Pour over any remaining vinaigrette and serve immediately, while the fish is still warm and all the elements of the salad remain sprightly and crisp.

Creamy coleslaw

THIS SALAD MAKES A GENEROUS QUANTITY for a party, or the recipe can easily be halved. This version of the old favourite is pepped up with caraway seeds, soured cream and mustard powder. You can make the coleslaw 2 days in advance and keep it, covered, in the refrigerator. You'll find that a generous bowlful of this on any buffet table will disappear far more quickly than you expected.

SERVES	PREP	COOK
SERVES 8-10	15-20 MINS PLUS CHILLING	NONE

Ingredients

FOR THE SALAD

500g (1lb 2oz) carrots

1 white cabbage, weighing about 1.4kg (3lb)

1 onion, finely diced

FOR THE SOURED CREAM DRESSING

2 tbsp sugar

salt and pepper

250ml (8fl oz) soured cream

175ml (6fl oz) cider vinegar

2 tsp mustard powder

2 tsp caraway seeds

250ml (8fl oz) mayonnaise

PREPARE THE SALAD INGREDIENTS

1 **Trim and peel the carrots.** Using the coarse side of a grater, grate them all. Leave them in a bowl of iced water for half an hour; you wil find the carrot strips will crisp up. Drain them very well, then wrap in a clean tea towel and shake to remove all the excess water.

2 **Trim the cabbage** and discard any wilted leaves. Cut it into quarters then cut out and discard the core. Shred the leaves into a large bowl using a mandoline, discarding any thick ribs. Alternatively, shred the cabbage in a food processor, using the slicing blade.

MAKE THE DRESSING

3 **Put the sugar,** salt, pepper, soured cream, and cider vinegar in a bowl. Add the mustard powder and caraway seeds. Add the mayonnaise and whisk to combine. Taste for seasoning.

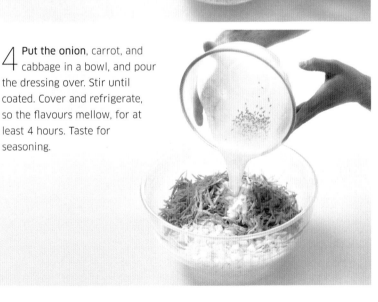

4 **Put the onion,** carrot, and cabbage in a bowl, and pour the dressing over. Stir until coated. Cover and refrigerate, so the flavours mellow, for at least 4 hours. Taste for seasoning.

FINISH THE SALAD

5 **Remove the coleslaw** from the refrigerator, and stir it once more to redistribute the dressing (you may find it has sunk to the bottom of the bowl in the refrigerator). Serve chilled.

Caesar salad

THE SUCCESS OF THIS CLASSIC DISH depends on crisp cos lettuce and the best quality Parmesan cheese, while the anchovies in the dressing are essential. The garlic croutons can be made 1 day in advance and stored in an airtight container.

SERVES	**PREP**	**COOK**
SERVES 6-8	20-25 MINS	2-3 MINS

Ingredients

FOR THE GARLIC CROUTONS

½ a day-old baguette

4 tbsp olive oil

3 garlic cloves, peeled

FOR THE DRESSING

6 anchovy fillets

3 garlic cloves, finely chopped

1 tbsp Dijon mustard

pepper

juice of 1 lemon

175ml (6fl oz) olive oil

FOR THE SALAD

1 cos lettuce, weighing about 1kg (2¼lb), leaves torn into pieces

1 egg

125g (4½oz) Parmesan cheese, freshly grated

MAKE THE GARLIC CROUTONS

1 **Cut the baguette** into 1cm (½in) slices, then into cubes. Heat the oil in a large frying pan. Add the garlic and bread and fry, stirring constantly, for 2-3 minutes, until golden. Tip the croutons on to kitchen paper to drain of any excess oil. Discard the garlic.

MAKE THE DRESSING

2 **Put the anchovy fillets** into a large salad bowl and crush them with a table fork. Add the garlic, mustard, pepper, and lemon juice and stir.

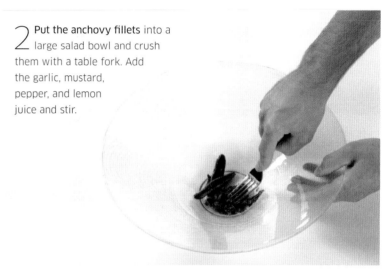

3 **Gradually whisk in the oil** so the dressing emulsifies and thickens slightly, and taste for seasoning.

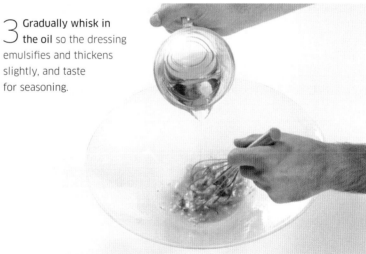

MAKE THE SALAD

4 **Add the lettuce** to the dressing and toss until well coated. Crack the egg into a small bowl, beat it with a fork, then add it to the leaves and dressing and toss together.

5 **Add half the croutons** and two-thirds of the Parmesan and toss again. Taste a piece of lettuce for seasoning, adding salt only if necessary; the cheese and anchovies are already salty. Serve the salad directly from the bowl and pass the remaining Parmesan and croutons separately.

Roast pepper and artichoke salad

ARTICHOKE HEARTS and roasted red peppers are delicious with the crunch of pine nuts. The blue cheese wafers here add a wonderful piquancy and, once tasted, will become a favourite accompaniment to all sorts of dishes.

SERVES	PREP	COOK
SERVES 8	40-45 MINS PLUS FREEZING	25-35 MINS

Ingredients

FOR THE CHEESE WAFERS

125g (4½oz) Stilton, Danish blue, or Roquefort cheese, chilled

125g (4½oz) Cambozola or Bavarian blue cheese, chilled

125g (4½oz) butter, at room temperature

175g (6oz) plain flour

FOR THE DRESSING

4 tbsp balsamic vinegar

2 tbsp Dijon mustard

salt and pepper

175ml (6fl oz) olive oil

FOR THE SALAD

3 red peppers

60g (2oz) pine nuts

leaves from 1 head of lollo rosso

leaves from 1 round lettuce

250g (9oz) spinach leaves

180g (6oz) jar artichoke heart in oil, drained

MAKE THE CHEESE WAFER DOUGH

1 Cut the cheeses into chunks, discarding the rind, and allow to come to room temperature. Beat the butter in a bowl until softened, then add the blue cheese.

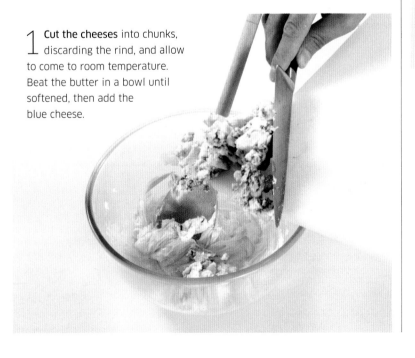

2 Beat the chunks of cheese into the butter with the wooden spoon, until they are evenly blended in and the mixture is creamy and smooth.

3 Add the flour and stir with a wooden spoon just until the dough comes together into a ball.

ROLL AND FREEZE THE CHEESE WAFER DOUGH

4 Set a 30x30cm (12x12in) piece of baking parchment on a work surface. Transfer the dough to the paper and spread it as evenly as possible along the length.

5 Roll the paper tightly around the dough, shaping it into a cylinder 4cm (1½in) in diameter. Twist the ends of the paper to seal. Put the dough in the freezer for 1-2 hours, until firm.

MAKE THE DRESSING

6 Whisk the balsamic vinegar, mustard, and salt and pepper together in a small bowl. Gradually whisk in the oil so the vinaigrette emulsifies and thickens slightly.

ROAST THE PEPPERS

7 **Heat the grill** and set the red peppers on the rack. Grill about 10cm (4in) from the heat, turning, for about 10-12 minutes, until black and blistered all over. Put them in a plastic food bag, seal, and leave until cool enough to handle.

8 **Peel off the skin,** then halve each pepper and cut out and discard the core, white pith that runs along the ribs, and seeds. Cut the flesh into even strips.

TOAST THE PINE NUTS

9 **Put the pine nuts** into a dry frying pan and place over a medium heat, shaking and watching constantly, until golden and toasted but not burned. Remove to a plate and set aside. Do not leave the pine nuts in the pan to cool, as they will continue to cook and may scorch. Any burning of the pine nuts will mar their flavour.

BAKE THE CHEESE WAFERS

10 **Preheat the oven** to 180°C (350°F/Gas 4). Cut 6 slices, each about 5mm (¼inch) thick, from the cheese wafer dough, using a thin-bladed knife dipped in hot water. Space out on a baking sheet. Re-wrap and return the remaining dough to the freezer.

11 **Bake the wafers** for 6-8 minutes, until lacy and golden brown. Allow to cool slightly, then carefully transfer to a wire rack lined with kitchen paper. Allow the baking sheet to cool, slice more of the dough, and continue baking the cheese wafers.

ASSEMBLE AND SERVE THE SALAD

12 **Put all the leaves** in a large salad bowl and add the peppers. Toss with the vinaigrette and sprinkle with pine nuts. Top with the artichoke hearts, arrange a few wafers on top and serve the rest alongside.

Greek salad

A **CLASSIC, DEEPLY REFRESHING** combination that needs very ripe, flavourful tomatoes. Make sure you use very tasty, pungent black olives, and an aromatic, strong extra-virgin olive oil for the dressing, for the best results.

SERVES	PREP	COOK
SERVES 6–8	25–30 MINS PLUS STANDING	NONE

Ingredients

FOR THE HERB VINAIGRETTE

3 tbsp red wine vinegar

salt and pepper

125ml (4fl oz) extra-virgin olive oil

leaves from 3–5 mint sprigs, finely chopped

leaves from 3–5 oregano sprigs, finely chopped

leaves from 7–10 parsley sprigs, finely chopped

FOR THE SALAD

2 small cucumbers

1kg (2¼lb) tomatoes

1 red onion

2 green peppers, cored, deseeded, and diced

125g (4½oz) Kalamata or other Greek olives

175g (6oz) feta cheese, cubed

MAKE THE HERB VINAIGRETTE

1 Whisk together the vinegar, salt, and pepper. Gradually whisk in the oil so the vinaigrette emulsifies and thickens slightly. Add the herbs, then whisk again and taste for seasoning.

PREPARE THE CUCUMBER

2 Peel the cucumbers and cut each in half lengthways. Scoop out the seeds with a teaspoon. Discard the seeds.

3 Cut them lengthways into 2–3 strips, then into 1cm (½in) slices.

PREPARE THE OTHER VEGETABLES

4 With the tip of a small knife, core the tomatoes. Cut each one into 8 wedges, then cut each wedge in half. Peel and trim the red onion and cut into very thin rings. Gently separate the concentric circles within each ring with your fingers.

ASSEMBLE THE SALAD

5 Put the cucumbers, tomatoes, onion rings, and peppers in a large bowl. Briskly whisk the dressing, pour it over and toss thoroughly. Add the olives and feta and gently toss again. Taste for seasoning. In Greece, olives would be left whole, but you may prefer to stone them. Allow the flavours to mellow for about 30 minutes before serving.

Warm salad of wild mushrooms

WILD MUSHROOMS ARE A TRUE DELICACY calling for the simplest preparation. To make expensive wild mushrooms go further, you can replace half of the amount with field mushrooms for this salad.

SERVES	PREP	COOK
SERVES 4	25-30 MINS	8-10 MINS

Ingredients

FOR THE VINAIGRETTE

2 tbsp red wine vinegar

½ tsp Dijon mustard

salt and pepper

3 tbsp vegetable oil

3 tbsp walnut oil

FOR THE SALAD

375g (13oz) mixed wild mushrooms, such as chanterelles, oyster mushrooms, and ceps

30-45 g (1-1½oz) butter

2 shallots, finely diced

leaves from 1 small head of frisée

leaves from 1 small head of radicchio

75g (2½oz) rocket

leaves from 1 small bunch of parsley, chopped

MAKE THE VINAIGRETTE

1 **In a bowl,** whisk together the vinegar, mustard, and salt and pepper. Gradually whisk in the vegetable and walnut oils so the vinaigrette emulsifies and thickens slightly. Taste for seasoning.

PREPARE THE MUSHROOMS

2 **Wipe the wild mushrooms** with damp kitchen paper. Trim the stalks and remove woody portions.

3 **Place the mushrooms on** a chopping board and cut them into medium pieces.

COOK THE MUSHROOMS AND FINISH THE SALAD

4 **Heat the butter** in a frying pan until foaming. Add the shallots and cook, stirring occasionally, for 2-3 minutes, until soft. Add the mushrooms and salt and pepper. Cook, stirring, for 5-7 minutes, until the mushrooms are tender and all the liquid has evaporated. Stir in the parsley and taste for seasoning, adjusting if necessary.

5 **Briskly whisk the vinaigrette** to re-emulsify it, then pour it over the salad leaves in a bowl and toss them well until all are coated. Taste for seasoning. Divide the salad leaves between 4 plates and spoon over the mushrooms from the pan. Serve at once while the salad remains crisp and the mushrooms are still warm from the stove.

Prawn, courgette, and saffron salad

SHELLFISH AND SAFFRON have an extraordinary affinity, which is celebrated in this dish. In fact, so successful has the combination always been that a very similar recipe to this was recorded 600 years ago in Italy.

SERVES	PREP	COOK
SERVES 6	30-35 MINS PLUS MARINATING	6-10 MINS

Ingredients

1 large pinch of saffron threads

3 lemons

6 garlic cloves, coarsely chopped

4 tbsp white wine vinegar

salt and pepper

250ml (9fl oz) olive oil

4 tbsp capers, drained

500g (1lb 2oz) courgettes, halved and sliced

18 raw, unpeeled jumbo prawns

MAKE THE MARINADE AND **MARINATE** THE COURGETTES

1 Put the saffron in a bowl and pour over 2 tbsp hot water. Leave for 5 minutes. Squeeze in the juice from 2 of the lemons and add the garlic, vinegar, salt, pepper, olive oil, and capers. Stir, lightly crushing the capers to extract their flavour. Put the courgettes into a shallow non-metallic dish and spoon over two-thirds of the marinade. Toss, cover and refrigerate for 3-4 hours. Cut the remaining lemons into wedges and set aside for serving.

PREPARE AND **MARINATE** THE PRAWNS

2 Hold each prawn, underside-up, on a chopping board. Leaving the tail end intact, cut each in half to open in a butterfly shape.

3 Pull out and discard the dark intestinal vein running along the back of each prawn. Rinse the prawns under cold, running water then place on kitchen paper and pat dry.

4 Put the prawns into another non-metallic dish, spoon the remaining marinade over and toss to coat. Cover and refrigerate for 3-4 hours.

COOK THE COURGETTES AND PRAWNS

5 **Heat a frying pan,** then add the courgettes along with all their marinade. Simmer, stirring, for 3–5 minutes, just until the slices are tender but still retain a little bite. Meanwhile, heat the grill and oil the grill rack. Take each prawn from the marinade and set it, cut-side up, on the rack. Brush each with a little marinade and spoon over the capers, retaining some marinade to brush over the prawns while grilling.

6 **Grill the prawns** about 5cm (2in) from the heat for 3–4 minutes, until pink and sizzling fiercely, brushing with the reserved marinade once or twice during cooking to keep them as moist and juicy as possible. Do not overcook the prawns, or they will be tough. You will find that they cook in very little time. Slice the remaining lemon into thin wedges.

7 **Pile the warm courgettes** into the centre of 6 warmed plates, moistening them with some of the marinade, and spread them out to make an attractive bed. Arrange the hot, butterflied prawns on top and serve with the lemon wedges.

 VARIATION: Marinated prawn and mushroom salad

A simple antipasto

1 Prepare the marinade as directed, omitting the saffron. Butterfly and devein the unpeeled prawns as directed. Marinate the butterflied prawns as directed, using one-third of the marinade.

2 Omit the courgettes. Wipe the caps of 375g (13oz) button or field mushrooms, trim the stalks, and cut any large mushrooms into quarters. Bring a small pan of salted water to a boil, add the mushrooms and simmer for 5–7 minutes. Drain very well, then add the mushrooms to the remaining marinade, stir, cover, and refrigerate for 3–4 hours.

3 Using a slotted spoon, divide the mushrooms among 6 plates, discarding the marinade. Grill the prawns as directed, add to the plates and serve immediately.

Spiced seafood salad

THIS TANGY THAI DISH is light and refreshing, just perfect for summer. When served immediately, the flavour is delicate; if left overnight, it becomes a little more pungent. Choose the version that suits your palate best.

SERVES	PREP	COOK
SERVES 4	30-40 MINS	12-15 MINS

Ingredients

FOR THE SALAD

250g (9oz) small squid, cleaned

250g (9oz) large scallops, trimmed

salt

250g (9oz) boneless white fish steak or fillet

250g (9oz) raw, shelled large prawns

small lettuce leaves, to serve

FOR THE DRESSING

4 kaffir lime leaves, or finely grated zest of 1 lime

2 garlic cloves, finely chopped

1 green chilli, finely chopped

1 stalk lemongrass, peeled, crushed, and thinly sliced

juice of 3 large limes, plus more if needed

4 tbsp fish sauce, plus more if needed

2 tbsp sugar

PREPARE THE SEAFOOD

1 **Cut the squid bodies** into 1cm (½in) wide rings. Cut the tentacles into 2-3 pieces if large. Cut the scallops horizontally into 2 rounds. Line a tray with kitchen paper. Fill a large saucepan with 5cm (2in) of water, add a pinch of salt and bring to a boil. Reduce the heat, add the squid and simmer for about 2 minutes, until opaque and starting to curl. Remove and drain on the kitchen paper. Repeat with the white fish.

2 **Add the prawns** to the simmering water and cook for 1-2 minutes, or just until they turn pink. Remove and drain on the kitchen paper. Repeat with the scallop slices.

MAKE THE DRESSING AND ASSEMBLE THE SALAD

3 **Cut out any hard central veins** from the lime leaves, if necessary. Very finely dice the leaves. Put the lime leaves, garlic, chilli, lemongrass, lime juice, fish sauce, and sugar in a small bowl. Stir until the sugar dissolves.

4 **Put the squid, scallops, and prawns** in a large bowl. Pour the dressing over the seafood. Toss the mixture to coat. Remove any skin from the white fish then add it, tossing gently to break into large pieces. Taste for seasoning, adding more lime juice or fish sauce if necessary.

5 **Arrange a bed of lettuce leaves** on individual plates, then mound a pile of the dressed seafood on top.

Cucumber-chilli salad

DELICIOUS WITH GRILLED OR BARBECUED DISHES. The longer it's left to marinate, the spicier it will be, but even if you like a milder dish, do give it at least 1 hour to allow the flavours to meld. This is an incredibly useful recipe to have in your repertoire, and you may well find yourself making it all the time to accompany rich meat dishes.

SERVES	PREP	COOK
SERVES 4	15-20 MINS	NONE

Ingredients

125g (4½oz) caster sugar, or to taste

½ tsp salt, or to taste

125ml (4fl oz) rice vinegar, or to taste

1 cucumber

1 hot red chilli

MAKE THE MARINADE AND PREPARE THE CUCUMBER

1 Pour 125ml (4fl oz) water into a small pan and tip in the sugar and salt. Place over a medium heat and stir until the sugar dissolves, then bring to a boil. Remove from the heat, stir in the vinegar and let cool.

2 **Peel and trim the cucumber.** Cut it lengthways in half, and scoop out the seeds with a teaspoon. Cut the halves across into thin slices.

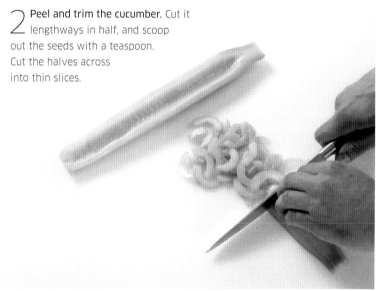

PREPARE THE CHILLI

3 **Wearing rubber gloves,** cut the chilli lengthways in half, discarding the core. Scrape out the seeds and cut away the fleshy white ribs from each chilli half. Cut each half lengthways into very thin strips

MAKE AND MARINATE THE SALAD

4 **Combine the cucumber,** chilli, and vinegar mixture in a bowl. Cover and marinate in the refrigerator for at least 1 and up to 4 hours. Taste just before serving, adding more salt, sugar, or vinegar to taste.

Melon and mint salad

THE SWEETLY KITSCH PRESENTATION used here will add fun to any summer meal. This refreshing salad, with its sweet and savoury dressing, is ideal to accompany cold meats on a picnic. It can be made up to 6 hours ahead and kept, covered and without the dressing, in the refrigerator.

SERVES
SERVES 6

PREP
15–20 MINS,
PLUS CHILLING

COOK
NONE

Ingredients

FOR THE SALAD

2 small orange- or yellow-fleshed melons, such as cantaloupe, total weight about 1.4kg (3lb)

1 medium green-fleshed melon, such as honeydew, weighing about 1.4kg (3lb)

375g (13oz) cherry tomatoes

1 bunch of mint

FOR THE DRESSING

75ml (2½fl oz) port

juice of 2 lemons

2 tbsp honey

salt and pepper

PREPARE THE MELONS

1 **Halve the melons,** scoop out the seeds with a spoon and discard.

2 **Using a melon baller,** cut balls from the flesh of each melon into a large bowl.

PREPARE THE SALAD INGREDIENTS

3 **Remove the stalks** from the cherry tomatoes. Immerse in a saucepan of boiling water very briefly, just until the skins start to split, then plunge into a bowl of cold water. When cold, peel off the skins. Add the tomatoes to the melon.

4 **Strip the mint leaves** from the stalks, reserving some sprigs for garnish. Pile the mint leaves on a board and coarsely chop. Add the mint to the melon and tomatoes.

MAKE THE DRESSING AND DRESS THE SALAD

5 **Put the port** in a bowl. Add the lemon juice, honey, salt, and pepper and whisk. Taste for seasoning. Pour the dressing over the melon, tomatoes, and mint. Stir gently, and taste for seasoning, adding more of any of the dressing ingredients if you like. Cover the bowl and refrigerate, so the flavours mellow, about 1 hour. Serve in melon shells for extra kitsch value, or in pretty bowls, decorated with the reserved mint sprigs.

Avocado, grapefruit, and Parma ham

GREAT FLAVOUR AND TEXTURE contrasts, with the sweet and silky Parma ham against the bitter rocket and sharp grapefruit. As ever when using avocado, be sure it is completely covered with citrus juice – in this case, grapefruit – to prevent any unattractive discolouration.

   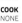

SERVES	PREP	COOK
SERVES 4	25–30 MINS	NONE

Ingredients

FOR THE POPPY-SEED VINAIGRETTE

½ small onion

3 tbsp red wine vinegar

1 tbsp honey

½ tsp mustard powder

¼ tsp ground ginger

salt and pepper

150ml (5fl oz) vegetable oil

1 tbsp poppy seeds

FOR THE SALAD

4 grapefruit

125g (4½oz) Parma ham

2 avocados

175g (6oz) rocket leaves

MAKE THE VINAIGRETTE

1 **Grate the onion** into a bowl, add the vinegar, honey, mustard powder, ginger, salt, and pepper and whisk. Gradually whisk in the oil so the vinaigrette emulsifies and thickens slightly. Stir in the poppy seeds and taste for seasoning.

PREPARE THE GRAPEFRUIT

2 **With a vegetable peeler,** peel half of the zest from 1 grapefruit, leaving behind the white pith. Cut into very fine julienne strips. Half-fill a small saucepan with water and bring to a boil. Add the grapefruit julienne, simmer 2 minutes, drain and set aside.

3 **Slice off the top and base of the grapefruits.** Cut away the zest, pith and skin, following the curve of the fruit. Holding each grapefruit over a bowl, cut out the segments, cutting down between the membranes. Release the segments into the bowl. Discard any seeds, cover, and refrigerate.

PREPARE THE SALAD INGREDIENTS

4 **Cut the Parma ham** into 2.5cm (1in) strips, cutting off and discarding any fat from the slices. Cut lengthways around each avocado, through to the stone. Twist and pull the halves apart. With a chopping movement, embed the blade of a knife into the stone, lift it free, and discard.

5 **Peel the avocados** and slice lengthways. Brush the slices on all surfaces with grapefruit juice so they do not discolour. Be sure to be punctilious about this, to avoid any of your diners receiving an ugly, browning slice.

ASSEMBLE THE SALAD

6 **Briskly whisk the dressing.** Toss the rocket with one-third of it, taste for seasoning, then divide between 4 plates. Arrange the grapefruit, Parma ham, and avocado on top. Spoon over the remaining vinaigrette and sprinkle with grapefruit julienne.

Gado-gado

THE PEANUT SAUCE can be made spicy or sweet, as you prefer. Feel free to use this recipe as a blueprint, adding whatever fresh vegetables are in season. This is a version to make in winter, using the produce of the cooler months. The vegetables can be blanched and the peanut sauce made 1 day ahead and kept, covered, in the refrigerator.

SERVES	PREP	COOK
SERVES 8	35-45 MINS	20-25 MINS

Ingredients

FOR THE SALAD

florets from 1 small cauliflower

salt and pepper

500g (1lb 2oz) carrots, cut into 5cm (2in) batons

375g (13oz) beansprouts

300g (10oz) tofu

500g (1lb 2oz) cucumbers, cut into 5cm (2in) batons

3 eggs

1 tbsp vegetable oil

FOR THE PEANUT SAUCE

125ml (4fl oz) vegetable oil

250g (9oz) unsalted peanuts

1 onion, finely chopped

3 garlic cloves, finely chopped

½ tsp crushed chillies

1 tbsp soy sauce

juice of 1 lime

2 tsp brown sugar

200ml (7fl oz) canned coconut milk

PREPARE THE VEGETABLES AND TOFU

1 **Cut any large cauliflower** florets in half. Bring a large saucepan of salted water to a boil. Add the florets and boil for 5-7 minutes, just until tender. Drain.

2 **Put the carrots** in a saucepan of cold, salted water. Bring to a boil and simmer for 3-5 minutes, just until tender. Drain.

3 **Put the beansprouts** in a bowl. Cover with boiling water and let stand, 1 minute. Drain. Drain the tofu then cut into 1cm (½in) cubes.

MAKE THE OMELETTE

4 **Beat the eggs** and seaon to taste. Heat the oil in a frying pan. Pour in the eggs, tilting to make an even layer. Cook over medium heat for 2 minutes, until the edge is slightly crispy and pulls away from the side.

5 **Turn and cook** for about 30 seconds, until firm. Slide on to a chopping board, let it cool slightly, then roll it up loosely and cut across the width into curled strips.

MAKE THE PEANUT SAUCE

6 **Heat half the oil** in a frying pan. Add the peanuts and cook, stirring, for 3-5 minutes, until brown. Transfer to a food processor and pulse-chop until slightly chunky.

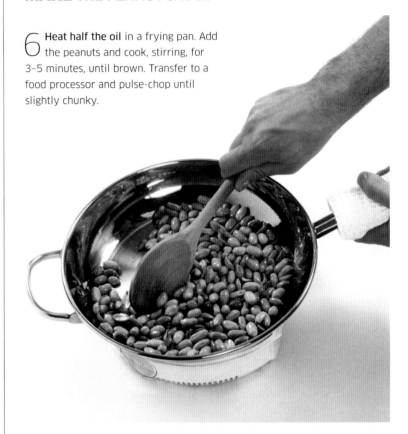

7 **Heat the remaining oil** in the frying pan and cook the onion, stirring, for 2-3 minutes, until lightly brown. Add the garlic and chillies, and cook until golden. Add the soy sauce and lime juice. Remove from the heat. Stir in the brown sugar and ground peanuts.

8 Gradually add the coconut milk to the peanut sauce, and stir until smooth and creamy. Season to taste. Arrange the bean sprouts on a serving platter, or on individual plates, and top with the carrots, cucumbers, tofu cubes, and cauliflower. Garnish with the omelette curls and serve the peanut sauce in a small bowl on the side.

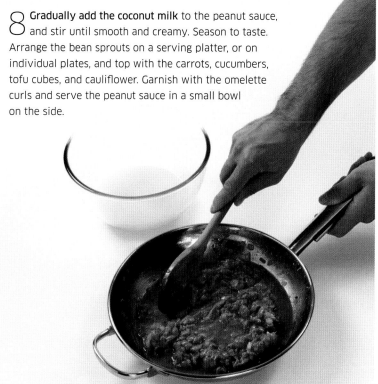

VARIATION: Bird's nest salad with peanut sauce

Crunchy red cabbage and French beans add brilliant colour to this version of Gado-gado.

1 Omit the cauliflower, carrots, cucumbers, omelette, and tofu. Peel 500g (1lb 2oz) potatoes, cut them into even-sized chunks and add to a pan of well-salted water. Cover, and bring to a boil. Simmer for about 15 minutes until tender, drain, then cut into 1cm (^{1}/$_2$in) cubes. Make the peanut sauce as directed in the main recipe.

2 Trim 375g (13oz) French beans and cut them into 2.5cm (1in) slices. Cook in boiling water for 5 minutes, or until just tender, then drain very well. Trim half a head of red cabbage, cut it in half and remove the core from each piece. Set the cabbage halves cut side down on a board and finely shred. Discard any thick ribs.

3 Cook the cabbage in boiling, salted water, for 1 minute only. Drain and toss, while still hot, with 4 tbsp red wine vinegar. Prepare the beansprouts as directed in the main recipe, then divide them evenly among 8 plates. Top with the red cabbage. Arrange the French beans in the centre, then pile the potatoes on top. Add a spoonful of the peanut sauce to the potatoes, and provide the rest on the side.

Red cabbage and bacon salad

A HEARTY FIRST COURSE for winter, or a tasty lunch for 4. The contrasts in taste, texture, and colour are wonderful, especially with the addition here of crumbled, creamy blue Roquefort cheese. Just eating this salad will make you feel healthy and more invigorated.

SERVES	PREP	COOK
SERVES 6	20-25 MINS PLUS MARINATING	5 MINS

Ingredients

FOR THE VINAIGRETTE

4 tbsp red wine vinegar, plus more if needed

1 tbsp Dijon mustard

salt and freshly ground black pepper

175ml (6fl oz) olive oil

FOR THE SALAD

½ head red cabbage (about 750g/1lb 10oz), cored and finely shredded

4 tbsp red wine vinegar

250g (9oz) lardons or thick streaky bacon rashers

leaves from 1 small cos lettuce, chopped

90g (3oz) Roquefort cheese, crumbled

PREPARE THE VINAIGRETTE

1 **Combine the vinegar,** mustard, and a pinch of salt. Grind in the pepper. Gradually whisk in the oil so the vinaigrette emulsifies and thickens. Taste for seasoning.

PREPARE THE CABBAGE

2 **Transfer the shredded cabbage** to a large bowl. Boil the vinegar in a small saucepan, then pour over the cabbage and toss. Pour 2 litres (3½ pints) boiling water over and let stand for 3-4 minutes, until slightly softened. Drain thoroughly, then return it to the large bowl.

3 **Toss the cabbage** with enough vinaigrette to moisten it well. Taste for seasoning, adding more vinegar if necessary. Cover and marinate for 1-2 hours.

PREPARE THE SALAD

4 **If using bacon rashers,** cut into strips about 10 minutes before serving. Fry the lardons or bacon strips in a frying pan, stirring occasionally, for 3-5 minutes, or until crisp and the fat is rendered. Spoon the hot bacon and its pan juices over the cabbage, reserving some bacon pieces for garnish. Toss them together.

5 **Arrange a bed of lettuce** on each of 6 plates. Spoon the remaining dressing over the lettuce. Mound the red cabbage and bacon mixture over the top. Top the salads with the crumbled blue cheese and reserved bacon and serve at once.

Celeriac rémoulade with carrot salad

YOU'LL FIND THIS UNPRETENTIOUS autumn dish on the menu of every French bistro. Both salads can be prepared and tossed in their dressings up to 1 day ahead. Store them, covered, in the refrigerator. The flavours will mellow and deepen. Try chopped walnuts or apple, or even some toasted sesame seeds, in place of the raisins in the carrot salad.

SERVES SERVES 6	**PREP** 25–30 MINS PLUS CHILLING	**COOK** 1–2 MINS

Ingredients

FOR THE CARROT SALAD

3 tbsp cider vinegar

1 tsp sugar

salt and pepper

75ml (2½fl oz) light olive oil

500g (1lb 2oz) carrots, coarsely grated

90g (3oz) raisins

FOR THE CELERIAC SALAD

1 celeriac, weighing about 750g (1lb 10oz)

175ml (6fl oz) mayonnaise

2 tbsp Dijon mustard, or to taste

MAKE THE CARROT SALAD AND DRESSING

1 **Whisk the vinegar** with the sugar, salt, and pepper. Gradually whisk in the oil, so the vinaigrette emulsifies and thickens slightly. Taste for seasoning. Add the carrots to the dressing, then the raisins. Toss everything together, and taste for seasoning. Cover and refrigerate for at least 1 hour.

PREPARE THE CELERIAC

2 **Place the celeriac** on a chopping board, and slice away all the thick, knobbly peel. Cut into thin slices, then into fine, even strips.

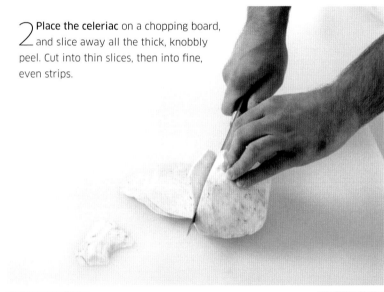

3 **Put the celeriac strips** in a saucepan of cold, salted water, and bring to a boil. Simmer for 1–2 minutes, until tender, but still retaining bite, then drain.

DRESS THE SALAD

4 **Mix the mayonnaise,** salt, pepper, and 2 tbsp mustard in a bowl. Taste, adding more mustard if you like. Add the celeriac, toss, then taste for seasoning. Cover, and refrigerate for at least 1 hour. Arrange the celeriac and carrot salads in individual bowls.

Spring rice salad

ASPARAGUS AND SMOKED SALMON make a perfect marriage with the sweet, aniseed taste of a tarragon dressing in this recipe. If you make this in April, when the asparagus is young and the stalks slender, they will not need to be peeled before cooking. The rice salad can be made 1 day in advance and kept, covered, in the refrigerator, but make sure it is brought to room temperature – and the rice fluffed up with a fork – before serving.

SERVES SERVES 4-6	**PREP** 20-25 MINS, PLUS CHILLING	**COOK** 15-20 MINS

Ingredients

FOR THE SALAD

salt and pepper

1 lemon

200g (7oz) long-grain rice

250g (9oz) asparagus

3 celery sticks

250g (9oz) sliced smoked salmon

FOR THE DRESSING

3 tbsp tarragon vinegar

2 tsp Dijon mustard

175ml (6fl oz) flavourless vegetable oil

COOK THE RICE AND MAKE THE VINAIGRETTE

1 Bring a large saucepan of salted water to a rolling boil. Squeeze the juice from half the lemon into the water, then add the lemon half as well to flavour the water. Add the rice, stir and bring back to a fast boil. Simmer just until tender, stirring occasionally to separate the grains and ensure they do not stick to the base of the pan. It should take about 10–12 minutes. Taste a grain to make sure it is tender before removing from the heat. There should be no hard core in the centre.

2 Meanwhile, make the vinaigrette. Put the vinegar, salt, and pepper in a small bowl. Add the mustard and whisk together well. Gradually whisk in the oil in a thin stream so the vinaigrette emulsifies and thickens slightly. Taste for seasoning and set aside. You can make this dressing in advance and keep it, in a sealed jar in the refrigerator, for up to 1 week. Shake the jar well before using to re-emulsify the vinaigrette..

3 Drain the rice, discard the lemon half, then place in a sieve and rinse with cold water to wash away the starch and drain again thoroughly. Repeat a couple of times more. This rinsing process is very important for rice that is to be served cold, as too much starch will make the grains stick together in clumps, which are unpleasant to eat. You are aiming for fluffy clouds of rice. Transfer to a large bowl. Squeeze and reserve the juice from the remaining lemon half.

PREPARE THE ASPARAGUS

4 With a vegetable peeler, strip away the tough outer skin from the asparagus stalks and trim off the woody ends. Tie the stalks in 2 equal bundles with kitchen string.

5 Bring a large saucepan of salted water to a boil, add the asparagus and simmer for 5–7 minutes, just until tender when pierced with the tip of a small knife.

6 Drain the asparagus and discard the strings. Trim off and reserve about 5cm (2in) of the asparagus tips. Cut the stalks into 1cm (½in) pieces.

ASSEMBLE THE SALAD

7 Peel the strings from the celery sticks with a vegetable peeler, then dice each stick quite finely. Cut the smoked salmon slices into even 1cm (½in) strips.

8 Briskly whisk the vinaigrette to re-emulsify it, and pour it over the rice, reserving 1-2 tbsp. Stir the rice well to distribute the dressing evenly, and fluff it up with a fork to separate the grains. Add the asparagus, celery, smoked salmon, and reserved lemon juice.

9 Toss all the ingredients together and taste for seasoning. Cover and refrigerate for at least 1 hour to allow the flavours to mingle together. Before serving, let the rice salad come to room temperature. Brush the asparagus tips with the reserved dressing and arrange on top of the rice salad. Serve in bowls.

 VARIATION: Rice salad with smoked trout and peas

Vivid green peas and red tomatoes add colour.

1 Omit the smoked salmon and asparagus. Cook the rice and make the vinaigrette as directed. Simmer 125g (4½oz) shelled, fresh green peas or frozen peas for 3–5 minutes, just until tender. Drain.

2 Using a small knife, peel the skin from 2 smoked trout (weighing 250g/9oz each), lift off the fillets, discarding the bones, and flake the flesh, checking for any remaining small bones as you do so.

3 Cut 375g (13oz) cherry tomatoes in half. Assemble the salad as directed and taste for seasoning. Transfer to a broad, shallow serving bowl and arrange the tomatoes on top.

Festive wild rice salad

THIS TASTES EVEN BETTER after standing for a few hours, so it is an ideal buffet party dish for Christmas time. You can prepare the wild rice salad 1 day ahead and keep it, covered, in the refrigerator. Let it come to room temperature before adding the smoked turkey and serving.

SERVES	PREP	COOK
SERVES 8	30-35 MINS PLUS STANDING	¾-1¼ HRS

Ingredients

FOR THE SALAD

salt and pepper

375g (13oz) wild rice

60g (2oz) pecans

375g (13oz) sliced smoked turkey breast

FOR THE CRANBERRY DRESSING

175g (6oz) fresh cranberries

50g (1¾oz) sugar

1 orange

4 tbsp cider vinegar

2 shallots, very finely chopped

125ml (4fl oz) flavourless vegetable oil

PREPARE THE RICE, CRANBERRIES, AND PECANS

1 Put 1.5 litres (2¾ pints) water in a large saucepan with 1 tsp salt and bring to a boil. Stir in the rice, cover, and simmer for about 1 hour, or until tender. Drain, cool, then tip into a large bowl.

2 Preheat the oven to 190°C (375°F/Gas 5). Spread the cranberries in a baking dish, sprinkle with sugar and bake in the heated oven for 10-15 minutes, until they start to pop. Let cool in the dish.

3 Spread the pecans on a baking sheet and bake for 5-8 minutes, stirring occasionally, until toasted, then coarsely chop.

PREPARE THE ORANGE JULIENNE

4 With a vegetable peeler, peel the zest from the orange, leaving behind the pith. Cut the zest into very fine julienne strips.

5 Bring a small saucepan of water to a boil and add the orange julienne. Simmer for 2 minutes, then drain and finely chop. Set aside. Squeeze the juice from the orange into a bowl.

PREPARE THE DRESSING AND **ASSEMBLE** THE SALAD

6 Add the vinegar, shallots, salt, and pepper to the orange juice. Gradually whisk in the oil so the dressing emulsifies and thickens slightly. Taste for seasoning. Add the cranberries, leaving their juice behind, and stir.

7 If necessary, remove the skin from the smoked turkey breast. Add the pecans, orange zest, and two-thirds of the dressing to the rice. Toss and let stand for 1 hour, for the flavours to combine. Taste for seasoning. To serve, transfer the rice salad to a platter, arrange the turkey on top and spoon over the remaining cranberry dressing.

Lacquered chicken salad

FRESH ROOT GINGER gives an Asian sparkle to this salad. When buying fresh root ginger, choose firm hands with no wrinkles and check that the broken part of the root is moist, to get the freshest specimens. If you can't find the rice wine for the marinade, use sherry instead.

SERVES	PREP	COOK
SERVES 4	25-30 MINS PLUS MARINATING	10-15 MINS

Ingredients

FOR THE SALAD

4 boneless, skinless chicken breasts, total weight about 750g (1lb 10oz)

leaves from 1 cos lettuce, shredded

125g (4½oz) bean sprouts

90g (3oz) baby sweetcorn, halved lengthways

FOR THE MARINADE AND DRESSING

1cm (½in) piece of fresh root ginger, peeled and finely chopped

1 garlic clove, finely chopped

45g (1½oz) soft brown sugar

2 tbsp Dijon mustard

3 tbsp rice wine

3 tbsp sesame oil

salt and pepper

4 tbsp soy sauce

125ml (4fl oz) vegetable oil

MARINADE THE CHICKEN

1 **Lightly score** the top of each chicken breast and set them in a shallow, non-metallic dish.

2 **Combine the ginger,** garlic, soft brown sugar, mustard, 1 tbsp each of the rice wine and sesame oil, and pepper in a bowl. Pour in the soy sauce and stir. Remove and reserve 4 tbsp, then pour the rest of the marinade over the chicken, cover, and refrigerate for 1–2 hours, turning 3–4 times.

PREPARE THE DRESSING AND BEANSPROUTS

3 **Add the remaining rice wine** and sesame oil to the reserved marinade and mix. Gradually whisk in the vegetable oil, so the dressing emulsifies and thickens slightly. Taste for seasoning and set aside, or refrigerate, tightly sealed, for up to 12 hours. Put the bean sprouts in a bowl. Cover generously with boiling water and let stand for 1 minute. Drain, rinse with cold, running water, and drain again.

GRILL THE CHICKEN AND FINISH THE SALAD

4 **Heat the grill** and oil the grill rack. Put the chicken on the rack and brush with the marinade. Grill about 7.5cm (3in) from the heat, brushing often with marinade, for 5–7 minutes, until well browned.

5 **Turn the breasts** over. Brush them with more marinade. Grill for a further 5–7 minutes, until they are well browned, glossy, and tender. Put them on a chopping board and cut diagonally into slices.

6 **Add the bean sprouts** and sweetcorn to the lettuce. Briskly whisk the dressing again and pour it over the salad. Toss and taste for seasoning. Arrange the salad attractively on a serving plate, top with the chicken, and serve while still hot.

Tortilla bean salad

A RIOT OF COLOUR with a vibrant chilli dressing. This is a Tex-Mex style of food, and best suited to the hot months of the year. You could also use black beans, for an even more dramatic-looking bowlful. Don't be too timid with the chillies, as beans can take a lot of seasoning and will soak up much of the heat. Wearing rubber gloves to prepare the chillies will protect your hands.

SERVES	PREP	COOK
SERVES 6-8	25-30 MINS PLUS CHILLING	1-1½ HRS

Ingredients

FOR THE CHILLI VINAIGRETTE

1 small bunch of coriander

125ml (4fl oz) cider vinegar

½ tsp ground cumin

3 green chillies

125ml (4fl oz) flavourless oil, plus more for tortillas and baking sheet

FOR THE SALAD

4 cobs of fresh sweetcorn, or 300g (10oz) canned, drained, or defrosted sweetcorn kernels, rinsed

1 red pepper

1 green pepper

1 yellow pepper

750g (1lb 10oz) tomatoes

2 x 400g (14oz) cans red kidney beans, rinsed

salt and pepper

6 corn tortillas

¼ tsp cayenne pepper

MAKE THE CHILLI VINAIGRETTE

1 Strip the coriander leaves from the stalks and finely chop them. Whisk together the vinegar, cumin, salt, and pepper.

2 Cut the chillies in half lengthways, discarding the cores. Scrape out the seeds and cut away the fleshy white ribs. Cut into fine dice. Add the chillies to the whisked dressing ingredients.

3 Gradually whisk in the oil so the vinaigrette emulsifies and thickens slightly. Stir in the coriander, reserving a little for garnish; taste for seasoning.

PREPARE THE VEGETABLES AND TOSS THE SALAD

4 If using fresh sweetcorn cobs, remove the husks and silks. Bring a large saucepan of water to a boil, add the sweetcorn, and cook at a lively bubble for 5-7 minutes.

5 Lift one of the sweetcorn cobs from the pan: it is cooked if the kernels pop out easily when tested with the point of a knife. Drain, let cool a little, and cut off the kernels. Core and seed all the peppers, and dice.

6 Core the tomatoes and score an "X" on the base of each. Immerse in boiling water until the skins start to split. Plunge them into cold water. Peel the tomatoes, then cut in half; squeeze out the seeds, and coarsely chop.

7 In a large bowl, combine the kidney beans, sweetcorn, tomatoes, peppers, and chilli vinaigrette. Gently toss the salad and taste for seasoning. Cover and refrigerate for at least 1 hour.

GRILL THE TORTILLAS AND FINISH THE SALAD

8 Just before serving, heat the grill and oil a baking sheet. Brush the tortillas with oil and season with salt and cayenne pepper, then slice them into triangles.

9 Spread the tortilla triangles on the baking sheet. Grill, 10cm (4in) from the heat, for 4–6 minutes, until golden brown and crisp, stirring occasionally so they colour evenly.

10 Divide the salad among 6–8 deep plates and top with the tortilla triangles. Sprinkle the reserved chopped coriander over the top, if you like. Serve chilled or at room temperature.

VARIATION: Red bean, sweetcorn, and onion salad

With cheesy tortilla triangles.

1 Omit the peppers from the salad. Prepare the sweetcorn, tomatoes, and the chilli vinaigrette dressing as directed in the main recipe. Dice 1 large, sweet red onion. Trim and thinly slice 2 spring onions, including some of their aromatic green tops.

2 Assemble the salad as directed, cover and refrigerate for at least 1 hour. Meanwhile, heat the grill. Grate 90g (3oz) mild Cheddar cheese. Arrange 6 corn tortillas on a baking sheet. Brush them with 1 tbsp oil and grill for 2–3 minutes, until crisp.

3 Sprinkle the tortillas with the cheese, cayenne pepper, and salt and grill for 1–2 minutes, until the cheese has melted. Watch carefully so they do not scorch and blacken, as this will make them bitter. Cut each tortilla into 6 triangles. Spoon the salad on to a large serving plate and garnish with coriander leaves, if you like. Serve the crispy tortilla triangles separately.

Tabbouleh with cacik

WARMED PITTA BREAD makes a fitting and delicious accompaniment to these "mezze" salads. Mezze are little dishes of vegetables, salads, olives, and such like that are the standard opening for a meal all over the Middle East.

SERVES	**PREP**	**COOK**
SERVES 6-8	35-40 MINS PLUS CHILLING	NONE

Ingredients

200g (7oz) bulghur wheat

2 small cucumbers, seeded and diced

salt and pepper

500g (1lb 2oz) tomatoes, peeled, deseeded and chopped

3 spring onions, chopped

leaves from 1 bunch of parsley, chopped

juice of 3 lemons

125ml (4fl oz) olive oil

leaves from 2 bunches of mint, chopped

3 garlic cloves, finely chopped

½ tsp ground coriander

¼ tsp ground cumin

500ml (16fl oz) plain yogurt

TO SERVE

125g (4½oz) black olives

6-8 pitta breads

PREPARE THE SALAD AND CACIK INGREDIENTS

1 **Put the bulghur** in a large bowl and pour over enough cold water to cover generously. Let soak for 30 minutes, then drain through a sieve and squeeze out any remaining water with your fist.

2 **Put the cucumber** in a colander, sprinkle with salt and stir to mix. Leave it for 15-20 minutes, to draw out the bitter juices, then rinse under cold, running water. Let drain.

MAKE THE TABBOULEH AND CACIK

3 **For the tabbouleh,** in a large bowl, combine the bulghur, tomatoes, spring onions, parsley, lemon juice, olive oil, two-thirds of the mint, and plenty of salt and pepper. Mix and taste for seasoning then cover and chill in the refrigerator for at least 2 hours.

4 **Make the cacik:** put the cucumbers in a bowl and add the garlic, remaining mint, ground coriander, ground cumin, salt, and pepper. Pour in the yogurt. Stir to combine and taste for seasoning. Chill in the refrigerator, to allow the flavours to blend, for at least 2 hours.

5 **Warm the pitta breads** in a low oven for 3-5 minutes, then remove and cut into strips. Take the salads from the refrigerator and allow to come to room temperature, then arrange them in separate bowls with the warm pitta bread fingers alongside.

Pear, fennel, and walnut salad

GORGONZOLA DRESSING CONTRASTS well with the sweet pears and aniseed flavor of the fennel. This salad really needs to be assembled right at the last minute, to retain the freshness and vibrancy of the pears and walnuts.

SERVES	PREP	COOK
SERVES 6	30–35 MINS	NONE

Ingredients

FOR THE SALAD

60g (2oz) walnut pieces

1 large fennel bulb

3 ripe pears

1 lemon

FOR THE DRESSING

125g (4½oz) Gorgonzola cheese

4 tbsp red wine vinegar

salt and pepper

75ml (2½fl oz) olive oil

TOAST THE WALNUTS AND MAKE THE DRESSING

1 **Preheat the oven** to 180°C (350°F/Gas 4). Spread the walnuts on a baking sheet and toast them in the heated oven for 5–8 minutes until crisp, stirring occasionally so they toast evenly.

2 **Cut the rind** from the Gorgonzola and crumble with your fingers or crush with the tines of a fork. Put two-thirds into a bowl, add the red wine vinegar, salt and pepper, and whisk together.

3 **Gradually whisk in the oil** so the dressing emulsifies and thickens slightly. Stir in the remaining cheese so a few larger pieces are left intact, and taste for seasoning. Cover and chill in the refrigerator.

PREPARE THE FENNEL

4 **Trim the stalks,** root end, and any tough outer pieces from the fennel. Reserve any fronds for decoration. Cut the fennel bulb in half lengthways.

5 **Set each fennel** half flat-side down on the chopping board and slice it lengthways.

PREPARE THE PEARS

6 **Peel the pears,** halve lengthways, and remove the core. Set each half cut-side down and cut lengthways into thin slices. Cut the lemon in half and squeeze lemon juice over the pear slices, tossing to coat.

7 **On individual plates,** arrange the pear and fennel slices and spoon on the Gorgonzola dressing. Scatter some toasted walnuts over each serving and decorate with fennel fronds

Salade Lyonnaise

A DRESSING OF RED WINE VINEGAR and bacon enlivens this warm spinach salad. It is a favourite in Lyon, which claims to be the gastronomic capital of France. For a more substantial dish, top with a warm poached egg, breaking the yolk into the dressing as you eat.

SERVES	PREP	COOK
SERVES 6	30-35 MINS	20-25 MINS

Ingredients

FOR THE CROUTES

½ baguette

3 tbsp olive oil

1 garlic clove

FOR THE SALAD

2 eggs

500g (1lb 2oz) fresh spinach

250g (9oz) lardons or streaky bacon rashers, chopped

75ml (2½fl oz) red wine vinegar

MAKE THE CROUTES

1 **Preheat the oven** to 200°C (400°F/Gas 6). Cut the baguette into 5mm (¼in) slices. Brush both sides of each slice with oil and set on the baking sheet. Bake for 7–10 minutes, until toasted and golden brown, turning once.

2 **Cut the garlic clove** in half. Rub one side of each slice of bread with the cut side of the garlic. Set the croutes aside.

PREPARE THE SALAD INGREDIENTS

3 **Hard-boil and shell** the eggs. Tear the spinach leaves into large pieces and put in a bowl. Separate the egg yolks from the whites by gently pulling the whites apart. Chop the whites. Put the yolks in a sieve set over a bowl; work them through with the back of a metal spoon.

DRESS THE SALAD

4 **Heat a frying pan,** add the bacon and cook, stirring, for 3–5 minutes, until it is crisp and the fat is rendered. Add to the spinach and toss vigorously for 30 seconds, until the spinach is slightly wilted.

5 **Pour the vinegar** into the frying pan. Bring it to a boil, stirring, and boil it for about 1 minute, until reduced by one-third. Pour over the spinach and bacon and toss together well.

6 **Pile the salad** on to 6 individual plates. Sprinkle each serving evenly with the chopped egg white and sieved yolk, and serve at once, with a pile of the croutes on the side.

Waldorf chicken salad

A CONTEMPORARY TAKE ON A CLASSIC, with yogurt in the dressing for lightness. This salad is a great way to use up leftover roast chicken, which saves poaching the chicken breasts. The recipe can be made up to 6 hours ahead and kept, covered, in the refrigerator. Be sure to bring it back up to room temperature before serving.

SERVES	PREP	COOK
SERVES 6	25–30 MINS PLUS CHILLING	25–35 MINS

Ingredients

FOR THE POACHING LIQUID

4 celery sticks, with leaves if possible

1 onion, peeled and quartered

1 carrot, peeled and quartered

10–12 black peppercorns

1 bouquet garni, made with 5–6 parsley stalks, 2–3 thyme sprigs, and 1 bay leaf

FOR THE SALAD

4 skinless, boneless chicken breasts, total weight about 750g (1lb 10oz)

125g (4½oz) walnut pieces

500g (1lb 2oz) tart, crisp apples

juice of 1 lemon

175ml (6fl oz) plain yogurt

175ml (6fl oz) mayonnaise

salt and pepper

POACH THE CHICKEN

1 **Trim the tops** and leaves from the celery (reserve the sticks), and put the trimmings in a wide, shallow pan with the onion, carrot, peppercorns, bouquet garni, and salt. Bring to a boil and simmer for 10–15 minutes. Add the chicken and simmer for a further 10–12 minutes, turning once, until the juices run clear when the meat is pierced at its thickest point.

2 **Remove from the heat,** and cool the chicken in the poaching liquid for 10–15 minutes, then put on kitchen paper to drain. With your fingers, pull the chicken into slivers about 5cm (2in) long. The meat will be juicier than if you were to cut it.

PREPARE THE SALAD

3 **Preheat the oven** to 180°C (350°F/Gas 4). Spread the walnut pieces on a baking sheet and bake for 5–8 minutes, until crisp, stirring occasionally so that they toast evenly. Peel and slice the celery sticks.

4 **Cut the top** and bottom ends from the apples, halve, core, then dice the flesh. Put in a large bowl, pour over the lemon juice, and toss to coat. Add the chicken, celery, yogurt, mayonnaise, and two-thirds of the walnuts, to the apple. Season and stir until combined. Taste for seasoning, cover, and chill for 1 hour. Coarsely chop the remaining walnuts. Spoon the salad into individual bowls, and sprinkle with the reserved walnuts.

Asian noodle salad

A FANTASTIC SPICY DRESSING really lifts this dish. Use this recipe as a blueprint: omit the prawns and add tofu if you have vegetarian guests, or replace the prawns with cooked chicken, pork, ham, or spicy Chinese sausage to ring the changes. This is a very convenient dish, as the flavours only benefit from getting to know each other in the refrigerator for up to 1 day.

SERVES SERVES 6	**PREP** 30-35 MINS PLUS MARINATING
COOK 6-9 MINS	

Ingredients

FOR THE DRESSING

2cm (¾in) piece of fresh root ginger

2 fresh green chillies

2 garlic cloves

2 tsp sugar

salt and pepper

4 tbsp rice wine vinegar

125ml (4fl oz) soy sauce

4 tbsp flavourless oil

2 tbsp sesame oil

FOR THE SALAD

250g (9oz) thin egg noodles

175g (6oz) mangetout

4 spring onions

75g (2½oz) roasted unsalted peanuts

1 small bunch of coriander

375g (13oz) cooked, peeled prawns

MAKE THE DRESSING AND **COOK** THE NOODLES

1 **With a small knife,** peel the skin from the root ginger. Slice the ginger, cutting across the fibrous grain. Crush each slice with the flat of the knife, then finely chop the slices.

2 **Core, seed, and dice the chillies.** Set the flat side of a knife on top of each garlic clove and strike it with your fist. Discard the skin and finely chop the garlic. Put the crushed ginger, chillies, garlic, sugar, pepper, and vinegar in a bowl. Pour in the soy sauce. Gradually whisk in the oils so the sauce emulsifies and thickens slightly. Taste for seasoning.

3 **Fill a large pan with water,** bring to a boil and add salt. Add the noodles and simmer for 4-6 minutes, or according to package directions, just until they are tender but still chewy. Stir them occasionally to prevent sticking.

4 **Drain the noodles** in the colander, rinse with hot water, and drain again thoroughly.

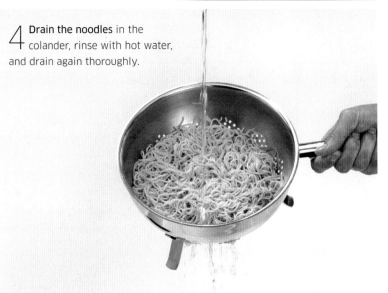

DRESS THE NOODLES AND PREPARE THE SALAD INGREDIENTS

5 Transfer the noodles to a large bowl. Briskly whisk the dressing, pour it over the warm noodles and toss until well coated. Set aside for at least 1 hour to marinate and allow the flavour to mellow.

6 Trim the stem end from each mangetout, then pull the string from the edge of the pods. Trim the other end. Cook in boiling salted water for 2–3 minutes, until tender but still crisp. Drain, rinse with cold water and drain again. Cut each diagonally into 2–3 slices.

7 Trim the spring onions and cut into thin diagonal slices, including some of the green tops. Coarsely chop the peanuts. Strip the coriander leaves from the stalks, pile the leaves on a chopping board and chop them coarsely.

8 Add the mangetout, spring onions, two-thirds of both the chopped peanuts and coriander, and all of the prawns to the noodles. Toss thoroughly. Taste for seasoning. It may be unnecessary to add salt because soy sauce is salty. Mound the salad on to a serving plate and top with the remaining chopped peanuts and coriander.

VARIATION: Thai noodle salad

A great way to use up leftover pork.

1 Make the dressing: omit the ginger and rice wine vinegar. Chop the garlic and fresh chillies. Coarsely chop 1 stalk of lemongrass and squeeze the juice from 1 lime. Whisk together the soy sauce, lime juice, garlic, chillies, lemongrass, sugar, and pepper. Gradually whisk in the oils. Taste for seasoning.

2 Cook and drain the noodles as directed and toss them in the dressing. Omit the prawns and mangetout. Cut 250g (9oz) cooked pork into thin strips. Chop the peanuts and coriander. Coarsely chop 7–10 basil sprigs. Drain a 250g (9oz) can of sliced water chestnuts.

3 Toss the noodles and dressing with the pork, water chestnuts, spring onions, all the chopped peanuts, and the herbs. Cover, and let stand, at least 1 hour. Divide among 6 plates. Garnish each serving with a basil sprig, if you like.

Steak salad with red onions

INSPIRED BY THE STEAK SANDWICH! Thick wedges of crusty French baguette would be fabulous alongside. Even the most ardent salad-dodgers will adore this hearty dish. The steak is marinated for the best flavour before grilling.

SERVES	PREP	COOK
SERVES 4	20–30 MINS PLUS MARINATING	6–12 MINS

Ingredients

625g (1lb 6oz) rump steak

250ml (9fl oz) vegetable oil

3 tbsp Worcestershire sauce

dash of Tabasco sauce, or to taste

salt and pepper

2 garlic cloves, chopped

500g (1lb 2oz) red onions, in 1cm (½in) slices

90g (3oz) mushrooms, trimmed and thinly sliced

1 lollo rosso lettuce

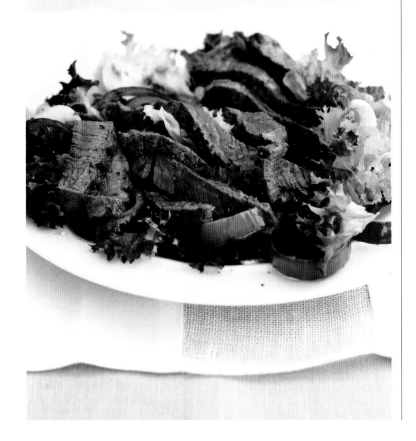

PREPARE THE MARINADE AND STEAK

1 **Trim the meat** of fat and sinew. With the point of a knife, lightly score both sides in a lattice pattern and lay it in a shallow, non-metallic dish.

2 **In a bowl,** whisk together the oil, Worcestershire sauce, Tabasco sauce, salt, and pepper. Set aside 125ml (4fl oz). Stir the garlic into the remaining dressing and pour over the steak. Cover, and leave to marinate in the refrigerator, turning several times, for at least 3 or up to 12 hours for maximum flavour and tenderness.

PREPARE THE VEGETABLES

3 **Insert a cocktail stick** into the side of each onion slice to hold it together during cooking. Toss the mushrooms very well with half the reserved dressing, being sure to coat them entirely.

4 **Twist off and discard** the root end from the lettuce. Immerse the leaves in plenty of cold water for 15–30 minutes, then dry thoroughly. Coarsely shred the leaves and put them in a large bowl.

GRILL THE STEAK AND ONIONS

5 **Heat the grill.** Lay the steak on the grill rack. Set the onion slices around it and brush with the marinade. Grill 7.5cm (3in) from the heat, allowing 3–4 minutes for rare, 5–6 minutes for medium, then turn and repeat.

6 **Press the steak** with a finger to test: it will feel quite spongy if rare; it will resist slightly if medium. Divide the lettuce and mushrooms evenly among 4 plates.

ASSEMBLE THE SALAD

7 **Cut the steak** into thin diagonal slices and arrange on the lettuce and mushrooms. Take the cocktail sticks from the onion slices, separate the rings, and arrange some over each serving.

German potato salad

THE PIQUANT CARAWAY DRESSING makes this salad great with cooked meats. It is inspired by recipes that came from the Black Forest in Germany, where few dishes are complete without ham, or sausage, or both!

SERVES	PREP	COOK
SERVES 6-8	25-30 MINS PLUS CHILLING	15-20 MINS

Ingredients

FOR THE SALAD

1.4kg (3lb) red-skinned new potatoes

salt and pepper

150g (5½oz) thinly sliced smoked ham

leaves from 7-10 parsley sprigs, chopped

FOR THE DRESSING

1 small red onion, very finely chopped

3 tbsp red wine vinegar

3 tbsp soured cream

2 tbsp hot mustard

2 tsp caraway seeds

250ml (9fl oz) flavourless vegetable oil

COOK THE POTATOES

1 **Scrub the potatoes** under cold, running water but do not peel. Cut any larger potatoes into 2-4 pieces. Put in a large saucepan with plenty of cold, salted water, cover, and bring to a boil. Simmer for 15-20 minutes, just until tender, then drain.

MAKE THE DRESSING AND DRESS THE POTATOES

2 **Put the onion** in a bowl with the vinegar, soured cream, mustard, salt, and pepper. Sprinkle in the caraway seeds. Whisk together just until mixed, then gradually whisk in the oil so the dressing emulsifies and thickens slightly. Taste for seasoning and set aside.

3 **While still warm, cut the potatoes** into 1cm (½in) slices. Transfer to a large bowl. Briskly whisk the dressing, then pour it over the warm potatoes. Stir gently to thoroughly coat and leave to cool.

4 **Trim the fat** from the ham, then cut into 1cm (½in) strips. Add the ham to the potatoes. Sprinkle three-quarters of the parsley over the top. Stir, taste for seasoning, cover, and refrigerate for at least 1 hour.

5 **Transfer the salad** to a large platter or into individual plates or shallow bowls, and sprinkle evenly with the remaining chopped parsley. Serve at room temperature.

Pasta and mussel salad

THE SPIRAL FUSILLI PASTA absorbs this gorgeous, tart dressing wonderfully, though hollow shells or macaroni would be good too. The pasta perfectly complements the texture of the mussels. This can be made 1 day ahead, covered, and refrigerated.

SERVES SERVES 4-6	**PREP** 30-35 MINS	**COOK** 8-10 MINS

Ingredients

FOR THE HERB DRESSING

4 shallots

3 garlic cloves

1 bunch of tarragon

1 bunch of parsley

2 lemons

salt and pepper

175ml (6fl oz) olive oil

FOR THE SALAD

1kg (2¼lb) mussels

175ml (6fl oz) dry white wine

250g (9oz) fusilli pasta spirals

3 spring onions, trimmed and sliced

MAKE THE HERB VINAIGRETTE

1 **Peel and finely dice** the shallots. Finely chop the garlic. Strip the tarragon and parsley leaves from the stalks, and finely chop.

2 **Squeeze the juice** from each of the lemons; there should be about 75ml (2½fl oz) juice. If you first roll the lemons on a hard surface, you will be able to extract more juice.

3 **Whisk together the lemon juice,** half the shallots, the garlic, salt, and pepper. Gradually whisk in the oil, so the dressing emulsifies and thickens slightly. Whisk in the herbs. Taste for seasoning and set aside.

PREPARE AND COOK THE MUSSELS

4 **Scrape each mussel** with a small knife to remove any barnacles, then detach and discard any weed or 'beard'. Scrub under cold, running water; discard any with broken shells or those that do not close when tapped.

5 **Put the wine,** remaining shallots, and plenty of pepper, in a large saucepan. Bring to a boil and simmer for 2 minutes. Add the mussels, cover, and cook over high heat for 4-5 minutes, stirring occasionally, just until the mussels open.

6 **Transfer the mussels** to a large bowl, discarding the cooking liquid. Leave until they are cool enough to handle. Discard any that have not opened at this point.

7 **With your fingers,** remove the mussels from their shells, reserving 4-6 mussels in their shells. Pull off and discard the rubbery ring from around each shelled mussel, and put them in a large bowl.

DRESS THE MUSSELS AND COOK THE PASTA

8 **Briskly whisk** the herb vinaigrette, and pour it over the mussels.

9 **Stir gently,** so all the mussels are well coated with dressing. Cover and refrigerate, while cooking the pasta.

10 **Fill a large pan** with water, bring to a boil, and add ½ tsp salt. Add the pasta, and simmer for 8-10 minutes, until tender but still chewy, or according to package directions. Stir occasionally to keep from sticking. Drain, rinse with cold water, and drain again.

11 **Tip the pasta** into the bowl of mussels and dressing. Sprinkle the spring onions over the pasta, add salt and pepper, toss well, and taste for seasoning. Arrange on 4–6 plates. Garnish each serving with a reserved mussel in its shell, adding a lemon slice and tarragon sprig, if you like.

 ## VARIATION: Pasta and scallop salad

One for when you're feeling flush!

1 Omit the mussels and wine. Chop the garlic, 2 shallots, the tarragon, and parsley, as directed. Snip 1 bunch of chives. Make the dressing as directed, using half the chopped garlic, 1 lemon, and 125ml (4fl oz) olive oil. Whisk in the herbs with 3 tbsp double cream, and taste for seasoning.

2 Prepare 500g (1lb 2oz) scallops in place of the mussels, and cut large scallops into 2 rounds. Heat 1 tbsp olive oil in a frying pan. Add the scallops with the remaining garlic, and sprinkle with salt and pepper. Sauté, turning once, for 1–2 minutes each side, until brown and slightly crisp.

3 Cook 250g (9oz) spinach pasta and slice the spring onions as directed. Drain the pasta. Toss with the spring onions, scallops and dressing. Taste for seasoning and serve at room temperature.

Warm salmon and orange salad

A RICH DISH, with cream and Grand Marnier dressing. The velvety bed of lamb's lettuce adds a touch of astringency to cut through the dressing, while segments of refreshing orange and toasted hazelnuts give great bursts of flavour and texture contrasts to this exciting salad. If you don't have any sherry vinegar in the cupboard, use white wine vinegar instead.

SERVES	PREP	COOK
SERVES 6	35-40 MINS	6-12 MINS

Ingredients

FOR THE DRESSING

4 oranges

60g (2oz) skinned hazelnuts

salt and pepper

2 tbsp sherry vinegar

1 tbsp Grand Marnier

2 tbsp double cream

125ml (4fl oz) hazelnut oil

FOR THE SALAD

500g (1lb 2oz) salmon fillet

1 tbsp vegetable oil

250g (9oz) lamb's lettuce

MAKE THE DRESSING

1 **Preheat the oven** to 180°C (350°F/Gas 4). Peel and segment the oranges, squeezing the leftover orange membranes over a bowl to catch the remaining juice. Cover and refrigerate. Spread the hazelnuts on a baking sheet and toast for 5-10 minutes, until lightly browned, stirring occasionally. Let cool, then chop the nuts coarsely.

2 **Put 3 tbsp of the orange juice** in a bowl (reserve the rest) and add salt, pepper, vinegar, Grand Marnier, and cream. Stir, then gradually whisk in all but 2 tbsp of the hazelnut oil, so the dressing emulsifies and thickens slightly. Add the hazelnuts, stir, and taste for seasoning.

PREPARE THE SALMON

3 **With a filleting knife,** trim off any cartilage from the salmon. If necessary, pull out any pin bones with tweezers.

4 **Holding the fish steady** with one hand, tail facing away from you and working towards it, use a filleting knife to cut 12 even slices, each about 5mm (¼in) thick. Leave any skin behind.

COOK THE SALMON

5 **Sprinkle the salmon** with salt and pepper. Heat the vegetable oil in a frying pan. Cook the salmon for 1-2 minutes each side, until lightly browned. Brush with 2 tbsp orange juice and the remaining hazelnut oil.

6 **Toss the lamb's lettuce** with half the dressing and the orange segments and arrange on 6 plates with 2 warm salmon slices. Sprinkle over the remaining dressing.

Cobb salad

A CALIFORNIAN CLASSIC. A wonderful main course salad that will satisfy with the smooth textures of avocado and Roquefort cheese against crispy bacon bits, mild chicken, and crunchy cos lettuce leaves. Tarragon vinaigrette brings the whole dish together.

SERVES SERVES 4-6	**PREP** 20-25 MINS	**COOK** 5 MINS

Ingredients

FOR THE SALAD

1.8kg (4lb) whole cooked chicken or 500g (1lb 2oz) cooked skinless, boneless chicken

6 unsmoked back bacon rashers, sliced

2 avocados

juice of 1 lemon

1 shallot, finely chopped

500g (1lb 2lb) large cos lettuce or Little Gem lettuces, leaves sliced into strips

2 large tomatoes, cored and sliced

90g (3oz) Roquefort or other blue cheese, crumbled

FOR THE VINAIGRETTE

4 tbsp red wine vinegar

2 tsp Dijon mustard

½ tsp salt

¼ tsp pepper

175ml (6fl oz) vegetable oil

leaves from 3 tarragon sprigs, finely chopped

PREPARE THE CHICKEN

1 If using a whole cooked chicken, remove the meat from the bones, discarding all skin and any gristle, and cut into thin slices.

MAKE THE VINAIGRETTE

2 Put the vinegar, mustard, salt, and pepper in a small bowl and whisk. Add the oil in a steady stream, whisking constantly. The dressing will emulsify and thicken slightly.

3 Stir the tarragon in to the dressing and taste for seasoning.

COOK THE BACON

4 In a small frying pan, cook the bacon strips until golden and crispy, and the fat has rendered. Remove with a slotted spoon and drain on kitchen paper to blot off any excess fat.

PREPARE THE AVOCADO

5 Cut lengthways around the avocados, remove the stone, peel, and thinly slice. Toss the slices gently with lemon juice to prevent discolouration.

ASSEMBLE THE SALAD

6 Toss the chicken, shallot, and lettuce with a little dressing. Arrange in bowls with all the other ingredients, drizzling with more vinaigrette.

Meat-free

A rich variety of recipes
for vegetarians and
vegetable lovers

Greek-style vegetables

THE FLAVOURS WILL MELLOW in the refrigerator if you make these up to 2 days in advance. This piquant dish is great on the side of a rich main course, or as an appetizer. Adapt it to include other vegetables to take the recipe through the seasons.

SERVES	PREP	COOK
SERVES 6-8	25-30 MINS	25-30 MINS

Ingredients

FOR THE SPICE BAGS AND COOKING LIQUID

15g (½oz) coriander seeds

1 tbsp black peppercorns

4 bay leaves

5-7 thyme sprigs

3-4 parsley sprigs

2 tbsp tomato purée

750ml (1¼ pints) vegetable stock or water, plus more if needed

juice of 1 lemon

4 tbsp dry white wine

FOR THE VEGETABLES

24 baby onions

4 tbsp vegetable oil

4 tbsp olive oil

500g (1lb 2oz) button mushrooms, trimmed

400g (14oz) can tomatoes

salt and pepper

500g (1lb 2oz) fennel bulbs, sliced

45g (1½ oz) raisins

PREPARE THE INGREDIENTS

1 **Combine** the coriander seeds, black peppercorns, bay leaves, thyme and parsley sprigs. Halve the spice mixture and tie each portion up in a small piece of muslin.

2 **Make the cooking liquid:** whisk the tomato purée, half the vegetable stock or water, the lemon juice, and white wine in a bowl.

3 **Put the baby onions** in a bowl, cover with hot water, and let stand for 2 minutes. Drain and peel, leaving a little of the root attached.

COOK THE ONIONS AND MUSHROOMS

4 **Heat half the vegetable oil** and half the olive oil in a sauté pan. Add half the baby onions and sauté for about 3 minutes, until lightly browned. Add the mushrooms, a spice bag, and the tomatoes.

5 **Pour in half the cooking liquid;** there should be enough almost to cover the vegetables. Add salt. Bring to a fast boil over high heat. Stir occasionally, adding a little stock or water as the liquid evaporates. Cook for 25-30 minutes, until tender to the tip of a knife.

COOK THE ONIONS AND FENNEL

6 **Heat the remaining oils** in another sauté pan and sauté the remaining onions until lightly browned. Put in the second spice bag, remaining cooking liquid and salt. Add the fennel and bring to a fast boil over high heat.

7 **Continue boiling,** for 10-12 minutes, then add the raisins and stir. Cook for 15-20 minutes, until tender when pierced with a knife. Remove the spice bags from both mixtures and taste for seasoning.

Mixed pickled vegetables

THIS ASSORTMENT OF FRESH VEGETABLES tossed in a golden turmeric sauce is often served as part of a Malaysian meal. It will enliven any stir-fry, curry, or Asian noodle dish, adding crunch and a pleasing sweet-sour flavour.

SERVES	PREP	COOK
SERVES 8-10	1½-2½ HRS	10 MINS

Ingredients

FOR THE VEGETABLES

1 cucumber

3 large carrots

florets from ½ small cauliflower

30 French beans, trimmed

250g (9oz) wedge of green cabbage, cored and finely shredded

45g (1½oz) roasted unsalted peanuts

FOR THE PICKLING SAUCE

6 unsalted roasted macadamia nuts

2 garlic cloves, finely chopped

6 shallots, diced

4cm (1½in) piece of fresh galangal or root ginger, finely chopped

1½ tsp ground turmeric

2 hot red chillies, finely chopped

4 tbsp oil

100g (3½oz) sugar

1 tsp salt

125 ml (4fl oz) rice vinegar

PREPARE AND BLANCH THE VEGETABLES

1 **Peel the cucumber** and cut in half lengthways, and scoop out the seeds. Cut lengthways into 5mm (¼in) strips, then into 5cm (2in) sticks. Cut the carrots into sticks as well. Cut any large cauliflower florets in half.

2 **Fill a wok** 5cm (2in) deep with water and bring to a boil. Add the carrots, cauliflower, and beans. Simmer for 2-3 minutes, until tender but still crisp, then add the cucumber and cabbage for 1 minute. Drain well.

MAKE THE PICKLING SAUCE

3 **Finely chop** the macadamia nuts. (Asians use native kemiri nuts, often called candlenuts. Macadamias have a similar rich flavour and texture.)

4 **Pound the nuts**, garlic, shallots, galangal, turmeric, and chillies in a mortar and pestle, adding one ingredient at a time and pounding well after each addition. Alternatively, work the ingredients to a paste in a food processor.

PICKLE THE VEGETABLES

5 **Heat a wok** over medium heat until hot. Drizzle in the oil to coat the sides and bottom. When the oil is hot, add the chilli-nut paste and stir for 3-5 minutes, until slightly thickened and the spices are fragrant.

6 **Stir in the sugar**, salt, and vinegar; bring to a boil. Remove the wok from the heat and add the vegetables, tossing to coat. Transfer to a bowl, and cover. Let stand, about 1 hour at room temperature or at least 2 hours in the refrigerator. Coarsely chop the peanuts and sprinkle on top.

Tomato tagliatelle with artichokes

THIS FLAVOURFUL PASTA can be made, dried, and stored, loosely wrapped, in the refrigerator for up to 48 hours. Use a good extra virgin olive oil so the flavour of the finished dish is intense. Walnuts complement the artichokes in the sauce perfectly in this recipe.

SERVES	PREP	COOK
SERVES 4-6	50-60 MINS PLUS DRYING	3-4 MINS

Ingredients

FOR THE PASTA DOUGH

300g (10oz) strong plain flour, plus more if needed

3 eggs

1 tbsp vegetable oil

1 tsp salt

2½ tbsp tomato purée

FOR THE SAUCE

6 large canned or frozen artichoke hearts

5 tbsp extra virgin olive oil

2 shallots, finely chopped

4 garlic cloves, finely chopped

3 tbsp dry white wine

salt and pepper

leaves from 1 small bunch of parsley, chopped

45g (1½oz) walnut halves, roughly chopped

30g (1oz) grated Parmesan cheese

MAKE THE PASTA

1 **Sift the flour** on to a work surface. With your fingers, make a well in the centre.

2 **Add the eggs**, oil, salt, and tomato purée. Gradually mix in the flour to make a firm dough and press into a ball. Knead for 5-10 minutes, until elastic.

3 **Cut the dough** into 3 or 4 pieces and roll through a pasta machine, ending at the second narrowest setting and the wider of the machine's cutters. Toss the tagliatelle gently with a little flour, coil in bundles and leave for 1-2 hours on a floured tea towel.

MAKE THE SAUCE

4 **Thickly slice** the artichoke hearts. Heat the olive oil in a frying pan. Add the shallots and garlic and sauté gently for about 1 minute, until soft but not brown. Add the artichokes and white wine and simmer for 2-3 minutes. Season to taste. Stir only very gently, to avoid breaking up the artichokes.

COOK THE PASTA AND FINISH THE DISH

5 **Fill a large pan** with water, bring to the boil and add 1 tbsp salt. Add the tagliatelle and simmer for 2-3 minutes, until tender but still chewy, stirring to prevent sticking. Drain and add the tagliatelle to the pan of artichoke mixture and toss over moderate heat until the pasta is hot and evenly coated with olive oil.

6 **Pile the pasta** on to a warmed serving dish and sprinkle evenly with the parsley and walnuts. Finish by sprinkling with most of the Parmesan cheese, offering the remainder on the side.

VARIATION: Tomato tagliatelle with Jerusalem artichokes and walnuts

A delicious, wintry alternative for an underused vegetable.

1 Make the tagliatelle as directed.

2 Replace the artichoke hearts with 500g (1lb 2oz) Jerusalem artichokes. Peel and simmer for 15-20 minutes, until tender.

3 Drain the Jerusalem artichokes, slice, and simmer in wine as directed for artichoke hearts. Finish the dish as directed.

Herbed aioli platter

A SPECTACULAR DISH, popular with everyone, and known as "le grand aioli" in France. In Marseille, this recipe is traditionally served on Ash Wednesday. For those who eat fish, add squid or salt cod, if you like. Because this dish relies on the quality of the vegetables, choose only the freshest and perkiest you can find, substituting any of the vegetables listed here with those that look at their peak. Be careful not to boil the eggs for too long; they are best just slightly moist inside, and will be spoiled if their yolks are ringed with grey.

SERVES	PREP	COOK
SERVES 8	50-60 MINS	65-70 MINS

Ingredients

FOR THE EGGS AND VEGETABLES

8 eggs

8 globe artichokes

1 lemon

500g (1lb 2oz) baby carrots

4 fennel bulbs

500g (1lb 2oz) new potatoes

500g (1lb 2oz) asparagus

FOR THE HERBED AIOLI

2 garlic cloves, or to taste

salt and pepper

5-7 tarragon and parsley sprigs

1 large egg yolk

1 tsp Dijon mustard

275ml (9fl oz) extra virgin olive oil

275ml (9fl oz) vegetable oil

lemon juice, to taste

COOK THE EGGS AND MAKE THE HERBED AIOLI

1 **Put all the eggs** in a pan of cold water, bring to a boil and simmer for 8 minutes. Drain, plunge into cold water to stop the cooking, then peel. Set aside in cold water.

2 **Crush the garlic** with 1 tsp salt in a pestle and mortar, then strip the herb leaves from the stalks and crush them, too, in the mortar. It doesn't matter if the paste is not completely smooth, but the herbs should have broken down a little. Mix the egg yolk and mustard in a small bowl.

3 **Very slowly trickle the oils** into the egg yolk, whisking constantly, until the mixture emulsifies, then whisk in the remaining oils in a slow but steady stream until you have a glossy, wobbly mayonnaise. Stir in the garlic and herbs and season with lemon juice, salt, and pepper, to taste. Cover and set aside until serving, or refrigerate for up to 1 day.

PREPARE THE ARTICHOKES

4 **Prepare the artichoke hearts** as directed on page 52. Cut them into quarters, rubbing with lemon juice to prevent discolouration.

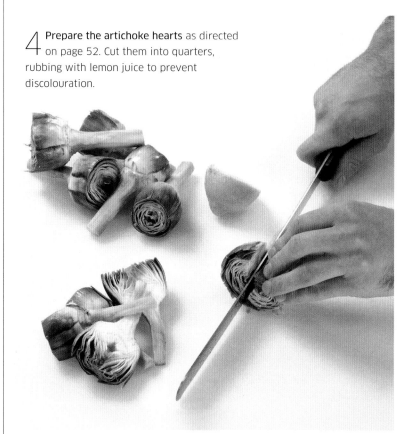

5 **Bring a saucepan of water** to the boil, add salt, then the artichokes and weigh them down with a heatproof plate. Simmer for about 15-20 minutes, until tender.

6 **Drain and allow to cool,** then scoop out the hairy chokes from each artichoke.

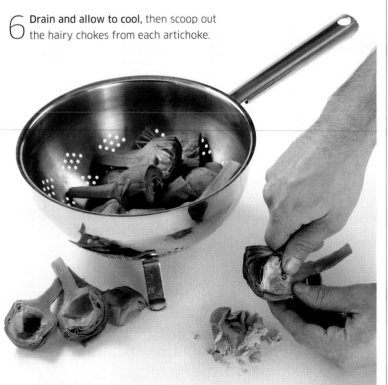

7 **Trim any green tops** from the baby carrots, leaving about 5mm (¼in) of green. Scrape the carrots to remove the thin skin. Put them in a saucepan of cold water, add salt, and bring to a boil. Simmer until just tender, 8-10 minutes, then drain.

PREPARE THE REMAINING VEGETABLES

8 **Trim the tops and bases of the fennel bulbs** to remove stalks and any dry ends. Discard any tough outer pieces. Cut each bulb lengthways into quarters. Bring a saucepan of water to a boil, add salt, then the fennel, and simmer until just tender, 12-15 minutes. Drain.

9 **Scrub the potatoes** and cut larger ones in half, so they are all about the same size. Put in a saucepan of cold water, add salt, and bring to a boil. Simmer until they are just tender, 12-15 minutes. Drain.

10 **With a vegetable peeler,** strip away the tough skin at the bottom of each asparagus stalk. Trim off any woody ends. With kitchen string, tie into bundles of 5-7 spears. Bring a shallow pan of water to a boil, add salt, then the asparagus and simmer for 5-6 minutes, until just tender. Drain.

11 **Drain and dry the hard-boiled eggs** and cut them in half. Arrange the vegetables on a large serving platter with the eggs. Serve at room temperature with the bowl of aioli.

Tempura

DELICIOUS JAPANESE FRITTERS with a lively dipping sauce. Tempura was actually introduced to Japan by Portuguese missionaries as a way to cook fish. Today, an authentic version is mainly based on vegetables. Meat and fish may be added and fried in the same way, for carnivores. Each piece of tempura must be dry and crisp, so ensure the oil is at the correct temperature before adding the vegetables (it's best to use a thermometer).

SERVES	PREP	COOK
SERVES 6-8	45-50 MINUTES	3-5 MINUTES

Ingredients

FOR THE VEGETABLES

1 head of broccoli

2 courgettes

125g (4½oz) mangetout

8 spring onions

2 sweet potatoes, total weight about 300g (10oz)

250g (9oz) shiitake mushrooms

125g (4½oz) canned water chestnuts

vegetable oil, for deep-frying

60g (2oz) plain flour, for dredging

FOR THE DIPPING SAUCE

60g (2oz) piece of daikon (white radish)

2.5cm (1in) fresh root ginger

125ml (4fl oz) sake

125ml (4fl oz) light soy sauce

FOR THE BATTER

2 eggs

300g (10oz) plain flour

PREPARE THE VEGETABLES

1 **Cut the broccoli florets** from the main stalk (discard the thick stalk). Cut any large florets in half straight through their stems. Trim the courgettes and cut them diagonally into 5mm (¼in) even slices. Trim the tops and tails from the mangetout and pull away any tough strings you find from the edges of the pods.

2 **Trim the spring onions** and cut each into 7.5cm (3in) lengths, discarding any thin, dark green ends or any discoloured outer leaves. Peel the sweet potatoes, making sure to remove all the "eyes", halve them lengthways then cut horizontally into 5mm (¼in) thick slices. Make sure the sweet potato slices are no thicker than this, or they may not cook through in the deep-fryer.

3 **Wipe the shiitakes** with damp kitchen paper, then trim off and discard any woody stalks. Cut any large mushrooms in half vertically, straight through the stalk. Drain and rinse the water chestnuts and slice them into thick discs.

MAKE THE DIPPING SAUCE AND BATTER

4 **Peel and grate the daikon.** Peel and slice the ginger, then crush each slice with the flat of a knife and very finely chop it.

5 **Mix the sake** and soy sauce together. Add the daikon and ginger and set aside.

6 **Lightly beat the eggs** in a large bowl and stir in 600ml (1 pint) cold water.

7 **Sift the** flour. Add it to the egg mixture and lightly whisk just until combined. The consistency should be slightly lumpy.

COAT AND FRY THE VEGETABLES

8 **Heat the oil** in a deep-fat fryer until it is hot enough to brown a cube of fresh bread in 40 seconds. If using a deep-fat thermometer, it should register 190°C (375°F). Heat the oven to very low, to keep the vegetables warm.

9 **Pour the batter** into a large, shallow dish. Put the flour for dredging in another shallow dish. Toss the broccoli florets in the flour to coat each evenly and lightly.

10 **Dip the vegetable pieces** in the batter so they are completely coated. Lift out the florets with a fork and drain off any excess batter. Lower the pieces gently into the hot oil. Do not crowd the pan; instead cook in small batches.

11 **Deep-fry until crisp** (it should take 3–5 minutes), turning once during cooking. With a slotted spoon, transfer the broccoli to a baking sheet lined with several layers of kitchen paper. Keep warm in the oven.

12 **Cook the other vegetables** in the same way, flouring them, then coating with batter, deep-frying, and transferring to the lined baking sheet to keep warm. Arrange the deep-fried vegetables on a serving platter. Warm the sauce in a saucepan just until hot, and taste for seasoning. Serve it in small bowls alongside the tempura.

Three-cheese Swiss chard crêpes

A VIVACIOUSLY FLAVOURED DISH for a cold day, indulgently filled with Gruyère, feta, and goat's cheese. Make sure your crêpes are as thin and lacy as possible, so that the dish isn't heavy. Most greens can be substituted for the Swiss chard in the recipe: try spinach, or even pak choi, if you prefer.

SERVES	**PREP**	**COOK**
SERVES 6	1 HR PLUS STANDING	20-25 MINS

Ingredients

FOR THE BATTER

125g (4½oz) plain flour

½ tsp salt

3 eggs

250ml (9fl oz) milk

3-4 tbsp vegetable oil

FOR THE FILLING

750g (1lb 10oz) Swiss chard

30g (1oz) butter

2 garlic cloves, finely chopped

3 shallots, finely chopped

90g (3oz) soft goat's cheese

125g (4½oz) feta cheese

salt and pepper

ground nutmeg

FOR THE CREAM SAUCE

250ml (9fl oz) milk

30g (1oz) butter

2 tbsp plain flour

125ml (4fl oz) double cream

ground nutmeg

30g (1oz) Gruyère cheese, coarsely grated

MAKE THE CRÊPES

1 **Sift the flour** and salt into a bowl, and make a well in the centre. Pour the eggs into the well, and whisk until just mixed. Add half the milk and whisk, drawing in the flour to make a paste. Stir in half of the remaining milk. Cover and let stand for 30-60 minutes. Stir in the remaining milk until the batter is the consistency of thin cream.

2 **Heat about 1 tbsp oil** in a pan until very hot; pour off the excess. Pour in a small ladle of batter, rotating and shaking the pan to coat the bottom evenly. Fry quickly for 1-2 minutes, until set on top and brown underneath. Loosen the crêpe, then flip it over with a palette knife, and cook for 30-60 seconds, until brown on the other side.

3 **Transfer the crêpe** to a plate. Continue making crêpes, adding oil to the pan as necessary, until all the batter is used, to make a total of 12. Pile them on the plate so that they stay moist and warm.

PREPARE THE SWISS CHARD

4 **Trim the root** from the Swiss chard, and discard any tough stalks and leaves. Thoroughly wash the stalks and leaves. Cut off the green leaves around the stalks. Using a vegetable peeler, remove any strings from the outer sides of the stalks, and set aside.

5 **Cut the stalks** into 1cm (½in) slices. Bring a large pan of water to a boil, add salt and the leaves, and simmer for 2-3 minutes, until tender. Drain, then chop.

MAKE THE FILLING

6 **Heat the butter** in a large frying pan. Add the garlic and shallots, and cook until soft but not brown. Add the chard stalks; sauté for 3-5 minutes, stirring, until just tender. Add the chard leaves; sauté for 2-3 minutes, stirring, until all moisture has evaporated. Remove the pan from the heat.

7 **Crumble the goat's cheese** into the chard mixture, then crumble in the feta. Season to taste with salt, pepper, and a pinch of nutmeg. Stir to mix, then set aside.

FILL AND BAKE THE CREPES

8 **Preheat the oven** to 180°C (350°F/Gas 4). Butter a shallow baking dish. To make the cream sauce: scald the milk in a saucepan. Melt the butter in another saucepan, over medium heat. Whisk in the flour, and cook for 30-60 seconds, until foaming.

9 **Remove from the heat** and let cool slightly, then whisk in the hot milk. Return to the heat and cook, whisking, until it boils and thickens. Whisk in the cream. Season with salt, pepper, and a pinch of nutmeg, and simmer for 2 minutes. Remove from the heat, cover, and keep warm.

10 **Put 2 spoonfuls of filling** on to one half of the paler side of a crêpe. Fold the crêpe in half, then in half again, to form a triangle. Arrange in the dish, then continue. Spoon over the sauce. Sprinkle with the Gruyère. Bake for 20-25 minutes, until bubbling and brown. Serve hot from the dish.

 VARIATION: Crêpes with wild mushrooms and herbs

Juicy and delicious.

1 Make the crêpes as directed. Wipe 250g (9oz) fresh shiitake mushrooms with a damp paper towel, trim the stalks, and halve any large mushrooms. Cut into 1cm (½in) slices. Clean 250g (9oz) button mushrooms, trim the stalks even with the caps, then slice.

2 Melt the butter, add the garlic, shallots, and shiitake and button mushrooms, and sauté for about 5 minutes, until the liquid has evaporated, stirring constantly. Set aside a few mushrooms for garnish. Chop the leaves from several sprigs of parsley, tarragon, and chives.

3 Make the white sauce as directed, saving the cream to add later, then stir in the herbs. Mix half the sauce with the mushrooms, put in each crêpe, fold in 2 sides, and roll up into cylinders. Arrange in the baking dish. Add the cream to the remaining herb sauce, and pour it over. Bake as directed, sprinkling with the reserved mushrooms just before serving.

Fusilli with pesto

PESTO SAUCE IS A REAL TREAT to have on hand and this is how to make it for yourself, to serve as an appetizer. It's so much better than the pesto you can buy that it's almost like a different sauce. Make it in a pestle and mortar, if you prefer, though you will need strong arms and a little more patience.

SERVES	PREP	COOK
SERVES 6-8	10-15 MINS	8-10 MINS

Ingredients

60g (2oz) basil

6 garlic cloves, peeled

45g (1½oz) pine nuts

125g (4½oz) grated Parmesan cheese

175ml (6fl oz) olive oil

salt and pepper

500g (1lb 2oz) fusilli pasta

cherry tomatoes, to serve (optional)

MAKE THE PESTO

1 **Strip the leaves** from the basil and put in a food processor with the garlic, pine nuts, Parmesan, and about 3 tbsp of the olive oil.

2 **Purée until smooth,** scraping down the sides of the bowl as necessary. With the blade turning, slowly pour in the remaining oil through the feed tube, until the pesto emulsifies. Season to taste.

COOK THE PASTA

3 **Fill a large pan** with cold water, bring it to the boil and add 1 tbsp salt. Add the pasta and simmer for 8-10 minutes, until tender but still chewy, or according to packet instructions, stirring occasionally to prevent the pasta spirals from sticking together. Drain the pasta thoroughly in a colander, shaking to remove any excess water.

FINISH THE DISH

4 **Put the pesto sauce** in a mixing bowl and tip in the pasta. Toss with 2 spoons or large forks until the pasta is evenly coated with pesto. Pile on to plates and decorate with a few cherry tomatoes, if you like, or more basil sprigs. Serve hot or warm.

Summer frittata with ratatouille

WHILE THE EGGS COOK slowly in this Italian-style omelette, you can sit back and enjoy a glass of wine. Use any vegetables you have to hand to make the filling, which can be prepared up to 24 hours ahead and kept, tightly covered, in the refrigerator. Cook the frittata just before serving.

SERVES	PREP	COOK
SERVES 3-4	20-25 MINS	20-25 MINS

Ingredients

6 eggs

salt and pepper

15–30g (½–1oz) butter

FOR THE FILLING

1 small aubergine

1 courgette

4 tbsp olive oil, plus more if needed

1 green pepper, sliced into strips

1 onion, thinly sliced

250g (9oz) tomatoes, peeled, deseeded and chopped, or 1 x 200g (7oz) can chopped tomatoes

2 garlic cloves, finely chopped

leaves from 5–7 thyme sprigs, plus a few sprigs to decorate

½ tsp ground coriander

1 large bouquet garni (10–12 parsley stalks, 4–5 thyme sprigs and 2 bay leaves)

PREPARE THE RATATOUILLE

1 **Trim the aubergine** and cut into 1cm (½in) chunks. Cut the courgette into 1cm (½in) slices. Put the aubergine and courgette on a tray and sprinkle generously with salt. Leave for 30 minutes, then place in a colander, rinse and pat dry with kitchen paper.

2 **Heat about half the oil** in a frying pan. Add the aubergine to the pan and stir-fry for 3-5 minutes, until browned. Transfer to a bowl with a slotted spoon. Repeat with the courgette slices.

3 **Add the green pepper** to the pan with a little more oil and stir-fry until limp; remove to the bowl. Heat about 1 tbsp more oil in the pan, add the onion and sauté for 2-3 minutes, until lightly browned.

4 **Return the aubergine,** courgette, and pepper to the pan and add the tomatoes, garlic, salt, pepper, thyme, coriander, and the bouquet garni. Stir until mixed. Cover and cook for 10-15 minutes, until tender. Remove and discard the bouquet garni. Let cool.

COOK THE FRITTATA

5 **Whisk the eggs** in a bowl until completely mixed. Stir in the ratatouille mixture and season with salt and pepper.

6 **Wipe the frying pan;** melt the butter over medium heat until foaming, then add the egg mixture. Reduce the heat, cover and cook very gently for 20-25 minutes, until the centre is set and the base is cooked and lightly browned when you lift the edge.

7 **Invert the frittata** onto a large warmed plate and decorate with the reserved thyme sprigs. Cut the frittata into wedges for serving.

Buddha's delight

A VISIT TO AN ASIAN STORE will be required for the ingredients, but it's worth it. Chinese vegetarian cooking originated in Buddhist monastery kitchens. The monks abstain from meat so protein-packed tofu is used in this typical dish.

SERVES	PREP	COOK
SERVES 4	40–50 MINS PLUS SOAKING	15–20 MINS

Ingredients

30g (1oz) dried Chinese black mushrooms	250g (9oz) lotus root
	2 tbsp lemon juice
45g (1½oz) dried tiger lily buds	6 large fresh water chestnuts
15g (½oz) dried tree ears	3 tbsp rice wine, plus more if needed
50g (1¾oz) cellophane noodles	3 tbsp light soy sauce, plus more if needed
175g (6oz) baby sweetcorn	2 tsp dark sesame oil
	2 tbsp cornflour
250g (9oz) mangetout	250g (9oz) firm tofu
	4 tbsp groundnut oil
	3 garlic cloves, finely chopped

PREPARE THE VEGETABLES

1 **Put the black mushrooms,** tiger lily buds, and tree ears in separate bowls. Add enough warm water to each bowl to cover, and let soak, about 30 minutes. Put the cellophane noodles in a bowl and cover with warm water. Let soak until soft, about 30 minutes.

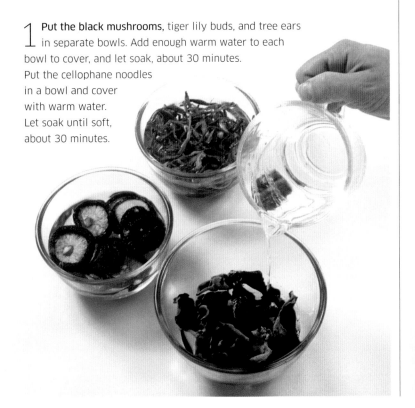

2 **Trim the baby sweetcorn** and cut each diagonally in half. Trim the end from each mangetout and pull the string from down the side of the pod. Repeat at the other end, pulling the string from the other side.

3 **With a cleaver,** scrape the skin from the lotus root and slice across into 1cm (½in) rounds. Put the lotus root and the lemon juice in a bowl of cold water to prevent discolouration.

PREPARE THE REMAINING INGREDIENTS

4 With a small knife, cut the peel from the water chestnuts, dropping them into a bowl of cold water as you work. Remove them from the water, slice into rounds, then return the slices to the water.

5 Drain the tiger lily buds and tree ears and rinse well to remove any grit. Drain and squeeze dry. Cut off and discard the tough ends of the tiger lily buds and tree ears. If the tree ears are large, cut into 5cm (2in) pieces.

6 Drain the cellophane noodles in a colander, then cut into 12.5cm (5in) lengths. Drain the black mushrooms, reserving the liquid. Trim off the woody stalks, then slice the mushroom caps.

7 Line a sieve with kitchen paper and set it over a measuring jug. Strain 175ml (6fl oz) of the mushroom soaking liquid into the jug; the kitchen paper will remove any grit. Discard the remainder.

8 In a bowl, combine the mushroom liquid, rice wine, soy sauce, sesame oil, and half the cornflour, and stir until the cornflour has dissolved into the liquid and it is smooth, with no lumps.

CUT AND FRY THE TOFU

9 Set the tofu on a chopping board and cut it diagonally twice from corner to corner to make 4 triangles. Cut each triangle in half to make 8 triangles. Pat each dry on kitchen paper.

10 Put the remaining cornflour on a plate. Dip the tofu into the cornflour, turning and patting the triangles lightly to coat them evenly. Heat a wok over high heat until very hot.

11 Drizzle in the oil to coat the bottom and sides. Heat until very hot, then add the tofu and fry for 6–8 minutes, until golden brown, turning. Transfer to a plate and keep warm. Reduce the heat to medium.

STIR-FRY THE VEGETABLES

12 Drain the lotus root and water chestnuts. Add them to the wok with the baby sweetcorn, and stir-fry for 3–4 minutes, until the lotus root begins to soften. Add the mangetout and garlic and stir-fry for about 1 minute longer, taking care the garlic doesn't burn.

13 Add the tiger lily buds, black mushrooms, and tree ears and stir-fry for about 1 minute. Stir the cornflour mixture again, then add it to the wok. Bring to a boil, stir-frying until the mixture thickens; it should take 1–2 minutes. Add the noodles and stir-fry until very hot. Taste for seasoning, adding more rice wine or soy sauce if needed.

14 Transfer the vegetables and noodles to a warmed serving dish or into individual bowls, and carefully arrange the fried tofu triangles on top of the crisp, aromatic vegetables.

Artichokes stuffed with olives

A WONDERFUL PROVENÇAL WAY to eat artichokes, simmered with white wine and served with a fantastic and tasty rich red pepper sauce. In France, this preparation of the vegetable is known as "à la barigoule".

SERVES	PREP	COOK
SERVES 4	50-55 MINS	40-45 MINS

Ingredients

FOR THE ARTICHOKES

4 globe artichokes, total weight about 1.4kg (3lb)

½ lemon

salt and pepper

250ml (9fl oz) white wine

FOR THE STUFFING

4 slices of white bread

45g (1½oz) butter

3 small onions, finely chopped

6 garlic cloves, finely chopped

250g (9oz) mushrooms, finely chopped

250g (9oz) Parma ham, cut into strips

2 anchovy fillets, finely chopped

175g (6oz) stoned black olives, finely chopped

leaves from 2-3 thyme sprigs

ground allspice

FOR THE RED PEPPER SAUCE

750g (1lb 10oz) red peppers

2 tbsp olive oil

400g (14oz) can chopped tomatoes

1 garlic clove, chopped

2 spring onions, chopped

leaves from 1 small bunch of basil, chopped, plus 4 sprigs for garnish

PREPARE THE ARTICHOKES

1 **Snap the stalk** from each artichoke so the fibres are pulled out with the stalk. Trim the base of each so they sit flat, and rub the cut surfaces with the lemon half to prevent discolouration. Trim the outer leaves with kitchen scissors to remove the pointed tips.

2 **Cut off** about 2cm (¾in) from the pointed top of each artichoke. Rub all cut surfaces with lemon. Fill a casserole with water, bring to a boil and add salt. Add the artichokes. Weigh them down with the heatproof plate to submerge. Simmer until almost tender and a leaf can be pulled out with a slight tug, 25-30 minutes.

3 **Lift out the artichokes** with a slotted spoon and set them upside-down on a wire rack placed over a tray to drain. When cool enough to handle, remove the inner leaves by twisting them out with your fingers.

4 **With a teaspoon,** scoop out the hairy choke from each to make a neat cavity for the stuffing.

MAKE THE STUFFING

5 Trim and discard the crusts from the bread. Work the bread slices in a food processor to form crumbs. Melt the butter in the frying pan, add the onions and garlic, and cook, stirring, until soft but not brown.

6 Stir in the mushrooms, Parma ham, anchovies, and olives, then remove from the heat. Add the breadcrumbs, thyme, and a large pinch of allspice and mix thoroughly. Season to taste with pepper.

STUFF AND BAKE THE ARTICHOKES

7 Preheat the oven to 180°C (350°F/Gas 4). Fill the centre of each artichoke with stuffing. Tie a piece of kitchen string around each to hold the leaves together. Put the artichokes in a casserole and pour in the wine.

8 Put the casserole over high heat, bring to a boil and reduce by half; it should take about 5 minutes. Pour in enough water to half-cover the artichokes and add salt and pepper. Bring back to a boil and cover.

9 Transfer to the oven. Bake, basting occasionally with the wine and juices, until tender and a central leaf can be pulled out easily. It should take 40-50 minutes, depending on the size of the artichokes.

MAKE THE SAUCE

10 Heat the grill. Set the peppers on a rack about 10cm (4in) from the heat and grill, turning, until black and blistered. Seal in a plastic bag and let cool. Peel, then core and scrape out the seeds. Cut into chunks.

11 Heat the olive oil in a frying pan. Add the peppers, tomatoes, garlic, spring onions, and basil and cook, stirring occasionally, for 15-20 minutes, until thickened. Pour into a food processor and purée until still slightly chunky. Season to taste.

12 Discard the strings from the artichokes and put on individual plates. Spoon some sauce around the base of each, garnish with a basil sprig, if liked, and pass the remaining sauce separately.

Mexican cheese-stuffed peppers

POBLANO CHILLIES are traditionally used in this dish as they are large and mild; do use them if you can find them. Green peppers make an excellent substitution in this recipe, which is known in Mexico as "chiles rellenos".

SERVES	PREP	COOK
SERVES 4	30–35 MINS, PLUS STANDING	45–50 MINS

Ingredients

FOR THE PEPPERS

8 large green peppers

2 onions

2 tbsp vegetable oil, plus more for the dish

500g (1lb 2oz) mild Cheddar cheese

2 tsp dried oregano

salt and pepper

FOR THE TOMATO SALSA

leaves from 1 small bunch of coriander, finely chopped

500g (1lb 2oz) tomatoes, peeled, deseeded and finely chopped

2 garlic cloves, finely chopped

2 large onions, finely chopped

2 green chillies, deseeded and finely chopped

juice of 1 lemon

1 tsp Tabasco sauce

FOR THE CUSTARD

3 eggs

125ml (4fl oz) milk

½ tsp dried oregano

ROAST, PEEL, AND STUFF THE PEPPERS

1 **Heat the grill** and set the whole peppers on a rack about 10cm (4in) from the heat. Grill them, turning once or twice, for 10–12 minutes, until the skin is black and blistered. Wrap in plastic bags and let cool.

2 **Peel off the skin,** then rinse under cold running water and pat dry with kitchen paper. Cut out the core from the centre of each pepper, then scrape out and discard the seeds with a teaspoon.

3 **Chop the onions.** Heat the vegetable oil in a frying pan, add the onions and cook, stirring, until soft but not brown. Let cool. Grate the cheese and put it in a bowl. Add the oregano, salt, pepper, and onions and mix well. Taste for seasoning.

4 **Oil the baking dish.** Spoon the cheese-onion mixture into each pepper and put the peppers sideways in the dish. They should fit snugly.

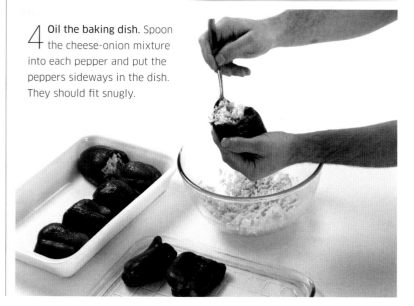

MAKE THE SALSA

5 Set aside some coriander for serving. Mix the chopped tomatoes, garlic, onions, chillies, lemon juice, remaining coriander, and Tabasco and season to taste with salt. Let stand for at least 30 minutes.

BAKE THE PEPPERS

6 Heat the oven to 180°C (350°F/Gas 4). Make the custard: whisk together the eggs, milk, oregano, salt, and pepper. Pour it around the peppers and bake for 45-50 minutes.

7 Decorate the salsa by sprinkling evenly with the reserved coriander leaves, scatter a spoonful of it over each pepper and serve the rest in a bowl on the side.

 VARIATION: Red peppers stuffed with sweetcorn

A really pretty dish.

1 Cook 2 corn cobs in a large pan of boiling water for 15-20 minutes, until the kernels pop out easily when tested with the point of a knife. Drain and cut the kernels from the cob. Or use a drained large can of sweetcorn.

2 Make the tomato salsa as directed in the main recipe. Peel, core, and deseed 8 red peppers as directed. Make the cheese filling as directed and stir in the sweetcorn.

3 Stuff the peppers and arrange them upright in individual baking dishes, 2 peppers to each dish. Pour in the custard and bake as directed.

Stir-fried Thai vegetables

ALMOST ANY CRISP VEGETABLE is excellent stir-fried; the textures stay firm and the colours vivid. There's only really one firm rule for a stir-fry: you have to be organised. All the component parts must be chopped and close to hand before you start, as the cooking must be done very quickly and at the last possible minute before serving.

SERVES	**PREP**	**COOK**
SERVES 4	30-35 MINS	15-20 MINS

Ingredients

300g (10oz) long-grain rice

salt

30g (1oz) dried oriental mushrooms, or other dried wild mushrooms

60g (2oz) skinned unsalted peanuts

175g (6oz) beansprouts

1 stalk lemongrass

3 tbsp fish sauce (*nam pla*)

2 tbsp oyster sauce

1 tsp cornflour

1 tsp sugar

3 tbsp vegetable oil

2 garlic cloves, finely chopped

2 dried red chillies

1 cauliflower, cut into florets

1 red pepper, cut into strips

500g (1lb 2oz) bok choi, trimmed and shredded

175g (6oz) mangetout, trimmed

leaves from 3-5 basil sprigs

BOIL THE RICE

1 Cook the long-grain rice in boiling salted water for 10-12 minutes, until barely tender. Drain in a colander, rinse with cold running water to wash away the starch, and let drain thoroughly. Meanwhile, prepare the vegetables. Butter a baking dish and enough foil to cover the dish.

PREPARE THE VEGETABLES

2 Preheat the oven to 190°C (375°F/Gas 5). Put the dried mushrooms in a bowl, pour over warm water to cover, and set aside to soften, about 30 minutes, then drain and slice.

3 Scatter the peanuts on a baking sheet and toast in the oven until brown, 5-7 minutes, then coarsely chop. Turn the oven to its lowest possible setting. Rinse the beansprouts in a colander. Trim the lemongrass. Slice the stalk lengthwise in half, then cut across to chop it.

4 Spread the rice evenly in the buttered baking dish, gently fluffing up the grains to separate them with a fork, and cover with the sheet of buttered foil. Keep the rice warm in the very low oven while you cook the stir-fry.

STIR-FRY THE VEGETABLES

5 Put the fish sauce, oyster sauce, cornflour, sugar, and lemongrass in a small bowl and whisk together.

6 Heat the oil in a wok. Add the garlic and chillies and stir-fry for 30 seconds, until fragrant. Add the cauliflower, red pepper, beansprouts, and bok choi and cook for 3 minutes, stirring constantly. Tip in the mushrooms and mangetout and stir-fry for 3 minutes more.

7 Add the basil leaves and fish sauce mixture to the vegetables and stir-fry for a final 2 minutes. Taste and season with more fish sauce, oyster sauce, and sugar, if needed. Remove the chillies and discard. Pile the rice on warmed plates. Spoon the vegetables and sauce over, and sprinkle with peanuts.

VARIATION: Chinese stir-fried vegetables

Best served with boiled Chinese noodles.

1 Prepare the mushrooms, bok choi, and beansprouts as directed in the main recipe; omit the cauliflower, mangetout, and red pepper. Omit the peanuts; toast 45g (1½ oz) flaked almonds in the oven for 3–5 minutes instead. You must be sure to watch very carefully, as flaked almonds can go from toasted to burned very quickly.

2 Cut the florets from 1 head of broccoli. Drain 60g (2oz) canned bamboo shoots and rinse 60g (2oz) baby sweetcorn. Slice the green parts only of 2 spring onions. Omit the fish sauce mixture. For the sauce, whisk together 3 tbsp rice wine, 2 tbsp soy sauce, 2 tsp sesame oil, 1 tsp cornflour, and a pinch of sugar.

3 Heat the oil in a wok, add the broccoli and bok choi and stir-fry for 2–3 minutes. Add the mushrooms and baby corn and stir-fry for 2 minutes more. Add the soy sauce mixture, bamboo shoots, beansprouts, and spring onions and cook, stirring, for 2 minutes. The sauce should thicken slightly. Continue to turn all the vegetables very well, so that everything is evenly cooked. Season with more rice wine, soy sauce, sesame oil, and sugar, if needed, and sprinkle with the toasted almonds.

Gratin dauphinois

WONDERFULLY RICH, and simply superb. Floury baking potatoes work best in this dish; look for the widely available Maris Piper or King Edward varieties. They are simmered in milk to keep them as sweet as possible before being cooked with double cream. If it is more convenient, you can assemble the gratin up to the point of baking, then keep it, covered, in the refrigerator for 1 day. Bake it just before serving.

SERVES SERVES 6-8	**PREP** 30-40 MINS	**COOK** 20-25 MINS

Ingredients

750g (1lb 10oz) potatoes

600ml (1 pint) milk

freshly grated nutmeg

salt and pepper

300ml (10fl oz) double cream

1 garlic clove

45g (1½oz) Gruyère cheese, coarsely grated

PREPARE THE POTATOES

1 **Peel the potatoes.** With a mandolin or knife, cut them into 3mm (⅛in) slices. Cover the slices with a wet tea towel, so that they do not discolour. Do not soak them in water; this would remove the starch that gives the gratin its creamy consistency.

PRE-COOK THE POTATOES

2 **Bring the milk to a boil** in a saucepan, stirring occasionally so it does not burn. Season it with a little grated nutmeg, salt, and pepper. Add the potatoes and cook, stirring occasionally, for 10-15 minutes, until just tender.

3 **Drain the potatoes** in a colander. Discard the milk, or save it for another use, such as soup, if you like.

ASSEMBLE AND BAKE THE GRATIN

4 **Return the potatoes** to the saucepan, and pour in the cream. Bring to a boil and simmer, stirring occasionally, for 10-15 minutes, until very tender. Taste for seasoning. Preheat the oven to 190°C (375°F/Gas 5).

5 **Peel the garlic clove,** cut it in half, and use the cut side to rub the bottom and sides of a 1.5 litre (2¾ pint) baking dish. Brush the bottom and sides of the dish with melted butter.

6 **Layer the potatoes** and cream in the dish, then sprinkle with the cheese. Bake for 20-25 minutes, until golden brown. Test with a small knife; the blade should feel hot when withdrawn. Serve the gratin dauphinois hot, directly from the baking dish.

Roast pepper lasagne

THIS RECIPE IS EASILY DOUBLED or tripled, and freezes well. You can assemble the dish, cover, and refrigerate for up to 2 days before baking. If you are pushed for time, use shop-bought roasted peppers in jars instead of roasting your own.

SERVES	PREP	COOK
SERVES 8	1½ HRS	35–45 MINS

Ingredients

FOR THE TOMATO SAUCE

2 x 400g (14oz) cans tomatoes

6 garlic cloves, finely chopped

leaves from 1 bunch of basil, chopped

leaves from 7–10 oregano sprigs, chopped

leaves from 1 bunch of flat-leaf parsley, chopped

salt and pepper

FOR THE LASAGNE

4 red peppers

4 green peppers

2 tbsp olive oil

750g (1lb 10oz) mushrooms, thinly sliced

1kg (2¼lb) ricotta cheese

pinch of ground nutmeg

375g (13oz) lasagne

175g (6oz) freshly grated Parmesan cheese

MAKE THE SAUCE

1 **Put the tomatoes,** half the garlic, and two-thirds of the herbs in a shallow pan. Season. Cook over medium heat, stirring occasionally, for 25–35 minutes, until thickened. Ladle into a food processor, and purée until smooth.

PREPARE THE VEGETABLES AND PASTA

2 **Heat the grill.** Set the peppers on a rack 10cm (4in) from the heat and grill, turning, until blackened. Put in a plastic bag, seal, and cool. Peel off the skins. Halve the peppers, and scrape out the cores and seeds. Cut into 1cm (½in) strips.

3 **Heat the oil** in a frying pan. Add the mushrooms with the remaining garlic and cook, stirring, for 10–12 minutes, until the liquid evaporates. Put the ricotta, remaining herbs, nutmeg, salt, and pepper in a bowl. Stir until thoroughly combined.

4 **Fill a large pan** with water and bring to a boil. Add 1 tbsp salt, and the lasagne, a sheet at a time. Simmer for 8–10 minutes, or according to package directions, until tender. Drain thoroughly on a tea towel.

FINISH THE LASAGNE

5 **Heat the oven** to 180°C (350°F/Gas 4). Brush a baking dish with oil. Spread 3–4 tbsp of tomato sauce in the dish; cover with a layer of lasagne sheets, overlapping slightly.

6 **Spread on a quarter of the ricotta,** then a quarter of the mushrooms and peppers. Spoon over a fifth of the remaining tomato sauce, and Parmesan. Continue to make 4 layers, finishing with lasagne on top. Cover with the remaining sauce and Parmesan. Bake the lasagne for 35–45 minutes, until bubbling and golden brown.

Aubergine cannelloni

CHOOSE BROAD AUBERGINES so you have big slices for filling with lots of luscious mozzarella and ricotta cheeses. These cannelloni can be baked up to 2 days ahead. Cover and chill, then reheat them in the oven for 20 minutes.

SERVES	**PREP**	**COOK**
SERVES 4-6	40-45 MINS PLUS STANDING	50-60 MINS

Ingredients

FOR THE AUBERGINES

4 aubergines, total weight about 1.4kg (3lb)

salt and pepper

4 tbsp olive oil

250g (9oz) mozzarella cheese

250g (9oz) ricotta cheese

leaves from 1 bunch of basil, plus a few sprigs for serving

30g (1oz) Parmesan cheese, grated

FOR THE SAUCE

75ml (2½fl oz) olive oil

3 onions, finely chopped

5 garlic cloves, finely chopped

90ml (3fl oz) tomato purée

1 bouquet garni

3 x 400g (14oz) cans chopped tomatoes

granulated sugar

PREPARE THE AUBERGINES

1 **Trim the aubergines** and cut them lengthways into 1cm (½in) slices. Lay on a non-metallic tray, in 1 layer, and sprinkle generously on both sides with salt. Leave 30 minutes. Preheat the oven to 190°C (375°F/Gas 5).

2 **Rinse the aubergine** slices with cold water and dry on kitchen paper. Lightly brush one side of each slice with olive oil and set oil-side down on baking sheets. Brush the tops with more oil.

3 **Bake the aubergine** slices in the oven, turning once, for about 20 minutes, until tender and lightly browned. Do not cook them for too long or they will be too soft to handle.

MAKE THE SAUCE

4 **Heat the oil** in a frying pan, add the onions, and cook over medium heat, stirring occasionally, for 3-4 minutes, until soft but not brown. Add the garlic, tomato purée, bouquet garni, tomatoes, a pinch of sugar, salt, and pepper. Cover and cook over very low heat, about 10 minutes.

5 **Uncover the frying pan** and continue cooking the tomato sauce, stirring occasionally, for about 15 minutes, until thick. Lift out and discard the bouquet garni. Taste for seasoning and adjust if necessary.

FILL THE CANNELLONI

6 **Spread one-third of the tomato sauce** in the bottom of a baking dish, about 23x32cm (9x13in). Cut the mozzarella into 1cm (½in) sticks.

7 **Spread a slice of aubergine** with 1 tbsp ricotta. Put a basil leaf at one end, set a mozzarella stick on top and sprinkle with pepper. Roll up the aubergine slice.

8 Transfer the roll to the baking dish and repeat with the remaining aubergine slices, ricotta, basil, and mozzarella cheese. Spoon over the remaining tomato sauce and sprinkle with Parmesan. Bake until very hot and bubbling, 20–25 minutes. Serve on warmed plates.

VARIATION: Aubergine feuilles

Lots of layers of luscious vegetables and molten cheese make this dish into an impressively tall, stacked plate.

1 Trim the aubergines and cut them into 1cm (¹⁄₂in) rounds. There should be 36 rounds. Spread them on a large, non-metallic tray, sprinkle with salt and leave for 25 minutes, then rinse, dry and bake with olive oil as directed. Make the tomato sauce as directed, cooking 5 minutes longer to make it thicker. Let it cool to tepid. Cut 300g (10oz) mozzarella cheese into 24 slices, each about 5mm (¹⁄₄in) thick.

2 Stir the ricotta cheese into half the cooled tomato sauce and taste for seasoning. Pull the basil leaves from the stalks, saving 6 sprigs for garnish. Oil a baking sheet. Spread a large aubergine round with the tomato and cheese filling, top with a slice of mozzarella and 2 basil leaves, then add a smaller round of aubergine. Repeat the layers, finishing with an even smaller piece of aubergine.

3 Secure the "feuilles" with a cocktail stick so they hold together during cooking. Transfer to the baking sheet and continue with the remaining aubergine rounds and filling. Bake in the heated oven until very hot and the mozzarella has melted, about 12 minutes. Reheat the remaining tomato sauce and spoon it on to 6 warmed plates. Set the hot feuilles on top. Remove the cocktail sticks and decorate with sprigs of basil.

Courgette tian

TIAN IS THE PROVENÇAL NAME for a shallow earthenware dish, as well as for a vegetable mixture, held together with eggs and cooked rice. Try to use small courgettes for this recipe, as they tend to have a more concentrated flavour than the larger, more watery examples. Use this recipe as a blueprint for other vegetables; all are equally delicious and make a satisfying vegetarian dish. For carnivores, this is also an excellent side dish with roast lamb or chicken.

SERVES	PREP	COOK
SERVES 6	30–35 MINS	20–30 MINS

Ingredients

75ml (2½ fl oz) olive oil

1kg (2¼lb) courgettes, in 5mm (¼in) slices

salt and pepper

65g (2¼oz) long-grain rice

2 onions, thinly sliced

3 garlic cloves, finely chopped

leaves from 5–7 flat-leaf parsley sprigs, finely chopped

60g (2oz) Parmesan cheese, grated

3 eggs

PREPARE THE COURGETTES

1 **Heat one-third of the oil** in a large frying pan. Add the courgettes, salt, and pepper, and cook over medium heat, stirring occasionally, for 10–15 minutes, until tender and evenly browned. Spread the slices out over a large plate to cool.

PREPARE THE REMAINING INGREDIENTS

2 **Bring a saucepan of salted water** to a boil, add the rice, and bring back to a boil. Simmer for 10–12 minutes, until just tender, stirring once or twice to prevent the grains sticking to the bottom of the pan. Drain the rice in a colander, rinse with cold water to remove some of the starch, and drain again thoroughly. Let the rice cool for 8–10 minutes, then stir with a fork to separate the grains.

3 **Heat half the remaining oil** in the frying pan, add the onions and garlic, and cook over medium heat, stirring occasionally, for 3–5 minutes, until soft but not coloured.

ASSEMBLE AND BAKE THE TIAN

4 **Preheat the oven** to 180°C (350°F/Gas 4). Brush a 1.5 litre (2¾ pint) baking dish with oil. Coarsely chop the cooled courgettes.

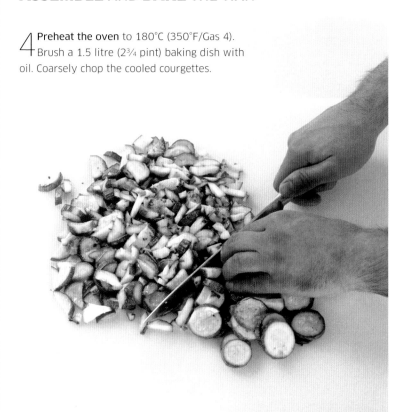

5 **In a large bowl,** combine the courgettes, onion mixture, parsley, rice, and Parmesan. Stir to mix, then taste for seasoning. Crack the eggs into a bowl and beat to mix. Stir them into the vegetable mixture with the wooden spoon.

6 **Spread the mixture** in the baking dish, and sprinkle with the remaining oil. Bake the tian in the heated oven for 10–15 minutes, until set. Increase the oven temperature to 200°C (400°F/Gas 6), and bake for 10–15 minutes longer, until brown. Serve hot, or at room temperature, from the baking dish.

 VARIATION: Spinach and mushroom tian

A tasty alternative.

1 Omit the courgettes, rice, and parsley. Trim the crusts from 2 slices of white bread, and work to fine crumbs in a food processor. Cook 1kg (2¼lb) spinach in a large saucepan of salted water for 1–2 minutes, until wilted. Drain, leave until cool enough to handle, then squeeze with your fist to remove any excess water. Chop coarsely. Wipe 375g (13oz) mushrooms, trim the stalks even to the caps (discard the base of the stalks), then thinly and evenly slice the caps.

2 Heat 2 tbsp olive oil in a large frying pan, and cook the onions and garlic as directed in the main recipe. Add the mushrooms and sauté for 5 minutes. Add the spinach, salt, and pepper, and cook, stirring occasionally, until all the liquid has been released and has then evaporated; it should take about 5 minutes. Make sure the pan is dry, or the tian will be soggy after baking. Let cool, then stir in the Parmesan. Taste for seasoning and adjust if necessary. Prepare a baking dish as directed.

3 Beat the eggs, then stir them evenly into the vegetable mixture. Spoon into the prepared baking dish, and sprinkle with the breadcrumbs and 2 tbsp olive oil. Bake as directed in the main recipe.

Mixed vegetable curry

TRY THIS WITH A RAITA of diced cucumber and plain yogurt, seasoned with salt and a pinch of cumin. There are a lot of spices used here, but each one is important for the total balance of the dish, and all are widely available. Replace some of the coconut milk in the curry with water for a lighter dish.

SERVES	PREP	COOK
SERVES 6-8	45-50 MINS	25-35 MINS

Ingredients

400g (14oz) basmati rice

salt

FOR THE SPICE MIXTURE

6 dried red chillies

12 cardamom pods

3 tbsp coriander seeds

1 tbsp cumin seeds

½ tsp mustard seeds

2 tsp each fenugreek seeds, ground turmeric, and ground ginger

FOR THE VEGETABLES

4 each onions, potatoes, and carrots

1 cauliflower

500g (1lb 2oz) French beans

75ml (2½ fl oz) vegetable oil

1 cinnamon stick

6 cloves

3 garlic cloves, finely chopped

4 large tomatoes, peeled and deseeded

250g (9oz) shelled fresh or defrosted frozen peas

2 x 400g (14oz) cans coconut milk

MAKE THE SPICE MIXTURE

1 Split the dried red chillies and discard the seeds. Crush the cardamom pods in a mortar and pestle and discard the pods, keeping the seeds in the mortar.

2 Put the chillies in a small frying pan with the coriander seeds and cumin seeds and toast over medium heat for about 2 minutes, stirring constantly to prevent burning, until browned and very fragrant. Set aside.

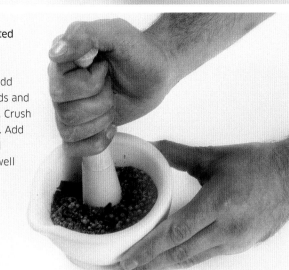

3 Put the toasted spices in the mortar with the cardamom and add the mustard seeds and fenugreek seeds. Crush to a fine powder. Add the turmeric and ginger, and stir well to mix.

PREPARE THE VEGETABLES

4 Dice the onions, then peel and cut each potato into 1cm (½in) dice. Put them in a bowl of water to prevent discolouration. Trim the florets from the cauliflower, then cut the florets into small pieces. Chop the carrots into 1cm (½in) slices, then trim the beans and cut into 5cm (2in) pieces.

MAKE THE CURRY

5 Heat the oil in the sauté pan, add the cinnamon stick and cloves, and cook for 30-60 seconds, until fragrant. Add the onions and garlic and sauté quickly, stirring to soften and cook evenly, until beginning to colour.

6 Add the spice mixture and cook over low heat, stirring constantly, for about 2-3 minutes. Drain the potatoes and add to the pan with the carrots, cauliflower, French beans, tomatoes, peas, and salt to taste. Sauté for 3-5 minutes, until thoroughly coated with spices.

7 Add the coconut milk and stir. Cover the pan and simmer for 15–20 minutes, until the vegetables are tender and the sauce is thick and rich. Remove and discard the cloves and cinnamon. Taste for seasoning.

COOK THE RICE

8 Put the rice in a large bowl, cover generously with cold water, and let soak for 2–3 minutes, stirring occasionally. Drain in a colander, rinse with cold water, and drain thoroughly.

9 Put the rice in a saucepan with 850ml (scant 1½ pints) water and a pinch of salt. Bring to a boil, then cover and simmer for 10–12 minutes, until just tender. Remove from heat and leave covered for at least 5 minutes, then gently stir the rice to fluff it. Serve the curry and rice hot on warmed plates.

 VARIATION: Winter vegetable curry

Use seasonal vegetables in the colder months.

1 Prepare the curry spice mixture, onions, garlic, potatoes, carrots, and cauliflower as directed; omit the green beans, tomatoes, and peas. Discard the seeds from 500g (1lb 2oz) pumpkin, cut into 7.5cm (3in) pieces and peel. Dice the flesh.

2 Trim, peel, and dice 3 turnips. Trim 250g (9oz) Brussels sprouts. Sauté the onions and garlic with the curry spice mixture. Add the prepared vegetables and continue with the curry as directed, simmering it for 15–20 minutes.

3 Spread the rice in a large, shallow serving bowl and add the vegetable curry. Serve hot.

Pumpkin stew

A HEARTY MEAL with an eye-popping presentation. Shown here ladled out into an individual serving bowl, the stew is best served inside a pumpkin. Take it to the table to make a real impact on your guests.

SERVES	PREP	COOK
SERVES 8	50-60 MINS	2½-3 HOURS

Ingredients

1 pumpkin, weighing about 5kg (11lb)

1 celeriac, weighing about 750g (1lb 10oz)

juice of ½ lemon

4 tomatoes, total weight about 500g (1lb 2oz)

125g (4½oz) butter

3 leeks, cut into 2.5cm (1in) slices

2 garlic cloves, finely chopped

30g (1oz) plain flour

500ml (16fl oz) vegetable or chicken stock, plus more if needed

salt and pepper

cayenne

2 celery sticks, peeled, cut into 1cm (½in) slices

5 turnips, total weight about 500g (1lb 2oz), in 2.5cm (1in) dice

1 butternut squash, weighing about 750g (1lb 10oz), in 2cm (¾in) dice

1 courgette, in 2.5cm (1in) dice

leaves from 3-5 thyme sprigs

PREPARE THE PUMPKIN SHELL

1 **Preheat the oven** to 170°C (325°F/ Gas 3). Cut around the stalk end of the pumpkin at an angle and pull off the round "lid". Set the lid aside.

2 **Using your hands,** scoop out the seeds with all the fibrous threads and discard them. Put the pumpkin in a baking dish. Pour enough boiling water into the pumpkin to fill it. Replace the stalk end and bake for 1½-2 hours, until the flesh is just tender.

3 **Ladle out and discard** the cooking water. With a large spoon, scoop out the flesh, leaving the shell about 1cm (½in) thick. Set the shell aside. Cut the flesh into chunks and purée in a food processor until smooth.

PREPARE THE CELERIAC AND TOMATOES

4 Peel the celeriac with a sharp knife, being careful not to remove too much of the flesh with the skin. Take care, as the skin is tough and a slip of the knife could be painful. Cut the flesh into 2.5cm (1in) cubes. Put the cubes of celeriac in a large bowl of water along with the lemon juice, to prevent discolouration.

5 Cut the cores from the tomatoes and score an "x" on the base of each. Immerse them in boiling water until the skin starts to split, then plunge into a bowl of cold water. Peel off the skin. Cut in half and squeeze out the seeds, then cut each half into quarters. Alternatively, simply use 1 x 400g (14oz) can chopped tomatoes. If tomatoes are not beautifully ripe and in season, the latter is usually the best choice.

MAKE THE STEW

6 Heat the butter in a casserole, add the leeks and garlic and soften over low heat, stirring occasionally, for 3–5 minutes. Add the flour and cook, stirring, for 1–2 minutes, until foaming.

7 Stir in the stock and pumpkin purée. Drain the celeriac and add it to the pot with salt, pepper, and cayenne to taste. Bring to a boil and simmer gently for 20 minutes. Add the celery and turnips and simmer for 20 minutes longer, until beginning to soften.

8 Add the squash and courgette, tomatoes, and thyme and simmer for 10 minutes longer. Taste for seasoning and adjust if necessary. Set the pumpkin shell on a large, robust serving plate, and ladle in the steaming hot stew. Provide warmed bowls for your guests.

Baked polenta with wild mushrooms

YOU CAN PREPARE THIS A DAY AHEAD up to the end of step 5, and refrigerate, then bake on the day. It is a hugely tempting and comforting dish, with the slight sweetness of polenta and the melting, unctuous cheese and mushrooms. Make it on a cold winter's day to warm both bodies and souls.

SERVES	PREP	COOK
SERVES 6	40-45 MINS PLUS CHILLING	20-25 MINS

Ingredients

FOR THE POLENTA

1 tbsp salt

375g (13oz) fine polenta

FOR THE WILD MUSHROOM STEW

250g (9oz) fresh wild mushrooms

375g (13oz) button mushrooms

3 tbsp olive oil

3 garlic cloves, finely chopped

leaves from 5-7 thyme or rosemary sprigs

125ml (4fl oz) dry white wine

250ml (9fl oz) vegetable stock or water

4 tbsp double cream

salt and pepper

250g (9oz) fontina cheese, sliced

MAKE THE POLENTA

1 **Sprinkle 2 baking sheets** with water. Bring 1.5 litres (2¾ pints) water to a boil in a saucepan and add the salt. Over medium heat, slowly whisk in the polenta in a thin, steady stream.

2 **Cook,** stirring, for 10-15 minutes, until thick enough to pull away from the pan. It should be soft and smooth. Spread on the baking sheets in a layer about 30cm (12in) square. Cool, then chill for 1 hour until very firm.

MAKE THE MUSHROOM STEW

3 **Wipe all the mushrooms** with damp kitchen paper and trim the stalks. Cut the wild mushrooms into slices and the common mushrooms into halves, or quarters if large.

4 **Heat the oil** in the frying pan. Add all the mushrooms, the garlic, and thyme or rosemary and cook, stirring, for 5-7 minutes, until the mushrooms are tender and the liquid has evaporated.

5 **Add the wine,** simmer for 2-3 minutes, then the stock and cook until reduced by half. Pour in the cream; cook until the liquid thickens. Season.

ASSEMBLE THE DISH

6 **Preheat the oven** to 220°C (425°F/ Gas 7). Brush a 23x33cm (9x13in) baking dish with oil. Cut the chilled polenta into 6 x 10cm (4in) squares; reserve the trimmings. Arrange half the squares in the dish in a single layer.

7 **Spoon half the mushroom stew** over, then half the fontina. Repeat with another layer of polenta and mushrooms. Top with the remaining fontina. Bake for 20-25 minutes, until the cheese has melted, and serve very hot.

Perfect pasta and cheese

GROWN-UP MACARONI CHEESE! The wild and domestic mushrooms in the pasta make this a sophisticated take on the old favourite, but use all button mushrooms if you want a more economical dish. A tomato salad is all you need on the side.

SERVES	PREP	COOK
SERVES 6	30-35 MINS	25-30 MINS

Ingredients

FOR THE PASTA

15g (½oz) butter

3 shallots, finely chopped

3 garlic cloves, finely chopped

125g (4½oz) mixed wild mushrooms, sliced

125g (4½oz) button mushrooms, sliced

salt and pepper

375g (13oz) penne pasta

FOR THE TOPPING AND CHEESE SAUCE

2 slices of white bread

1 small bunch of chives, snipped

250g (9oz) sharp Cheddar cheese, grated

1 litre (1¾ pints) milk

1 slice of onion

6 black peppercorns

1 bay leaf

30g (1oz) butter

2 tbsp plain flour

freshly grated nutmeg

PREPARE THE MUSHROOMS

1 **Melt the butter** in a sauté pan, add the shallots, and stir for 1 minute, until soft. Add the garlic, mushrooms, salt, and pepper. Cook, stirring, for 3-5 minutes, until the liquid has evaporated and the mushrooms are tender.

MAKE THE TOPPING

2 **Discard the crusts** from the bread, and break down to coarse crumbs in a food processor. Combine with a quarter of the chives, and 30g (1oz) of the cheese. Set aside.

MAKE THE SAUCE

3 **Scald the milk** in a saucepan with the onion slice, peppercorns, and bay leaf. Remove from the heat and leave for 10 minutes. Melt the butter in another pan, and whisk in the flour. Remove from the heat, and strain in two-thirds of the milk. Return to the heat, and whisk until it boils.

4 **Grate a little nutmeg** into the sauce, season well, and simmer for 2 minutes. Remove from the heat, and add the remaining cheese. Gradually whisk in the remaining milk. Taste for seasoning.

FINISH THE DISH

5 **Preheat the oven** to 180°C (350°F/Gas 4). Fill a large pan with water, bring to a boil, and add 1 tbsp salt. Add the pasta, and simmer for 5-7 minutes. Drain. Butter a 2 litre (3½ pint) dish. Mix the pasta with the sauce, mushrooms, and remaining chives. Spoon into the dish, and sprinkle over the topping. Bake for 25-30 minutes, until bubbling and golden.

Vegetable couscous

COUSCOUS LOOKS AND COOKS LIKE A GRAIN, though in fact it is made from a wheat-flour dough. It is a very popular dish in France, where Algerian and Moroccan immigrants have settled for a century, bringing their delicious food with them. This version is served in the Algerian style, with the broth separate from the fragrant vegetables and fluffy couscous. If you can find the Moorish spice blend *ras-el-hanout*, add a teaspoon of it to the broth at the same time as the ginger and turmeric. You'll need 16 bamboo skewers.

SERVES	PREP	COOK
SERVES 8	35-40 MINS PLUS MARINATING	30-35 MINS

Ingredients

FOR THE VEGETABLE BROTH

large pinch of saffron threads

2kg (4½lb) mixed vegetables: 2 leeks, 2 courgettes, 2 carrots, 2 turnips, 1 onion, 3 tomatoes

2 tbsp olive oil

2 litres (3½ pints) chicken stock

400g (14oz) can chickpeas

1 bouquet garni

1 tsp each ground ginger, turmeric, and paprika

salt and pepper

FOR THE VEGETABLE KEBABS

2 courgettes

2 red peppers

250g (9oz) mushrooms

5-6 small onions, total weight about 375g (13oz)

leaves from 1 small bunch of coriander, finely chopped

leaves from 4-6 thyme sprigs

125ml (4fl oz) olive oil

250g (9oz) cherry tomatoes

1 tsp ground cumin

FOR THE COUSCOUS

500g (1lb 2oz) couscous

45-60g (1½-2oz) butter

MAKE THE VEGETABLE BROTH

1 **Put the saffron** in a small bowl and pour over 3-4 tbsp hot water. Set aside to steep while you prepare the vegetables. Wash the leeks very well and cut them into strips. Cut the courgettes, carrots, and turnips into slices. Dice the onion.

2 **Peel, deseed, and coarsely chop** the tomatoes. Heat the oil in a large saucepan, add the onion and stir for 2-3 minutes, until they are soft but not brown. Add the tomatoes and cook for about 5 minutes, until the mixture has thickened.

3 **Add the chicken** stock, courgettes, carrots, turnips, leeks, chickpeas, and bouquet garni. Stir in the ginger, turmeric, paprika, saffron with its liquid, and salt and pepper.

4 **Bring to a boil** and simmer for 15-20 minutes until the vegetables are just tender to the point of a knife. Discard the bouquet garni, taste the broth for seasoning, and set aside.

MAKE THE KEBABS

5 **Trim the courgettes.** Cut each lengthways into quarters, then into chunky pieces. Cut the peppers into large squares. Cut the mushrooms in halves or quarters if large, or leave them whole if they are small.

6 **Cut the onions** into quarters, leaving on a little root to hold them together. Set aside 1-2 tbsp of the herbs; put the remainder in a small bowl, and mix in the olive oil.

7 **Put the mushrooms,** courgettes, red peppers, onions, and tomatoes in a large bowl. Pour the herb and olive oil mixture over the vegetables. Toss to coat, and leave to marinate for 1-2 hours at room temperature. Meanwhile, soak 16 bamboo skewers in water.

GRILL THE KEBABS AND PREPARE THE COUSCOUS

8 **Heat the grill.** Thread the vegetables on to the skewers. Scrape any herbs from the bowl and brush them on the kebabs. Set on the baking sheet, and grill about 7.5cm (3in) from the heat for about 5 minutes, until browned. Turn and grill on the other side for about 5 minutes longer, until browned and tender.

9 **While the kebabs are grilling,** prepare the couscous: put it in a large bowl and pour over 500ml (16fl oz) boiling water, stirring quickly with a fork. Let the couscous sit for about 5 minutes, until plump. The quantity of water required may vary with the type of couscous you use, so check the package directions.

10 **Add the butter,** salt, and pepper to the couscous. Stir and toss with the fork to fluff the grains and incorporate the butter. Taste for seasoning. Reheat the vegetable broth if necessary and transfer it to serving bowls. Pile the couscous on to warmed plates. Sprinkle the kebabs with salt, pepper, and cumin. Arrange the skewers on the couscous; serve with fiery *harissa* (Moroccan hot sauce), if liked.

Stuffed veggies with walnut sauce

TRY USING OTHER GRAINS such as buckwheat instead of bulghur wheat, if you prefer. The garlicky walnut sauce which forms the accompaniment here is a deliciously useful one to know, and can be used to go with any grilled or barbecued vegetables.

SERVES	PREP	COOK
SERVES 4	40-45 MINS PLUS STANDING	15-20 MINS

Ingredients

FOR THE VEGETABLES

4 large tomatoes

salt and pepper

4 red or Spanish onions

2 large courgettes

250g (9oz) bulghur wheat

3 tbsp olive oil, plus more for dish and foil

2 celery sticks, peeled and thinly sliced

4 garlic cloves, finely chopped

125g (4½oz) fresh shiitake or button mushrooms, chopped

leaves from 4-6 tarragon sprigs, chopped

leaves from 4-6 parsley sprigs, chopped

FOR THE WALNUT-GARLIC SAUCE

leaves from 4-6 parsley sprigs

4 garlic cloves, peeled

75g (2½oz) walnut halves

250ml (9fl oz) walnut oil

PREPARE THE VEGETABLES

1 **Core the tomatoes** and cut a slice from the top of each. Scoop out the seeds and flesh, leaving a 1cm (½in) wall of flesh. Scrape the seeds from the scooped-out flesh; reserve the flesh for the stuffing. Season the inside of the tomatoes and set them upside-down on kitchen paper for 30 minutes.

2 **Peel the onions.** Cut a flat slice from the top and a thin slice from the root end of each so it will sit flat. Put in a saucepan and cover with water. Add salt, put on the lid, and bring to a boil. Simmer for 10-15 minutes, until barely tender. Drain on kitchen paper. Hollow out the onions, leaving a 1cm (½in) wall, pushing out the core with your fingers. Reserve the cores for the stuffing.

3 **Trim the courgettes** and cut them lengthways in half. Fill a saucepan with water, bring to a boil, add salt, then the courgettes. Simmer for 3-5 minutes. Drain in a colander and rinse with cold water. Scoop out and discard the seeds, leaving a 1cm (½in) shell of flesh.

MAKE THE STUFFING

4 **Put the bulghur** in a large bowl, pour on 750ml (1¼ pints) boiling water, cover and let stand for 30 minutes, until plump. Drain off any excess water. Chop the reserved onion cores and the tomato flesh.

5 **Heat the oil** in a frying pan. Add the celery, garlic, and chopped onion and cook, stirring, for 2-3 minutes, until soft but not brown. Add the mushrooms, season and cook for about 5 minutes, until the liquid has evaporated. Stir in the chopped tomato and cook until the liquid evaporates, about 2 minutes more. Add the chopped herbs and taste for seasoning. Mix the sautéed vegetables into the bulghur. Taste for seasoning.

STUFF AND BAKE THE VEGETABLES

6 **Preheat the oven** to 190°C (375°F/Gas 5). Oil a large baking dish. Spoon the stuffing into the onions, courgettes, and tomatoes. Spread the remaining stuffing over the bottom of the dish and arrange the vegetables on top. Cover with oiled foil, and bake for 15–20 minutes, until tender.

MAKE THE SAUCE

7 **Put the parsley,** garlic, walnuts, and 2 tbsp cold water in a food processor and purée to a paste. Season with salt and pepper. With the blade turning, gradually add the walnut oil. Taste for seasoning.

8 **Arrange a tomato,** an onion, and a courgette half, with extra stuffing from the baking dish, if you like, on 4 warmed plates. Serve the walnut-garlic sauce on the side.

VARIATION: Vegetable trio with carrot-rice stuffing

Carrot makes a colourful addition here.

1 Prepare the vegetables as directed. Cook 250g (9oz) long-grain white rice in boiling salted water until barely tender; it should take 10–12 minutes, or according to the packet instructions. Drain in a colander and rinse with cold running water to remove some of the starch.

2 Peel and coarsely grate 2 carrots. Make the stuffing as directed, using the rice in place of the bulghur wheat and stirring in the grated carrot just before stuffing the vegetables.

3 Stuff and bake the vegetables as directed and serve with the walnut-garlic sauce. Decorate with sprigs of fresh tarragon.

Broccoli and mushroom quiche

LOOK FOR BROCCOLI with firm, juicy stalks that still seem moist, as it will be the freshest. When purple-sprouting broccoli is in season in early spring, use it here instead of the regular broccoli; it will be sweeter but with a more assertive flavour and a stronger colour. Try to choose mushrooms with good flavour; the large, flat-capped field or Portobello mushrooms are good, as well as being reasonably priced.

SERVES	PREP	COOK
SERVES 6-8	45–50 MINS PLUS STANDING	30–35 MINS

Ingredients

FOR THE PASTRY

200g (7oz) plain flour

1 egg yolk

½ tsp salt

100g (3½ oz) unsalted butter

FOR THE FILLING

1–2 heads of broccoli, total weight about 500g (1lb 2oz)

salt and pepper

30g (1oz) butter

175g (6oz) mushrooms, sliced

2 garlic cloves, finely chopped

ground nutmeg

FOR THE CUSTARD

3 eggs, plus 2 egg yolks

375ml (12fl oz) milk

250ml (9fl oz) double cream

60g (2oz) Parmesan cheese, grated

ground nutmeg

MAKE THE PASTRY

1 **Sift the flour** on to a work surface and make a well in the centre. Put the egg yolk, salt, and 3 tbsp water in the well. Wrap the butter in baking parchment and pound it with a rolling pin or meat mallet to soften it slightly, then add it to the well.

2 **With your fingers,** work the flour into the other ingredients until coarse crumbs form. Press the dough lightly into a ball. If it's too dry, sprinkle with a little more water.

3 **Lightly flour a work surface,** then knead the pastry for 1–2 minutes, or until it is very smooth and peels away from the work surface in one piece. Shape into a ball, wrap it tightly with cling film, and chill for about 30 minutes until firm.

LINE THE TIN

4 **Preheat the oven** to 220°C (425°F/Gas 7). Butter a 25cm (10in) fluted flan tin. Lightly flour a work surface and roll out the dough to a 30cm (12in) round. Drape over the tin. Gently lift the edge of the dough with one hand and press it well into the bottom edge of the tin.

5 **Roll the rolling pin** over the top of the tin, pressing down to cut off the excess.

6 **With your forefingers** and thumb, press the dough evenly up the side, from the bottom, to increase the height of the dough rim. Prick the shell with a fork to prevent air bubbles from forming during baking. Chill for at least 15 minutes, until firm.

BLIND BAKE THE PASTRY

7 Line the pastry with a double thickness of foil, pressing it well into the bottom edges of the tin. If necessary, trim the foil so it stands about 4cm (1½in) above the sides of the tin. Spread an even layer of dried beans, baking beans, or raw rice on to the foil to weigh down the pastry, and stop it from rising while it is baking.

8 Bake the pastry dough shell until it is set and starting to turn golden brown; it should take about 15 minutes, but check after 12 by lifting up a corner of the foil and looking at the pastry underneath. When it is ready, remove the foil and all the beans or rice and reduce the oven temperature to 190°C (375°F/Gas 5). Continue baking the pastry shell until it is lightly browned all over. It should only take about 5 minutes, but check after 3 minutes, and turn the tin around if the pastry shell looks as though it is browning unevenly.

COOK THE BROCCOLI AND MUSHROOMS, AND ASSEMBLE THE QUICHE

9 Cut the florets from the broccoli stalk, then slice the stalk lengthwise into sticks. Half-fill a saucepan with water and bring to a boil. Add salt, then the broccoli. Cook until just tender; it should only take about 3–5 minutes. Drain.

10 Melt the butter in a frying pan, add the mushrooms and garlic and sauté until the mushrooms have first given out all their liquid, and then all that liquid has evaporated.

11 Whisk together the eggs, egg yolks, milk, cream, grated cheese, salt, pepper, and a pinch of nutmeg. Spread the mushrooms in the pastry shell. Arrange the broccoli on top. Ladle the cheese custard over to fill almost to the rim. Bake for 30–35 minutes, until browned and the custard has a slight wobble in the centre when shaken. Serve hot or at room temperature.

Polenta with vegetable stew

A WONDERFULLY SUBSTANTIAL meal. This is actually better if you make the vegetables the day before and refrigerate; the flavours will marry and the whole stew become far more succulent. Reheat just before serving. Creamy polenta is an ideal comfort food, and makes a great change from potatoes or rice as a filling side dish; add extra butter for a more indulgent treat. Once cooked, polenta can be flavoured with cheese and herbs – experiment to find your favourite combination.

SERVES SERVES 6-8	**PREP** 40 MINS	**COOK** 50 MINS

Ingredients

FOR THE POLENTA

1 tbsp salt

450g (1lb) fine polenta

45g (1½oz) butter

FOR THE VEGETABLE STEW

2 aubergines

2 courgettes

salt and pepper

400g (14oz) can plum tomatoes

1 bunch of basil

4 tbsp olive oil, plus more if needed

3 onions, sliced

4 garlic cloves, finely chopped

1 red pepper, sliced

1 yellow pepper, sliced

1 green pepper, sliced

PREPARE THE POLENTA

1 Bring 2 litres (3½ pints) of water to a boil in a large, very heavy-based saucepan and add the salt. Over medium heat, slowly whisk in the polenta in a thin, steady stream, keeping a whirling eddy in the pan until all the grain has been added. Whisk constantly to avoid lumps; the polenta mixture should remain completely smooth throughout cooking.

2 Cook, stirring occasionally, until the polenta is thick enough to hold a shape and pulls away from the side of the pan; it should take 15–20 minutes. Make sure it does not threaten at any time to catch on the base of the pan, as the scorched taste will spoil the dish. Meanwhile, make the vegetable stew.

3 Taste the polenta; it should have no remaining taste of raw corn. If it does, continue to cook for 5 minutes more, than taste again. Cover, keep warm and set aside while you finish making the vegetable stew.

PREPARE THE AUBERGINES AND COURGETTES

4 **Trim the ends** from the aubergines and cut into 2.5cm (1in) chunks. Trim the courgettes, cut lengthways in half, then into 1cm (½in) slices.

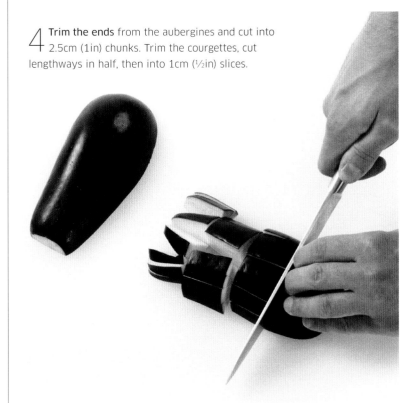

5 **Put the aubergines and courgettes** on a large plate or tray and sprinkle generously with salt. Let stand to draw out the bitter juices, 30 minutes.

6 Rinse the aubergines and courgettes with cold water and pat dry with kitchen paper.

COOK THE VEGETABLE STEW

7 Drain the canned tomatoes, reserving the juice, and chop. Strip the basil leaves from the stalks, reserving 6-8 sprigs for decoration, and coarsely chop.

8 Heat the olive oil in a sauté pan. Add the onions and garlic, and cook, stirring, for 3-5 minutes, until softened but not brown. Make sure that the garlic does not turn brown, as that will impair the flavour of the finished dish. Stir in the sliced peppers, then the aubergine chunks, and cook for 2-3 minutes longer, stirring constantly, until everything is just beginning to become tender.

9 Add the courgettes and continue cooking, stirring often, until all the vegetables are just tender to the point of a knife; it should take 7-10 minutes. Add more oil if the pan starts to dry out at any stage. Stir in the tomatoes with any of their juice, and add salt and pepper generously; the vegetables will be at their best if very well seasoned. Simmer, stirring occasionally, for 12-15 minutes, until the stew has thickened.

FINISH THE POLENTA

10 Beat the butter into the polenta until evenly mixed. Serve a golden pile of the polenta on warmed plates with the vegetable stew, and sprinkle with the reserved basil.

Potato and blue cheese filo pie

BASED ON THE GREEK SPINACH PIE, *spanokopita*, but with an indulgent twist to the filling. This is an excellent dish to make ahead for a mid-week meal as it can be prepared entirely, up to the point of baking, then wrapped tightly in clingfilm and refrigerated for 2 days. Bake it just before serving.

SERVES	PREP	COOK
SERVES 6	35-40 MINS	45-55 MINS

Ingredients

1kg (2¼lb) potatoes, very thinly sliced

125g (4½oz) crumbly blue cheese

175g (6oz) butter

500g (1lb 2oz) package filo pastry

4 shallots, finely diced

leaves from 4-5 parsley sprigs, finely chopped

leaves from 4-5 tarragon sprigs, finely chopped

leaves from 4-5 chervil sprigs, finely chopped

salt and pepper

3-4 tbsp soured cream

PREPARE THE FILLING

1 **Bring a saucepan of water** to a boil, add the potatoes, and simmer for 5 minutes. Drain, and set aside to cool. Crumble the cheese.

CUT THE FILO

2 **Preheat the oven** to 180°C (350°F/ Gas 4). Melt the butter in a saucepan. Brush a 28cm (11in) springform tin with a little of the butter. Lay a damp tea towel on a work surface, and unroll the filo pastry sheets on to the towel.

3 **Using the tin** as a guide, cut through the pastry sheets to leave a 7.5cm (3in) border around the tin. Reserve the trimmings. Cover the sheets and the pastry trimmings with a second damp towel.

4 **Put a filo sheet** on a third damp tea towel and brush with butter, then press into the tin. Repeat with another sheet, putting it in the tin at a right angle to the first. Continue until half the filo is used.

5 **Arrange half the potatoes** in the tin, sprinkling with half the cheese, chopped shallots, herbs, salt, and pepper. Repeat, then pour over the soured cream.

6 **Cover the pie** with the remaining filo, buttering and layering as before. Cut a 7.5cm (3in) hole from the centre, so the filling shows through. Scrunch up and arrange the filo trimmings on top. Bake for 45-55 minutes, until golden brown. Serve in wedges, with salad leaves on the side.

Spaghetti primavera

THE YOUNGER THE VEGETABLES you can get your hands on, the better and sweeter this dish will be. Their beautiful pale greens and oranges epitomize the colours of spring. During the season, add asparagus tips, baby fennel bulbs, or tiny, new broad beans, as you prefer. This is a wonderfully light dish for the first of the warmer evenings.

SERVES	PREP	COOK
SERVES 4	45–50 MINS	10–12 MINS

Ingredients

2 courgettes, in 1cm (½in) dice

salt and pepper

2 carrots, in 1cm (½in) dice

210g (7½oz) shelled fresh peas

500g (1lb 2oz) spaghetti

45g (1½oz) butter

175ml (6fl oz) double cream

30g (1oz) grated Parmesan cheese

PREPARE THE VEGETABLES AND PASTA

1 **Bring a saucepan** of water to the boil. Add the courgettes and salt and cook for 2–3 minutes, until barely tender to the tip of a knife. Drain very well, then blot dry on kitchen paper. Set aside on fresh kitchen paper, to ensure the blanched courgettes are not at all soggy when added to the spaghetti sauce.

2 **Put the carrots** in a saucepan, cover with cold water, add salt and bring to the boil. Simmer for 5 minutes, or until just tender, then drain, rinse with cold water and set aside. Bring a clean saucepan of salted water to the boil. Add the peas and simmer for 3–8 minutes, depending on their size and age, until tender. Drain, rinse with cold water and set aside. It is necessary briefly to boil (or blanch) the vegetables separately, because each cooks at a different rate. In a dish such as this, which is all about showing off vegetables at the peak of their sweetness, each must be perfectly cooked.

3 **Fill a very large pan with water,** bring to the boil and add 1 tbsp salt. It may seem a lot, but the water in which you boil pasta must always be very salty. Add the spaghetti and simmer for 10–12 minutes, stirring to prevent sticking, until tender but still chewy. Drain it very well.

FINISH THE DISH

4 Meanwhile, heat the butter in a large saucepan, add the courgette and carrot dice, and the peas, and sauté for 1 minute.

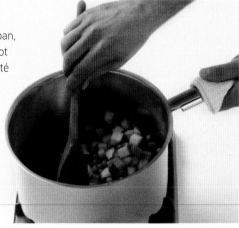

5 Add the cream, stir well and bring to a simmer. Take the pan from the heat, add the spaghetti and toss well. Add the Parmesan and toss again. Serve on warmed plates, sprinkled with pepper.

Onion and Roquefort quiche

THE SECRET TO THIS DISH is that the onions should be cooked to a melting softness. Often, people are put off quiche because they are used to rubbery offerings. Success and true succulence come when the custard comes from the oven wobbly, not solid.

SERVES	PREP	COOK
SERVES 6-8	40-50 MINS PLUS CHILLING	30-35 MINS

Ingredients

FOR THE PASTRY

200g (7oz) plain flour, plus more to dust

1 egg yolk

½ tsp salt

100g (3½ oz) unsalted butter, plus more for the tin

FOR THE FILLING

2-3 thyme sprigs

500g (1lb 2oz) onions

30g (1oz) unsalted butter, plus more for foil

salt and pepper

1 egg

1 egg yolk

125ml (4fl oz) milk

1 pinch of ground nutmeg

4 tbsp double cream

175g (6oz) Roquefort cheese

MAKE THE PASTRY

1 **Sift the flour** on to a work surface and make a well in the centre. Put the egg yolk, salt, and 3 tbsp water in the well.

2 **Using a rolling pin,** pound the butter to soften it slightly, then add it to the well in the flour. Using your fingertips, work the ingredients in the well until thoroughly mixed.

3 **With your fingers,** work the flour into the other ingredients until coarse crumbs form. Press the dough into a ball.

4 **Lightly flour the work surface,** then blend the dough by pushing it away from you with the heel of your hand for 1-2 minutes, until it is very smooth and peels away from the work surface in 1 piece. Shape into a ball, wrap it tightly and chill for about 30 minutes, until firm.

LINE THE TIN

5 **Butter a 25cm (10in) flan tin.** Lightly flour a work surface. Roll out the chilled dough to a 30cm (12in) round. Roll up the dough around the rolling pin and drape it over the tin, so that it hangs over the edge.

6 **Gently lift** the dough and firmly press it into the tin. Roll the rolling pin over the top of the tin, pressing down to cut off the excess dough.

7 **With your forefingers** and thumb, press the dough evenly up the side, to increase the height of the dough rim. Prick the bottom lightly with a fork to prevent air bubbles. Chill again for at least 15 minutes, until firm.

BLIND BAKE THE PASTRY

8 **Preheat the** oven to 220°C (425°F/Gas 7). Line the pastry dough shell with foil, pressing it well into the bottom edge. Trim the foil if necessary so it stands about 4cm (1½in) above the edge of the tin.

9 **Half-fill the** foil with baking beans or raw rice to weigh down the dough. Bake the shell for about 15 minutes, until set and starting to brown.

10 **Remove the** foil and beans and reduce the oven temperature to 190°C (375°F/Gas 5). Continue baking for 5-8 minutes longer, until lightly browned. Remove from the oven.

PREPARE THE FILLING

11 **Strip the thyme leaves** from the stalks. Slice the onions. Melt the butter in a frying pan. Add the onions and thyme and season with salt and pepper. Butter a piece of foil, press it on top and cover with the lid. Cook very gently, stirring occasionally, for 20-30 minutes, until very soft but not brown.

12 **Meanwhile,** make the custard: put the egg, egg yolk, milk, salt, pepper, and a pinch of ground nutmeg into a bowl. Pour in the double cream. Whisk until thoroughly mixed.

13 Crumble the cheese into the onions; stir until melted. Let cool slightly. Using the back of a wooden spoon, spread the mixture evenly into the pastry shell. Place the tin on a baking sheet. Ladle the custard over the onion mixture to fill the shell almost to the rim, and gently mix in with a fork.

BAKE AND SERVE THE QUICHE

14 Bake in the hot oven for 30-35 minutes, just until lightly browned and a skewer inserted into the centre of the custard comes out clean. Watch it carefully through the oven door - but avoid opening the oven - and do not overcook, or the custard will become dry and rubbery. The custard should retain a slight wobble when the tin is gently shaken. Let cool slightly in the tin before unmoulding.

15 Remove the quiche from the tin and place on a serving plate. Serve warm or at room temperature, cut in wedges. (Never serve quiche cold from the refrigerator; the texture will be hard and unpleasant.) A refreshingly astringent salad of chicory, watercress, and tomatoes makes a delicious accompaniment, and cuts through the richness of the creamy blue cheese filling.

Aubergine Parmigiana

A WELL-LOVED CLASSIC dish, big, hearty, and immensely satisfying for even the keenest appetites. This dish is also a good way to introduce aubergines to people who haven't tried them before, as the immensely comforting layers of cheese, tomato sauce, and sweet vegetables is sure to win over even the most stubborn doubter.

SERVES	PREP	COOK
SERVES 8	45-50 MINS PLUS STANDING	40-50 MINS

Ingredients

FOR THE PARMIGIANA

4 aubergines

salt and pepper

175ml (6fl oz) olive oil

leaves from 1 bunch of basil, shredded

125g (4½oz) freshly grated Parmesan cheese

500g (1lb 2oz) mozzarella cheese, diced

FOR THE TOMATO SAUCE

2.5kg (5½lb) tomatoes

3 onions, finely chopped

5 garlic cloves, finely chopped

leaves from 5-7 oregano sprigs, coarsely chopped

3 tbsp tomato purée

1 pinch of sugar

1 bouquet garni, made with 5-6 parsley stalks, 2-3 thyme sprigs, and 1 bay leaf

PREPARE THE AUBERGINES AND SAUCE

1 **Trim the stalk ends** from each of the aubergines and cut them widthways into 1cm (½in) slices. Lay them in a shallow dish and sprinkle with salt. Let stand for 30 minutes to draw out the moisture and any bitter juices.

2 **Cut the cores** from the tomatoes and score an "X" on the base of each. Immerse in boiling water for 8-15 seconds, until the skins start to split, then plunge into cold water to stop the cooking. Peel off the skins, halve, squeeze out the seeds, then coarsely chop the flesh.

3 **Heat 3 tbsp of the oil** in a sauté pan, add the onions and cook over medium heat, stirring occasionally, for 3-4 minutes, until soft but not brown. Add the tomatoes, garlic, oregano, tomato purée, salt, pepper, sugar, and bouquet garni, then stir to combine.

4 **Cover the pan** and simmer over very low heat for 15 minutes. Uncover and continue cooking, stirring occasionally, until thick, about 15 minutes longer. Discard the bouquet garni and taste for seasoning.

5 **Rinse the aubergine slices** well in a colander under cold running water, to remove the salt. Dry the slices thoroughly on kitchen paper. Preheat the oven to 180°C (350°F/Gas 4).

ASSEMBLE AND BAKE THE PARMIGIANA

6 **Oil 2 baking sheets.** Lay the aubergine slices on the sheets and brush with oil. Bake just until tender, turning once and brushing again with oil. It should take 20-25 minutes in total.

7 **Spread about one-quarter of the tomato sauce** over the bottom of a baking dish. Arrange one-third of the aubergine slices on top of the sauce in rows, overlapping them slightly. Cover with about a third of the basil, a quarter of the Parmesan, and a quarter of the mozzarella.

8 Repeat layering the sauce, aubergine, basil, Parmesan, and mozzarella to form 3 layers. Top with the remaining tomato sauce, mozzarella and Parmesan. Bake in the oven for 20–25 minutes, until bubbling and lightly browned on top. Leave to stand for 15 minutes, then serve.

 VARIATION: Tian of Mediterranean vegetables

Named after the traditional Provençal earthenware dish.

1 Omit the tomato sauce and mozzarella. Trim and slice 6 small aubergines (total weight about 1kg/2¼lb) and 3 large courgettes (total weight about 750g/1lb 10oz). Salt the slices and rinse as directed in the main recipe. Thinly slice 6 large onions. Heat 2 tbsp olive oil in a large frying pan and add the onions, salt, and pepper. Cover with foil and cook over low heat, stirring occasionally, for 20 minutes, or until soft and just beginning to turn brown.

2 Peel, seed, and chop 1.5kg (3lb 3oz) of tomatoes. Strip the leaves from 1 bunch of thyme. Cook the tomatoes and three-quarters of the thyme leaves in the pan, uncovered, as directed; it should take about 10 minutes longer to become a thick sauce.

3 Brush eight 15cm (6in) gratin dishes with oil. Spread most of the tomato mixture in each dish, reserving about 120ml (4fl oz). Cover with the aubergines and courgettes, alternating in a spiral pattern. Sprinkle each dish with 1 tsp olive oil, the remaining thyme, salt, and pepper. Bake for about 15 minutes. Add a spoonful of the reserved tomato mixture to the centre of each dish. Sprinkle with another 1 tsp oil and 1 tbsp Parmesan cheese. Continue baking the tians for about 10 minutes, until they are completely tender when pierced with a knife.

Flemish vegetable tart

A QUICK BRIOCHE DOUGH makes a sumptuous crust for this unusual vegetable tart, which is really a hearty alternative to pizza. You can choose to cook the tart in a frying pan, if you like, for a more rustic effect. Don't be worried about making brioche: this version is very easy indeed, and has the advantage that it can be made the day ahead and refrigerated, wrapped in clingfilm, overnight.

SERVES	PREP	COOK
SERVES 8	50–55 MINS PLUS RISING	40–45 MINS

Ingredients

FOR THE DOUGH

9g (⅓oz) fresh yeast, or 1½ tsp dried yeast

250g (9oz) strong plain flour, more if needed

1 tsp salt

3 eggs

125g (4½oz) unsalted butter, softened

FOR THE FILLING

500g (1lb 2oz) mushrooms

4 carrots

2 turnips

90g (3oz) unsalted butter

8–10 spring onions, finely sliced

salt and pepper

4 eggs

250ml (9fl oz) double cream

¼ tsp ground nutmeg

2 **With your fingertips,** work the ingredients in the well until thoroughly mixed. Draw in the flour – using a pastry scraper if you like – and work into the other ingredients with your fingertips to form a smooth dough; add more flour if it is very sticky.

3 **Knead the dough** on a floured work surface, lifting it up and throwing it down until it is very elastic and resembles chamois leather; it will take about 10 minutes. Work in more flour as necessary, so that the dough is slightly sticky but peels easily from the work surface.

MAKE THE BRIOCHE DOUGH

1 **Crumble or sprinkle the yeast** over 2 tbsp lukewarm water in a small bowl and let stand for 5 minutes. Lightly oil a medium bowl. Sift the flour on to a work surface with the salt. Make a well in the centre and add the yeast and eggs.

4 **Add the butter,** and pinch and squeeze to mix it into the dough, then knead for 3–5 minutes, until smooth again. Shape into a ball and put into the oiled bowl. Cover with clingfilm and refrigerate for about 1 hour. Or, if it's more convenient, leave to rise overnight in the refrigerator.

PREPARE THE VEGETABLES

5 Wipe the mushrooms clean with damp kitchen paper and trim the stalks level with the caps. Set each mushroom stalk-side down on a chopping board and cut into very thin strips.

6 Peel and trim the carrots and turnips, then cut them into very fine julienne strips. Melt the butter in a saucepan. Add the carrot strips and cook gently for about 5 minutes, stirring occasionally. Add the mushrooms and turnips and season with salt and pepper.

7 Press a piece of buttered foil over the vegetables. Cover with the lid of the pan and cook for about 10 minutes, until tender, stirring occasionally. The vegetables should gently steam without browning. Remove from the heat, add the spring onions and taste for seasoning.

LINE THE DISH

8 Butter a 30cm (12in) flan dish. Knead the brioche dough lightly to knock out the air. Lightly flour a work surface, then roll out the dough to a round 7.5cm (3in) larger than the dish. Roll the dough around the rolling pin and drape it over the dish.

9 Gently lift the edges of the dough with one hand and press it well into the bottom and edge of the flan dish with the other hand. Roll the rolling pin over the top of the dish, pressing down to cut off excess dough. With your forefinger and thumb, press the dough evenly up the side, from the bottom, to increase the height of the dough rim.

FILL AND BAKE THE TART

10 Heat the oven to 200°C (400°F/Gas 6). Spread the vegetable mixture evenly in the dough case. Whisk together the eggs, double cream, salt, pepper, and nutmeg until evenly mixed, then pour this custard over the vegetables in the flan dish.

11 Fold the top edge of the dough rim over the filling to form a border. Let rise in a warm place until puffed up; this will take 20–30 minutes, though it can take a little longer on a cool day. Bake until the brioche case is very brown and the custard set but retaining a slight wobble when tested with a knife; it will take 40–45 minutes. If the top gets too brown before the tart is ready, cover it with foil. Serve hot or at room temperature.

Three-pepper pizza with cheese

FOR A SPICY FLAVOUR HERE, the dough is made with black pepper. Choose peppers that are brightly coloured and firm, with no soft spots, and add finely sliced chillies instead of the cayenne, if you prefer (sprinkle the pizza with the chillies when it has just 5 minutes left to bake).

SERVES	PREP	COOK
SERVES 4-6	1¼ HRS PLUS STANDING	20-25 MINS

Ingredients

FOR THE DOUGH

1½ tsp dried yeast, or 9g (⅓oz) fresh yeast

2 tbsp olive oil, plus more for the bowl

375g (13oz) strong plain flour, plus more if needed

½ tsp ground black pepper

salt

FOR THE TOPPING

4 tbsp olive oil

2 onions, thinly sliced

2 red peppers, cut into strips

1 green pepper, cut into strips

1 yellow pepper, cut into strips

3 garlic cloves, finely chopped

1 small bunch of any herb, such as rosemary, thyme, basil, or parsley, or a mixture, leaves finely chopped

cayenne, to taste

175g (6oz) mozzarella cheese

MAKE THE DOUGH

1 **Sprinkle or crumble the yeast** over 2-3 tbsp of lukewarm water, and let stand for about 5 minutes, until dissolved. Lightly oil a large bowl.

2 **Sift the flour** on to a work surface, then add the black pepper and ¼ tsp salt. Make a well in the centre and add the yeast mixture, 250ml (9fl oz) lukewarm water, and the 2 tbsp olive oil. Work the ingredients in the well with your fingertips until thoroughly mixed.

3 **Draw in the flour,** and work into the other ingredients with your fingertips to form a smooth dough; add more flour if the dough is very sticky. Knead until elastic, shape into a ball, and leave to rise for an hour.

PREPARE THE TOPPING

4 **Heat 1 tbsp of oil** in a frying pan, add the onions, and cook, stirring, for 2-3 minutes, until soft but not brown. Transfer to a bowl and set aside.

5 **Add the remaining oil** to the pan, then the peppers, garlic, and half the herbs. Season with salt and cayenne. Sauté, stirring, for 7-10 minutes, until softened but not brown. Taste for seasoning: it should be quite spicy. Let cool. Slice the mozzarella.

ASSEMBLE THE PIZZA

6 **Preheat the oven** to 230°C (450°F/Gas 8). Put a baking sheet near the bottom of the oven to heat. Generously flour a second baking sheet.

7 **Knead the dough** lightly to knock out the air, then shape into a ball. Lightly flour a work surface. Roll the dough into a round. Pull and slap it until the round is 1cm (½in) thick.

8 **Transfer the dough** round to the floured baking sheet, and press up the edge to form a shallow rim, if you like.

BAKE THE PIZZA

9 Spread the onions, and then the peppers, evenly on the pizza base, leaving a 2cm (¾in) border all around the edge, so it can become golden in the oven. Spoon any remaining oil from the frying pan over the peppers, and top them evenly with the slices of mozzarella. Let the assembled pizza stand in a warm place for 10-15 minutes, until the dough has puffed up well around the edges. Don't leave it for any longer, as it should be baked as soon as possible to retain maximum flavour.

10 With a sharp, jerking movement, slide the pizza on to the heated baking sheet at the bottom of the oven. (But don't be so exuberant that it splatters on the rear wall!) Bake the pizza until browned all over, and the cheese has melted into beautiful, tempting pools. It should take 20-25 minutes to cook, but it will depend on how fast your oven tends to be. Sprinkle the pizza evenly with the reserved herbs, and cut it into generous wedges to serve.

 VARIATION: Three-pepper calzone with cheese

The pizza recipe is made into a turnover; this will serve 4 people.

1 Make the pizza dough as directed. Prepare the topping as directed, and mix the onions and pepper strips together. Divide the dough into 4 equal pieces. Roll and pull each piece into a square about 1cm (½in) thick.

2 Spoon the pepper mixture onto a diagonal half of each square, leaving a 2.5cm (1in) border. Arrange the mozzarella slices on top. Moisten the edge of each square with water, and fold one corner over to meet the other, forming a triangle.

3 Pinch the edges together to seal. Put the triangles on the floured baking sheet and let rise (prove) for 30 minutes. Whisk 1 egg with ½ tsp salt, and brush over the calzone. Bake for 15-20 minutes, until golden brown. Brush each with a little olive oil, and serve.

One-pot dishes

All-in-one meals that almost cook themselves

Scallop and sweetcorn chowder

A LUXURIOUS AMERICAN CLASSIC. A wonderful dish for a special occasion that marries the sweetness of both the shellfish and sweetcorn with salty bacon. Oyster crackers, available from some specialist delicatessens, are the traditional accompaniment. If you can find them, allow diners to crumble them over their own bowl.

SERVES SERVES 6-8	**PREP** 25-30 MINS	**COOK** 15-20 MINS

Ingredients

4 cobs sweetcorn

750g (1lb 10oz) small scallops

250g (9oz) streaky bacon rashers, cut into strips

2 onions, thinly sliced

500g (1lb 2oz) new potatoes

1 bay leaf

salt and pepper

750ml (1¼ pints) fish stock

250ml (9fl oz) single cream

500ml (16fl oz) milk

paprika

PREPARE THE CHOWDER INGREDIENTS

1 **Hold each sweetcorn cob** vertically on a chopping board and cut from the tip down to remove the kernels. Put them in a small bowl. Working over the bowl, with the back of the knife, scrape the pulp and milk from each cob.

2 **If necessary,** discard the tough, crescent-shaped membrane at the side of each scallop. Make sure there is no black intestinal vein running around the edge of the shellfish. If you find one, peel it off and discard.

COOK THE CHOWDER BASE

3 **Heat a large saucepan,** add the bacon and fry for 3-5 minutes, stirring until the fat has rendered. With a slotted spoon, transfer the bacon to a plate lined with kitchen paper.

4 **Reduce the heat,** then add the onions and cook, stirring frequently, for 3-5 minutes, until soft and translucent. With a slotted spoon, transfer the onions to the lined plate. Discard any remaining fat from the pan.

FINISH THE CHOWDER

5 **Add the potatoes** to the pan with the bay leaf, salt, and pepper. Pour in the stock. Bring to a boil and simmer gently for 7-10 minutes, until the potatoes are slightly soft when pierced with the tip of a knife.

6 **Return most of the bacon and onions** to the pan with the sweetcorn kernels and pulp, cream, and milk. Bring to a boil and simmer for 7-10 minutes, until the potatoes are tender. Add the scallops. Bring back to a simmer, then discard the bay leaf, ladle into warmed bowls, and sprinkle with paprika and the reserved onion and bacon.

Hunter's chicken

THE ITALIAN WAY to cook a bird after a shoot. In Italy, the dish is called *alla cacciatora*, meaning "hunter's style". Add sage instead of rosemary, if you prefer. The slight bitterness of braised escarole makes a flavoursome accompaniment and must be made just before serving. The chicken can be made 2 days ahead and refrigerated in the sauce.

SERVES	**PREP**	**COOK**
SERVES 4	20-25 MINS	45-60 MINS

Ingredients

salt and freshly ground black pepper

1.5kg (3lb 3oz) chicken, jointed into 8 pieces

4 tbsp olive oil

1 onion, diced

4 garlic cloves, finely chopped

1 rosemary sprig

1 bay leaf

4 tbsp dry white wine

125ml (4fl oz) chicken stock, plus more if needed

1 head of escarole, weighing about 750g (1lb 10oz)

COOK THE CHICKEN

1 **Season the chicken** all over. Heat half the oil in a sauté pan over medium heat. Add the thighs and drumsticks, skin side down, and sauté for about 5 minutes, until they begin to brown. Add the breast pieces, and cook gently for 10-15 minutes, until very brown. Turn and brown the other side.

2 **Add the onion** and half the garlic, letting them fall to the bottom of the pan. Continue cooking gently until they are soft and golden brown, about 10 minutes. Add the rosemary, bay leaf, wine, stock, salt, and pepper and stir. Cover and simmer until tender, 15-20 minutes.

SAUTÉ THE ESCAROLE

3 **Meanwhile,** trim the root end of the escarole. Discard any tough, green outer leaves, then wash well. Cut into 8 wedges through the core. Heat the remaining oil in a frying pan. Add the rest of the garlic with the escarole, 4 tbsp water, salt and pepper. Bring to a boil, then cover and simmer gently for 10-20 minutes, turning occasionally. Test the escarole is tender by piercing near the core with a knife. The liquid should have evaporated so the leaves are lightly glazed with oil.

4 **Remove the chicken pieces** from the pan and arrange on warmed individual plates. Discard the bay leaf and rosemary from the sauce, and taste for seasoning; adjust if necessary.

5 **Arrange the escarole** next to the chicken, tucking large leaves under small ones to make neat packages. Spoon the sauce over the chicken and serve with crusty bread.

Monkfish and white wine stew

THE DELICATE FLAVOUR of monkfish here is highlighted by white wine, and the sauce is given a velvety consistency with the addition of a kneaded butter and flour paste, known as beurre manié. Make the stew up to the end of step 4 a day ahead.

SERVES	PREP	COOK
SERVES 6	45–50 MINS	25–30 MINS

Ingredients

FOR THE STEW

750g (1lb 10oz) skinned monkfish fillets

salt and pepper

2 leeks

500g (1lb 2oz) small courgettes

75g (2½oz) butter, at room temperature

2 shallots, diced

2 garlic cloves, finely chopped

250g (9oz) mushrooms, trimmed and quartered

leaves from 3–5 thyme sprigs

1 bay leaf

250ml (9fl oz) dry white wine

500ml (16fl oz) fish stock

3 tbsp flour

leaves from 1 small bunch of parsley, chopped

FOR THE CROUTES (optional)

6 slices of white bread

45g (1½oz) butter

3 tbsp vegetable oil

PREPARE THE FISH AND VEGETABLES

1 **If necessary,** cut away the thin membrane that covers the monkfish. Rinse and pat dry with kitchen paper. Holding each fillet steady, cut into 1cm (½in) diagonal slices. Season with salt and pepper.

2 **Trim the leeks.** Slit them lengthways, then cut diagonally into 1cm (½in) pieces. Wash the leeks thoroughly under cold running water to remove any remaining grit or soil. Drain well.

3 **Trim the courgettes** and cut them into 5cm (2in) pieces. Cut each piece lengthways into quarters.

SIMMER THE BROTH AND MAKE THE CROUTES

4 **Melt 30g (1oz) of butter,** and sauté the shallots, garlic, and leeks for 3–5 minutes. Add the mushrooms, thyme, bay, wine, and stock, cover and simmer for 10–15 minutes. Add the courgettes and cook for 8–10 minutes..

5 **Cut the crusts** from the bread, then cut into triangles. Melt the butter and oil in a frying pan. Add the bread in batches and fry for 1 minute on each side, until golden. Drain on kitchen paper.

COOK THE FISH AND THICKEN THE STEW

6 **Add the monkfish** to the broth with water, if necessary, so that the fish is barely covered, and stir very gently to combine. Too vigorous stirring may make the fish fall apart.

7 **Cover the pan,** bring back to a boil, and simmer for 3–5 minutes, until the fish is tender when tested with a fork.

8 **Fork together the remaining butter** with the flour to form a smooth paste. Add to the broth, stir to combine and simmer for 2 minutes.

9 **Discard the bay leaf,** stir in half the parsley and taste for seasoning. Serve in a warmed tureen, sprinkled with the remaining parsley, and serve with the croutes, if you like.

 VARIATION: Monkfish and red wine stew

Wonderfully unusual and full-flavoured

1 Omit the garlic, leeks, parsley, thyme, courgettes and white wine. Prepare the monkfish, shallots, and mushrooms as directed. Make the croutes as directed. Cook the shallots in butter for 1 minute, until soft. Add 500ml (16fl oz) red wine and simmer until reduced by half.

2 Meanwhile, peel 250g (9oz) pickling onions. Melt 30g (1oz) butter in a frying pan, add the onions and cook for 5–8 minutes, until golden. Add the mushrooms and cook for 3–5 minutes, until the liquid evaporates and the mushrooms are tender.

3 Add 500ml (16fl oz) fish stock and 1 bay leaf to the red wine. Add the monkfish and cover. Simmer for 3–5 minutes, until tender. Stir in the onions and mushrooms and thicken the stew as directed. Serve on warmed plates.

Paella

A DISH TO FEED A CROWD, so invite family and friends. This Spanish recipe of saffron-flavoured rice with chicken, prawns, mussels and chorizo is named after the paellera in which it is traditionally cooked. Of course, most kitchens won't have one of those in the cupboard, so just use your broadest frying pan. It is important that the ingredients are not piled up too deeply in the pan; they should form a relatively shallow layer for the best results.

SERVES	PREP	COOK
SERVES 8-10	1 HOUR	40-45 MINS

Ingredients

2 large pinches of saffron threads

500g (1lb 2oz) raw, unpeeled jumbo prawns

1kg (2¼lb) mussels

750g (1lb 10oz) chicken thighs, on the bone if preferred, diced

salt and pepper

4 tbsp olive oil

250g (9oz) chorizo sausage, in 1cm (½in) slices

2 large onions, diced

2 red peppers, sliced

750g (1lb 10oz) paella or other short-grain rice

3 garlic cloves, finely chopped

2 x 400g cans chopped tomatoes

375g (13oz) French beans, in 1cm (½in) slices

1-2 tbsp chopped parsley

PREPARE THE INGREDIENTS

1 **Put 3-4 tbsp boiling water** in a small bowl and sprinkle in the saffron threads. Leave to soak for at least 15 minutes; the saffron will give up its beautiful yellow-orange colour and subtle aromas during this time, meaning it will flavour the stew more highly later.

2 **Leaving the prawns in their shells**, pull off and discard the legs. Twist each prawn tail and pull it off very gently to remove the dark intestinal vein (this is attached to the tail and should emerge from along the back of the prawns). Rinse them as swiftly as possible under running water and dry very well; never leave prawns sitting in water as they will soak it up, adversely affecting their texture.

3 **Scrub the mussels** under cold running water with a small stiff brush. Scrape the shells with an old, blunt knife to remove any barnacles. Pull off and discard any weeds or 'beards' from the shells. Discard any mussels that have broken shells or that do not close when tapped on the side of the kitchen sink.

COOK THE PAELLA

4 **Season the chicken.** Heat the oil in a 30-35cm (12-14in) paella pan and sauté the chicken, turning, for 10-12 minutes, until brown. Transfer to a plate. Add the chorizo to the pan and sauté for 1-2 minutes on each side, until browned. Transfer to the plate with a slotted spoon.

5 **Add the onion** and red pepper to the pan; cook for 5-7 minutes, stirring occasionally, until soft. Stir in the rice and cook for 2-3 minutes, until the grains absorb the oil and all the other flavours.

6 **Stir in 1.5 litres (2¾ pints) water,** the garlic, the saffron with its soaking liquid, and plenty of salt, and pepper. Push the chicken pieces down into the rice. Scatter the chorizo slices over, followed by the tomatoes, beans, prawns and mussels. Bring to a boil.

7 **Simmer,** uncovered, for 25-30 minutes, until all the liquid has evaporated and the rice is tender but slightly chewy. Do not stir, or the rice will become sticky. If the rice is undercooked, add a little more water and simmer a few minutes longer. Remove from the heat and discard any mussels that have not opened. Cover with a tea towel and let stand for 5 minutes. Sprinkle with parsley and serve.

 VARIATION: Seafood paella

Squid replaces the chicken in this version.

1 Omit the French beans and chicken. Prepare the saffron, onions, garlic, tomatoes, and chorizo as directed in the main recipe, substituting green peppers for red and using the same weight of clams in place of the mussels. Cut the prawns in half to open in a butterfly shape. Remove the dark intestinal vein.

2 Rinse 375g (13oz) cleaned squid and drain it well. Cut the tentacles from the bodies and cut them into 2-3 pieces if large, or leave whole if small. Cut the body into 1cm (½in) rings.

3 Cook the chorizo, onions, peppers, and rice as directed. Pour in the water, arrange the chorizo over the rice, followed by the prawns, tomatoes, squid, 125g (4½oz) shelled fresh or defrosted peas, and finally the clams. Cook and serve as directed.

Seafood and tomato cioppino

A HEARTY DISH created by Italian immigrants to San Francisco in the 19th century. Make sure you cook this fragrant dish with care, as the crabs, mussels, and scallops will toughen if overcooked.

SERVES	**PREP**	**COOK**
SERVES 4	45-50 MINS	20-25 MINS

Ingredients

4 tbsp olive oil

2 large onions, diced

1 tbsp tomato purée

3 x 400g (14oz) tins chopped Italian plum tomatoes

3 garlic cloves, finely chopped

pinch of cayenne pepper

salt and pepper

1 bouquet garni, made with 5-6 parsley stalks, 2-3 thyme sprigs, and 1 bay leaf

500ml (16fl oz) dry white wine

2 whole cooked crabs, total weight about 1.4kg (3lb)

750g (1lb 10oz) mussels

500g (1lb 2oz) skinned white fish fillets

250g (9oz) small scallops

leaves from a small bunch of parsley, finely chopped

MAKE THE TOMATO BROTH

1 **Heat the oil** in a saucepan, add the onions and cook for 3-5 minutes, until soft and translucent. Add the tomato purée, tomatoes, garlic, cayenne, salt, pepper, and bouquet garni.

2 **Pour in the white wine.** Cover the pan and simmer gently, stirring occasionally, for about 20 minutes. The sauce should thicken slightly and release its aromas.

PREPARE THE CRABS

3 **Set the crabs,** back down, on a chopping board. Twist off the legs and reserve. Holding the crab body steady, twist off the claws at the bottom joint.

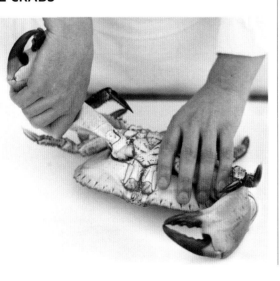

4 **Using crab crackers,** or the back of a heavy knife, crack the claws, leaving them whole and taking care not to crush the meat. If the legs are large, crack them also; discard them, or use to make stock if they are small.

5 **Open the body:** with your fingers, lift off and discard the "apron" flap from the centre of the shell. With your thumbs, push along the perforation to crack the central section of the shell under the tail and prise it apart.

6 **Gently pull the body** from the shell. Scrape out any soft brown meat from the shell and reserve in a bowl. Pull off and discard the soft gills from the body. Crack the body in half. Pick out the meat from the body with the end of a teaspoon. Add to the crab meat in the bowl and reserve.

PREPARE THE REMAINING FISH

7 **Scrub the mussels** thoroughly under cold running water with a small stiff brush. Discard any with broken shells or that do not close when tapped against the side of the kitchen sink. Scrape with an old, blunt knife to remove any barnacles. Pull off and discard any weeds or 'beards' from the shells with your fingers.

8 **Rinse the fish fillets** under cold running water and dry. Set on a chopping board and cut into chunky 5cm (2in) pieces. If necessary, discard the tough crescent-shaped membrane at the side of each scallop (though these are usually trimmed off before the scallops are sold). Make sure the scallops have no black or brownish intestinal vein running around the edge; if they do, pull it off and discard.

COOK THE CIOPPINO

9 **Discard the bouquet garni** from the broth. Taste; it should be peppery. Pack the fish into the bottom of a casserole in an even layer, then the scallops. Arrange the crab meat, legs, and claws, and the mussels on top.

10 **Ladle the hot tomato broth** over the seafood and add water, if necessary, so the seafood is just covered. Cover the casserole with the lid and bring to a boil. Simmer for 3–5 minutes, until the mussels have opened and the white fish flakes easily with a fork.

11 **Discard any mussels** that have not opened. Taste for seasoning. Serve the cioppino in warmed bowls, with a crab claw in each bowl. Sprinkle with the parsley. Serve immediately, with slices of sourdough bread.

Chicken paprika with dumplings

GOOD-QUALITY HUNGARIAN PAPRIKA is the key to this dish. Caraway seed dumplings are delicious with the chicken, as well as being an aid to the digestion. Steamed, crisp green beans or sugarsnap peas would provide the ideal crunch and freshness alongside. The chicken paprika can be prepared 1 day ahead and kept, covered, in the refrigerator; add the soured cream and make the dumplings just before serving. As this dish is already so highly seasoned and flavoured, use water instead of chicken stock if you prefer.

SERVES	PREP	COOK
SERVES 4-6	40-45 MINS	35-40 MINS

Ingredients

FOR THE DUMPLINGS

100g (3½oz) plain flour

¼ tsp baking powder

½ tsp salt

2 tsp caraway seeds

2 eggs

FOR THE CHICKEN

1.6kg (3½lb) chicken, jointed into 8 pieces

salt and pepper

2 tbsp vegetable oil
1 large onion, diced
2 garlic cloves, finely chopped
2 tbsp paprika, plus more to taste
1 tbsp plain flour
400g (14oz) can chopped tomatoes
500ml (16fl oz) chicken stock, plus more if needed
125ml (4fl oz) soured cream

PREPARE THE DUMPLINGS

1 **Sift the flour,** baking powder, and salt together into a large bowl, lifting the sieve high above the bowl in order to aerate the flour particles as they float down. Mix in the fragrant caraway seeds well, so they are distributed evenly through the flour and the dumplings will each receive their portion. Make a well in the centre.

2 **In a small bowl,** whisk the eggs together until broken down. Add them to the well with about 120ml (4fl oz) water. Gradually draw in the flour to the wet ingredients from the inside out, and stir until it is all combined. Add more water if it is dry; the dough should be moist but not soft or sticky. Cover and refrigerate.

COOK THE CHICKEN PAPRIKA

3 **Preheat the oven** to 180°C (350°F/Gas 4). Season the chicken pieces. Heat the oil in the casserole on top of the stove. Working in batches, if necessary, add the chicken to the casserole, skin-side down, and brown well for about 5 minutes.

4 **Turn the chicken** and brown the other side. Transfer to a plate and set aside. Add the onion to the casserole and cook over medium heat, stirring occasionally, for 2-3 minutes, until soft. Add the garlic and continue cooking for 3-5 minutes longer.

5 **Stir in the paprika.** Cook very gently, stirring occasionally, for about 5 minutes. Stir in the flour, then add the tomatoes, stock, salt and pepper; bring to a boil. Return the chicken, cover and cook in the heated oven for 35-40 minutes, until the chicken is tender.

COOK THE DUMPLINGS

6 **Fill a shallow saucepan** with salted water and bring to a boil. Take 2 small spoons, dip them first in the boiling water, then use them to shape the dumpling dough into 2cm (¾in) balls; drop the balls into the boiling water. Cook the dumplings in batches so the saucepan is not crowded.

7 **Cover the pan,** and simmer for 7-10 minutes, until the dumplings are firm and cooked in the centre. Using a slotted spoon, transfer the dumplings to a plate lined with kitchen paper.

FINISH AND SERVE THE CHICKEN PAPRIKA

8 **Transfer the chicken pieces** to a platter and keep warm. Stir the soured cream into the sauce and taste for seasoning. Add the dumplings to the casserole and turn each to coat in sauce. Cover and cook very gently for about 2 minutes.

9 **Divide the chicken** evenly among warmed plates; cover with the paprika sauce and add the dumplings, making sure all your diners receive the same number.

Chicken and beer stew

THE DARKER THE BEER, the richer this dish will be. Mashed potatoes would be good on the side and, naturally, you can guess what is the best drink to serve. If prepared up to the end of step 8 and refrigerated overnight, not only will the flavours blend together more harmoniously, but it will be easier to skim all the fat from the top of the dish. Bring to room temperature and reheat on top of the stove before serving.

SERVES	PREP	COOK
SERVES 4-6	25-30 MINS	50-55 MINS

Ingredients

1 chicken, weighing about 1.6kg (3½lb)

salt and pepper

30g (1oz) butter

2 tbsp vegetable oil

750g (1lb 10oz) onions, thinly sliced

30g (1oz) plain flour

3-4 tbsp Cognac

500g (1lb 2oz) mushrooms, quartered

1 bouquet garni, made with 5-6 parsley stalks, 2-3 thyme sprigs and 1 bay leaf

2 tsp juniper berries, gently crushed

750ml (1¼ pints) beer

4 tbsp double cream

leaves from 1 small bunch of parsley, finely chopped

JOINT THE CHICKEN

1 With a sharp knife, cut down between one leg joint and the body. Twist the leg sharply outwards to break the joint, then cut through it and pull the leg from the body. Repeat for the other leg.

2 Slit closely along both sides of the breastbone to loosen the meat, then split the breastbone. Turn the bird over on to its breast and cut along one side of the backbone. The bird is now divided in half.

3 Cut the backbone and rib bones in one piece from the breast half where they are still attached, leaving the wing joints attached to the breast.

4 Cut each breast in half diagonally so a portion of breast meat is included with the wing. Cut each leg in half through the joint between thigh and drumstick. Cut off any sharp bones.

COOK THE STEW

5 **Season the chicken** pieces. Heat the butter and oil in a casserole until foaming, and add the chicken, skin-side down. Brown them well for about 5 minutes. Turn and brown the other side. Transfer the chicken to a plate.

6 **Add the onions** and cook, stirring occasionally, for 10–15 minutes, until soft and well browned. Sprinkle with the flour and cook, stirring, for 1–2 minutes, until the flour is just lightly browned. Return the chicken to the pan in a single layer.

7 **Add the Cognac.** Standing well back, set the alcohol alight with a lighted match. Baste the chicken with the Cognac until the flames subside; it should take 20–30 seconds.

8 **Add the mushrooms,** bouquet garni, and crushed juniper berries. Pour in the beer, bring to a boil, cover and simmer for 40–50 minutes, until the chicken is tender when pierced and the juices run clear.

9 **Discard the bouquet garni** and skim off excess fat from the surface with a large metal spoon. Stir in the cream and bring back just to a boil. Taste for seasoning and adjust if needed, then sprinkle with the parsley.

 ## VARIATION: Chicken with Cognac

This version increases the amount of Cognac and replaces the beer with chicken stock.

1 Omit the mushrooms, onions, beer, juniper berries, cream, and parsley. Joint the chicken as directed in the main recipe. Put 500g (1lb 2oz) pickling onions in a bowl, cover them with boiling water and let stand for 2 minutes. Remove and peel off the skins.

2 Brown the chicken as directed; set aside. Add the onions to the casserole and cook, stirring, for 5–7 minutes, until golden brown. Transfer to a bowl. Sprinkle the flour into the casserole and cook for 1–2 minutes, stirring to amalgamate the flour with all the juices in the casserole and to 'cook out' the flour's raw taste. Return the chicken to the pot and increase the heat to medium-high, continuing to stir so the flour does not scorch.

3 Add 250ml (9fl oz) Cognac and bring to a boil. Set alight, standing well back, and baste as directed until the flames subside. Add 250ml (9fl oz) chicken stock, the onions, bouquet garni, salt, and pepper and cook as directed. Discard the bouquet garni and taste for seasoning.

Rabbit Provençal

A WONDERFUL DISH, with tomatoes baked slowly in the oven. Herbes de Provence is one of the few dried herbs that it is still worth buying: the mixture includes wild thyme, savory, and fennel, and is wonderfully aromatic. As with all dried herbs, make sure to use them quickly or they lose their aroma.

SERVES	PREP	COOK
SERVES 4	35-40 MINS	3-3½ HOURS

Ingredients

FOR THE RABBIT

1 rabbit, weighing about 1.4kg (3lb), cut into 8 pieces

2 shallots, chopped

250ml (8fl oz) dry white wine

4 tbsp olive oil

2 tbsp herbes de Provence

1 tbsp plain flour

250ml (8fl oz) chicken stock

5-7 thyme sprigs

FOR THE TOMATOES

1 tbsp olive oil

6 plum tomatoes, total weight about 500g (1lb 2oz)

salt and pepper

MARINATE THE RABBIT

1 In a shallow, non-metallic dish wide enough to hold the rabbit pieces in 1 layer, combine the rabbit, shallots, white wine, half the oil, and the herbes de Provence.

2 Add the rabbit and turn until coated. Cover and refrigerate for 2-3 hours, to marinate. Meanwhile, bake the tomatoes.

BAKE THE TOMATOES

3 Preheat the oven to 130°C (250°F/Gas ½). Brush a grill rack with oil. Core the tomatoes and cut each lengthways into 3 slices. Put them in a bowl with the oil, salt and pepper, and toss to coat.

4 Arrange the tomato slices on the grill rack and bake for 2–2½ hours, until slightly shrivelled. Transfer to a plate and increase the oven temperature to 190°C (375°F/Gas 5).

FINISH THE DISH

5 Take the rabbit from the marinade; reserve the marinade. Season the rabbit with salt and pepper. Heat half the remaining oil in a casserole. Add half the rabbit and cook for 5 minutes, until browned. Transfer to a plate, add the remaining oil, and brown the remaining rabbit.

6 Return all the rabbit and sprinkle with the flour. Cook for 2-3 minutes, then stir in the marinade and stock. Cover and bake for 50-55 minutes, stirring occasionally, until very tender. Return the tomatoes to the oven for the last 10 minutes, to heat through. Strip the thyme leaves from the stems. Serve the rabbit and tomatoes sprinkled with the thyme.

Hungarian beef goulash

TRUE HUNGARIAN PAPRIKA, aromatic and piquant, makes a great difference to this recipe. Find it in specialist food shops. If you have no luck, you may want to add more paprika to the goulash, to taste, in step 2. You can make this dish up to 2 days ahead, cover, and refrigerate.

SERVES 4   PREP 25-30 MINS   COOK 2½-3 HOURS

Ingredients

FOR THE GOULASH

1 tbsp vegetable oil

60g (2oz) smoked bacon, diced

6 onions, total weight about 750g (1lb 10oz), chopped

2 tbsp paprika

750g (1lb 10oz) braising steak, cut into 4cm (1½in) cubes

2 garlic cloves, finely chopped

½ tsp caraway seeds

2 tomatoes, cored, seeded and chopped

2 green peppers, sliced

salt and pepper

125ml (4fl oz) soured cream (optional)

FOR THE DUMPLINGS

1 egg

45g (1½oz) plain flour

COOK THE GOULASH

1 **Heat the oil** in a casserole, add the bacon and cook, stirring, for 3-5 minutes, until it is lightly browned and the fat has rendered. Stir in the onions. Cut a piece of foil to fit the casserole, then cover the mixture and add the lid. Cook over low heat, stirring occasionally, for 20-25 minutes until the onions are soft and translucent.

2 **Preheat the oven** to 180°C (350°F/ Gas 4). Stir the paprika into the onions and bacon and cook for 2 minutes longer; don't let the paprika scorch. Add the steak, garlic, caraway seeds, and 500ml (16fl oz) water and stir. Bring to a boil, stirring, then cover and cook in the oven until the beef is almost tender, 1-1½hours.

FINISH THE GOULASH

3 **Stir the tomatoes and peppers** into the goulash. Season to taste. Cover and cook for 30-45 minutes longer, until the meat is very soft and the stew rich and thick. Taste for seasoning.

MAKE AND COOK THE DUMPLINGS

4 **Lightly beat the egg** in a small bowl. Put the flour and a pinch of salt in another bowl, then stir in the egg.

5 **Transfer the goulash** to the top of the stove and heat to boiling. Using 2 teaspoons, drop spoonfuls of the dumpling mixture into the goulash and simmer for 5-7 minutes, until cooked through.

6 **Ladle the goulash and dumplings** into warmed soup bowls. Top each serving with a spoon of soured cream, if you like.

Poule au pot

A COMPLETE MEAL: you'll find this classic French dish becomes a real favourite. Mastering this recipe will also add to your repertoire the piquant sauce *gribiche*, which is a wonderful accompaniment here but also works marvels with fish and seafood, or even with offal.

SERVES	PREP	COOK
SERVES 4-6	1 HR	1¼-1½ HRS

375g (13oz) carrots

375g (13oz) turnips

60g (2oz) vermicelli

Ingredients

FOR THE POULE AU POT

1 large chicken, weighing about 2kg (4½lb)

salt and pepper

1 onion

1 clove

1 bouquet garni, made with 5-6 parsley stalks, 2-3 thyme sprigs, and 1 bay leaf

4 litres (7 pints) chicken stock, plus more if needed

1kg (2¼lb) leeks

FOR THE SAUCE GRIBICHE

2 eggs

juice of ½ lemon

1 tsp Dijon mustard

2 tbsp dry white wine

250ml (9fl oz) vegetable oil

1 tbsp drained capers, finely chopped

3 gherkins, finely chopped

leaves from 5-7 parsley sprigs, finely chopped

1 small bunch of chives, finely snipped

COOK THE CHICKEN

1 **Truss the chicken,** and season. Trim the root and stalk from the onion, peel and stud it with the clove. Put the chicken in a casserole. Add the bouquet garni and onion; pour in enough stock to cover the chicken by about three-quarters. Bring to a boil, cover and simmer for 45 minutes.

2 **Trim the leeks,** discarding the roots and tough green tops. Slit them lengthways, wash thoroughly under cold water, and cut into 7.5cm (3in) lengths. Put them on a large piece of muslin, gather up the edges, and tie securely with string to make a bundle.

3 **Trim the carrots** and cut into 7.5cm (3in) lengths. Tie them in a piece of muslin as for the leeks. Peel the turnips and cut into 2.5cm (1in) cubes. Tie them in muslin in the same way as the leeks and carrots.

4 **Add the vegetable bundles** to the chicken with more stock, so they are covered. Cover and simmer for 25-30 minutes longer, until the chicken and vegetables are cooked.

MAKE THE SAUCE GRIBICHE

5 **Boil the eggs** for 10 minutes. Drain, cool, and shell them. Separate the yolks from the whites by gently pulling them apart. Cut the whites into strips and finely chop.

6 **Put the yolks** in a small sieve set over a bowl and work them through, using the back of a spoon. Scrape away the yolk clinging to the bottom of the sieve.

7 **Add the lemon juice** to the egg yolks with the mustard, salt, pepper, and white wine; whisk until combined. Gradually pour in the oil, whisking constantly. It will emulsify and thicken slightly. Add the chopped egg whites, capers, gherkins, and herbs; whisk together to combine. Taste for seasoning.

FINISH THE DISH

8 **Transfer the chicken** to a board, and remove the trussing string. Carve the chicken: cut down between one leg and the body. Turn the bird on its side, and cut around the oyster meat so it remains attached to the thigh. Twist the leg sharply to break the joint, then cut through and pull the leg from the body.

9 **Halve the leg** by cutting through the joint, using the line of fat on the underside as a guide. Repeat for the other leg. Cut horizontally above one wing joint, through to the breastbone, so you will be able to carve whole slices from the breast. Cut off the wing. Repeat with the other wing.

10 **Carve the breasts** in slices parallel to the ribcage. Put all the chicken pieces on a heatproof plate, cover with foil, and keep warm in a very low oven. Remove the vegetables from the broth with a slotted spoon and keep warm, still in their muslin.

11 **Strain the broth** into the saucepan, bring to a boil, and simmer for 10-20 minutes. With a large metal spoon, skim off as much fat as possible from the top, and taste for seasoning. Add the vermicelli to the boiling broth and simmer, just until tender. It will take 3-5 minutes, or according to package instructions.

12 **Meanwhile,** cut the string from the bundles of carrots, leeks, and turnips, unwrap them, and discard the muslin. Add to the chicken, gently mixing so everything is evenly spread, and continue to keep warm until ready to serve.

13 **Mix the chicken and vegetables** into the broth and remove from the heat. Stir very gently, then add to warmed bowls, making sure each diner gets a fairly even amount of chicken, vegetables, and vermicelli. Serve the *sauce gribiche* separately.

Turkey mole

A DELECTABLE BLEND of hot spices and dark chocolate combine in this famous Mexican dish. If you are unfamiliar with the recipe, it could seem a rather odd combination, but do try it because it is absolutely delicious and will soon become part of your regular repertoire. Don't let the rather long ingredients list put you off making this recipe; it is definitely worth the effort. Make sure you use the best quality dark chocolate.

SERVES	PREP	COOK
SERVES 8	45–50 MINS	1¼–1¾ HRS

Ingredients

FOR THE STEW

1.6kg (3½lb) boneless turkey thighs

salt and pepper

4 tbsp vegetable oil

1 celery stick, roughly chopped

2 onions, quartered

4 garlic cloves, peeled

1 tsp black peppercorns

1 carrot, roughly chopped

FOR THE MOLE MIXTURE

45g (1½oz) 70 per cent cocoa solids chocolate

1 slice of stale white bread

1 stale corn tortilla

400g (14oz) can chopped tomatoes

175g (6oz) blanched almonds

75g (2½oz) raisins

30g (1oz) chilli powder

1 tsp each ground cloves, coriander, and cumin

¼ tsp ground aniseed

2 tsp ground cinnamon

30g (1oz) sesame seeds

COOK THE TURKEY

1 **Season the turkey.** Heat half the oil in the casserole. Add the turkey pieces, skin-side down. Brown the turkey well, turning occasionally, for 10–15 minutes.

2 **Add 1 litre (1¾ pints) water,** the celery, 4 onion quarters, 1 garlic clove, the peppercorns, and carrot. Bring to a boil, cover, and simmer until the turkey is very tender when pierced, 45–60 minutes.

PREPARE THE MOLE PURÉE

3 **Break the chocolate** into pieces. Tear the bread and tortilla into pieces. Put the tomatoes in a food processor with the remaining onion and garlic, bread, tortilla, almonds, raisins, chilli powder, cloves, coriander, cumin, aniseed, cinnamon, and half the sesame seeds. Work to a smooth purée.

ASSEMBLE THE MOLE

4 **Remove the casserole** from the heat, transfer the turkey to a plate and let cool slightly. Strain the cooking liquid into a bowl, discarding the vegetables. Remove the skin and any fat from the turkey and pull the meat into bite-sized pieces with your fingers.

5 **Heat the remaining oil** in the casserole. Add the mole purée and cook, stirring constantly with the wooden spoon for about 5 minutes, until thick and dark. Add the chocolate and cook, stirring, to melt, for about 5 minutes longer.

6 **Pour in the cooking liquid,** season with salt, and stir. Simmer for 25-30 minutes, until the sauce begins to thicken. Meanwhile, toast the remaining sesame seeds for 2-3 minutes in a dry frying pan until lightly browned. Return the turkey to the casserole and simmer for 10-15 minutes longer, until the sauce is thick enough to coat the back of a spoon. Taste for seasoning. Serve in warmed individual bowls with white rice. Sprinkle with the toasted sesame seeds.

VARIATION: Pork mole

Sweet pork and soured cream make a delectable version of the Mexican dish.

1 Omit the turkey, celery, carrots, and black peppercorns. Peel and quarter 1 onion. Peel 3 garlic cloves. Make the mole purée as directed in the main recipe. Cook the purée and chocolate, substituting 1 litre (1¾ pints) water for the turkey cooking liquid. Simmer until the sauce has thickened; this should take 25-30 minutes. It should be thick enough to coat the back of a spoon.

2 Trim the excess fat from 8 pork chops (weighing about 175g/6oz each) and season both sides of each. Heat 2 tbsp oil in a large frying pan and brown the chops well over high heat for 1-2 minutes on each side. Add the chops to the hot mole sauce, cover and cook very gently until completely tender when pierced with the tip of a knife; it will take 1-1¼ hours.

3 Toast the sesame seeds as directed. Taste the mole for seasoning and adjust if necessary. Divide the pork and sauce among 8 warmed plates, or serve on a large warmed platter, sprinkle with the toasted sesame seeds, and top each serving with 1 tbsp soured cream. Serve with plenty of fluffy white rice.

Poussins with plums and cabbage

THE UNDERLYING SWEETNESS OF PLUMS works wonders in this dish. The dish can be made 1 day ahead and kept, covered, in the refrigerator. Reheat the birds with the cabbage, add the remaining plums and thicken the sauce just before serving.

SERVES SERVES 6	**PREP** 35-40 MINS	**COOK** 1¼-1½ HRS

Ingredients

6 poussins, each weighing about 500g (1lb 2oz)

salt and pepper

1 Savoy cabbage, weighing about 1.4kg (3lb), cored and coarsely shredded

1 onion

1 clove

2 tbsp vegetable oil

250g (9oz) streaky bacon rashers, sliced

750g (1lb 10oz) purple plums, halved and stoned

1 bouquet garni

250ml (9fl oz) dry white wine

500ml (16fl oz) chicken stock or water

2 tsp arrowroot

TRUSS THE BIRDS FOR EVEN COOKING

1 **Season the insides** of the poussins with salt and pepper. Hold one bird, breast-side down, on a work surface, tuck the neck skin under the bird, and cover with the wings.

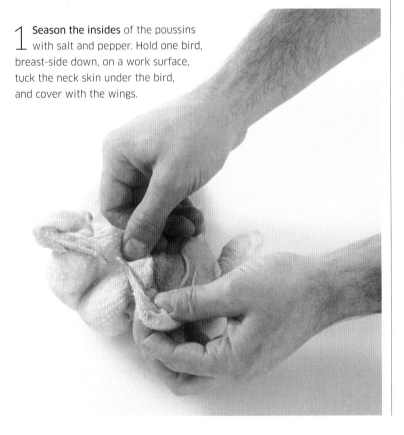

2 **Turn the bird over** and pass a length of string under the tail end of the bird; tie a secure knot over the leg joints. Bring the strings along the sides of the body, between the breast and the legs, and loop them around the legs.

3 **Turn the bird over** so it is breast-side down again and tie the strings tightly under the body. Bring both ends of the string down between the sides of the body and the insides of the wings.

4 **Tie the wing bones** at the neck opening so they are tucked securely under the body. Repeat the process with the remaining poussins and set aside.

BLANCH THE CABBAGE

5 Fill a large pan with salted water and bring to a boil. Add the cabbage, return to a boil and simmer for 2 minutes until beginning to soften. Drain thoroughly in a colander.

ASSEMBLE AND BAKE THE DISH

6 Preheat the oven to 180°C (350°F/Gas 4). Peel the onion and stud it with the clove. Heat the oil in the casserole. Season the birds with salt and pepper. Brown them on all sides, turning, for 5–10 minutes. Transfer to a plate. Reduce the heat and let the casserole cool slightly.

7 Add the bacon and cook, stirring, for 3–5 minutes, until the fat has rendered. Spoon off all but 2 tbsp of fat. Stir in half the cabbage, and spread it evenly. Add the poussins and two-thirds of the plums.

8 Add the clove-studded onion and bouquet garni. Cover with the remaining cabbage and pour over the wine and stock. Cover and bake for 45–55 minutes, until the birds are cooked and the juices run clear when the thighs are pierced.

9 Discard the onion and bouquet garni. Transfer the birds to a chopping board; remove the strings. Taste the cabbage mixture for seasoning. With a slotted spoon, transfer the cabbage to a warmed large serving dish. Set the birds on top, cover with foil and keep warm.

FINISH THE DISH

10 Add the remaining plums to the cooking liquid and simmer for 5–8 minutes, until just tender. Lift them out with a slotted spoon and arrange them with the poussins and cabbage in the centre of the dish.

11 Boil the liquid until well-flavoured and reduced by about half; it should take 5–10 minutes. Stir the arrowroot and 1 tbsp water together to form a smooth paste with no lumps. Whisk enough of the paste into the liquid so it thickens to lightly coat the back of a spoon. Taste for seasoning, adjusting if necessary.

12 Spoon some sauce over each of the poussins, just to moisten the birds, and serve the rest separately in a warmed gravy boat for your diners to help themselves.

Chicken and prawn laksa

NOODLES AND TOFU add extra body to this aromatic recipe. For vegetarians, add more tofu and soaked dried oriental mushrooms and omit the meat and shellfish, or for more carnivorous souls add chunks of spicy sausage and pork.

SERVES	PREP	COOK
SERVES 6	35–40 MINS	30–35 MINS

Ingredients

750g (1lb 10oz) skinless, boneless chicken breasts

salt and pepper

500g (1lb 2oz) raw prawns

3 dried red chillies, or to taste

6 shallots, peeled and coarsely chopped

3 garlic cloves, peeled

1½ tsp ground turmeric

1 tbsp ground coriander

5cm (2in) piece of fresh root ginger, peeled, sliced, and crushed

250g (9oz) tofu

125g (4½oz) thin rice noodles

2 tbsp vegetable oil

250g (9oz) beansprouts

400ml (14fl oz) can coconut milk

1 small bunch of spring onions, thickly sliced

POACH THE CHICKEN

1 **Bring 750ml (1¼ pints) of water** to a boil in a saucepan and add the chicken breasts, salt, and pepper. Simmer for 12–15 minutes, or until tender when pierced at the thickest portion and the juices run clear.

2 **With a slotted spoon,** transfer the chicken to a chopping board. Reserve the poaching liquid.

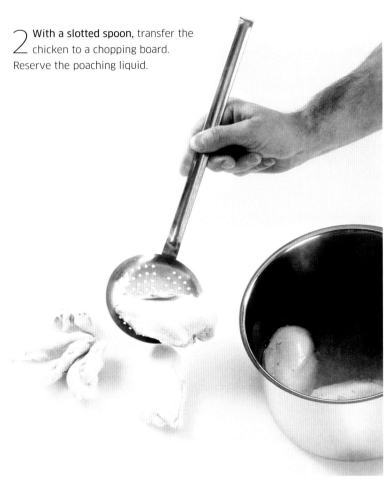

3 **When the chicken is cool,** halve each breast lengthways, then cut across into 2.5cm (1in) pieces.

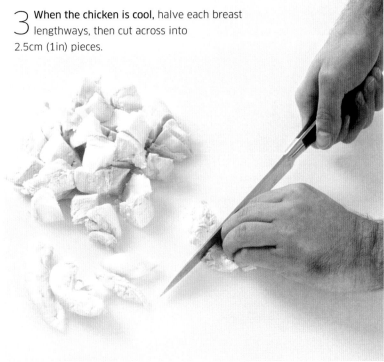

PREPARE THE OTHER INGREDIENTS

4 **Make a shallow cut** along the back of each prawn and remove and discard the dark intestinal vein that runs along its length with the tip of a sharp knife.

5 **Put the dried chillies** in a bowl and pour over hot water to cover. Soak for 5 minutes, then drain, cut in half, and scrape out and discard the seeds and white ribs.

6 **In a food processor,** combine the shallots, garlic, chillies, ground turmeric, coriander and ginger; work to a smooth paste. If the mixture is very thick, add 2-3 spoonfuls of the chicken poaching liquid.

7 **Drain the tofu** in a colander and discard the liquid. Cut it into 1cm (½in) cubes, being careful not to break up the pieces.

8 **Fill a large pan** with salted water and bring to a boil. Add the noodles and remove from the heat. Allow to soften for 3-5 minutes, until tender but still slightly chewy. Stir occasionally to prevent them sticking. Drain.

ASSEMBLE THE DISH

9 **Heat the oil** in a wok. Add the puréed ingredients, and cook gently, stirring constantly, for 1-2 minutes, or until you can clearly smell all the fragrant aromas. Add the chicken to the wok and continue cooking, stirring constantly, for 1-2 minutes longer, turning to make sure the chicken is coated all over in the aromatics. Stir in the reserved poaching liquid from the chicken and simmer until the sauce is rich and thickened. Expect it to take 20-25 minutes.

10 **Add the prawns** and simmer, stirring occasionally, just until they begin to lose their transparency and turn pink; it should only take 3-5 minutes and you should not cook them further or they will become tough. Add the tofu, beansprouts, and noodles. Pour in the coconut milk and stir. Simmer very gently for about 5 minutes, until the flavours combine. Stir in half the spring onions. Taste for seasoning, adding more salt and pepper if you think it necessary. Divide the laksa between 6 warmed bowls and sprinkle with the remaining spring onions.

Duck with turnips and apricots

WIDE NOODLES are the perfect accompaniment to this dish. Sweet Madeira wine adds a wonderful flavour and depth to the sauce. If you don't have any chicken stock to hand, you can use water here instead. It's a great recipe for entertaining, as it is rich enough to taste like a special treat, and it can be made 1 day ahead and kept, covered, in the refrigerator. Reheat it gently on top of the stove. You can, of course, ask your butcher to joint the bird for you, but it is easy to do yourself.

SERVES	PREP	COOK
SERVES 4	35-40 MINS	1½-2 HRS

Ingredients

1 duck, weighing about 1.8kg (4lb)

12-16 pickling onions

500g (1lb 2oz) turnips

salt and pepper

1 tbsp vegetable oil

15g (½oz) butter

2 tbsp plain flour

175ml (6fl oz) dry white wine

500ml (16fl oz) chicken stock, plus more if needed

1 bouquet garni, made with 5-6 parsley stalks, 2-3 thyme sprigs and 1 bay leaf

2 shallots, finely chopped

1 tsp granulated sugar

175g (6oz) stoned dried apricots

4 tbsp Madeira wine

JOINT THE DUCK

1 **Trim the excess fat** and skin from the duck. Using a thin, sharp knife, cut down between a leg and the body of the duck. Twist the leg sharply outwards to break the joint, cut through it, and cut the whole leg from the body. Repeat with the other leg.

2 **Cut each leg in half** at the joint between the thigh and the drumstick, using the line of white fat on the underside as a guide.

3 **Slit closely along both sides** of the breastbone to loosen the skin and meat from the bone. With poultry shears or a sharp knife, cut along the breastbone, to split it lengthwise in half.

4 **Turn the bird over,** and cut away the rib bones and backbone in one piece, from the breast, leaving the breast pieces with the wing joints attached. Discard the back and rib bones, or use them to make stock. Cut each breast piece diagonally in half, so a portion of breast meat is left with the wing joint. Cut off any sharp bones.

PREPARE THE VEGETABLES

5 **Put the pickling onions** in a bowl, cover with boiling water, and let stand for 2 minutes. Peel them, leaving a little of the root attached.

6 **Trim the ends** from the turnips, and peel them using a vegetable peeler. Cut small turnips into quarters, and larger ones into eighths. With a small knife, trim off the sharp edges, so they are rounded.

COOK THE STEW

7 **Preheat the oven** to 180°C (350°F/Gas 4). Season the duck. Heat the oil and butter in a casserole, and add the duck, skin-side down. Brown well over low heat for 20-25 minutes. Turn and brown the other side more quickly (for only about 5 minutes). Set aside.

8 **Transfer all but 2-3 tbsp fat** from the casserole to a frying pan. Return the casserole to the heat. Add the flour and cook, stirring constantly, for 1-2 minutes, until lightly browned but not burnt.

9 **Add the white wine,** stock, bouquet garni, salt, pepper, and shallots. Bring the mixture to a boil, and return the duck. Cover and cook in the oven for 40-45 minutes.

10 **Meanwhile,** heat the duck fat in the frying pan over a medium heat. Add the onions, turnips, sugar, salt and pepper, and cook, shaking the frying pan occasionally, for 5-7 minutes, until all the vegetables are evenly browned and beginning to become caramelized from the sugar. Make sure they do not scorch, as this may taint the flavour of the dish.

11 **Remove the stew** from the oven; add the onions, turnips, and apricots. Stir in more stock if the sauce is very thick and the ingredients are not covered (or add water to cover, if necessary). Cover with the lid and return to the oven for 20-25 minutes longer, until the duck and vegetables are tender.

12 **Skim off any fat** from the surface with a wide, shallow spoon. Stir in the Madeira, bring just to a boil on top of the stove, taste for seasoning, and adjust if needed. Serve on warmed individual plates, on a bed of wide noodles if you like.

Cassoulet

A QUICK VERSION OF DUCK CONFIT makes this complex but superb dish far more speedy to prepare than the traditional version. Save it for a very cold spell, when the warming, rich plateful of mixed meats and beans will be greeted by a welcoming and grateful chorus.

SERVES	PREP	COOK
SERVES 8	50-55 MINS PLUS MARINATING	1¾-2¼ HRS

Ingredients

FOR THE QUICK DUCK CONFIT

1 duck, weighing about 1.8kg (4lb), jointed into 8 pieces

1 tsp black peppercorns

3-5 thyme sprigs

3 bay leaves

3 tbsp sea salt flakes

1 tbsp vegetable oil

15g (½oz) butter

FOR THE CASSOULET

250g (9oz) streaky bacon rashers, cut into strips

750g (1lb 10oz) boneless lamb shoulder, in 5cm (2in) dice

375g (13oz) pork sausages

375g (13oz) onions, chopped

2 x 400g (14oz) cans chopped plum tomatoes

175ml (6fl oz) dry white wine

1.5 litres (2¾pints) chicken stock

4 garlic cloves, finely chopped

1 bouquet garni made with 5-6 parsley stalks, 3 thyme sprigs, and 1 bay leaf

1 tbsp tomato purée

salt and pepper

375g (13oz) garlic poaching sausages

4 x 400g (14oz) cans white beans

60g (2oz) dried breadcrumbs

MAKE THE CONFIT

1 **Remove the backbone** from the duck pieces, if necessary. Put the peppercorns in a plastic bag and crush with a rolling pin. Strip the thyme leaves from the stalks. Crush the bay leaves with your fingers. Combine the peppercorns, thyme, and bay in a bowl.

2 **Rub each piece of duck** with some sea salt and put the pieces into a non-metallic bowl. Sprinkle with the peppercorn mixture. Cover with clingfilm and refrigerate for 8-12 hours. Rinse the duck with cold water, then wipe with kitchen paper.

3 **Heat the oil** and butter in a casserole. Add the duck pieces, skin-side down, and brown well over low heat for 20-25 minutes, so the fat is thoroughly melted. Turn and brown the other side more quickly (only for about 5 minutes). Set aside. Spoon off and discard all but 2 tbsp of fat from the casserole.

COOK THE MEATS AND VEGETABLES

4 **Preheat the oven** to 190°C (375°F/Gas 5). Heat the casserole with the reserved duck fat, add the bacon and fry, stirring, for 3-5 minutes, until the fat is rendered. Transfer to a bowl with a slotted spoon.

5 **Season the lamb.** Add the lamb in batches to the casserole and cook over high heat, stirring, for 3-5 minutes, until evenly browned. Transfer to the bowl. Add the sausages to the casserole and brown all over. Transfer to a plate. Discard all but 2 tbsp fat. Add the onions and cook for 3-5 minutes, until soft.

6 **Return the lamb** to the casserole with the bacon and duck. Add the tomatoes, white wine, and two-thirds of the stock and stir to dissolve the pan juices. Stir in the garlic, bouquet garni, tomato purée, and salt and pepper. Bring to a boil on top of the stove, skimming occasionally. Cover and bake in the oven for 1-1¼ hours, until almost tender.

7 Meanwhile, put the poaching sausages into a pan with water to cover. Bring just to a boil. Simmer very gently for 20-25 minutes, until a skewer inserted in a sausage is warm to the touch. Do not boil or the sausages will burst. Drain, slit the skins with the knife, then peel and cut into 2cm (¾in) slices.

ASSEMBLE THE CASSOULET

8 **Drain the beans** in a colander. Rinse with cold water and drain again thoroughly. Add both kinds of sausage and the beans to the casserole. Stir and bring just to a boil on top of the stove. It should be very moist but not soupy. If necessary add more stock or water. Discard the bouquet garni and taste for seasoning.

9 **Sprinkle evenly with the breadcrumbs** and return the casserole to the oven. Bake, uncovered, for 20-25 minutes, until a beautifully crisp layer of golden crust forms on top of the cassoulet and the lamb beneath has become very tender.

10 **Serve the cassoulet** directly from the casserole, giving each diner a combination of lamb, duck, and sausages. Sprinkle with chopped parsley, if you like.

Italian beef braised in red wine

A FAVOURITE DISH in northern Italy. Barbera is the preferred wine, but substitute any good-quality dry red. When cooking with wine, it is very important to use a bottle you would also like to drink; you will taste a bad wine if you use it in a dish. Ovens did not find their way into many Italian kitchens until after World War II, so this dish was cooked on top of the stove, and you can do so too, if you prefer.

SERVES	PREP	COOK
SERVES 6	15-20 MINS	4-4½ HRS

Ingredients

1 rolled silverside of beef, weighing about 1.8kg (4lb)

2 tbsp olive oil

1 small onion, chopped

1 small carrot, in 5mm (¼in) dice

1 celery stick, peeled and diced

500ml (16fl oz) dry red wine

1 tbsp tomato purée

500ml (16fl oz) beef stock, plus more if needed

2-3 thyme sprigs

salt and pepper

ASSEMBLE THE DISH

1 **Preheat the oven** to 150°C (300°F/ Gas 2). With a sharp knife, trim any excess fat and sinew from the beef. Heat the oil in a casserole. Add the beef and brown well on all sides, turning. Transfer to a plate and set aside. Add the onion, carrot, and celery, and cook, stirring, for 3-5 minutes, until the vegetables are soft.

2 **Add the red wine,** stir to dissolve the pan juices, and bring to a boil. Stir in the tomato purée and return the beef. Add enough stock to come halfway up the meat. Add the thyme, season, and bring to a boil. Cover the casserole tightly.

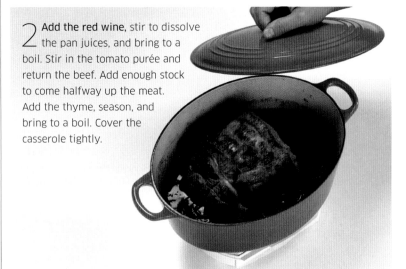

BRAISE THE BEEF

3 **Cook in the oven** for 4-4½ hours, until the meat is very tender when pierced with a fork. Turn the meat 3-4 times during cooking, and add more stock if the casserole seems dry. Make sure the liquid remains at a simmer, not boiling, so the beef does not cook too quickly and become tough.

FINISH THE DISH

4 **Transfer the meat** to a chopping board and cover with foil to keep warm. Boil the liquid until thickened and reduced to about 250ml (9fl oz). Discard the thyme and taste the liquid for seasoning.

5 **Carve the meat** into neat slices on a chopping board. Arrange the beef slices on warmed plates. Spoon a little of the red wine sauce over, and serve the rest separately.

Lamb chops champvallon

DATING BACK to the reign of Louis XIV and attributed to one of his mistresses! Apparently, she created it in an attempt to stay in the king's good graces. The dish will certainly please your diners, with its succulent chops baked in the oven between layers of sliced potatoes and onions, which absorb all the delicious meaty flavours.

SERVES	PREP	COOK
SERVES 6	25–30 MINS	2–2¼ HOURS

Ingredients

6 lamb loin chops, each 2.5cm (1in) thick, total weight about 1kg (2¼lb), trimmed

salt and freshly ground black pepper

1 tbsp vegetable oil

500g (1lb 2oz) onions, thinly sliced

1.1kg (2½lb) baking potatoes

leaves from 1 small bunch of thyme, plus a few sprigs for garnish

3 garlic cloves, finely chopped

1 litre (1¾ pints) chicken or beef stock, plus more if needed

PREPARE THE INGREDIENTS

1 **Trim off** any excess fat from the lamb chops and season both sides. Heat the oil in a large frying pan, add the chops, and cook over high heat for 1–2 minutes each side, until well browned. Remove to a plate and set aside.

2 **Pour** off all but about 1 tbsp of fat from the pan. Add the onions and cook over medium heat, stirring, for 3–5 minutes, until soft and translucent. Remove the pan from the heat.

3 **Peel the potatoes** and cut into very thin slices. In a large bowl, gently stir the potato slices with the softened onions, thyme leaves, salt, and pepper.

ASSEMBLE AND BAKE THE DISH

4 **Preheat the oven** to 180°C (350°F/ Gas 4). Brush a 23x32cm (9x13in) baking dish with oil. Spread half the potato mixture in the dish and sprinkle with the garlic.

5 **Arrange the chops** on top. Cover with the remaining potato, arranging the slices neatly in rows. Pour over enough stock to come just to the top of the potatoes. Bake, uncovered, for 2 hours, or until the lamb and potatoes are tender when pierced.

6 **Divide the chops,** potatoes, and onions among 6 warmed plates and spoon over a little cooking liquid. Decorate with a sprig of thyme.

Lamb dhansak

FRESH MANGO RELISH is optional but it makes a colourful accompaniment to this curry. Traditionally, dhansak would be made with three different types of lentils and loads of vegetables. This version is simpler, but no less tasty for that. It can be made 2 days ahead and kept, covered, in the refrigerator.

SERVES	PREP	COOK
SERVES 6	40-45 MINS	1½-1¾ HRS

Ingredients

FOR THE CURRY

1 large aubergine

salt and pepper

2cm (¾in) piece of fresh root ginger

4 tbsp vegetable oil

750g (1lb 10oz) boned shoulder of lamb, cut into 2.5cm (1in) dice

1 large onion, finely chopped

5 garlic cloves, finely chopped

2 tsp each ground cumin, coriander, and turmeric

1 pinch of cayenne pepper

1 tbsp plain flour

175g (6oz) green lentils

1 small cauliflower, cut into florets

FOR THE MANGO RELISH

1 dried red chilli

1 large mango, weighing about 500g (1lb 2oz)

leaves from 7-10 coriander sprigs, finely chopped

5mm (¼in) piece of fresh root ginger, finely chopped

PREPARE THE AUBERGINE AND GINGER

1 Trim the aubergine and cut into 2.5cm (1in) chunks. Put them in a colander and sprinkle generously with salt. Let stand for about 30 minutes, to draw out some of the juices and soften slightly. Rinse under cold running water and drain well. Pat dry with kitchen paper.

2 Using a small knife, peel the skin from the fresh root ginger. Slice the ginger, cutting across the fibrous grain. Crush each slice with the flat of the knife, then finely chop the slices.

COOK THE CURRY

3 Heat two-thirds of the oil in a large casserole. Add some of the lamb and season. Cook over high heat for 3-5 minutes, stirring so the pieces brown evenly on all sides. Transfer to a bowl. Brown the rest of the lamb in the same way.

4 Add the remaining oil to the casserole, then add the aubergine and cook, stirring occasionally, for 5-7 minutes, until brown. With a slotted spoon, transfer to a separate bowl.

5 Add the onion to the casserole; cook, stirring occasionally, for 7-10 minutes, until golden brown. Stir in the garlic and ginger and cook for 2-3 minutes longer, until softened and fragrant.

6 Stir in the ground cumin, coriander, turmeric, and cayenne; cook, stirring constantly, for 1-2 minutes, until thoroughly combined. Return the lamb with any juices. Sprinkle with the flour and cook, stirring, for about 1 minute.

7 Stir in 1 litre (1¾ pints) of water and bring to a boil. Lower the heat, cover, and simmer gently, stirring occasionally, for 30 minutes. Stir in the lentils and cook for 15 minutes longer.

8 Stir in the aubergine, cauliflower, and 500ml (16fl oz) more water; continue simmering, stirring often, for 50-60 minutes, until completely tender. Add more water during cooking if the curry seems dry. Meanwhile, make the mango relish.

MAKE THE MANGO RELISH

9 Put the dried chilli in a small bowl and cover with hot water. Let soften for 5 minutes, then drain. Cut lengthways in half, discard the core, scrape out the seeds and chop very fine. Cut the mango lengthways into 3 pieces, slightly off-centre so the knife just misses the stone.

10 With a small knife, slash the cut side of the mango pieces in a lattice, at 5mm (¼in) intervals, just cutting through the flesh. Holding the mango flesh upwards, carefully push the peel with your thumbs to turn it inside out, opening out the cuts.

11 **Cut the cubes** of mango away from the skin into a bowl. In a small bowl, combine the mango, chilli, coriander, salt, pepper, and ginger, and stir until mixed. Taste for seasoning, cover and chill, 30 minutes. Serve with the curry.

 VARIATION: Chicken dhansak

The same spices enhance chicken, chickpeas and vegetables.

1 Omit the lamb, cauliflower, and lentils. Prepare the aubergine as directed. Sprinkle 1 medium chicken, jointed into 8 pieces, with salt and pepper. Heat the oil in a large casserole, add the chicken, skin-side down, and brown well for 5–7 minutes, Turn and brown the other side, then transfer to a plate.

2 Brown the aubergine as directed. Drain a 400g (14oz) can of chickpeas. Cook the curry as directed, adding a 400g (14oz) can of chopped plum tomatoes and 1 litre (1¾ pints) water. Return the chicken to the casserole, cover and simmer for 20 minutes.

3 Add the aubergine and chickpeas, then continue cooking for 15–20 minutes, until the chicken is tender when pierced. Taste for seasoning and serve with cucumber raita and naan bread.

Brunswick stew

A COLONIAL AMERICAN DISH using lots of Southern ingredients – such as smoked bacon, beans, sweetcorn, and hot pepper – this was originally made with squirrel! Brunswick county in North Carolina and the county of the same name in Virginia both claim this famous recipe. It will freeze well for up to 3 months.

SERVES	PREP	COOK
SERVES 4-6	25-35 MINS	2-2½ HRS

Ingredients

1.5kg (3lb 3oz) chicken, jointed into 6 pieces

500g (1lb 2oz) smoked bacon hock

1 tbsp dark soft brown sugar

1 bouquet garni

1 onion, chopped

3 celery sticks, trimmed and thinly sliced

400g (14oz) can chopped tomatoes

200g (7oz) fresh, or thawed frozen, or canned sweetcorn

375g (13oz) potatoes

1 tsp dried chilli flakes

250g (9oz) shelled fresh or thawed frozen broad beans, peeled

salt and pepper

COOK THE CHICKEN AND HAM

1 **Put the chicken joints** in a casserole with the bacon hock and pour in enough water to cover. Add the sugar and bouquet garni. Bring to the boil and skim well with a slotted spoon.

2 **Cover and simmer** gently until the chicken joints are almost tender when pierced; it will take about 1 hour.

3 **Lift out the chicken** with a slotted spoon and reserve it. Remove the casserole from the heat and set aside.

FINISH THE STEW

4 **Bring the chicken liquid** in the casserole back to the boil. Add the onion, celery, and tomatoes and simmer, stirring often, for 20–30 minutes. Make sure the heat is very gentle; the liquid should be only barely bubbling. Add the sweetcorn and simmer for 10 minutes longer. Meanwhile, cut the potatoes into chunks and put them in a saucepan of salted water. Bring to the boil, cover and simmer for 15–20 minutes, until tender. Drain, then mash until very smooth (an old-fashioned potato ricer does the best job of getting potatoes really smooth).

5 **Stir the potatoes,** chilli flakes, and beans into the stew and season to taste, remembering that the heat of the chillies will mellow, if you are cooking this dish in advance. Return the chicken to the casserole and simmer, stirring often, until all the meats and vegetables are very tender, about 15 minutes longer.

6 **Lift out the bacon.** Using a fork and knife, pull the meat from the bones in large pieces, discarding the skin and fat. Shred the meat into chunky bits and stir it back into the stew. The sauce should be thick but, if it is too sticky (which it may be, depending on the potatoes you used), add a little more water to thin it out. Discard the bouquet garni and taste for seasoning.

 VARIATION: Chicken with kidney beans and garlic sausage

A colourful and spicier version.

1 Soak 500g (1lb 2oz) dried red kidney beans in enough cold water to cover them by 10cm (4in), leave overnight (or for at least 6 hours), then drain. Put the beans in a pot and add 1 onion stuck with a clove and a bouquet garni. Cover with fresh water and bring to a boil. Boil for at least 5 minutes, then reduce the heat and simmer for 25 minutes. Now add salt (adding salt before this will toughen the beans), and simmer for 45 minutes longer.

2 When the beans are ready, drain them into a colander, discarding the bouquet garni and the onion. Thickly slice a 375g (13oz) piece of garlic sausage, discarding the skin.

3 Prepare and cook the chicken as directed in the main recipe. Omit the broad beans and sweetcorn. Add the kidney beans to the casserole with the onion, tomatoes, and celery, and simmer until the beans are nearly tender. It should take about 30 minutes. Thicken the stew with the potatoes as directed in the main recipe, and add the sausage when you return the chicken to the stew.

Portuguese pork and clams

THIS COMBINATION of rich pork and salty clams – and indeed any pork with shellfish – has been enjoyed for centuries in Portugal and Spain. The dish really benefits from a squeeze of lemon at the end, so do encourage your diners to add some. You can make this dish to the end of step 4 up to 2 days in advance. Keep it, covered, in the refrigerator, then gently reheat the stew and cook the clams, following the instructions in step 5, just before serving.

SERVES	PREP	COOK
SERVES 6-8	30-35 MINS PLUS MARINATING	2-2½ HOURS

Ingredients

FOR THE MARINADE

2 garlic cloves, finely chopped

1 bay leaf, crumbled

1½ tbsp paprika

salt and pepper

3 tbsp olive oil

375ml (13fl oz) dry white wine, plus more if needed

FOR THE STEW

1.4kg (3lb) boned loin of pork, cut into 2.5cm (1in) cubes

1kg (2¼lb) clams, such as amandes

1 large onion, thinly sliced

2 garlic cloves, finely chopped

400g (14oz) can tomatoes

1 tbsp tomato purée

dash of Tabasco sauce, more to taste

1 lemon, cut into wedges, to serve

leaves from 1 bunch of parsley, chopped

MARINATE THE PORK

1 Put the garlic, bay leaf, paprika, plenty of black pepper, 1 tbsp oil, and the wine into a non-metallic bowl, then whisk to combine all the ingredients. Add the pork and mix well with its marinade. Cover and refrigerate for 24 hours, stirring occasionally so that all the cubes of pork come into contact equally with the marinade.

PREPARE THE CLAMS

2 Scrub the clams under cold running water with a stiff brush to remove any grit, sand, or seaweed, and discard any with broken shells, or that do not tightly close when tapped. As with any shellfish, if in any doubt about a clam, discard it. It's really not worth the risk of serving it up and poisoning your diners.

FINISH THE STEW

3 Preheat the oven to 180°C (350°F/Gas 4). Lift the meat from the marinade with a slotted spoon and pat dry with kitchen paper. Heat the remaining oil in a large casserole. Add the pork, in batches, and brown well on all sides. Transfer to a bowl.

4 Reduce the heat and add the onion and garlic. Cover and cook very gently for 20-25 minutes, until the onion is very soft and brown. Add the tomatoes, tomato purée, Tabasco, and pork. Pour in the marinade and stir. Cover and cook in the oven for 1½-1¾ hours, until tender when pierced. Add more wine if the stew becomes dry.

5 **Arrange the clams** on top of the pork, cover with the lid, and cook in the oven for 15–20 minutes longer, until the clams open. Discard any clams that are still closed after cooking. Transfer to a warmed serving bowl. Sprinkle with chopped parsley. Serve the lemon wedges in a separate bowl.

 VARIATION: Chilean pork and beans

To save time, use canned kidney beans instead.

1 Omit the marinade and clams. Put 375g (13oz) dried red kidney beans in a bowl. Cover with water and let soak overnight. Drain and rinse. Put the beans in a saucepan, cover with fresh water, and boil for 10 minutes. Reduce the heat, cover, and simmer for 1 hour, or until almost tender but still slightly firm. Drain well.

2 Meanwhile, prepare the garlic and onion as directed. Core, seed and dice 1 hot green chilli and 2 green peppers. Peel 500g (1lb 2oz) each of yams and sweet potatoes, then cut them into 2.5cm (1in) cubes. Chop the leaves from a few sprigs each of parsley, coriander, and oregano. Brown the pork; cook the onions and garlic as directed. Return the pork to the pan. Add the tomatoes, tomato purée, herbs, and 500ml (16fl oz) water. Cover, and cook until the pork is just tender, 1¼–1½ hours. Add the vegetables, beans, and 750ml (1¼ pints) more water to cover.

3 Cook, stirring occasionally, until tender; this could take 40-45 minutes longer. Transfer the stew to the top of the stove, stir in 2 tbsp red wine vinegar, and simmer, uncovered, for 5 minutes. Taste for seasoning (you may want more herbs or seasoning, as beans need a lot) and serve in warmed bowls with rice or flour tortillas.

Navarin of lamb

THE BRIGHT FLAVOURS of young, melting lamb marry perfectly with vivid baby vegetables in this springtime stew. The secret is to cook the lamb until it is soft enough to fall from a fork, while only lightly cooking the vegetables.

SERVES	PREP	COOK
SERVES 6	45–50 MINS	2–2¼ HRS

Ingredients

500g (1lb 2oz) baby onions

2 tbsp vegetable oil

750g (1lb 10oz) boneless lamb shoulder, in 2.5–4cm (1–1½in) dice

salt and pepper

2 tbsp plain flour

1 tbsp tomato purée

2 garlic cloves, finely chopped

1 bouquet garni made with 5–6 parsley stalks, 2–3 thyme sprigs, and 1 bay leaf

500ml (16fl oz) chicken or lamb stock

375g (13oz) tomatoes

250g (9oz) baby carrots

250g (9oz) turnips

250g (9oz) French beans

750g (1lb 10oz) small new potatoes

150g (5½oz) fresh or frozen peas (optional)

leaves from 4–5 parsley sprigs, finely chopped

PREPARE THE ONIONS

1 **Put the baby onions** in a bowl, cover with boiling water, and let stand for 2 minutes. Drain, then peel. Heat the oil in a casserole. Add the onions and stir for 5–7 minutes, until golden. Remove and set aside.

SIMMER THE LAMB

2 **Season the lamb** with salt and pepper and add to the casserole, in batches if necessary. Cook over high heat, stirring occasionally, for 3–5 minutes until evenly browned. With a slotted spoon, transfer to a bowl.

3 **Return all the cooked lamb** to the pan, sprinkle with the flour, then stir to mix. Cook over medium heat, stirring occasionally, for 2–3 minutes, until the flour is browned.

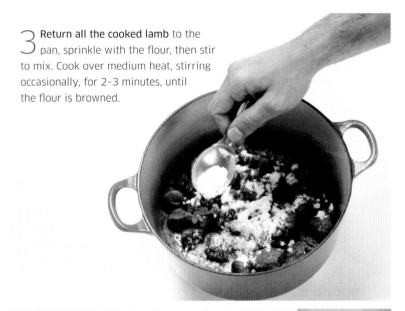

4 **Let the casserole cool slightly**, then stir in the tomato purée, garlic, and bouquet garni. Pour in enough stock to just cover, stir, and bring to a boil. Cover with a lid and simmer for 1 hour.

PREPARE THE VEGETABLES

5 **Core the tomatoes** and score an "X" on the base of each. Immerse in boiling water until the skins start to split (8–15 seconds). Plunge at once into cold water. When cool, peel off the skins, cut in half, squeeze out the seeds, then coarsely chop.

6 **If the baby carrots have green tops**, trim them, leaving a little of the green, then scrape to remove the thin skin. Peel the turnips. Cut them into quarters or wedges, depending on their size, and trim off sharp edges with a small knife.

7 **Snap the ends off the beans** and cut into 2.5cm (1in) pieces. Peel the potatoes and put them into a bowl of cold water to prevent discolouration.

FINISH THE NAVARIN

8 **With a slotted spoon**, transfer the meat to a large bowl, then skim the fat from the sauce with a broad, shallow spoon. Strain the sauce back over the meat, then return both the meat and sauce to the casserole. Taste for seasoning, adjusting if necessary.

9 **Drain the potatoes** and add them to the casserole with the turnips, onions, tomatoes, and carrots. Pour in more stock to almost cover the meat and vegetables. Cover and simmer for 20-25 minutes, until the potatoes are tender to the point of a knife.

10 **Add the peas, if using, and beans** to the stew and simmer until they are just tender. Be sure not to cook the navarin for any longer than necessary to cook the vegetables through; they should retain their fresh crunch and bright colours. Taste for seasoning, and adjust if necessary. The sauce should be glossy and lightly thickened. Ladle the meat and vegetables on to warmed plates, moisten with the sauce, and sprinkle with parsley.

VARIATION: Lamb ratatouille

Tasty Mediterranean vegetables add to the flavours.

1 Omit the baby onions, tomato purée, bouquet garni, carrots, turnips, French beans, potatoes, parsley, and peas. Brown the lamb as directed, using olive oil, then add the stock and simmer for 1¼ hours.

2 Trim 1 aubergine and cut into 2.5cm (1in) chunks. Put into a colander and sprinkle with salt. Let stand for 30 minutes. Meanwhile, chop 3 garlic cloves. Peel, seed, and chop 500g (1lb 2oz) tomatoes. Slice 1 green and 1 red pepper. Thinly slice 1 large onion. Rinse the aubergine chunks and pat dry.

3 Heat 3 tbsp olive oil in a frying pan. Add the onions and garlic and cook, stirring, for 3-5 minutes, until soft. Stir in the peppers and cook for 2-3 minutes. Add the aubergine and cook, stirring, until just tender (7-10 minutes). Add the tomatoes. Add the vegetables and 125ml (4½fl oz) chicken or lamb stock to the meat. Cook covered for 15 minutes, then cook uncovered for 20 minutes longer, until tender and well flavoured.

Provençal daube of beef

THE RICH, INTENSE AROMA of this dish is hard to beat. The beef is marinaded in all the aromas of the Mediterranean – oranges, red wine, and herbs – before being very slowly braised with lots of black olives. A truly delicious classic. You will need to start a day or two before your meal, to allow the beef a good long marinating time. If you can find salt pork, substitute it here for half the amount of bacon rashers in the recipe.

SERVES	PREP	COOK
SERVES 6-8	45-50 MINS PLUS MARINATING	3½-4 HRS

Ingredients

FOR THE MARINADE

1 orange

2 garlic cloves, finely chopped

500ml (16fl oz) red wine

2 bay leaves

3-4 sprigs each of rosemary, thyme, and parsley

10 peppercorns

2 tbsp olive oil

FOR THE STEW

1kg (2¼lb) braising steak, cut into 4cm (1½in) cubes

500g (1lb 2oz) piece of smoked streaky bacon, cut into 5mm (¼in) lardons

400g (14oz) can tomatoes

2 onions, sliced

2 carrots, sliced

175g (6oz) mushrooms, trimmed and sliced

200g (7oz) good-quality, stoned black olives

250ml (9fl oz) beef stock or water

salt and pepper

45g (1½oz) butter

3 tbsp plain flour

MARINATE THE BEEF

1 **Peel the zest** from the orange in wide strips. Combine the orange zest, garlic, red wine, bay leaves, rosemary, thyme, parsley, and peppercorns in a non-metallic bowl. Add the beef and mix well. Pour the olive oil on top. Cover tightly and refrigerate, turning occasionally, for 24-48 hours.

PREPARE THE BACON

2 **Put the bacon** in a saucepan of water, bring to a boil and blanch for 5 minutes. Drain in a colander and rinse with cold water. This removes excess salt from the large amount of bacon in the recipe.

COOK THE STEW

3 **Preheat the oven** to 150°C (300°F/Gas 2). Remove the beef pieces from the marinade, place on kitchen paper on a large plate and pat dry; set aside. Strain the marinade. Reserve the liquid and tie the flavouring ingredients in a piece of muslin.

4 **Spread the bacon** on the bottom of a casserole and cover with the beef. Layer the tomatoes and onions on top. Continue layering with the carrots, mushrooms, and olives. Pour in the strained marinade and stock and season with pepper. Add the bag of flavourings.

5 **Bring to a boil** on top of the stove, then cover the casserole, transfer to the heated oven, and cook for 3½-4 hours, stirring occasionally. The beef is ready when it is tender enough to crush in your fingers. Top up with more stock or water if it seems dry.

FINISH THE DISH

6 Make a beurre manié (kneaded butter): using a fork, crush the butter on a small plate until smooth, softened and easy to work. Work in the flour with the fork until the paste is smooth. This is an excellent technique to have in your repertoire, as the paste can be used to thicken any robust stew whose sauce is too thin for your taste (more delicate concoctions should not be thickened with it, though; reduce their sauces instead over a high heat).

7 Transfer the casserole to the top of the stove and scoop out the flavouring bag with a slotted spoon. Discard the flavouring bag. Add the beurre manié to the casserole in small pieces, stirring so each bit melts and thickens the sauce. Do not rush this process, as you want to cook out the taste of raw flour from the butter. Simmer for 2 minutes, then taste for seasoning. Serve in warmed dishes or bowls. Decorate with a few rosemary sprigs, if you like.

 VARIATION: Provençal lamb stew with green olives

Here, more traditional lamb replaces the beef.

1 Cut 1kg (2¼lb) boned lamb shoulder into large cubes, using a sharp knife. Marinate the lamb for 24–48 hours as directed in the main recipe.

2 Prepare the bacon and vegetables as directed, using green olives instead of black. Cook the stew as directed.

3 Make the beurre manié and finish the dish as directed, sprinkling a little chopped thyme on each serving, if you like. This stew can be made up to 2 days ahead and kept, covered, in the refrigerator. Bring to room temperature, then reheat on top of the stove until hot through and bubbling.

Beef with barley and mushrooms

BARLEY IS A TASTY GRAIN that used to be completely overlooked, unless one was making Scotch broth. Today it has made a well-deserved comeback, and is now a fashionable grain, adding body and earthy flavour to all sorts of dishes. For a treat, use wild mushrooms.

SERVES	PREP	COOK
SERVES 6-8	30-35 MINS	2¼-2½ HRS

Ingredients

3 tbsp vegetable oil

1.4kg (3lb) braising steak, in 5cm (2in) dice

625g (1¼lb) onions, thinly sliced

salt and pepper

1 bouquet garni, made with 5-6 parsley stalks, 2-3 thyme sprigs, and 1 bay leaf

1 litre (1¾ pints) beef stock, plus more if needed

375g (13oz) carrots, sliced

4 celery sticks, peeled and sliced

200g (7oz) pearl barley

500g (1lb 2oz) mushrooms, trimmed and sliced

leaves from 2-3 parsley sprigs, finely chopped (optional)

PREPARE THE INGREDIENTS

1 **Preheat the oven** to 180°C (350°F/Gas 4). Heat the oil in a casserole on top of the stove until hot. Add half the beef (it should sear when it hits the pan) and brown well. Transfer to a bowl. Brown the remaining beef in the same way.

2 **Add the onions** with a little salt and pepper. Cook over medium heat, stirring, for 5-7 minutes, until lightly browned. Return the beef, add the bouquet garni, salt, and pepper. Pour in the stock and stir.

COOK THE STEW

3 **Cover the casserole** and transfer to the heated oven. Cook, stirring occasionally, for about 1½ hours, then add the carrots, celery, and barley. Stir in more stock or water, if necessary, to keep the casserole moist.

4 **Cover and continue cooking** for 40-45 minutes longer, until the meat and vegetables are tender when pierced. The barley should be tender but still slightly chewy. About 10 minutes before the end of cooking, stir in the mushrooms.

5 **Discard the bouquet garni** and taste the stew for seasoning. Serve in warmed individual bowls, sprinkled with the parsley, if you like. Pass crusty bread alongside.

Spring veal blanquette

TO RETAIN THE WHITENESS of the rich sauce, be careful that nothing browns during the cooking of this classic French dish. Replace some of the total weight of meat with veal breast, for extra richness. Boiled white rice is the traditional accompaniment, though steamed new potatoes are also delicious.

SERVES	PREP	COOK
SERVES 6	45-50 MINS	1½-2¼ HRS

Ingredients

FOR THE VEAL

1.5kg (3lb 3oz) boned veal shoulder, in 5cm (2in) cubes

1 onion

1 clove

1 bouquet garni, made with 5-6 parsley stalks, 2-3 thyme sprigs and 1 bay leaf

salt and white pepper

1.5 litres (2¾ pints) chicken stock or water, plus more if needed

500g (1lb 2oz) pickling onions

1 large fennel bulb, thinly sliced, fronds reserved

500g (1lb 2oz) baby carrots, peeled

FOR THE SAUCE

45g (1½oz) butter

30g (1oz) plain flour

juice of ½ lemon

freshly grated nutmeg

2 egg yolks

125ml (4fl oz) double cream

SIMMER THE VEAL

1 **Put the diced veal** into a saucepan and cover with cold water. Bring to a boil, reduce the heat and simmer, skimming often, for 5 minutes. Drain the veal, rinse with cold water, and drain again. Trim the onion and peel it. Stud the onion with the clove.

2 **Transfer the veal** to a casserole. Add the clove-studded onion, bouquet garni, salt, and white pepper, and pour in the stock or water. Cover, bring to a boil and simmer very gently, skimming occasionally, until the meat is almost tender. Expect this to take up to 1 hour.

FINISH THE BLANQUETTE

3 **Put the pickling onions** in a bowl. Pour over hot water to cover and let stand for 2 minutes. Drain and peel. Discard the onion and the bouquet garni from the casserole. Add the pickling onions, fennel, and carrots, with more stock or water, if needed, so that everything is covered. Continue simmering for 20-30 minutes, until the veal and vegetables are tender.

MAKE THE SAUCE

4 **Remove the veal** and vegetables. Strain the liquid into a saucepan and simmer for 10-20 minutes, until well flavoured and reduced by about half. Melt the butter in the casserole. Whisk in the flour and cook for 30-60 seconds, until foaming. Cool slightly. Whisk in the cooking liquid and return to the heat, whisking constantly, for 3-5 minutes, until it boils and thickens. Simmer for 10-15 minutes, until it coats the back of a spoon.

5 **Return the veal and vegetables** to the sauce and season to taste with the lemon juice, salt, white pepper, and nutmeg. Gently heat the blanquette for 7-10 minutes longer, so the flavours blend. In a bowl, whisk together the egg yolks and cream, then whisk in a few spoonfuls of the hot sauce. Stir this mixture back into the stew and heat gently for 1-2 minutes, until the sauce thickens slightly. Serve immediately, sprinkled with fennel fronds.

Chicken pot pies with herb crust

A **DELICIOUS RECIPE** with a tasty scone topping. Best of all, no accompaniments are needed. The filling can be prepared 1 day ahead and kept, covered, in the refrigerator. Bring it to room temperature before topping and cooking. The scone dough should be made shortly before baking. You will need ovenproof individual casserole dishes.

SERVES	PREP	COOK
SERVES 4-6	25-35 MINS	22-25 MINS

Ingredients

FOR THE CHICKEN

1 litre (1¾ pints) chicken stock

3 carrots, sliced

750g (1lb 10oz) large potatoes, diced

3 celery sticks, thinly sliced

175g (6oz) peas

500g (1lb 2oz) cooked skinless, boneless chicken

60g (2oz) butter

1 onion, chopped

30g (1oz) flour

175ml (6fl oz) double cream

ground nutmeg

salt and pepper

leaves from 1 small bunch of parsley, chopped

1 egg

FOR THE TOPPING

250g (9oz) plain flour

1 tbsp baking powder

1 tsp salt

60g (2oz) butter

leaves from 1 small bunch of parsley, chopped

150ml (5fl oz) milk, more if needed

MAKE THE HERB SCONE TOPPING

5 **Sift the flour** into a large bowl with the baking powder and salt and make a well in the centre. Add the butter, cut into small pieces with two knives.

6 **Rub the mixture** with your fingertips until it forms fine crumbs, lifting and crumbling to aerate it. Add the parsley, make a well in the centre, add the milk and cut in quickly with a knife to form coarse crumbs. Add a little more milk if it seems dry.

7 **Mix the dough** with your fingers just until it comes together. Turn on to a floured surface and knead lightly for a few seconds until smooth. Pat the dough out to 1cm (½in) thick. Cut out rounds with a 8.5cm (3½in) pastry cutter or glass. Pat out the trimmings and cut additional rounds, for a total of 4-6.

MAKE THE FILLING

1 **Heat the stock** to boiling in a large saucepan. Add the carrots, potatoes, and celery and simmer for 3 minutes. Add the peas and simmer for about 5 minutes until all the vegetables are tender.

2 **Drain the vegetables** in a colander, reserving the stock. Cut the chicken into slivers and put in a bowl. Add the vegetables.

3 **Melt the butter** in a small saucepan over moderate heat. Add the onion and cook for 3-5 minutes, until softened but not browned. Sprinkle the flour over the onions and cook, stirring, for 1-2 minutes.

4 **Stir in 500ml (16fl oz) stock and heat**, whisking, until the sauce comes to the boil and thickens. Simmer for 2 minutes, then add the cream and a pinch of nutmeg and taste for seasoning. Pour the sauce over the chicken and vegetables, add the parsley, and mix gently.

ASSEMBLE AND BAKE THE PIES

8 Preheat the oven to 220°C (425°F/Gas 7). Divide the chicken filling evenly among 6 individual ovenproof dishes, making sure the vegetables are well distributed between them. Place a scone round on top of each pie (it's nice if the scone is positioned slightly off-centre, so you can see some of the creamy filling beneath). Lightly beat the egg with pinch of salt in a small bowl and brush the rounds with this glaze.

9 Bake the pies in the heated oven for 15 minutes. Reduce the heat to 180°C (350°F/Gas 4) and continue baking until the scone crust is golden brown and the filling is piping hot and bubbling. You need to cook at this lower temperature so that the filling heats through completely. It should take 7–10 minutes longer, but keep an eye on it. If the scone topping threatens to scorch, cover the pies loosely with a sheet of foil.

 VARIATION: Large chicken pot pie

The scone topping gives this pie a cheerful appearance.

1 Prepare the filling exactly as directed in the main recipe. Instead of baking in individual dishes, spoon the filling into a medium ovenproof dish, or a shallow soufflé dish, depending on preference.

2 Omit the chopped parsley from the scone dough and add chopped sage, thyme, or tarragon, as you prefer, instead. Cut the patted-out dough into 8 rounds, using a 6cm (2½in) pastry cutter.

3 Arrange the rounds evenly over the filling, then glaze the scones and bake the pie, allowing 15 minutes at 220°C (425°F/Gas 7) then 20–25 minutes at 180°C (350°F/Gas 4). The filling should be bubbling hot and give off delicious aromas.

Peppery Tuscan beef

ITALIAN CUISINE at its simple best. Chianti is the wine of Tuscany, but you can use any good-quality, full-bodied red wine. Here, sage-flavoured *fettunta* – rustic bread toasts – are served alongside. They must be made just before serving, but the beef itself will benefit from being prepared ahead and kept, covered, in the refrigerator; the flavours will mellow. Gently reheat it on top of the stove.

SERVES	PREP	COOK
SERVES 6	35-40 MINS PLUS MARINATING	2-2½ HRS

Ingredients

5-6 sage sprigs

2 tbsp freshly ground black pepper

300ml (10fl oz) olive oil

1.4kg (3lb) braising steak, in 5cm (2in) dice

125g (4½oz) pancetta lardons

1 large onion, diced

6 garlic cloves

400g (14oz) can chopped tomatoes

2 bay leaves

250ml (9fl oz) beef stock, plus more if needed

500ml (16fl oz) red wine

salt

500g (1lb 2oz) loaf crusty Italian peasant-style bread

PREPARE THE SAGE OIL AND MARINATE THE BEEF

1 **Chop the leaves** from 2 of the sage sprigs, and put them in a small bowl. Don't be tempted to add more sage, as it is a strong flavour and can easily overpower a dish. In a large bowl, combine half the black pepper with all but 3 tbsp of the oil. Ladle one-quarter of this into the bowl with the chopped sage, and set it aside for the *fettunta*. This dish contains an awful lot of black pepper, but it is all necessary for the recipe. So don't be too timid and add less pepper, you will find it mellows and lends an incredible depth of flavour to the beef once marinated and braised.

2 **Add the beef** to the bowl with the black pepper and oil mixture. Stir until every piece of the beef is well coated, then cover tightly with clingfilm and refrigerate, stirring occasionally to redistribute the marinade, for 8-12 hours. Unfortunately, this step cannot be rushed, so make sure you can prepare the dish a day ahead; after all, it will only take about 5 minutes. The beef needs this long amount of marinating time in order to absorb all the pepper flavour. You will find the texture of the meat also becomes wonderfully tender during its bath in oil.

COOK THE STEW

3 **Chop the remaining** sage leaves. Remove the meat from the marinade with a slotted spoon, and transfer to a plate lined with kitchen paper. Pat dry. Heat half the remaining oil in a large pan over high heat, add half the meat and brown well on all sides for 3-5 minutes.

4 **Transfer the meat** to a bowl with a slotted spoon. Add the remaining oil to the pan, and brown the rest of the beef in the same way. Reduce the heat to medium, add the pancetta and cook, stirring occasionally, for 2-3 minutes, until the fat has rendered.

5 **Add the onion** and cook, stirring, for 3-5 minutes longer, until softened. Return the beef with 5 of the garlic cloves, finely chopped, the tomatoes, bay leaves, sage, remaining black pepper, stock, and wine. Bring to a boil, stirring. Cover, reduce the heat and simmer for 1¾-2 hours, until very tender, stirring occasionally.

6 **During cooking,** add more stock or water if the stew seems dry. The beef is ready when it is tender enough to crush in your fingers. Discard the bay and taste for seasoning. If the sauce is thin, increase the heat and boil, uncovered, until it has reduced and concentrated.

MAKE THE SAGE FETTUNTA

7 **Meanwhile,** heat the oven to 190°C (375°F/Gas 5). Cut the bread into fairly even 1cm (½in) slices. Cut any large slices in half. Set them on a baking sheet, spaced well apart so they do not steam rather than toast, and brush each generously, on both sides, with the sage-flavoured oil, then sprinkle the slices evenly with salt.

8 **Bake the bread** in the oven until toasted; it should take about 7–10 minutes. Turn it once during this time, so both sides become evenly golden brown. Cut the reserved garlic clove in half. Rub each bread slice all over with the cut side of the garlic clove, and transfer to a wire rack. You will find the toasted surface of the bread acts like a "grater" for the garlic, and that almost all of the clove disappears on to the bread. Discard any remaining garlic. Spoon the beef into a warmed serving dish. Serve the delicious, crispy *fettunta* alongside.

Japanese one-pot yosenabe

YOU WILL NEED A TABLETOP BURNER and a suitable pot that fits on top. An attractive flameproof casserole would serve perfectly. Food simmered at the table is common in northern Japan, and this recipe is simmered in the country's mother stock, called dashi. If you can't find Japanese rice wine, you can use dry sherry instead.

SERVES	PREP	COOK
SERVES 4	40–50 MINS PLUS STANDING	5–7 MINS

Ingredients

FOR THE DIPPING SAUCE

juice of 1 lemon

4 tbsp sweet Japanese rice wine

2.5cm (1in) piece of dried kelp

1 tsp dried bonito flakes

75ml (2½fl oz) Japanese soy sauce

FOR THE SOUP STOCK

10cm (4in) piece of dried kelp

1 tsp dried bonito flakes

2 tbsp Japanese soy sauce

2 tbsp sweet Japanese rice wine

salt

FOR THE POT

250g (9oz) fresh shirataki noodles or 60g (2oz) dried cellophane noodles

250g (9oz) firm tofu, in 2.5cm (1in) dice

1 large carrot, in 3mm (⅛in) slices

½ Chinese cabbage, sliced

4 spring onions, in 5cm (2in) pieces

4 fresh shiitake mushrooms, sliced

2 skinless boneless chicken breasts

8 clams, such as Venus

4 large oysters

MAKE THE DIPPING SAUCE AND SOUP STOCK

1 **For the dipping sauce,** combine the lemon juice, rice wine, dried kelp, bonito flakes and soy sauce in a bowl. Let stand at room temperature for at least 1 hour or up to 24 hours.

2 **For the stock,** pour 1 litre (1¾ pints) cold water into a large saucepan, and add the kelp. Bring to a boil, then immediately remove and discard the kelp. Remove the pan from the heat.

3 **Sprinkle the dried bonito flakes** evenly over the surface of the kelp-infused water. Let the stock stand for 3–5 minutes, until the flakes settle to the bottom (the time it takes will depend on the thickness and dryness of the flakes). Line a sieve with dampened muslin.

4 **Strain the stock** through the muslin into the pot in which you are serving the meal. Add the soy sauce and sweet rice wine. Stir and taste for seasoning, adding salt if necessary.

PREPARE THE INGREDIENTS

5 **Bring a large saucepan of water to a boil.** Add the shirataki noodles and boil for 1 minutes, until firm but still chewy, stirring occasionally. If using cellophane noodles, soak them in warm water for 30 minutes. Drain and cut into 12.5cm (5in) lengths.

6 **Arrange the tofu,** vegetables, and noodles on a large plate or tray. Cover tightly and chill. Slice the chicken breasts in half lengthways, then into 2.5cm (1in) pieces. Cover and chill.

PREPARE THE CLAMS AND OYSTERS

7 **Scrub and rinse the clams.** With a tea towel, grip a clam, keeping the hinge between your thumb and fingers. Press the cutting edge of an oyster knife between the halves opposite the hinge. Push in the knife and rotate the blade to pry the shell open. Cut the muscle from the top and bottom shells and discard the top shell.

8 **Scrub and rinse the oysters.** With a folded tea towel in one hand, grip an oyster. Holding the oyster knife in your other hand, insert the point of the blade next to the hinge of the shell. Twist to pry the shell open. Cut the top muscle of the oyster from the shell and discard the top shell.

9 **Using the blade** of the oyster knife, cut loose the muscle from the lower half of the shell. Repeat with the remaining oysters. Arrange the chicken in a bowl, and the clams and oysters on the half-shell on a serving platter.

FINISH THE DISH

10 **Line a sieve** with muslin. Strain the dipping sauce into a measuring jug and pour it into 4 small bowls, so each diner has their own. Set your chosen flameproof pot on a table-top burner. Pour in the stock and slowly bring it to a boil over medium heat.

11 **When the stock** is simmering, add the chicken and carrot. Cook until the chicken is firm and the carrot slices almost tender. It will only take 2-3 minutes.

12 **Add half the tofu,** vegetables, and noodles and cook until the vegetables are tender; again, it should take just 2-3 minutes. Add the oysters and clams, without their shells, and cook just until the edges of the oysters start to curl.

13 **Guests can help themselves,** using chopsticks to dip the ingredients into the sauce before eating. When the pot is empty, replenish it with the remaining ingredients and cook until tender. When these are finished, ladle the remaining broth into bowls and serve.

Boeuf à la Bourguignonne

FEW FRENCH DISHES are better known, and with good reason, than this classic from Burgundy. The secret of a successful pot roast – the technique used in this dish – is using well-aged beef, so find a good butcher. Try to use a hearty red wine, such as pinot noir, to add substance to the sauce. The dish can be made up to 3 days ahead and kept, covered, in the refrigerator. The flavour will improve.

SERVES	**PREP**	**COOK**
SERVES 6-8	25-30 MINS	3½-4 HRS

Ingredients

1 onion	250ml (9fl oz) red wine
2 cloves	salt and pepper
1 beef topside, weighing 1.4-1.6kg (3-3½lb)	250ml (9fl oz) beef stock, plus more if needed
3 tbsp olive oil	16-20 pickling onions
1 carrot, peeled and quartered	250g (9oz) piece of smoked streaky bacon, cut into 5mm (¼in) lardons
1 bouquet garni, made with 5-6 parsley stalks, 2-3 thyme sprigs, and 1 bay leaf	250g (9oz) mushrooms, sliced

COOK THE POT ROAST

1 Preheat the oven to 160°C (325°F/Gas 3). Peel the onion and stud with the cloves. If necessary, roll the beef topside into a neat shape and, using string, tie at 2.5cm (1in) intervals to hold the shape.

2 Heat 2 tbsp of the oil in a casserole until very hot. Add the meat (it should sizzle) and brown it well on all sides. Remove the casserole from the heat, take out the meat and discard all but 2 tbsp of fat from the casserole.

3 Replace the meat in the casserole, and add the clove-studded onion, carrot, bouquet garni, red wine, salt (not too much, as the bacon will be salty), and pepper. Cover and cook in the oven for 30 minutes.

4 Pour in the stock and stir well. Cook for about 3 hours, turning the meat 3 or 4 times, and add more stock if too much liquid evaporates.

PREPARE THE GARNISH

5 Put the pickling onions in a bowl, pour over hot water to cover and let them stand for 2 minutes to help loosen the skins. Drain, and peel. Heat the remaining oil in a frying pan.

6 Add the bacon to the pan and fry for 3–5 minutes, until browned and the fat has rendered. Transfer to a bowl. Add the pickling onions to the pan and cook, stirring occasionally, for 3–5 minutes, until lightly browned. Add to the bacon using a slotted spoon.

7 Add the mushrooms to the frying pan and cook, stirring occasionally, for 2–3 minutes, until they are tender and their liquid has evaporated. Transfer them to the bowl containing the bacon and onions.

FINISH THE DISH

8 Remove the meat from the casserole. Strain the cooking liquid, discarding the flavourings. If the liquid is too thin, return it to the casserole and boil until reduced and slightly thickened. Return the meat to the casserole and add the bacon, pickling onions, and mushrooms. Cover and continue cooking for 30 minutes, or until very tender.

9 Transfer the meat to a chopping board. Skim off and discard any fat from the cooking liquid and taste it for seasoning. Remove and discard the strings from the beef, then cut into 12 thick slices.

10 Arrange the beef on warmed plates. Spoon the garnish and a little of the cooking liquid over and serve the remainder separately. Decorate each plate with fresh thyme sprigs, if you like.

Lamb shanks in red wine

PERFECT FOR A CHILLY DAY. You will need to start this dish at least 1 day ahead, so you have enough time to marinate the lamb. Shanks are cheap, so it's worth doubling this recipe and freezing some for another time. Defrost it in the refrigerator overnight, then reheat on top of the stove.

SERVES	PREP	COOK
SERVES 6	45–50 MINS PLUS MARINATING	2½-2¾ HRS

Ingredients

FOR THE MARINADE

2 tsp black peppercorns

2 tsp juniper berries

4 shallots, roughly chopped

2 garlic cloves, peeled

2 onions, quartered

2 carrots, roughly sliced

1 bouquet garni, made with 5-6 parsley stalks, 2-3 thyme sprigs, and 1 bay leaf

2 tbsp red wine vinegar

750ml (1¼ pints) dry red wine

FOR THE LAMB

6 lamb shanks, total weight about 1.8kg (4lb)

3 tbsp vegetable oil

30g (1oz) plain flour

750ml (1¼ pints) beef stock, plus more if needed

salt and pepper

30g (1oz) butter

1 celeriac, weighing about 500g (1lb 2oz), in 1cm (½in) dice

250g (9oz) mushrooms, quartered

3 tbsp redcurrant jelly

1 bunch of watercress, to garnish (optional)

MARINATE THE MEAT

1 **Combine the black peppercorns** and juniper berries in a plastic bag. Holding the end of the bag closed, crush them with a rolling pin. Alternatively, crush them in a mortar and pestle. They don't have to be finely ground, so a coarse texture is fine in this case.

2 **In a saucepan,** combine the peppercorns, juniper berries, shallots, garlic, onions, carrots, bouquet garni, and vinegar. Pour in the red wine, bring to a boil, and simmer for about 2 minutes so the flavours meld together. Transfer the marinade and vegetables to a shallow dish, so it loses its heat rapidly, and set aside to cool completely.

3 **Trim off and discard any excess fat** and sinew from the lamb shanks. Add the shanks to the dish, and stir to coat with the marinade. (First ensure that the marinade is cold, or the meat may turn sour.) Cover and refrigerate, turning occasionally to redistribute the marinade evenly around the shanks, for 1-2 days.

ASSEMBLE AND COOK THE STEW

4 **Preheat the oven** to 180°C (350°F/Gas 4). Put the lamb shanks on a plate lined with kitchen paper and pat dry. Reserve the bouquet garni. Drain the vegetables in a sieve set over a bowl. Reserve the vegetables and marinade separately. Heat half the oil in a casserole. Add three lamb shanks, and brown well on all sides over high heat for 3-5 minutes.

5 **Transfer the lamb** to a bowl. Heat the rest of the oil and brown the remaining shanks in the same way. Add the vegetables and cook, stirring frequently, for 5-7 minutes, until they start to brown. Sprinkle with the flour and cook, stirring, for 3-5 minutes more, until the flour has been absorbed and the vegetables are lightly browned.

6 **Stir in the reserved marinade,** scraping the bottom of the pan to dissolve the pan juices. Add the lamb with any juices, the bouquet garni, stock, salt, and pepper. Cover and cook in the oven, turning occasionally, for 2-2¼ hours, until tender. If the sauce evaporates rapidly during cooking, add more stock.

COOK THE CELERIAC AND MUSHROOMS

7 Melt the butter in a frying pan, add the celeriac and season. Cook, stirring occasionally, for 8-10 minutes, until tender. Transfer to a bowl. Add the mushrooms to the pan. and cook for 3-5 minutes, until all the liquid has evaporated and they are tender. Add to the bowl with the celeriac.

8 Transfer the lamb shanks from the casserole to a plate, and keep warm. Ladle the sauce into a sieve set over a large pan, reserving some of the more attractive pieces of shallot and carrot. Press the remaining vegetables with a ladle to extract the juices.

FINISH THE SAUCE

9 Whisk the redcurrant jelly into the sauce with plenty of pepper. Bring back to a boil and simmer for 20-30 minutes, until reduced by half.

10 Add the mushrooms, celeriac, reserved carrot and shallot, and taste for seasoning. It should be fruity, but piquant with pepper. Return the lamb and heat for 5-10 minutes, until very hot. Return the lamb. Divide among warmed plates, and decorate with sprigs of watercress, if you like.

 VARIATION: Venison stew with pears

Wonderfully rich and sweet.

1 Omit the lamb shanks. Prepare the marinade as directed in the main recipe. Trim the fat and sinew from 1.6kg (3½lb) venison stew meat, and cut it into fairly even 4cm (1½in) cubes. Marinate the meat and vegetables as directed. Continue as directed, cooking the venison until tender; it should take 1¼-1½ hours.

2 Meanwhile, peel and core four firm ripe pears, and cut each half into thirds. Sprinkle with the juice of one lemon to prevent discolouration, and toss to coat. Remove the venison from the sauce and set it aside, keeping it warm. Strain the sauce into a saucepan, and whisk in the redcurrant jelly with plenty of pepper.

3 Add the pears, bring back to a boil, and simmer for 6-8 minutes, until tender. Remove the pears. Continue simmering the sauce for 5-10 minutes. until it has thickened slightly. Return the venison and pears and bring back just to a boil. Transfer to a warmed tureen.

French beef and herb potato pie

AN UPDATE OF A FRENCH CLASSIC. The recipe was originally designed as a way to use up the remains of a beef roast. If you would like to be thrifty and use leftover beef, add it to the gravy 10 minutes before the end of step 3, to heat through and absorb all the other flavours.

SERVES	PREP	COOK
SERVES 6	45–50 MINS	35–40 MINS

Ingredients

FOR THE BEEF

4 garlic cloves

75ml (2½fl oz) olive oil

1 large onion, diced

1kg (2¼lb) minced beef

salt and pepper

400g can chopped tomatoes

250ml (8fl oz) beef stock

125ml (4fl oz) dry white wine

FOR THE POTATOES

1kg (2¼lb) potatoes

1 bunch of basil

1 bunch of parsley

250ml (8fl oz) milk, plus more if needed

COOK THE MINCED BEEF

1 Remove the skins from the garlic cloves, and discard. Finely chop 2 of the cloves. Heat one-third of the oil in a sauté or frying pan. Add the onion and cook, stirring, until soft but not brown, 3–5 minutes.

2 Add the chopped garlic, minced beef, salt, pepper and tomatoes. Reduce the heat and cook very gently, stirring occasionally, for 10–12 minutes, until the meat is brown.

3 Stir in the stock and wine. Simmer over very low heat, stirring from time to time, for 25–30 minutes, until most of the liquid has evaporated but the meat is still very moist. Do not cook the meat too fast or it will be tough.

MAKE THE HERB MASHED POTATOES

4 Peel the potatoes and cut each into 2–3 pieces, depending on size. Put them in a saucepan with plenty of cold water and add salt. Cover and bring to a boil. Simmer for 15–20 minutes, until tender when pierced with a knife.

5 Meanwhile, strip the basil and parsley leaves from the stalks. Put the leaves and the 2 whole garlic cloves in a food processor. Work with the remaining oil to form a purée, scraping the side of the bowl occasionally.

6 Drain the potatoes, return them to the saucepan and mash. Add the herb purée. Scald the milk in another saucepan.

7 Gradually beat the milk into the potatoes over medium heat, and stir for 2–3 minutes, until the potatoes just hold a shape. Season to taste.

ASSEMBLE AND BAKE THE PIE

8 **Preheat the oven** to 190°C (375°F/Gas 5). Brush a large, shallow baking dish with oil. Taste the meat for seasoning, then spoon it, with any of its liquid, into the baking dish. Cover with an even layer of the herb potatoes and smooth the top with the back of a spoon, making sure the potatoes go right to the edges of the dish and no meat or sauce shows through.

9 **Make a scalloped pattern** on the herb potatoes with the tip of a dessert spoon or the tines of a fork. Dip the spoon or fork into a bowl of hot water set close to hand once or twice during the process, so the potato does not stick to it.

10 **Transfer the pie** to the heated oven and bake until the top is golden brown, the edges bubbling with gravy, and the tip of a skewer inserted in the centre for 30 seconds is hot to the touch when withdrawn; it should take 35–40 minutes. Cut the pie into 6 portions and transfer to warmed plates.

 VARIATION: Old Emily's Shepherd's Pie

Many of us were brought up on this!

1 Omit the beef, wine, garlic, basil, parsley, olive oil, and tomatoes. Cut 2 carrots into 5mm (¼in) cubes. Heat 1 tbsp vegetable oil in a large sauté or frying pan; sauté the carrots and onions until soft, 3–5 minutes; lower the heat to cool the pan.

2 Brown 1kg (2¼lb) minced lamb very gently. Add 250ml (8 floz) beef stock or water, with 1 sprig each thyme and rosemary; simmer as directed. Discard the herbs and taste for seasoning. Meanwhile, peel and cook 1kg (2¼lb) potatoes as directed. Drain, mash them and stir in 45g (1½oz) butter. Beat in the hot milk as directed. Season to taste.

3 Brush 6 heatproof bowls with melted butter and fill them with the lamb. Divide the mashed potatoes among the bowls and make a design on the top with a fork. Bake in the oven as directed until golden brown.

Home
from work

Simple but scintillating
dishes to make in a hurry

Sole fillets in wine vinegar

MARINATE THE NIGHT BEFORE you want to eat. This is an old Italian dish dating from before domestic kitchens had refrigeration, so pickling was a common method of preserving. If you would prefer a milder marinade, use just half the quantity of vinegar and an equal amount of white wine.

SERVES	PREP	COOK
SERVES 4-6	30-35 MINS PLUS MARINATING	6-8 MINS

Ingredients

FOR THE SOLE

90ml (3fl oz) olive oil

1 large onion, thinly sliced

salt and pepper

250ml (9fl oz) red wine vinegar

45g (1½oz) raisins

500g (1lb 2oz) sole fillets

30g (1oz) plain flour

30g (1oz) pine nuts

FOR THE SALAD

juice of ½ orange

3 tbsp olive oil

250g (9oz) rocket

PREPARE THE MARINADE

1 **Heat a third of the oil** in a pan. Add the onion, salt, and pepper, cover, and cook for 15 minutes, until soft. Uncover, increase the heat, and cook until caramelized. Add the vinegar and raisins. Boil for 2 minutes. Set aside.

COOK THE FISH

2 **Rinse the sole** and pat dry. Cut the fillets across into 5cm (2in) pieces. Spread the flour on a large plate and season. Add some of the fish and turn to coat. Transfer to a second plate, and coat the remaining fish pieces.

3 **Heat the remaining oil** and add the sole. Cook over medium-high heat for 1-2 minutes, until browned. Turn and fry for 1-2 minutes, until the flesh just flakes when tested with a fork. Drain on kitchen paper and cool completely.

MARINATE THE FISH

4 **Spread the sole** in a baking dish, and cover with the vinegar mixture.

5 **Sprinkle with the pine nuts.** Cover tightly and leave to marinate in the refrigerator for 12 hours, or up to 24 hours. Remove it from the refrigerator 1 hour before serving.

PREPARE THE SALAD

6 **Pour the orange juice** into a bowl and season. Gradually whisk in the oil so the vinaigrette emulsifies and thickens slightly. Taste for seasoning. Add the rocket and toss. Serve with the sole and spoon on the marinade.

Grilled pepper-stuffed mussels

SO DELICIOUS that you'll want to make it everyday food. This light dish is perfect for a special romantic meal. To make it even quicker to prepare, use roast peppers from a jar rather than roasting them yourself, but be sure to drain them thoroughly.

SERVES	**PREP**	**COOK**
SERVES 4	25–30 MINUTES	1–2 MINUTES

Ingredients

1 small bunch of flat-leaf parsley

1 large red pepper

2 slices of white bread

2 garlic cloves, peeled

2 tbsp olive oil

salt and pepper

24 large mussels, total weight about 750g (1lb 10oz)

250ml (9fl oz) dry white wine

lemon wedges, to serve

MAKE THE TOPPING

1 **Reserving a few sprigs** for decoration, strip the parsley leaves from the stalks, keeping leaves and stalks separate.

2 **Heat the grill.** Set the pepper on a rack about 10cm (4in) from the heat and grill, turning, for 10–12 minutes, until black all over. Seal in a plastic bag and let cool, then peel, scrape out the seeds and ribs, and cut into strips.

3 **Trim and discard the crusts** from the bread. Cut the bread into cubes and work them in a food processor to form crumbs. Add the parsley leaves, garlic, oil, and red pepper. Work to a purée and season.

PREPARE THE MUSSELS

4 **Clean the mussels** (see p41). Discard any that have broken shells or do not close when tapped. Put the wine and parsley stalks in a saucepan. Bring to a boil and simmer for 2 minutes. Add the mussels.

5 **Cover and cook** over high heat, stirring once, for 2–3 minutes, until the mussels open. Transfer to a large bowl with a slotted spoon. Discard any that have not opened.

STUFF THE MUSSELS

6 **Heat the grill.** Remove the top shell from each mussel, and discard the rubbery ring surrounding the meat.

7 **Spoon a little topping** on to each mussel. Set the mussels in their bottom shells, in a baking dish. Grill for 1–2 minutes, until very hot and the topping is heated through. Serve with lemon wedges and parsley sprigs, if you like.

Pinwheel chicken with goat's cheese

THE PRETTY HERBAL GREEN FILLING makes a spiral pattern when sliced. You can make the chicken the night before, refrigerate, and reheat in simmering water for 10 minutes. This means you can have your beautifully presented dinner on the table in a flash – perfect for a mid-week supper for friends.

SERVES
SERVES 4

PREP
30-40 MINS

COOK
15-20 MINS

Ingredients

FOR THE CHICKEN

4 large skinless, boneless chicken breasts, total weight about 750g (1lb 10oz)

125g (4½oz) goat's cheese

2-3 tbsp single cream, if necessary

leaves from 1 small bunch of basil, finely chopped

leaves from 1 small bunch of parsley, finely chopped

leaves from 3 thyme sprigs

juice of ½ lemon

salt and pepper

FOR THE TOMATO BUTTER SAUCE

3 shallots, finely chopped

250ml (9fl oz) dry white wine

125g (4½oz) butter

1 tbsp tomato purée

PREPARE THE CHICKEN BREASTS

1 **Split each chicken breast** open by slicing three-quarters of the way through. Place it between 2 sheets of dampened baking parchment. Pound lightly with a rolling pin until the chicken is of an even thickness.

MAKE THE STUFFING

2 **Put the goat's cheese** in a bowl and mash with a fork (harder cheese may be crumbled by hand), discarding any rind. If the cheese is too dry, soften it with cream. Add the herbs and lemon and mix. Taste for seasoning.

STUFF THE CHICKEN

3 **Peel the top sheet** of baking parchment from each breast. With a palette knife, evenly spread a quarter of the herb and goat's cheese filling in the centre of each. Loosen the breast from the paper.

4 **Roll the chicken breast** up into a neat cylinder, beginning with a long side of the chicken.

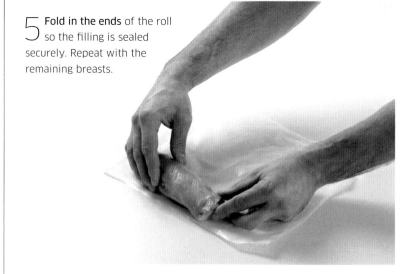

5 **Fold in the ends** of the roll so the filling is sealed securely. Repeat with the remaining breasts.

COOK THE CHICKEN

6 **Cut a piece of foil** to wrap generously around a rolled breast. Put it on the work surface, shiny-side down. Set the breast on the foil. Roll up the stuffed breast in the foil neatly and tightly, smoothing the foil to keep it taut. Twist the ends of the foil firmly to form a tight cylinder, sealing in the ends. Repeat the process for the remaining rolled breasts.

7 **Half fill a wide pan with water** and bring to the boil. With a slotted spoon, put the packages in the water and simmer until a skewer inserted in the centre is hot to the touch, about 15 minutes. Keep the chicken warm in its foil in the pan of hot (not boiling) water.

MAKE THE SAUCE

8 In a small saucepan, boil the shallots and wine with a small pinch each of salt and pepper until reduced to a syrupy glaze. Off the heat, whisk in the butter, a few small pieces at a time, whisking constantly and moving the pan on and off the heat. Do not boil; the butter should thicken the sauce creamily without melting to oil.

9 Whisk in the tomato purée and taste for seasoning. Butter sauces are delicate, and separate easily if overheated. To keep the sauce warm, set the saucepan in another pan of warm, not hot, water. Whisk occasionally but never leave for more than 30 minutes.

FINISH THE DISH

10 Remove the chicken rolls from the pan with a slotted spoon and carefully unwrap them on kitchen paper to absorb any water. Cut them into diagonal slices about 1cm (½in) thick. Spoon the sauce on to warmed individual plates, arrange the pinwheel slices on top and serve.

 VARIATION: Pinwheel chicken Italienne

With Parma ham and fontina cheese.

1 Prepare and pound the chicken breasts as directed in the main recipe. Trim 4 large, or 8 small, slices of Parma ham to the same size as the flattened breasts. Set the ham on the chicken evenly, so that each mouthful will contain the same amount of ham and chicken.

2 Cut a 125g (4½oz) piece of fontina cheese into thin slices, discarding the rind. Lay the cheese along one long side of each breast. Fontina melts beautifully, which is delicious, but does mean you will need to be punctilious about rolling the chicken so that there is a minimal chance of leaking. Roll up as directed in the main recipe, wrap in foil, and poach the breasts.

3 Prepare the butter sauce, omitting the tomato purée. For an attractive presentation, strain the sauce to separate the shallots, then garnish with the shallots and steamed, finely diced courgettes to add colour.

Milanese veal escalopes

A NORTHERN ITALIAN CLASSIC. It is very important, when frying this dish, that the escalopes have a lot of room in the frying pan. If they are too close together, they will steam instead of fry and you will not get the wonderfully crisp crust.

SERVES	PREP	COOK
SERVES 6	20–25 MINS	4–12 MINS

Ingredients

FOR THE VEAL

6 veal escalopes, total weight about 375g (13oz)

30g (1oz) plain flour

salt and pepper

2 eggs

60g (2oz) dried breadcrumbs

60g (2oz) grated Parmesan cheese

30g (1oz) butter

2 tbsp olive oil, plus more if needed

1 lemon, sliced, to serve

FOR THE SAUTÉED PEPPERS

2 tbsp olive oil

1 garlic clove, finely chopped

1 small green pepper, sliced

1 small red pepper, sliced

leaves from 7–10 oregano sprigs, finely chopped, plus more to serve

PREPARE THE VEAL ESCALOPES

1 **If necessary,** flatten the veal: put 2 veal escalopes between 2 sheets of baking parchment. Lightly pound to 3mm (⅛in) thick with a rolling pin. Repeat with the remaining slices.

COAT THE VEAL

2 **Season the flour** with salt and pepper and sift it on to a sheet of baking parchment.

3 **Lightly beat the eggs** in a shallow dish. Mix the breadcrumbs and Parmesan together in a small bowl and spread on another sheet of baking parchment.

4 **Lay each veal slice** in the seasoned flour to coat, then turn and coat the other side.

5 **Using 2 forks,** dip each slice in the egg and coat it thoroughly on both sides. Finally, press the veal into the breadcrumb and cheese mixture and coat both sides evenly. Put each slice on a plate. Refrigerate, uncovered, while you sauté the peppers.

SAUTÉ THE PEPPERS

6 Heat the oil in a medium frying pan. Add the garlic, pepper, salt and pepper, and sauté, stirring occasionally, until softened, 7–10 minutes. Remove from the heat, add the oregano and taste for seasoning; keep warm while frying the escalopes.

FRY THE VEAL AND SERVE

7 Heat half the butter and 1 tbsp oil in a large frying pan, or divide the total amount of butter and oil between 2 frying pans. Add 2–3 escalopes to a pan and fry over medium-high heat until golden brown, 1–2 minutes. They should not touch or they will stick together. Reduce the heat if the crumbs threaten to scorch at any time.

8 Turn and continue cooking until brown and no longer pink in the centre. It should take about 1–2 minutes, but cut into an escalope with a sharp knife to check (served it with the other side uppermost). Transfer the cooked veal to a plate lined with kitchen paper to blot off the excess fat and keep warm. If you used just 1 pan, add the remaining butter and oil and make sure it gets hot before frying the remaining veal, adding more oil if necessary. Be sure not to add too much oil, as the escalopes should remain crisp and not soggy.

9 Transfer the escalopes to warmed individual plates and garnish each with a few lemon slices and a sprig of oregano. Spoon the pepper strips alongside. Encourage your diners to squeeze lemon liberally over the veal; the combination is quite wonderful.

Turkish lamb kebabs

SUCCULENT GRILLED cylinders, perfect on a bed of tabbouleh (p108). These whip up in no time for the evening meal, but can also be made in the morning and refrigerated for an even speedier supper, as their flavours will improve.

SERVES	PREP	COOK
SERVES 6	30-35 MINS	10-15 MINS

Ingredients

FOR THE YOGURT SAUCE

1 large cucumber

1 tsp salt

500ml (16fl oz) Greek yogurt

1 garlic clove, finely chopped

FOR THE KEBABS

1 large onion

1kg (2¼lb) minced lamb

2 tsp ground cumin

salt and pepper

3 garlic cloves, finely chopped

leaves from 3-5 mint sprigs, finely chopped, plus more leaves for garnish

leaves from 3-5 parsley sprigs, finely chopped

olive oil

MAKE THE SAUCE

1 **Wipe and trim** the cucumber. Grate it, with the skin, into a large bowl. Stir in the salt. Set a colander over a bowl. Transfer the grated cucumber to the colander and let drain for 10 minutes, to draw out excess moisture.

2 **Put the yogurt** in a large bowl. Remove more water from the cucumber by squeezing it in your hand. Add the cucumber to the yogurt. Stir in the garlic with salt to taste. Cover and chill.

PREPARE THE KEBABS

3 **Cut the onion** into chunks and put into a food processor. Blend until finely chopped, then stir it into the minced lamb in a large bowl. Mix in the cumin, salt and pepper, garlic, and herbs. To test for seasoning, fry a spoonful of meat in the small frying pan until browned on both sides. Taste, and add more salt and pepper to the raw mixture if necessary.

COOK THE KEBABS

4 **Heat the grill** and set the rack 5cm (2in) from the heat. Wet your hands to make the mixture easier to work, and divide the mixture into 12. Roll each into a cylinder 2.5cm (1in) in diameter.

5 **Brush 6 metal skewers** and the grill rack with olive oil. Thread the meat on to the skewers, pressing them well into shape, and place on the grill rack. Brush with oil and grill for 5-7 minutes, until brown and sputtering.

6 **Turn the skewers** and grill the other side. The meat should remain juicy in the centre. Serve on a bed of tabbouleh, with the reserved mint leaves and the yogurt sauce.

Crisp salmon with coriander pesto

CRISPY BUT LIGHTLY COOKED, this is a wonderful way to cook fillets of salmon and bass, or any other rich fish. It is always useful to have a jar of pesto in the refrigerator and this recipe will keep for 2 days, if the surface is covered with a thin layer of oil to keep it from the air. Surprisingly, this pesto will also freeze very successfully.

SERVES	PREP	COOK
SERVES 4	5–10 MINS	10–15 MINS

Ingredients

4 x 175g (6oz) salmon fillets, with skin

3 tbsp vegetable oil

1 lemon

2 tsp sea salt

coriander leaves, to serve

FOR THE PESTO

leaves from 1 large bunch of coriander

2–3 garlic cloves

2 tbsp pine nuts

75ml (2½fl oz) olive oil

30g (1oz) grated Parmesan cheese

salt and pepper

MAKE THE PESTO

1 **Put the coriander** in a food processor with the garlic, pine nuts, and 2 tbsp olive oil. Add the Parmesan. With the blade turning, slowly pour in the remaining oil in a steady stream. Continue working the pesto until it thickens and emulsifies. Season to taste, scrape into a bowl, and cover.

PREPARE THE SALMON

2 **If necessary,** pull out any bones from the salmon with tweezers. Cut off any fatty or bony edges and trim the fillets neatly. Rinse the salmon under cold water then pat dry with kitchen paper. Brush the skin side of each fillet with some vegetable oil.

COOK THE SALMON

3 **Heat the remaining oil** in a frying pan until hot. Add the salmon, skin side down.

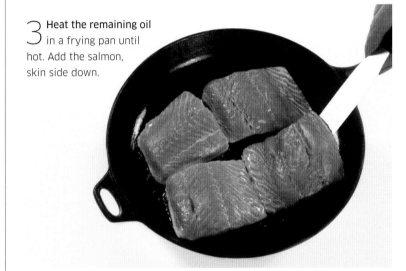

4 **Cook over medium heat** until the skin is crispy. Then increase the heat to high, turn and brown the sides and top of each fillet very quickly. The top should remain slightly soft, showing it is rare. Slice the lemon into wedges. Serve the salmon on warmed plates, sprinkle with sea salt and spoon on some coriander pesto. Decorate with lemon wedges and coriander leaves.

Oriental halibut en papillote

EACH DINER OPENS A PAPER CASE and savours the aroma as it is freshly released, the dish having lost none of its delicious fragrance on the journey from the oven. Though the flavourings here are Chinese in origin, the method of cooking food in paper parcels is French. Noodles and stir-fried crisp vegetables would be excellent alongside.

SERVES	PREP	COOK
SERVES 4	15–20 MINS	10–12 MINS

Ingredients

125g (4½oz) mangetout, trimmed

30g (1oz) black fermented Chinese beans, or 2 tbsp black bean sauce

4 garlic cloves, finely chopped

2.5cm (1in) piece fresh root ginger, finely chopped

3 tbsp light soy sauce

2 tbsp dry sherry

½ tsp granulated sugar

1 tbsp sesame oil

2 tbsp vegetable oil

1 egg

½ tsp salt

4 x 175g (6oz) skinned halibut fillets or steaks

4 spring onions, thinly sliced

PREPARE THE MANGETOUT AND ORIENTAL SEASONING

1 **Half-fill a saucepan** with salted water and bring to the boil. Add the mangetout and simmer for 1–2 minutes. Drain. If you have found fermented black beans, rinse them with cold water and drain. Coarsely chop three-quarters of them.

2 **Combine** the garlic, ginger, whole and chopped black beans or black bean sauce, soy sauce, sherry, sugar, and sesame oil in a bowl. Stir well to mix, then set aside.

PREPARE THE PAPER CASES

3 **Fold a sheet of baking parchment** (about 30x34.5cm/12x15in) in half and draw a curve with a pencil to make a heart shape when unfolded. It should be large enough to leave a 7.5cm (3in) border around a fish fillet.

4 **Cut out the heart shape** with scissors. Repeat to make 4 paper hearts. Open each out and brush with the vegetable oil, leaving a border about 2.5cm (1in) wide at the edges.

5 **Put the egg** and salt in a small bowl and beat together. Brush this egg glaze evenly on the border of each of the paper hearts.

FILL THE PAPER CASES

6 **Preheat the oven** to 200°C (400°F/Gas 6). Rinse the fish fillets and pat dry with kitchen paper. Arrange a quarter of the mangetout on 1 side of each paper heart and set a halibut fillet on top.

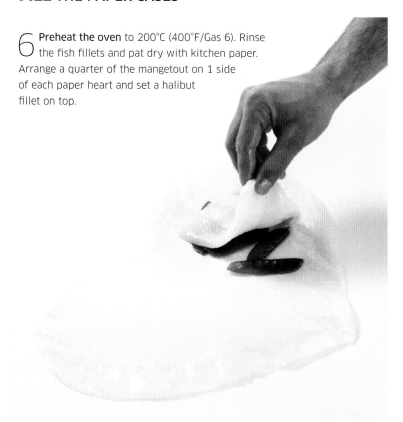

7 **Spoon a quarter of the oriental seasoning** on top of each fillet and sprinkle with a quarter of the spring onions. Fold the paper over the fish and run your finger along the edge to stick the 2 sides of paper together. Make small pleats to seal the edges.

8 Twist the 'tails' of each paper case to seal them, so that the filling does not ooze out during baking. Lay the cases on a baking sheet and bake for 10–12 minutes, until puffed and brown. Transfer to warmed plates, allowing each guest to open their own aromatic fish package.

 VARIATION: Thai-style halibut en papillote

Beautifully piquant with chillies and lime.

1 Omit the mangetout and the oriental seasoning. Put 25g (1oz) dried Chinese black mushrooms in a bowl of warm water and soak for 30 minutes, until plump. Drain and slice if they are very large. Finely chop the fresh root ginger and 2 garlic cloves. Slice 2 spring onions. Very finely chop 1 green chilli, removing the seeds if you would prefer a milder dish (leave them in if you like a bit of heat). Strip the leaves from 5 basil sprigs. Peel and slice 1 lime. Squeeze the juice from a second lime.

2 Put the mushrooms, chopped garlic, 1 tbsp soy sauce, 1 tsp sugar, and 120ml (4fl oz) water in a small saucepan and boil for 5–7 minutes, until all the liquid has just evaporated. Make sure the pan does not boil dry, or the garlic will burn in the hot sugar. Stir in the ginger, chilli, basil leaves, 2 tsp fish sauce (*nam pla*; you'll find it is widely available in most supermarkets) and the lime juice.

3 Prepare the paper cases and fish as directed. Set the fish on the paper cases, evenly spoon over the mushroom mixture, then sprinkle with the spring onions. Put a lime slice on top of each pile and season well with pepper. Seal and pleat the paper cases and bake as directed. If you like, accompany each serving with a fine ribbon pasta, tossed with more shredded basil and diced mushrooms.

Steak au poivre

THE LONGER YOU CAN LEAVE THE STEAK to marinate in the peppercorns the better and more intense the flavour will be, so start it off before you leave home in the morning. Chips made at home are a thousand times better than any you can buy, especially when they are fried twice, as in this recipe. It really is worth having a go at making them for a treat, even if you don't deep-fry often.

SERVES	PREP	COOK
SERVES 4	25–30 MINS	10–15 MINS

Ingredients

1 sirloin steak, 5cm (2in) thick, weighing about 1kg (2¼lb)

3 tbsp black peppercorns

1kg (2¼lb) potatoes

1 tbsp vegetable oil, plus more for deep-frying

30g (1oz) butter

salt

FOR THE SAUCE

125ml (4fl oz) brandy

125ml (4fl oz) double cream

MARINATE THE STEAKS

1 **Trim any excess fat** and sinew from the steak. With a small knife, slash diagonally through the fat to the beef at 4cm (1½in) intervals. This will prevent the steak curling while cooking. Now slice the steak into 4 portions.

2 **Put the peppercorns** into a plastic bag and crush with a rolling pin.

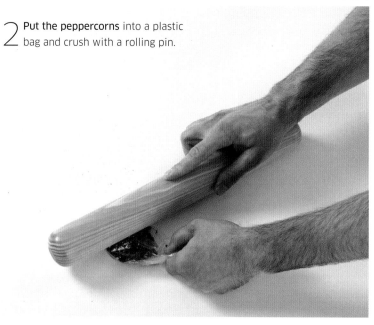

3 **Put the steaks** into a shallow dish and press the crushed peppercorns on to both sides. Cover and leave to marinate. Meanwhile, prepare the potatoes.

PREPARE THE POTATOES AND FRY THEM FOR THE FIRST TIME

4 **Peel the potatoes**. Square off the sides of each and cut into 1cm (½in) sticks. Put them into a bowl of cold water to remove the starch, and leave to soak for 30 minutes.

5 **Heat the vegetable oil** in a deep-fat fryer to 180°C (350°F). To test the oil temperature without a thermometer, drop in a cube of bread: it should turn golden in 1 minute.

6 **Remove the potatoes** from the bowl of water, drain them in a colander, and dry on kitchen paper so that the oil does not splatter. Dip the frying basket into the hot oil to prevent the potatoes sticking. Lift the basket from the oil, put in a third of the potatoes, and carefully lower into the oil.

7 **Fry until tender** when pierced with the tip of a knife and just starting to brown; it should take 7–9 minutes. Remove the basket and let the potatoes drain over the fryer for 1–2 minutes. Transfer to a large plate. Repeat for the remaining potatoes.

COOK THE STEAKS, FINISH FRYING THE POTATOES

8 Reheat the oil in the deep-fat fryer to 190°C (375°F). If you don't have a thermometer, test with a cube of bread: it should turn golden in about 30 seconds.

9 Heat 1 tbsp vegetable oil with the butter in a large frying pan. For a mild flavour, scrape off and discard the pepper from the steaks; for a stronger flavour, leave it on. Season the steaks with salt. Put the steaks into the pan, and fry over high heat for 2–3 minutes, until brown.

10 Turn the steak and continue cooking until the second side is brown, 2–3 minutes for rare steak, or 4–6 minutes for medium steak, depending on thickness. To test if it is done, press the centre with your finger. If it feels spongy, it is rare; if firm, it is well done. Remove the steak from the pan and cover with foil. Pour off the fat and discard.

11 Return a third of the potatoes to the basket and lower it into the hot oil. Continue frying for 1–2 minutes, until crisp and golden brown. Drain on kitchen paper. Repeat with the remaining potatoes.

MAKE THE SAUCE

12 Return the cooked steaks to the frying pan. Pour in the brandy and bring it to a boil. Stand back and hold a lighted match to the side of the pan to light the brandy. Baste the steaks with the pan juices - using a long-handled spoon - until the flames subside. It should only take about 20–30 seconds.

13 Transfer the steaks to a carving board and cover with foil to keep warm and allow the meat to rest and become incredibly tender. Add the cream to the frying pan and simmer, stirring to dissolve the pan juices. Taste for seasoning, and adjust if necessary, though it is unlikely you will need any more pepper! Either leave the steaks whole, or carve into generous slices about 2.5cm (1in) thick.

14 Divide the steaks among 4 warmed plates and spoon a little of the sauce on top. Serve the rest on the side. Sprinkle the chips lightly with salt and pile them beside the steaks. Serve with a sprig of watercress, if you like.

Mexican barbecued pork with salsa

MARINATE THE PORK in the morning for your evening meal. The barbecue sauce will make it taste smoky, as if it was cooked outdoors, even in the kind of weather that would extinguish the flames!

SERVES	PREP	COOK
SERVES 6	35-40 MINS PLUS MARINATING	40-50 MINS

Ingredients

FOR THE SALSA

375g (13oz) tomatoes

1 large onion, diced

1 garlic clove, finely chopped

leaves from 3-4 coriander sprigs, finely chopped

1 green chilli, finely chopped

1 yellow or red pepper, diced

1 lemon

Tabasco sauce

salt

FOR THE BARBECUE SAUCE

3 tbsp vegetable oil

1 large onion, diced

3 garlic cloves, finely chopped

1 green chilli, finely chopped

1 tbsp coriander seeds

2 x 400g (14oz) cans chopped tomatoes

4 limes

4 tbsp red wine vinegar

125ml (4fl oz) black treacle

FOR THE PORK

1kg (2¼lb) boned loin of pork

3 ripe avocados

1 lemon

3 corn tortillas

75ml (2½fl oz) vegetable oil, plus more if needed

MAKE THE SALSA

1 **Cut the cores** from the tomatoes and score an "X" on the base of each. Immerse in boiling water for 8-15 seconds, then plunge into cold water. Peel off the skin, cut in half, squeeze out the seeds and chop the flesh.

2 **Combine** the onion, garlic, coriander leaves, chillies, tomatoes, and peppers in a large bowl. Squeeze the lemon and pour in the juice. Season to taste with Tabasco sauce and salt, then cover and refrigerate.

MAKE THE BARBECUE SAUCE

3 **Heat the oil** in a sauté pan, add the onion, garlic, and chilli, and sauté, stirring, for 3-4 minutes, until soft but not brown. Add the coriander seeds and tomatoes. Squeeze the limes and pour in the juice. Cook, stirring, for about 15 minutes, until reduced and thickened. Add the vinegar, bring to a boil and reduce until thickened again.

4 **Stir in** the treacle and simmer the mixture 1-2 minutes longer. Season with salt. Let the sauce cool slightly, then purée it in a food processor and allow to cool completely. Slice the pork, cover with barbecue sauce, cover and refrigerate for 2-8 hours.

GRILL THE PORK

5 **Heat the grill.** Slice the avocados and brush with lemon juice. Cut the tortillas into strips. Heat the oil in a frying pan, add the tortillas and fry, turning once, until crisp. Keep warm on kitchen paper.

6 **Brush the grill rack** with oil. Take the pork from the barbecue sauce with tongs, allowing excess sauce to drip off, and put on the rack. Cook about 5cm (2in) from the heat for 5-7 minutes, until slightly charred. Turn, brush with sauce, and cook until well browned and no longer pink inside. Put the pork on to warmed plates. Spoon on some of the salsa and add the tortilla strips and avocado.

Devilled drumsticks

THESE ARE ALSO EXCELLENT cooked on a barbecue. The drumsticks are served with a warm potato salad; when choosing potatoes for salad, go for a variety with a waxy texture that will hold their shape, such as Charlotte.

SERVES	PREP	COOK
SERVES 4	20-25 MINS	35-40 MINS

Ingredients

FOR THE DEVIL MIXTURE

125g (4½oz) butter

2 tbsp mango chutney

2 tbsp tomato purée or ketchup

2 tbsp Worcestershire sauce

1 tsp ground nutmeg

½ tsp anchovy paste

salt and pepper

cayenne pepper or Tabasco sauce

FOR THE POTATO SALAD

2 tbsp red wine vinegar

½ tsp Dijon mustard

90ml (3fl oz) vegetable oil

750g (1lb 10oz) baby potatoes

leaves from a few parsley sprigs, finely chopped

a few chives, snipped

FOR THE CHICKEN

8 chicken drumsticks

vegetable oil for grill rack

MAKE THE DEVIL MIXTURE

1 **Melt the butter** gently in a small saucepan. Chop any large pieces of fruit in the chutney. Put the chutney in a small bowl and add the remaining devil ingredients, with a pinch of cayenne pepper or dash of Tabasco sauce, and the melted butter. Mix well and taste for seasoning.

MAKE THE POTATO SALAD

2 **Whisk together** the vinegar, mustard, oil, and a pinch each of salt and pepper. Put the potatoes in a saucepan of salted water and bring to the boil. Cover and simmer for 15-20 minutes, or until tender.

3 **Drain thoroughly,** then halve and immediately transfer to a large bowl. While they are still warm, add the herbs and pour over the dressing; mix gently. Cover with foil and keep warm.

PREPARE AND GRILL THE CHICKEN

4 **Heat the grill**. Brush the rack in the grill pan with oil. Cut the skin from the chicken drumsticks and pull it off. Slash the meat diagonally several times with the point of a knife. Brush some of the devil mixture over each, working it well into the cuts.

5 **Arrange the drumsticks** on the rack. Grill 7.5-10cm (3-4in) from the heat, turning once during cooking and basting frequently with the remaining devil mixture and any pan juices. Cook for 10-12 minutes on each side, until well browned and tender. Arrange the warm potato salad on plates, with the drumsticks alongside.

Oriental stir-fried chicken

THIS INVITES ENDLESS VARIATIONS, just always use fresh ingredients, finely cut. Make sure you prepare all the ingredients in advance, as the cooking time is swift and cannot be interrupted. For a properly "seasoned" wok, do not wash it after cooking. Instead, wipe it out with kitchen paper while still warm, then coat the inside surface with a thin layer of flavourless vegetable oil.

SERVES SERVES 4	**PREP** 15–20 MINS PLUS MARINATING	**COOK** 10–12 MINS

Ingredients

FOR THE STIR-FRY

30g (1oz) dried Chinese black mushrooms or other dried wild mushrooms

45g (1½oz) flaked almonds

1 onion

4 celery sticks

500g (1lb 2oz) head of broccoli

2 skinless, boneless chicken breasts, total weight about 375g (13oz)

90ml (3fl oz) vegetable oil

1 tsp sesame oil

FOR THE MARINADE

4 tbsp soy sauce

4 tbsp rice wine or dry sherry

2 tsp cornflour

PREPARE THE VEGETABLES AND ALMONDS

1 Put the mushrooms in a bowl, cover with 250ml (9fl oz) warm water and allow to soften for 30 minutes.

2 Preheat the oven to 190°C (375°F/Gas 5). Spread the almonds evenly on a baking sheet and toast for 6–8 minutes, until lightly browned.

3 Cut the onion in half lengthways. Cut each half into 4–5 wedges. Trim the celery and cut across, on the diagonal, into 1cm (½in) thick slices. Cut the broccoli head into very small florets.

4 Drain the mushrooms, reserving the liquid. Trim off any woody stalks, then slice. Strain the liquid through a sieve lined with kitchen paper to remove any sand or grit.

MARINATE THE CHICKEN

5 Cut each chicken breast on the diagonal into very thin slices (try to get 10–15 from each breast). In a bowl, mix the soy sauce, rice wine, and cornflour, stirring until the cornflour dissolves. Add the chicken and stir to coat. Marinate for about 15 minutes.

COOK THE STIR-FRY

6 Heat half the oil in a wok. Add the onion and celery and stir and toss over high heat for 1–2 minutes, until beginning to soften. Add the broccoli and fry, stirring and tossing, for 2–3 minutes. Add the mushrooms and cook for 2 minutes more.

7 Remove the vegetables from the wok to a bowl and set aside in a warm place. Wipe the wok with kitchen paper. Add the remaining oil to the wok and heat it.

8 Drain the chicken, reserving the marinade. Add the chicken to the wok and cook over high heat, stirring and tossing, for 2–3 minutes, until opaque. Return the vegetables to the wok, adding 4 tbsp of the mushroom soaking liquid.

9 **Pour the marinade liquid** into the wok and cook, stirring, for 2 minutes. Sprinkle with sesame oil, stir and taste for seasoning. Sprinkle with the almonds and serve in individual bowls, with noodles if you like.

 VARIATION: Sweet and sour stir-fried chicken

Pineapple gives sweetness to this old-fashioned favourite.

1 Prepare the chicken breasts as directed in the main recipe. For the marinade, reduce the amount of rice wine to 1 tbsp, and add 1 tbsp wine vinegar and 1 tbsp caster sugar to give a sweet and sour flavour to the final stir-fry sauce.

2 Omit the broccoli and mushrooms from the recipe and replace them with 4 rings of canned pineapple in fruit juice (not syrup), cut into small pieces for even cooking. Add whatever other vegetables you would prefer; 1 red and 1 yellow pepper, sliced, and 120g (4oz) mangetout, halved widthways, would make good additions to the recipe.

3 Finish the stir-fry as directed, adding 4 tbsp pineapple juice from the can instead of the mushroom soaking liquid to increase the sweetness of the dish. Serve with plain boiled rice and sprinkle with sesame seeds, if liked.

Fish plaits with warm vinaigrette

THESE LOOK FANCY, but can be put together speedily for a special after-work dinner. Here, the fish have been carefully unplaited to serve in a casual style; however, the 3 different-coloured skins of the fish look beautiful kept together in their braids for a more formal occasion. The herb-dotted vinaigrette marries with the dish wonderfully, and the whole – steamed over an aromatic court bouillon – is light and immensely appetizing for even the most jaded palates.

SERVES SERVES 6	**PREP** 35-40 MINS	**COOK** 8-10 MINS

Ingredients

FOR THE COURT BOUILLON

1 bouquet garni made with 5-6 parsley stalks, 2-3 thyme sprigs and 1 bay leaf

6 peppercorns

2 cloves

1 carrot, quartered

1 onion, quartered

FOR THE FISH

375g (13oz) red snapper fillets, with skin

375g (13oz) lemon sole fillets, with skin

375g (13oz) mackerel fillets, with skin

salt and pepper

FOR THE WARM VINAIGRETTE

125ml (4fl oz) red wine vinegar

2 tsp Dijon mustard

2 shallots, finely chopped

75ml (2½fl oz) olive oil

150ml (5fl oz) vegetable oil

leaves from 5-7 tarragon or thyme sprigs, finely chopped, plus more to garnish

leaves from 7-10 parsley or chervil sprigs, finely chopped, plus more to garnish

PREPARE THE COURT BOUILLON

1 **Combine** 1 litre (1¾ pints) water, the bouquet garni, peppercorns, cloves, carrot and onion in a pan over which you can fit a large steamer. Bring just to a boil and simmer for 20-30 minutes.

PREPARE THE FISH

2 **Rinse the fish** and pat dry with kitchen paper. Discard any bones and trim the fillets so they are roughly the same length. Cut each fillet into strips about 2cm (¾in) thick. You need 6 strips of each type of fish.

PLAIT AND STEAM THE FISH

3 **Take a strip each of** snapper, sole, and mackerel. Plait them together. Continue with the remaining fish. With a fish slice, transfer the plaits to the steamer and sprinkle with salt and pepper.

4 **Set the steamer over** the simmering court bouillon. Make sure there is at least 5cm (2in) of water underneath the steamer – if not, top up with boiling water.

5 **Cover and steam the fish for** 8-10 minutes, until it just flakes easily when tested with a fork.

MAKE THE VINAIGRETTE

6 In a small saucepan, whisk together the vinegar, mustard, and shallots. Add the olive oil, then the vegetable oil in a steady stream, whisking constantly so the vinaigrette emulsifies and thickens slightly. You may not need to add all the vegetable oil; stop when the consistency of the vinaigrette is as you would prefer. The shallots must be chopped very finely indeed, so they become an integral part of the vinaigrette, rather than intrusive lumps.

7 Heat gently until the vinaigrette is warm, whisking constantly. Remove from the heat and whisk in the herbs and salt and pepper to taste. Spoon the vinaigrette on to 6 warmed plates and put the fish plaits on top (unbraid them if you like, for a more casual presentation). Garnish with the reserved herb sprigs, which will serve as a vibrant and very green salad, and serve at once.

 VARIATION: Panache of steamed fish with warm sherry vinaigrette

A 'panache', or selection, of fish. French beans are a good accompaniment.

1 Make the court bouillon as directed. Rinse the fish fillets and pat dry. Cut into even diamonds. Steam as for the fish plaits, allowing 5–7 minutes, depending on thickness. You may have to steam in batches.

2 Meanwhile, prepare the warm vinaigrette as directed in the main recipe, substituting sherry vinegar for the red wine vinegar and walnut oil for the olive oil. Omit the herbs.

3 Arrange the fish on warmed plates, skin-side up. Spoon a little of the warm sherry vinaigrette over the fish and serve the remainder separately.

Russian beef sauté

BASED ON BEEF STROGANOFF. Fresh noodles are a good accompaniment. For a cheaper dish, substitute top sirloin for the fillet of beef; the slices are thinly enough cut that they shouldn't be tough. The mushrooms here are not strictly authentic, though they make a welcome addition. It is best to make this dish at the point of serving, as reheating may both curdle the cream and overcook the beef.

SERVES	PREP	COOK
SERVES 4	15-20 MINS	20-25 MINS

Ingredients

750g (1lb 10oz) fillet of beef

30g (1oz) butter, more if needed

2 tbsp vegetable oil

salt and pepper

2 onions, sliced

250g (9oz) mushrooms, sliced

1 tbsp plain flour

125ml (4fl oz) beef stock or water

2-3 tsp Dijon mustard

125ml (4fl oz) soured cream

leaves from 3-5 tarragon sprigs, chopped

PREPARE THE BEEF

1 **Trim the beef** of any fat or sinew. Cut the meat into 1cm (½in) slices. Cut each slice into 1cm (½in) strips, about 7.5cm (3in) long.

2 **Heat half the butter** and oil in a sauté pan, until starting to brown. Add half the beef, sprinkle with salt and pepper, and cook over very high heat, stirring, for 2-3 minutes, until well browned but still rare in the centre. Remove with a slotted spoon, and add more butter if the pan is dry. Brown the remaining beef in the same way.

BEGIN THE SAUTÉ

3 **Heat the remaining butter** and oil in the sauté pan, add the onions, separating the slices into rings, and sauté over medium heat for 5-7 minutes, until softened and browned, stirring occasionally. Transfer them to a bowl with the slotted spoon.

4 **Add the mushrooms** to the pan and sauté for 4-5 minutes, until all the moisture has evaporated. Stir in the flour, and cook for 1 minute. Pour in the stock and bring to a boil, stirring so the sauce thickens smoothly.

FINISH THE SAUTÉ

5 **Return the onions** to the pan, season, and simmer for 2 minutes. Stir in the mustard, and heat gently without boiling. If the mustard boils, the sauce will be bitter. Return the beef and its juices to the pan and heat through gently but thoroughly for 2-3 minutes. If the beef is overcooked, it will be tough.

6 **Stir in the soured cream,** and cook for about 1 minute longer. Taste for seasoning. Do not let the mixture get too hot or the soured cream may curdle. Serve immediately, with cooked fresh noodles. Sprinkle with the chopped tarragon.

Indonesian chicken satay

MARINATE THESE IN THE MORNING, for dinner. They are considered as street snacks in Indonesia, but make a wonderfully exotic main course with this spicy peanut sauce, a rice pilaf and a crisp salad; great to come home to after a hard day

SERVES	PREP	COOK
SERVES 6	15–20 MINS PLUS MARINATING	8–10 MINS

Ingredients

1.5kg (3lb 3oz) skinless, boneless chicken breasts

FOR THE MARINADE

3 shallots, finely chopped

2 garlic cloves, finely chopped

½ tsp chilli powder

2 tsp ground coriander

2 tsp ground ginger

3 tbsp soy sauce

2 tbsp distilled white vinegar

2 tbsp vegetable oil

FOR THE PEANUT SAUCE

1½ tbsp vegetable oil

175g (6oz) shelled, skinned raw peanuts

½ onion, sliced

1 garlic clove

½ tsp dried chilli flakes

2 tsp ground ginger

1 tsp brown sugar

1½ tbsp lemon juice

salt and pepper

PREPARE AND MARINATE THE CHICKEN

1 **Remove the tendon** from each chicken breast. Separate the fillet from each breast by lifting the end of the fillet, and pulling it towards you. With a sharp knife, cut each fillet in half lengthwise. Cut each breast into 7 thin strips on the diagonal, the same size as the strips of fillet.

2 **Put all the marinade ingredients** in a large bowl. Mix together with a metal spoon. Add the chicken strips, and mix until well coated with the marinade. Cover with clingfilm, and refrigerate for at least 3 hours or up to 12 hours.

MAKE THE PEANUT SAUCE

3 **Soak 18 bamboo skewers** in water for 30 minutes. Heat the oil in a pan. Add the peanuts and stir for 3–5 minutes, until brown. Transfer to a food processor. Add the onion, garlic, chilli, ginger, sugar, and lemon juice.

4 **Purée until very smooth,** scraping the bowl with the spatula as necessary. Blend in 375ml (12fl oz) hot water, adding enough to make a pourable sauce. Transfer to a saucepan, heat to boiling, and simmer for 2 minutes, stirring constantly. Season to taste. Remove from the heat and keep warm.

PREPARE AND COOK THE KEBABS

5 **Heat the grill.** Thread the chicken strips on to the skewers concertina fashion, using 3 strips per skewer, and twisting the strips slightly as you thread them. Brush the grill rack with oil. Arrange the chicken kebabs on the rack.

6 **Grill the kebabs,** about 5–7cm (2–3in) from the heat for 2–3 minutes, until browned. Turn and cook the other side. Arrange on plates with the warm peanut sauce. Accompany with a rice pilaf for a more substantial meal.

Southern fried chicken

SOAK THE CHICKEN the night before you want to eat this. An American favourite from the South, the chicken is soaked in milk to whiten the meat. The traditional accompaniment is mashed potatoes, enlivened if you like by a sprinkling of chopped herbs such as parsley or chives. The pan gravy served here may not be to everyone's tastes, though it is authentic; leave it out if it's not for you. The fried chicken is also delicious served cold on a picnic, with a potato salad and crisp green leaves.

SERVES	PREP	COOK
SERVES 4	10–15 MINS PLUS SOAKING	20–30 MINS

Ingredients

FOR THE CHICKEN

1.5kg (3lb 3oz) chicken, jointed into 8

500ml (16fl oz) milk, plus more if needed

250ml (8fl oz) vegetable oil for frying, plus more if needed

60g (2oz) plain flour

2 tsp pepper

1 lemon

FOR THE GRAVY (OPTIONAL)

2 tbsp flour

375ml (13fl oz) milk

salt and pepper

PREPARE THE CHICKEN

1 **Put the chicken** in a bowl and add enough milk to cover. Cover securely with clingfilm and refrigerate for 8–12 hours. With a slotted spoon, transfer the chicken joints to a dish. Discard the milk.

2 **Pour vegetable oil** into the frying pan to make a 2cm (¾in) deep layer. Heat over moderate heat until it measures 180°C (350°F) on a deep-fat thermometer. If you don't have one, drop in a cube of fresh bread: if it turns golden brown in 1 minute, the oil is ready.

3 **Mix the flour** and pepper in a shallow dish. Dip the chicken in the flour and pat off the excess with your hands to obtain an even coating.

FRY THE CHICKEN

4 **Gently add the chicken joints** to the pan, skin side down, taking care as the chicken may sputter. Fry for 3–5 minutes, until brown.

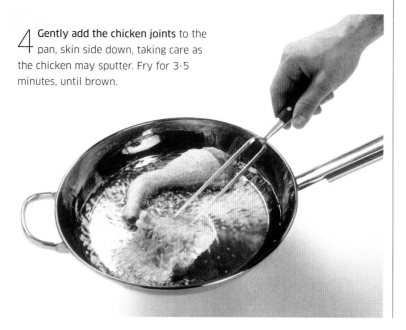

5 **Turn the chicken over** and reduce the heat to low.

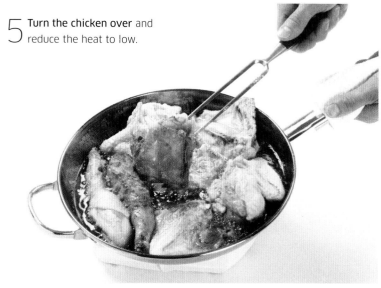

6 **Continue frying** for 20–25 minutes, until the chicken is brown and tender when pierced. If some pieces cook before others, remove them, pat dry with kitchen paper, and keep warm, uncovered or the crisp coating will soften.

MAKE THE GRAVY (OPTIONAL)

7 **Discard all** but about 2 tbsp of the fat from the frying pan. You can strain it carefully and keep it, refrigerated, for frying chicken again, but it should not be used more than twice or the flavour will begin to taint and stale. Evenly sprinkle the flour into the remaining fat in the pan. Cook, stirring with a large metal spoon, until browned. It should take 2-3 minutes to cook out the taste of the raw flour. Do not skip or hurry this step, as the taste of uncooked flour will spoil the sauce.

8 **Whisk in the milk** and simmer until the gravy is thickened. It should only take about 2 minutes. Taste and season the gravy to taste (you may want to add pepper) and strain into a gravy boat.

9 **Cut the lemon** into wedges. Arrange the chicken on a serving dish with some lemon wedges, for your diners to squeeze over as they prefer. A squeeze of lemon really lifts this dish, cutting through the richness of the fried chicken. A few crisp green leaves are lovely on the side.

 VARIATION: Bacon-fried chicken

The flavour of the bacon is wonderful and the gravy spiked with a little Tabasco.

1 Soak the chicken in milk as directed in the main recipe. Omit the vegetable oil for frying and sauté 8-12 bacon rashers until crisp and brown and all the fat has been released into the pan. Remove the bacon, leaving its fat in the pan, drain the rashers on kitchen paper, and keep warm.

2 Flour the chicken as directed, then cook it in the bacon fat and drain on kitchen paper, blotting carefully to remove excess grease. Prepare the pan gravy, adding a dash of Tabasco sauce, to taste, when seasoning.

3 Crumble the bacon and sprinkle it over the chicken when serving. This version of fried chicken is especially delicious with the authentic addition of a pan of cornbread (p386).

Griddled tuna steaks with salsa

MARINATE AS YOU WALK IN THE DOOR for dinner later, after you've relaxed with a bath and a glass of wine. The tart, lemony marinade sets off the rich fish perfectly, while the crisp salsa is the perfect foil. Always be careful, when cooking tuna, to sear the outsides while keeping the centre of the fish moist and slightly rare. Tuna is not at all good dry and overcooked.

SERVES	**PREP**	**COOK**
SERVES 4	25-30 MINS PLUS MARINATING	5-7 MINS

Ingredients

FOR THE MARINADE

2-3 thyme sprigs

2 tbsp vegetable oil

½ lemon

FOR THE TUNA AND SALSA

4 x 250g (9oz) tuna steaks

salt and pepper

4 tomatoes

1 red pepper

1 onion

1 bunch of coriander

200g canned sweetcorn, drained

2 limes

3-4 tbsp vegetable oil

MARINATE THE TUNA

1 **Strip the thyme leaves** from the stalks, letting them fall into a shallow, non-metallic dish. Add the oil to the dish.

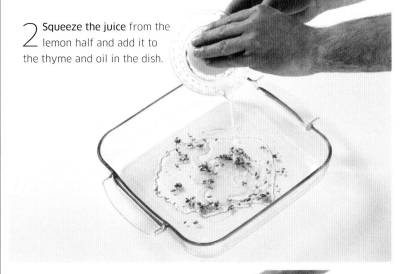

2 **Squeeze the juice** from the lemon half and add it to the thyme and oil in the dish.

3 **Rinse and pat dry the tuna** steaks. Season with salt and pepper, then put the tuna steaks in the marinade and turn to coat. Cover and refrigerate for 1 hour, turning occasionally. Meanwhile, make the salsa.

MAKE THE SALSA

4 **Cut the cores** from the tomatoes and score an "x" on the base of each. Immerse in a pan of boiling water until the skin starts to split, then plunge into cold water. Peel, cut in half and squeeze out the seeds. Coarsely chop the flesh.

5 **Core, deseed, and dice the pepper** and chop the onion. Strip the coriander leaves from the stalks and finely chop. Put the tomatoes, sweetcorn, coriander, onion, and pepper in a bowl. Squeeze 1 of the limes into the mixture and season. Leave to stand for the flavours to blend.

GRILL THE TUNA

6 **Heat a griddle pan.** Brush the griddle with oil, and add the tuna. While brushing each tuna steak with the marinade, cook for 2–3 minutes, without turning, until a steak comes away from the griddle without tearing. When you can lift off a steak, do so, and turn over each steak with tongs and brush with the remaining marinade. Griddle for 2–3 minutes more. The tuna should remain rare in the centre: flake with a knife, you should see a pinkish-red and translucent layer in the middle. Each steak should also feel slightly soft when gently pressed with the tongs. Be very careful not to overcook the fish.

7 **Cut the remaining lime** into wedges. Put the tuna - with its handsome griddle marks - on to 4 warmed plates. Serve the salsa in a bowl on the side, for everyone to help themselves. Arrange the lime wedges around and garnish with a few more coriander sprigs, if you like.

 VARIATION: Griddled swordfish with fennel and sun-dried tomatoes

Flavoured with aniseed liqueur.

1 Rinse and pat dry 4 x 250g (9oz) swordfish steaks. Marinate as directed. Omit the salsa. Slice 3 fennel bulbs. Melt 60g (2oz) butter in a saucepan, add the fennel, season and press a piece of buttered foil on top.

2 Cover and cook over low heat until very soft; it will take 40–45 minutes. Drain 60g (2oz) sun-dried tomatoes in oil and coarsely chop. Stir into the fennel with 1–2 tbsp aniseed-flavoured liqueur (such as Pernod). Cook for about 10 minutes, then season to taste.

3 Griddle the swordfish as directed and serve on warmed plates with the fennel mixture on the side.

Pork and ginger sukiyaki

MARINATE THE PORK soon after you walk in the door for dinner an hour or two later. If you can find the sweet Japanese rice wine, *mirin*, use it instead of the sweet sherry and sugar in this recipe, adding just 1 tbsp. You will find it in larger supermarkets and Asian stores. This is a great dish for a mid-week supper, as it's so quick to cook.

SERVES SERVES 6	**PREP** 15–20 MINS PLUS MARINATING	**COOK** 15–20 MINS

Ingredients

1kg (2¼lb) pork tenderloins

2.5cm (1in) piece fresh root ginger, coarsely chopped

125ml (4fl oz) saké

4 tbsp soy sauce

1 tbsp sweet sherry

1 tsp granulated sugar

60g (2oz) dried oriental mushrooms

10 spring onions

75ml (2½fl oz) vegetable oil, plus more if needed

cellophane noodles for serving (optional)

PREPARE AND **MARINATE** THE PORK

1 Trim the pork tenderloins of any fat and membrane. Cut diagonally across each to make thin, even slices. Combine the ginger, saké, soy sauce, sweet sherry, and sugar in a non-metallic bowl. Add the pork to the bowl and stir to coat. Cover and marinate for 1–2 hours in the refrigerator.

PREPARE THE REMAINING INGREDIENTS

2 Put the mushrooms in a bowl, and cover with warm water. Soak for about 30 minutes, until plump, then drain. Trim the spring onions, and cut diagonally into 4cm (1½in) pieces.

COOK THE SUKIYAKI

3 Heat 1 tbsp oil in a frying pan. Add the mushrooms and spring onions, and sauté over medium heat, stirring often, for 2–3 minutes, until they soften. Transfer to a large bowl. Drain the pork in a sieve, reserving the liquid.

4 Heat another tablespoon of oil in the pan. Add a quarter of the pork and sauté over very high heat, stirring constantly, for 2–3 minutes, until the meat is lightly coloured. Transfer to the bowl with the mushrooms and spring onions. Cook the remaining pork in batches, adding more oil as needed.

FINISH AND **SERVE** THE DISH

5 Pour the reserved marinade into the pan. Return the mushrooms, spring onions, and pork. Simmer for 1–2 minutes, until the meat is just heated through. Do not overcook, or the meat will be tough.

6 Taste and season with more sake, soy sauce, sherry, and sugar, if needed. Serve on warmed plates, with cellophane noodles, if you like.

Veal saltimbocca

SALTIMBOCCA literally means "jump into the mouth" in Italian. These take next to no time to prepare and, even better, can be prepared up to the end of step 2 before you leave for work in the morning. Layer them between sheets of baking parchment, cover tightly and refrigerate to cook quickly in the evening.

SERVES	PREP	COOK
SERVES 4	20–25 MINS	10–12 MINS

Ingredients

4 veal escalopes, total weight about 500g (1lb 2oz)

4 thin slices of Parma or cooked ham

12 sage leaves, plus more for garnish

60g (2oz) butter

75ml (2½fl oz) white wine

salt and pepper

PREPARE THE SALTIMBOCCA

1 **Put a veal** escalope between 2 sheets of baking parchment. Pound it to a thickness of about 3mm (⅛in), with a rolling pin. Peel the parchment away from the meat. Cut the veal into 3 pieces. Trim away any rind and excess fat from 1 of the Parma ham slices. Cut the slice into 3 pieces.

2 **Lay a sage leaf** on each escalope, and top with a piece of ham. Put a piece of baking parchment over the veal and ham, and pound gently to press the ham on to the meat. Peel off the parchment carefully, so the ham and sage adhere to the meat. Prepare the remaining escalopes in the same way.

COOK THE SALTIMBOCCA

3 **Heat the butter** in a frying pan. Add a few of the saltimbocca to the pan, and brown over medium heat for about 2 minutes. Take care; veal escalopes cook very quickly, and will be tough if overcooked. Turn each saltimbocca and brown the other side for 1–2 minutes. As the saltimbocca are cooked, transfer them to a plate, and keep them warm.

4 **Add the wine** to the pan and heat to boiling, stirring to dissolve the pan juices. Season to taste. (You may not need salt because the Parma ham is quite salty.)

5 **Transfer the saltimbocca** to a warmed platter or individual plates, using a palette knife. Spoon the sauce around the veal, and garnish with a few chopped sage leaves, if you like.

Five-spice fillet of salmon

YOU CAN USE INDIAN SPICES, instead of Chinese five-spice, if you prefer, though the aroma and flavour of fennel is completely delicious. Try it even on a professed aniseed hater (without telling them). They will love it. This is a fabulous dish to make after a bad day at work; chopping is incredibly therapeutic, and preparing this meal is a great way to vent your frustrations.

SERVES	PREP	COOK
SERVES 4	30–35 MINS	20–25 MINS

Ingredients

FOR THE VEGETABLES AND FISH

375g (13oz) carrots

750g (1lb 10oz) courgettes

750g (1lb 10oz) leeks

60g (2oz) butter, plus more if needed

salt and pepper

4 x 175g (6oz) skinless salmon fillets

2 tbsp dry white wine

FOR THE SPICE MIXTURE

1 tbsp Chinese five-spice powder

1 tbsp ground fennel seed

1 pinch of cayenne pepper

PREPARE THE VEGETABLE JULIENNE

1 **Peel and trim the carrots.** Cut them into 7.5cm (3in) lengths and square off the sides. Cut each piece lengthways into fine slices. Stack the slices and cut lengthways into fine julienne.

2 **Trim the courgettes** and cut them into 7.5cm (3in) lengths. Cut off the peel, including about 3mm (⅛in) of flesh.

3 **Cut the slices of peel** lengthwise into fine strips. Discard the interior pieces. Trim the leeks, discarding the roots and tough green tops. Cut into 7.5cm (3in) lengths, then cut lengthways in half. Fan each half slightly, and cut lengthways into thin julienne. Wash very thoroughly in a colander.

4 **Melt half the butter** in a sauté pan. Add the leeks, carrots, salt, and pepper. Press a piece of buttered foil on top, cover, and cook gently, stirring occasionally, for about 10 minutes. Add the courgette, cover with the foil, and cook until tender, stirring occasionally, for 8–10 minutes. Remove from the heat and transfer to a baking dish in an even layer.

PREPARE THE SALMON

5 Preheat the oven to 200°C (400°F/Gas 6). Rinse the salmon and dry with kitchen paper. Combine the five-spice powder, fennel, cayenne, and a pinch of salt. Sprinkle the spices on to a sheet of baking parchment. Coat the sides of each piece of salmon with the spice mixture, patting the fish gently with your hands so it is evenly coated.

COOK THE DISH

6 Heat the remaining butter in the sauté pan. Cook the salmon over high heat, turning once with a palette knife, for 1–2 minutes on each side. Transfer to a baking dish.

7 Sprinkle each piece of salmon with a little white wine. Bake the salmon and vegetables in the heated oven for 20–25 minutes. When done, the salmon flesh should just flake when tested with a fork.

8 Pile the vegetable julienne on warmed individual plates and set one piece of salmon on top of each. Decorate with lemon slices, if you like.

 VARIATION: Salmon fillets with mushroom and leek julienne

The spice coating is omitted here, to show off the pretty pink of the salmon flesh.

1 Omit the courgettes, carrots, and spice mixture. Cut the leeks as directed in the main recipe. Wipe 375g (13oz) mushrooms, trim the stalks even with the caps, and thinly slice the caps. Stack the slices on the chopping board and cut into very thin strips.

2 Cook the leeks as directed, add the mushrooms, and continue cooking, uncovered, until all the liquid has evaporated (the mushrooms will emit a lot of liquid, and then this has to be boiled off, or it will make the dish watery); it should take about 5–8 minutes longer.

3 Transfer the vegetables to individual baking dishes. Rinse the salmon as directed, season with salt and pepper and set 1 piece in each dish of vegetables. Sprinkle each piece of fish with a little white wine and bake as directed in the main recipe.

Malaysian fried rice noodles

ESPECIALLY POPULAR on the Malaysian island of Penang. Traditionally, this dish would be made with fresh rice noodles – do use them if you can find them in Asian stores – but the dried variety work just as well. If you need a meal really quickly in the evening, this is the one for you. You can speed it up even more if you chop all the ingredients in the morning and store them separately, tightly covered, in the refrigerator.

SERVES	PREP	COOK
SERVES 4	30-40 MINS	8-12 MINS

Ingredients

250g (9oz) dried wide rice sticks

3 Chinese pork sausages, or 175g (6oz) smoked ham

250g (9oz) raw large prawns

3 eggs

4 tbsp oil

3 small onions, sliced into thin rings

3-4 red chillies, finely chopped

2 garlic cloves, finely chopped

125g (4½oz) beansprouts

3 tbsp light soy sauce, plus more if needed

4 tbsp chicken stock

2 spring onions, sliced diagonally

SOAK THE RICE STICKS

1 Put the rice sticks in a bowl and cover generously with warm water. Let soak until soft, about 30 minutes or according to packet instructions, stirring every so often, while you prepare the remaining ingredients. When the rice sticks have soaked for long enough, thoroughly drain them in a colander, shaking well, then fork them through to separate the strands and set aside.

PREPARE THE OTHER INGREDIENTS

2 With a cleaver, cut the Chinese sausages diagonally into thin slices. If using smoked ham instead, cut it into generous 2.5cm (1in) sticks. Devein the prawns: run a very sharp knife along the back of each prawn, then lift out and discard the dark intestinal vein with the tip of a knife. It is very important to do this each time you prepare prawns, as the vein can be gritty and unpleasant in the mouth. If you have had no time to do so beforehand, prepare the other ingredients now and place them separately in small bowls near to the stove top, as everything must be chopped and readily to hand once you start stir-frying. It is a rapid process and cannot be stopped and started. Bear this in mind every time you make a stir-fried dish, as a little preparation results in a very quick cooking time and a crisper, more satisfying meal.

MAKE THE STIR-FRY

3 Beat the eggs in a bowl. Heat a wok over medium heat until hot. Drizzle in 1 tbsp of the oil to coat the bottom and sides. When the oil is hot, pour in the eggs and stir at once until they are scrambled in small pieces; it will take just 1–2 minutes. Transfer to a bowl.

4 Increase the heat to medium-high and add the remaining oil. When hot, add the onions and stir-fry, tossing, for 3-4 minutes, until they start to brown. Add the chillies, garlic, and Chinese sausages and stir-fry until fragrant, about 30 seconds.

5 **Add the** prawns to the wok and stir-fry until they just turn pink, 1–1½ minutes. Increase the heat to high. Add the beansprouts, rice sticks, soy sauce, and chicken stock and stir-fry for 2–3 minutes, until the ingredients are just wilted.

6 **Add the eggs** to the other ingredients and stir for 1 minute, until thoroughly mixed and very hot. Taste and add more soy sauce, if necessary. Transfer to warmed plates and sprinkle with the spring onions. Serve at once.

Pan-fried mackerel in rolled oats

A TRADITIONAL SCOTTISH RECIPE. For true authenticity (and lots of added flavour), use lard or bacon drippings instead of oil. The accompanying mustard sauce is a very welcome and piquant contrast to the rich fish. These days, both mackerel and oats are classified as "super foods". Add the lemon wedges and hot, sinus-clearing mustard, and this dish is a true cold-weather winner.

SERVES	PREP	COOK
SERVES 6	15–20 MINS	8–12 MINS

Ingredients

FOR THE FISH

6 large mackerel fillets

salt and pepper

75ml (2½fl oz) vegetable oil, plus more if needed

wedges of lemon and watercress sprigs, to serve

TO COAT THE FISH

2 eggs

30g (1oz) plain flour

175g (6oz) rolled oats

FOR THE MUSTARD SAUCE

60g (2oz) butter

2 tbsp plain flour

juice of ½ lemon

1 tbsp Dijon mustard, or to taste

PREPARE THE MACKEREL AND COATING

1 **Rinse the mackerel** and pat dry. Beat the eggs in a dish. Sift the flour on to a sheet of baking parchment. With your fingers, combine the rolled oats, salt and pepper on a second sheet of baking parchment.

COAT THE FISH

2 **Turn each mackerel** fillet in the flour to coat evenly.

3 **Dip the mackerel** in the egg, then coat in oats. Set aside on a plate.

MAKE THE SAUCE

4 **Melt a third of the butter.** Add the flour and whisk to a paste until foaming. Whisk in 300ml (½ pint) boiling water. The sauce will thicken. Return to the heat and whisk for 1 minute. Remove from the heat, add the remaining butter, and whisk. Add the lemon juice and mustard and season.

FRY THE MACKEREL

5 **Line a baking sheet** with kitchen paper. Heat the oil in a large frying pan. Add half the fish and cook for 2–3 minutes on each side, until crisp and golden. Transfer to the baking sheet and keep warm while you cook the remaining fish. Serve with lemon wedges, watercress, and the sauce.

Tex-Mex chicken

A MEAL IN ITSELF. Tortilla chips are the best accompaniment. This is great to make on a warm summer evening after a hard day; the crisp, fresh flavours will lift the spirits wonderfully. It takes next to no time to whip up, especially as it contains cooked chicken, and is great for using up leftovers.

SERVES
SERVES 4-6

PREP
20-25 MINS

COOK
NONE

Ingredients

FOR THE DRESSING

4 tbsp red wine vinegar

2 tsp Dijon mustard

½ tsp salt

¼ tsp pepper

175ml (6fl oz) vegetable oil

leaves from 3 tarragon sprigs, finely chopped

FOR THE SALAD

500g (1lb 2oz) cooked skinless, boneless chicken, sliced

1 shallot, finely chopped

500g (1lb 2oz) large cos or Little Gem lettuce, sliced

2 large tomatoes, sliced

175g (6oz) drained canned sweetcorn

1 red pepper, cored, seeded, and diced

1-2 chillies, finely chopped, to taste

MAKE THE VINAIGRETTE AND DRESS THE SALAD

1 **Put the vinegar**, mustard, salt, and pepper in a small bowl and whisk. Add the oil in a thin stream, whisking constantly so the dressing emulsifies and thickens slightly.

2 **Stir the tarragon** into the dressing and taste for seasoning. Combine the chicken and shallot in a large bowl with 3-4 tbsp of the dressing. Put the lettuce in another large bowl. Add 3-4 tbsp of the dressing and toss.

ASSEMBLE THE SALAD

3 **Arrange the lettuce** on individual plates and mound the chicken on top. Arrange the tomatoes around the edges of the plates and spoon the sweetcorn on top.

4 **Scatter the red pepper** on top of the chicken and drizzle over the remaining vinaigrette. With a fork, sprinkle lightly with the chopped chilli and serve.

Saltimbocca of salmon

A VARIATION on the traditional veal dish (see p253), slices of salmon are marinated in olive oil and herbs (do so as you walk in the door), wrapped around succulent smoked salmon, and cooked to beautiful, toothsome bundles.

SERVES
SERVES 4-6

PREP
20-25 MINS
PLUS MARINATING

COOK
1-2 MINS

Ingredients

FOR THE SALTIMBOCCA

1kg (2¼lb) fresh salmon fillet, with skin

5-7 basil sprigs

250g (9oz) sliced smoked salmon

45g (1½oz) butter

salt and pepper

FOR THE MARINADE

juice of ½ lemon

175ml (6fl oz) olive oil

3-4 thyme sprigs

2 bay leaves

FOR THE TOMATO-BASIL GARNISH

4 tomatoes, total weight about 625g (1lb 6oz)

small bunch of basil

2 tbsp olive oil

pinch of granulated sugar

PREPARE AND MARINATE THE SALMON

1 **Rinse the salmon** and pat dry with kitchen paper. If necessary, pull out any pin bones with tweezers. With the tail facing away from you and working towards it, use a filleting knife to cut 12 diagonal slices, as thin and even as possible. Leave the skin behind.

2 **Put the lemon juice** and oil in a shallow dish. Strip the thyme leaves from the stalks and add to the dish with pepper. Crush the bay leaves into the dish.

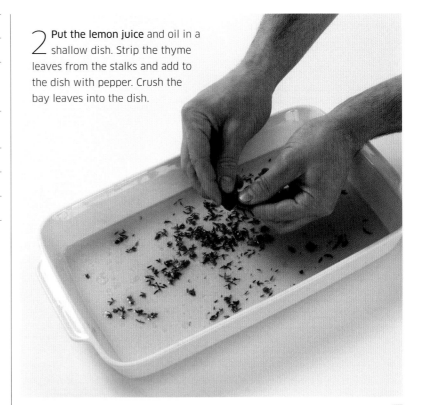

3 **Add the salmon slices,** cover and marinate in the refrigerator for 1 hour.

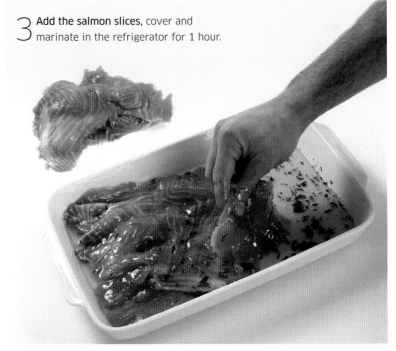

MAKE THE TOMATO-BASIL GARNISH

4 **Cut the cores** from the tomatoes. Cut an "x" in their bases. Immerse in boiling water for 8-15 seconds, until the skin starts to split, then plunge into cold water. Peel, cut in half and squeeze out the seeds, Chop the flesh.

5 **Strip the basil leaves** from their stalks and coarsely chop. Mix the tomatoes with the oil and basil and season, adding sugar to taste. Let stand to marinate at room temperature for 30-60 minutes.

ROLL AND COOK THE SALTIMBOCCA

6 **Lift the salmon slices** from the marinade and pat dry with kitchen paper. Strip the basil leaves from their stalks. Cut the smoked salmon slices into pieces the same size as the fresh salmon.

7 **Arrange a piece of smoked salmon** on top of each of the fresh salmon slices. placing it as centrally as possible so the flavours of fresh and smoked salmon are consistent throughout each bite. Put a basil leaf in the centre of each piece of smoked salmon. Roll up the saltimbocca as you would a Swiss roll, staring from the longest side and progressing carefully and gently, and secure shut with a cocktail stick.

8 **Heat the butter** in a frying pan and add a batch of the salmon saltimbocca, leaving space around each piece. Cook over high heat, turning, until lightly browned on all sides. It should take 1-2 minutes, but watch carefully; you must not overcook the salmon or it will lose its vibrant and tempting juiciness.

9 **Remove from the pan** and keep warm while you cook the remaining saltimbocca. Remove the cocktail sticks. Arrange the salmon rolls on warmed plates and serve with the tomato-basil garnish.

Curried chicken with saffron rice

AN UNUSUAL DRESSING thickened with cottage cheese and flavoured with chutney. Saffron rice provides a brilliant background. The curry dressing, saffron rice, tomatoes and vinaigrette can all be prepared 1 day ahead, and kept covered, separately, in the refrigerator, so the dish is very quick and easy to whip up in the evening.

SERVES	**PREP**	**COOK**
SERVES 4-6	25-35 MINS	20-30 MINS

Ingredients

FOR THE SAFFRON RICE

large pinch of saffron

300g (10oz) long-grain rice

3 celery sticks, thinly sliced

FOR THE CURRY DRESSING

90ml (3fl oz) vegetable oil

1 small onion, finely chopped

1 tbsp curry powder

4 tbsp tomato juice

4 tbsp red wine vinegar

2 tsp apricot jam

2 tbsp lemon juice

250g (9oz) cottage cheese

salt and pepper

FOR THE CHICKEN

1.8kg (4lb) whole cooked chicken

3 tbsp lemon juice

175ml (6fl oz) vegetable oil

500g (1lb 2oz) cherry tomatoes

½ tsp paprika

PREPARE THE SAFFRON RICE

1 **Put the saffron** and a pinch of salt in a large saucepan along with 600ml (1 pint) water. Bring to a boil and simmer for 2 minutes. Stir in the rice and bring back to a boil. Cover and simmer for 15-20 minutes, until tender. Let cool for 5-10 minutes, then taste for seasoning. Set aside.

MAKE THE CURRY DRESSING

2 **Heat 1 tbsp oil** in a small saucepan over moderate heat. Add the onion and sauté for about 2 minutes, until soft but not brown, stirring occasionally. Add the curry powder and cook gently for 2 minutes, stirring.

3 **Add the tomato juice** and vinegar and simmer until reduced by half. Stir in the jam. Let the mixture cool, then transfer to a food processor or blender. Blend until smooth. Add the lemon juice and cottage cheese and blend until smooth. With the blades turning, pour in the remaining oil. Taste for seasoning.

PREPARE THE CHICKEN

4 **Cut down** between the leg and body of the chicken. Twist the leg sharply outwards to break the joint, then cut through it and pull the leg from the body. Repeat for the other leg. Slit along one side of the breastbone. Using your fingers and a knife, loosen the breast meat and remove in one piece. Repeat on the other side.

5 **With your fingers**, pull away the wishbone and the meat adhering to it. Pull off any remaining meat from the chicken carcass. Pull off the skin from the breasts and discard it. Pull the meat into shreds with your fingers and pile on a dish.

6 **Using your fingers** and the point of the knife, tear and cut the meat from the leg bones. Trim away the tendons and discard the skin. Shred the meat with your fingers and add to the plate. There should be about 500g (1lb 2oz).

FINISH THE RICE

7 **Stir the celery** gently into the cooled saffron rice, to give it a nice crisp and varied texture. Transfer the rice to a bowl. Make a vinaigrette: put the lemon juice, salt, and pepper in a small bowl and whisk in the oil in a thin stream, so the dressing emulsifies and thickens slightly. Pour three-quarters of the vinaigrette on to the rice and toss together gently until it is evenly coated in the dressing.

8 **Mix the cherry tomatoes** gently with the remaining vinaigrette dressing. In another bowl, toss the chicken with half the curry dressing. Pile the saffron rice in the centre of a platter and arrange the chicken evenly on top. Sprinkle with paprika and garnish with cherry tomatoes to add a juicy fruitiness. Serve the remaining curry dressing alongside, for your diners to help themselves.

 VARIATION: Chicken with tarragon dressing and rice

A natural pairing.

1 Prepare the chicken as directed in the main recipe, cutting the chicken into slices rather than tearing it into shreds. Prepare the rice salad as directed, but omit the saffron.

2 Replace the curry dressing with this dressing: purée 250g (9oz) cottage cheese in a food processor or blender with 1 tbsp tarragon vinegar. Chop the leaves from 1 bunch of tarragon and stir it into the puréed cottage cheese. Season to taste.

3 Arrange the rice and chicken on individual plates and garnish with a few more tarragon sprigs.

Sautéed liver and onions

THIS DELICIOUS RECIPE is a classic Venetian dish. The onions can be cooked the night before if you want to get ahead, as it is important they are properly caramelized and that takes a little patience. However, it's easy enough to fry onions while you relax with a glass of wine, and talk to your family.

SERVES	PREP	COOK
SERVES 6	15–20 MINS	35–40 MINS

Ingredients

FOR THE LIVER AND ONIONS

90ml (3fl oz) olive oil

1kg (2¼lb) large onions, sliced

salt and pepper

750g (1lb 10oz) calf's liver

FOR THE MASHED POTATOES

635g (1lb 6oz) potatoes

4 tbsp milk

60g (2oz) butter

PREPARE THE ONIONS

1 **Heat two-thirds** of the oil in a frying pan. Add the onions with a little salt and pepper, and cover with foil. Cook over low heat, stirring occasionally, for 25–30 minutes, until very soft.

2 **Remove the foil** from the onions, increase the heat to medium-high, and cook, stirring constantly, for 5–7 minutes, until golden and caramelized but not burned. Transfer to a bowl with a slotted spoon, leaving any excess oil in the pan.

PREPARE THE MASHED POTATOES

3 **Meanwhile,** peel the potatoes and cut into pieces. Put in a saucepan of salted water, cover, and bring to a boil. Simmer for 15–20 minutes, until tender. Drain the potatoes thoroughly. Return them to the pan, and mash them with a potato masher.

4 **Heat the milk** in a small saucepan. Add the butter, salt, and pepper and beat until mixed. Gradually add the hot milk to the potatoes, beating until light and fluffy. Taste for seasoning and keep warm.

PREPARE THE LIVER

5 **Slice the liver** about 5mm (¼in) thick, and season. Add the remaining oil to the frying pan, and heat over high heat. Add half the liver and cook for 45–60 seconds on each side, just until browned. It should be pink in the centre. Transfer to a plate and keep warm. Cook the remaining liver.

6 **Return the onions** to the pan with all the liver and stir quickly over high heat for 30–60 seconds, until very hot. Season with salt and pepper. Serve at once, with the mashed potatoes.

Tuna and bacon kebabs

A TART MARINADE sets these off perfectly. This is about the quickest and freshest meal you can make when you get home from work, and is packed with the vitamins that will see you through tomorrow, with none of the heaviness and assorted nasties usually found in a ready-prepared bought dinner.

SERVES	PREP	COOK
SERVES 8	20-25 MINS PLUS MARINATING	10-12 MINS

Ingredients

FOR THE KEBABS

1.25kg (2¾lb) skinned tuna fillet or steak

500g (1lb 2oz) cherry tomatoes

500g (1lb 2oz) streaky bacon rashers

vegetable oil

salt and pepper

FOR THE MARINADE

juice of 2 limes

2 tbsp olive oil

Tabasco sauce

FOR THE SPINACH AND MANGO SALAD

1 ripe mango

juice of 1 lime

¼ tsp Dijon mustard

75ml (2½fl oz) vegetable oil

250g (9oz) baby spinach leaves

PREPARE AND MARINATE THE TUNA

1 Rinse the tuna and pat dry with kitchen paper. Cut into 4cm (1½in) cubes. To make the marinade, whisk the lime juice with the oil, a dash of Tabasco, and a little salt and pepper in a large non-metallic bowl.

2 Add the tuna and toss until the pieces are well coated in the marinade. Cover and marinate for 30-60 minutes, storing in the refrigerator if your kitchen is warm.

PREPARE THE SALAD AND DRESSING

3 Peel the mango and cut off the 'cheeks'. Cut each cheek into neat slices. In a small bowl, whisk the lime juice with the mustard, salt, and pepper. Gradually whisk in the oil so the dressing emulsifies. Taste for seasoning.

ASSEMBLE AND GRILL THE KEBABS

4 Rinse and dry the cherry tomatoes. Cut the bacon rashers in half; each piece should be 6cm (2½in) long. Heat the grill. Soak 8 bamboo skewers in a shallow bowl of water, or brush 8 long metal skewers with oil.

5 Wrap a piece of bacon around each cube of tuna. Thread the fish and tomatoes loosely on to the skewers.

6 Set the kebabs on the grill rack and grill about 7.5cm (3in) from the heat until the bacon is crisp. Turn and repeat. The fish should be rare within; do not overcook or it will be dry.

7 Toss the spinach with most of the dressing and put in a salad bowl. Arrange the mango on top and sprinkle with the remaining dressing. Serve with the tuna kebabs.

Spicy, saucy fish

DELICIOUS WITH POPPADUMS. Serve boiled, aromatic basmati rice on the side. If monkfish proves too expensive, this dish is equally wonderful with grey mullet, huss, or red snapper, all of which are reasonably priced. A satisfying meal for a cold winter's night.

SERVES	PREP	COOK
SERVES 6	30–35 MINS	30–35 MINS

Ingredients

FOR THE SPICY SAUCE

1 apple

30g (1oz) butter

1 onion, finely chopped

1 tsp ground cumin

1 tsp ground coriander

½ tsp ground ginger

½ tsp ground cloves

¼ tsp cayenne pepper or ½ tsp crushed chillies

1½ tbsp cornflour

200ml (7fl oz) coconut milk

150ml (¼ pint) fish stock

FOR THE FISH

1kg (2¼lb) skinned monkfish fillets

4 tbsp vegetable oil

2 onions, thinly sliced

2 tbsp paprika

300ml (½ pint) fish stock

2 x 400g cans tomatoes

6 garlic cloves, finely chopped

4 bay leaves

2 celery sticks, peeled and thinly sliced

2 carrots, thinly sliced

salt and pepper

MAKE THE SPICY SAUCE

1 **Peel and core** the apple, then cut into 1cm (½in) dice. Melt the butter in a saucepan. Add the onion and apple and cook for 3–5 minutes, until soft but not brown.

2 **Add the cumin,** coriander, ginger, cloves and cayenne. Cook, stirring, over low heat, for 2–3 minutes. Put the cornflour in a small bowl. Add 2–3 tbsp of the coconut milk and blend to a smooth paste.

3 **Add the remaining coconut milk** and the stock to the saucepan and bring to a boil. Stir in the cornflour paste; the sauce will thicken at once. Remove from the heat, season to taste and set aside.

PREPARE THE MONKFISH

4 **Cut the membrane** (if any) from the monkfish, then rinse the fish and pat dry with kitchen paper. Cut into 2.5cm (1in) cubes.

COOK THE FISH STEW

5 **Heat the oil** in a casserole. Add the onions and cook for 3–5 minutes, until soft but not brown. Add the paprika and cook for about 1 minute, stirring to combine evenly with the onions.

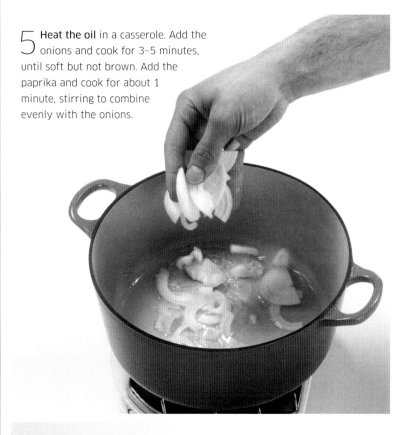

6 **Add the stock,** tomatoes, garlic, bay leaves, celery, and carrots. Season and bring to the boil. Reduce the heat and simmer until the liquid is reduced by a third; it should take 15–20 minutes.

7 **Add the spice sauce** and stir well, then bring back to a boil. Add the fish. Cover and simmer, stirring occasionally, for 12–15 minutes, until the fish flakes easily. Discard the bay leaves and taste for seasoning. Serve in warmed bowls.

 VARIATION: Spicy fish with mixed peppers

There's an added crunch to this version.

1 Make the spicy sauce as directed in the main recipe, omitting the apple. Prepare the vegetables as directed, omitting the carrots and celery. The apple, carrots and celery, which sweeten the main recipe, are replaced in this version with peppers, whose sweetness is tempered with a very slight bitter tang.

2 Cut out the core from 1 green, 1 red, and 1 yellow pepper (or whatever mixture of colours and flavours you prefer), then halve the peppers and scrape out the seeds. Cut away the white ribs from the inside. Set each pepper half cut-side down on a chopping board and press with the heel of your hand to flatten it slightly. Slice it lengthways into even, medium strips. Omit the monkfish. Prepare the same weight of haddock fillets, cutting them into 2.5cm (1in) cubes.

3 Cook the stew as directed, adding the peppers along with the tomatoes (remember that it could take a few minutes more for the peppers to soften fully; check them before you put in the fish). Add the fish and simmer very gently as directed in the main recipe. Snip a few chives and sprinkle over the top to serve.

Minute steak marchand du vin

THIS RECIPE INCLUDES delicious, mild roasted shallots, and garlic. If you omit them, this simplest of dishes takes just 15–20 minutes to make from start to finish. Add the roast alliums on other occasions, when you have more time. The most important piece of equipment to make a good steak is a cast-iron frying or griddle pan, because it distributes the heat evenly, with no hot spots. Cook 1cm (½in) thick individual steaks, rather than a big piece, if you would prefer (don't pound these).

SERVES SERVES 4	**PREP** 15–20 MINS	**COOK** 40–50 MINS

Ingredients

1 large bulb of garlic	250ml (9fl oz) red wine
vegetable oil	leaves from 2–3 thyme sprigs
salt and pepper	leaves from 1 small bunch of parsley, finely chopped
10 small shallots	30g (1oz) butter
750g (1lb 10oz) piece fillet of beef	

ROAST THE GARLIC AND SHALLOTS

1 **Preheat the oven** to 160°C (325°F/Gas 3). To separate the garlic cloves, crush the bulb, pushing down with the heels of your hands to exert pressure from the top. Break the separated garlic cloves apart, discarding the root, and remove any loose skin (or it could burn in the oven), but don't bother to peel them.

2 **Put the garlic cloves** in a small baking dish, add 1 tbsp oil, and sprinkle with salt and pepper. Stir until each garlic clove is evenly coated in oil and seasoning.

3 **Trim the roots,** and remove any papery or loose skin from the shallots, without peeling them. Put the shallots in a second baking dish, setting aside 2 to make the sauce later. Toss them with 2 tbsp oil, salt, and pepper, again ensuring they are evenly covered (any unoiled shallot or garlic skin is far more likely to scorch in the oven, which may risk tainting the flavour of the finished dish).

4 **Transfer the garlic** and shallots to the heated oven, placing them on a shelf towards the top. Roast the garlic for 30–35 minutes, and the shallots for 25–30 minutes, stirring occasionally, until both are sweet and tender. Finely chop the 2 reserved shallots for the sauce.

PREPARE AND FRY THE STEAKS

5 **Trim any fat** from the beef, and cut it into 1cm (½in) steaks, cutting the steaks slightly thicker at the narrower end of the fillet. You should have 8 steaks.

6 **Pound the thicker steaks** with the flat of a knife, so they resemble the larger steaks. Put the steaks on a plate, and sprinkle both sides with salt and pepper.

7 **Heat about 1 tbsp** oil in a heavy-based frying pan. Fry 4 steaks over moderately high heat for 1–2 minutes, until well browned. Turn and fry for 1–2 minutes more. The steaks are done when they yield if pressed with your finger. If firm, they are well done. Keep them warm while you fry the remaining steaks.

FINISH THE DISH

8 **Add the chopped shallots** to the pan and sauté, stirring for 1–2 minutes, until soft but not brown. Add the wine and thyme and bring to a boil, stirring to scrape up all the delicious savoury meat juices. Boil to slightly thicken and concentrate the flavour. It should take 3–5 minutes, and you must work quickly now as you should eat the steaks as soon as possible after cooking. Stir in most of the parsley and taste for seasoning. Add the butter and swirl the sauce, taking the pan on and off the heat, so that the butter thickens the sauce without melting into oil.

9 **Sprinkle the steaks** with the remaining parsley on individual plates. Arrange the garlic and shallots around the steaks for diners to peel themselves; their sweet, soft flesh is delicious when squashed on to pieces of crusty baguette and used as "butter". Serve with salad leaves and well-salted French fries, if you like.

 VARIATION: Minute steak Dijonnaise

A tangy sauce with white wine, tangy Dijon mustard, and cream.

1 Omit the roasted shallots and garlic. Put 20–24 pickling onions in a bowl, cover with hot water, and let stand for 2 minutes. Drain and peel with a small knife, leaving a little of the root to hold the onion together. Roast as for the shallots, sprinkling them with 1 tbsp sugar halfway through.

2 Chop 2 shallots. Prepare and fry the steaks as directed. Stir 250ml (9fl oz) dry white wine into the pan, and boil for 2–3 minutes, until reduced by half. Take the pan from the heat and stir in 1 tbsp Dijon mustard, and 2–3 tbsp double cream, omitting the butter. Taste for seasoning.

3 Put 1 or 2 steaks on each plate. Coat with the sauce, set the onions on the side, decorated with parsley sprigs, and serve with homemade game chips, if you like.

Grilled chicken thighs in yogurt

A MIDDLE EASTERN-STYLE DISH. Marinate the chicken in the morning for dinner. Yogurt plays two roles in this recipe: first it tenderizes the chicken; then it thickens and enriches the sauce. This can also be cooked on the barbecue. Serve it hot or at room temperature.

SERVES
SERVES 4

PREP
20-25 MINS
PLUS MARINATING

COOK
15-20 MINS

Ingredients

FOR THE CHICKEN

8 chicken thighs

250ml (9fl oz) plain yogurt

salt and pepper

vegetable oil for grill rack

FOR THE CORIANDER SAUCE

2 tbsp vegetable oil

1 onion, chopped

2 tbsp ground coriander

2 garlic cloves, finely chopped

250ml (9fl oz) plain yogurt

a few coriander sprigs

125ml (4fl oz) soured cream

PREPARE THE CHICKEN

1 **Put the chicken thighs** in a large bowl and pour over the plain yogurt. Season with salt and pepper to taste. Turn the thighs until well coated with yogurt, then cover the bowl tightly and refrigerate for 3-8 hours. Try not to leave it much longer, or it will have a woolly texture.

2 **Heat the grill.** Brush the grill rack with oil. Lift the chicken out of the bowl. Scrape off and discard the yogurt. Dry the chicken with kitchen paper, then arrange the thighs on the grill rack.

COOK THE CHICKEN

3 **Grill the chicken,** about 7.5cm (3in) from the heat, for 8-10 minutes, until very brown. Turn and continue grilling until the pieces are very brown and no pink juice runs out when they are pierced. It should take 7-10 minutes longer. Meanwhile, make the sauce.

MAKE THE CORIANDER SAUCE

4 **Heat the oil** in a saucepan and sauté the onion until soft and starting to brown. Add the ground coriander and garlic and continue cooking for 2-3 minutes, stirring constantly. Purée the onion mixture with the yogurt in a food processor. Add the coriander sprigs and process just until it is chopped.

5 **Return to the saucepan.** Pour in the soured cream, then season. Heat the sauce, stirring constantly. Taste for seasoning and keep warm. Do not let it boil or it will separate. Arrange 2 chicken thighs on each warmed plate and spoon the sauce around them.

Sautéed trout with hazelnuts

THE CRUNCHY TOPPING makes a delicious contrast to the soft-textured fish. This is about as quick as cooking gets, and produces a fresh, satisfying, and wholesome family dish. Serve with a rice pilaf (see p302) for a heartier meal. Mackerel would work equally well in this recipe, and is cheaper.

SERVES	PREP	COOK
SERVES 4	20–25 MINS	10–15 MINS

Ingredients

4 x 300g (10oz) trout, cleaned and scaled

60g (2oz) hazelnuts

2 lemons

20–30g (¾–1oz) plain flour

salt and pepper

125g (4½oz) butter

leaves from 5–7 parsley sprigs, chopped

PREPARE THE TROUT

1 **Cut the fins** from the trout, and trim the tails. Rinse inside and out, and pat dry with kitchen paper.

2 **Preheat the oven** to 180°C (350°F/Gas 4). Spread the hazelnuts on a baking sheet, and toast them for 8–10 minutes, until browned. While still hot, rub in a tea towel to remove the skins. Set aside.

3 **Trim the ends** from one lemon, halve and cut into thin semi-circles. Peel the second lemon, being sure to remove all the white pith, and cut into thin rounds. Remove any pips.

COOK THE TROUT

4 **Put the flour** on a large plate and season. Coat each trout in flour, patting to coat evenly. Heat half the butter in a large frying pan, until foaming. Add two of the trout, and brown over medium heat for 2–3 minutes.

5 **Turn and continue cooking** over low heat for 3–5 minutes. When ready, the trout will be browned, and the flesh will flake easily when tested with a fork. Keep warm while you cook the remaining fish in the rest of the butter.

FINISH THE DISH

6 **Add the hazelnuts** to the pan, and sauté over medium heat for 3–4 minutes, until golden brown, stirring. Stir in most of the parsley. Serve the fish on warmed plates, and spoon over the hazelnuts. Decorate with the lemon semi-circles and rounds, and sprinkle with the remaining parsley.

Food to share

Something special for friends and family

Lamb korma

FRAGRANT AND LUXURIOUS. A korma is a mild Indian curry. The flavour will improve if the dish is made up to 3 days ahead and kept, covered, in the refrigerator. The sauce may thicken, so add water when reheating, if necessary.

SERVES	PREP	COOK
SERVES 4-6	25-30 MINS	2½-3 HRS

Ingredients

FOR THE SPICE MIXTURE

5 cardamom pods

1 cinnamon stick

2 dried red chillies, deseeded

5 cloves

7 black peppercorns

2 tsp ground cumin

1 tsp ground mace

1 tsp paprika

FOR THE KORMA

125ml (4fl oz) vegetable oil

6 onions, sliced

2.5cm (1in) piece fresh root ginger, finely chopped

2 garlic cloves, finely chopped

1.4kg (3lb) boned lamb shoulder, in 2.5cm (1in) dice

250ml (9fl oz) plain yogurt

250ml (9fl oz) double cream

salt

leaves from 3-5 coriander sprigs, chopped

PREPARE THE SPICE MIXTURE

1 **Crush the cardamom pods** with the flat of a small knife, and extract the seeds with the tip.

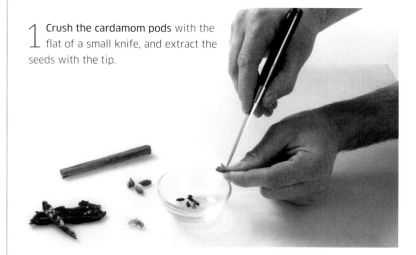

2 **Crush the cinnamon stick** with the end of a rolling pin. Put the chillies, cardamom seeds, cinnamon, cloves, and peppercorns in a mortar and crush them as finely as possible with the pestle. Stir in the cumin, mace, and paprika.

COOK THE KORMA

3 **Heat the oil** in a casserole. Add the onions and cook over low heat, stirring occasionally, for 20 minutes, until soft and golden brown. Stir in the ginger and garlic and cook for 2 minutes, until softened and fragrant.

4 **Add the spice mixture** and cook, stirring constantly, for 1-2 minutes, until thoroughly combined. Add the lamb and cook, stirring and tossing constantly, so it absorbs the flavour of the spices, for about 5 minutes.

5 **Add half the yogurt**, half the double cream, and a little salt, and bring almost to a boil. Reduce the heat, cover, and cook over very low heat for 2-2½ hours, until the meat is tender enough to crush with your finger. Stir occasionally. If the liquid evaporates too quickly, add a little water.

FINISH THE DISH

6 **Stir the remaining yogurt** and cream into the lamb. Taste for seasoning and heat until very hot. Transfer to warmed plates and sprinkle with coriander. Serve with rice.

Moroccan chicken tagine

ANY HEAVY CASSEROLE IS JUST AS GOOD if you don't have a tagine (an attractive North African earthenware vessel with a conical lid). If you don't want to joint the chicken yourself, simply buy it already jointed. Bear in mind that dark-meat chicken - such as leg or thigh pieces - take best to the long-cooking treatment they get in this recipe. Serve with couscous for true authenticity.

SERVES	PREP	COOK
SERVES 4	10-15 MINS	1½ HOURS

Ingredients

1.5kg (3lb 3oz) chicken	400g (14oz) can tomatoes
large pinch of saffron	2 tbsp honey
6 onions	2 tsp ground cinnamon
75g (2½oz) dried apricots	1 tsp ground ginger
	leaves from a few parsley sprigs, chopped
	salt and pepper
	125ml (4fl oz) olive oil

JOINT THE CHICKEN

1 **Cut down between the leg joint** and body on one side. Twist the bone sharply outwards to break the joint, then cut through it and pull the leg from the body. Repeat this procedure for the other leg.

2 **Slit the chicken closely** along both sides of the breastbone to loosen the meat, then split the breastbone with poultry shears.

3 **Turn the bird over** on to its breast and cut the rib bones and backbone from the breast in 1 piece, leaving the wing joints attached to the breast. The 2 breasts of the bird are now divided.

PREPARE THE INGREDIENTS

4 **Put the saffron** into a small bowl. Spoon over 3-4 tbsp boiling water. Set aside to soak. Thinly slice 4 of the onions and finely chop the remaining 2 onions. Cut the dried apricots into chunks using kitchen scissors or a knife.

COOK THE CHICKEN

5 **Preheat the oven** to 180°C (350°F/Gas 4). Put the chicken in a tagine or casserole. Cover with the sliced onions, then the tomatoes. Mix the chopped onions, saffron and its liquid, dried apricots, honey, cinnamon, ginger, parsley, salt, and pepper in a bowl. Add the oil. Spoon the mixture over the chicken.

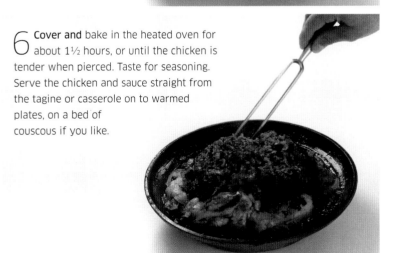

6 **Cover and** bake in the heated oven for about 1½ hours, or until the chicken is tender when pierced. Taste for seasoning. Serve the chicken and sauce straight from the tagine or casserole on to warmed plates, on a bed of couscous if you like.

Sea bass with herb butter sauce

AN IMPRESSIVE DISH to share. A herb butter sauce is a useful thing to know how to cook, as it makes an unctuous, rich emulsion that is an excellent embellishment to quick-cooked fish fillets. This recipe will work equally well with whole salmon trout or sea bream, but either way is one to keep for an auspicious occasion. It is important to keep a close eye on the roasting fish, as it is all too easy to overcook, which will spoil the firm texture.

SERVES	PREP	COOK
SERVES 4	40-45 MINS	30-40 MINS

Ingredients

FOR THE HERB BUTTER SAUCE

1 bunch of watercress

8 spinach leaves

leaves from 10-12 parsley sprigs

leaves from 10-12 chervil sprigs

1 lemon

1 garlic clove, peeled

2 anchovy fillets

2 tsp capers, drained

1 small gherkin

75g (2½oz) butter

3 tbsp olive oil

1 tsp Dijon mustard

FOR THE FISH

1 whole sea bass, weighing about 2kg (4½lb), cleaned and scaled

3-5 thyme sprigs

30g (1oz) butter

125ml (4fl oz) dry white wine

salt and pepper

MAKE THE SAUCE

1 **Set aside** half the watercress to decorate the finished dish. Bring a saucepan of well-salted water to a boil. Add the watercress, spinach, parsley, and chervil, and simmer for just 1-2 minutes, until tender. Drain well in a colander.

2 **Rinse the greens** with cold water until cool enough to handle, and drain again thoroughly. Squeeze the leaves in your fist, to remove all the excess water.

3 **Cut the lemon** lengthways in half. Set one half, flat-side down, on a chopping board, cut it across into thin slices, and reserve them for cooking the fish (discard the end slices, which will mostly be white pith). Squeeze all the juice from the remaining lemon half.

4 **In a food processor,** work the garlic, anchovy fillets, capers, and gherkin until finely and evenly chopped, with no large lumps. Add the butter, piece by piece, and work the mixture to a smooth purée. Tip in the greens and work again, until finely chopped.

5 **With the blade** turning, slowly pour in the olive oil. Add the lemon juice, mustard, and salt and pepper, and work again briefly. Taste for seasoning, then transer to a serving dish and set aside.

ROAST THE SEA BASS

6 **Preheat the oven** to 190°C (375°F/Gas 5). Cut the fins from the sea bass with scissors. Rinse thoroughly inside and out with cold water, and pat dry with kitchen paper.

7 **Slash the fish** diagonally 3-4 times on each side. The slashes should be about 1cm (½in) deep for heat to penetrate. Set the sea bass in a roasting tin, and tuck a sprig of thyme and a slice of lemon, into each slash.

8 Dot with the butter, and sprinkle with white wine, salt, and pepper. Roast, basting occasionally, until it just flakes easily when tested with a fork, and is no longer translucent in the centre. It could take 30 minutes, but check it, so it does not overcook. Remove the head to serve, with the sauce.

 VARIATION: Loire sea bass

Beurre blanc originated in Brittany, near the River Loire.

1 Omit the herb butter sauce. Roast 2 cleaned and scaled sea bass (each weighing about 1kg/2¼lb) as directed in the main recipe, replacing the thyme with an equal amount of tarragon. It will take 25–30 minutes, but check them often so that they do not overcook.

2 Meanwhile, dice 2 shallots. In a small heavy-based pan, combine 3 tbsp each of white wine vinegar and dry white wine with the shallots, then boil until reduced to about 1 tbsp. It will only take 3–5 minutes. Add 1 tbsp double cream, bring to a boil, and reduce the sauce again until only about 1 tbsp remains.

3 Cut 250g (9oz) cold butter into small, even pieces. Whisk the butter into the shallots, 1 piece at a time, waiting until the previous amount has melted before adding more. The sauce will emulsify and thicken slightly. Taste for seasoning. Cut each fish in half and remove the head and tail. Serve with the sauce on the side.

Coq au vin

THE FRENCH USE A BOILING FOWL or, best of all, the traditional cock bird. The more mature the chicken, the better the dish. The flavour will vary with the wine you use: a Rhône wine gives a rich dark sauce; a Loire wine a fruitier dish; a Burgundy makes a full-bodied sauce. You need to start the recipe 1 day ahead, to allow time for marinating.

SERVES	PREP	COOK
SERVES 4-6	30 MINS PLUS MARINATING	1½-1¾ HRS

Ingredients

FOR THE MARINADE

1 onion, thinly sliced

1 celery stick, thinly sliced

1 carrot, thinly sliced

1 garlic clove, peeled

6 black peppercorns

375ml (13fl oz) red wine

2 tbsp olive oil

FOR THE STEW

2kg (4½lb) chicken

1 tbsp vegetable oil

15g (½oz) butter

125g (4½oz) piece of bacon, diced

18-20 baby onions

250g (9oz) mushrooms, quartered

3 tbsp flour

500ml (16fl oz) chicken stock or water

1 garlic clove, finely chopped

2 shallots, finely chopped

1 bouquet garni

salt and pepper

JOINT AND MARINATE THE CHICKEN

1 **Put the onion,** celery, carrot, garlic clove, and peppercorns in a saucepan. Pour in the red wine and bring everything to a boil. Simmer for about 5 minutes, so all the flavours meld well together, then allow this marinade to cool completely. Putting it in a shallow dish with maximum surface area will mean the marinade cools far more rapidly.

2 **Joint the chicken** into eight pieces (see p184), or buy a pre-jointed chicken if you prefer. The chicken must be on the bone, and at least half of it should be dark meat, for the best results. Boneless white meat chicken pieces will disintegrate during cooking, and those that remain whole will become stringy, tough and dry, so save those chicken breasts for a more suitable, quick-cooked recipe. Put all the chicken pieces in a large bowl, pour over the cooled marinade, then spoon the olive oil over the top. Cover the bowl tightly with clingfilm and leave the chicken to marinate for 12-18 hours in the refrigerator, turning occasionally to redistribute the marinade and ensure all the pieces of chicken marinate evenly.

SAUTÉ THE CHICKEN

3 **Remove the chicken pieces** from the marinade, and pat them dry thoroughly with kitchen paper. Strain the marinade through the sieve over a bowl, and reserve both the liquid and the vegetables.

4 **Heat the oil** and butter in the casserole until foaming, add the bacon and fry until browned, and the fat has rendered. Remove the bacon with a slotted spoon.

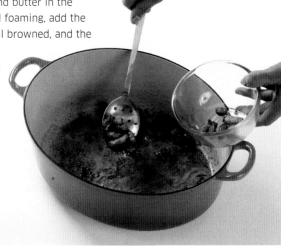

5 **Add the chicken** to the casserole, skin side down, and cook for about 10 minutes, until well browned. Turn and brown the other side, then remove.

PREPARE THE GARNISH

6 Put the baby onions in a bowl, cover with hot water and leave for 2 minutes. Remove the onions and peel them. Add the baby onions to the casserole, and sauté lightly until browned. Lift out with a slotted spoon and reserve. Add the mushrooms and sauté for 2-3 minutes, until tender. Remove the mushrooms with the slotted spoon and reserve.

FINISH THE COOKING

7 Discard all but about 2 tbsp of fat from the casserole, and add the reserved vegetables from the marinade. Cook over very low heat for 5 minutes, until softened. Sprinkle the flour over the vegetables and cook, stirring, for 2-3 minutes, until lightly browned.

8 Stir in the reserved marinade, stock, garlic, shallots, bouquet garni, salt, and pepper. Heat until boiling, stirring well. Replace the chicken, cover and simmer over low heat for 45-60 minutes, until just tender.

9 Transfer the chicken to a plate and keep warm in a low oven while you finish the dish. Pour the sauce into a bowl and scoop out and reserve a few attractive pieces of carrot. Wipe out the casserole with kitchen paper and add the baby onions. Strain the sauce over them through a sieve, pressing down with a small ladle or spoon to extract the maximum flavour and liquid from the vegetables.

10 Simmer over low heat for 5-10 minutes, until the baby onions are almost tender. Add the mushrooms and reserved carrots and continue to simmer for 2-3 minutes longer, until the sauce is reduced, and lightly coats the back of a spoon. (Draw your finger down the back of the spoon; it should leave a clear trail through the sauce.) Taste for seasoning, and adjust it if necessary.

11 Add the chicken pieces and bacon to the sauce and reheat gently for 3-4 minutes. Spoon the chicken and sauce from the casserole on to warmed plates or shallow bowls. Serve with steamed baby potatoes, or potatoes fried in butter and oil for a richer accompaniment. Crusty bread on the side is great for soaking up the delicious wine sauce.

Rack of lamb with parsley crumb

THE BREADCRUMBS GIVE A CRISP FINISH to this dish. A rack of lamb is among the more expensive cuts, so be sure to cook it correctly. Medium is really the best way, to keep the meat wonderfully juicy and accentuate the deep, herby flavour. Look for a small joint with creamy fat and a good dark colour to the meat, and be sure that the butcher has trimmed off the chine bone (backbone) that keeps the rack together; it is almost impossible to do it at home without butchers' knives (and muscles).

SERVES	PREP	COOK
SERVES 4	35-40 MINS	25-30 MINS

Ingredients

FOR THE LAMB

2 racks of lamb, weighing 750g-1kg (1lb 10oz-2¼lb) each, chine bones removed

2 garlic cloves

2 tbsp olive oil

4 slices white bread

45g (1½oz) butter

leaves from 1 small bunch of parsley, chopped

salt and pepper

FOR THE GRAVY

125ml (4fl oz) white wine

250ml (9fl oz) lamb, beef, or chicken stock

PREPARE THE RACKS OF LAMB

1 **Set a rack of lamb** on a chopping board, ribs upwards, and, with a sharp knife, cut out any sinew lying under the ribs. Turn the rack over. Cut away the small crescent of cartilage at one end.

2 **Make a small incision** under the thin layer of skin covering the fat. Using your fingers, pull off the skin. If you can't get a good grip, use a clean tea towel to help. Score through the fat and meat down to the rib bones, about 5cm (2in) from the ends of the bones.

3 **Turn the rack over.** Place it over the edge of the board and score down to the bone, about 5cm (2in) from the ends of the bones.

4 **Cut out the meat** between the bones, using the point of a knife. Scrape the bones clean. Be sure to scrape away all skin, or it will spoil the appearance of the roasted rack. Repeat for the second piece of meat.

ROAST THE LAMB

5 **Preheat the oven** to 230°C (450°F/Gas 8). Peel the garlic cloves with your fingers, then cut each into 4-5 thin slivers. Make several incisions in the lamb with the point of a knife, and push in the garlic.

6 **Transfer the racks** to a roasting tin, ribs downwards. Wrap the bones in foil to prevent them from burning. Spoon the oil over the lamb, and sprinkle with salt and pepper. Roast in the heated oven for 25-30 minutes, basting once or twice with the juices in the roasting tin. The meat will shrink away from the bones a little.

7 **Test the lamb** with a metal skewer: when inserted for 30 seconds, it will feel warm to the touch when withdrawn. A meat thermometer should register 60°C (140°F). This will give medium meat.

MAKE THE BREADCRUMB CRUST

8 **Trim the crusts** from the bread, and work the slices in a food processor to form crumbs. Melt the butter in a frying pan, add the breadcrumbs and cook, stirring, until just golden, 2-3 minutes. Stir in the parsley and season.

MAKE THE GRAVY

9 **When the lamb is cooked** to your taste, transfer the racks to a chopping board. Discard the foil used to cover the bones. Insulate the racks with more foil, and set aside to rest. This allows all the juices to flow back evenly through the meat, giving juicier lamb. Heat the grill.

10 **Discard the fat** from the roasting tin. Add the wine and boil until reduced by half, stirring to dissolve the roasting juices from the bottom of the tin. Add the stock, and boil for 5-7 minutes, until the gravy is well flavoured. Season to taste. Strain and keep warm until ready to serve. You can stir in 1-2 tsp cornflour, mixed with cold water until smooth, if you want a thicker gravy, though this thin sauce is more elegant.

FINISH THE DISH

11 **Press the breadcrumbs** on to the top surface of the lamb, and baste with the roasting juices. Grill, breadcrumb side up, until lightly browned. It should take 1-2 minutes, but watch that the breadcrumb coating does not scorch. Carve, and serve the gravy on the side.

Szechuan pepper chicken

A DISTANT COUSIN OF STEAK AU POIVRE (see p238) with aromatic, hot Szechuan pepper. This spice is a fabulous addition to your kitchen cupboard; its heat is not overpowering, but it does give a strangely pleasing tingling sensation to the mouth and lips. You'll find this recipe worryingly addictive...

SERVES	PREP	COOK
SERVES 4	20-25 MINS	40-50 MINS

Ingredients

30g (1oz) Szechuan pepper

1.5kg (3lb 3oz) chicken, jointed into 6 pieces

1 onion

1 tbsp vegetable oil

15g (½oz) butter

250ml (8fl oz) chicken stock

125ml (4fl oz) double cream

COAT THE CHICKEN

1 Toast the Szechuan pepper in a small dry pan over very low heat for 3–5 minutes, shaking until it smells aromatic. Put the pepper in a plastic bag and crush finely with a rolling pin (or crush in a mortar and pestle). Coat the chicken pieces with the pepper, patting to coat evenly. Set aside.

CHOP THE ONION

2 Peel the onion, leaving on the root to hold it together. Cut in half and lay one half on a chopping board. Make a series of horizontal cuts from the stalk to the root (cut just to the root of the onion but not through it).

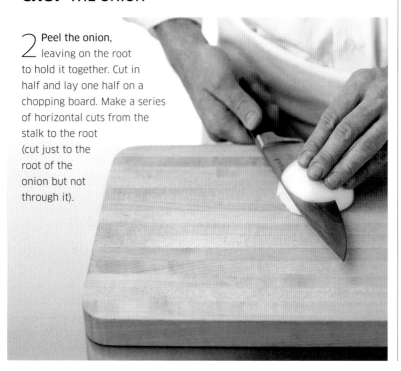

3 **Make** a series of lengthways vertical cuts, cutting just to the root but not through it. Try to tuck your fingertips under and use your knuckles to guide the blade.

4 **Slice** the onion across into fine dice, again keeping your fingers slightly tucked under to avoid any cuts.

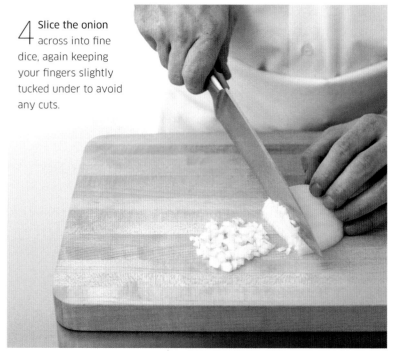

SAUTÉ THE CHICKEN

5 **Heat the oil** and butter in a sauté pan over moderate heat until foaming. Add the chicken legs, skin side down, and sauté for about 5 minutes, until they begin to brown. Add the breast pieces and continue cooking gently for about 10-15 minutes longer, until very brown. Turn and brown the other side.

6 **Push the chicken** to one side of the pan and add the onion to the other. Stir, scraping the pan, and sauté for about 3 minutes, until soft but not brown. Spread out the chicken again and add half the stock. Cover and cook for 15-25 minutes, until tender.

7 **To check if the chicken is cooked,** pierce the meat with a 2-pronged fork or the tip of a knife. The juices should run clear. If some pieces cook before others, remove them from the pan and keep warm.

MAKE THE SAUCE

8 **Remove all the chicken pieces** from the pan and keep warm in a very low oven, covered loosely with aluminium foil to keep in as much of the moisture as possible. Add the remaining stock to the pan, increase the heat to very high and boil the pan juices, stirring so they don't catch on the base of the pan, until they are reduced to a shiny glaze.

9 **Add the cream** and shake the pan gently to mix it well into the sauce, then bring to the boil once more, stirring, for 1–2 minutes, until it tastes rich and has slightly thickened. Taste for seasoning. Return all the chicken pieces to the pan and heat through gently for 1-2 minutes until piping hot and well combined with the sauce. Serve with a mixture of wild and white rices, and sprinkle with very finely sliced spring onion, if liked.

Sweet-sour duck with cherries

TART CHERRIES ARE KEY to this dish from Limousin, in central France, where cherries grow wild in the hedgerows. A mixture of caramel and red wine, added to the pan at the end of cooking, lends the sweet-sour flavour to the wonderful cherry sauce.

SERVES	PREP	COOK
SERVES 2-3	30-35 MINS	1¼-1½ HRS

Ingredients

1 duck, weighing about 1.8kg (4lb)

salt and pepper

1 tbsp vegetable oil

60g (2oz) granulated sugar

75ml (2½fl oz) red wine vinegar

375ml (13fl oz) rich chicken stock

375g (13oz) tart cherries, stoned

parsley sprigs, to serve (optional)

TRUSS THE DUCK

1 **Wipe the inside of the duck** with kitchen paper, and season inside and out. Pull off and discard any loose bits of fat. With a small knife, remove the wishbone to make the duck easier to carve later.

2 **Set the duck breast-side up.** Push the legs back and down. Push a trussing needle into the flesh at the knee joint, through the bird and out, through the other knee joint.

3 **Turn the duck** over. Pull the neck skin over the neck cavity, and tuck the wing tips over it. Push the needle through one of the wings into the neck skin. Continue under the backbone of the duck, to the other side. Repeat with the second wing.

4 **Turn the duck** on to its side. Pull the ends of the string firmly together, and tie them together securely. Turn the duck breast-side up. Tuck the tail into the cavity of the bird, and fold over the top skin. Push the needle through the skin.

5 **Loop the string** around one of the drumsticks, under the breastbone and over the other drumstick. Tie the ends of string together.

ROAST THE DUCK

6 **Preheat the oven** to 220°C (425°F/Gas 7). Heat the oil in a roasting tin. Set the duck on its side, and roast in the oven for 15 minutes. Turn the duck on to the opposite side and roast for another 15 minutes.

7 **Spoon the fat** from the roasting tin; discard it. Prick the skin all over to release the fat. Reduce the temperature to 190°C (375°F/Gas 5). Turn the duck on to its breast, and roast for 15 minutes longer. Discard any melted fat.

8 **Finally,** set the duck on its back, and continue roasting for 15-20 minutes longer, until the juices run clear. Transfer to a warmed platter, and cover with foil to rest and keep warm.

PREPARE THE CARAMEL VINEGAR SAUCE

9 Put 75ml (2½fl oz) water and the sugar into a small heavy-based saucepan, and heat gently until the sugar is dissolved, stirring occasionally. Increase the heat and boil, without stirring, until the syrup starts to turn golden. Reduce the heat, and cook to a deep golden caramel. Remove from the heat and let the bubbles subside.

10 Pour in the vinegar. Simmer, stirring occasionally, for 3-5 minutes, until the caramel is dissolved and the mixture is reduced by half. Remove from the heat and set aside.

11 In a medium saucepan, combine the caramel vinegar and the stock.

12 **Add the cherries** to the pan, and simmer for 3-5 minutes, until just tender. Transfer the cherries to a bowl with a slotted spoon.

FINISH THE DISH

13 **Discard any remaining fat** from the duck roasting tin. Add the caramel sauce and bring to a boil, stirring to dissolve the pan juices. Simmer until reduced by half.

14 **Strain the liquid** back into a saucepan. With a wooden spoon, press two-thirds of the cherries through a sieve into the liquid. Add the remaining cherries, bring to a boil, then season to taste.

15 **Discard the trussing string,** and carve the duck. Arrange the meat on warmed plates, and spoon over some of the cherry sauce. Decorate with parsley sprigs, if you like, and serve at once. Serve the remaining cherry sauce separately.

Sauté of chicken with mussels

UNUSUAL BUT QUITE DELICIOUS, and a distant cousin of paella (p178). The mussel juices lend an intense flavour. If you want to get ahead, the chicken can be sautéed up to the end of step 2 and kept with the wine sauce, tightly covered, in the refrigerator for up to 2 days. It's then very quick to finish the recipe for a mid-week dinner.

SERVES	PREP	COOK
SERVES 4	30-35 MINS	40-50 MINS

Ingredients

1.5kg (3lb 3oz) chicken, jointed into 6

30g (1oz) plain flour

salt and pepper

1 tbsp vegetable oil

15g (½ oz) butter

4 tbsp dry white wine

375g (13oz) French beans, trimmed

18-24 mussels, cleaned (p41)

125ml (4fl oz) chicken stock

1 small bunch of chives, snipped

SAUTÉ THE CHICKEN

1 **Dip the chicken** in the flour and seasoning and pat off the excess. Heat the oil and butter in a sauté pan over moderate heat, until foaming. Add the chicken legs, skin down, and sauté for about 5 minutes. Add the breasts, and cook gently for 10–15 minutes, until very brown. Turn and brown the other side.

2 **Add the wine.** Cover and cook for 10–20 minutes, until almost tender. To test, pierce the meat with a fork: the chicken should fall easily from the fork. If some pieces cook before others, remove them, and keep warm.

COOK THE FRENCH BEANS

3 **Bring a large saucepan** of salted water to the boil. Add the beans and cook for 5 minutes, until just tender (tiny, slender beans may take as little as 3 minutes).

4 **Drain the beans** in a colander, rinse under cold running water to stop them cooking, then leave them to drain again thoroughly.

FINISH THE DISH

5 **Set the mussels on top** of the chicken pieces in the sauté pan, cover, and cook for about 5 minutes, until the mussels open. Discard any mussels that haven't opened.

6 **Transfer the mussels** and chicken to a baking dish. Cover with foil, and keep warm in a low oven. Add the stock to the pan and boil for 3-5 minutes, until the sauce is reduced and slightly syrupy, stirring occasionally.

7 **Return the chicken,** mussels, and French beans to the sauté pan with the chives, and heat gently for 2-3 minutes. Taste for seasoning. Serve on warmed plates with the sauce spooned over and around.

Sauté of chicken with prawns

A SEEMINGLY UNUSUAL COMBINATION, but traditional in Burgundy. A dash of marc de Bourgogne, a favourite Burgundian spirit, adds a rich flavour, though brandy would be equally good. Make sure the prawns have been properly deveined before starting to cook this dish.

SERVES
SERVES 4-6

PREP
25-30 MINS

COOK
45-55 MINS

Ingredients

30g (1oz) butter

2 tbsp vegetable oil

375g (13oz) raw large prawns

1.8kg (4lb) chicken, cut into 8 pieces

salt and pepper

1 onion, finely chopped

2 shallots, finely chopped

2 garlic cloves, finely chopped

3 tbsp marc de Bourgogne, or brandy

200g (7oz) canned chopped tomatoes

1 tbsp tomato purée

1 bouquet garni made with 5-6 parsley stalks, 2-3 thyme sprigs, and 1 bay leaf

4 tbsp dry white wine

125ml (4fl oz) chicken stock

leaves from 4-6 parsley sprigs, finely chopped

COOK THE CHICKEN AND PRAWNS

1 **Heat the butter** and oil in a large sauté pan. Add the prawns and sauté over high heat, stirring occasionally, for 2-3 minutes, until the prawns turn pink and begin to lose their transparency. Remove them with a slotted spoon and set aside on a plate.

2 **Season the chicken pieces** and add them to the pan, skin-side down. Brown well over medium heat for 8-10 minutes. Turn and brown the other side for 3-5 minutes.

3 **Add the onion,** shallots, and garlic, letting them fall to the bottom of the pan. Cover and cook over low heat for 10 minutes, stirring occasionally, until the vegetables are tender but not browned.

FINISH THE SAUCE

4 **Pour in the marc de Bourgogne** and bring to a boil. Hold a lighted match to the side of the pan to set the alcohol alight. Baste until the flames subside. Add the tomatoes, tomato purée, bouquet garni, wine, stock, salt, and pepper, stir well, and bring to a boil.

5 **Cover and simmer,** turning, for 10-15 minutes, until tender. Transfer the chicken to a plate and cover with foil. Bring the sauce to a boil and simmer for 8-10 minutes, until thickened. Return the chicken and prawns and reheat, stirring, for 1-2 minutes. Discard the bouquet garni. Arrange on warmed plates. Spoon the sauce over, sprinkle with parsley, and serve at once.

Butterflied leg of lamb

BUTTERFLIED, A LEG OF LAMB CAN BE COOKED in a quarter of the time needed for a whole leg. The procedure is quite simple, especially if you follow these steps, so do give it a try. You'll find it an invaluable skill to possess during barbecue season, as a marinated, butterflied leg is a wonderful addition to the usual burgers and sausages.

SERVES	PREP	COOK
SERVES 6–8	35–40 MINS PLUS MARINATING	20–30 MINS

Ingredients

1 leg of lamb, weighing about 2.2kg (5lb)

2 tbsp olive oil

4 garlic cloves, finely chopped

leaves from 3–4 rosemary sprigs, chopped

leaves from 3–4 thyme sprigs

salt and pepper

3 tbsp red wine

BONE AND BUTTERFLY THE LAMB

1 **Trim the skin** and most of the fat from the lamb. Cut around the pelvic bone, freeing it at the joint and cutting through the tendons to the leg. Remove the pelvic bone. Grasp the tip of the shank bone, and cut all tendons at the base. Cut the meat away from the shank, keeping it in one piece. Locate the knee, and scrape away meat and fat to expose the joint.

2 **Cut the tendons** at the joint, and remove the shank bone. With the knife, gently release each end of the leg bone from the meat. Cut and scrape to clean the leg bone, easing it out as you work. Twist the bone and pull it out. Lift and carefully cut away the tendons from the meat.

3 **Insert the blade** of a sharp knife into the cavity left by the leg bone. Holding the blade horizontal, cut outwards to slit open one side.

4 **Lift up the flap** created by cutting open one side, and spread out the meat into a "butterfly" shape. Working from the centre, make a cut in the thick muscle so the leg can be opened out flat.

MARINATE AND GRILL THE LAMB

5 Brush the grill rack and both sides of the lamb with oil. Rub half the garlic and herbs into the top. Marinate for 1 hour at room temperature, or up to 4 hours in the refrigerator.

6 Heat the grill to high. Sprinkle the lamb with salt and pepper, and grill 7.5cm (3in) from the heat for 10–15 minutes, until brown and slightly charred. Turn the lamb over.

7 Sprinkle the lamb with the remaining garlic, herbs, salt, and pepper, and continue grilling for 10–15 minutes, until a skewer inserted in the thickest part for 30 seconds is warm to the touch when withdrawn. Remove the lamb from the rack, cover it loosely with foil, and let it rest in a warm place for 5 minutes; reserve the juices in the pan.

MAKE THE SAUCE

8 Add the red wine to the grill pan and heat on top of the stove, stirring to dissolve the pan juices. Cut the lamb in thick diagonal slices. Divide the slices between warmed plates, and spoon over the sauce. Serve with new potatoes.

 VARIATION: Butterflied loin of pork

Dijon mustard permeates the meat for flavour.

1 Butterfly a 1.4kg (3lb) boneless loin of pork: unroll the flap of meat left from boning, and set the pork on a chopping board, fat-side down. Make a horizontal slit in the meat, cutting almost through to the other side. Open it out like a book.

2 Press the loin into a flat rectangle, and cover with baking parchment. Pound with a rolling pin to tenderize and achieve an even thickness throughout the loin. Evenly brush the pork with 2 tbsp Dijon mustard on each side, and sprinkle with double the quantity of oil. Prepare double quantities of chopped garlic and herbs, then rub half into the top of the pork; marinate as directed in the main recipe.

3 Grill the pork 13cm (5in) from the heat for 12–15 minutes. Turn and sprinkle with the remaining garlic and herbs. Grill until a skewer inserted in the thickest part for 30 seconds is hot to the touch when withdrawn; it should take 12–15 minutes. Cut through the thickest part of the meat to double-check: the pork should have no trace of pink. Make the sauce as directed, replacing the red wine with white, and adding 2 tsp Dijon mustard.

Fillet of beef with mushrooms

A DISH FOR A SPECIAL OCCASION: lean, tender, and easy to carve. Here, a fillet is stuffed with an intensely flavoured "duxelles" of mushrooms, parsley, garlic, and bacon. The Madeira sauce adds an edge of depth and sweetness to complement the meat perfectly. Make sure you buy properly aged beef from a reputable butcher.

SERVES	PREP	COOK
SERVES 8-10	50-55 MINS PLUS COOLING	1-1¼ HRS

Ingredients

FOR THE BEEF

1 fillet of beef, 1.6kg (3½lb) trimmed weight

salt and pepper

2 tbsp vegetable oil

750ml (1¼ pints) beef stock

8-10 large button mushrooms

30g (1oz) butter

FOR THE STUFFING

2 shallots

125g (4½oz) streaky bacon

3 garlic cloves

500g (1lb 2oz) mushrooms

leaves from 1 bunch of parsley, finely chopped

juice of ½ lemon

1 tbsp arrowroot or cornflour

125ml (4fl oz) Madeira

1 bunch of watercress

PREPARE AND ROAST THE BEEF

1 **Preheat the oven** to 230°C (450°F/Gas 8). Tie a piece of string lengthways around the fillet. Using separate pieces of string, tie the roll across at 2.5cm (1in) intervals.

2 **Sprinkle the beef with salt** and pepper. Heat the oil in a large roasting tin on top of the stove until very hot, then brown the fillet well on all sides. Transfer the beef to the heated oven.

3 **Roast,** allowing 12-15 minutes for rare meat or 18-20 minutes for medium. For rare, a skewer inserted in the centre of the meat will be cool to the touch when withdrawn after 30 seconds; for medium, it will be warm. Or test with a meat thermometer: it will register 52°C (125°F) for rare meat and 60°C (140°F) for medium.

4 **Remove the beef,** let it cool, then chill it for at least 2 hours until cold. Discard any fat from the roasting tin. Add half the stock and bring to a boil, stirring to dissolve the juices in the tin. Strain the juices back into the remaining stock and set aside.

PREPARE THE STUFFING

5 **Peel the shallots** and cut into quarters. Slice the bacon rashers into 2.5cm (1in) pieces. Peel the garlic. Put the shallots, garlic, and bacon into a food processor and chop to a paste. Transfer to a frying pan.

6 **Wipe the mushroom caps** with damp kitchen paper and trim the stalks. Cut the caps into quarters. Chop them in the food processor, using the pulse button.

7 **Heat the shallot,** garlic, and bacon mixture in the frying pan, stirring, for 2-3 minutes, until the mixture begins to brown. Add the mushrooms, salt, and pepper and cook over high heat, stirring occasionally, for 10-15 minutes, until all the moisture has evaporated. Stir in the chopped parsley. Taste the stuffing for seasoning. Let it cool, then chill.

STUFF AND REHEAT THE BEEF

8 Preheat the oven to 220°C (425°F/Gas 7). When the fillet is cold, remove and discard the strings. Slice the beef at 1cm (½in) intervals, cutting not quite through the fillet so that the underside remains attached.

9 Set the fillet on top of a sheet of heavy-duty foil. With a palette knife, spread 1–2 tbsp of the stuffing between each slice and press the fillet back into its original shape.

10 Wrap the fillet in the foil, making a neat cylinder and twisting the ends to make handles. Set on a baking sheet and put in the oven. For rare beef, allow 15–20 minutes; a skewer inserted in the centre will be cool to the touch when withdrawn after 30 seconds and a meat thermometer will register 52°C (125°F). For medium, allow 20–25 minutes; the skewer will be warm when withdrawn and a thermometer will register 60°C (140°F).

FINISH THE DISH

11 Put the mushrooms in a frying pan with the butter, lemon juice, salt, pepper, and enough water to cover them partially. Fold a square of baking parchment in half then in half again to make a triangle. Fold over once or twice or more to form a slender cone. Holding the tip of the cone over the centre of the pan, cut the cone, using the edge of the pan as a guide. Unfold the round.

12 Butter the baking parchment round and place it over the mushrooms in the frying pan, buttered-side down (this piece of improvised cooking equipment is known as a "cartouche"). Simmer until the mushrooms are tender – it will take 15–20 minutes, but stir occasionally and check the mushrooms are not scorching on the base of the pan – then remove with a slotted spoon and keep warm.

13 Put the stock in the saucepan and add the mushroom cooking liquid. Bring to a boil and cook until it has reduced by half. Put the arrowroot or cornflour in a small bowl and stir in 2 tbsp of the Madeira to form a smooth paste.

14 Whisk the arrowroot paste into the stock. It will thicken at once, but keep whisking to avoid the formation of lumps. Stir in the remaining Madeira and taste the sauce for seasoning. Cut a slit in one end of the foil parcel surrounding the beef and carefully drain all of its juices into the sauce. Whisk to mix in the juices, then keep the sauce warm over very low heat while you serve the dish.

15 Carve the fillet into slices, following the slices you made earlier while stuffing the joint, and arrange them on a warmed platter or on individual warmed plates. Garnish with the sautéed mushroom caps and watercress, and pass the sauce separately.

Poussins in vine leaves

A DISH VERY CLOSE TO THE VINEYARD! The white wine in the sauce completes the theme. Poussins are a great idea to serve for a dinner party, as each bird makes a very substantial single portion and gives a feeling of generosity and plenty. The allspice and tarragon contained in the stuffing complement the dish perfectly and the recipe is always popular; you may find this soon becomes part of your regular repertoire.

SERVES	PREP	COOK
SERVES 4	45-50 MINS	60-80 MINS

Ingredients

FOR THE STUFFING

4 slices of white bread, crusts cut off

1 chicken liver

2 streaky bacon rashers, sliced

1 shallot, finely chopped

1 tbsp brandy

leaves from 3-5 tarragon sprigs, finely chopped

leaves from 3-5 parsley sprigs, finely chopped

1 pinch of ground allspice

FOR THE POUSSINS

4 poussins, each weighing about 500g (1lb 2oz)

8-12 preserved vine leaves

4 streaky bacon rashers

2 tbsp vegetable oil

1 tbsp brandy

250ml (9fl oz) dry white wine

250ml (9fl oz) chicken stock

salt and pepper

MAKE THE STUFFING

1 Roughly tear the bread into pieces and work them in a food processor to form crumbs. Trim any membrane from the chicken liver with a small knife, then coarsely chop the liver.

2 Put the bacon into a small frying pan and cook, stirring occasionally, for 3-5 minutes, until crisp and the fat has rendered. With a slotted spoon, transfer to a bowl.

3 Add the shallot to the pan and cook for 2-3 minutes, until soft. Add the chicken liver, sprinkle it with pepper, and cook, stirring, for 1-2 minutes, until brown. Pour in the brandy and simmer for 1 minute.

4 Combine the liver mixture with the bacon. Stir in the breadcrumbs, herbs, and allspice. Season the stuffing with pepper to taste; salt may not be needed as the bacon is salty.

STUFF AND TIE THE POUSSINS

5 Wipe the insides of the poussins with kitchen paper, and season inside and out with salt and pepper. Spoon one-quarter of the stuffing into the cavity of each bird.

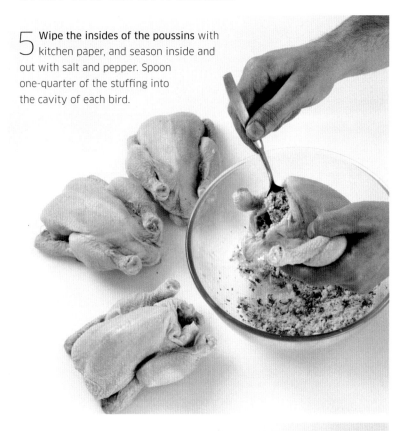

6 Rinse the vine leaves thoroughly in cold water. Drain in a colander. Place the leaves between sheets of kitchen paper and pat gently to dry.

7 Wrap **2 or 3 vine leaves** over the breast of each poussin, then top with a folded slice of bacon. Tie each poussin with string like a parcel.

COOK THE POUSSINS

8 **Preheat the oven** to 180°C (350°F/Gas 4). Heat the oil in a casserole on top of the stove. Add the poussins and brown all over, turning, for 5-10 minutes. Cover and transfer to the oven. Bake until tender, and a metal skewer inserted into the stuffing for 30 seconds is hot to the touch when withdrawn. It should take 45-55 minutes. Make sure the juices run clear when the skewer is removed; if there is any trace of pink, continue cooking for 5 minutes more and then test again.

9 **Transfer the poussins** to a warmed platter. Discard the trussing strings if liked (though they can look pretty as part of a rustic presentation), and cover with foil to keep warm. Spoon the fat from the casserole, then add the brandy and white wine.

10 **Bring to a boil and** simmer, stirring, until reduced by half. This should take 5-7 minutes. Add the stock and reduce again by half, it will take 5-7 minutes longer. Spoon the sauce through a sieve into a small bowl. Taste for seasoning.

11 **Set the poussins** on warmed plates and spoon over the wine sauce. Leave each guest to remove the string, if it has been left on, and their own wrappings of bacon and vine leaves. The leaves should not be eaten; they have already done their job by adding a subtle fragrance to the roasting birds.

Roast monkfish with two sauces

BOTH GARLIC AND CHILLI SAUCES show off this excellent, firm fish. The fillets are roasted whole, then sliced to serve, showing off their pristine white flesh. If monkfish is out of your budget, reasonably priced huss makes a good substitute.

SERVES	PREP	COOK
SERVES 6	25–30 MINS PLUS MARINATING	12–15 MINS

Ingredients

FOR THE MONKFISH

6 skinned monkfish fillets, total weight 1.4kg (3lb)

2 tbsp olive oil

leaves from 5–7 oregano sprigs, chopped

leaves from 5–7 thyme sprigs

salt and pepper

FOR THE GARLIC AND CHILLI SAUCES

45g (1½oz) butter

3 tbsp plain flour

8 garlic cloves, or to taste, peeled

4 eggs, hard-boiled and separated

125ml (4fl oz) olive oil

leaves from 6–9 parsley sprigs

2 red chillies

2 tsp tomato purée

cayenne pepper (optional)

MARINATE THE MONKFISH

1 **Rinse the fillets** with cold water, then pat dry with kitchen paper. Put them in a shallow dish and sprinkle with the oil, herbs, salt, and pepper. Toss so the fillets are coated. Cover and refrigerate for 2 hours.

MAKE THE SAUCES

2 **Melt the butter** in a saucepan. Whisk in the flour and cook for about 1 minute, until foaming. Take from the heat and whisk in 250ml (8fl oz) boiling water. The sauce will thicken at once. Return the saucepan to the heat and cook for 1 minute, whisking.

3 **Transfer the sauce** to a food processor. Add the garlic, hard-boiled egg yolks, salt, and pepper and purée until smooth. With the blades turning, pour in the oil in a thin stream, so the sauce thickens and becomes creamy. Taste for seasoning. Put half of the sauce in a bowl.

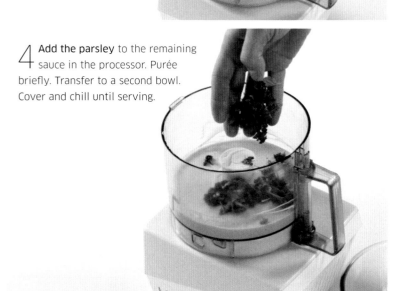

4 **Add the parsley** to the remaining sauce in the processor. Purée briefly. Transfer to a second bowl. Cover and chill until serving.

5 **Rinse out the food processor.** Core, deseed, and chop 1 chilli. Put in the processor. Add the tomato purée and reserved sauce. Purée until smooth. Season with cayenne, if you like. Transfer to a bowl, cover and chill. Core, deseed, and thinly slice the second chilli into rings.

ROAST THE FISH

6 Preheat the oven to 230°C (450°F/Gas 8). Line a baking sheet with aluminium foil. Arrange the monkfish fillets, side by side, on the foil, spacing them out evenly so they are not squashed together. Spoon the marinade from the dish over the fillets.

7 Roast the fillets in the heated oven, brushing occasionally with the juices which have collected on the foil, for 12-15 minutes, until they are browned and the fish is no longer rare in the centre (the flesh should just flake when tested with a fork).

8 Arrange the fish on warmed plates, and add a little of each sauce. Decorate with the rings of chilli, or thyme sprigs, if you like. Serve the remaining sauces separately. Roasted cherry tomatoes make welcome embellishments to the plates.

 VARIATION: Grilled monkfish escalopes with garlic and chilli sauces

A griddle will give great marks to the fish.

1 Rinse and pat dry the monkfish fillets. Holding each fillet steady, cut diagonal slices about 1cm (½in) thick, working towards the tail and keeping the slices as even as possible.

2 Marinate the fish as directed, using twice the amount of herbs. Meanwhile, make the sauces as directed. Omit the rings of chilli. Grill the escalopes about 7.5cm (3in) from the heat for 4 minutes; you won't need to turn them, or griddle them in a very hot griddle pan for 2 minutes each side.

3 Make pools of garlic and chilli sauces on warmed plates. Arrange the fish around the edge of each plate. Decorate with herbs.

Chinese roast duck

AROMATIC AND UNIVERSALLY POPULAR. This is traditionally made with a whole duck, head attached, as often seen hanging in the windows of Chinatown shops and restaurants. Luckily, a duck without its head can also be used! The duck can be dried, uncovered, overnight in the refrigerator.

SERVES	PREP	COOK
SERVES 4	45 MINS PLUS AIR-DRYING	1¾-2 HRS

Ingredients

FOR THE DUCK

1 duck, weighing about 2.25kg (5lb)

1 tbsp maltose or honey

FOR THE AROMATIC SEASONING

1 tsp Szechuan peppercorns

2 tbsp ground bean sauce or black bean sauce

1 tbsp Chinese rice wine or dry sherry

2 tsp caster sugar

½ tsp five-spice powder

2 tbsp light soy sauce

1 tsp oil

3 garlic cloves, finely chopped

2.5cm (1in) piece fresh root ginger, finely chopped

4 spring onions, sliced

leaves from 1 small bunch of coriander, chopped, plus more sprigs for serving, if liked

AIR-DRY THE DUCK

1 Rinse the duck thoroughly inside and out with cold water and pat dry with kitchen paper. Pull away and discard any fat from the body cavity. Tie heavy string around the flap of skin at the neck opening, looping it several times.

2 Half-fill a wok with water and bring to a boil. Hold the duck by the string and immerse it in the water. Using a ladle, pour water over the breast for 1 minute until the duck skin becomes taut. Remove the duck and pat dry with kitchen paper.

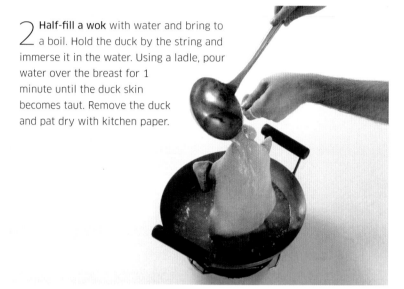

3 Hang the duck by the string in a cool (10–13°C/50–55°F), airy place. Place a dish underneath to catch any drips. Leave for about 2 hours, until the skin is dry. Drying time will vary depending on the weather.

PREPARE THE AROMATIC SEASONING

4 Heat a wok over medium heat until hot. Add the Szechuan peppercorns and cook, stirring, for 1–2 minutes, until they smoke slightly. Transfer to a small sturdy bowl or mortar and pound to a coarse powder.

5 Put the peppercorn powder in a bowl and add the bean sauce, rice wine, sugar, five-spice powder, and soy sauce. Stir together.

6 Heat the wok again, over medium heat, until very hot. Drizzle in the oil to coat the bottom and sides. Continue heating until the oil is very hot, then add the garlic, ginger, and spring onions, and stir-fry for about 30 seconds, until fragrant.

7 Add the sauce mixture and the coriander. Bring to a boil, then reduce the heat to low, and simmer for about 1 minute. Transfer to a bowl and let cool to room temperature.

SEASON AND ROAST THE DUCK

8 About 45 minutes before roasting the duck, put a bamboo skewer into a bowl of cold water and let soak. Preheat the oven to 200°C (400°F/Gas 6). Spoon the aromatic seasoning into the body cavity.

9 Overlap the skin to close the cavity and thread the skewer 2-3 times from the top of the cavity through both layers of skin, then through the tail. To close tightly, tie string around the tail and the top of the skewer to bring the tail up. Set the duck, breast-side up, on a rack set in a roasting tin. Roast in the heated oven for 15 minutes.

10 Meanwhile, combine the maltose or honey and 4 tbsp boiling water in a small bowl, stirring to dissolve the maltose completely. Remove the duck from the oven, and brush the maltose mixture generously all over the skin, being sure to cover it all.

11 Reduce the oven temperature to 180°C (350°F/Gas 4) and continue roasting, brushing every 15 minutes with the maltose mixture, until dark brown and the leg meat feels soft when pinched, 1½–1¾ hours.

12 Transfer the duck to a chopping board and let stand for about 15 minutes, then carefully remove the string and skewer. Set a sieve over a bowl. Pour the seasoning from the duck cavity into the sieve. Skim off and discard the fat; reserve the liquid.

13 Carve the duck and chop the pieces up into 2.5cm (1in) pieces with a cleaver. Arrange on a warmed platter, to resemble the original shape of the duck if you like. Pour the seasoning over and decorate the platter with sliced spring onions and coriander sprigs, if you want. Serve immediately.

Hindle Wakes chicken with prunes

TRADITION HAS IT that this dish was created to reward those who kept watch (or "wake") on the eve of a great festival in Yorkshire. Try to get hold of a mature chicken for this recipe, as it will respond better to the cooking process; a good butcher should be able to help you source the perfect bird. Really top-quality prunes will lift the whole dish, giving a deep, sweet, fruity quality to the sauce.

SERVES	PREP	COOK
SERVES 4	30 MINS PLUS SOAKING	1¼–1½ HRS

Ingredients

FOR THE STUFFING

250g (9oz) large stoneless prunes

125g (4½oz) butter

1 small onion, finely chopped

10 slices of white bread

leaves from 1 bunch of parsley, finely chopped

zest, finely grated, and juice of 1 lemon

125ml (4fl oz) chicken stock

FOR THE CHICKEN

1.8kg (4lb) boiling fowl, with liver if possible

2 carrots, quartered

1 bouquet garni

2 cloves

1 onion

2 garlic cloves

1 tsp black peppercorns

300ml (10fl oz) medium dry white wine

1.5 litres (2¾ pints) chicken stock or water

salt and pepper

FOR THE VELOUTÉ SAUCE

75g (2½ oz) butter

45g (1½ oz) flour

175ml (6fl oz) double cream

lemon juice, to taste

PREPARE THE STUFFING

1 **Put the prunes** in a bowl and cover with hot water. Allow to soak for about 1 hour, until softened and plump, then drain. Set aside 8–12 of the firmest to be stuffed; chop the rest.

2 **Heat half the butter** in a small saucepan, add the onion and fry for 2–3 minutes, until soft but not brown. Cut any membrane from the chicken liver, if using, then chop it. Stir the liver into the onion and cook for 1–2 minutes, until brown. Turn into a bowl.

3 **Break up the bread** and work it in a food processor to make crumbs. Melt the remaining butter in a small saucepan. Add the chopped prunes, breadcrumbs, parsley, and lemon zest to the bowl. Stir in the chicken stock, lemon juice, and melted butter. Season well to taste. Set aside.

POACH THE CHICKEN

4 **Put the chicken** into a casserole. Add the carrots and bouquet garni. Stick the cloves into the onion, and add to the casserole with the garlic and peppercorns. Add the white wine with enough stock to cover the chicken above its legs.

5 **Bring to a boil,** skimming well, then cover and simmer over low heat, skimming occasionally, for 1¼–1½ hours. Turn halfway through. The chicken is done when the thigh meat is tender, and no pink juice runs out when it is pierced. Remove from the casserole, wrap in foil, and keep warm. Reserve the cooking liquid.

COOK THE PRUNES AND STUFFING

6 **Preheat the oven** to 190°C (375°F/Gas 5). Fill the whole prunes with stuffing. Butter a baking dish. Spread the remaining stuffing in it. Arrange the stuffed prunes on top and cover with foil. Bake for 30–40 minutes. Take out and keep warm.

MAKE THE VELOUTÉ SAUCE

7 **Skim off and discard any fat** from the cooking liquid. Boil the liquid until reduced by half. Strain and measure it: there should be about 750ml (1¼ pints). Add more stock or water if necessary. Discard the vegetables and bouquet garni.

8 **Melt the butter** in a medium saucepan. Whisk in the flour. Cook the mixture for 1–2 minutes, until foaming but not browned, whisking well.

9 **Add the cooking liquid** and whisk constantly, until the sauce comes to the boil and thickens. Add the cream and simmer for 2 minutes. Take from the heat, stir in lemon juice and seasoning to taste, and keep warm. Carve the chicken, arrange on warmed plates and coat with sauce. Place a serving of stuffing next to it and pass the remaining sauce separately.

Chicken Pojarski

ONCE A FAVOURITE of the Russian royal family, and said to be named after the innkeeper who invented it. If you don't want to deep-fry the Pojarski, simply omit step 4 and bake them in the oven for a lighter dish. You can prepare them up to the end of step 3 a day in advance, cover, and refrigerate.

SERVES	PREP	COOK
SERVES 4	35-40 MINS	40-50 MINS

Ingredients

FOR THE CHICKEN

6 individual brioches, total weight about 250g (9oz)

125ml (4fl oz) milk

420g (15oz) skinless, boneless chicken breasts

3 tbsp double cream

ground nutmeg

salt and pepper

30g (1oz) seasoned flour

1 egg

vegetable oil, for deep-frying

FOR THE SAUCE

2 tbsp vegetable oil

1 small onion, chopped

125g (4½oz) mushrooms, sliced

1 x 400g (14oz) can tomatoes

1 tbsp tomato purée

1 garlic clove, finely chopped

1 bouquet garni

a pinch of sugar, to taste

PREPARE THE CHICKEN

1 Cut 4 of the brioches into dice and set aside. Break apart the remaining brioches and put them in a small bowl. Pour the milk over and soak for 5 minutes. Squeeze any excess milk from the brioches.

2 Cut the chicken into chunks. Work it through the fine blade of a mincer with the soaked brioches. Beat the cream into the minced chicken mixture with a pinch of nutmeg and salt and pepper. To test the mixture for seasoning, fry a little piece in the frying pan and taste; it should be well seasoned, so add more salt and pepper if required.

SHAPE AND COOK THE POJARSKI

3 With wet hands, shape into 4 balls and flatten slightly. Dip them in the flour and pat off the excess. Beat the egg and brush on to the rounds, draining off any excess. Coat the balls in diced brioches to completely cover. Chill, uncovered, for 30 minutes.

4 Preheat the oven to 190°C (375°F/Gas 5). Heat the oil in a deep-fat fryer to 180°C (350°F) (a cube of bread should turn golden in 1 minute). Add 1-2 Pojarski and fry until brown, 2-3 minutes. With a slotted spoon, transfer to a baking sheet. Fry the remaining Pojarski in the same way.

BAKE THE POJARSKI AND MAKE THE SAUCE

5 Bake in the heated oven for 25-30 minutes, until a skewer inserted in the centre is hot to the touch when withdrawn. If they brown too quickly, cover them loosely with foil.

6 Meanwhile, heat half the vegetable oil in a sauté pan, add the onion and mushrooms, and cook for 2-3 minutes, until brown. Stir in the tomatoes, tomato purée, garlic, bouquet garni, salt, pepper, and sugar, and cook, stirring occasionally, until fairly thick, 8-10 minutes. Serve with the Pojarski.

Roast leg of pork with orange

THIS IS EASY TO ADAPT for a cooked ham or gammon on the bone (bake for 1 hour only). This dish is also excellent cold, so worth making in its entirety (as it's a cheap cut) even if you don't have a crowd to feed. The leftovers are almost more delicious than the hot dish itself!

SERVES	PREP	COOK
SERVES 8-10	20-25 MINS	3½-4 HRS

Ingredients

FOR THE PORK

1 leg of pork, weighing about 4.5kg (10lb)

8 oranges

1 tbsp Dijon mustard

180g (6oz) dark soft brown sugar

20 cloves

1 bunch of watercress

FOR THE SAUCE

4 tbsp Grand Marnier

½ tsp grated nutmeg

½ tsp ground cloves

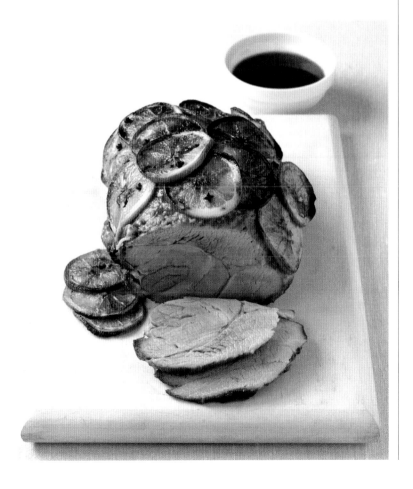

ROAST THE PORK

1 **Preheat the oven** to 180°C (350°F/Gas 4). Wipe the pork with kitchen paper, then set it in a roasting tin. Halve 6 of the oranges and squeeze out the juice. There should be about 500ml (16fl oz).

2 **Pour some of the orange juice** over the pork and roast in the heated oven for 3–3½ hours, pouring more orange juice over about every 30 minutes to keep it moist. Slice the remaining oranges, discarding any pips.

3 **To test if the pork is cooked,** insert a metal skewer for 30 seconds near the centre of the leg; it should be warm to the touch when withdrawn. A meat thermometer should show 77°C (170°F).

GLAZE THE PORK

4 **Take the pork** from the oven and let it cool slightly. Increase the heat to 200°C (400°F/Gas 6). Cut through the skin around the bone end of the joint. With a knife, peel the skin from the fat, starting from the wider end of the joint.

5 **Mix the mustard** and sugar together. Spread and press over the pork. Overlap the orange slices over the joint. Stud each piece with a clove. Roast for 30–45 minutes, basting with the juices every 10 minutes. Transfer to a warmed serving platter. Remove the orange slices and arrange next to the pork. Cover with foil and keep warm.

MAKE THE SAUCE

6 **Pour the Grand Marnier** into the roasting tin. Bring to a boil and whisk to dissolve the juices. Add the nutmeg and cloves and mix them in. Transfer to a sauce boat.

7 **Carve the pork** on to warmed plates with the orange slices, adding a little watercress, if you like. Pass the sauce separately.

Monkfish Americaine

A FIRM, LOBSTER-LIKE TEXTURE has made monkfish hugely popular, and so enough of a treat to impress your friends. The richness of the sauce used here, with its tomato, garlic and Cognac, makes it a suitable dish for the colder months.

SERVES	PREP	COOK
SERVES 4-6	45-50 MINS	35-40 MINS

Ingredients

1.4kg (3lb) piece of monkfish, on the bone

2 onions, chopped

125ml (4fl oz) white wine or juice of ½ lemon

1 tsp peppercorns

3-5 parsley sprigs

30g (1oz) plain flour

salt and pepper

2 tbsp olive oil

125g (4½oz) butter

FOR THE AMERICAINE SAUCE

3-4 tarragon sprigs

1 carrot, in 1cm (½in) dice

2 garlic cloves, finely chopped

400g can chopped plum tomatoes

150ml (¼ pint) white wine

3 tbsp Cognac

pinch of cayenne pepper (optional)

1 bouquet garni

4 tbsp double cream

1 tbsp tomato purée

pinch of sugar (optional)

FOR THE PILAF

2 tbsp vegetable oil

1 onion, chopped

300g (10oz) long-grain rice

PREPARE THE MONKFISH

1 **If necessary,** skin the monkfish: using a filleting knife, cut and release the black skin, then pull it off.

2 **Cut away the thin membrane** that covers the fish, cutting close to the flesh with a filleting knife, and pulling the membrane away with your fingers. Cut along one side of the backbone to remove 1 fillet. Repeat the process on the other side. Rinse the fillets with cold water and pat dry with kitchen paper.

3 **With a sharp, heavy knife,** cut the bone in pieces and reserve the pieces for the fish stock.

4 **Cut each fillet** into 1cm (½in) slices. Slightly flatten each slice into escalopes with the side of a knife.

MAKE THE STOCK AND PREPARE THE SAUCE INGREDIENTS

5 Put half the chopped onions in a large saucepan and add the fish bones, wine, peppercorns, parsley and 500ml (16fl oz) water. Bring slowly to a boil, then simmer, uncovered, for 20 minutes. Never cook fish stock for any longer than this, or it may become bitter. Strain into a bowl and cool. You should have about 500ml (16fl oz) of fish stock.

6 Strip the tarragon leaves from the stalks and pile them on a chopping board. Coarsely chop the leaves and reserve for garnish. Set aside the stalks for the sauce.

COOK THE PILAF

7 Heat the oil in a heavy-based saucepan, add the onion, and cook stirring, for 1–2 minutes, until soft but not brown. Add the rice and cook, stirring, for 2–3 minutes, until the oil has been absorbed and the rice looks a little more translucent.

8 Pour in 750ml (1¼ pints) water, season and bring to a boil. Cover, reduce the heat, and simmer for about 20 minutes, or until all the liquid has been absorbed and the rice is tender. Let stand, still covered, 10 minutes, then stir with a fork to fluff up the grains.

COOK THE FISH AND MAKE THE SAUCE

9 Meanwhile, put the flour on a plate and season. Lightly coat the fish slices, patting to cover evenly. Heat the oil and a quarter of the butter in a sauté pan, add half the fish and sauté, turning once, for 2–3 minutes, until brown on both sides. Transfer to a plate. Sauté the remaining fish in the same way.

10 Add the carrot, garlic, and the remaining onion to the pan and cook, stirring to mix in the browned flour from the bottom of the pan, for 3–5 minutes, until soft but not brown.

11 Add the tomatoes, wine, Cognac, tarragon stalks, salt and pepper and a pinch of cayenne pepper, if you like. Tie the bouquet garni to the pan handle. Pour in the stock. Bring to a boil and simmer for 15–20 minutes, until slightly thickened.

12 Sieve the sauce into a large saucepan, pressing with a ladle to extract all the liquid. Boil for 5–10 minutes, until thickened. Whisk in the cream and tomato purée. Taste, adding a pinch of sugar if it is too acidic.

13 Add the monkfish slices to the sauce and simmer for 5–10 minutes, until just tender. Take the saucepan from the heat and add the remaining butter, in small pieces, shaking so the butter melts into the sauce. Serve the monkfish, sprinkled with the chopped tarragon, on warmed plates. Accompany with the rice pilaf.

Yellow flower pork

A STIR-FRIED PORK and egg mixture from northern China, wrapped in thin pancakes. Stir-fried dishes that contain eggs are known as "mu shu" in China, after the fragrant yellow flower of that name (this dish would be called mu shu rou). If you don't have any Chinese rice wine, use dry sherry instead.

SERVES SERVES 4	**PREP** 35–45 MINS PLUS SOAKING	**COOK** 15–20 MINS

Ingredients

FOR THE PANCAKES

250g (9oz) plain flour, plus more to dust

1 tbsp dark sesame oil

4 tbsp hoisin sauce

FOR THE FILLING

45g (1½oz) dried Chinese mushrooms

250g (9oz) boneless loin of pork

2 tsp cornflour

2 tbsp light soy sauce, plus more if needed

2 tbsp Chinese rice wine

2 tsp dark sesame oil

3 eggs

3 tbsp flavourless oil

30g (1oz) bamboo shoots

2 spring onions, in 5cm (2in) slices

MAKE THE PANCAKE DOUGH

1 **Sift the flour** into a large bowl and make a well in the centre. Slowly pour 175ml (6fl oz) boiling water into the well, mixing until the water is absorbed and the mixture forms a rough mass.

2 **Let stand until cool** enough to handle. Gather the dough together and press into a ball. Turn on to a lightly floured surface and knead for about 5 minutes, adding more flour as necessary, until smooth and elastic. Cover loosely with a tea towel and let rest for 30 minutes.

PREPARE THE FILLING

3 **Put the mushrooms** in a bowl and cover with 250ml (9fl oz) warm water; let soak for 30 minutes. Trim off any fat from the pork. Cut it across into 5mm (¼in) slices. Cut each slice into 3mm (⅛in) strips.

4 **Drain the mushrooms,** reserving the liquid. Trim off the hard, woody stems, then slice the caps. Line a sieve with kitchen paper and hold it over a measuring jug. Pour in the mushroom soaking liquid to strain; reserve 125ml (4fl oz) of the mushroom liquid.

5 **Put the cornflour** into a small bowl. Add the reserved mushroom liquid and mix until smooth; then stir in the soy sauce, rice wine, and sesame oil. In a small bowl, beat the eggs.

MAKE THE PANCAKES

6 **On a lightly floured surface,** roll the dough into a cylinder about 30cm (12in) long. Dust a cleaver or broad knife with flour, and cut the cylinder into 12 equal pieces. Cover the pieces with a dampened tea towel.

7 **Roll each piece of dough** into a ball. Flatten each ball to make a 7.5cm (3in) round and cover with the dampened tea towel. Brush 1 side of each round lightly with sesame oil. Press the oiled sides of 2 rounds together to form 6 pairs. Lightly flour a work surface and rolling pin. Roll out each pair of rounds into a thin pancake, about 17.5cm (7in) in diameter.

8 **Heat a wok** until very hot. Add 1 pancake and cook until blistered and puffed, about 1 minute. Turn and cook the other side, pressing down until brown spots appear on the underside, about 30 seconds. Remove, then peel the halves apart to make 2 very thin pancakes. Repeat with the remainder. Once the pancakes are cooked, stack them on a plate; cover with a dampened tea towel to keep warm.

STIR-FRY THE FILLING

9 **Heat the wok** over medium heat until hot. Drizzle in 1 tbsp oil to coat the sides. When the oil is hot, pour in the eggs. Cook to form a thin omelette, set in the centre and slightly crisp around the edge.

10 **Carefully turn the omelette.** Cook for 15–30 seconds, until the other side is lightly browned. Slide on to a chopping board and let cool slightly. Roll up loosely and cut across into 5mm (¼in) strips.

11 **Reheat the wok** over high heat. Drizzle in the remaining oil and continue heating until very hot. Add the pork and cook for 2–3 minutes, stirring and tossing, until no longer pink.

12 **Add the mushrooms** and bamboo shoots and stir-fry until mixed and heated through. Stir the cornflour mixture again, then pour it into the pork mixture.

13 **Stir-fry until the vegetables** are hot and the sauce thickens, about 2 minutes. Add the spring onions and omelette and taste, adding more soy sauce if needed. Stir-fry for 1 minute. Spoon into a warmed serving dish. Arrange the pancakes on a plate. Put the hoisin sauce in a small bowl. Each guest spreads sauce on a pancake, tops it with some filling, and rolls it up.

Sole turbans with wild mushrooms

AN OLD-FASHIONED CLASSIC, well worth reviving for today's palates. The mushroom mousse can be made up to 1 day ahead and kept, covered, in the refrigerator. Bake the sole turbans just before serving. The choice of mushrooms is entirely down to your taste and budget; substitute cultivated mushrooms for some of the total if you like, but do try to use a few wild mushrooms as well for their gutsy, earthy flavours.

SERVES
SERVES 4

PREP
20-25 MINS
PLUS CHILLING

COOK
35-45 MINS

Ingredients

FOR THE WILD MUSHROOM MOUSSE

30g (1oz) butter, plus more for dishes and foil

150g (5½oz) wild mushrooms, sliced

salt and pepper

1 egg, plus 1 egg yolk

1 tbsp Madeira

leaves from 2-3 coriander sprigs, chopped

125ml (4fl oz) double cream

FOR THE SOLE AND SAUCE

6 skinless lemon sole fillets, total weight about 500g (1lb 2oz)

125ml (4fl oz) dry white wine

125g (4½oz) butter, chilled

leaves from 3-5 coriander sprigs, finely chopped, plus more for garnish

MAKE THE WILD MUSHROOM MOUSSE

1 **Heat the butter** in a frying pan. Add the mushrooms with salt and pepper. Cook, stirring constantly, until the mushrooms have given up their liquid, and it has all evaporated. It may take 3-5 minutes, but do persevere, as otherwise the mousse will be soggy. Remove from the heat and let the mushrooms cool slightly.

2 **Put the mushrooms** in a food processor and purée them. With the blade turning, add the whole egg and egg yolk. Purée until smooth. Add the Madeira and coriander, and purée just until combined.

3 **Season,** then transfer to a bowl. Cover and chill for about 1 hour. Fold the cream into the mushroom mixture. Preheat the oven to 190°C (375°F/Gas 5). Brush the inside of a soufflé dish with melted butter.

4 **Transfer the chilled mousse** to the prepared dish. Set it in a baking dish. Pour in sufficient hot water to come halfway up the side of the soufflé dish. Bake for 20-25 minutes, until just set when lightly pressed. Reduce the oven temperature to 180°C (350°F/Gas 4).

PREPARE THE SOLE TURBANS

5 **Rinse the sole fillets** and carefully pat dry with kitchen paper. Cut them lengthways in half. Shape each fillet half into a 7.5cm (3in) ring, skinned-side in, tail end around the outside. Secure with cocktail sticks. Brush a shallow baking dish with melted butter, then arrange the sole in the dish.

6 **Fold the top of a piping bag,** fitted with a large star nozzle, over your hand to form a collar. Spoon in the mousse. Twist the top of the bag, then pipe the mousse in a swirl into each sole ring to fill completely.

7 **Carefully pour the white wine** around the sole turbans in the baking dish. Butter a piece of foil and use to cover. Bake for 15-20 minutes, until the fish is white and opaque, and the mousse is firm. Keep the sole warm, and reserve the cooking liquid. Remove the cocktail sticks.

MAKE THE CORIANDER SAUCE

8 Cut the chilled butter into small even-sized pieces. Pour the cooking liquid from the dish into a small frying pan. Place over a high heat and boil until it is reduced right down to only about 2 tbsp of strongly flavoured liquid. Take the pan from the heat and add the butter, a little at a time, whisking constantly. The sauce should thicken a little more each time another piece of butter is added. Do not stop whisking, or the emulsified sauce will split. If it cool too much, return it to a very gentle heat for a moment.

9 Whisk in the coriander and taste the sauce for seasoning; you may want more salt, pepper, wine, or even a touch of Madeira, to marry in with the flavours of the mushroom mousse (though if you choose the latter 2 options, cook off the alcohol by boiling in a separate pan before whisking into the sauce and continuing). Pour the sauce over and around the sole turbans to enrich the dish. Garnish with some finely chopped coriander leaf, if you like.

 VARIATION: Turbans of plaice with spinach mousse

Lovely bright greens and reds here, with a tomato-butter sauce.

1 Bring a large pan of water to a boil, add salt, then 750g (1lb 10oz) trimmed spinach, and blanch for 1 minute. Drain in a colander, rinse with cold water, and squeeze to remove all water.

2 Make the mousse as directed, replacing the mushrooms with spinach and omitting the Madeira. Add a pinch of ground coriander with the salt and pepper. Replace the sole with 6 plaice fillets, weighing about 500g (1lb 2oz), and prepare and shape as directed.

3 Fill the plaice rings with the spinach mousse and bake as directed. Make the sauce, omitting the coriander. Whisk in 1 tbsp tomato purée after the butter. Serve on warmed plates with the butter sauce.

Leg of lamb with roasted garlic

THE FLAVOURS OF GARLIC and shallots sweeten and mellow when they are slowly roasted. The garlic will soften to a delicious purée that tastes wonderful spread either on the meat, or on a piece of crusty baguette served alongside. Make sure you get hold of really good-quality meat for this simple recipe, as the lamb takes centre stage.

SERVES
SERVES 8

PREP
15-20 MINS

COOK
1¼-2 HRS

Ingredients

1 small leg of lamb, weighing about 2.25kg (5lb)

2 heads of garlic

500g (1lb 2oz) shallots

5-7 thyme sprigs

2 tbsp olive oil

salt and pepper

125ml (4fl oz) dry white wine

250ml (9fl oz) chicken or beef stock

PREPARE THE INGREDIENTS

1 **Preheat the oven** to 230°C (450°F/Gas 8). Trim all but a thin layer of fat from the lamb. With the heel of your hand, press sharply down on the heads of garlic to loosen the cloves. Separate the cloves, and discard the root and any loose skin.

2 **With a small knife,** trim the tops and roots from the shallots but do not peel them. Strip the thyme leaves from half the sprigs, and reserve the remaining sprigs for garnish.

ROAST THE LAMB AND VEGETABLES

3 **Put the lamb** into a roasting tin and spoon over the oil. Sprinkle with thyme leaves, salt, and pepper. Roast in the heated oven for 10-15 minutes, until browned.

4 **Reduce the oven temperature** to 180°C (350°F/Gas 4). Add the garlic and shallots to the roasting tin with 125ml (4fl oz) water and stir to mix.

5 **Continue cooking,** basting often, and adding more water if necessary, for 1-1¼ hours for rare meat or 1¼-1½ hours for medium. Remove the lamb from the tin, cover with foil, and keep warm. Remove the garlic and shallots, cover and keep warm. Let the lamb stand for 10-15 minutes.

6 **Discard the fat** from the tin. Add the wine and bring to a boil, stirring to dissolve the pan juices. Simmer for 3–5 minutes. Stir in the stock, and continue simmering for 2–3 minutes longer. Taste for seasoning. Carve the meat and serve with the garlic, shallots, and gravy, sprinkling with the reserved thyme.

VARIATION: Leg of lamb with potatoes

Before every home had an oven, this French dish would have been cooked by the local baker.

1 Omit the shallots, water, and wine. Peel four garlic cloves. Finely chop two and cut the other two into thin slivers. Make incisions in the lamb and insert the slivers. Thinly slice 500g (1lb 2oz) onions and 1kg (2¼lb) potatoes. Strip the thyme from the stalks, and mix with the potatoes.

2 Heat 2 tbsp oil in a frying pan and soften the onions and garlic. Stir the onions into the potatoes with a pinch of nutmeg, salt, and pepper. Preheat the oven to 230°C (450°F/Gas 8). Brown the lamb as directed. Transfer to a plate. Spread the potatoes over the dish. Add 500ml (16fl oz) beef stock. Set the lamb on top, lower the heat to 180°C (350°F/Gas 4), and continue roasting as directed.

3 If necessary, remove the lamb, keep warm, and continue baking the potato mixture until golden. Carve the lamb and serve with the potatoes and gravy.

Poached salmon, watercress sauce

POACHING IN AN AROMATIC COURT BOUILLON is the ideal way to cook a whole salmon, adding flavour and keeping it moist. This is a great dish to impress, and makes a stunning centrepiece for a cold table. If you prefer, omit the watercress from the sauce and instead add a mixture of fragrant herbs: tarragon, parsley, dill, or chervil are all delicious with salmon. Experiment with the sauce to find a version that suits your palate: here, it is lightened with yogurt, but you may prefer a richer sauce with the addition of mayonnaise, or even soured cream for an extra layer of tangy flavour.

SERVES	PREP	COOK
SERVES 4-6	25-30 MINS	15-20 MINS

Ingredients

FOR THE COURT BOUILLON

1 onion, sliced

1 carrot, sliced

6 peppercorns

250ml (8fl oz) dry white wine

1 bouquet garni made with 5-6 parsley stalks, 2-3 thyme sprigs and 1 bay leaf

FOR THE FISH

1.8kg (4lb) salmon, scaled and trimmed

salt and pepper

FOR THE WATERCRESS SAUCE

250ml (8fl oz) double cream

250ml (8fl oz) plain yogurt

1 bunch of watercress, trimmed and chopped

Tabasco sauce

1 lemon

MAKE THE COURT BOUILLON

1 **Combine the onion**, carrot, peppercorns, wine, 1.5 litres (2¾ pints) water, and 1 tsp salt in a roasting tin. Add the bouquet garni. Bring to a boil and simmer for 20 minutes. Let cool.

PREPARE AND POACH THE SALMON

2 **With a filleting knife**, working inside the belly of the fish, slit between the ribcage bones and flesh as carefully as possible. Work towards the backbone, loosening the flesh from the bones on both sides of the ribcage without cutting through the skin. It is a tricky job, but just do the best you can and work as neatly as possible.

3 **Using scissors**, snip the backbone at the head to release it. Pull the bone out. Snip the bone at the tail end to release it there, too. Cut the bone into pieces and reserve. With tweezers, remove any visible bones that remain in the cavity of the fish, then run your fingers along the inside to check they have all been removed. Rinse the fish inside and out, and pat dry with kitchen paper.

4 **Add the reserved pieces** of bone to the cold court bouillon. Sprinkle the inside of the fish with salt and pepper. Cut and fold a piece of foil slightly larger than the fish, and lay the fish on it. Set it in a large, deep roasting tin so the body of the fish is in the liquid.

5 **If necessary**, add water to the court bouillon so the fish is completely immersed. Cover the roasting tin with foil and bring the liquid very slowly to a boil; this should take about 15 minutes. Simmer for 1 minute, then let the salmon cool to tepid in the liquid.

MAKE THE SAUCE

6 **Whip the cream** until soft peaks form. In another bowl, whisk the yogurt until smooth. Add the yogurt to the cream and stir gently to mix. Add the watercress and a dash of Tabasco. Squeeze the juice from the lemon and add to the sauce. Stir the sauce until evenly blended. Add salt and pepper to taste. Cover the bowl and chill until ready to serve.

FINISH THE SALMON

7 **Holding the ends** of the foil, carefully lift the salmon out of the liquid; let drain. Lift the fish off the foil. Using a small knife, slit the skin neatly around the head. Repeat around the tail.

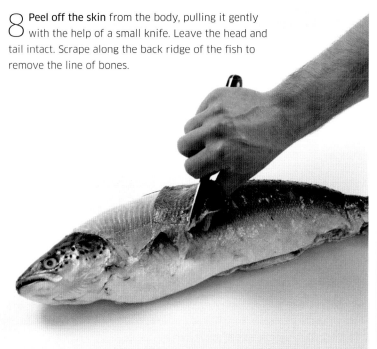

8 **Peel off the skin** from the body, pulling it gently with the help of a small knife. Leave the head and tail intact. Scrape along the back ridge of the fish to remove the line of bones.

9 **Using a small knife**, gently scrape off any dark flesh from the length of the salmon. Carefully transfer the fish to a platter. Serve the watercress sauce in a bowl on the side.

Beef rendang

AN INTENSELY FLAVOURED Indonesian speciality, originally made with water buffalo. It can be made up to 2 days ahead and kept, covered, in the refrigerator. Bring to room temperature, then reheat on top of the stove before serving.

SERVES
SERVES 6

PREP
40-50 MINS

COOK
3½-4 HRS

Ingredients

FOR THE CURRY PASTE

2.5cm (1in) piece cinnamon stick

12 cloves

2 stalks lemongrass, trimmed and roughly chopped

6 shallots, quartered

7.5cm (3in) piece fresh root ginger, roughly chopped

6 garlic cloves, peeled

6 red chillies, finely chopped

1 tsp ground turmeric

FOR THE RENDANG

3 x 400g (14oz) cans coconut milk

4 bay leaves

1.4kg (3lb) beef chuck steak, in 5cm (2in) cubes

1½ tsp salt

PREPARE THE CURRY PASTE

1 **Crumble or break** the cinnamon stick into small pieces and put them in a mortar with the cloves. Pound them with the pestle until coarsely crushed.

2 **Put the cinnamon** and cloves in the food processor with the remaining curry paste ingredients. Process to a coarse paste. If the mixture is very thick, add about 4 tbsp of the coconut milk.

MAKE THE CURRY

3 **Combine the curry paste** and coconut milk in a wok and stir until well mixed. Add the bay leaves and bring to a boil over high heat, stirring occasionally.

4 **Reduce the heat** to medium and cook the sauce, stirring occasionally, for about 15 minutes. Add the beef and salt, stir, and return to a boil over high heat. Reduce the heat to medium and simmer, uncovered, stirring occasionally, for 2 hours.

FINISH THE CURRY

5 **Reduce the heat** to very low and continue cooking for 1½-2 hours, until the beef is tender and the sauce quite thick. Stir frequently to prevent sticking.

6 **Skim off all the fat.** Taste the curry and add salt if necessary. It will be very thick and rich. Towards the end of cooking, oil will separate from the sauce and the beef will fry in it. Arrange a bed of cooked rice on warmed plates or shallow bowls, and spoon the curried beef on top.

Osso bucco

A CLASSIC DISH from Milan. A zesty mixture called "gremolata" is sprinkled on top just before serving. This dish is traditionally served with a risotto made with saffron and Parmesan cheese, which is delicious though very rich.

SERVES	PREP	COOK
SERVES 4-6	30-35 MINS	1½-2 HRS

Ingredients

FOR THE STEW

400g(14oz) can Italian plum tomatoes

30g (1oz) plain flour

salt and pepper

4-6 pieces of veal shin with bones, about 1.8kg (4lb)

2 tbsp vegetable oil

30g (1oz) butter

1 carrot, thinly sliced

2 onions, finely chopped

250ml (9fl oz) white wine

1 garlic clove, finely chopped

zest of 1 orange, finely grated

125ml (4fl oz) chicken or veal stock, plus more if needed

FOR THE GREMOLATA

leaves from 1 small bunch of parsley, finely chopped

zest of 1 lemon, finely grated

1 garlic clove, finely chopped

PREPARE THE INGREDIENTS

1 **Preheat the oven** to 180°C (350°F/Gas 4). Tip the canned tomatoes into a sieve set over a bowl and drain off as much liquid as possible. Transfer the tomatoes to a chopping board and coarsely chop.

2 **Put the flour** on a large plate, season with salt and pepper, and stir to combine. Lightly coat the veal pieces with the seasoned flour, patting to ensure the flour adheres.

BRAISE THE VEAL

3 **Heat the oil** and butter in a sauté pan, add the veal pieces, in batches if necessary so the pan is never crowded, and brown thoroughly on all sides. Transfer to a plate with a slotted spoon.

4 **Discard all but 2 tbsp fat** from the pan. Add the carrot and onions and cook, stirring occasionally, until soft. Add the wine and boil until reduced by half. Stir in the tomatoes, garlic, orange zest, salt, and pepper. Lay the veal on top.

5 **Pour in the stock**, cover the pan and cook in the oven for 1½-2 hours, until very tender. Add more stock during cooking if the pan gets dry. The sauce should be thick and rich. If necessary, boil to reduce and thicken it.

MAKE THE GREMOLATA

6 **Mix the parsley**, lemon, and garlic in a small bowl. Put the veal on warmed plates, spoon the sauce on top and sprinkle with the gremolata.

Korean grilled beef (bulgogi)

A GREAT MEAL FOR ENTERTAINING; guests grill their own meat in a table-top burner. These hot pickled vegetables (*kimchee*) are served with most Korean meals, and need to be started 4 days ahead of your meal.

SERVES
SERVES 4

PREP
50 MINS
PLUS MARINATING

COOK
10 MINS

Ingredients

FOR THE PICKLED VEGETABLES

½ small Chinese cabbage (about 250g/9oz)

100g (3½oz) salt

1 tbsp chilli powder or 1 tsp cayenne

2 tbsp fish sauce

1 tsp sugar

4 garlic cloves, finely chopped

4 spring onions, chopped

2.5cm (1in) piece fresh root ginger, finely chopped

10cm (4in) piece of daikon, weighing about 175g (6oz), cut into 3mm (⅛in) strips

FOR THE BULGOGI

625g (1lb 6oz) piece of beef fillet

1 tbsp sesame seeds

4 spring onions, chopped

3 garlic cloves, finely chopped

2 tsp Japanese rice wine

3 tbsp Korean or Japanese soy sauce

2 tbsp sugar

1 tbsp dark sesame oil

¼ tsp freshly ground black pepper

oil for brazier or grill rack

boiled long-grain white rice, to serve

PREPARE THE PICKLED VEGETABLES

1 **Rinse the cabbage.** Put 1 litre (1¾ pints) water and all but ¼ tsp of the salt in a large bowl and stir until the salt has dissolved. Add the cabbage and weight it with a plate to keep it covered. Let soak for 8–10 hours.

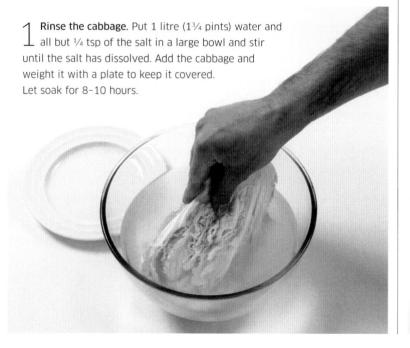

2 **In a bowl,** mix the chilli powder or cayenne with the fish sauce, sugar, and remaining salt. Add the garlic, spring onions, ginger, and daikon and stir until the mixture is red in colour.

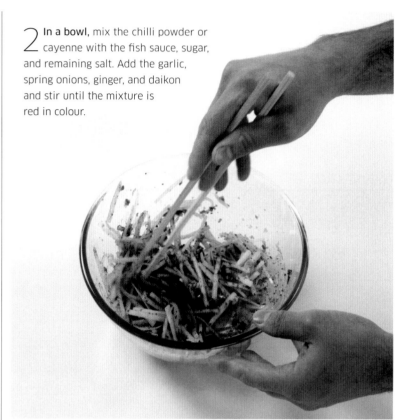

3 **Drain the cabbage,** rinse, and squeeze to remove the moisture. Pack the daikon mixture between each leaf, then push the cabbage into a jar. Pour any leftover daikon on top. Cover and leave in a cool place to ferment for at least 3 days. Each day, open the jar to release any gas, and push the cabbage down into the liquid. After 3 days, taste a cabbage leaf to test if it is sufficiently sour. When it's ready, cut it into 2.5cm (1in) slices and refrigerate until ready to serve.

PREPARE, MARINATE, AND **GRILL** THE BEEF

4 Wrap the piece of beef and freeze it for about 1 hour. Heat a frying pan over medium-high heat. Add the sesame seeds and cook, stirring, for 1–2 minutes, until golden brown. Transfer to a spice grinder and work until fine but not reduced to a paste. (Or crush in a pestle and mortar.)

5 Combine the spring onions, garlic, toasted sesame seeds, rice wine, 2 tbsp water, soy sauce, sugar, sesame oil, and pepper in a bowl and stir well to mix.

6 When the beef is partially frozen, cut it across the grain into 5mm (¼in) slices. Arrange the slices, overlapping, on a large plate. Pour the marinade over to cover each slice evenly, cover tightly and let marinate at room temperature for about 1 hour.

7 Lightly oil the cooking surface of a table-top brazier. Heat over high heat until sizzling hot. Arrange as many slices of beef as will fit in a single layer on the brazier (though do not squash them too tightly together), or allow each of your guests to do so for themselves. Cook until the beef is well-browned (about 1 minute). Turn and brown the other side for about 1 minute longer. The beef slices should remain pink in the centre though be well browned and even crusty on the outside.

8 Each guest takes a slice of beef directly from the brazier, to eat with a portion of the pickled vegetables and some plain boiled rice. Do not be scared that the pickles will be unpopular; you'll find that most people, once they have discovered kimchee, become worryingly addicted to it. Continue cooking the remaining beef when the first batch is finished, until it is all used up, allowing guests to take as much as they want.

Pork loin with garlic and rosemary

THE ITALIAN NAME for this recipe, *arista*, translates as "the best" – what more is there to say? This pork dish, with its pungent stuffing, is also delicious served at room temperature, so any leftovers will find a warm welcome. Make sure you do not cook it too long, as pork loin is lean and should remain juicy, not dry, once carved.

SERVES
SERVES 6-8

PREP
15-20 MINS

COOK
1-1½ HRS

Ingredients

10 garlic cloves, peeled

leaves from 1 small bunch of rosemary

2 tsp black peppercorns

salt

2 tbsp olive oil

1.4kg (3lb) boned loin of pork

MAKE THE STUFFING

1 **Put the garlic** in a food processor. Add the rosemary, peppercorns, and salt. Pulse-blend until finely chopped, or coarse, as you prefer.

PREPARE AND STUFF THE PORK

2 **Preheat the oven** to 200°C (400°F/Gas 6). Brush a roasting tin with olive oil. Make a deep horizontal slit through the meat, almost to the other side, and spread half the garlic and rosemary stuffing over. Fold the flap back, and reshape the loin.

ROAST THE PORK

3 **Using separate pieces of string,** tie the pork at 2.5cm (1in) intervals to hold its shape during cooking. Set in the prepared tin and spread the remaining stuffing over the outside. Sprinkle with olive oil.

4 **Roast until it starts** to brown (20-25 minutes). Remove from the oven and pour 125ml (4fl oz) water over the pork.

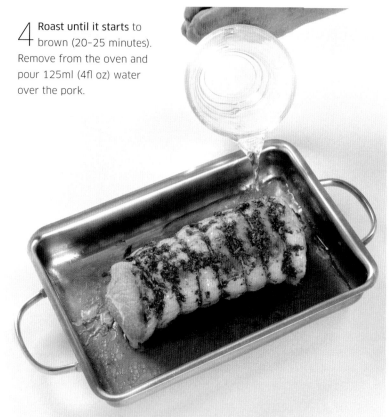

5 **Turn the meat** over. Continue roasting for 45-60 minutes longer, turning 2 or 3 times so it browns evenly, and adding more water when the tin becomes dry.

6 **The pork is cooked** when a skewer inserted into its centre for 30 seconds is very hot to the touch when withdrawn. Transfer to a chopping board, cover with foil, and stand for 10 minutes to allow the juices to be reabsorbed before carving.

FINISH THE DISH

7 **Spoon out** and discard some of the fat from the roasting tin. Add 100ml (3½fl oz) water and boil, stirring, to dissolve the juices in the roasting tin. Taste for seasoning. As you gain in cooking confidence, you may feel you want to flavour the gravy in a more complex way. The first step is to substitute chicken stock for the water used in this simple version. You may also want to add white wine, or even Madeira, for a sweeter result. Any alcoholic liquids used in the gravy must be boiled for long enough to evaporate all traces of the alcohol, or the flavour of the sauce will be tainted. You can easily find out whether you have boiled off the alcohol by tasting carefully as you cook.

8 **Discard the strings** from the pork, being careful not to pull the loin apart, and cut the meat into fairly even slices, each about a generous 1cm (½in) thick. Arrange the slices on a warmed serving dish or serve them straight on to warmed plates; spooning over the cooking juices. Steamed green vegetables make a lovely accompaniment; sweet leeks and broad beans are particularly appropriate with the succulent pork.

Bouillabaisse

A DELICIOUS SOUP for a special occasion. Purists maintain that a true bouillabaisse cannot be made anywhere but in the Mediterranean. However, you can create an excellent version based on local fish, with fabulous flavours.

SERVES	**PREP**	**COOK**
SERVES 8-10	50-55 MINS PLUS MARINATING	50-60 MINS

Ingredients

FOR THE BOUILLABAISSE

1.4 kg (3 lb) mixed white fish, cleaned, on the bone, with heads

1kg (2¼lb) mixed oily fish, cleaned, scaled, on the bone

2 large pinches of saffron

5-6 garlic cloves

125ml (4fl oz) olive oil

1 orange

2 onions, thinly sliced

2 leeks, thinly sliced

2 celery sticks, thinly sliced

1 fennel bulb, thinly sliced

400g (14oz) can chopped tomatoes in thick juice

leaves from 10-12 parsley sprigs, chopped

1 bouquet garni

1 tbsp tomato purée

1 tbsp Pernod or other aniseed-flavoured liqueur

FOR THE CROUTES

1 baguette

olive oil, to brush

FOR THE CHILLI MAYONNAISE

1 red chilli, deseeded

4 garlic cloves, peeled

salt and pepper

175ml (6fl oz) mayonnaise

1 tsp tomato purée

cayenne pepper (optional)

PREPARE THE FISH, MARINADE, AND STOCK

1 **Rinse the fish** inside and out, drain, and pat dry. Keeping the white and oily fish separate, cut all the fish into 5cm (2in) chunks. Reserve the heads and tails for the stock (rinse the heads thoroughly).

2 **Put 1 large pinch of saffron** in a small bowl and add 2 tbsp boiling water. Let soak for 10 minutes. Peel and finely chop 2 garlic cloves. Combine the saffron, its liquid, the chopped garlic, and 3 tbsp olive oil in a bowl.

3 **Put the white** and oily fish separately in 2 large non-metallic bowls. Add half the marinade to each. Toss, cover, chill, and marinate for 1-2 hours.

4 **Meanwhile,** make the stock: put the fish heads and tails in a large saucepan, add water barely to cover, and bring to a boil. Simmer for 20 minutes. Pour through a sieve into a bowl and set aside.

PREPARE THE BROTH

5 **Peel a wide strip of zest** from the orange with a vegetable peeler. Peel and coarsely chop the remaining garlic cloves. Soak the remaining pinch of saffron in 3-4 tbsp boiling water for 10 minutes.

6 **Heat the remaining oil** in a casserole. Add the onions, leeks, celery, and fennel. Cook, stirring, for 5-7 minutes. Add the tomatoes, orange zest, garlic, and parsley to the casserole.

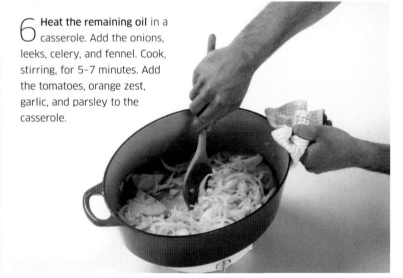

7 **Tie the bouquet garni** to the handle of the casserole. Pour in the stock. Add the saffron with its liquid and season. Bring to a boil. Simmer for 30-40 minutes, until thickened and the flavour is mellow, stirring occasionally.

MAKE THE CROUTES AND MAYONNAISE

8 **Preheat the oven** to 180°C (350°F/Gas 4). Cut the baguette into 2cm (¾in) slices and place them on a baking sheet, spacing them evenly apart. Brush each slice lightly with oil, using a pastry brush. Turn and brush the other side as well. Bake in the hot oven until the slices are light brown. It should take 10–12 minutes, but check often, turning the baking sheet, so all the slices brown evenly and none of them threaten to scorch. Remove any slices that brown before the rest.

9 **To make the mayonnaise,** put the chilli, garlic, and salt and pepper into the bowl of a food processor and pulse-blend until everything is finely chopped. Add the mayonnaise and the tomato puree and work until the mayonnaise is smooth. Taste and add cayenne pepper, if you like, though be cautious as the sauce should be pungent but not fierily hot. Chill, covered, until ready to serve.

FINISH THE BOUILLABAISSE

10 **Bring the broth back** to a boil. Add the oily fish and boil fiercely for 7 minutes. Shake the casserole from time to time to prevent the mixture from sticking to the base of the pan; do not stir or the pieces of fish will disintegrate.

11 **Add the white fish.** Set the most delicate types of fish on top, so they will receive the least heat. Continue boiling until the fish just flakes easily with a fork; it should take 5–8 minutes. If necessary, add more water so the fish remains covered, but don't add too much or the broth will be watery; it should remain highly flavoured.

12 **Discard the bouquet garni** and orange zest from the broth and whisk in the tomato purée and Pernod. Taste for seasoning. Ladle the broth into a soup tureen and serve at once, with the croutes and chilli mayonnaise.

Poussins with mushroom sauce

PERFECT FOR A ROMANTIC DINNER. Once split and flattened, the birds will remain moist naturally under the grill because the bones disperse the heat. If you are using a large chicken, you will need to baste it more frequently. A pair of poultry shears will make the job of splitting the birds far easier; though sturdy kitchen scissors can be used. A bigger chicken to serve 2 can be used in place of the poussins This is even more delicious if you serve the birds with a glass of the same wine you used in the mushroom sauce.

SERVES	PREP	COOK
SERVES 2	30–40 MINS	35–40 MINS

Ingredients

FOR THE POUSSINS

2 poussins

oil for the grill rack

30g (1oz) butter

salt and pepper

1 tbsp Dijon mustard

15g (½oz) dried breadcrumbs

bunch of watercress, to garnish

FOR THE MUSHROOM SAUCE

60g (2oz) butter

15g (½oz) flour

150g (5½oz) mushrooms, sliced

2 shallots, finely chopped

1 garlic clove, finely chopped

4 tbsp medium dry white wine

4 tbsp white wine vinegar

1½ tbsp Dijon mustard, or to taste

375ml (13fl oz) chicken stock

SPLIT AND FLATTEN THE POUSSINS

1 **Set one bird breast side down** on a board. With poultry shears, cut along each side of the backbone and discard it. Trim any flaps of skin and cut off the wing tips.

2 **Force the bird open** and snip the wishbone. Wipe the inside of the bird with kitchen paper. Turn breast up with the legs turned in. With the heel of your hand, push down sharply on the breast to break the breastbone and flatten the bird.

3 **Make a small cut** in the skin between the leg and breastbone and tuck in the leg knuckles.

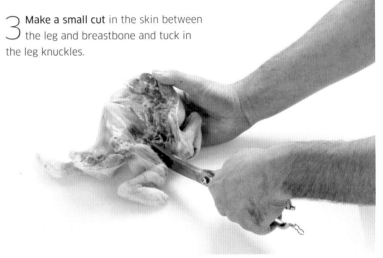

4 **Thread a skewer** through the wings of the bird to hold it flat. Thread a second skewer through the legs. Repeat the procedure for the second bird.

COOK THE POUSSINS

5 Heat the grill. Brush the grill rack generously with oil. Melt the butter in a small saucepan and keep it close to hand for basting. Brush the poussins evenly with half the melted butter and sprinkle with salt and a good amount of pepper.

6 Put the poussins on the grill rack, skin side up. Grill them about 7.5cm (3in) from the heat for about 15 minutes, basting once with butter during this time. Turn, brush the underside of the birds with the remaining butter and grill for another 10 minutes.

7 Turn again so the birds are breast side up once more. Brush the skin with the mustard then sprinkle evenly with the breadcrumbs. Grill, skin side up, until tender, about 10 minutes longer. If they brown too quickly, or the breadcrumbs threaten to scorch, lower the rack further from the heat.

MAKE THE MUSHROOM SAUCE

8 In a shallow dish, mash half the butter with the flour until soft. Melt half the remaining butter in a saucepan. Add the mushrooms and cook, stirring occasionally, for 3-5 minutes, until tender and lightly browned.

9 Melt the remaining butter in another saucepan, add the shallots and garlic, and cook until softened. Add the wine and vinegar and simmer until reduced to about 2 tbsp.

10 Add the mustard and stock and stir to combine. Stir in the mushrooms and simmer for 5 minutes. Whisk in the flour paste a small piece at a time, until the sauce lightly coats the back of a spoon. Season to taste.

11 Remove the skewers from the poussins. Arrange the birds on warmed plates and decorate with sprigs of watercress, if you like. Spoon on a little sauce and serve the rest separately.

Trout with orange-mustard glaze

GRILLED WHOLE FISH is a dream for the cook, quick to prepare, and easy to present. Small fish are best because their bones keep them moist and their skin protects them from the intense heat of the grill. You could barbecue the fish for this dish, but do not use strongly-flavoured wood for the fuel, as it can overpower the trout. The glaze can be made up to 1 week ahead and kept, covered, in the refrigerator.

SERVES	PREP	COOK
SERVES 6	15–20 MINUTES	20–30 MINS

Ingredients

FOR THE TROUT

6 trout, each weighing 375g (13oz), cleaned through the gills

6–8 tarragon sprigs

3–4 tbsp vegetable oil, for grill rack

3 large sweet onions, in 1cm (½in) slices

250g (9oz) mushrooms, trimmed

3 ripe tomatoes, cored and halved

FOR THE ORANGE AND MUSTARD GLAZE

4 tbsp Dijon mustard

2 tsp honey

juice of 2 oranges

4 tbsp vegetable oil

salt and pepper

PREPARE THE FISH

1 Make sure your fishmonger cleans the fish through the gills; if its stomach is slit, it may curl. Rinse inside and out and pat dry with kitchen paper. Slash diagonally 3–4 times on both sides. Make the slashes about 1cm (½in) deep to allow heat to penetrate.

2 Strip the tarragon leaves from the stalks, then tuck a leaf in each slash. Set the fish aside in a cool place.

MAKE THE GLAZE

3 Whisk the Dijon mustard and honey together in a bowl until smooth and liquid in consistency, then whisk in the orange juice until it is evenly combined. Gradually pour in the oil, whisking constantly until the glaze emulsifies and thickens slightly. Season with salt and pepper. Taste for seasoning; you may find you want to add more mustard, honey, or orange. Adjust the balance of flavourings until they suit your palate perfectly (though be careful not to add too much mustard, as it could overpower the taste of the delicate fish).

GRILL THE VEGETABLES AND FISH

4 Heat the grill. Brush the rack generously with oil. Arrange the onion slices and mushrooms on the rack. Brush with a little of the glaze and season. Grill about 7.5cm (3in) from the heat, brushing with more glaze and turning, allowing about 3 minutes for the mushrooms and 5–7 minutes for the onions; they should be slightly charred. Remove and keep warm.

5 Cook the tomatoes skin-side towards the heat for 5–7 minutes, or until warmed through and the skin is slightly charred; do not turn. Remove and keep warm.

6 Place the fish on the rack (in 2 batches if necessary). Brush with glaze; sprinkle with salt and pepper. Grill for 4–7 minutes, until browned.

FINISH AND SERVE THE DISH

7 Carefully turn the fish, being careful not to tear the skin, and brush each generously with more of the glaze. Continue grilling until the flesh just flakes easily when tested with a fork and there is no opaque flesh near the spine (serve the fish with the tested side downwards for the neatest presentation). They could take anything from 4–7 minutes more to cook, depending on the thickness of the fish and the strength of the grill. As a general guide, for every 2.5cm (1in) of a fish at its thickest part, allow 10 minutes cooking, whether on a barbecue or under a grill. (If cooking on a barbecue, make sure the fish is placed over a coolish part or it will burn on the outside before the flesh is cooked through.) Place the fish on warmed plates and serve with a stack of the grilled vegetables. Spoon any remaining glaze over the fish.

 VARIATION: Grilled cod steaks with maître d'hotel butter

Try to use farmed fish rather than the endangered wild cod.

1 Omit the glaze. Finely chop 1 shallot and 8–10 parsley stalks. Cream 75g (2½oz) butter. Mix in the shallot and parsley, the juice of ½ lemon, salt, and pepper. Spoon the butter on to a piece of baking parchment and shape into a roll, twisting the ends to seal. Refrigerate until firm.

2 Rinse and dry 6 cod steaks. Brush with 3–4 tbsp olive oil, season and grill for 3–5 minutes on each side. After turning, brush with more olive oil and sprinkle with more salt and pepper.

3 Set a slice of the maître d'hôtel butter on top of each cod steak and serve.

Very garlicky sautéed chicken

THE FLAVOUR OF GARLIC mellows as it cooks, and it acts as a thickening agent for the sauce. This sauté has a piquant sauce made from red wine vinegar and chopped tomatoes. Don't worry if the amount of garlic seems excessive; all your guests will love the bold flavours of this dish. Herb and other flavoured vinegars can be used in this recipe, each will add its own distinctive taste. If you choose balsamic vinegar, use only half the quantity.

SERVES	PREP	COOK
SERVES 4	15-20 MINS	1-1¼ HRS

Ingredients

1.5kg (3lb 3oz) chicken, jointed into 6 pieces, or 6 chicken joints

salt and pepper

1 tbsp vegetable oil

90g (3oz) butter

15 garlic cloves

250ml (9fl oz) red wine vinegar

1 tbsp tomato purée

1 bouquet garni

2 tomatoes, coarsely chopped

250ml (8fl oz) chicken stock

SAUTÉ THE CHICKEN AND GARLIC

1 **Season the chicken** with salt and pepper. Heat the oil and 15g (½oz) of the butter in a sauté pan over moderate heat until foaming. Add the chicken legs, skin side down, and sauté for about 5 minutes, until they begin to brown.

2 **Add the chicken breasts** and continue cooking gently for 10-15 minutes, until very brown. Turn and brown the other side.

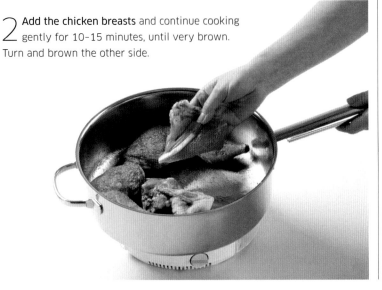

3 **Add the unpeeled garlic cloves**. Shake the pan gently to distribute the garlic in among the chicken joints, then cover and cook over low heat for 20 minutes.

ADD THE OTHER INGREDIENTS

4 **Stir in the vinegar** and simmer, uncovered, until reduced by half; it will take about 10 minutes to get to this stage. Add the tomato purée to the pan and stir to mix with the juices, scraping the base of the pan with a wooden spoon to incorporate all the chicken flavours. Cook the tomato purée briefly to eliminate any raw taste, making sure it does not stick to the pan or the flavour of the sauce will be spoiled. Add the bouquet garni and tomatoes to the pan and mix into the chicken.

5 **Cover again** and simmer for 5-10 minutes longer, until the chicken joints are tender when pierced with a 2-pronged fork and the juices run clear. If there is any trace of pink in the juices, return the chicken to the pan for a few minutes longer before testing again. If some joints are done before others, remove them from the pan, put them on a plate, loosely cover with foil, and keep them warm in a very low oven; overcooking the chicken will result in tough meat.

MAKE THE GARLIC AND VINEGAR SAUCE

6 Remove all the chicken from the pan and keep warm in a very low oven. Add the stock to the juices in the pan and boil for 3–5 minutes, stirring occasionally, until well reduced and concentrated in flavour, again scraping the base of the pan with a wooden spoon to release all the flavour. Strain the sauce through a sieve back into the saucepan, pressing hard on the garlic to extract the pulp.

7 Cut the remaining butter into small pieces. Bring the sauce back to a boil, then remove from the heat and add the butter, a few pieces at a time, whisking constantly and moving the pan on and off the heat. You should see the sauce beginning to thicken, and develop a glossy sheen. Do not boil; the butter should make the sauce creamy and rich without melting to oil, as it will if it boils. Taste for seasoning. Arrange the chicken on warmed plates and spoon over a generous amount of the sauce, serving the remaining sauce on the side.

 VARIATION: Very garlicky sautéed guinea fowl with blackberries

A gamier bird, the flavours here are sharpened by tangy berries.

1 Joint the guinea fowl into 6 pieces, or get your butcher to do it for you. Brown the pieces as directed in the main recipe, then add the garlic.

2 Omit the red wine vinegar. Stir in 120ml (4fl oz) sherry vinegar and reduce as directed, then add the bouquet garni. Omit the tomato purée and tomatoes. Simmer as directed until the guinea fowl is cooked through, then remove the pieces and keep them warm.

3 Add the stock to the pan and reduce as directed, and strain the sauce back into the pan, pressing on the garlic. Add the butter. Pick through 120g (4oz) blackberries, washing them only if they are dirty. Add the berries to the sauce and heat them through. Taste for seasoning; you may need a pinch of sugar if the berries are very tart. Serve with the guinea fowl pieces.

Comfort food

Hearty, homely, and deeply nourishing dishes

Rib of beef with Yorkshire pudding

AS TRADITIONAL AS IT GETS, and irresistible with the crisp, golden Yorkshire puddings. Carving a rib of beef takes a little skill: set the joint upright on a carving board and, holding it steady with a carving fork, cut away the rib bones at the base of the meat, removing as little beef as possible as you do so. With the joint on its side, carve into even slices.

SERVES	PREP	COOK
SERVES 6-8	25-30 MINS	1¾-2¼ HRS

Ingredients

FOR THE YORKSHIRE PUDDING

180g (6oz) plain flour

2 eggs, beaten

300ml (10fl oz) milk

vegetable oil, if needed

FOR THE BEEF AND GRAVY

2kg (4½lb) beef rib roast (2 ribs)

salt and pepper

1-2 tbsp plain flour

500ml (16fl oz) beef stock

MAKE THE BATTER

1 **Sift the flour** into a large bowl. Make a well in the centre and add the eggs, with some salt and pepper.

2 **Slowly whisk in the milk,** drawing in the flour to make a smooth paste. Stir in 90ml (3fl oz) water. Cover with a tea towel, and let stand at room temperature for at least 15 minutes.

PREPARE AND ROAST THE BEEF

3 **Meanwhile,** preheat the oven to 230°C (450°F/Gas 8). Sprinkle the meat with salt and pepper, and set it in a large roasting tin, ribs pointing up. Roast for 15 minutes. Reduce the oven temperature to 180°C (350°F/Gas 4). Continue roasting for 50 minutes for rare beef, or 65 minutes for medium-done, basting often.

4 **When the meat is rare,** a metal skewer inserted into the centre for 30 seconds will be cool to the touch when withdrawn (a meat thermometer will show 52°C/125°F). When medium-done, the skewer will be warm (a meat thermometer will show 60°C/140°F).

5 **Transfer the meat** to a board, cover loosely with foil and leave in a warm place, while you make the Yorkshire pudding and gravy. Tilt the baking dish, and spoon off the fat with a large metal spoon. Reserve the fat.

MAKE THE YORKSHIRE PUDDINGS

6 Increase the oven temperature to 230°C (450°F/Gas 8). Pour a teaspoon of the beef fat into each of 12 Yorkshire pudding, or deep bun, tins, topping up with vegetable oil if necessary. Heat in the oven for about 5 minutes until very hot. Pour in the batter to half-fill each of the tins; it should sizzle as it hits the hot fat. Bake in the hot oven for 15-20 minutes, until puffed and golden brown. Do not open the oven during this time, or the Yorkshire puddings may sink.

7 Meanwhile, make the gravy: stir 1-2 tbsp plain flour into the juices in the roasting tin and cook, stirring, for 2-3 minutes, until very brown. Add the beef stock. Bring to a boil, stirring, and simmer for 2 minutes. Strain and season to taste.

8 Carve the joint (see the recipe introduction) and arrange on warmed plates, with the Yorkshire puddings and vegetables of your choice. Serve the gravy separately.

 VARIATION: Rib of beef pebronata

With a Corsican tomato and red pepper sauce.

1 Prepare and roast the beef as directed in the main recipe. Meanwhile, finely chop 1 onion and 4 garlic cloves. Chop the leaves from 3 sprigs each thyme and parsley. Roast, peel, and core 3 red peppers.

2 Heat 2 tbsp olive oil and sauté the onion, garlic and herbs. Stir in 2 x 400g (14oz) cans chopped tomatoes, season, and cook for 25 minutes. Heat another 2 tbsp oil in a second pan and add the red pepper, 1 bay leaf, and 4 juniper berries. Cook for 10 minutes. Stir in 2 tbsp plain flour, then the tomato mixture. Simmer for 10 minutes, until thick. Stir in 250ml (9fl oz) red wine.

3 Cover the beef and let rest, as directed in the main recipe. Spoon off the fat from the roasting tin. Stir a further 250ml (9fl oz) red wine into the tin and bring to a boil. Strain into the pebronata sauce and serve with the carved beef.

Chilli con carne

IN TEXAS, YOU WILL NEVER FIND RED BEANS in a chilli; they are served on the side, as in this authentic recipe. Do mix them in with the meat, if you prefer. This is great to have in hand for a cold night; it will keep for 3 days in the refrigerator. For a real Texan touch, serve it with cornbread (p386).

SERVES	PREP	COOK
SERVES 6	35-40 MINUTES	2-2½ HOURS

Ingredients

3 garlic cloves

2-4 dried red chillies

3 tbsp vegetable oil, plus more if needed

1.4kg (3lb) braising steak, in 1cm (½in) cubes

3 onions, chopped

2 x 400g (14oz) cans chopped tomatoes

leaves from 5-6 oregano sprigs, chopped or 1 tbsp dried oregano

2 tbsp chilli powder

1 tbsp paprika

2 tsp ground cumin

1-2 tsp Tabasco sauce, or to taste

salt and pepper

1 tbsp fine cornmeal (polenta)

2 x 400g (14oz) cans red kidney beans

PREPARE THE GARLIC AND CHILLI

1 Set the flat side of a knife on top of each garlic clove, and strike it with your fist. Discard the skin and finely chop the garlic.

2 Trim and split the chillies lengthways. Discard the seeds, then finely chop or crumble them. The seeds are the hottest part; if you like your chilli extra hot, you can leave them in.

COOK THE CHILLI

3 Heat half the oil in a casserole, add about a quarter of the beef, and cook over high heat, stirring, until browned. Using a slotted spoon, transfer the meat to a plate. Brown the remaining beef cubes in 3 batches, adding more oil as needed.

4 Return all the browned meat, with the juices, to the casserole. Add the onions, garlic, and tomatoes, and cook, stirring, for 8-10 minutes, until the onions are just soft.

5 Pour in 500ml (16fl oz) water, and stir into the casserole with the chillies, oregano, chilli powder, paprika, cumin, Tabasco sauce, salt, and pepper. Bring just to a boil, then cover and simmer for about 2-2½ hours, until the meat is very tender, stirring occasionally.

6 About 30 minutes before the end of cooking, stir in the cornmeal. At the end of cooking, the chilli should be thick and rich. Taste for seasoning, and serve it hot from the casserole, with boiled white long-grain rice, and bowls of warmed red kidney beans alongside for each diner.

Herbed roast chicken

THIS IS A CLASSIC, juicy roast chicken, with herbs inside for flavour. Though it is a simple dish, you will find it is everyone's favourite meal. The butter used in cooking the chicken goes into the gravy so the more butter you use, the richer the gravy will be! Roast potatoes – crisp on the outside and tender within – are the perfect accompaniment. Use the very best chicken you can afford.

SERVES	PREP	COOK
SERVES 4-6	20-30 MINS	1-1¼ HRS

Ingredients

2kg (4½lb) chicken

salt and pepper

2-3 large thyme sprigs

2-3 large rosemary sprigs

1 bay leaf

60-75g (2-2½oz) butter

500ml (16fl oz) chicken stock

PREPARE THE CHICKEN

1 **Preheat the oven** to 220°C (425°F/Gas 7). Wipe the inside of the chicken with kitchen paper. Remove the wishbone for easier carving. Season the chicken inside and out. Put the herbs inside the chicken.

2 **Set the bird breast** up and push the legs back and down. Insert a metal skewer near the knee joint and push through the bird and out through the other leg. Turn the bird breast down. Pull the neck skin over the cavity and tuck the wing tips over it.

3 **Push a second skewer** through both sections of the wing, through the neck and out through the other wing. Tie the ends of the legs together with kitchen string.

ROAST THE CHICKEN

4 **Put the chicken** in a roasting tin, breast up. Cut the butter into slices and arrange them on the breast. Roast in the heated oven for 1-1¼ hours, basting with the juices in the tin every 10-15 minutes.

5 **Turn the chicken** on to its breast to keep it moist after it starts to brown. Return it breast up about 15 minutes before the end of cooking. Transfer to a carving board and cover with foil to keep warm.

MAKE THE GRAVY AND SERVE

6 **Add the stock** to the roasting tin and boil over high heat, stirring to dissolve the juices. Continue boiling until thoroughly reduced and concentrated. Taste for seasoning, then strain through a sieve into a gravy boat or serving bowl. Serve with the carved chicken.

Lamb chops in paper with fennel

CHOPS ENCLOSED IN BAKING PARCHMENT steam in their own juices, using the minimum fat for the maximum flavour. The paper parcels puff up and turn golden brown in the oven and, when opened, release wafts of delicious, gentle aniseed aroma.

SERVES SERVES 4	**PREP** 25–30 MINS	**COOK** 35–40 MINS

Ingredients

1kg (2¼lb) fennel bulbs

4 tbsp olive oil

2 garlic cloves, finely chopped

400g (14oz) can chopped tomatoes

3 tbsp pastis

salt and pepper

4 lamb loin chops, each 2.5cm (1in) thick, total weight about 625g (1lb 6oz)

melted butter, to brush

1 egg

PREPARE THE FENNEL

1 Trim off and discard the fennel stalks and root, alnog with any tough outer layers from the bulb. Reserve some green fronds for decoration. Thinly slice each fennel bulb.

2 Heat half the oil in a frying pan, add the fennel and garlic, and sauté for 6–8 minutes, until the fennel begins to soften.

3 Add three-quarters of the tomatoes, the pastis, salt, and pepper to the pan and cook, stirring occasionally, for 20-25 minutes, until the mixture is thick, and most of the moisture has evaporated. Taste for seasoning.

PREPARE THE LAMB

4 Meanwhile, cut the "tail" from each chop and season. Heat the remaining oil in another frying pan, add the chops and tails, and cook over high heat for 1-2 minutes, until well browned. Turn and brown the other side.

5 Fold a large sheet of baking parchment measuring about 30x37.5cm (12x15in) in half, and draw a curve to make a heart shape when unfolded, large enough to leave a 7.5cm (3in) border around a chop.

MAKE THE PAPER CASES

6 Cut out the heart shape with scissors. Repeat to make 4 paper hearts. Open out and brush each one with melted butter, leaving a border of about 2.5cm (1in) unbuttered.

7 Beat the egg with ½ tsp salt. Brush the egg glaze on the unbuttered border of each paper heart.

FILL THE PAPER CASES AND BAKE

8 Heat the oven to 190°C (375°F/Gas 5). Spoon a bed of the fennel mixture on 1 half of a paper heart.

9 Set a lamb chop and tail on top of the fennel mixture. Spoon a little of the reserved tomato over, and lay a fennel frond on top.

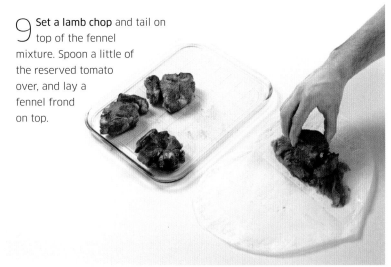

10 Fold the paper over the filling and run your fingers along the edge to stick the 2 sides of the heart together. Make small pleats to seal the edges of the paper case.

11 **Twist the ends** of the paper case to finish. Repeat the process with the remaining ingredients to make 4 paper parcels. Place on a baking sheet and bake for 10–14 minutes, until puffed and brown. Serve at once, allowing each diner to open their own parcel.

 VARIATION: Lamb chops in paper cases with leeks

This version is sweet flavoured and scented with herbs.

1 Omit the fennel. Trim 500g (1lb 2oz) leeks, discarding the root and tough green tops. Slit lengthways, wash thoroughly, drain well, and slice.

2 Strip the leaves from 3–5 rosemary or thyme sprigs, setting aside 4 small sprigs. Finely chop the leaves. Heat the oil in a frying pan and add the garlic, leeks, and all the tomatoes with 125ml (4fl oz) dry white wine, salt, and pepper. Continue as directed, omitting the pastis. Stir in the herbs at the end of cooking.

3 Brown the lamb chops, make the paper cases, and fill as directed, topping each chop with a reserved herb sprig. Bake and serve immediately.

Indonesian fried rice (nasi goreng)

WONDERFULLY RESTORATIVE and a good way to use up leftover cooked rice. This dish, from Java, is seasoned with hot chillies and sweet soy sauce. You can cook the rice and make the chilli-onion paste 1 day ahead; keep them separate, covered, in the refrigerator. Done like this, it is a great way to prepare for a very quick-to-make evening meal. Leave out the chicken and prawns and add mixed vegetables and tofu for a vegetarian version.

SERVES SERVES 4	**PREP** 40-45 MINS PLUS STANDING	**COOK** 10-15 MINS

Ingredients

250g (9oz) long-grain white rice

3 tbsp oil, plus more for the tray

1 onion, finely chopped

1 garlic clove, coarsely chopped

1 tsp dried prawn paste

1 tsp crushed chillies

2 eggs

125g (4½oz) raw, peeled large prawns

1 skinless, boneless chicken breast, weighing about 175g (6oz), very thinly sliced

2 spring onions, thinly sliced

2 tbsp sweet soy sauce, or 2 tbsp dark soy sauce plus 1 tbsp brown sugar, more if needed

COOK THE RICE

1 **Put the rice** in a large bowl, cover with cold water, and stir with your fingertips until the water has turned a milky white. Pour off the water. Repeat once or twice until the water is fairly clear. Drain in a sieve.

2 **Put the drained rice** in a saucepan and add 500ml (16fl oz) water. Bring to a boil over high heat. Stir, cover, then reduce the heat to low and simmer until all the water has been absorbed and the rice is tender; it should take about 15 minutes.

3 **Remove from the heat** and let the rice stand, without lifting the lid, for 15 minutes. Uncover, and stir to fluff it up. Lightly oil a baking sheet. Transfer the rice to the sheet and spread it out evenly so the steam can escape. Let it cool to room temperature.

MAKE THE CHILLI-ONION PASTE

4 **In a mortar,** pound the chopped onion with a pestle until pulpy. Add the garlic, prawn paste, and crushed chillies and pound until the mixture forms a coarse paste. Alternatively, purée the ingredients in a food processor. Set the paste aside.

MAKE THE OMELETTE STRIPS

5 **Beat the eggs** in a small bowl. Heat a wok over medium heat until hot. Drizzle in 1 tbsp of the oil to coat the bottom and sides of the wok. Continue heating until hot, then pour in the eggs.

6 **Quickly tilt the wok** so that the egg spreads over the bottom in an even layer. Cook for 1-2 minutes, until set in the centre and slightly crisp around the edge. Turn the omelette. Cook until the other side is lightly browned (15-30 seconds). Slide the omelette on to a chopping board. Let cool slightly. Roll it up loosely and cut into 1cm (½in) strips.

PREPARE THE PRAWNS

7 **Make a** shallow cut along the back of each prawn with a small, sharp knife and remove the dark intestinal vein. Rinse the prawns and pat them dry with kitchen paper.

STIR-FRY THE CHICKEN AND PRAWNS

8 **Heat the wok** over medium-high heat. Drizzle in 1 tbsp oil to coat the bottom and sides. When the oil is hot, stir in the chilli-onion paste; cook for about 30 seconds, until fragrant.

9 **Increase the heat** to high. Add the chicken slices and stir-fry for 2-3 minutes, until they are opaque.

10 **Add the prawns** and stir-fry until they turn pink, about 1–2 minutes. Using the spatula, transfer the chicken and prawns from the wok to a bowl and keep warm.

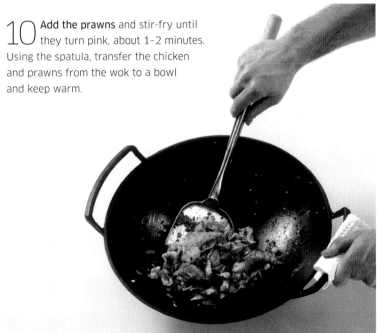

FINISH THE DISH

11 **Reduce the heat** to medium. Heat the remaining oil in the wok. Add the cooled rice and stir-fry until each grain is separate. You will need to keep turning it over and over with a flat spoon or a wok spatula, but be very gentle so the grains remain whole and do not begin to break up into a mush. Cover and cook the rice until it softens; this should only take about 3 minutes, stirring once or twice to prevent it from browning at the bottom of the wok.

12 **Add the spring onion**, sweet soy sauce, and a little salt, and stir-fry for about 1 minute longer until the flavourings are well dispersed throughout the rice. Return the omelette strips, chicken, and prawns to the wok; stir-fry over high heat until thoroughly combined and very hot all the way through, being very gentle so as not to break up any of the component parts. This should take about 2–3 minutes, but continue for as long as is necessary to get all the ingredients piping hot and steaming, continuing to stir so that nothing catches or browns at the bottom of the wok. Taste for seasoning, adding more soy sauce, if needed. The dish should be intensely flavoured with a good kick from the chilli. Serve at once.

Perfect fish and chips

DOUBLE-FRIED CHIPS are fluffy within and crisp without. The light beer batter makes the crust extra brittle and delicious. The traditional accompaniment to the dish is tartare sauce, and the recipe here beats anything you can buy in a jar hands down, so do give it a try.

SERVES	PREP	COOK
SERVES 4	45-50 MINS PLUS STANDING	20-25 MINS

Ingredients

FOR THE TARTARE SAUCE

125ml (4fl oz) mayonnaise

1 hard-boiled egg, coarsely chopped

1 tsp drained capers, chopped

2 gherkins, coarsely chopped

1 small shallot, finely chopped

leaves from 2-3 parsley sprigs, chopped

leaves from 2-3 chervil or tarragon sprigs, chopped

FOR THE FISH AND CHIPS

6 potatoes, total weight about 750g (1lb 10oz)

vegetable oil for deep-frying

30g (1oz) plain flour

salt and pepper

4 skinned cod fillets, total weight 750g (1lb 10oz)

1 lemon, cut into wedges, to serve

FOR THE BATTER

1½ tsp dried yeast (or 9g/⅓oz fresh yeast)

150g (5½oz) plain flour

1 tbsp vegetable oil

175ml (6fl oz) bitter ale

1 egg white

MAKE THE TARTARE SAUCE

1 Mix together the mayonnaise, egg, capers, gherkins, shallot, and herbs, and taste for seasoning. Cover the refrigerate until serving.

PREPARE THE POTATOES AND BATTER

2 Peel the potatoes and, with a knife, square off the sides and ends of each. Cut lengthways into 1cm (½in) sticks. Put in a bowl of cold water to soak for 30 minutes. This removes starch, so the chips will be crisp when fried. Meanwhile, sprinkle the dried or crumble the fresh yeast over 4 tbsp warm water and let stand for about 5 minutes, until dissolved.

3 Sift the flour and a pinch of salt into a large bowl and make a well in the centre. Add the yeast mixture, oil, and two-thirds of the beer; stir to form a smooth paste. Stir in the remaining beer. Do not overmix. Let the batter stand in a warm place for 30-35 minutes, until it has thickened and become frothy, showing the yeast is working.

PART-FRY THE CHIPS

4 While the batter is standing, heat the vegetable oil in a deep-fat fryer until it is at 180°C (350°F) on an oil thermometer. Drain the potatoes, transfer to kitchen paper and pat dry.

5 Dip the empty frying basket in the hot oil (this will prevent the potatoes sticking). Lift the basket out of the oil and add the potatoes. Carefully lower the basket back and deep-fry for 5-7 minutes, until just tender when pierced with the tip of a knife, and just starting to brown. Lift out and let drain over the deep fryer, then tip on to a plate lined with kitchen paper.

COAT AND DEEP-FRY THE FISH

6 Heat the oven to low. Heat the oil to 190°C (375°F). Put the flour on a plate and season with salt and pepper. Coat the pieces of fish with the flour, patting with your hands so they are evenly coated.

7 Beat the egg white in a medium metal bowl until stiff peaks form when the whisk is lifted. Gently fold the whisked egg white into the batter, using a wooden spoon, until combined.

8 Using a 2-pronged fork, dip a piece of fish in the batter, turning to coat thoroughly. Lift out the fish and hold it over the bowl for 5 seconds so excess batter can drip off.

9 Carefully lower the fish into the hot oil and deep-fry, turning once, until golden brown and crisp, 6–8 minutes depending on the thickness of the fillets. Coat and deep-fry the remaining fish, 1 or 2 pieces at a time.

FINISH THE CHIPS

10 As the fish is deep-fried, transfer to a baking sheet lined with kitchen paper so that excess oil is absorbed. Keep the fish warm in the oven, loosely covered with aluminium foil to keep in the moisture.

11 Put the partially cooked chips back in the frying basket and deep-fry for 1–2 minutes more, until very hot and golden brown. Drain on kitchen paper to soak up any excess oil from the chips.

12 Divide the fish and chips among warmed plates. Sprinkle the chips with a little salt to add flavour. Decorate the plates with the lemon wedges and serve at once, accompanied by the tartare sauce.

Onion confit and gorgonzola pizzas

ONIONS AND GORGONZOLA are delicious together, topping a crust made crunchy with polenta. To make an onion confit, sliced red onions are cooked very slowly in their own juices, with red wine added for colour and another depth of flavour.

SERVES	PREP	COOK
MAKES 6	40–45 MINS PLUS RISING	15–20 MINS

Ingredients

FOR THE DOUGH

1½ tsp dried yeast or 10g (⅓oz) fresh yeast

250g (9oz) unbleached strong white flour, plus more if needed

75g (2¾oz) polenta (fine yellow cornmeal), plus more for the foil

1 tsp salt

2 tbsp olive oil

FOR THE TOPPING

2 tbsp olive oil

750g (1lb 10oz) red onions, thinly sliced

2 tsp sugar

pepper

4 tbsp red wine

leaves from 5–7 oregano sprigs, finely chopped

175g (6oz) gorgonzola cheese

MAKE THE DOUGH

1 **In a small bowl,** sprinkle or crumble the yeast over 4 tbsp lukewarm water. Let stand for about 5 minutes until dissolved, stirring once.

2 **Put the flour** on to a work surface with the polenta and salt. Make a large well in the centre and add 150ml (5fl oz) lukewarm water, the oil and dissolved yeast.

3 **With your fingertips,** work the ingredients in the well until thoroughly mixed. Draw in the flour mixture, working it into the other ingredients with your hand to form a smooth dough. It should be soft and slightly sticky.

4 **Sprinkle the dough** and your hands with flour, and begin to knead by holding the dough with one hand and pushing it away from you with the other. Give the dough a quarter turn and knead for 5–7 minutes, until it is very smooth, elastic, and forms a ball. If the dough sticks while kneading, flour the work surface.

5 **Brush a large bowl** with oil and put in the dough, flipping it so the surface is lightly oiled. Cover with a damp tea towel, or clingfilm, and let rise in a warm place until doubled in bulk (1–1½ hours). To test the dough, press it gently but firmly with your forefinger. If the dough holds the impression of your finger, it has risen sufficiently.

MAKE THE RED ONION CONFIT

6 **Heat the oil** in a frying pan. Add the onions, sugar, salt, and pepper. Cook over medium heat, stirring often, for 5–7 minutes, until the onions are soft and lightly brown.

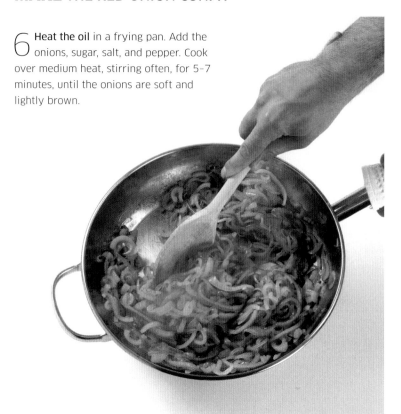

7 **Add the wine** and continue cooking until it has evaporated. Reduce the heat, press a piece of foil on top of the onions, and cover with a lid.

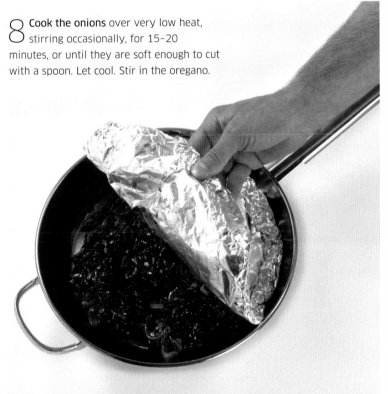

8 **Cook the onions** over very low heat, stirring occasionally, for 15-20 minutes, or until they are soft enough to cut with a spoon. Let cool. Stir in the oregano.

ASSEMBLE AND **BAKE** THE PIZZAS

9 **Preheat the oven** to 230°C (450°F/Gas 8). Put 2 baking sheets on separate racks in the bottom half of the oven to heat. Cut six 23cm (9in) squares of foil, and sprinkle each generously with polenta.

10 **Turn the dough** on to a lightly floured work surface and knead with your hand just to knock out the air. Cover the dough, and let rest for about 5 minutes.

11 **With your hands**, roll the dough into a cylinder about 5cm (2in) in diameter. Cut the cylinder in half, and then cut each half into 3 equal pieces. Shape the pieces of dough into balls.

12 **Roll a ball of dough** into an 18cm (7in) round. Transfer the round to 1 of the squares of foil. Repeat to shape the remaining dough. Press up the edges of the rounds with your fingertips to form shallow rims, if you like. Spread the rounds with the onion confit.

13 **Top the rounds with cheese**, and let rise in a warm place for about 15 minutes, until the dough is puffed. Bake the pizzas, on the foil, on the baking sheets, for 15-20 minutes, until lightly browned and crisp. Switch the baking sheets after 7 minutes so the pizzas brown evenly.

14 **Serve the pizzas** hot from the oven. Brush the crusts with olive oil, and top with the oregano sprigs, if you like.

Cold chicken and ham pie

A FOND MEMORY FROM CHILDHOOD. The tasty butter and lard crust encases a plentiful, juicy filling. This is wonderful to take on a picnic, served with chutney and a crisp green salad. It can be made up to 3 days ahead and kept refrigerated.

SERVES	PREP	COOK
SERVES 8-10	50-60 MINS PLUS COOLING	1½ HRS

Ingredients

FOR THE PASTRY

500g (1lb 2oz) plain flour

2 tsp salt

75g (2½oz) butter

75g (2½oz) lard

FOR THE FILLING

4 skinless, boneless chicken breasts, total weight about 750g (1lb 10oz)

375g (13oz) lean boneless pork

1 lemon

9 eggs

1 tsp dried thyme

1 tsp dried sage

ground nutmeg

salt and pepper

375g (13oz) cooked lean ham

butter for the pan

MAKE THE PASTRY

1 **Sift the flour** and salt into a large bowl. Make a well in the centre. Put the butter and lard in the well and cut them into small pieces with round-bladed knives. Rub with your fingertips until it forms fine crumbs.

2 **Make a well** in the centre again, add 150ml (¼ pint) water and mix quickly with a knife to form crumbs. If the mixture seems dry, add 1-2 tbsp more water. Mix with your fingers; it should be soft but not sticky.

3 **Turn the dough** on to a floured surface and knead lightly with the heel of your hand for 5-10 seconds, until smooth. Wrap the dough in clingfilm and chill for 30 minutes in the refrigerator.

MAKE THE FILLING

4 **Cut 2 of the chicken breasts** and the pork into chunks. Work the pork and chicken chunks through the fine blade of a mincer, or work in a food processor (not too finely). Put the minced meats in a large bowl.

5 **Grate the zest** from half of the lemon on to the minced meats. With a fork, beat 2 eggs; add to the minced meats with the thyme, sage, nutmeg, salt, and pepper. Beat the filling until it pulls from the side of the bowl.

6 **To test for seasoning,** fry a piece in a pan, and taste. It should be well seasoned, so add more salt and pepper if required. Cut the reserved chicken breasts and ham into 2cm (¾in) cubes and stir into the filling.

LINE THE TIN

7 **Butter the bottom a**nd side of a 20-23cm (8-9in) springform tin. Cut off about three-quarters of the dough and shape it into a ball; keep the remaining dough covered. On a floured surface, roll out the ball of dough into a 5mm (¼in) thick circle large enough to line the tin with dough left to overhang.

8 **Loosely roll the dough** around the rolling pin and unroll it over the tin. Do not stretch the dough or it will shrink during baking. Ease the dough into the tin, pressing it well into the bottom and side. Try to avoid pleats in the side. Trim the edges of the dough with scissors, leaving about 1cm (½in) overhanging. Add the trimmings to the remaining dough.

ASSEMBLE AND BAKE THE PIE

9 **Put 6 eggs in a saucepan** of cold water, bring to the boil and simmer for 10 minutes. Run cold water into the pan to stop the cooking, then allow the eggs to cool. Drain the eggs; tap them on a work surface to crack the shells all over, then peel. Preheat the oven to 200°C (400°F/Gas 6).

10 **Spread half the filling** in the pastry case. Arrange the eggs on top, gently pushing them into the filling. Cover with the remaining chicken mixture, ensuring all the gaps are filled. Fold over the trimmed dough overhang. Beat the remaining egg with pinch of salt for the glaze. Brush the edge of the dough with egg glaze.

11 **Roll out the remaining dough** to a circle about 5mm (¼in) thick. Set the tin on top and cut around the base to form a lid of dough the diameter of the tin. Lay the lid over the filling and press the edges of dough together to seal.

12 **Using a metal skewer,** poke a hole in the lid and insert a roll of foil to form a chimney, so the steam can escape during baking. Use the pastry trimmings to decorate the top, if you wish, glaze with beaten egg, and bake for 1 hour, until golden brown. Reduce the heat to 180°C (350°F/Gas 4) and bake for 30 minutes, until very brown. Allow to cool, discard the foil chimney and chill for 3-4 hours. Unmould and allow to come to room temperature before serving.

Roast leg of lamb with haricot beans

A GOOD ROAST LEG OF LAMB is unbeatable for flavour and succulence. This recipe comes from Brittany, and is accompanied by the haricot beans for which that region is famous. It's worth the effort of soaking dried beans for their superior texture.

SERVES
SERVES 6-8

PREP
35-40 MINS
PLUS SOAKING

COOK
1½-2 HRS

Ingredients

FOR THE BEANS

500g (1lb 2oz) dried haricot beans

1 onion

2 cloves

1 carrot, quartered

1 bouquet garni

2-3 parsley sprigs (optional)

FOR THE LAMB

2.7kg (6lb) leg of lamb

2 garlic cloves

1 onion, quartered

1 carrot, quartered

3 tbsp olive oil

leaves from 2-3 rosemary sprigs, chopped

salt and pepper

125ml (4fl oz) white wine

250ml (9fl oz) lamb stock or water, plus more if needed

SOAK AND COOK THE BEANS

1 Put the haricot beans in a bowl, pour in cold water to cover, and let soak overnight.

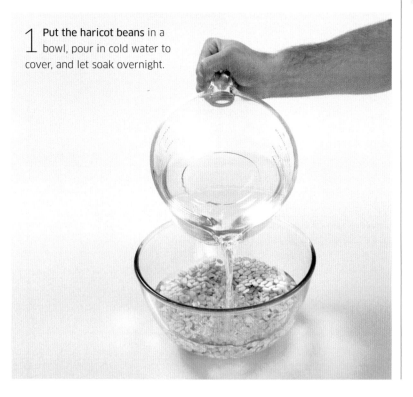

2 **Peel the onion** and stud with the cloves. Drain the beans and put them in a casserole; add the clove-studded onion, carrot, bouquet garni, and enough fresh water to cover by at least 2.5cm (1in).

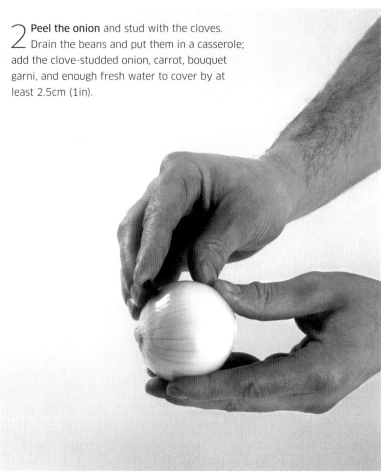

3 **Bring to a boil,** cover and simmer, skimming as necessary, for 1½-2 hours. Add hot water, as needed, to keep the beans covered. Season halfway through cooking. When cooked, the beans should be tender, but not mushy. Remove the onion, carrot, and bouquet garni, and discard.

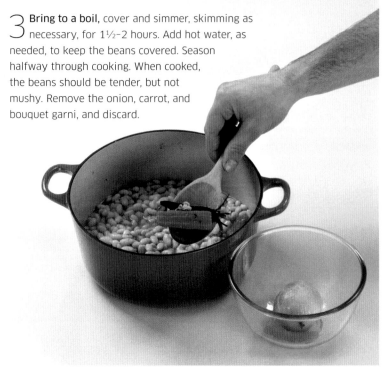

PREPARE AND ROAST THE LAMB

4 Preheat the oven to 230°C (450°F/Gas 8). Trim any skin and fat from the lamb. Peel the garlic and cut each clove into 4–5 thin slivers. Make several shallow incisions in the lamb with the point of a small knife. Insert the slivers of garlic.

5 Put the onion and carrot in a roasting tin. Set the lamb on top. Pour the oil over the lamb and sprinkle with the rosemary, salt, and pepper. Sear in the heated oven for 10–15 minutes, until browned.

6 Reduce the oven temperature to 180°C (350°F/Gas 4) and roast, basting often, 1–1¼ hours for rare meat or 1¼–1½ hours for medium. When rare, a skewer inserted for 30 seconds will be cool to the touch when withdrawn. A meat thermometer will show 52°C (125°F). When the meat is medium, the skewer will be warm and a meat thermometer will show 60°C (140°F).

FINISH THE DISH

7 Transfer the lamb to a warmed serving platter. Cover with foil and let it stand for 10–15 minutes, for the meat to rest and the juices to settle (this "resting" time makes for the most succulent meat). Make the gravy. Discard the excess fat from the roasting tin, leaving the carrot and onion.

8 Add the wine to the tin and boil until it has reduced by half. Add the stock and boil, stirring to dissolve the juices from the bottom of the tin, until the gravy is concentrated and well flavoured. It will take 5–10 minutes. Keep warm over a gentle heat.

9 Reheat the beans if necessary. Finely chop the parsley and sprinkle it on the beans, if you like. Carve the tender lamb into thin slices and arrange them on warmed plates. Spoon a mound of the beans next to it. Serve the gravy separately.

Chicken en cocotte with Parmesan

COOKED IN A COVERED CASSEROLE to keep moist and with a simple, piquant sauce sharpened with lemon and given richness from cream. These small chickens are incredibly moist. Serve them with a selection of crisply cooked vegetables. The chickens can be cooked and kept with their pan juices, covered, in the refrigerator up to 24 hours. Reheat them for about 20 minutes in an oven preheated to 180°C (350°F/Gas 4), then make the sauce just before serving.

SERVES	PREP	COOK
SERVES 4	15-20 MINUTES	45-55 MINUTES

Ingredients

FOR THE CHICKEN

2 x 1kg (2¼ b) chickens

salt and pepper

2 lemons

45g (1½oz) butter

FOR THE CHEESE SAUCE

125ml (4fl oz) chicken stock

125ml (4fl oz) double cream

1 tsp cornflour or arrowroot

30g (1oz) grated Parmesan cheese

TRUSS THE CHICKENS

1 **Wipe the inside of the birds** with kitchen paper and season inside and out. With a small knife, remove the wishbone. Set each bird breast up and push the legs back and down. Insert a threaded trussing needle at the knee joint and push it through the bird and out through the other knee joint.

2 **Turn the bird over** so it is breast down. Pull the neck skin over the cavity and tuck the wing tips over it. Push the needle through both sections of 1 wing and into the neck skin. Continue under the backbone of the bird to the other side. Push the needle through the second wing in the same way, through both wing bones.

3 **Turn the bird on to its side**. Pull the ends of the string firmly together and tie them securely. Turn the bird breast up. Tuck the tail into the cavity of the bird and fold over the top skin. Push the needle through the skin.

4 **Loop the string** around 1 drumstick, under the breastbone and over the other drumstick. Tie the ends of the string together. Repeat with the other bird. Chickens hold a better shape and are easier to carve if you truss them.

COOK THE CHICKENS

5 **Heat the oven** to 190°C (375°F/Gas 5). Pare the zest from the lemons with a vegetable peeler, then cut the pieces into fine julienne, discarding any of the bitter white pith.

6 **Melt the butter** in the casserole. Add 1 chicken and brown it on all sides for 5-10 minutes. Transfer it to the platter and brown the second chicken. Return the first chicken to the casserole. Add the lemon zest and cover. Cook in the oven, turning occasionally so they cook evenly.

7 **After 30-40 minutes**, lift the birds with a carving fork. The juices that run out should not be pink. Transfer the birds to a board, cover with foil and keep them warm.

8 **Remove the excess fat** from the casserole and discard.

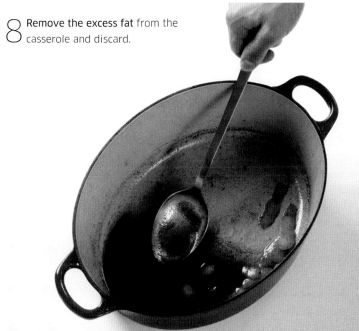

MAKE THE CHEESE SAUCE

9 **Add the stock t**o the casserole and bring to the boil, stirring to dissolve the pan juices. Boil for about 5 minutes, until well reduced. Strain it into a saucepan. Add the cream and whisk to mix, then bring just to a boil.

10 **Stir the cornflour** or arrowroot and 1 tbsp water together in a small bowl to form a smooth paste. Whisk in enough of the paste to thicken the sauce. It should lightly coat the back of a spoon.

11 **Take the sauce** from the heat and whisk in the Parmesan. Taste for seasoning. Keep warm.

FINISH THE CHICKEN

12 **Discard the trussing strings** from the chickens. Set a bird breast up on the board. Slice closely along the breastbone with a thin, sharp knife to loosen the meat. Cut along 1 side of the breastbone with poultry shears. Turn the bird over; cut along each side of the backbone and discard it. Repeat with the other bird. Set each chicken half on a warmed serving plate and spoon over the sauce.

Spicy tomato-bacon pasta

RED CHILLI BRINGS WARMTH to this dish. On the whole, Italians don't use a lot of chilli, but this arrabbiata sauce is an exception. The sauce can be made up to 2 days ahead, covered and refrigerated. Reheat it on top of the stove and cook the pasta just before serving.

SERVES
SERVES 6

PREP
35-40 MINS

COOK
30-40 MINS

Ingredients

125g (4½oz) thick-cut bacon rashers, sliced, or bacon lardons

375g (13oz) mushrooms, trimmed and sliced

2 garlic cloves, finely chopped

1 red chilli, deseeded and finely diced

leaves from 5-7 oregano sprigs, finely chopped

2 x 400g (14oz) cans chopped plum tomatoes

salt and pepper

500g (1lb 2oz) pasta quills

30g (1oz) butter

60g (2oz) grated Parmesan cheese

MAKE THE SAUCE

1 **Put the bacon** into a frying pan. Fry over low heat, stirring occasionally, for 5-7 minutes, until the bacon is lightly browned and the fat is rendered. Spoon off all but 3 tbsp of the fat. Increase the heat and add the mushrooms. Cook, stirring, for 3-5 minutes, until mushrooms have softened and most of the liquid has evaporated.

2 **Add the garlic,** chilli, oregano, chopped tomatoes, salt, and pepper. Bring to a boil, cover and simmer, stirring occasionally, for 25-30 minutes, until thick and rich. If necessary to thicken the sauce, continue to cook, uncovered, for a few minutes longer. Taste the sauce for seasoning.

COOK THE PASTA

3 **Fill a large pan** with cold water, bring to a boil, and add 1 tbsp salt. Add the pasta quills. Simmer until *al dente*, tender but still chewy, stirring occasionally. It should take 5-8 minutes, or cook according to the package directions. Drain in a colander.

FINISH THE DISH

4 **Put the quills** into a warmed serving bowl, and add the butter. Toss together until well coated. Spoon over the sauce and half the cheese. Toss together, then sprinkle over a little more Parmesan. Serve immediately, with the remaining cheese.

Pork chops with mustard sauce

WONDERFULLY COMFORTING, especially with mashed potatoes or buttered tagliatelle. Use a frying pan that will hold the pork chops snugly. If the pan is too big, the simmering liquid will not cover them sufficiently and they will dry out and may become tough. Use good-quality Dijon mustard here.

SERVES	PREP	COOK
SERVES 4	20-25 MINS	50-60 MINS

Ingredients

4 x 175g (6oz) pork chops	250ml (9fl oz) dry white wine
salt and pepper	250ml (9fl oz) chicken stock or water, plus more if needed
125g (4½oz) streaky bacon rashers, sliced	1 bouquet garni
	4 tbsp double cream
30g (1oz) butter	1 tbsp Dijon mustard, or to taste
1 tbsp plain flour	leaves from 5-7 parsley sprigs, finely chopped

PREPARE THE PORK CHOPS

1 **Trim excess fat** from the chops and sprinkle them with pepper. Heat the bacon in a frying pan and cook, stirring occasionally, for 3-5 minutes, until crisp and the fat has rendered. With a slotted spoon, remove from the pan and drain on kitchen paper.

2 **Discard all** but 1 tbsp of the bacon fat. Heat the butter with the remaining bacon fat until foaming. Add the chops and brown well over medium heat for about 5 minutes. Turn and brown the other side. Remove from the pan and set aside.

COOK THE CHOPS

3 **Remove the pan** from the heat and let cool slightly, then sprinkle in the flour, and cook, stirring, for 2-3 minutes. Whisk in the wine and stock or water. Add the bouquet garni and pepper and bring to a boil. Return the chops and bacon to the pan. Cover and simmer, stirring occasionally, for 5-10 minutes, until tender when pierced with a fork.

FINISH THE DISH

4 **Transfer the pork chops** to a plate and keep warm. Add the cream to the pan and bring just to a boil. Return the chops to the pan and heat gently for 2-3 minutes, so that the flavours blend.

5 **Arrange the chops**, bones pointing upwards, on a warmed platter. Taste the sauce for seasoning, whisking in more mustard if you like. Spoon the sauce over the chops, then sprinkle with the parsley.

Fisherman's pie

A HEARTY HOT MEAL and a traditional favourite. You'll find that everyone loves a good fish pie, and there are never any leftovers. One of the best ever dishes for entertaining, it can be made 1 day ahead and kept, covered, in the refrigerator.

SERVES	PREP	COOK
SERVES 6	35–45 MINS	20–30 MINS

Ingredients

625g (1lb 6oz) potatoes

salt and pepper

1 litre (1¾ pints) plus 4 tbsp milk

60g (2oz) butter

1 small onion

10 peppercorns

2 bay leaves

750g (1lb 10oz) skinned haddock fillets

90g (3oz) butter, plus more for the dish

60g (2oz) plain flour

leaves from 5–7 parsley sprigs, chopped

3 eggs, hard-boiled

125g (4½oz) cooked, peeled prawns

MAKE THE MASHED POTATO

1 **Wash and peel the potatoes.** Cut them into pieces. Half-fill a saucepan with water, add salt, then the potatoes, and bring to a boil. Simmer for 15–20 minutes, until tender. Drain thoroughly, then mash.

2 **Heat 4 tbsp milk** in a small saucepan. Add the butter, salt, and pepper and stir until mixed. Pour the hot milk mixture into the potatoes. Beat over medium heat for a few minutes, until fluffy. Taste for seasoning. Set aside.

COOK THE FISH

3 **Peel and quarter the onion.** Pour the remaining milk into a sauté pan, then add the peppercorns, bay leaves, and onion quarters.

4 **Bring to a boil,** then remove from the heat. Cover and let stand in a warm place to infuse for about 10 minutes.

5 **With a sharp knife,** cut each of the fillets across into pieces. Add the fish to the milk, cover and simmer for 5–10 minutes, depending on thickness; it should flake easily when tested with a fork .

6 **Transfer the fish** to a large plate, using a slotted spoon; reserve the cooking liquid. Let the fish cool, then flake with a fork.

MAKE THE SAUCE

7 Gently melt the butter in a saucepan over medium heat. Whisk in the flour and cook for 30-60 seconds, until foaming. Remove from the heat. Pour the reserved fish cooking liquid through a sieve into the butter and flour mixture.

8 Whisk the liquid into the sauce, then return to the heat and cook, whisking constantly, until the sauce boils and thickens. Season with salt and pepper and simmer for 2 minutes. Stir in the parsley.

ASSEMBLE AND BAKE THE PIE

9 Preheat the oven to 180°C (350°F/Gas 4). Melt some butter and use it to butter a 2 litre (3½ pint) pie dish. Coarsely chop the hard-boiled eggs. Ladle a third of the sauce into the bottom of the dish.

10 Spoon the flaked haddock on top of the sauce, in an even layer. Cover with the remaining sauce, then distribute the prawns evenly on the surface. Sprinkle the chopped hard-boiled eggs over the top.

11 Spread the mashed potatoes on top, so it is covered completely. Bake in the heated oven for 20-30 minutes, until the potato topping is brown and the sauce bubbles around the edge. Serve hot from the dish, on to warmed plates.

 VARIATION: Individual fish crumbles

Rolled oats and Parmesan cheese add texture and flavour to this version of fish pies.

1 Follow the main recipe, replacing the potato topping with crumble topping. To make the crumble, sift 150g (5½oz) plain flour into a bowl. Cut 90g (3oz) butter into small pieces in the flour. Rub in the butter with your fingertips, lifting the mixture up so it is aerated as it floats back down into the bowl, until the mixture resembles fine crumbs. Make sure there are no large pieces of butter remaining in the mixture.

2 Chop the leaves from 3-5 additional parsley sprigs. Stir 40g (1½oz) rolled oats into the butter and flour, with the additional chopped parsley, 1 tbsp grated Parmesan cheese (or to taste), salt, and pepper. Stir together gently but very well, until all the flavours are evenly distributed throughout the crumble topping.

3 Butter 6 individual casserole dishes or large ramekins and layer the ingredients as directed in the main recipe. Sprinkle the crumble topping evenly over the pies and bake them for 20-25 minutes. If necessary, brown the individual fish crumbles under the grill for 1-2 minutes more, until golden and the sauce bubbles around the edges, being careful not to scorch the crumble.

Cabbage with chestnut and pork

AN OLD FAVOURITE, ideal for a cold day. It is far easier than you might imagine to assemble the dish, and everyone loves the rich stuffing. A tomato and mushroom sauce is the perfect complement.

SERVES
SERVES 6

PREP
35–40 MINS

COOK
50–60 MINS

Ingredients

FOR THE CABBAGE

1.4kg (3lb) head of Savoy cabbage

salt and pepper

125g (4½oz) lean, boneless pork

1 onion

2 slices of white bread

60g (2oz) butter

2 celery sticks, peeled and thinly sliced

500g (1lb 2oz) canned or vacuum-packed unsweetened chestnuts, chopped

leaves from 10 parsley sprigs, chopped

10–12 sage leaves, finely chopped

finely grated zest of 1 lemon

2 eggs

FOR THE SAUCE

2 tbsp vegetable oil

1 small onion, finely chopped

500g (1lb 2oz) tomatoes, chopped

1 tbsp tomato purée

1 garlic clove, finely chopped

1 bouquet garni

granulated sugar

125g (4½oz) mushrooms, sliced

PREPARE THE CABBAGE

1 **Cut the outside leaf** from the base of the cabbage stalk, and carefully peel the leaf from the head, being careful not to tear it. Repeat, until you have removed the ten largest cabbage leaves. Wash the leaves very well in cold water to remove any soil or grit.

2 **Bring a large saucepan** of water to a boil. Add salt, then immerse the ten large cabbage leaves in the water and blanch for 1 minute, to soften them. With a slotted spoon, transfer the leaves to a bowl of cold water to stop the cooking.

3 **Trim and discard** the stalk from the remaining cabbage head, and cook it in the boiling water for 3–4 minutes. Transfer it to a bowl of cold water to stop the cooking. When cool, remove and drain thoroughly, stalk-end down, in the colander.

4 **When the leaves are cool,** drain and carefully pat each dry with kitchen paper. Remove and discard the thick rib at the centre of each large cabbage leaf with a sharp knife. Slice the cabbage head in half. Cut a wedge around the core in each half of cabbage and remove and discard it. Shred the leaves reasonably fine.

MAKE THE STUFFING

5 **Cut the pork** into 2–3 pieces and the onion into quarters. Work the pork and onion through the fine blade of a mincer, or in a food processor.

6 **Trim and discard** the crusts from the bread. Work to crumbs in a food processor. Melt the butter in a frying pan, add the shredded cabbage, and cook, stirring, for 7–10 minutes, until tender. Transfer to a large bowl.

7 **Put the minced pork** and onion into the frying pan with the celery. Cook, stirring occasionally, until the minced pork is crumbled and brown; it should take 5–7 minutes.

8 **Add the breadcrumbs,** chestnuts, chopped herbs, lemon zest, salt, and pepper to the shredded cabbage. Add the pork and stir well together. Taste for seasoning. Lightly beat the eggs and stir into the stuffing.

STUFF AND COOK THE CABBAGE

9 **Line a large bowl** with a damp tea towel. Arrange 9 blanched cabbage leaves in an overlapping layer around the inside. Allow about 5cm (2in) of the leaves to extend above the rim. Set the last leaf in the bottom of the bowl. Spoon in the stuffing, then press it down gently.

10 **Fold the ends** of the cabbage leaves over, to enclose the chestnut stuffing completely.

11 Gather the ends of the cloth over the top of the cabbage, and tie them together with a piece of the string to make a tight ball.

12 Bring a large pan of water to a boil. Immerse the stuffed cabbage in the water, and set a heatproof plate on top to weigh it down. Simmer for 50–60 minutes, until a skewer inserted in the centre for 30 seconds comes out hot to the touch.

MAKE THE SAUCE

13 Heat half the oil in a frying pan. Add the onion and cook, stirring, for 2–3 minutes, until soft. Stir in the tomatoes, tomato purée, garlic, bouquet garni, salt, pepper, and a pinch of sugar, and cook, stirring occasionally, for 8–10 minutes, until fairly thick.

14 Sieve the tomato mixture into a bowl, pressing down to extract the pulp. Wipe the frying pan, heat the remaining oil, and sauté the mushrooms until tender. Stir in the tomato sauce and taste for seasoning.

15 Lift the cabbage from the pan, drain and let cool slightly. Unwrap and set it, stalk down, on a warmed plate. Cut into wedges to serve. Serve the sauce separately.

Baked rigatoni with meatballs

A PERENNIAL FAMILY FAVOURITE. Italians would use finger-length macaroni called mezzani, but other shapes of pasta tubes, such as penne, make a fine alternative. This is a very convenient recipe as the whole dish can be baked 1 day ahead, covered, and kept refrigerated. Reheat it in an oven at 190°C (375°F/Gas 5) for 20 minutes.

SERVES	PREP	COOK
SERVES 6-8	45-50 MINS	30-40 MINS

Ingredients

FOR THE SAUCE AND PASTA

2 x 400g cans chopped plum tomatoes

3 garlic cloves, finely chopped

leaves from 1 bunch of basil, chopped

salt and pepper

375g (13oz) rigatoni

FOR THE MEATBALLS

500g (1lb 2oz) lean minced beef

125g (4½oz) grated Parmesan cheese

leaves from 3-5 flat-leaf parsley sprigs, chopped

juice of ½ lemon

1 egg

3 tbsp olive oil, plus more for the dish

MAKE THE TOMATO-BASIL SAUCE

1 **Put the tomatoes** in a frying pan and add two-thirds of the garlic, basil, and salt. Stir over medium heat for 10-12 minutes, until thickened. Transfer to a food processor, and purée. Set aside. Wipe the frying pan clean.

MAKE THE MEATBALLS

2 **Put the minced beef,** a quarter of the Parmesan, the parsley, remaining garlic, lemon juice, salt, and pepper in a bowl. Add the egg. Mix all the ingredients in the bowl with your hands until they are thoroughly combined.

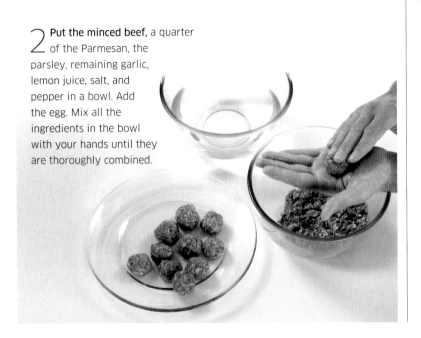

3 **Test the mixture for seasoning:** heat 1 tbsp oil in a frying pan, add a small spoon of meat mixture, and fry until brown on both sides. Taste and adjust the seasoning of the remaining mixture, if necessary. Shape the mixture into meatballs about 2cm (¾in) in diameter, wetting the palms of your hands so shaping the meat is easier.

4 **Heat the remaining oil** in the frying pan. Add the meatballs, making sure they are not crowded. (If necessary, fry them in batches.) Fry the meatballs briskly, turning, for 2-4 minutes, until they are brown on the outside and still pink inside. Transfer to a large plate with a slotted spoon. Set aside.

MAKE THE PASTA AND BAKE

5 **Preheat the oven** to 190°C (375°F/Gas 5). Brush the inside of a 2 litre (3½ pint) deep baking dish or souffle dish lightly with a little olive oil.

6 **Fill a large saucepan** with water, bring to a boil, and add 1 tbsp salt. Add the pasta to the pan and simmer for 8–10 minutes, until *al dente*, tender but still chewy, or according to package directions. Stir occasionally to keep from sticking.

7 **Drain the pasta** in a colander, rinse with hot water, and drain again thoroughly. Return the pasta to the saucepan and pour in the tomato-basil sauce. Gently stir the pasta and sauce together, until the pasta is well coated.

8 **Spoon about a third** of the pasta and sauce into the prepared dish, and level the surface. Spoon half the meatballs on top. Sprinkle with a third of the remaining cheese. Top with half the remaining pasta, and then the rest of the meatballs. Sprinkle with half the remaining Parmesan.

9 **Add the remaining pasta** and top with the remaining Parmesan. Bake in the heated oven for 30–40 minutes, until very hot and the top is browned. Let stand for about 15 minutes, so the flavours blend together. Sprinkle with a little shredded basil, if you like, and serve warm.

---

§§§ **VARIATION:** Baked ziti with mozzarella and olives

Anchovies spice the sauce in this version.

1 Chop eight anchovy fillets very finely. Make the tomato sauce as directed in the main recipe, adding the chopped anchovies to the tomatoes with the garlic. You will find the anchovies disappear as they will 'melt' into the sauce. Omit the basil and the meatballs. Stone 195g (6¾oz) oil-cured black olives. Cut 250g (9oz) mozzarella cheese into small, fairly even cubes. Oil the dish as directed.

2 Cook 375g (13oz) chunky ziti as for the pasta in the main recipe, or according to the package directions, and drain thoroughly. Layer the pasta, sauce, and fillings as directed, using the olives in place of the meatballs and the mozzarella cubes in place of the Parmesan, spreading it throughout the dish and using it as a topping as well.

3 Bake as directed for 20–25 minutes, until the pasta dish is very hot, golden brown and bubbling, and the cheese has melted. Set aside to rest for about 15 minutes, then serve on warmed plates. The piquancy given from the olives and anchovies is delicious next to the creamy, sweet mozzarella.

Aunt Sally's meat loaf

A TRUE AMERICAN CLASSIC, great with mashed potatoes and ketchup or cranberry sauce. It makes an excellent dish for family gatherings, as it can be made 2 days ahead and kept, covered, in the refrigerator. Reheat it for 20 minutes in an oven preheated to 180°C (350°F/Gas 4) for a hot dish, though this is also excellent sliced and served cold as part of a buffet spread.

SERVES	PREP	COOK
SERVES 4–6	25–30 MINS	1–1½ HRS

Ingredients

175g (6oz) spinach

salt and pepper

375g (13oz) streaky bacon rashers

2 eggs

6 slices of white bread

750g (1lb 10oz) minced beef

250g (9oz) minced veal

1 large onion, finely chopped

4 garlic cloves, finely chopped

leaves from 3–4 thyme sprigs

leaves from 3–4 rosemary sprigs, chopped

1 tbsp Worcestershire sauce

PREPARE THE INGREDIENTS

1 **Remove the tough ribs** and stalks from the spinach. Wash it well in a sink of water, then repeat, until all traces of grit and soil are gone. Half-fill a saucepan with water and bring to a boil. Add salt, then the spinach and simmer for 2–3 minutes, just until tender. Do not overcook, or the spinach will lose its vivid colour and the flavour will dull.

2 **Drain the spinach** in a colander, rinse with cold water to stop the cooking and retain the bright green colour, and drain again thoroughly. Squeeze the spinach hard between your hands to remove all excess water from the leaves, then chop.

3 **Cut the bacon** into tiny strips, reserving 4 neat rashers for the top of the meat loaf. Lightly beat the eggs in a small bowl until evenly blended. Trim off and discard the crusts from the bread. Work the bread slices in the food processor or a blender, using the pulse button, until they form even crumbs, then tip them into a large bowl that is big enough to comfortably hold all the remaining ingredients.

MIX AND BAKE THE MEAT LOAF

4 **Preheat the oven** to 180°C (350°F/Gas 4). Add the minced meat, chopped spinach, onion, garlic, thyme, rosemary, Worcestershire sauce, salt, and pepper to the large bowl and mix.

5 **Add the beaten eggs** and lightly mix them in. To test for seasoning, fry a spoonful of the mixture in a frying pan until browned on both sides. Taste it and add more seasoning to the remaining mixture if necessary.

6 **Transfer** to a 23x13x7.5cm (9x5x3in), or 900g (2lb), loaf tin, pressing it down and patting with a wooden spoon to smooth the top. Arrange the reserved bacon rashers on top of the meat loaf.

7 **Bake the meat loaf** in the heated oven for 1-1¼ hours, until a skewer inserted in the centre for 30 seconds comes out hot to the touch. Let it stand at least 10 minutes in the tin to reabsorb the juices and become easier to slice. Run a knife around the edge, unmould the meat loaf and cut into slices.

 VARIATION: Pork loaf with apricots

A sweet yet savoury version.

1 Soak 150g (5½oz) dried apricots in hot water to cover until plump. It should take about 15 minutes, but can be left for longer as they will only plump up more. Coarsely chop three-quarters of the volume of apricots and cut the rest in half.

2 Prepare the meat loaf ingredients as directed, omitting the spinach and bacon, and substituting minced pork for minced beef.

3 Put half the meat loaf mixture in the pan and spread the chopped apricots on top. Cover with the remaining meat and arrange the apricot halves on top. Bake and finish as directed in the main recipe. Take care that the apricots on top of the loaf do not threaten to burn; if they do, cover with a layer of foil.

Spinach gnocchi in tomato cream

THESE NEVER FAIL to please. The shape of the gnocchi, which are made with potato for a light texture, ensures that they both cook evenly and hold on to the sauce well. The tomato sauce can be made to the end of step 2 up to 1 day ahead and kept, tightly covered, in the refrigerator. Add the cream and bake the spinach gnocchi just before serving the dish.

SERVES	PREP	COOK
SERVES 6-8	50-55 MINS	30-40 MINS

Ingredients

FOR THE SAUCE

45g (1½oz) butter, plus more for the dish

1 small onion, finely chopped

1 carrot, finely chopped

1 celery stick, finely chopped

2 x 400g (14oz) cans chopped plum tomatoes

salt and pepper

250ml (8fl oz) double cream

1 pinch of ground nutmeg

FOR THE GNOCCHI

1kg (2¼lb) baking potatoes

250g (9oz) fresh or 150g (5½oz) defrosted spinach

125g (4½oz) plain flour, plus more if needed

MAKE THE SAUCE

1 Melt the butter in a frying pan. Add the onion, carrot, and celery, and cook over medium heat, stirring, for 7-10 minutes, until tender.

2 Add the tomatoes to the pan with any juice, salt, and pepper, and simmer, stirring occasionally, for 25-35 minutes, until thick. Transfer to a food processor and purée until smooth. Wipe the frying pan clean.

MAKE THE GNOCCHI

3 Peel the potatoes, and cut each one into several pieces. Put them in a saucepan of cold, salted water, cover and bring to a boil. Simmer for 15-20 minutes, until very tender when pierced with the tip of a knife.

4 Drain the potatoes until completely dry. If the potatoes seem at all moist, spread them on a baking sheet and let dry in a low oven with the door open for 5-10 minutes. Mash the potatoes in the pan until there are no lumps remaining.

5 Prepare the fresh spinach, if using: discard the tough ribs and stalks, then wash the leaves. Bring another saucepan of cold, salted water to a boil. Add the spinach and simmer for 1-2 minutes. Drain the spinach, rinse with cold water, and drain again.

6 Squeeze the cooked fresh spinach, or defrosted spinach, in your fist to remove all excess water. Purée the spinach in a food processor, or chop it finely with a sharp knife.

7 Add the spinach to the potatoes with the flour, salt, and pepper, and mix together well. Taste for seasoning. Transfer to a lightly floured work surface, and knead lightly to form a dough, working in a little more flour to bind the mixture, if necessary.

8 To test the consistency, roll a 2cm (¾in) ball of dough, drop it into a saucepan of simmering water, and cook until it floats to the surface. If the gnocchi falls apart, add about 2 tbsp more flour to the dough, then test again. If the gnocchi holds, shape the remaining dough.

SHAPE AND COOK THE GNOCCHI

9 Divide the dough into 12 equal pieces. Lightly flour your hands; roll each piece into a cylinder about 1cm (½in) in diameter. Then cut each into logs 2cm (¾in) long. Lightly flour a baking sheet. Hold a fork in one hand with the concave side towards you. With the thumb of your other hand, roll each piece of dough along the prongs, then drop on to the baking sheet.

10 Preheat the oven to 220°C (425°F/Gas 7). Butter a baking dish. Heat a large pan of salted water to boiling. Add a quarter of the gnocchi. Cook, stirring occasionally, for 1-2 minutes, until they float to the surface.

11 Transfer the gnocchi to drain on paper towels, then place in the baking dish. Continue cooking the gnocchi in batches.

ASSEMBLE AND BAKE THE DISH

12 Reheat the sauce in a frying pan until it is piping hot, but not boiling. Remove from the heat, and evenly stir in the cream. Do not heat the sauce on the stove top again after this point, or it may separate. Season to taste with salt, pepper, and a little nutmeg. If your tomatoes were not very sweet, you may also find you need to add a pinch of sugar, so check it and see what you would prefer.

13 Spoon the sauce evenly over the gnocchi in the baking dish, making sure some runs under the dumplings as well as on top. This will prevent the gnocchi from sticking to the dish when in the oven. Bake in the heated oven until very hot and the top is starting to brown; it should only take about 5-7 minutes. Check that the dish is hot all the way to the centre: insert a metal skewer right to the middle of the dish; the tip should be very hot to the touch when withdrawn. Serve the gnocchi immediately on to warmed plates, sprinkled with chopped flat-leaf parsley to add a splash of colour, if you like.

Chicago deep-dish pizza

A HEARTY PIZZA, dating back to 1940s Chicago. Not only will the kneading prove enormously therapeutic, but the pizza's generous depths of Italian sausage and melting mozzarella could have been designed to soothe the soul. The dough can be made, kneaded, and left to rise in the refrigerator overnight, if it's more convenient.

SERVES	PREP	COOK
SERVES 6-8	35-40 MINS PLUS RISING	20-25 MINS

Ingredients

FOR THE DOUGH

2½ tsp dried yeast, or 15g (½oz) fresh yeast

500g (1lb 2oz) unbleached strong white flour, plus more if needed

2 tsp salt

3 tbsp olive oil, plus more for the bowl and pan

2-3 tbsp polenta (fine yellow cornmeal)

FOR THE SAUCE

375g (13oz) mild Italian sausage

1 tbsp olive oil

3 garlic cloves, finely chopped

2 x 400g cans chopped plum tomatoes

pepper

leaves from 7-10 flat-leaf parsley sprigs, chopped

175g (6oz) mozzarella cheese

MAKE THE DOUGH

1 **In a small bowl,** sprinkle or crumble the yeast over 4 tbsp lukewarm water. Let stand until dissolved for about 5 minutes, stirring once.

2 **Put the flour** on to a work surface with the salt. Make a large well in the centre and add the dissolved yeast, 300ml (½ pint) lukewarm water, and the oil. With your fingertips, work the liquid ingredients in the centre of the well until thoroughly and evenly mixed. Begin to draw in the flour.

3 **Continue to draw in the flour** and work it into the other ingredients, to form a smooth dough. It should be soft and slightly sticky.

4 **Sprinkle the dough** and your hands with flour, and begin to knead by holding the dough with 1 hand, and pushing it away from you with the other. Peel the dough from the surface, give it a quarter turn, and knead for 5-7 minutes, until very smooth, elastic and forms a ball. If the dough sticks while kneading, flour the work surface.

5 **Brush a large bowl** with oil. Put the dough in the bowl and flip it so the surface is lightly oiled. Cover with a damp tea towel and let the dough rise in a warm place for 1-1½ hours, until doubled in bulk.

MAKE THE SAUCE

6 **Slit the side** of each sausage and push out the meat, discarding the casing. Heat the oil in a sauté pan. Add the sausage meat, and fry over medium-high heat, breaking up the meat with the wooden spoon, for 5-7 minutes, until cooked. Reduce the heat to medium, remove the meat from the pan, and pour off all but 1 tbsp of the fat.

7 **Stir the garlic** into the pan and fry for about 30 seconds, until fragrant. Return the sausage and stir in the tomatoes, salt, pepper, and all but 1 tbsp of the parsley.

8 **Cook, stirring occasionally,** for 10-15 minutes, until the sauce has thickened. Remove the sauce from the heat, taste for seasoning, and let cool completely. Chop or tear the mozzarella into small chunks.

ASSEMBLE AND BAKE THE PIZZA

9 **Brush a 35cm (14in) pizza pan,** or 2 x 23cm (9in) cake tins, with oil. Sprinkle the polenta in the pan or tins, and turn it to coat the bottom and side, then turn upside down and tap to remove the excess. Turn the dough on to a lightly floured work surface and knock out the air for 15-20 seconds. Cover, and let rest for about 5 minutes.

10 **Shape the dough** into a loose ball. With a rolling pin, roll the ball into a round or rounds to fit your pan or tins. Working carefully, wrap the dough around the rolling pin and drape it over the pan or tins.

11 **With your hands,** press the dough into the bottom of the pan or tins, and 2.5cm (1in) up the side, to form a rim.

12 **Cover with a dry tea towel,** and let rise for about 20 minutes. Preheat the oven to 230°C (450°F/Gas 8). Heat a baking sheet in the oven. Spread the sauce over the dough, leaving a border. Sprinkle over the cheese and remaining parsley. Bake for 20–25 minutes, until crisp and golden.

Spiced lamb pies

A LEAVENED DOUGH WRAPPED around a delicious lamb filling, similar to snacks found all around the Middle East. The filling can be prepared, covered and refrigerated up to 1 day ahead. You can also make the dough in an electric mixer fitted with a dough hook, to save kneading.

SERVES	PREP	COOK
MAKES 12	40-45 MINS PLUS RISING	20-25 MINS

Ingredients

FOR THE DOUGH

1 tsp dried yeast, or 6g (⅕oz) fresh yeast

2 tsp olive oil, plus more for bowl and baking sheet

1 tsp salt

60g (2oz) strong wholemeal flour

250g (9oz) unbleached strong, white flour, plus more if needed

FOR THE FILLING

2 tbsp olive oil

375g (13oz) minced lamb

salt and pepper

3 large garlic cloves, finely chopped

1cm (½in) piece of fresh root ginger, finely chopped

1 onion, finely chopped

½ tsp ground coriander

¼ tsp ground cumin

¼ tsp ground turmeric

large pinch of cayenne pepper

2 tomatoes, peeled, deseeded, and chopped

leaves from 5-7 coriander sprigs, finely chopped

MAKE THE DOUGH AND LET IT RISE

1 **In a bowl**, sprinkle the yeast over 4 tbsp warm water. Let stand, stirring once, for 5 minutes. Put the yeast, 250ml (8fl oz) lukewarm water, oil, and salt in a bowl. Mix in the wholemeal with half the strong white flour.

2 **Add the remaining** strong white flour, 60g (2oz) at a time, mixing after each addition, until the dough pulls away from the side of the bowl. Turn on to a floured work surface.

3 **Holding the dough** with one hand, press firmly down into the dough with the heel of your other hand, pushing away from you. Peel it from the work surface in one piece, fold it over, and give it a quarter turn.

4 **Continue kneading** the dough, until very smooth and elastic. If the dough sticks while kneading, flour the work surface. Press the dough with your finger; it will spring back when it has been sufficiently kneaded.

5 **Wash a large bowl** and brush it with oil. Put the dough in the bowl, and flip it, so the surface is lightly oiled. Cover with a damp tea towel and let rise in a warm place for 1-1½ hours, until doubled in bulk.

PREPARE THE FILLING

6 **Heat the oil** in a sauté pan. Add the lamb, season and stir over medium-high heat, until evenly browned. With a slotted spoon, transfer to a bowl. Reduce the heat to medium, and pour off all but 2 tbsp of the fat.

7 **Add the garlic** and ginger and fry for 30 seconds, until fragrant. Add the onion and stir until soft. Add the ground coriander, cumin, turmeric, cayenne, lamb and tomatoes, cover and cook for 10 minutes, until thickened.

8 **Remove the pan** from the heat. Stir in the chopped coriander leaves and taste for seasoning. Let the filling cool, then taste again: it should be well seasoned, so adjust if necessary.

SHAPE THE PIES

9 **Brush two baking sheets** with oil. Turn the dough onto a lightly floured work surface, and knock out the air for 15-20 seconds. Cover the dough. Let rest for about 5 minutes.

10 **Cut the dough** in half. Shape one piece into a cylinder about 5cm (2in) in diameter. Cut into six pieces, and cover them. Repeat to shape and divide the remaining dough.

BAKE THE PIES

13 **Cover the pies** with a clean, dry tea towel, and let rise in a warm place until they have puffed up once more. It should take about 20 minutes, but will depend on the weather, humidity, and the temperature of the room, so be patient and experiment until your knowledge increases. Do not give up and bake them before they have properly risen! Meanwhile, preheat the oven to 230°C (450°F/Gas 8).

14 **Bake the pies** in the heated oven until the bottoms are golden brown and ring hollow when tapped with a finger. It will take 10-15 minutes. Serve the pies warm from the oven, with a spoonful or two of Greek yogurt on the side, if you like.

11 **Shape a piece of dough** into a ball. With a rolling pin, roll into a 10cm (4in) round. Spoon some of the lamb into the centre of the round, leaving a 2.5cm (1in) border. Lift the dough up and over the filling, to form a triangular parcel.

12 **Pinch the edges with** your fingers to seal. Place the pie on a prepared baking sheet. Repeat to shape and fill the remaining dough.

Spinach-stuffed veal

A STUFFING OF SPINACH, Parmesan, and walnuts enlivens this Italian favourite. If you like, you can substitute beef, pork, chicken, or turkey for the veal here. The rolls can be cooked up to 2 days ahead, covered and refrigerated, or they can be frozen. Their flavour will mellow.

SERVES	PREP	COOK
SERVES 4	45–50 MINS	30–40 MINS

Ingredients

FOR THE STUFFING

500g (1lb 2oz) fresh or 300g (10½oz) frozen and defrosted spinach

2 tbsp olive oil

8 garlic cloves, finely chopped

45g (1½oz) walnuts, chopped

30g (1oz) grated Parmesan cheese

salt and pepper

freshly grated nutmeg

FOR THE VEAL

8 veal escalopes, total weight about 625g (1lb 6oz)

2 tbsp olive oil, plus more if needed

1 onion, thinly sliced

1 carrot, thinly sliced

2 celery sticks, thinly sliced

250ml (9fl oz) dry white wine

250ml (9fl oz) chicken stock, plus more if needed

MAKE THE STUFFING

1 **If using fresh spinach**, trim and wash it. Bring a saucepan of water to the boil, add the spinach and simmer for 1–2 minutes, then drain. Squeeze either fresh or defrosted spinach to remove excess water, then chop.

2 **Heat the oil** in a frying pan, and add the spinach. Stir until any moisture has evaporated. Remove from the heat, add half the garlic, the walnuts, Parmesan, salt, pepper, and nutmeg. Stir well, and taste for seasoning.

MAKE THE VEAL ROLLS

3 **If necessary,** flatten the escalopes: put the veal slices between two sheets of baking parchment. Gently pound to 3mm (⅛in) thick with a rolling pin. Lay one escalope on a work surface and season. Spread about one-eighth of the spinach stuffing on top.

4 **Roll up the meat**, tucking in the ends. Repeat with the remaining escalopes and stuffing. Tie up the rolls in neat packages, or secure each with a wooden toothpick, threading it in and out along the seam.

COOK THE VEAL

5 **Heat the olive oil** in a sauté pan, and add the veal rolls. Cook over high heat, turning occasionally, until well browned on all sides, 2–3 minutes. Transfer to a plate and set aside; slice to serve when the sauce is ready.

6 **Stir the onion** and remaining garlic into the pan, and cook until softened. Add the carrot and celery. Reduce the heat and cook for 8–10 minutes, until tender. Pour in the wine, bring to a boil and simmer to reduce by half.

7 **Return the veal** to the pan, and add the stock. Cover and simmer for 30–40 minutes, until tender. Strain the liquid into a saucepan, reserving the vegetables, and boil until reduced to 175ml (6fl oz); taste and serve.

Prawn risotto

SMOOTH AND CREAMY, but slightly firm to the bite. Perfect for a cold night. You have to stir a risotto constantly, to release the starch from the grains of rice and achieve the blissfully smooth texture, but the results are well worth it. Serve it the moment it is ready.

SERVES	PREP	COOK
SERVES 6	15-20 MINS	25-30 MINS

Ingredients

500g (1lb 2oz) small or medium raw prawns

90ml (3fl oz) olive oil

2 garlic cloves, finely chopped

leaves from 1 small bunch of flat-leaf parsley, chopped

salt and pepper

4 tbsp dry white wine

1 litre (1¾ pints) fish or chicken stock

1 onion, finely chopped

420g (15oz) arborio rice

PREPARE THE PRAWNS AND COOKING LIQUID

1 **Make a shallow cut** along the back of each prawn with a small knife, and remove the dark intestinal vein. Heat a third of the oil in a saucepan, and add the peeled prawns, garlic, parsley, salt, and pepper.

2 **Cook, stirring,** just until the prawns turn pink (a matter of 1-2 minutes). Pour in the wine and stir thoroughly. Transfer the prawns to a bowl; set aside. Simmer the liquid in the pan for 2–3 minutes, until reduced by three-quarters. Add the stock and 250ml (9fl oz) water, and heat to boiling. Keep the liquid simmering.

MAKE THE RISOTTO

3 **Heat half the remaining oil** in a large saucepan. Add the onion and cook, stirring, for 2–3 minutes, until soft but not brown. Add the rice, and stir until shiny and coated with oil. Ladle in just enough of the simmering liquid to cover the rice.

4 **Stir the rice** constantly until all the liquid is absorbed. Add more liquid just to cover the rice and simmer, stirring, until completely absorbed. Continue adding liquid to the rice in this way. Stop when the rice is *al dente*: just tender, but firm to the bite; it should take 25–30 minutes.

FINISH THE DISH

5 **Stir in the prawns** and the remaining olive oil, and season with salt and pepper, to taste (you may not need much salt). Spoon the risotto into warmed bowls, and serve immediately.

Ham with prunes in a wine sauce

PRUNES ADD SWEETNESS TO THIS DISH, from the Chablis region of France. A white Chablis is the obvious choice for the sauce, though any good-quality flinty dry white will do. It may sound like an unusual dish, but it is deeply comforting. Serve with mashed potatoes on a cold night.

SERVES	PREP	COOK
SERVES 6	40–45 MINS	20–25 MINS

Ingredients

FOR THE VINEGAR AND CARAMEL SYRUP

100g (3½oz) caster sugar

125ml (4fl oz) red wine vinegar

FOR THE SAUCE

135g (5oz) stoned prunes

4 tbsp marc de Bourgogne, or brandy

45g (1½oz) butter

4 shallots, finely chopped

2 tbsp plain flour

250ml (9fl oz) dry white wine

250ml (9fl oz) chicken or beef stock

½ tsp black peppercorns, coarsely crushed

salt

125ml (4fl oz) double cream

1kg (2¼lb) piece of cooked ham

MAKE THE VINEGAR AND CARAMEL SYRUP

1 Gently heat the sugar with 125ml (4fl oz) water in a heavy-based saucepan until dissolves. Increase the heat and boil, without stirring, until the syrup starts to turn golden at the edge.

2 Reduce the heat, and cook until the syrup becomes a deep golden caramel. Remove the saucepan from the heat, and let the bubbles subside.

3 Slowly add the vinegar, standing well back to avoid the strong fumes and spluttering syrup. Simmer, stirring occasionally, for 5–8 minutes, to dissolve the caramel and reduce by half. Remove from the heat.

PREPARE THE SAUCE

4 Halve the prunes, and put them in a small saucepan with the marc or brandy. Heat gently for 5-8 minutes, or until they plump up. Using a slotted spoon, transfer the prunes to a plate; reserve the delicious, fruity and boozy liquid.

5 Melt the butter in a medium saucepan. Add the shallots and cook, stirring occasionally, for 3-5 minutes, until softened but not browned. Stir in the flour and cook for 30-60 seconds, until foaming; stir constantly, so the flour does not catch on the bottom of the pan. Remove the saucepan from the heat, and let cool slightly.

6 Whisk in the wine, return to the heat, and simmer for 1 minute. Add the stock, prune soaking liquid, crushed peppercorns, and salt. Simmer, whisking constantly, for 10-12 minutes, until the sauce thickens and lightly coats the back of a spoon.

7 Whisk the vinegar and caramel syrup into the sauce, and continue simmering, until it is again thick enough to coat the back of a spoon; it should take 5-10 minutes longer. Be gentle, as you don't want the caramel to darken any further. Stir in the cream. Reserving a few prunes for garnish, add the rest to the pan, and taste for seasoning.

FINISH THE DISH

8 Preheat the oven to 180°C (350°F/Gas 4). Brush a gratin dish with melted butter, to keep the ham from sticking to the dish. Cut the ham into 6 equal slices with a finely serrated or very sharp knife, making sure to err on the side of thick, generous slices. Remember this is supposed to be comfort food, after all.

9 Arrange the ham slices evenly in the dish, overlapping them slightly. Ladle over the rich wine sauce to coat every slice of ham, bearing in mind that any uncoated pieces are more likely to catch and burn in the oven. Bake in the heated oven until the dish is hot all the way through and the sauce is gently bubbling. It should take 20-25 minutes, but check occasionally that the ham is not scorching on the top; this dish should have a sweet, mellow flavour and it may be tainted by any charring. If you see that the top is threatening to burn before the dish is hot all the way through, cover it loosely with a sheet of foil.

10 Garnish the ham with the reserved prune halves, and serve from the gratin dish with mashed or parsley potatoes, if you like. Due to the sweetness of the ham and prunes, mashed potatoes flavoured with a little Dijon mustard, to cut through the richness, would make an excellent accompaniment.

Country terrine

A RICH MIXTURE, deeply reassuring to have at hand in the refrigerator in case of unexpected guests or hunger pangs. Even better, it can be made up to 5 days ahead and kept, covered, in the refrigerator. The flavour will only improve.

SERVES	PREP	COOK
SERVES 8-10	1¼ HRS PLUS CHILLING	1¼-1½ HRS

Ingredients

1 thick slice cooked ham, weighing about 125g (4½oz)

2 tbsp brandy

salt and pepper

15g (½oz) butter

1 onion, very finely chopped

2 garlic cloves, finely chopped

leaves from 2-3 thyme sprigs

125g (4½oz) chicken livers, trimmed and chopped

625g (1lb 6oz) minced pork, part fat, part lean

250g (9oz) minced veal

¼ tsp ground allspice

pinch of ground nutmeg

pinch of ground cloves

2 eggs

250g (9oz) fat bacon rashers

1 bay leaf

45g (1½oz) plain flour

8-10 gherkins, to serve

crusty bread, to serve

MARINATE THE HAM

1 Place the slice of cooked ham on a chopping board and slice it into long strips about 1cm (½in) wide. Combine the ham, brandy and salt and pepper in a bowl. Cover and let marinate for 1 hour. Meanwhile, prepare the remaining ingredients.

MAKE THE TERRINE MIX

2 Melt the butter in a frying pan, add the onion and cook, stirring occasionally, for 3-5 minutes, until soft and brown. Turn into a bowl; let cool.

3 Add the garlic, thyme, chicken livers, minced pork, minced veal, allspice, nutmeg, cloves, and salt and pepper. Mix with a wooden spoon. Crack the eggs into a small bowl, beat to mix, then add them to the meat. Add the marinade from the ham.

4 Beat the mixture for 1-2 minutes, until it draws from the side of the bowl. Wipe the frying pan with kitchen paper. Add a little of the meat and fry for 1-2 minutes, until browned on both sides. Taste, and add more spices and salt and pepper if needed. It should be quite spicy.

ASSEMBLE AND BAKE THE TERRINE

5 Preheat the oven to 180°C (350°F/Gas 4). Set aside a third of the bacon and use the rest to line the bottom and longer sides of a 30x7.5x7.5cm (12x3x3in) terrine mould.

6 Spoon half the meat mixture into the terrine, then arrange the ham strips lengthways, end to end, on the top. Spread on the remaining meat mixture, fold over the bacon overhanging the sides, then top with the reserved bacon and bay leaf. Cover.

7 Put the flour and 2-3 tbsp water into a small bowl and mix together to make a soft smooth paste. Using your fingers, seal the gap between the rim of the mould and the lid with the paste.

8 Set the mould in a roasting tin. Add boiling water to come halfway up the sides. Bring this water bath to a boil on top of the stove, then carefully transfer the terrine in the tin to the oven.

9 Bake for 1¼–1½ hours, until a metal skewer inserted into the terrine for 30 seconds is hot to the touch when withdrawn. Remove the terrine from the water bath and let it cool to tepid. Remove the lid, cover the terrine, and set a 500g (1lb 2oz) weight on top. Chill for at least 1 day to allow the flavours to mellow.

FINISH THE TERRINE

10 With a metal spoon, scrape away and discard any fat from the top of the terrine. Dip a small knife into hot water and run it around the sides of the terrine to make it easter to turn out.

11 Holding the terrine mould with both hands, turn out the terrine on to a chopping board. Cut into slices about 1cm (½in) thick. Arrange the slices on plates or a large platter and serve with gherkins and crusty bread.

 VARIATION: Game terrine

Try this with pheasant or rabbit instead of venison.

1 Omit the ham, veal, and gherkins. Cut a 125g (4½oz) piece of venison into chunky strips, each about 1cm (½in) wide. Crush 3 juniper berries. Combine the juniper, brandy, and salt and pepper in a bowl. Add the venison strips and marinate as directed for the ham in the main recipe.

2 Make the meat mixture as directed, using 250g (9oz) minced venison in place of the veal and adding 60g (2oz) shelled pistachio nuts with the minced meat. The pistachios give this terrine beautiful flashes of bright green and crunches of texture. Cook a small portion of the meat mixture as directed, then taste for seasoning. Correct it if necessary, adding more pistachios if that would suit your palate.

3 Assemble the terrine, lining the mould with the 250g (9oz) bacon rashers and replacing the ham with the venison strips. Bake and unmould the terrine and slice as directed.

Steak and wild mushroom pie

AS COMFORTING as it gets. A quick puff pastry recipe is incredibly useful to have in your repertoire, very easy once you get the hang of it, and pleasingly impressive to your diners. But do substitute bought puff pastry if you're short of time.

SERVES	PREP	COOK
SERVES 4-6	50-55 MINS PLUS CHILLING	2½-3 HRS

Ingredients

FOR THE QUICK PUFF PASTRY

250g (9oz) plain flour

salt and pepper

175g (6oz) unsalted butter

1 egg, to glaze

FOR THE FILLING

500g (1lb 2oz) mixed wild mushrooms, sliced, or 75g (2½oz) dried wild mushrooms

35g (1¼oz) plain flour

1kg (2¼lb) braising steak, cut into 2.5cm (1in) cubes

900ml (1½ pints) beef stock or water, plus more if needed

4 shallots, finely chopped

leaves from 6 parsley sprigs, finely chopped

PREPARE THE QUICK PUFF PASTRY

1 **Sift the flour** and ½ tsp salt into a bowl. Rub in a third of the butter to form coarse crumbs. Make a well in the centre and pour in 100ml (3½fl oz) water; mix to a rough dough. Form a ball, wrap, and chill for 15 minutes.

FINISH THE PASTRY

2 **Roll out the dough** on a lightly floured surface to a 15x38 cm (6x15in) rectangle. Cut the remaining butter into small pieces, then dot the pieces over two-thirds of the dough rectangle. Fold the unbuttered dough over half of the buttered portion.

3 **With both hands,** fold the dough again so the butter pieces are completely enclosed in layers of dough. Turn the folded dough over and press the edges with the rolling pin to seal. Wrap and chill the dough 15 minutes.

4 **Roll out the dough** to a 15x45cm (6x18in) rectangle, keeping the corners square. Work quickly, moving the dough on the floured surface so that it does not stick. Fold the rectangle in thirds again, so it forms a square, bringing the final fold towards you.

5 **Turn the dough** 90° so that the folded edge is to your left. Gently press the seams with the rolling pin to seal. This completes the first 'turn'. Repeat from step 4, to complete a second turn, then wrap tightly and chill for 15 minutes. Give the dough 2 more turns and chill for another 15 minutes.

PREPARE THE FILLING

6 **Preheat the oven** to 180°C (350°F/Gas 4). If using dried mushrooms, soak in a bowl of warm water for about 30 minutes, until they are plump. Drain thoroughly, slice any large mushrooms, and continue as for fresh mushrooms.

7 **Season the flour** with salt and pepper. Toss the steak in the flour to coat, discarding the excess. Put the floured cubes into a casserole. Pour in the stock. Add the mushrooms and shallots and stir well so all the ingredients and flavours are well combined. Bring to a boil on top of the stove, stirring constantly both to evenly warm the ingredients and to prevent any of the mixture sticking to the bottom of the casserole.

8 **Cover the casserole** and transfer to the heated oven. Cook, stirring occasionally, until the meat is tender enough to crush with your finger and the sauce is the consistency of single cream, 2–2¼ hours. The meat should be almost covered with gravy. If necessary, add additional stock or water during cooking.

9 **Stir in the parsley** and season to taste with salt and pepper. Spoon the pie filling into a 2 litre (3½ pint) pie dish with a pie funnel in the centre. Let cool completely. Increase the oven heat to 220°C (425°F/Gas 7).

FINISH AND BAKE THE PIE

10 **Lightly flour a work surface** and roll out three-quarters of the chilled dough to a rough shape at least 2.5cm (1in) larger than the dish. Trim the edges and cut a strip the width of the dish rim from the edge of the dough.

11 **Using a pastry brush,** brush the flat rim of the pie dish with a little water, just to moisten. Lay the strip of dough on the rim of the dish and press it down on to the rim. Lightly beat the egg with ½ tsp salt and brush the strip of dough with egg glaze.

12 **Roll the large piece of dough** around the rolling pin and drape it over the pie. Do not stretch the dough. With your fingertips, press the dough firmly to seal it to the strip of dough on the rim of the pie dish. Trim off any excess to make a neat finish.

13 **Brush the top** of the pie with the egg glaze. Cut a hole in the centre of the dough lid, over the funnel, to allow steam to escape. Use the pastry trimmings to decorate the pie, if you like, and glaze any decorations with egg, too.

14 **Chill the pie** for 15 minutes, then bake it in the heated oven for 25–35 minutes, until the top is golden brown. If the top browns too quickly, cover it with foil. Serve the pie hot from the dish.

Scallops with lemon-herb potatoes

BECAUSE SOMETIMES YOU JUST NEED TO TREAT YOURSELF! Scallops are expensive, so this is a dish to reserve for a special occasion. Because of their cost – but mostly due to their exquisite texture and flavour – scallops need to be cooked very carefully. Overcooked scallops will be dry and rubbery, whereas properly seared scallops are juicy, silky in texture, and bursting with saline flavours. Everything must be cooked just before serving for the best results.

SERVES	PREP	COOK
SERVES 6	45–50 MINS	20 MINS

Ingredients

FOR THE LEMON-HERB POTATOES

500g (1lb 2oz) potatoes

salt and pepper

4–6 parsley sprigs

4–6 tarragon sprigs

60g (2oz) butter

finely grated zest of 1 lemon

75ml (2½fl oz) milk, plus more if needed

FOR THE SCALLOPS

500g (1lb 2oz) large scallops

30g (1oz) plain flour

30g (1oz) butter

2 tbsp oil

lemon wedges and rocket leaves, to serve

PREPARE THE MASHED POTATOES

1 **Peel the potatoes** and cut into pieces. Put them in a saucepan of cold salted water, cover and bring to a boil. Simmer for 15–20 minutes, until tender.

2 **Strip the parsley** and tarragon leaves from the stalks.

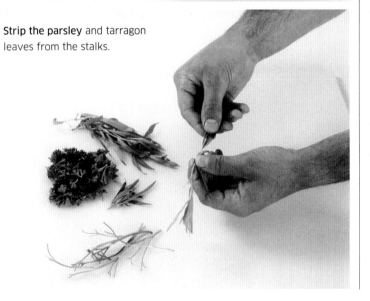

3 **Put the butter,** herb leaves, and lemon zest in a food processor. Purée until the herbs are chopped finely.

4 **When the potatoes are tender,** drain and return to the pan. Carefully mash the potatoes and beat in the herb purée over low heat until smooth. Season, cover with the milk, and keep warm in a low oven.

PREPARE AND SAUTÉ THE SCALLOPS

5 If necessary, discard the tough, crescent-shaped membrane at the side of each scallop. Put the flour on a plate and season. Roll the scallops in the flour and pat off the excess.

6 Heat the butter and oil in a frying pan. Sauté the scallops, turning them once, until just crisp and brown, 2–3 minutes.

FINISH THE DISH

7 Meanwhile, stir the milk into the potatoes, adding 2–3 tsp more, if needed. Remove the scallops from the pan and squeeze in the juice of half a lemon. Arrange the mashed potatoes and scallops on warmed serving plates and spoon over the pan juices. Serve at once, with the lemon wedges and rocket leaves.

 VARIATION: Poached scallops in cider sauce

Served in the shells with piped mashed potato.

1 Cook the potatoes as directed. Make the herbed butter, omitting the lemon zest and adding 2 garlic cloves. Mash the potatoes and spoon into a piping bag fitted with a star nozzle. Pipe them around the edges of 6 scallop shells.

2 Prepare the scallops as directed. Dice 2 shallots and squeeze the juice from 2 lemons. Put them in a saucepan with 120ml (4fl oz) each cider and white wine and 250ml (8fl oz) water. Add the scallops and heat to simmering. Poach for 30 seconds, then remove from the heat,

3 Reduce the scallop liquid to 250ml (9fl oz) and whisk in 2 tbsp plain flour, then 2 egg yolks beaten with 120ml (4fl oz) double cream. Return the scallops to the sauce, spoon them in the shells and grill for 3 minutes.

Quiche Lorraine

SERVE WARM or at room temperature, but never very hot as the custard will be too soft. This famous recipe, from Lorraine in eastern France, is as contentious as most of the traditional Gallic repertoire. Purists say it should be flavoured only with bacon, but the Gruyère cheese used in this version adds another welcome layer of flavour. The pastry can be made up to 2 days ahead and kept, tightly wrapped, in the refrigerator.

SERVES	PREP	COOK
SERVES 6	45–50 MINS PLUS CHILLING	30–35 MINS

Ingredients

FOR THE PÂTE BRISÉE DOUGH

175g (6oz) plain flour, plus more to dust

1 egg yolk

½ tsp salt

90g (3oz) unsalted butter

FOR THE FILLING

250g (9oz) thick-cut bacon rashers, sliced

500ml (16fl oz) single cream

1 pinch of ground nutmeg

salt and pepper

1 egg yolk plus 3 eggs

75g (2½oz) Gruyère cheese, grated

MAKE THE PÂTE BRISÉE DOUGH

1 **Sift the flour** on to a work surface and make a well in the centre. Put the egg yolk, salt, and 3 tbsp cold water into the well. Using a rolling pin, pound the butter to soften it slightly, then add it to the well in the flour. With your fingertips, work the ingredients in the well together gently, until thoroughly mixed.

2 **Draw in the flour** and work it into the other ingredients until coarse crumbs form, trying to work the dough as little as possible so the pastry will be light and tender. Press the dough lightly into a ball. If the crumbs seem a little dry, sprinkle them with a very little more water before pressing the dough together.

3 **Lightly flour the work surface**, then blend the dough by pushing it away from you with the heel of your hand. Gather it up and continue to blend until it is very smooth and peels away from the work surface in one piece. It should only take 1–2 minutes to get to this stage. Try not to overwork it, or it will be tough; stop as soon as it forms a homogenous whole. Shape it gently into a ball, wrap tightly in clingfilm, and chill in the refrigerator until firm. It will take at least 30 minutes, or you can chill it for up to 2 days, if that is more convenient.

LINE THE TIN

4 **Brush a 25cm (10in) tin** with removable base with melted butter. Lightly flour a work surface. Roll out the chilled dough into a 30cm (12in) round. Wrap the dough around the rolling pin and unroll it so that it drapes over the tin and hangs over the edge. Do not stretch the dough or it will shrink when baked.

5 **Gently lift the edge** of the dough with one hand and press it well into the bottom edge of the tin with the forefinger of the other hand. Roll the rolling pin over the top of the tin, pressing down to cut off the excess dough.

6 **With your forefingers and thumb**, press the dough evenly up the side, from the bottom, to increase the height of the dough shell. Prick the bottom of the shell lightly with a fork to prevent air bubbles from forming during baking. Chill for at least 15 minutes, until firm.

BAKE THE PASTRY SHELL BLIND

7 **Preheat the oven** to 200°C (400°F/Gas 6). Put a baking sheet into the oven to heat. Line the pastry shell with a double thickness of foil, pressing it well into the bottom. Trim if necessary so it stands about 4cm (1½in) above the edge of the tin. Spread a layer of dried beans or rice over the foil to weigh down the dough while it is baking.

8 **Place the tin** on the baking sheet and bake the pastry shell in the heated oven for about 10 minutes, until set and the rim starts to brown. Carefully remove the foil and beans or rice.

9 Reduce the oven temperature to 190°C (375°F/Gas 5). Continue baking for 5-8 minutes longer, until the pastry is lightly browned. Remove the pastry shell from the oven and let cool slightly. Leave the oven on.

MAKE THE FILLING AND BAKE THE QUICHE

10 Put the bacon into a frying pan and cook for 3-4 minutes, stirring occasionally, until lightly browned. Using a slotted spoon, lift the bacon out of the frying pan and transfer to kitchen paper to drain. Put the cream, nutmeg, and salt and pepper into a bowl. Add the egg yolk and eggs and whisk until thoroughly mixed.

11 Sprinkle the bacon and cheese evenly over the bottom of the pastry shell. Set the tin on the hot baking sheet in the oven. Whisk the custard mixture and ladle it carefully over the bacon and cheese. Bake the quiche in the heated oven for 30-35 minutes, until lightly browned and the custard is lightly set.

12 Let the quiche cool slightly on a wire rack, then set the tin on a bowl to loosen and remove the side. Transfer to a chopping board or serving platter. Serve warm or at room temperature.

Home-made straw and hay pasta

GREEN AND WHITE FETTUCCINE REPRESENT straw and hay, and pasta is very soothing to make on a quiet afternoon. It is far easier than you think; all you need is a pasta machine and a little time, and everyone will be immeasurably impressed that you made it yourself, so you'll get an ego boost too!

SERVES	PREP	COOK
SERVES 6	55-60 MINS PLUS STANDING	10 MINS

Ingredients

FOR THE PLAIN FETTUCCINE

150g (5½oz) strong plain flour, plus more if needed

2 eggs

FOR THE SPINACH FETTUCCINE

2 tbsp defrosted spinach

220g (8oz) strong plain flour, plus more if needed

2 eggs

FOR THE SAUCE

60g (2oz) butter

1 small onion, finely chopped

250g (9oz) mushrooms, trimmed and sliced

salt and pepper

125g (4½oz) cooked ham, sliced into strips

100g (3½oz) shelled fresh or defrosted peas

250ml (9fl oz) double cream

1 pinch of ground nutmeg

60g (2oz) freshly grated Parmesan cheese, to serve

MAKE THE PLAIN AND SPINACH PASTA DOUGHS

1 For the plain pasta, sift the flour on to a work surface in a mound. With your fingers, make a well in the centre. Lightly beat the eggs with a fork, and add to the well, with ½ tsp salt.

2 Gradually mix in the flour from the sides to make a firm dough. If the dough is sticky, add more flour. As you mix, use a palette knife to scrape up any dough that sticks to the work surface. The dough may appear dry and floury at first, but will become more moist as the flour absorbs the eggs.

3 On a floured work surface, press the dough into a ball. Knead it with the heel of your hand to blend. Cover the dough with a bowl, and leave to rest for 1 hour. Meanwhile, make the spinach pasta dough.

4 For the spinach pasta dough, squeeze the defrosted spinach to remove all the water, then finely chop. Make as for the plain dough, adding the spinach with the eggs and salt. Leave the dough to rest, covered with a bowl, for 1 hour.

5 Cut each ball of dough into three or four roughly equal pieces, and set your pasta machine rollers to their widest setting.

MAKE THE FETTUCCINE

6 Flour one piece of dough lightly, and feed it through the rollers of the machine. Fold the dough strip into thirds to make a square, then feed it through the machine again, dusting with flour if it sticks. Repeat this folding and rolling process 7-10 times, until the dough is smooth and elastic.

7 Tighten the pasta machine rollers one notch, and feed the dough through them. Continue rolling the pasta dough, tightening the rollers one notch each time, ending with the narrowest setting. Lightly dust the dough with flour if necessary, so it does not stick. The dough will be satiny smooth and no longer crack at the sides as it comes out of the rollers.

8 Hang the pasta sheet over a clean broom handle and let dry for 5-10 minutes, until it has a leathery look. Meanwhile, knead and roll the remaining pieces of dough, and hang them over the broom handle. With a knife or scissors, cut the sheets of dough into lengths of about 30cm (12in).

MAKE THE SAUCE

10 **Heat half the butter** in a large frying pan. Add the onion and cook, stirring occasionally, for 3-5 minutes, until soft. Add the mushrooms with salt and pepper, and continue cooking for 5-7 minutes, until the liquid has completely evaporated.

11 **Add the ham**, peas, and cream to the onions and mushrooms. Stir and heat to boiling, then simmer for 1-2 minutes, until slightly reduced. Add the ground nutmeg and taste for seasoning.

COOK THE PASTA AND FINISH THE DISH

12 **Fill a large pan** with water, bring to a boil and add 1 tbsp salt. Add the fettuccine and simmer for 1-2 minutes, until just tender but still chewy, stirring occasionally to prevent sticking. Drain thoroughly.

13 **Melt the remaining butter** in the pan, and add the fettuccine. Toss over medium heat, then add the sauce and toss for 1-2 minutes, until coated and very hot. Take from the heat, sprinkle generously with some of the Parmesan, and toss again. Pile the pasta in warmed bowls, and serve with the remaining Parmesan.

9 **Fit the handle** into the wider of the machine's cutters, and feed one sheet of dough through the machine. As the fettuccine strips emerge, catch them on your hand. Toss with a little flour, then coil loosely into a bundle. Repeat with the remaining pasta sheets. Let dry for 1-2 hours.

Sole bonne femme

AN OLD-FASHIONED CLASSIC and the most delicious of fish dishes. The bones from the filleted sole are used to make the stock, which itself is the basis for the recipe's creamy sauce. The fish stock can be prepared 4 hours ahead and chilled.

SERVES	PREP	COOK
SERVES 4	30–35 MINS	25–30 MINS

Ingredients

FOR THE FISH STOCK

Heads and bones from 2 Dover sole

1 onion, sliced

3–5 parsley sprigs

1 tsp peppercorns

250ml (9fl oz) white wine or juice of 1 lemon

FOR THE FISH

15g (½oz) butter

250g (9oz) mushrooms, sliced

salt and pepper

2 shallots, finely chopped

2 Dover sole, 1kg (2¼lb) each, filleted, heads and bones reserved for the stock

FOR THE VELOUTÉ SAUCE

30g (1oz) butter

2 tbsp plain flour

3 tbsp double cream

3 egg yolks

juice of ½ lemon, or to taste

MAKE THE FISH STOCK

1 **Cut the washed fish heads** and bones into 4–5 pieces with a strong knife. Put in a medium saucepan. Add the onion, 500ml (16fl oz) water, parsley, and peppercorns. Pour in the wine.

2 **Bring to a boil** and simmer for about 20 minutes, skimming occasionally with a large, flat spoon. Pour the stock through a sieve into a second saucepan. Do not season; the flavours will intensify when it is reduced.

POACH THE SOLE

3 **Preheat the oven** to 180°C (350°F/Gas 4). Melt the butter in a frying pan; add the mushrooms, salt, pepper, and 3–4 tbsp water. Cover with buttered foil and cook for 5 minutes, until tender. Set aside.

4 **Butter a baking dish** and sprinkle the shallots over the bottom. Fold each sole fillet in half, skinned side inwards, and arrange on the shallots, tail upwards. Season. Ladle enough stock over to half-cover. Top with buttered foil. Poach the fish in the oven for 15–18 minutes, until it just flakes easily when tested with a fork. With a fish slice, transfer to kitchen paper to drain, reserving the cooking liquid. Keep the fillets warm while making the sauce.

MAKE THE SAUCE

5 **Add the fish cooking liquid** with the shallots to the remaining stock; boil until reduced to 375ml (12fl oz). Melt the butter in a separate saucepan. Whisk in the flour. Cook for 1–2 minutes, until foaming. Remove the pan from the heat and let cool slightly.

6 **Strain the reduced stock** into the butter and flour mixture. Bring to a boil, whisking constantly until thickened. Reduce the heat and let simmer for 5 minutes. Remove the sauce from the heat. Add the mushrooms with their cooking liquid, and stir to mix. Whisk the cream and egg yolks in a small bowl.

7 **Ladle a little of the hot sauce** into the cream and egg-yolk mixture and whisk to mix. Stir the cream mixture into the remaining sauce in the pan.

8 **Return to the heat** and cook gently, stirring, for 2-3 minutes, or until it thickens enough to coat the back of the spoon (your finger will leave a trail). Do not boil or it will curdle. Remove from the heat. Add lemon juice, salt and pepper to taste. Heat the grill. Arrange 2 fillets on each of 4 flameproof plates. Ladle the sauce over. Grill for 1-2 minutes, until lightly browned and glazed. Serve at once.

VARIATION: Fillets of sole with mushrooms and tomatoes

A colourful variation.

1 Peel, deseed, and finely chop 2 tomatoes. Prepare the sole, fish stock, and mushrooms as directed. Poach the sole fillets as directed, adding the tomatoes to the baking dish with the shallots.

2 Strip the leaves from 10-12 parsley sprigs and finely chop. Make the sauce, adding the fish cooking liquid to 125ml (4½fl oz) white wine instead of the remaining stock. Pour the reduced liquid into the butter and flour mixture without straining. When the sauce thickens, whisk in 1½ tbsp tomato purée.

3 Add the chopped parsley with the mushrooms and their liquid. Ladle the sauce over the fish arranged on flameproof plates and grill as directed.

Bread

Loaves, buns, and rolls
made easy

Split-top white bread

A STAPLE RECIPE for novice and practiced bakers alike. The flour "sponge" used here is a fermented batter that adds a characteristic flavour and improves the texture of the bread. The loaves are rich in taste, and have an even, tender crumb. White loaves are best on the day of baking, but can be frozen very successfully. The dough can also be made, kneaded, and refrigerated to rise overnight.

SERVES	PREP	COOK
MAKES 2 LOAVES	2½-3 HRS PLUS FERMENTING	35-40 MINS

Ingredients

FOR THE SPONGE

2½ tsp dried yeast, or 15g (½oz) fresh yeast

125g (4½oz) unbleached, strong white flour, plus more to sprinkle

FOR THE BREAD

500ml (16fl oz) milk, plus more to glaze

750g (1lb 10oz) unbleached, strong white flour, plus more if needed

1 tbsp salt

PREPARE THE SPONGE

1 **In a small bowl,** sprinkle or crumble the yeast over 4 tbsp taken from 250ml (9fl oz) lukewarm water. Let stand for about 5 minutes, until dissolved, stirring once. Put the yeast and remaining water into a large bowl. Stir in the flour and mix vigorously, using your hand as a paddle, for 30-60 seconds.

2 **Sprinkle the sponge** with about 2 tbsp flour, covering most but not all of the surface. Cover the bowl with a damp tea towel, and let the sponge ferment in a warm place until the bubbles break through the flour; it will take anything from 30-60 minutes, depending on the heat of the room, the weather, or even the humidity. Even the most experienced bakers find the time hard to estimate, as each batch of flour is different.

MAKE THE DOUGH

3 **Meanwhile,** bring the milk just to a boil, and let it cool to lukewarm. When the sponge has risen, add the milk and mix it in with your hand. Stir in half the flour and the salt, and mix well with your hand. Add the remaining flour, 125g (4½oz) at a time, mixing well after each addition. Keep adding flour until the dough pulls away from the side of the bowl in a ball. It should be soft and slightly sticky. You may not need to use all the flour, so stop adding it when you feel the dough has the correct texture.

KNEAD THE DOUGH AND LET IT RISE

4 **Turn the dough** on to a floured work surface. Sprinkle the dough and your hands with flour, and begin to knead by holding the dough with one hand, and pushing it away from you with the other.

5 **Continue to knead** by peeling the dough from the surface. Give the dough a quarter turn, and knead for 8-10 minutes, until it is very smooth, elastic, and forms a ball. If the dough sticks while kneading, flour the work surface.

6 **Wash a large bowl** and brush it with melted butter. Put the kneaded dough in the bowl, and flip it so the surface is lightly buttered. Cover the bowl with a damp tea towel, and let the dough rise in a warm place for 1-1½ hours, until doubled in bulk.

SHAPE THE LOAVES

7 Brush 2 x 20x10x5cm (8x4x2in) loaf tins with melted butter. Turn the dough on to a lightly floured work surface, and knead with your hand for 15–20 seconds, just to knock out the air. Cover the dough and let rest for about 5 minutes.

8 Cut the dough in half. Cover one piece while shaping the other. Flour your hands, and pat the dough into a 25x20cm (10x8in) rectangle. Starting with a long side, roll into a cylinder. With the cylinder seam-side up, fold the ends over, making it the length of the tin.

9 Drop the loaf, seam-side down, into one of the prepared tins. Repeat to shape the remaining dough. Cover the tins with a dry tea towel, and let the loaves rise in a warm place for 45 minutes, until the tins are just full.

GLAZE AND BAKE THE LOAVES

10 Preheat the oven to 220°C (425°F/Gas 7). Brush the loaves with milk. With a very sharp knife or scalpel, make a slash about 1cm (½in) deep in each loaf. Bake for 20 minutes, and then lower the heat to 190°C (375°F/Gas 5) and bake for 15–20 minutes longer, until well browned.

11 Remove the loaves from the tins. Turn them over and tap the bottoms with your knuckles. The bread should sound hollow and the sides should feel crisp when pressed. Let the loaves cool completely.

 VARIATION: Cinnamon swirl bread

Each slice reveals a dark spiral of spice.

1 Make and knead the dough, and let it rise as directed in the main recipe. Brush two loaf tins very well with melted butter. In a small bowl, combine 1 tbsp ground cinnamon with 100g (3½oz) sugar. Set 2 tsp of the mixture aside for the glaze. Melt 45g (1½oz) unsalted butter in a small saucepan and let it cool completely.

2 Knock the air out of the dough, and let rest as directed in the main recipe. Cut the dough in half, and cover one piece while shaping the other. Roll the dough into a 30x20cm (12x8in) rectangle. Brush with some of the melted butter, and sprinkle with half the cinnamon and sugar mixture. This will combine to give a moist and delicious spiral seam throughout the loaves. Starting with a short end, roll the rectangle into an even cylinder and pinch the seam and ends to seal them together. Drop the loaf, seam-side down, into one of the prepared tins. Repeat to shape the remaining dough into another cinnamon swirl loaf.

3 Cover the loaves, and let rise as directed. Do not let the loaves rise longer than directed, or the cinnamon swirl may separate. Heat the oven to 220°C (425°F/Gas 7). Brush each loaf evenly with melted butter, sprinkle with the remaining cinnamon and sugar, and bake as directed in the main recipe. Serve warm, or toasted and spread with butter.

Wholemeal bread

STONE-GROUND WHOLEMEAL FLOUR varies from mill to mill and batch to batch so experiment with this recipe, using various flours and adding more or less water. A little white flour has been added to this recipe to bring the crumb of the loaf a lighter texture. Don't feel bound to shape the dough into these cottage loaves. Make them into long ovals or normally shaped sandwich rectangles, if it suits your purpose better. This bread is best eaten on the day it is baked, though it freezes very successfully.

SERVES	PREP	COOK
MAKES 2 LOAVES	35–40 MINS PLUS RISING	40–45 MINS

Ingredients

60g (2oz) unsalted butter

3 tbsp honey

1 tbsp dried yeast, or 20g (¾oz)

fresh yeast

1 tbsp salt

125g (4½oz) unbleached strong white flour, plus more if needed

625g (1lb 6oz) stone-ground wholemeal flour

MAKE THE DOUGH AND LET IT RISE

1 **Melt the butter** in a small saucepan. Stir in 1 tbsp of the honey, along with 4 tbsp taken from 500ml (16fl oz) lukewarm water, in a small bowl until mixed. Sprinkle or crumble the yeast over the honey and water mixture and let stand for about 5 minutes until dissolved, stirring once.

2 **Put the melted butter,** remaining honey and water, dissolved yeast and salt into a large bowl. Stir in the white flour with half of the wholemeal, and mix with your hand.

3 **Add the remaining wholemeal flour,** 125g (4½oz) at a time, mixing well after each addition. Keep adding wholemeal flour until the dough pulls away from the side of the bowl in a ball. It should be soft and slightly sticky.

4 **Turn the dough** on to a floured work surface. Sprinkle it with white flour, and begin to knead by holding the dough with one hand and pushing it away from you with the other. Give the dough a quarter turn and knead for 8–10 minutes, until it is very smooth, elastic, and forms a ball. If the dough sticks while kneading, flour the work surface.

5 **Wash out the large bowl** and brush it with melted butter. Put the kneaded dough in the bowl, and flip it so the surface of the dough is lightly buttered. Cover the bowl with a damp tea towel and let the dough rise in a warm place for 1–1½ hours, or until doubled in bulk.

SHAPE AND BAKE THE LOAVES

6 **Once the dough has doubled** in bulk, brush a baking sheet with melted butter. Turn the dough on to a lightly floured work surface and knead with your hand just to knock out the air. Cover the dough and let rest for about 5 minutes.

7 **Cut the dough** into 3 equal pieces. Cut 1 piece in half. Cover 1 large and 1 small piece of dough with a tea towel while shaping the others. Shape 1 large piece of dough into a loose ball. Fold the sides over to the centre, turning and pinching to make a tight round ball. Flip the ball, seam-side down, on to the prepared baking sheet.

8 **Shape 1 small piece** of dough into a ball. Fold the sides over to the centre, turning and pinching to make a tight round ball. Set it, seam-side down, on top of the first ball. With a finger, press through the centre of the 2 balls down to the bottom of the baking sheet and rotate your finger to enlarge the hole slightly. Repeat to shape the remaining 2 balls of dough.

9 **Cover the loaves** with a tea towel and leave in a warm place for about 45 minutes, or until doubled in bulk. Meanwhile, preheat the oven to 190°C (375°F/Gas 5). Bake the loaves for 40-45 minutes, until well browned. Turn them over and rap with your knuckles; They should sound hollow. Transfer to a wire rack until completely cool.

 VARIATION: Double wheat bread

Bulghur wheat adds flavour to this bread baked in flower pots.

1 Put 125g (4½oz) bulghur in a bowl and cover with water. Soak for 30 minutes, then drain, pressing to extract excess water. Melt the butter and dissolve the yeast as directed. Put the bulghur in a large bowl. Add the melted butter, dissolved yeast, and salt. Stir in the white and wholemeal flours, knead, and let rise as directed.

2 Preheat the oven to 150°C (300°F/Gas 2). Soak 2 x 750ml (1¼ pints) clean clay flower pots in water for 5 minutes. Put in the oven to dry. Repeat this process twice. Knock the air out of the dough and let rest. Cut it in half, and shape each piece into a ball. Drop into the prepared flower pots and let rise until the pots are just full; it should take about 45 minutes.

3 Preheat the oven to 190°C (375°F/Gas 5). Bake as directed. Remove the loaves from the pots to test if they are ready: the bread should sound hollow when tapped. Serve the bread in the flowerpots, if you like.

Sourdough bread

THIS BREAD HAS A WONDERFUL TANG, and is worth the trouble of making the "starter", which must be assembled 3–5 days ahead of time. You may find, as have many bakers, that creating the perfect sourdough bread becomes a bit of an obsession... The tightly wrapped loaves will freeze very successfully.

SERVES	PREP	COOK
MAKES 2 LOAVES	45–50 MINS PLUS RISING	40–45 MINS

Ingredients

FOR THE SOURDOUGH STARTER

1 tbsp dried yeast, or 20g (³⁄₄oz) fresh yeast

250g (9oz) unbleached strong white flour

FOR THE SPONGE

250g (9oz) unbleached strong white flour, more to sprinkle

FOR THE DOUGH

1½ tsp dried yeast, or 10g (⅓oz) fresh yeast

375g (13oz) unbleached strong white flour, plus more for bowls

1 tbsp salt

vegetable oil, for the bowl

polenta (fine yellow cornmeal) for the baking sheet

MAKE THE SOURDOUGH STARTER

1 This starter can be used within 3–5 days. Let the starter ferment for a day at room temperature, then use or refrigerate as directed below. Discard it if mould appears, or if it gives off a bad (rather than sour) odour.

2 In a large jar, sprinkle the yeast over 500ml (16fl oz) lukewarm water. Let stand for 5 minutes, stirring once. Stir in the flour, cover, and ferment in a warm place for 24 hours. It will be frothy with a distinct, sour aroma.

3 Stir the starter, cover, and stir each day for 2–4 days. Use or refrigerate. Replenish after each use. If a recipe calls for 250ml (9fl oz) starter, use it as directed. Then stir in 125g (4½oz) flour and 250ml (9fl oz) water.

MAKE THE SPONGE

4 Pour 250ml (9fl oz) lukewarm water into a large bowl, and spoon in 250ml (9fl oz) sourdough starter. Stir in the flour and mix vigorously with your hand for 30–60 seconds.

5 Sprinkle the sponge with 3 tbsp flour, cover the bowl with a damp tea towel, and let ferment in a warm place for 5–8 hours, or overnight. If you prefer a more sour flavour, let the sponge ferment overnight.

MAKE AND KNEAD THE DOUGH AND LET IT RISE

6 In a bowl, sprinkle the yeast over 4 tbsp lukewarm water. Let stand 5 minutes. Add to the sponge, and mix. Mix in half the flour and the salt. Add the remaining flour, 60g (2oz) at a time, mixing after each addition.

7 Turn the dough on to a floured work surface. Sprinkle the dough and your hands with flour. Knead for 8–10 minutes, until it is very smooth, elastic, and forms a ball, flouring the work surface if necessary.

8 Wash a large bowl. Brush it with oil. Put the kneaded dough in the bowl and flip it, so it is lightly oiled. Cover the bowl with a damp tea towel, and let the dough rise in a warm place for 1–1½ hours, until doubled in bulk.

SHAPE AND BAKE THE LOAVES

9 Line 2 x 20cm (8in) bowls with cotton cloth, and sprinkle generously with flour. Turn the dough on to a lightly floured work surface and knock out the air. Cover, and let rest for 5 minutes.

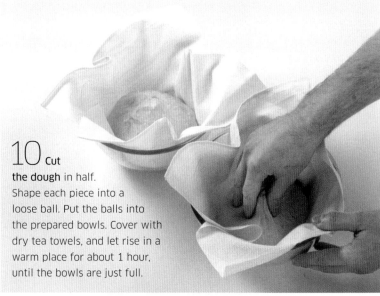

10 Cut the dough in half. Shape each piece into a loose ball. Put the balls into the prepared bowls. Cover with dry tea towels, and let rise in a warm place for about 1 hour, until the bowls are just full.

11 **Preheat the oven** to 200°C (400°F/Gas 6). Set a roasting tin to heat on the floor of the oven or on the lowest oven rack. Sprinkle 2 baking sheets with polenta. Turn the loaves on to the prepared baking sheets. With a very sharp knife, cut 3 slashes, 1cm (½in) deep, on the top of each loaf, then make 3 more to form a criss-cross pattern.

12 **Put the loaves** in the heated oven. At once, drop ice cubes into the hot roasting tin, then bake the loaves for 20 minutes. Lower the heat to 190°C (375°F/Gas 5), and continue baking for 20–25 minutes longer, until well browned. Turn the loaves over, and tap the bottoms with your knuckles. The bread should sound hollow, and the sides should feel crisp, when pressed. Let the loaves cool on a wire rack.

Cornbread

A TRADITIONAL AMERICAN LOAF baked in a cast-iron frying pan and studded with sweetcorn kernels. It is easily cut into wedges and can be served from the pan, if you like. The crust is deliciously crisp, and the bread is a brilliant accompaniment to baked hams or Southern Fried Chicken (p248).

SERVES	PREP	COOK
SERVES 8	15–20 MINS	20–25 MINS

Ingredients

2 fresh corn cobs, or 200g (7oz) defrosted and drained sweetcorn kernels

60g (2oz) unsalted butter

150g (5½oz) polenta (fine yellow cornmeal)

125g (4½oz) unbleached strong white flour

50g (1¾oz) sugar

1 tbsp baking powder

1 tsp salt

2 eggs

250ml (9fl oz) milk

MAKE THE BATTER

1 **Preheat the oven** to 220°C (425°F/Gas 7). If using fresh corn, hold each cob vertically and cut away all the kernels, from the tip down, with a sharp knife. Turn and continue cutting, removing as many whole kernels as possible.

2 **Put all the kernels** into a small bowl and, working over the bowl, use the back of a knife to scrape each cob and remove the deliciously sweet corn pulp. Mix this in with the kernels.

3 **Brush a 23cm (9in) flameproof cast-iron frying pan** with melted butter. Melt the butter for the batter in a small saucepan.

4 **Sift the polenta,** flour, sugar, baking powder, and salt into a large bowl, and make a well in the centre. Add the sweetcorn kernels to the well. In a medium bowl, whisk the eggs, melted butter, and milk until thoroughly combined. Pour three-quarters of the milk mixture into the well in the flour, and begin to stir.

FINISH AND BAKE THE BREAD

5 **Gradually draw in the dry ingredients,** adding the remaining milk mixture, and stirring to make a smooth batter. Do not overstir the batter or the bread will be heavy.

6 **Pour the cornbread batter** into the prepared frying pan and brush the top generously with melted butter. Bake for 20–25 minutes, until the bread starts to shrink from the side of the pan and a metal skewer inserted in the centre comes out clean. Let the cornbread cool slightly on a wire rack. Serve warm.

Sesame grissini

BREADSTICKS IN THE SICILIAN STYLE. The Italian tradition has it that the breadsticks should be pulled to the length of the baker's outstretched arm, though there's no need to go that far (and who has an oven big enough to cook them?). Sesame seeds are immensely popular in Sicilian food, and provide a great crunch and depth of flavour to the recipe.

SERVES	PREP	COOK
MAKES 32	40-45 MINS PLUS RISING	15-18 MINS

Ingredients

2½ tsp dried yeast, or 15g (½oz) fresh yeast

425g (15oz) unbleached strong white flour, plus more if needed

1 tbsp sugar

2 tsp salt

2 tbsp olive oil

45g (1½oz) sesame seeds

MAKE AND KNEAD THE DOUGH AND LET IT RISE

1 **In a small bowl,** sprinkle or crumble the yeast over 4 tbsp taken from 300ml (10fl oz) lukewarm water. Let stand for about 5 minutes until dissolved, stirring once. Put the flour on to a work surface with the sugar and salt. Make a large well in the centre and add the dissolved yeast, remaining water, and oil.

2 **With your fingertips,** draw in the flour and work it into the other ingredients to form a smooth dough. It should be soft and slightly sticky. Sprinkle the dough and your hands with flour, and knead for 5-7 minutes, until the dough is very smooth and elastic, and forms a ball.

3 **Cover the dough** with a damp tea towel and let rest for about 5 minutes. Flour your hands and pat the dough into a rectangle on a well-floured work surface. With a rolling pin, roll the dough to a 40x15cm (16x6in) rectangle, pressing evenly so the breadsticks will be uniform in thickness. Brush the dough lightly with oil.

4 **Cover the** dough with the damp tea towel, and let rise for 1-1½ hours, or until doubled in bulk. (Rising time will depend on the temperature of the room.) Meanwhile, preheat the oven to 220°C (425°F/Gas 7).

CUT AND BAKE THE BREADSTICKS

5 **Brush 3 baking sheets with oil.** Gently lift the dough to prevent it from sticking to the work surface. Lightly brush with water. Sprinkle with the sesame seeds and press them down gently into the surface. With a sharp knife, cut the dough across into 32 strips, each about 1cm (½in) wide.

6 **Stretch 1 strip of dough** to the width of a baking sheet. Set it on 1 of the prepared baking sheets, letting the dough come just to the edges. Repeat with the remaining strips, arranging them 2cm (¾in) apart. Bake for 15-18 minutes, until golden and crisp. Transfer to a wire rack and let cool completely.

Multi-grain breakfast bread

A HEARTY BREAD with rolled oats, wheat bran, and polenta, the texture of this recipe is softened with buttermilk. This bread is best on the day of baking, but can be tightly wrapped and kept for up to 2 days, or it can be frozen successfully. Sunflower seeds add crunch, but you can use any of your favourite seeds instead, or a mixture, if you prefer. You could even use finely crushed bran cereal flakes in place of the wheat bran, for the perfect breakfast loaf.

SERVES	PREP	COOK
MAKES 2 LOAVES	45–50 MINS PLUS RISING	40–45 MINS

Ingredients

75g (2½oz) sunflower seeds

425ml (15fl oz) buttermilk

2½ tsp dried yeast, or 15g (½oz) fresh yeast

45g (1½oz) rolled oats

45g (1½oz) wheat bran

75g (2½oz) polenta (fine yellow cornmeal), plus more for the baking sheet

45g (1½oz) soft brown sugar

1 tbsp salt

250g (9oz) strong wholemeal flour

250g (9oz) unbleached strong white flour, plus more if needed

1 egg white, to glaze

MAKE THE DOUGH

1 **Preheat the oven** to 180°C (350°F/Gas 4). Spread the seeds on a baking sheet, and toast in the heated oven for 5–7 minutes, until lightly browned, stirring occasionally, so they colour evenly. Let cool, then coarsely chop.

2 **Pour the buttermilk** into a saucepan. Heat just to lukewarm (too hot, and it will curdle). Sprinkle or crumble the yeast over 4 tbsp lukewarm water, and set aside for 2 minutes. Stir gently, then leave for 2–3 minutes more, until completely dissolved.

3 **Put the sunflower seeds,** rolled oats, wheat bran, polenta, brown sugar, and salt in a large bowl. Add the dissolved yeast and buttermilk, and mix with your hand. Stir in the wholemeal flour with half of the strong white flour, and mix well with your hand.

4 **Add the remaining strong white flour,** 60g (2oz) at a time, mixing well after each addition. Keep adding strong white flour until the dough pulls away from the side of the bowl in a ball. It should be soft and slightly sticky.

KNEAD THE DOUGH AND LET IT RISE

5 Turn the dough on to a floured work surface. Sprinkle the dough and your hands with strong white flour. Knead by holding the dough with one hand, and pushing it away from you with the other. Peel the dough from the surface, give it a quarter turn, and knead for 8–10 minutes, until it is very smooth, elastic, and forms a ball. If the dough sticks while kneading, flour the work surface.

6 Wash a large bowl and brush it with melted butter. Put the kneaded dough in the bowl and flip it, so the surface is lightly buttered. Cover the bowl with a damp tea towel, and let rise in a warm place for 1½–2 hours, until doubled in bulk.

SHAPE AND BAKE THE LOAVES

7 Sprinkle 2 baking sheets with polenta. Turn the dough on to a lightly floured work surface, and knead with your hand just to knock out the air. Cover the dough, and let rest for about 5 minutes.

8 With a sharp knife, cut the dough in half. Flour your hands and pat one piece of dough into a rough 38x10 cm (15x4in) rectangle, leaving the corners rounded. Fold the rectangle in half, gently pressing the halves together. Transfer to 1 of the prepared baking sheets, and repeat to shape the remaining dough.

9 Cover with a dry tea towel, and let the loaves rise in a warm place for about 1 hour, until doubled in bulk. You may find that this takes slightly longer; it will depend on the weather, the humidity, the temperature of the room, and even of the qualities of the batch of flour you have used (flours will differ from batch to batch). Meanwhile, preheat the oven to 190°C (375°F/Gas 5). Make the glaze: beat the egg white just until frothy. Brush the loaves with the glaze.

10 Bake the loaves in the heated oven until well browned. It will take 40–45 minutes. To test if they are ready, turn the loaves over and tap on the bottoms with your knuckles. The bread should sound hollow, and the sides should feel crisp. Transfer to a wire rack and let cool completely. This bread is completely delicious for breakfast, with eggs and bacon, or just thickly spread with good butter.

Baguette

THE MOST RENOWNED of French breads. It is left to rise three times for an open crumb and yeasty flavor – well worth it! Once you have fallen in love with home-made baguettes (and you will), you may want to invest in a baguette frame. We have shown you how to use that equipment here, though it is by no means necessary to own one in order to make this wonderful bread.

SERVES
MAKES 3

PREP
40-45 MINS
PLUS RISING

COOK
25-30 MINS

Ingredients

2½ tsp dried yeast, or 15g (½oz) fresh yeast

500g (1lb 2oz) unbleached strong white flour, plus more if needed

2 tsp salt

MAKE AND KNEAD THE DOUGH AND LET IT RISE

1 In a small bowl, sprinkle or crumble the yeast over 4 tbsp taken from 425ml (15fl oz) lukewarm water. Let stand for about 5 minutes until dissolved, stirring once. Put the flour on to a work surface with the salt. Make a large well in the centre of the flour and add the dissolved yeast and remaining water. With your fingertips, work the ingredients in the well.

2 Gradually draw in the flour and work it into the liquid ingredients with your hand to form a smooth dough. It should be soft and slightly sticky. Sprinkle the dough with flour and begin to knead by holding the dough with one hand and pushing it away from you with the other. Continue for 5-7 minutes, until very smooth, elastic and forms a ball.

3 Brush a large bowl with melted butter. Put the kneaded dough in the bowl, and flip it so the surface is lightly buttered. Cover the bowl with a damp tea towel and let rise in a warm place for 2-2½ hours, until tripled in bulk. Turn the dough on to a lightly floured work surface and knead with your hand just to knock out the air. Return it to the bowl, cover and let rise for 1-1½ hours, or until doubled in bulk.

4 For the next stage, use a baguette frame if you are planning on making baguettes often. Otherwise, use a cotton cloth and baking sheet, and flour generously. Pleat the cloth between the baguettes, and let rise. To bake, roll the loaves from the cloth on to the baking sheet.

SHAPE AND BAKE THE BAGUETTES

5 Sprinkle the baguette frame or cloth with flour. Turn the dough on to a lightly floured work surface and knead with your hand just to knock out the air. Cover and let rest for about 5 minutes. With a sharp knife, cut straight down through the dough, dividing it into 3 equal pieces.

6 Cover 2 pieces of dough while shaping the other. Flour your hands and pat 1 piece of dough into an 18x10cm (7x4 in) rectangle. Starting with a long side, roll the rectangle into a cylinder, pinching and sealing it with your fingers as you go. With the palms of your hands, roll the cylinder, stretching it until it is a stick about 40cm (16in) long.

7 **Put the shaped loaf** into the prepared baguette frame or cloth. Repeat to shape the remaining dough. Cover the frame with a dry tea towel, and let the dough rise in a warm place for about 1 hours or until doubled in bulk. Meanwhile, preheat the oven to 220°C (425°F/ Gas 7). Set a roasting tin to heat on the floor (or lowest rack) of the oven. With a scalpel, make 3 long, slightly diagonal slashes, 5mm (¼in) deep, in each loaf.

8 **Put the frame** holding the loaves into the heated oven, or roll the loaves from the cloth into the oven. At once drop 10-15 ice cubes into the hot roasting tin. Bake for 25-30 minutes, until well browned. Turn them over and tap the bottoms with your knuckles. The bread should sound hollow and the sides should feel crisp. Let cool completely.

Focaccia with rosemary

THIS MOIST ITALIAN BREAD is at its simplest and best in this recipe. Its shape, and the ingredients with which it is flavoured, differ from region to region. It can be sweet or savoury, is most often baked, but sometimes fried. These days you can buy all sorts of flavoured focaccias, but they do not always add much to the original. This is a good-tempered dough, and can be made, kneaded, and left in the refrigerator to rise overnight. Shape the dough, let it come to room temperature, then bake as directed.

SERVES	PREP	COOK
SERVES 6-8	30-35 MINS PLUS RISING	15-20 MINS

Ingredients

leaves from 5-7 rosemary sprigs	2 tsp salt
1 tbsp dried yeast, or 20g (¾oz) fresh yeast	90ml (3fl oz) olive oil
	¼ tsp freshly ground black pepper
425g (15oz) unbleached strong white flour, plus more if needed	

MAKE AND KNEAD THE DOUGH AND LET IT RISE

1 **Finely chop** two-thirds of the rosemary leaves. Reserve the remaining whole rosemary leaves for topping the focaccia. In a small bowl, sprinkle the dried or crumble the fresh yeast over 4 tbsp taken from 300ml (½ pint) lukewarm water. Let stand for about 5 minutes until dissolved, stirring once.

2 **Put the flour** on to a work surface with the salt. Make a large well in the centre of the mound and add the chopped rosemary, dissolved yeast, 4 tbsp of the oil, the freshly ground pepper, and the remaining water. With your fingertips, work together all the ingredients in the well until they are thoroughly mixed.

3 **Gradually draw in the flour** and work it into all the other ingredients with your hand to form a smooth dough. It should be soft and sticky. Do not be tempted to add more flour to dry it out as you want a moist loaf after baking. Sprinkle the dough and your hands with flour and knead, lifting the dough up and throwing it down for 5-7 minutes, until it is very smooth, elastic, and forms a ball. This bread can be made in a food processor using the dough hook attachment, but making it by hand is very satisfying and more than a little therapeutic

4 **Brush a large bowl** with olive oil. Put the kneaded dough in the bowl and flip it so the surface is lightly oiled. Cover the bowl with a damp tea towel and let rise in a warm place for 1-1½ hours, or until doubled in bulk. Alternatively, let the dough rise in the refrigerator overnight, loosely covered with clingfilm, ensuring no strong flavours can taint the mixture (it is best to ensure the refrigerator contains no pungent foods).

SHAPE AND BAKE THE FOCACCIA

5 **Generously brush** a 38x23cm (15x9in) Swiss roll tin with olive oil. Turn the dough on to a lightly floured work surface and knead to knock out the air. Cover and let rest for about 5 minutes.

6 **Transfer the dough** to the tin. With your hands, flatten the dough to fill the tin evenly. Cover with a dry tea towel, and let rise in a warm place for 35-45 minutes, until puffed. Meanwhile, preheat the oven to 200°C (400°F/Gas 6). Brush the dough with the remaining oil, then top with the reserved rosemary leaves.

7 **With your fingertips,** poke the dough all over to make deep dimples. Bake for 15–20 minutes, until crisp-crusted underneath and lightly browned on top. Transfer to a wire rack and let cool slightly. Cut or break the focaccia into pieces, and serve warm as a snack, or as an appetizer at an informal supper.

 VARIATION: Focaccia with sage

1 Omit the rosemary and the freshly ground black pepper. Finely chop the leaves from 3–5 sage sprigs, discarding the stalks. (Do not be tempted to add more sage, as it is a strong flavour and can easily overpower). Make the focaccia dough, adding the chopped sage to the well in place of the rosemary. Knead the dough, and let rise as directed in the main recipe. Brush a baking sheet evenly with olive oil.

2 Knock the air out of the dough, and let rest as directed. With a rolling pin and your hands, roll and pull the dough into a rough 35cm (14in) oval. Transfer to the oiled baking sheet.

3 With a scalpel or very sharp knife, make diagonal slashes through the dough to resemble the veins of a leaf, pulling the slits apart slightly with your fingers. If your knife if not very sharp, the dough will tear and the loaf will not rise so well. The focaccia will bake to a beautiful leaf shape. Let the dough rise as directed in the main recipe, then brush it evenly with 1 tbsp well-flavoured olive oil. Bake as directed. This is delicious with a herbed roast loin of pork, or simply with good-quality ham.

Seeded rye bread

A CRUSTY LOAF full of flavour, accented by aromatic caraway seeds. Rye flour is darker than wheat flour and low in gluten, so here it is mixed with strong white flour (slightly higher in gluten) to lighten the texture of the loaf. Rye bread is best eaten on the day of baking, but can be tightly wrapped and kept for up to 2 days, or it freezes very successfully. You can make this loaf in an electric mixer fitted with a dough hook, or in a food processor, if you would rather not knead it by hand.

SERVES	PREP	COOK
MAKES 1 LOAF	35–40 MINS PLUS RISING	50–55 MINS

Ingredients

2½ tsp dried yeast, or 15g (½oz) fresh yeast

1 tbsp black treacle

1 tbsp vegetable oil

1 tbsp caraway seeds

2 tsp salt

250ml (9fl oz) lager

250g (9oz) rye flour

175g (6oz) unbleached strong white flour, plus more if needed

polenta (fine yellow cornmeal), for the baking sheet

1 egg white, to glaze

MAKE AND KNEAD THE DOUGH AND LET IT RISE

1 **In a small bowl,** sprinkle or crumble the yeast over 4 tbsp lukewarm water. Let stand for about 5 minutes, until dissolved, stirring once. Put the dissolved yeast, black treacle, oil, two-thirds of the caraway seeds, and the salt into a large bowl. Pour in the lager. Stir in the rye flour and mix everything together well with your hand.

2 **Add the strong white flour,** 60g (2oz) at a time, mixing well after each addition, until the dough pulls away from the side of the bowl in a ball. It should be soft and slightly sticky. Turn on to a floured surface. Sprinkle the dough with flour, and knead for 8–10 minutes, until it is very smooth, elastic, and forms a ball.

3 **Wash out the large bowl** and brush it with oil. Put the kneaded dough in the bowl, and flip it so the surface is lightly oiled. Cover the bowl with a damp tea towel and let rise in a warm place for 1½–2 hours, or until about doubled in bulk.

SHAPE AND BAKE THE LOAF

4 **Sprinkle a baking sheet** with polenta. Turn the dough on to a lightly floured work surface and knead just to knock out the air. Cover and let rest for about 5 minutes. Flour your hands and pat the dough into an oval about 25cm (10in) long.

5 **Gently roll the dough back** and forth on the work surface, exerting more pressure on the ends to taper them. Transfer the loaf to the baking sheet. Cover with a dry tea towel, and let rise in a warm place for about 45 minutes, or until doubled in bulk. Meanwhile, preheat the oven to 190°C (375°F/Gas 5).

 VARIATION: Horseshoe rye bread

1 Omit the caraway seeds. Make and knead the dough, and let it rise as directed. Sprinkle a baking sheet with polenta. Knock the air out of the dough, and let rest as directed. Flour your hands and pat the dough into a 25x20cm (10x8in) rectangle.

2 Starting with a long side, roll the rectangle into a cylinder, pinching and sealing it with your fingers as you go. With the palms of your hands, roll the cylinder until it is about 45cm (18in) long and of an even thickness. Transfer the cylinder, seam-side down, to the baking sheet, then curve the ends around to form a horseshoe shape.

3 Cover the loaf and let rise as directed. Heat the oven to 190°C (375°F/Gas 5). Make the glaze and brush the loaf with egg white as directed. With a scalpel, make a slash, 5mm (¼in) deep, along the top, following the curve of the loaf. Bake the loaf, and let cool as directed.

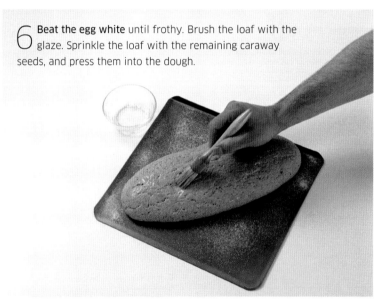

6 **Beat the egg white** until frothy. Brush the loaf with the glaze. Sprinkle the loaf with the remaining caraway seeds, and press them into the dough.

7 **With a scalpel,** make 3 diagonal slashes, about 5mm (¼in) deep, in the top of the loaf. Bake until well browned, 50–55 minutes. Turn the loaf over and tap the bottom with your knuckles. The bread should sound hollow and the sides should feel crisp. Transfer to a wire rack and let cool completely. This is especially good with cheese, cooked meats, and coleslaw.

Dinner rolls

AN EGG-ENRICHED DOUGH, easy to shape. You can shape the rolls however you like, though an assortment of different forms looks very nice in a basket. The dough can be made, shaped, and frozen ahead of time. Defrost, then bake just before serving. Freshly baked rolls also freeze well.

SERVES	PREP	COOK
MAKES 16	45–55 MINS PLUS RISING	15–18 MINS

Ingredients

FOR THE ROLLS

150ml (9fl oz) milk

60g (2oz) unsalted butter

2 tbsp sugar

2½ tsp dried yeast, or 15g (½oz) fresh yeast

2 eggs

2 tsp salt

550g (1¼lb) unbleached strong white flour, plus more if needed

FOR THE GLAZE

1 egg yolk

poppy seeds, to sprinkle (optional)

MAKE AND KNEAD THE DOUGH AND LET IT RISE

1 Put the milk into a saucepan, and bring just to a boil. Pour 4 tbsp of the milk into a small bowl, and let cool to lukewarm. Meanwhile, cut the butter into pieces. Add the butter and sugar to the remaining milk in the pan, stirring occasionally, until the butter is melted. Let cool to lukewarm.

2 Sprinkle the yeast over the 4 tbsp milk and let stand, stirring once, for about 5 minutes, until dissolved. In a large bowl, beat the eggs just until mixed. Add the cooled sweetened milk, salt, and dissolved yeast.

3 Stir in half the flour and mix well with your hand. Add the remaining flour, 60g (2oz) at a time, mixing well after each addition. Keep adding flour until the dough pulls away from the side of the bowl in a ball. It should be soft and slightly sticky.

4 Turn the dough on to a floured work surface. Knead for 5–7 minutes, until it is very smooth, elastic, and forms a ball. If the dough sticks while kneading, flour the work surface.

5 Wash a large bowl and brush it with melted butter. Put the dough in the bowl, and flip it so the surface is lightly buttered. Cover with a damp tea towel and let rise in a warm place for 1–1½hours, until doubled in bulk,.

6 Brush two baking sheets with melted butter. Turn the dough onto a lightly floured work surface and knead to knock out the air. Cover and let rest for about 5 minutes. Cut the dough in half. With your hands, roll one piece of the dough into a cylinder about 5cm (2in) in diameter. Cut the cylinder into eight equal pieces. Repeat with the remaining dough.

SHAPE THE ROLLS

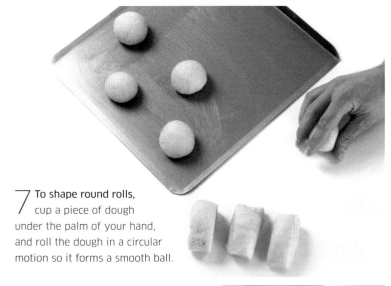

7 To shape round rolls, cup a piece of dough under the palm of your hand, and roll the dough in a circular motion so it forms a smooth ball.

8 For a baker's knot, roll a piece of dough into a long rope. Shape into a figure of eight, and tuck the ends through the holes.

9 For a twist, roll a piece of dough into a long rope, fold it in half and twist. Arrange on a baking sheet and press down the ends.

10 **For a snail,** roll a piece of dough into a long rope and wind it around in a spiral, tucking the end underneath. Arrange eight rolls on each baking sheet. Cover with a dry tea towel and let rise in a warm place for about 30 minutes, until doubled in bulk.

BAKE THE ROLLS

11 **Meanwhile,** preheat the oven to 220°C (425°F/Gas 7). Make the glaze: beat the egg yolk with 1 tbsp water just until it looks frothy. Brush the rolls with the glaze, sprinkle evenly with poppy seeds, if you like, then bake until the rolls are golden brown. It should take just 15–18 minutes, but do check them often (without opening the oven door), as their small size means they can scorch easily. As your baking confidence increases, experiment by sprinkling with different seeds (try sesame, or sunflower), or add a swirl of pesto, anchovy, or tomato purée to a "snail" roll before twisting it into its final spiral shape.

12 **Turn over the rolls** and tap the bottoms with your knuckles to test if they are ready. They should sound hollow. Allow to cool slightly and release any steam on a wire rack, then serve the rolls warm, piled in a basket, with plenty of good butter for spreading.

Onion and walnut crown

WONDERFUL FLAVOURS from the south-west of France come together in this simple white loaf. The onions are first sautéed, and the walnuts toasted, before being kneaded into the dough. This bread is perfect to go alongside a cheeseboard, ideally accompanied by a glass of mellow red wine, for a simple – though very classy – weekend lunch. It freezes very successfully.

SERVES	PREP	COOK
MAKES 1 LARGE LOAF	40-45 MINS, PLUS 1¾-2¼ HOURS	45-50 MINUTES

Ingredients

425ml (15fl oz) milk, plus more to glaze

2½ tsp dried yeast, or 15g (½oz) fresh yeast

2 tbsp vegetable oil, plus more for the bowl and baking sheet

2 tsp salt

500g (1lb 2oz) unbleached strong white flour, plus more if needed

1 large onion, finely chopped

pepper

60g (2oz) walnut pieces

MAKE AND KNEAD THE DOUGH AND LET IT RISE

1 **Bring the milk** just to a boil. Pour 4 tbsp of the milk into a small bowl and let it cool to lukewarm. Sprinkle or crumble the yeast over the 4 tbsp milk and let stand for about 5 minutes, stirring once, until dissolved.

2 **Put the dissolved yeast,** remaining milk, half the oil, and the salt into a large bowl. Stir in half the flour and mix well with your hand. Add the remaining flour, 60g (2oz) at a time, mixing well after each addition, until the dough pulls away from the side of the bowl in a ball. It should be soft and slightly sticky.

3 **Turn the dough** on to a floured work surface. Sprinkle the dough and your hands with flour, and knead for 5-7 minutes, until very smooth, elastic, and forms a ball. If the dough sticks while kneading, flour the work surface.

4 **Wash out the large bowl** and brush it with melted butter. Flip the dough in the bowl so it is lightly buttered. Cover with a damp tea towel and let rise in a warm place for 1-1½ hours, or until doubled in bulk.

PREPARE THE ONION AND WALNUTS

5 **Preheat the oven** to 180°C (350°F/Gas 4). Heat the remaining oil in a frying pan. Add the onion with salt and pepper and cook, stirring, for 5-7 minutes, or until soft and light brown. Taste for seasoning and leave to cool.

6 **Spread the walnut pieces** on a baking sheet and toast in the heated oven, stirring occasionally, for 8-10 minutes, until lightly browned. Let the nuts cool, then coarsely chop them.

SHAPE THE CROWN

7 **Brush a baking sheet** with oil. Turn the dough on to a lightly floured work surface and knead with your hand to knock out the air. Cover and let rest for about 5 minutes. Knead the onion and walnuts into the dough until evenly blended. Cover and let rest, about 5 minutes longer.

8 **Shape the dough** into a loose ball. Fold the sides over to the centre, turning and pinching to make a tight round ball. Flip the ball, seam-side down, on to the work surface. Make a hole in the centre of the ball with two fingers. With your fingers, enlarge the hole, turning to make an even ring. Gradually enlarge the ring to a diameter of 25-30cm (10-12in).

9 **Lift the ring** on to the prepared baking sheet. Cover with a dry tea towel and let rise in a warm place for about 45 minutes, or until doubled in bulk. Meanwhile, preheat the oven to 200°C (400°F/Gas 6). Brush the ring with milk. With kitchen scissors, snip around the top of the ring in a zig-zag design.

10 **Bake the loaf** in the heated oven for 45–50 minutes, until well browned. Turn the loaf over and tap the bottom with your knuckles. The bread should sound hollow and the sides should feel crisp when pressed. Transfer the bread to a wire rack and let cool completely.

Pesto garland bread

A FRAGRANT AND BEAUTIFUL LOAF. The rye-flavoured dough is rolled into a cylinder, then cut before baking to reveal spirals of the pesto filling. This bread is best fresh, but it can be baked 1 day ahead and the flavour will mellow. Store it wrapped in foil, then warm in a low oven before serving.

SERVES	PREP	COOK
MAKES 1 LOAF	35–40 MINS PLUS RISING	30–35 MINS

Ingredients

FOR THE BREAD

2½ tsp dried yeast, or 15g (½oz) fresh yeast

125g (4½oz) rye flour

300g (10oz) unbleached strong white flour, plus more if needed

2 tsp salt

FOR THE FILLING

leaves from 1 large bunch of basil

3 garlic cloves, peeled

3 tbsp olive oil

30g (1oz) pine nuts, coarsely chopped

60g (2oz) freshly grated Parmesan cheese

freshly ground black pepper

MAKE AND KNEAD THE DOUGH AND LET IT RISE

1 **In a small bowl,** sprinkle or crumble the yeast over 4 tbsp taken from 300ml (10fl oz) lukewarm water. Let stand for about 5 minutes, until dissolved, stirring once.

2 **Put the rye flour,** and half the strong white flour in the bowl of a food processor, with the salt. Combine the dissolved yeast and remaining water and pour in, pulse-blending just until mixed. Add the remaining flour, 60g (2oz) at a time. Mix after each addition, until the dough pulls away from the bowl in a ball. It should be soft and slightly sticky.

3 **Continue working** the dough until it is very smooth and elastic; it will take 60 seconds longer. Turn the dough on to a lightly floured work surface, and remove the blade. Shape into a ball. Brush a large bowl with oil, put in the dough, and flip so it is lightly oiled. Cover with a damp tea towel and let rise in a warm place for 1–1½ hours, until doubled in bulk.

MAKE THE PESTO

4 **Put the basil** in a food processor or blender with the garlic. Work until coarsely chopped. With the blades turning, gradually add the oil until smooth. Transfer the pesto mixture to a bowl and stir in the pine nuts, Parmesan, and plenty of black pepper. Taste for seasoning.

SHAPE AND BAKE THE LOAF

5 **Brush a baking sheet** with oil. Turn the dough on to a lightly floured work surface, and knead to knock out the air. Cover and let rest for about 5 minutes. Flatten the dough, then roll it into a 40x30cm (16x12in) rectangle with a rolling pin. Use your hands to shape the rectangle.

6 **With a spatula,** spread the pesto evenly over the dough, leaving a 1cm (½in) border. Starting with a long end, roll up the rectangle into an even cylinder. Running the length of the cylinder, pinch the seam firmly together. Do not seal the ends.

7 **Transfer the cylinder,** seam-side down, to the prepared baking sheet. Curve the cylinder into a ring, overlapping and sealing the ends. With a sharp knife, make a series of deep cuts around the ring, about 5cm (2in) apart. Pull the slices apart slightly, and twist them over to lie flat. Cover with a dry tea towel, and let rise in a warm place for about 45 minutes, until doubled in bulk. Meanwhile, preheat the oven to 220°C (425°F/Gas 7).

8 Brush the loaf with oil and bake for 10 minutes. Reduce the heat to 190°C (375°F/Gas 5), and continue baking for 20–25 minutes longer, until well browned. Carefully transfer to a wire rack and let cool slightly.

VARIATION: Sun-dried tomato spiral

A gutsy, intensely flavoured bread.

1 Make the dough, and let it rise as directed in the main recipe. Drain 75g (2½oz) oil-packed sun-dried tomatoes, reserving 2 tbsp of the oil; then coarsely chop the tomatoes. Chop the pine nuts. Peel and finely chop 2 garlic cloves. Strip the leaves from 5–10 basil sprigs and finely chop.

2 Put the sun-dried tomatoes in a small bowl with the pine nuts, garlic, basil, and the grated Parmesan cheese. Stir in 1 tbsp of the reserved tomato oil, and season with plenty of black pepper. Brush a 20cm (8in) round cake tin with the remaining oil. Sprinkle 1–2 tbsp polenta in the tin, and turn it to coat the bottom and side; turn the tin upside down, and tap to remove excess cornmeal.

3 Knock the air out of the dough, and let rest as directed. Roll the dough into a rectangle, spread the filling and shape a cylinder. Flip so it is seam-side down, curve it into a spiral and tuck the end underneath. Drop it into the tin, cover, and let rise as directed. Bake as directed, allowing 25–30 minutes at 190°C (375°F/Gas 5). Unmould and let cool.

Irish soda bread

This has a surprisingly light, almost cake-like texture. Stone-ground flour makes a great difference to the flavour, and it takes very little time to make. As an added bonus, it requires no kneading, so is a wonderfully effort-free loaf. It is best eaten warm from the oven, with lots of butter and either very good mature cheese or jam.

SERVES	PREP	COOK
MAKES 1 LOAF	10-15 MINS	35-40 MINS

Ingredients

500g (1lb 2oz) stoneground strong wholemeal flour

1½ tsp bicarbonate of soda

1½ tsp salt

500ml (16fl oz) buttermilk, plus more if needed

MAKE THE DOUGH

1 **Preheat the oven** to 200°C (400°F/Gas 6). Brush a baking sheet with melted butter. Sift the flour, bicarbonate of soda, and salt into a large bowl, tipping the bran from the sieve into the bowl. Mix with your hand to combine the dry ingredients, and make a well in the centre.

2 **In a steady stream,** pour the buttermilk into the centre of the well. With your hand, quickly draw the flour into the buttermilk to make a soft dough. It should be slightly sticky. Do not overwork the dough or the bread will be heavy. Add a little more buttermilk if the dough seems dry.

SHAPE AND BAKE THE LOAF

3 **Turn the dough** on to a lightly floured work surface, and quickly shape it into a round loaf. Put the loaf on the prepared baking sheet and pat it down with the palms of your hands to form a round, about 5cm (2in) high.

4 **With a scalpel** or a very sharp knife, make an "x", 1cm (½in) deep, in the top of the loaf. This is the traditional decoration for this bread, and the deep slashes allow steam to escape during baking.

5 **Bake the loaf** in the heated oven for 35-40 minutes, until brown. Turn the loaf over and tap the bottom with your knuckles. The bread should sound hollow. Transfer the bread to a wire rack and let cool slightly.

6 **Cut the bread** into slices or wedges and serve warm, with plenty of butter. Soda bread is a traditional accompaniment to soup or stew, and also makes very good toast.

Buttermilk scones

ONE OF THE SIMPLEST and best teatime treats. Buttermilk adds flavour and makes the lightest scones. Serve these hot, with generous toppings of butter, jam, and clotted cream, if you like. The only drawback to the recipe is that they must be made and eaten on the same day, though that shouldn't prove too taxing!

SERVES
MAKES 8-10

PREP
15-20 MINS

COOK
12-15 MINS

Ingredients

60g (2oz) unsalted butter

250g (9oz) unbleached strong white flour

2 tsp baking powder

½ tsp salt

2 tbsp caster sugar

175ml (6fl oz) buttermilk, plus more if needed

MAKE THE DOUGH

1 **Preheat the oven** to 220°C (425°F/Gas 7). Brush a baking sheet with melted butter. Sift the flour, baking powder, and salt into a medium bowl. Stir in the sugar. Add the butter and cut it into small pieces using 2 round-bladed knives (this keeps the butter cool).

2 **Rub the mixture** with your fingertips until it forms fine crumbs, lifting and crumbling to aerate it. Work quickly so the warmth of your hands does not melt the butter. In a slow, steady stream, pour the buttermilk into the centre of the well.

3 **Quickly toss the flour mixture** and buttermilk with a fork to form crumbs. Do not overmix the dough or the scones will be heavy. Add a little more buttermilk if the crumbs seem dry.

4 **Stir the mixture** just until the crumbs hold together and form a dough. It is important not to work this dough any more than absolutely necessary, for the best results, so take care.

SHAPE AND BAKE THE SCONES

5 **Turn the dough** on to a floured work surface and knead lightly for 3-5 seconds. Don't be tempted to make the dough smooth. The rougher the dough remains, the lighter the scones will be. Pat the dough out to a round, 1cm (½in) thick. Cut out rounds with a 7cm (2¾in) pastry cutter, patting out the trimmings and cutting additional rounds until all the dough has been used.

6 **Arrange the scones** 5cm (2in) apart on the baking sheet. Bake for 12-15 minutes, until lightly browned. Pile the scones in a basket and serve them hot with jam, butter, and clotted cream.

Pitta bread

A MIDDLE EASTERN BREAD, delicious when stuffed with salad. The cumin seeds in the dough add a subtle crunch and pungent flavour, but the breads will be equally delicious if you don't have any, or prefer to leave them out. If you would rather not knead the bread by hand, it can be made in a food processor fitted with a dough hook, or in a heavy-duty electric mixer.

SERVES	PREP	COOK
MAKES 6	20–30 MINS PLUS RISING	5 MINS

Ingredients

1 tsp dried yeast, or 6g (⅕oz) fresh yeast

2 tsp olive oil

1 tsp salt

60g (2oz) strong wholemeal flour

250g (9oz) unbleached strong white flour, plus more if needed

2 tsp cumin seeds

MAKE AND KNEAD THE DOUGH AND LET IT RISE

1 In a small bowl, sprinkle or crumble the yeast over 4 tbsp taken from 250ml (9fl oz) lukewarm water. Let stand for about 5 minutes until dissolved, stirring once.

3 Add the remaining strong white flour, 60g (2oz) at a time, mixing well after each addition. Keep adding flour until the dough pulls away from the side of the bowl in a ball. It should be soft and slightly sticky. Turn the dough on to a floured work surface, and knead until very smooth and elastic.

2 Put the dissolved yeast, remaining water, oil, and salt in a large bowl. Stir in the wholemeal flour with half of the strong white flour and the cumin seeds, and mix well with your hand.

4 Wash a large bowl and brush it with oil. Put the kneaded dough in the bowl, and flip it, so the surface is lightly oiled. Cover the bowl with a damp tea towel, and let rise in a warm place for 1-1½ hours, until doubled in bulk.

SHAPE THE PITTA BREADS

5 Generously flour 2 baking sheets. Turn the dough on to a lightly floured work surface, and knead with your hand just to knock out the air. Cover the dough and let rest for about 5 minutes. Shape the dough into a cylinder about 5cm (2in) in diameter, then cut the cylinder into 6 pieces.

6 Take 1 piece of the dough, and cover the rest while you work. Shape the piece of dough into a ball, then roll the ball into an 18cm (7in) round or oval with a rolling pin. Transfer the round to a prepared baking sheet. Repeat to shape the remaining dough. Cover the pitta breads with a dry tea towel, and let rise in a warm place for about 20 minutes, until puffed. Meanwhile, preheat the oven to its maximum setting.

7 Put an additional baking sheet in the oven to heat. With a palette knife, gently loosen the rounds or ovals from 1 of the baking sheets. Slide the loosened rounds all at once on to the heated baking sheet in the oven, and bake them until puffed; it should only take about 5 minutes. You only want the tops to be tinged with brown; they should not be golden or crispy, so err on the side of undercooked rather than overcooked. Crisped pitta breads will be impossible to fill.

8 Transfer the cooked breads to a wire rack, and brush the tops lightly with water, in order to keep the very thin pittas moist as they cool. Bake the remaining rounds or ovals from the second baking sheet. Brush any excess flour from the bottom of each pitta, and serve while still warm: break each open, and stuff with salad.

Potato-chive monkey bread

BREAD MADE WITH MASHED POTATO has a soft crust and moist centre, and is an American favourite. Potato bread is delicious warm from the oven, but the dough can be made, kneaded, and left to rise in the refrigerator overnight. Shape the dough, let it come to room temperature, then bake as directed.

SERVES	PREP	COOK
MAKES 1 LOAF	50-55 MINS PLUS RISING	40-45 MINS

Ingredients

250g (9oz) potatoes

2½ tsp dried yeast, or 15g (½oz) fresh yeast

125g (4½oz) unsalted butter, plus more for the bowl and mould

1 large bunch of chives, snipped

2 tbsp sugar

2 tsp salt

425g (15oz) unbleached strong white flour, plus more if needed

PREPARE THE DOUGH

1 **Peel the potatoes** and cut them into 2-3 pieces. Put them in a saucepan with plenty of cold water, cover, and bring to a boil. Simmer gently for 15-20 minutes, or just until the potatoes are tender when pierced with the tip of a knife.

2 **Drain the potatoes,** reserving 250ml (9fl oz) of the cooking liquid. Mash the potatoes well, ensuring there are no lumps. Let the reserved liquid and potatoes cool. In a small bowl, sprinkle or crumble the yeast over 4 tbsp lukewarm water. Let stand for about 5 minutes until dissolved, stirring once.

3 **Melt half the butter** in a saucepan. Put the reserved potato liquid, mashed potato, dissolved yeast, and melted butter into a large bowl. Add the snipped chives, sugar, and salt and mix with your hand, until all the ingredients are evenly spread through the mixture.

4 **Stir in half the flour** and mix well with your hand. Add the remaining flour, 60g (2oz) at a time, mixing well after each addition. Keep adding flour until the dough pulls away from the side of the bowl in a ball. It should be soft and slightly sticky.

KNEAD THE DOUGH AND LET IT RISE

5 **Turn the dough** on to a floured work surface. Sprinkle the dough and your hands with flour and knead for 5-7 minutes, until it is very smooth and elastic, and forms a ball. If the dough sticks while kneading, flour the work surface sparingly.

6 **Wash out the large bowl** and brush it with melted butter. Put the dough in the bowl and flip it so the surface is lightly buttered. Cover with a damp tea towel and let the dough rise in a warm place for 1-1½ hours, or until doubled in bulk.

SHAPE AND BAKE THE LOAF

7 **Brush a 1.7 litre (3 pint) ring mould** with melted butter. Melt the remaining 60g (2oz) butter and pour it into a shallow dish. Turn the dough on to a lightly floured work surface and knead just to knock out the air. Cover and let rest for about 5 minutes. Flour your hands and pinch off walnut-sized pieces of dough, making about 30 pieces.

8 **Roll each piece of dough** between the palms of your hands to shape into smooth balls. Put a few balls of dough into the dish of melted butter and turn them with a spoon until coated.

9 **Transfer the balls** of dough to the prepared mould. Repeat with the remaining dough. Cover the mould with a dry tea towel and let rise in a warm place for about 40 minutes, until the mould is full. Preheat the oven to 190°C (375°F,/Gas 5).

10 **Bake the loaf** in the heated oven for 40–45 minutes, until golden brown and the bread starts to shrink from the side of the mould. Let cool slightly on a wire rack, then carefully unmould. With your fingers, pull the bread apart while still warm. It is delicious with roast chicken.

 VARIATION: Soured cream and dill potato bread

1 Omit the melted butter for coating, and omit the chives. Strip the leaves from 5–7 dill sprigs and coarsely chop. Prepare the potatoes and make the dough, using 60g (2oz) butter and adding the dill in place of the chives. Knead, and let rise as directed.

2 Brush a ring mould with melted butter. Put 75ml (2½fl oz) soured cream into a small bowl in place of the melted butter for coating. Knock the air out of the dough, and rest as directed. Cut the dough in half. Roll the pieces of dough into cylinders about 5cm (2in) in diameter. Cut each into 4 pieces. Lightly flour the work surface. Roll a piece of dough into a smooth ball. Drop it into the mould.

3 Brush the sides and top of the ball of dough with the soured cream. Repeat with the remaining dough, arranging the balls evenly in the mould. Let the loaf rise as directed. Heat the oven to 190°C (375°F/Gas 5). Bake, cool, and unmould the bread as directed.

Walnut, bacon, and herb kugelhopf

FROM ALSACE, the most easterly province of France, this egg-rich bread is traditionally baked in a ring mould to give the characteristic shape. Make sure that your walnuts and bacon are of the best quality, as they will give the bread its definite taste. Buy walnuts from France, if you can, for the sweetest and most delicious results. The bread freezes successfully; make sure that you get it into the freezer as soon as it is completely cold.

SERVES	PREP	COOK
MAKES 1 LOAF	45–50 MINS PLUS RISING	45–50 MINS

Ingredients

150ml (5fl oz) milk

150g (5½oz) unsalted butter

1 tbsp sugar

1 tbsp dried yeast, or 20g (¾oz) fresh yeast

3 eggs

500g (1lb 2oz) unbleached strong white flour

1 tsp salt

60g (2oz) walnut halves

125g (4½oz) thick-cut bacon rashers, sliced

3–5 sage sprigs, chopped

3–5 thyme sprigs, chopped

MAKE AND KNEAD THE DOUGH AND LET IT RISE

1 **Bring the milk** just to a boil, pour 4 tbsp into a bowl and let cool to lukewarm. Cut the butter into pieces. Add the butter and sugar to the milk in the pan and stir until melted.

2 **Sprinkle the yeast** over the 4 tbsp milk and let stand for 5 minutes until dissolved, stirring once. Beat the eggs just until mixed. Sift the flour and salt into a large bowl. Make a well in the centre and add the dissolved yeast, eggs, and the cooled sweetened milk.

3 **With your fingertips,** work the ingredients in the well until thoroughly mixed. Gradually draw in the flour and work it into the other ingredients with your hand to form a smooth dough.

4 **Beat the dough:** cupping your hand like a spoon, lift the dough, then let it fall back into the bowl with a slap. Continue beating for 5–7 minutes, until very elastic. Do not be tempted to add more flour; it should be very sticky. Cover the bowl with a damp tea towel and let rise in a warm place for 1–1½ hours, or until doubled in bulk.

PREPARE THE OTHER INGREDIENTS

5 Brush a 1 litre (1¾ pint) kugelhopf or ring mould with melted butter. Freeze the mould until the butter is hard (about 10 minutes) then butter it again. Set 5 walnut halves aside for decoration and coarsely chop the rest.

6 Cook the bacon in a frying pan, stirring occasionally, for 3-4 minutes, until lightly browned. With a slotted spoon, transfer the bacon to kitchen paper and let drain.

FINISH AND BAKE THE KUGELHOPF

7 Beat the dough lightly with your hand to knock out the air. Add the herbs, chopped walnuts, and bacon and beat with your hand until well combined. Arrange the reserved walnut halves in a circle in the bottom of the prepared mould, placing them rounded-side down.

8 Drop the dough into the mould, filling it evenly. Cover with a clean, dry tea towel and let the dough rise in a warm place until it comes just above the top of the mould. It should take about 30-40 minutes, but it will depend on the heat of the room, or even the humidity of the atmosphere. Sometimes it can take a lot longer, depending on the flour used (flour can vary greatly). Preheat the oven to 190°C (375°F/Gas 5) when the bread has risen to the required height.

9 Bake the kugelhopf in the heated oven until puffed and very brown, and the bread starts to shrink from the side of the mould. It should take 45-50 minutes. Watch carefully so that the bread does not scorch, as this will taint the flavour. Let it cool slightly. Unmould the bread on to a wire rack and let cool completely. Serve the kugelhopf as an accompaniment to soups or simple salads.

Small brioches

A CLASSIC FRENCH BREAD, rich with eggs and butter. You'll need 10 x 7.5cm (3in) brioche moulds. You can choose whether or not to place a round "head" on top of each brioche; it is traditional, but the golden, shining domes are just as beautiful if you leave them off. The dough can be made up to the end of step 5, kneaded, and left in the refrigerator to rise overnight. Let the dough come to room temperature, knead in the butter, and finish the brioche as directed.

SERVES MAKES 10	PREP 45–50 MINS PLUS RISING	COOK 15–20 MINS

Ingredients

FOR THE BRIOCHES

2½ tsp dried yeast, or 15g (½oz) fresh yeast

5 eggs

375g (13oz) unbleached strong white flour, plus more if needed

2 tbsp sugar

1½tsp salt

175g (6oz) unsalted butter, softened, plus more for the bowl and moulds

FOR THE GLAZE

1 egg

½ tsp salt

MAKE AND KNEAD THE DOUGH AND LET IT RISE

1 **In a small bowl,** sprinkle or crumble the yeast over 2 tbsp lukewarm water. Let stand for about 5 minutes, until dissolved, stirring once. In another small bowl, beat the eggs with a fork just until mixed.

2 **Sift the flour** on to a work surface with the sugar and salt. Make a large well in the centre, and add the eggs and dissolved yeast. With your fingertips, work the ingredients in the well until thoroughly mixed.

3 **Gradually draw in the flour,** and work it into the other ingredients with your hand to form a smooth dough. It should be soft and sticky. Sprinkle the dough with flour and knead, lifting the dough up and throwing it down, for 8–10 minutes, until it is very elastic and resembles chamois leather.

4 **Work in more flour,** so the dough is slightly sticky; it will become less sticky while kneading, so add flour sparingly. Brush a bowl with butter. Put in the dough and roll it against the side, so the surface is lightly buttered.

5 **Cover the bowl** with a damp tea towel, and let rise in a warm place for 1–1½ hours, until doubled in bulk. Alternatively, put the covered bowl of dough in the refrigerator, and leave it up to 8 hours or overnight. It will rise slowly during that time.

KNEAD IN THE BUTTER

6 **Brush 10 x 7.5cm (3in) brioche moulds** with melted butter. Set the moulds on a baking sheet. Turn the dough onto a lightly floured work surface, and knead with your hand to knock out the air. Cover the dough and let rest for about 5 minutes.

7 **Knead in the softened butter,** pinching and squeezing the dough with both hands. Knead the dough on the floured work surface for 3–5 minutes, until smooth again. Cover, and let rest for 5 minutes more.

SHAPE AND BAKE THE BRIOCHES

8 **Divide the dough** in half. Roll one piece of dough into a cylinder about 5cm (2in) in diameter. Cut the cylinder into five pieces. Repeat to shape and divide the remaining dough. Lightly flour the work surface. Cup each piece of dough under the palm of your hand and roll the dough so it forms a smooth ball.

9 **Pinch about one-quarter** of each ball between your thumb and forefinger, almost dividing it from the remaining dough, to form the head. Holding the head, lower each ball into a mould, twisting and pressing the head on to the base of the brioche.

10 **With your forefinger,** press down 2–3 times around the head to seal it to the base of the brioche. Cover the moulds with a dry tea towel, and let rise in a warm place for about 30 minutes, until the moulds are full and the dough is puffed. Meanwhile, preheat the oven to 220°C (425°F/Gas 7).

11 **Lightly beat the egg** with the salt. Brush the brioches with egg glaze. Bake the brioches in the heated oven for 15–20 minutes, until puffed and brown. Unmould one of the brioches, turn it over and tap the bottom; it should sound hollow. Let the brioches cool slightly, then unmould. Transfer to a wire rack and let cool completely. Brioches make a special breakfast or afternoon tea, served plain, or with jam.

Yule bread

IF YOU WANT TO EAT THIS BREAD at Christmas, you will need to make it 1 month before, to give it time to moisten and mellow. Eat it with a well-aged Stilton cheese. To store the loaf, wrap it first in baking parchment, and then in foil, and seal it in an airtight container. It will be fine for up to 4 weeks, and you won't have to worry about it.

SERVES	PREP	COOK
MAKES 1 LARGE LOAF	50-55 MINS, PLUS RISING	60-65 MINS

Ingredients

1 English breakfast tea bag	2 eggs
90g (3oz) sultanas	530g (1lb 3oz) unbleached strong white flour, plus more if needed
90g (3oz) currants	½ tsp ground cinnamon
45g (1½oz) candied orange peel	½ tsp ground cloves
	3 tbsp granulated sugar
2½ tsp dried yeast, or 15g (½oz) fresh yeast	1 tsp salt
	125g (4½oz) unsalted butter, plus more for the bowl and tin
	2 tbsp fine brown sugar crystals, to glaze

MAKE THE DOUGH

1 **Bring 300ml (½ pint) of water** to a boil. Take from the heat, add the tea bag and let soak for 5 minutes. Put the sultanas and currants in a medium bowl. Discard the tea bag. Pour over the warm tea, and let the fruit soak for 10-15 minutes, until plump.

2 **Strain the fruit,** reserving the tea. Chop the candied orange peel. Set all the fruit aside. In a small bowl, sprinkle or crumble the yeast over 4 tbsp lukewarm water. Let stand for about 5 minutes, until dissolved, stirring once. In another small bowl, beat the eggs with a fork just until mixed.

3 **Sift the flour,** cinnamon, and cloves into a large bowl, and add the sugar and salt. Make a well in the centre and add the reserved tea, eggs and dissolved yeast. Work the ingredients in the well until thoroughly mixed.

4 **Gradually draw in the flour,** and work it into the other ingredients with your hand, to form a smooth dough. It should be soft and slightly sticky. Turn on to a floured work surface. Knead for 5-7 minutes, until it is very smooth, elastic, and forms a ball.

5 **Wash a large bowl.** Brush the bowl with melted butter. Put the dough in the bowl, and flip it so that the surface is lightly buttered. Cover the bowl with a damp tea towel, and let the dough rise in a warm place for 1-1½ hours, until doubled in bulk.

KNEAD IN THE BUTTER AND SHAPE THE LOAF

6 **Brush a 23x12x7.5cm (9x5x3in) loaf tin** with melted butter. Turn the dough on to a lightly floured work surface and knead to knock out the air. Cover and let rest for about 5 minutes. Knead in the softened butter, pinching and squeezing the dough with both hands. Knead the dough on the floured work surface for 3-5 minutes, until smooth again. Cover and let rest for about 5 minutes longer.

7 **Knead the sultanas,** currants, and candied orange peel into the dough until evenly blended. Cover and let rest for about 5 minutes. Flour your hands and pat the dough into a 25x20cm (10x8in) rectangle, on the floured work surface. Starting with a long side, roll the rectangle into a cylinder, sealing it with your fingers as you go.

8 **Roll the cylinder,** stretching it until it is about 45cm (18in) long. Working with the cylinder seam-side up, fold the ends over to meet, making it the length of the tin. Drop the loaf, seam-side down, into the tin. Cover with a dry tea towel and let rise in a warm place for about 45 minutes, until the tin is just full.

9 Put the sugar crystals in a plastic bag. Crush them with a rolling pin; they should be rather fine. Preheat the oven to 200°C (400°F/Gas 6). Brush the top of the loaf with water. Sprinkle the loaf with the sugar crystals, spreading them evenly over the surface.

BAKE THE LOAF

10 Bake the loaf on the center shelf of the oven until it puffs up and begins to brown; it will take about 15 minutes. Reduce the heat to 180°C (350°F/Gas 4) and continue baking until a metal skewer inserted in the centre comes out clean. It should take 45–50 minutes longer. This is a long baking time, so if the top of the bread browns too quickly before it is fully baked (which is quite likely), cover it loosely with a sheet of aluminium foil to protect the surface from scorching. Be sure to check the bread, without opening the oven door, frequently, so that it does not threaten to burn. If your oven is particularly fast, it may help to put a small ovenproof bowl of water on to the bottom rack, to keep the air inside the oven moist; this can help prevent scorching.

11 Remove the bread from the tin. To check if it is ready, turn it over and firmly tap the bottom with your knuckles. The bread should sound hollow, and the sides should feel crisp when gently squeezed. Transfer the bread to a wire rack and let it cool completely. This is good for breakfast, served plain or toasted, and spread with butter. Or eat it with a full-flavoured, mature cheese; it's especially good with blue cheese, as a festive snack or as a savoury, after the main course.

Chocolate bread

A DELICIOUS DESSERT BREAD. Try it spread with mascarpone and eaten with a glass of red wine. The recipe comes from Italy, and is a cousin of the more famous panettone. It is very important to use good-quality chocolate for the best flavour. This is a wonderful bread to serve when you have a house full of guests; it's unlikely they will have seen its like before, and everyone loves it.

SERVES	PREP	COOK
MAKES 1 LOAF	35–40 MINS PLUS RISING	45–50 MINS

Ingredients

2½ tsp dried yeast, or 15g (½oz) fresh yeast

15g (½oz) unsalted butter, softened

30g (1oz) cocoa powder

500g (1lb 2oz) unbleached strong white flour

2 tsp salt

60g (2oz) sugar

125g (4½oz) good-quality dark chocolate

MIX AND KNEAD THE DOUGH IN A FOOD MIXER

1 **In a small bowl,** sprinkle or crumble the yeast over 4 tbsp taken from 375ml (13fl oz) lukewarm water. Let stand for 5 minutes, until dissolved, stirring once. Put the dissolved yeast, softened butter and cocoa powder into the food mixer bowl. Pour in the remaining water and mix with the paddle on low speed to combine.

2 **Add half the flour** to the bowl with the salt and sugar, and beat with the paddle just until combined. Add the remaining flour, 60g (2oz) at a time, beating after each addition. Keep adding flour until the dough pulls away from the side of the bowl in a ball. It should be soft and slightly sticky.

3 **Attach the dough hook.** On medium speed, knead the dough for 3–5 minutes, until very smooth and elastic. If necessary, add more flour while kneading. If the dough climbs up the hook, stop the machine, and push the dough back down.

4 **Remove the kneaded dough** from the dough hook, and shape it into a ball. Brush a large bowl with melted butter. Put the dough in the bowl and flip it so the surface is lightly buttered. Cover with a damp tea towel and let rise in a warm place for 1–1½ hours, or until doubled in bulk.

FINISH THE DOUGH

5 **Brush a 1.5 litre (2¾ pint) soufflé dish** with melted butter. Set aside. Cut the chocolate into large chunks, then coarsely chop them. Chill the chocolate, so it won't melt when kneaded into the dough. Once the dough has risen, turn it from the bowl on to a lightly floured work surface.

6 **Knead the dough** with your hand just to knock out the air. Cover and let rest for about 5 minutes. Knead the chopped chocolate into the dough until evenly blended. Cover and let rest again for about 5 minutes more. Shape the dough into a loose ball. Fold the sides over to the centre, turning and pinching to make a tight round ball.

7 **Carefully put the ball of dough,** seam-side down, into the prepared dish. Cover with a dry tea towel and let rise in a warm place until the soufflé dish is just full. It should take about 45 minutes. Meanwhile, preheat the oven to 220°C (425°F/Gas 7).

BAKE THE LOAF

8 **Brush the loaf** with water and lightly sprinkle with sugar to glaze. Bake for 20 minutes. Reduce the heat to 190°C (375°F/Gas 5) and bake for 25-30 minutes longer, until well browned. Remove the loaf from the dish. Turn it over and tap the bottom. The bread should sound hollow, and the sides should feel crisp. Using a dry tea towel, carefully transfer the bread to a wire rack and let cool completely.

 VARIATION: Chocolate and orange rolls

Grated orange zest adds a wonderful tang to this bread.

1 Omit the cocoa powder. Finely grate the zest of 2 oranges, making sure to include none of the bitter white pith. Make the dough, adding the orange zest to the softened butter and liquid ingredients in place of the cocoa powder. Knead and let the dough rise as directed in the main recipe. Chop and chill the chocolate. Brush 2 baking sheets with melted butter.

2 Knock the air out of the dough and let it rest for about 5 minutes. Knead in the chocolate and let the dough rest again, for about 5 minutes more. Cut the dough in half. Roll 1 piece of dough into a cylinder about 5cm (2in) in diameter. Cut the cylinder into 4 pieces. Shape and divide the remaining dough. Lightly flour a work surface. Roll each piece of dough into a smooth ball. Set the ball on a prepared baking sheet. Shape the remaining pieces. Cover and let rise in a warm place until the rolls have doubled in bulk. It will probably take about 30 minutes.

3 Preheat the oven to 220°C (425°F/Gas 7). Glaze the rolls as directed, and bake them in the heated oven for 15 minutes, until they begin to brown. Reduce the heat to 190°C (375°F/Gas 5) and bake until well browned and the rolls sound hollow when tapped. It could take 15-20 minutes longer, but keep a close eye on them so that the rolls do not scorch. Cover them with foil if they threaten to do so. Makes 8 rolls.

Pies, tarts, and cakes

Sweet baked goodies, for dessert or with tea

Blackberry and apple pie

BECAUSE THEY RIPEN TOGETHER in early autumn, blackberries and apples are a popular combination. Traditionally, cooking apples are used, but this recipe contains eating apples for their sweeter flavour. Serve the pie warm, with double cream. The shortcrust pastry dough can be made up to 2 days ahead and kept, tightly wrapped with clingfilm, in the refrigerator. The pie itself is best eaten on the day it is baked, but that shouldn't prove too difficult to achieve!

SERVES	PREP	COOK
SERVES 4-6	35-40 MINS PLUS CHILLING	50-60 MINS

Ingredients

FOR THE PASTRY

215g (7½oz) plain flour

1½ tbsp caster sugar (optional)

¼ tsp salt

45g (1½oz) white vegetable fat, chilled

60g (2oz) unsalted butter, chilled

FOR THE FILLING

500g (1lb 2oz) blackberries

1 lemon

875g (1lb 15oz) eating apples

150g (5½oz) caster sugar, or to taste

MAKE THE PASTRY

1 **Sift the flour**, sugar, if using, and salt into a medium bowl. Cut the chilled vegetable fat and butter into pieces, and add it to the flour mixture; then cut the fats into the mixture with 2 round-bladed table knives to keep the mixture as cool as possible. (You can use your hands, but this will warm up the pastry, which should be avoided.)

2 **Rub in the fat** with your fingertips until the mixture forms coarse crumbs, lifting and crumbling to help aerate it. Try to make this process as quick as possible, to avoid warming up the pastry mixture. Sprinkle 3-4 tbsp cold water over the mixture, 1 tbsp at a time, and mix in with a fork. Stop as soon as the crumbs begin to cling together in moist clumps. Do not use too much water, or the dough will be sticky and the pastry may be tough once baked.

3 **Continue mixing** the pastry with the fork, to keep the mixture cool and prevent the fat from melting, until the crumbs are moist enough to start sticking together. Press the dough lightly into a ball - again being very careful not to let it come into too much contact with your warm palms - then wrap it tightly, and chill until firm in the refrigerator. It will take at least 30 minutes, but can be chilled for up to 3 days, if this is more convenient.

PREPARE THE PIE FILLING

4 **Pick over the blackberries**; wash them only if dirty. Squeeze the lemon and set the juice aside. Peel the apples with a vegetable peeler. Cut out the stalk and flower ends from each apple.

5 **Halve 1 apple**, and scoop out the core from each half with a teaspoon or a melon baller, ensuring all the hard fibres and membranes are removed. Repeat for the remaining apples.

6 **Set 1 apple half**, cut-side down, on the chopping board. Cut it lengthways in half, then slice it across into 6 equal chunks. Repeat for the remaining apple halves. Put the apples in a bowl. Add the lemon juice and all but 2 tbsp of the sugar; toss to combine.

7 **Add the blackberries** to the apple chunks and toss again lightly. Taste the fruit mixture, adding more sugar if necessary. How much you will need depends whether the apples are sweet or tart.

ASSEMBLE THE PIE

8 **Lightly flour a work surface**. Roll out the dough, and trim to a shape 7.5cm (3in) larger than the top of your chosen pie dish. The dish can be any shape as long as it has a 1 litre (1¾ pint) capacity. Reserve the trimmings.

9 **Invert the pie dish** on to the pastry. Cut a 2cm (¾in) strip from the edge of the dough, leaving a shape 4cm (1½in) larger than the dish. Place a pie funnel in the centre and spoon the fruit around it into a mound.

10 **With a pastry brush**, lightly moisten the edge of the pie dish with cold water. Lift the strip from around the dough and transfer it to the edge of the pie dish, pressing it down firmly. Brush the strip with cold water.

11 **Roll up the pastry** around the rolling pin and unroll it over the filling. Press the edge down on to the dough strip to seal it. With the tip of a small knife, cut a hole in the dough over the pie funnel, to allow steam to escape. Trim the edges; use the trimmings to decorate the pie, if you like.

BAKE THE PIE

12 **Chill the pie** until firm, about 15 minutes. Meanwhile, preheat the oven to 190°C (375°F/Gas 5). Bake the pie for 50-60 minutes, until the pastry is lightly browned and crisp, and the apples are tender when pierced with a metal skewer. Remove from the oven and sprinkle with the reserved sugar. Serve hot or warm, with double cream, if you like.

Lemon meringue pie

TART LEMON CURD WITH SWEET MERINGUE PEAKS is a combination few can resist. It's not surprising that this pie has achieved international fame. The pastry shell can be baked and the lemon curd made 1 day ahead.

SERVES
SERVES 6-8

PREP
45-50 MINS
PLUS CHILLING

COOK
30-35 MINS

Ingredients

FOR THE PASTRY

215g (7½oz) plain flour

¼ tsp salt

90g (3oz) white vegetable fat

1½ tbsp caster sugar (optional)

FOR THE LEMON CURD

5 lemons

3 egg yolks

2 eggs

125g (4½oz) unsalted butter

150g (5½oz) caster sugar

FOR THE ITALIAN MERINGUE

100g (3½oz) caster sugar

3 egg whites

MAKE THE PASTRY AND BAKE BLIND

1 **Sift the flour** and salt into a bowl. Cut in the fat with 2 knives. With your fingertips, rub in the fat until the mixture forms coarse crumbs. Add the sugar, if using. Mix in 3-4 tbsp cold water, 1 tbsp at a time. When the crumbs stick together, press lightly into a ball, wrap, and chill for 30 minutes.

2 **Brush a 23cm (9in) pie dish** with melted butter. On a floured surface, roll the pastry into a round 5cm (2in) larger than the dish. Using the rolling pin, drape the dough over the dish. Gently lift the edge of the pastry with your fingertips and press it well into the bottom and up the side of the pie dish. Press to seal any cracks.

3 **Using kitchen scissors** or a round-bladed table knife, trim the dough so that it extends 1cm (½in) out from the edge of the dish. Fold under the excess pastry to make a thicker edge. Flute the edge of the pastry shell: press your thumbs together diagonally into it to make a ridge. Continue around the edge in this way until the fluting is completed.

4 **Prick the bottom of the pastry shell** with a fork to prevent air bubbles forming during cooking. Chill for about 15 minutes, until firm. Meanwhile, preheat the oven to 200°C (400°F/Gas 6). Heat a baking sheet in the oven. Line the pastry with a double thickness of foil, pushing well into the bottom. Half-fill with dried beans or rice. Bake on the baking sheet for about 15 minutes, until set and the rim starts to brown.

5 **Remove the foil** and beans, and reduce the oven temperature to 190°C (375°F/Gas 5). Bake for 5-10 minutes longer, until golden. Transfer to a wire rack and let cool before adding the filling. Leave the oven on and the baking sheet in the oven.

MAKE THE LEMON CURD

6 **Finely grate the zest** from 2 of the lemons on to baking parchment. Set aside. Halve all the lemons. Squeeze the juice and strain it into a measuring jug. There should be about 250ml (8fl oz). Whisk the egg yolks with the whole eggs until evenly mixed together. Cut the butter into small pieces.

7 **Put the sugar,** zest, and butter into a heavy-based saucepan. Add the lemon juice. Whisk over fairly low heat for 2-3 minutes, until the sugar has dissolved. Off the heat, whisk in the beaten eggs until evenly combined with the lemon mixture.

8 **Return to the heat and cook gently,** so the curd thickens slowly and does not curdle, stirring constantly with a wooden spoon, for 4-6 minutes, or until it is thick enough to coat the back of the spoon.

9 Sieve the lemon curd into a bowl to remove any bits of egg or zest and set aside to cool. Spoon the lemon curd into the pastry shell. Bake on the baking sheet for 10-12 minutes, just until the mixture starts to set. Transfer to a wire rack and let cool, then chill. The curd will set further when cold.

MAKE THE MERINGUE AND FINISH THE PIE

10 Heat the sugar in 75ml (2½fl oz) water until dissolved. Boil, without stirring, until it reaches hard ball stage (120°C/248°F on a sugar thermometer, or until a small spoonful forms a firm, pliable ball).

11 Meanwhile, put the egg whites into a metal bowl and whisk with an electric mixer or by hand. Begin whisking slowly, but increase the speed when the egg whites become foamy and white. Continue whisking the egg whites until stiff peaks form when the beaters are lifted.

12 Gradually pour the hot sugar syrup into the beaten egg whites, beating constantly. Be sure to pour the syrup directly into the egg whites so that it does not stick to the side of the bowl. Continue beating for about 5 minutes, until the meringue is cool and stiff.

13 Heat the grill. With a palette knife, spread the meringue over the filling to cover (or pipe it on, if you prefer). Grill the pie 7.5cm (3in) from the heat for 1-2 minutes, until the meringue is golden brown. Transfer to a serving platter and serve from the pie dish while the meringue is warm and the filling is chilled. Cut it into wedges with a knife dipped in hot water to cut cleanly.

Rhubarb and strawberry tart

TART RHUBARB AND SWEET STRAWBERRIES go into this wonderful pie, which is delicious warm or at room temperature. Ice cream would make a good accompaniment. The pastry can be made up to 2 days ahead and kept, tightly wrapped, in the refrigerator. The pie is best eaten on the day it is baked. Make this in late spring, when both rhubarb and strawberries are at their best.

SERVES	PREP	COOK
SERVES 6-8	30-35 MINS PLUS CHILLING	50-55 MINS

Ingredients

FOR THE PASTRY

330g (11oz) plain flour

½ tsp salt

150g (5½oz) white vegetable fat

2 tbsp caster sugar (optional)

FOR THE FILLING

375g (13oz) strawberries

1 orange

1kg (2¼lb) rhubarb, sliced

250g (9oz) caster sugar

¼ tsp salt

30g (1oz) plain flour

15g (½oz) unsalted butter

FOR THE GLAZE

1 tbsp milk

1 tbsp caster sugar

MAKE THE PASTRY AND LINE THE PIE DISH

1 **Sift the flour** and salt into a bowl. Add the fat, cutting it with 2 round-bladed knives. With your fingertips, rub the fat into the flour until the mixture forms coarse crumbs, lifting and crumbling the mixture to help aerate it. Add the sugar, if using. Sprinkle 6-7 tbsp cold water over the mixture, 1 tbsp at a time, mixing lightly with a fork. When the crumbs start sticking together, press the dough lightly into a ball, wrap it tightly, and chill until firm, about 30 minutes.

2 **Brush a 23cm (9in) pie dish** with melted butter. Lightly flour a work surface. Roll out two-thirds of the dough into a round, 5cm (2in) larger than the top of the dish. Using the rolling pin, drape the pastry over the dish. Gently lift the edge of the dough and press it well into the bottom and up the side of the pie dish.

3 **Lift the dish** and trim the pastry even with the outer edge of the dish, using a table knife. Reserve the trimmings. Chill the pastry shell for about 15 minutes, until firm.

PREPARE THE FILLING

4 **Hull the strawberries,** washing only if dirty. Halve or quarter them according to size. Using the medium grid of a grater, grate the zest from the orange on to a sheet of baking parchment.

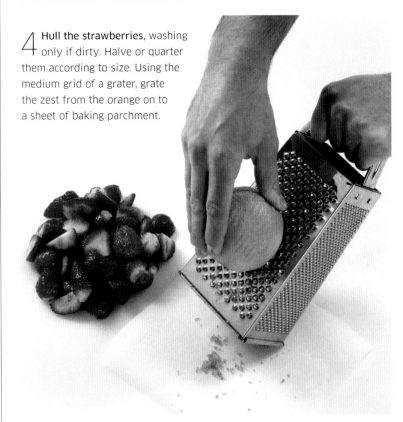

5 **In a bowl,** combine the rhubarb, orange zest, sugar, salt, and flour, and stir to mix. Add the strawberries and toss gently. Spoon the fruit mixture into the lined pie dish, doming it slightly. Cut the butter into small pieces and dot the pieces over the filling.

FINISH AND BAKE THE PIE

7 Use the pastry trimmings to decorate the top of the pie, if you like. With a small knife, cut steam vents around the top crust of the pie. (If you don't do this, the pastry topping may become a little soggy while baking, as it will soak up all the moisture from the fruit.) Scallop the edge of the pie, if you like: place the forefinger of one hand on the edge of the dough, pointing outwards. With the forefinger and thumb of your other hand, push the dough inwards to form scallops. Repeat around the pie.

8 Brush the top crust with milk, and sprinkle evenly with the sugar. Chill the pie until firm; it should take about 15 minutes. Meanwhile, preheat the oven to 220°C (425°F/Gas 7). Put a baking sheet in the centre of the oven to heat up.

9 Bake the pie on the baking sheet in the oven, 20 minutes. Baking on a hot metal baking sheet will mean the base of the pie is in instant contact with direct heat from the moment it goes into the oven, so the bottom crust will be as crisp as possible. Reduce the oven temperature to 180°C (350°F/Gas 4). Bake until the rhubarb is tender when pierced with a skewer through a steam vent, and the crust is browned. It should take 30–35 minutes longer. If the top crust threatens to scorch before the pie is ready, cover it loosely with a sheet of foil and continue to bake until the fruit is completly tender. Transfer to a wire rack, and let cool. Serve in generous slices, with ice cream or pouring cream.

6 Brush the edge of the pastry shell with cold water. Roll out the remaining dough into a 28cm (11in) round. Wrap it around the rolling pin and drape it over the filling. With a small knife, trim the top crust even with the bottom crust. Press the edges together to seal them.

Pear pie with walnut pastry

IN THIS SPECIALITY from central France, wedges of pear are sandwiched between a double crust of walnut pastry. The pastry dough can be made up to 2 days ahead and kept, tightly wrapped, in the refrigerator. Serve the pie warm, with crème fraiche or whipped cream.

SERVES
SERVES 6-8

PREP
35-40 MINS
PLUS CHILLING

COOK
35-40 MINS

Ingredients

FOR THE WALNUT PASTRY

60g (2oz) walnut pieces

135g (4¾oz) caster sugar

250g (9oz) plain flour, plus more if needed

150g (5½oz) unsalted butter

1 egg

½ tsp salt

1 tsp ground cinnamon

FOR THE FILLING

1 lemon

875g (1lb 15oz) pears

½ tsp freshly ground black pepper

1 tbsp caster sugar

MAKE THE WALNUT PASTRY DOUGH

1 Put the walnut pieces in a food processor. Add about half the sugar, and finely grind. Sift the flour on to a work surface, add the ground walnut and sugar mixture, then make a large well in the centre of the ingredients. Using the rolling pin, pound the butter to soften it slightly.

2 Put the egg, remaining sugar, butter, salt, and ground cinnamon into the well. With your fingertips, work the ingredients in the well until they are all thoroughly mixed together. Draw in the flour, working it into the other ingredients with your fingers, until coarse crumbs form.

3 Press the dough gently into a ball. It should be quite soft, but if it is too sticky, add a little more flour. Sprinkle the work surface lightly with flour. Knead the dough for 1-2 minutes, until it is very smooth and peels away from the work surface in one piece. Shape into a smooth ball, wrap tightly, and chill for 1 hour, until firm.

LINE THE TIN

4 Brush a 23cm (9in) flan tin with removable base, with melted butter. Lightly flour the work surface. Roll out two-thirds of the chilled dough into a 28cm (11in) round. Rewrap and return the unrolled dough to the refrigerator. Wrap the rolled dough around the rolling pin. Gently drape it over the tin.

5 Gently press the dough into the bottom of the tin. Roll the rolling pin over the top, pressing down to cut off excess dough. Add the trimmings to the reserved portion of dough and return to the refrigerator. With your thumbs, press the dough evenly up the tin side to increase the height of the shell. Chill for about 1 hour, until very firm.

PREPARE THE PEARS

6 Squeeze the juice from the lemon. Peel the pears with a vegetable peeler. Using the tip of a small knife, cut out the stalk and flower ends from each pear.

7 Cut each pear into quarters, then scoop out the central stalks and cores with a small knife, being sure to remove all the hard fibres and working gently to keep the pear quarters intact.

8 **Put the pear wedges** into a bowl. Add the black pepper and the lemon juice. Toss until the pear wedges are coated. The lemon juice will stop the fruit from discolouring.

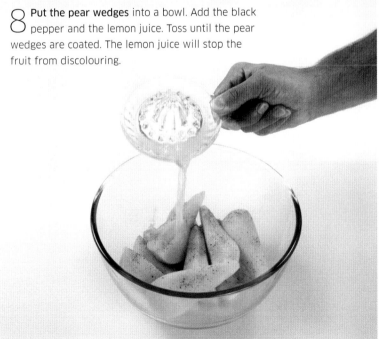

FILL AND **BAKE** THE PIE

9 **Shaking off any excess lemon juice**, arrange the pear wedges evenly in a cartwheel pattern on the bottom of the pastry shell. Roll out the remaining dough into a 25cm (10in) round; stamp out a 5cm (2in) round from the centre, using a cutter or a glass as a guide. This will provide very crisp pastry and allow a tantalizing glimpse into the pie filling.

10 **Wrap the dough** around the rolling pin, and drape it carefully over the pear wedges. With a small sharp knife, trim the top round even with the filled pastry shell, using the tin as a guide. Press the dough edges together firmly with the back of a fork to seal the top and bottom of the pastry shell together.

11 **Brush the top** of the pie with water and sprinkle evenly with the sugar. Chill the pie until firm; it should take about 15 minutes. Meanwhile, preheat the oven to 190°C (375°F/Gas 5). Heat a baking sheet in the oven. Put the pie on the baking sheet so the heat starts to cook the pastry base immediately, and bake the pie until the pastry is browned, and the pears are tender when pierced with a metal skewer, 35–40 minutes. If the top crust threatens to scorch before the pie is ready, cover it loosely with foil and continue to bake until the fruit is completely tender.

Almond and raspberry tart

NOW A VIENNESE SPECIALITY, this tart of buttery almond pastry and raspberry filling probably originated in the town of Linz, in Austria. It is ideal for entertaining, as it actually mellows, becoming more delicious, if it is baked a day or 2 ahead and stored in an airtight container. Sprinkle with icing sugar only about 30 minutes before serving, or it will sink into the pastry and may make it soft.

SERVES SERVES 6-8	**PREP** 30–35 MINS PLUS CHILLING	**COOK** 40–45 MINS

Ingredients

FOR THE ALMOND PASTRY DOUGH

1 lemon

175g (6oz) whole blanched almonds

125g (4½oz) plain flour, plus more if needed

½ tsp ground cinnamon

1 pinch of ground cloves

125g (4½oz) unsalted butter

1 egg yolk

100g (3½oz) caster sugar

¼ tsp salt

FOR THE FILLING

375g (13oz) raspberries

125g (4½oz) caster sugar

1–2 tbsp icing sugar

MAKE THE ALMOND PASTRY DOUGH

1 **Grate the zest** from the lemon on to a piece of baking parchment. Halve the lemon, and squeeze about 1½ tbsp juice. Put the whole almonds in a food processor, and add half the flour to prevent them from becoming oily. Finely grind.

2 **Sift the remaining flour** on to a work surface, with the cinnamon and cloves. Mix in the nuts, then make a well. Pound the butter to soften it. Put the butter, egg yolk, sugar, salt, lemon juice, and zest into the well.

3 **Using your fingertips,** work the ingredients in the well until thoroughly mixed. Draw in the flour and work it into the other ingredients, until coarse crumbs form. Press the dough into a ball, adding a little more flour if it is sticky. Lightly flour the work surface.

4 **Blend the dough** by pushing it away from you with the heel of your hand. Then gather it up and continue to blend for 1–2 minutes, until it is very smooth, and peels away from the work surface in 1 piece. Shape into a ball, wrap tightly, and chill for 1–2 hours, until firm. Meanwhile, make the filling.

MAKE THE RASPBERRY FILLING

5 Pick over the raspberries; wash them only if dirty. Put the sugar and raspberries in a saucepan. Cook, stirring, for 10–12 minutes, until they form a thick pulpy jam. Set aside to cool.

6 With the back of a wooden spoon, press half of the fruit pulp through a sieve set over a bowl to remove the seeds. Stir in the remaining pulp, leaving in its seeds for a little texture.

LINE THE TIN AND FINISH THE TART

7 Brush a 23cm (9in) flan tin with removable base with melted butter. Lightly flour a work surface; roll out two-thirds of the dough into a 28cm (11in) round. Rewrap and chill the remaining dough.

8 Wrap the dough around the rolling pin, then drape it over the tin and press it into the bottom. Roll the rolling pin over the top to cut off the excess dough. Reserve the trimmings. With your thumbs, press the dough evenly up the side of the flan tin to increase the height of the shell.

9 Spread the filling in the shell. Roll out the remaining dough; trim to a 15x30cm (6x12in) rectangle. Reserve the trimmings. Cut the dough into 12x1cm (½in) strips. Arrange half the strips across the tart, about 2cm (¾in) apart. Turn the tart 45°, and arrange the remaining strips diagonally over the first to form a lattice. Trim the overhanging dough strips.

10 Roll out all the dough trimmings thinly. Cut 3–4x1cm (½in) strips, with a patterned edge if you like. Brush the edge of the tart with cold water. Press the strips around the edge. Chill for about 15 minutes, until firm. Meanwhile, preheat the oven to 190°C (375°F/Gas 5), and heat a baking sheet.

11 Bake the tart on the baking sheet for 15 minutes, until the pastry begins to brown. Reduce the oven temperature to 180°C (350°F/Gas 4) and continue baking for 25–30 minutes longer, until the tart is golden brown and just beginning to shrink from the side of the tin.

12 Transfer the tart to a wire rack, and let cool slightly. Set the tin on a bowl and remove the side. Slide the tart on to the wire rack. Let cool completely. About 30 minutes before serving, dust with icing sugar.

Bavarian plum tart

BAVARIA IS FAMOUS for its cakes and tarts. In this recipe, a quick version of brioche forms the base. Juice from the fruit mingles with the custard filling to bring about a deliciously moist result. The amount of sugar you need depends on the sweetness of the plums. Apricots or greengages are also delicious in this tart.

SERVES	**PREP**	**COOK**
SERVES 8-10	35-40 MINS PLUS RISING	50-55 MINS

Ingredients

FOR THE BRIOCHE DOUGH

1½ tsp dried yeast, or 9g (⅓oz) fresh yeast

375g (13oz) plain flour, more if needed

2 tbsp caster sugar

1 tsp salt

3 eggs

125g (4½oz) unsalted butter

FOR THE FILLING

875g (1lb 15oz) purple plums

2 tbsp dried breadcrumbs

2 egg yolks

100g (3½oz) caster sugar

60ml (2fl oz) double cream

MAKE THE BRIOCHE DOUGH

1 Sprinkle or crumble the yeast over 60ml (2fl oz) lukewarm water in a small bowl. Let stand for 5 minutes, until dissolved. Lightly oil a medium bowl. Sift the flour on to the work surface. Make a well in the centre and add the sugar, salt, yeast mixture, and eggs.

2 With your fingertips, work the ingredients in the well until they are thoroughly mixed. Work in the flour to form a soft dough; add more flour if it is very sticky. Knead on a floured work surface for 10 minutes, until very elastic. Work in more flour as needed so that the dough is slightly sticky but peels easily from the work surface.

3 Pound the butter with a rolling pin to soften it. Add the butter to the dough; pinch and squeeze to mix it in, then knead until smooth. Shape into a ball and put it into the oiled bowl. Cover, and let rise in the refrigerator for 1½-2 hours, until doubled in bulk. If more convenient, the dough can be left to rise overnight.

4 Brush a 28cm (11in) quiche dish with melted butter. Knead the chilled brioche dough lightly to knock out the air. Flour the work surface; roll out the dough into a 32cm (13in) round. Wrap the dough around the rolling pin and loosely drape it over the quiche dish.

5 Lift the edge of the dough with one hand and press it well into bottom and up the side of the dish with other hand. With a small knife, trim off the excess dough, using the rim of the dish as a guide. Sprinkle the breadcrumbs over the bottom of the dough shell. Preheat the oven to 220°C (425°F/Gas 7). Put a baking sheet in the oven to heat.

MAKE THE CUSTARD AND FINISH THE TART

6 Meanwhile, stone the plums. Cut each plum half into two. Arrange the plum wedges, cut side up, in concentric circles on the brioche shell. Let stand at room temperature for 30-45 minutes, until the edge of the dough is puffed. Put the egg yolks and two-thirds of the sugar into a bowl. Pour in the double cream. Whisk together.

7 Sprinkle the plum wedges with the remaining sugar and bake the tart on the baking sheet for 5 minutes. Reduce the heat to 180°C (350°F/Gas 4).

8 **Ladle the custard mixture** over the fruit, return the tart to the oven, and continue baking for 45-50 minutes longer, until the dough is browned, the fruit is tender, and the custard is set. Let the tart cool on a wire rack. Serve warm or at room temperature.

 VARIATION: Bavarian blueberry tart

Traditionally, bilberries would be used for this tart.

1 Omit the plums. Prepare the brioche dough as directed in the main recipe. Pick over 500g (1lb 2oz) blueberries; wash them only if they are dirty, as the added moisture will be unwelcome in the finished tart. Any that have to be washed must be gently and very thoroughly patted dry. Leave the fruit whole. Assemble the tart as directed. Make the custard as directed, using 60g (2oz) sugar, 4 egg yolks, and 125ml (4fl oz) double cream.

2 Sprinkle the blueberries with 2 tbsp sugar. Bake the tart for 5 minutes, as directed. Ladle the custard evenly over the blueberries and bake for 45-50 minutes longer. Keep an eye on it as it bakes and cover with foil if the surface of the custard or the berries threaten to scorch before the tart is fully cooked.

3 Just before serving, use a sieve to sprinkle the tart with 1-2 tbsp icing sugar. Serve the blueberry tart warm or at room temperature, cut into neat wedges.

Lemon tart

THIS RECIPE, WITH ITS FILLING OF CITRUS zest and juice in a smooth custard, is from the famous Maxim's restaurant in Paris. Candy the lemon slices at least 1 day, and up to 2 days, ahead, and keep them at room temperature. The dough can be made up to 1 day ahead and refrigerated, tightly wrapped.

SERVES SERVES 8	**PREP** 40–45 MINS	**COOK** 40–45 MINS

Ingredients

FOR THE CANDIED LEMON SLICES

2 lemons

250g (9oz) caster sugar

FOR THE PÂTE SUCRÉE DOUGH

215g (7½oz) plain flour, plus more if needed

90g (3oz) unsalted butter, plus more for the tin

60g (2oz) caster sugar

½ tsp vanilla essence

¼ tsp salt

3 egg yolks

FOR THE CUSTARD

1 orange

3 lemons

3 eggs, plus 1 egg yolk

150g (5½oz) caster sugar

CANDY THE LEMON SLICES

1 **Trim the ends** from the lemons. Cut each lemon into 3mm (⅛in) slices; discard any seeds and the small, pithy end slices of each fruit.

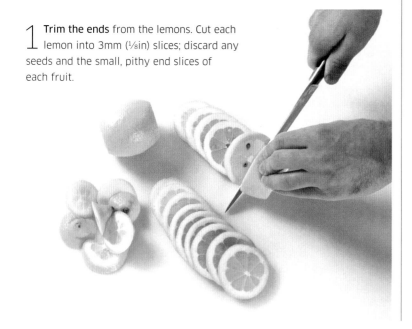

2 **Bring a saucepan of water** to a boil. Add the lemon slices, and simmer for 3 minutes, until they soften. With a slotted spoon, remove and let drain. Attach 3 lengths of kitchen string to an upturned round wire rack. Dissolve the sugar in 500ml (16fl oz) water in a wide shallow pan, then bring to a boil. Put the lemon slices on the rack, tie the strings together, and lower into the syrup.

3 **Press a round of greaseproof paper** on top. Bring slowly to a simmer, taking 10–12 minutes. Poach the lemon slices for about 1 hour, until tender to the bite. Add more water, if necessary, so the slices are always covered. Let the candied lemon slices cool in the syrup. Let stand, covered with the paper round, at room temperature, for 24 hours.

MAKE THE PÂTE SUCRÉE DOUGH

4 **Sift the flour** on to a work surface and make a well in the centre. Pound the butter with a rolling pin to soften it. Put the sugar, butter, vanilla, salt, and egg yolks into the well. Work the ingredients in the well until thoroughly mixed, then draw in the flour until coarse crumbs form.

5 **Press the crumbs** together to form a ball. If the dough is sticky, work in a little more flour. Lightly flour the work surface, and knead the dough for 1–2 minutes, until it is very smooth. Shape into a ball, wrap tightly and chill for about 30 minutes, until firm.

LINE THE TIN AND BAKE BLIND

6 **Brush a 25cm (10in) flan tin** with a removable base with melted butter. Lightly flour a work surface, and roll out the dough into a 30cm (12in) round. Wrap it around the rolling pin and drape it over the tin.

7 **Gently press the dough** into the tin. Roll the rolling pin over the top of the tin to cut off excess dough. With your thumbs, press the dough evenly up the side of the tin, from the bottom, to increase the height of the pastry rim. Chill for about 15 minutes, until firm.

8 **Preheat the oven** to 200°C (400°F/Gas 6), and put a baking sheet in the oven. Line the shell with foil. Half-fill with rice. Bake on the sheet for 10 minutes. Remove the foil and rice. Reduce the oven temperature to 190°C (375°F/Gas 5). Bake for 5 minutes, until pale brown. Leave the oven on.

MAKE THE FILLING, FILL, AND FINISH THE TART

9 **Grate the zest** from the citrus, then squeeze the juice. Put the eggs, yolk, and sugar in a bowl. Whisk in the zest and juice. Set the pastry shell on a baking sheet. Ladle in the filling, then bake for 25–30 minutes, until set.

10 **Transfer to a wire rack** and let cool slightly. Set the tart on a bowl and remove the side. Let cool. Lift the candied lemon slices from the syrup and drain. Using a palette knife, arrange the slices over the filling.

 VARIATION: Lime and cardamom tart

An exotic and exciting version.

1 Substitute 4 limes for 4 of the lemons; omit the sugar and water for candying. Make and chill the pastry dough, line the tin, and bake the shell blind as directed in the main recipe. Pare the zest from 1 lime. Cut it into very fine julienne strips. Bring a small saucepan of water to a boil, add the zest strips, and simmer to blanch for 2–3 minutes. Drain, rinse in cold water, and drain again thoroughly.

2 Grate the zest from 2 of the remaining limes and the lemon, then squeeze the juice from the lemon and all 4 limes; there should be 175ml (6fl oz) juice. Make the filling as directed in the main recipe, using the lime, lemon juice, and zest, and adding 150ml (¼ pint) double cream, and ½ tsp ground cardamom to the custard.

3 Bake, cool, and unmould the tart as directed. Sprinkle the edge of the tart with the lime julienne, and serve with sweetened whipped cream or crème fraîche.

Chocolate pie with crunchy crust

A VELVETY COMBINATION of dark chocolate and cream in a crisp, almond crust. The pastry recipe dates back to 18th-century England. The pie can be baked 1 day in advance. Keep it, covered, in the refrigerator and allow it to come to room temperature before serving. Omit the white chocolate decoration, if you prefer.

SERVES	PREP	COOK
SERVES 8	30-35 MINS	25-30 MINS

Ingredients

FOR THE CRUNCHY CRUST

60g (2oz) caster sugar

175g (6oz) blanched almonds

1 egg white

butter, for the tin

FOR THE FILLING

270g (10oz) good-quality plain chocolate

375ml (13fl oz) double cream

2 eggs plus 1 egg yolk

60g (2oz) white chocolate, to decorate

MAKE AND BAKE THE CRUST

1 **Put the sugar** and blanched almonds in a food processor, and finely grind. In a bowl, whisk the egg white just until frothy. Add the ground almond and sugar mixture. Stir with a wooden spoon to form a stiff paste. Shape it into a ball, wrap tightly, and chill for about 30 minutes, until firm.

2 **Melt a little butter** in a small saucepan, then brush it over a 25cm (10in) flan tin with removable base. Lightly flour a work surface, then lightly pound out the crust mixture with a rolling pin to flatten it.

3 **With the back of a spoon,** dipped into cold water, or with the heel of your hand, press the mixture into the tin, then push it well up the side. Chill for about 15 minutes, until firm. Preheat the oven to 180°C (350°F/Gas 4). Put a baking sheet in the oven to heat.

4 **Put the shell** on the sheet, and bake for 8-10 minutes, until lightly browned. Slide the shell on to a wire rack. Let the crust cool in the tin. Leave the oven on while you make the chocolate filling.

MAKE THE FILLING

5 **Chop the chocolate** and put it into a bowl. In a saucepan, bring the cream just to a boil. Pour the cream over the chocolate. Whisk until the chocolate has melted completely. Set aside to cool to tepid. Put the eggs and the egg yolk into another bowl, and whisk them together until mixed.

6 **Whisk the tepid chocolate** and cream mixture into the eggs. Carefully pour into the cooled shell. Put the tart on the baking sheet and bake in the oven for 15-20 minutes, until the filling begins to set, but is still soft in the centre. Let cool slightly on a wire rack, then carefully loosen the pastry from the side of the tin. Melt the white chocolate in a bain marie (see p472) and drizzle it on top to serve.

Rustic apple tart

EVERY FRENCH HOUSEWIFE has her own version of this tart, the recipe of which comes from Normandy, where they grow the best apples. The pastry dough can be made up to two days ahead, and kept tightly wrapped, in the refrigerator. The apple tart is at its best freshly baked.

SERVES	PREP	COOK
SERVES 6-8	40-45 MINS PLUS CHILLING	30-40 MINS

Ingredients

FOR THE PÂTE SUCRÉE DOUGH

175g (6oz) plain flour, more if needed

90g (3oz) unsalted butter, more for flan tin

60g (2oz) caster sugar

½ tsp vanilla essence

¼ tsp salt

3 egg yolks

FOR THE FILLING

1.4kg (3lb) cooking apples

30g (1oz) butter

1 tsp vanilla essence

60g (2oz) caster sugar, plus more to taste

juice of ½ lemon

FOR THE GLAZE

4 tbsp apricot jam

MAKE THE DOUGH AND PREPARE THE APPLES

1 **Make and chill** the pâte sucrée dough (see p430). Peel two-thirds of the apples, core them, and cut into dice.

2 **Melt the butter** in a frying pan. Add the apples, vanilla essence, and all but 2 tbsp of the sugar. Cook, stirring, for 10-15 minutes, until almost a purée. Taste, adding more sugar if needed. Let cool. Peel, core, and thinly slice the remaining apples. Sprinkle with the lemon juice, and toss to coat.

LINE THE TIN

3 **Brush a 25cm (10in) flan tin** with removable base, with melted butter. Lightly flour a work surface, and roll the dough into a 30cm (12in) round. Wrap it around the rolling pin, then push it into the tin, trimming any excess.

4 **Press the dough** evenly up the side, from the bottom, to increase the height of the shell. Chill for about 15 minutes, until firm. Preheat the oven to 200°C (400°F/Gas 6). Heat a baking sheet in the oven.

ASSEMBLE AND BAKE THE TART

5 **Spoon the cooled apple compote** over the pastry shell. Arrange the apple slices on top in concentric circles. Sprinkle with the remaining sugar.

6 **Bake on the baking sheet** in the oven for 15-20 minutes. Reduce the oven temperature to 180°C (350°F/Gas 4), and continue baking for 15-20 minutes longer, until the apple slices are tender and the rim is golden brown. Let cool slightly on a wire rack, then remove the tin.

7 **Let the tart cool.** Heat the jam with 1-2 tbsp water; work through a sieve. Brush it over the apples and pastry. Serve with crème fraîche.

Peach pie

THIS IS AN AMERICAN CLASSIC, and rightly so. Ripe, fresh peaches and their thick juices are enclosed in a pastry lattice for a succulent and indulgent pie that will leave your guests clamouring for second helpings. Choose peaches that are ripe, and full of juice, with no green tinge. It makes the perfect summer dessert, especially when served with vanilla ice cream. The pie can be made up to 2 days ahead and kept, covered, at room temperature, but is really best eaten on the day it is baked.

SERVES	PREP	COOK
SERVES 8	40–45 MINS PLUS CHILLING	40–45 MINS

Ingredients

FOR THE PASTRY DOUGH

250g (9oz) plain flour

½ tsp salt

125g (4½oz) white vegetable fat

75g (2½oz) unsalted butter

FOR THE FILLING

4–5 ripe peaches

30g (1oz) plain flour

150g (5½oz) granulated sugar, plus more if needed

salt

1–2 tbsp lemon juice (optional)

FOR THE GLAZE

1 egg

½ tsp salt

MAKE THE PASTRY DOUGH

1 **Sift the flour** and salt into a large bowl, using a sieve. Hold the sieve a fair distance above the bowl, and knock it with your free hand, so the flour travels through it.

2 **Add the fat** and butter, and cut them into the flour with a pastry blender, if you have one. A pastry blender will keep the pastry as cool as possible, as it avoids any contact with warm hands, but if you don't have one, use 2 round-bladed knives. Keep cutting, until the mixture forms coarse crumbs.

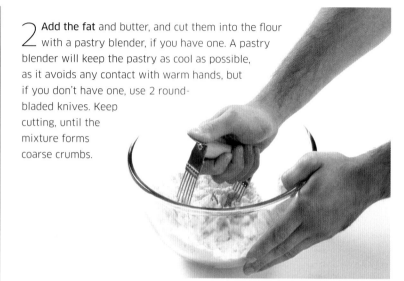

3 **Sprinkle with 3 tbsp water,** and continue blending until the dough can be gathered up into a ball. If the dough seems too dry, add more water, a little at a time. Continue kneading lightly for about 30 seconds, until mixed.

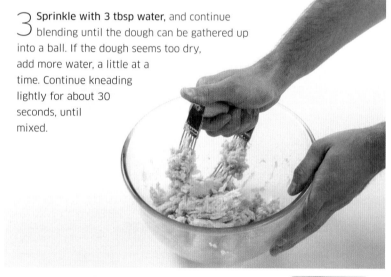

4 **Shape the dough** into a ball, handling it as little as possible. Then wrap it tightly in clingfilm, and chill it in the refrigerator for about 30 minutes, until firm.

LINE THE TIN

5 **Preheat the oven** to 200°C (400°F/Gas 6), and put in a baking sheet. Roll out two-thirds of the dough, about 5cm (2in) larger than a 23cm (9in) pie tin. Press the dough well into the tin. Chill for about 15 minutes, until firm.

PREPARE THE FILLING

6 **Immerse the peaches** in boiling water for 10 seconds, then transfer to a bowl of cold water. Halve the peaches, remove the stones, and peel off the skins. Cut the peaches into 1cm (½in) slices and put in a large bowl.

7 **Sprinkle the peaches** with the flour, sugar, a pinch of salt, and lemon juice, to taste. Carefully stir the peaches, then transfer them to the lined pie tin, with the juices in the bowl.

MAKE THE LATTICE

8 **Press any dough trimmings** into the remaining dough, and roll into a rectangle. Cut out 8 strips 1cm (½in) wide. Weave them into a lattice on top of the pie. Use the trimmings to make leaves, marking veins with a knife.

9 **Lightly beat** together the egg and salt, and use this to glaze the lattice and leaves. Bake for 40–45 minutes, until the pastry is golden brown, and the peaches soft and bubbling. Serve warm, with vanilla ice cream.

 ## VARIATION: Cherry pie

The most famous of American pies.

1 Stone 500g (1lb 2oz) cherries. Prepare the pie pastry dough and line the pie tin as directed in the main recipe. Stir the cherries with 200g (7oz) sugar, more if needed to taste, depending on how sweet or tart are your cherries. Add 45g (1½oz) flour to thicken the cherries, and ¼ tsp almond essence to add a subtle depth of flavour, if you like. Stir very well, so all the cherries are evenly coated in the flour mixture. Transfer these coated cherries to evenly cover the pastry in the pie tin.

2 Cut the pastry strips, using a fluted ravioli cutter, and use them to make a prettily-edged lattice as directed in the main recipe. Place the lattice carefully over the top of the cherry pie. Cut two more strips with the ravioli cutter, and lay them around the edge of the pie to cover the lattice ends neatly, pressing this strip down firmly to adhere both to the pastry rim and to the lattice strips.

3 Flute the edge of the pastry rim, pinching it with your fingers, as neatly as you possibly can. Brush with the egg and salt glaze, as directed. Bake the pie as directed in the main recipe, watching it carefully without opening the oven door to avoid any scorching of the pastry lattice. Serve at room temperature, or even slightly chilled, with scoops of vanilla ice cream or generous billowing piles of crème fraîche.

Normandy pear tart

THIS DELICIOUS TART has become a signature recipe of Normandy, where they grow some of the world's best pears. The sliced fruits are arranged like petals, and baked in a fragrant almond cream. The pears you choose should be ripe, or they will discolour during cooking.

SERVES
SERVES 6-8

PREP
40-45 MINS

COOK
40-45 MINS

Ingredients

FOR THE SWEET PASTRY DOUGH

175g (6oz) plain flour

3 egg yolks

60g (2oz) sugar

salt

75g (2½oz) unsalted butter

½ tsp vanilla essence

FOR THE ALMOND CREAM

125g (4½oz) whole blanched almonds

125g (4½oz) unsalted butter, at room temperature

100g (3½oz) caster sugar

1 egg plus 1 egg yolk

1 tbsp kirsch

2 tbsp plain flour

FOR THE PEARS

1 lemon

3-4 ripe pears

FOR THE GLAZE

150g (5½oz) apricot jam

2-3 tbsp kirsch or water

MAKE THE SWEET PASTRY DOUGH

1 **Sift the flour** on to a work surface. Make a well in the centre and add the egg yolks, sugar, and a pinch of salt. Using a rolling pin, pound the butter to soften it slightly. Add the butter to the well with the vanilla. Using your fingertips, work the ingredients in the well until thoroughly mixed.

2 **With your fingers,** work the flour into the other ingredients until coarse crumbs form. If they seem dry, add a little water. Lightly flour a work surface, then knead for 1-2 minutes. Wrap, and chill for 30 minutes.

LINE THE TIN

3 **Brush the inside** of a 23-25cm (9-10in) flan tin with butter. Unwrap the dough; roll on a lightly floured work surface to a round 5cm (2in) larger than the tin. Roll the dough around the rolling pin, then unroll it over the tin.

4 **Gently press the dough** into the tin. Leave a ridge of dough just inside the edge, to make a deep shell. Cut off the excess dough. With your thumb, press the dough up the side of the tin. Neaten the edge of the dough.

5 **With both forefingers and thumbs,** pinch the dough above the side of the tin to form a fluted edge. Prick the bottom with a fork, to prevent air bubbles. Chill for at least 15 minutes, until firm.

MAKE THE ALMOND CREAM

6 **Grind the almonds** in 2-3 batches, in a food processor. Take care not to overwork the nuts or their oil will be released, creating a paste rather than a "flour" of ground almonds.

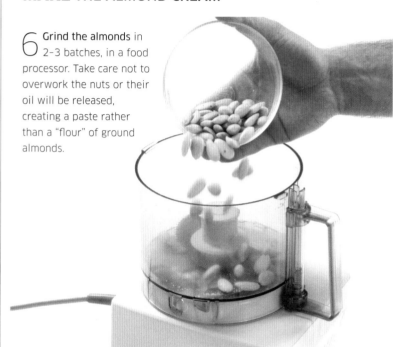

7 **With an electric mixer** or wooden spoon, cream the butter. Add the sugar, and continue beating for 2-3 minutes, until fluffy and light. Do not stop beating too soon, as you want the mixture to be as aerated as possible.

8 **Add the egg** and egg yolk to the mixture, 1 at a time, beating well after each addition. Add the kirsch, then stir in the ground almonds and flour with a spatula, just until everything is well blended. Go gently, to keep the mixture as light as you can.

PREPARE THE PEARS

9 **Cut the lemon** in half. Peel the pears, rubbing them all over with the cut lemon to prevent discolouration. Cut the pears lengthways in half. Neatly remove the cores, and rub all the cut surfaces with the cut lemon again.

10 **Set a pear half cut-side down** on a chopping board. Using a thin-bladed knife, cut it lengthways into thin slices. Repeat with all the remaining pear halves.

ASSEMBLE AND BAKE THE TART

11 **Preheat the oven** to 200°C (400°F/Gas 6). Heat a baking sheet near the bottom of the oven. Spoon the almond cream into the pastry shell, and spread it evenly with a palette knife.

12 **Transfer the pear** slices to the tart, arranging like the petals of a flower. Set the tin on the baking sheet, and bake for 12–15 minutes. Reduce the heat to 180°C (350°F/Gas 4), and bake for 25–30 minutes more.

13 **Meanwhile,** melt the jam with the kirsch in a small pan, work it through a sieve and reheat. Unmould the tart and transfer it to a plate. Brush the top with the glaze. Serve at room temperature.

Fig and mulled wine tart

FRESH FIGS, with their deep, red flesh and delicate flavor, call for the simplest treatment. Here, they are poached briefly in mulled wine syrup. If you can't get hold of a vanilla pod, use ½ tsp of vanilla extract instead. Do not buy or use anything labelled vanilla "essence"; it is made from synthetic ingredients and tastes very little like the real thing. This is a lovely tart to serve during later summer, when figs are at the peak of their season and so reasonably priced.

SERVES	**PREP**	**COOK**
SERVES 6-8	25-30 MINS, PLUS CHILLING	15-20 MINS

Ingredients

FOR THE POLENTA PASTRY

125g (4½oz) plain flour, plus more if needed

45g (1½oz) polenta (fine yellow cornmeal)

75g (2½oz) unsalted butter, plus more for the baking sheet and flan ring

1 egg

50g (1¾oz) caster sugar

¼ tsp salt

FOR THE LIGHT PASTRY CREAM

½ vanilla pod

250ml (8fl oz) milk

3 egg yolks

3 tbsp caster sugar

2 tbsp flour

10g (¼oz) unsalted butter

90ml (3fl oz) double cream

FOR THE FILLING

500g (1lb 2oz) purple figs

1 orange

1 lemon

1 nutmeg

100g (3½oz) caster sugar

5cm (2in) piece of cinnamon stick

2 whole cloves

1 tsp black peppercorns

500ml (16fl oz) dry red wine

MAKE THE DOUGH, LINE THE TIN, AND BAKE THE SHELL

1 **Sift the flour** on to a work surface. Add the polenta and make a well in the centre. Pound the butter with a rolling pin to soften it. Beat the egg to mix. Put the butter, egg, sugar, and salt into the well. With your fingertips, work the ingredients until thoroughly mixed.

2 **Draw in the flour** and polenta, and work them into the other ingredients with your fingers, until coarse crumbs form. Press the dough into a ball. If it is sticky, work in a little more flour.

3 **Lightly flour a work surface.** Knead the dough for 1-2 minutes, until it peels away from the surface. Shape into a ball, wrap tightly, and chill for 30 minutes, until firm. Preheat the oven to 190°C (375°F/Gas 5). Brush a 25cm (10in) springform tin with melted butter. Roll out the dough on a floured surface, into a 28cm (11in) round. Wrap around the rolling pin and drape over the tin.

4 **Gently press the dough** into the tin. Fold over the excess dough inside, to form a border. Chill for about 15 minutes, until firm. Bake the pastry for 15-20 minutes, until set and golden brown. Carefully slide the pastry round on to a wire rack, loosen the sides of the tin, and let cool.

MAKE THE LIGHT PASTRY CREAM

5 **Split the vanilla pod.** In a heavy-based pan, bring the milk to a boil with the pod. Remove from the heat, cover, and let stand for 10-15 minutes. Whisk the egg yolks and sugar until thick. Stir in the flour. Gradually stir in the hot milk until smooth. Pour back into the pan. Bring to a boil over medium heat, whisking constantly to keep it smooth, until thickened.

6 **Reduce the heat** and cook, still whisking, for about 2 minutes, until the pastry cream softens slightly. Remove from heat, and take out the vanilla pod. Transfer to a bowl. Rub the butter over surface of the cream to keep it from forming a skin, and chill for 30 minutes.

7 **Pour the double cream** into a chilled bowl, and whip until soft peaks form; cover and chill. Add the cream to the chilled pastry cream and fold together gently but thoroughly. Cover and chill. Meanwhile, make the syrup and poach the figs.

MAKE THE SYRUP AND POACH THE FIGS

8 **Prick each fig** two or three times with the tines of a fork, so that the syrup will penetrate the fruit. Pare the zest from the orange and lemon. Crush the nutmeg in a plastic bag with the rolling pin; it should be very aromatic.

9 **Put the zest** and nutmeg into a saucepan with the sugar, spices, and peppercorns. Add the wine. Heat, stirring, to dissolve the sugar. Bring just to a boil, then add the figs. Cover, and poach for 3–5 minutes, just until the figs are tender.

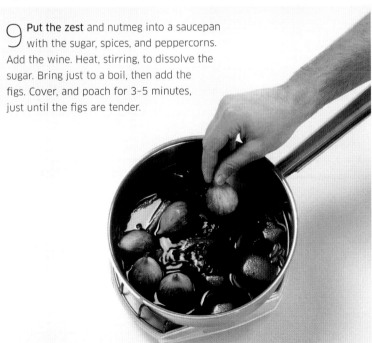

10 **Remove the figs** with a slotted spoon, allowing them to drain well, and let cool. Simmer the syrup for 25–30 minutes, until reduced to about 125ml (4fl oz). Strain and cool. Cut the stalks from the figs; cut the figs into halves. Now cut them nearly through into quarters, leaving them attached at the flower ends. Slide the pastry shell on to a serving plate. Spread the pastry cream over the pastry. Arrange the figs in concentric circles on top, and pull each half open slightly. Spoon 1–2 tbsp syrup over the figs. Just before serving, spoon the remaining syrup over.

Filo apricot turnovers

FILO IS A MULTI-PURPOSE DOUGH and not nearly as hard to work with as you might think. Here, it is folded into triangles to enclose a filling of fresh apricots, cooked with a spicy blend of cinnamon, nutmeg, and cloves. These light and flaky turnovers can be eaten with a knife and fork, or your fingers. They can be prepared up to the end of step 7, wrapped tightly and securely, and kept in the refrigerator for up to 2 days. They also freeze very well. Bake them just before serving.

SERVES MAKES 24	**PREP** 35-40 MINS	**COOK** 12-15 MINS

Ingredients

500g (1lb 2oz) apricots

1 lemon

200g (7oz) caster sugar

1 tsp ground cinnamon

ground nutmeg

ground cloves

225g (8oz) pack of filo pastry sheets

175g (6oz) unsalted butter

MAKE THE APRICOT FILLING

1 Cut each apricot in half around the stone. Using both hands, give a quick, sharp twist to each half to loosen it from the stone. Scoop out the stone with a knife and discard. Cut each half into 4-5 pieces. Grate the zest from half of the lemon on to a plate.

2 In a saucepan, combine the apricots, lemon zest, three-quarters of the sugar, the cinnamon, and a pinch each of nutmeg and cloves. Add 2 tbsp water. Cook gently, stirring occasionally, for 20-25 minutes, until the mixture thickens to the consistency of jam. Transfer to a bowl and let cool.

PREPARE THE FILO PASTRY

3 Preheat the oven to 200°C (400°F/Gas 6). Lay a tea towel on the work surface, and sprinkle it lightly with water. Unroll the filo pastry sheets on the towel, and cut them lengthways in half. Cover them with a second moistened towel.

4 Melt the butter in a small pan. Take a half sheet of dough from the pile and set it lengthways on the work surface. Lightly brush the left-hand side of the sheet with butter, and fold the other half over on top. Brush the strip of dough with more butter.

FILL, SHAPE, AND BAKE THE TURNOVERS

5 Spoon 1-2 tsp of the cooled filling onto the strip of dough about 2.5cm (1in) from one end. Do not put too much apricot filling in each turnover, or they will burst during cooking. Fold a corner of the dough strip over the filling to meet the other edge of dough, forming a triangle.

6 Continue folding the strip over and over, to form a triangle with the filling inside. Set the triangle on a baking sheet with the final edge underneath, and cover the baking sheet with a moistened tea towel. Make sure you have closed the corners tightly so the filling does not leak.

7 Continue making triangles with the remaining filo pastry sheets and filling, arranging them on baking sheets and keeping them covered with moistened tea towels.

8 Brush the top of each triangle with butter, and sprinkle with the remaining sugar. Bake in the heated oven for 12–15 minutes, until golden brown and flaky. With the palette knife, transfer the turnovers to a wire rack to cool slightly, and serve warm or at room temperature.

 VARIATION: Filo berry turnovers

Great for high summer, when a glut of berries brings down their usually high price.

1 Hull 250g (9oz) strawberries and pick over 175g (6oz) raspberries. Wash them only if dirty, as water will adversely affect their texture as well as introducing water into the filo pastry filling. Cut the strawberries in half or into quarters. Put all the fruit in a bowl, sprinkle with 60g (2oz) sugar and toss lightly to combine.

2 Fill each triangle with a scant 1 tbsp berries, being sure not to overfill the turnovers, or they will burst while baking. Brush with butter, sprinkle with sugar, and bake as directed in the main recipe.

3 Decorate each serving with whole raspberries and mint sprigs, if you like.

Tarte Tatin

THIS DESSERT WAS NAMED AFTER two impoverished gentlewomen from the French region of Sologne, who earned their living by baking their father's favourite apple tart. The secret of this upside-down tart lies in cooking the apples in the caramel itself, so it flavours deep inside the fruit. It is delicious served warm, with piles of sharp, refreshing crème fraîche to cut through the richness of the caramel. Make sure you use a heavy-based frying pan to make the best caramel.

SERVES	PREP	COOK
SERVES 8	45–50 MINS	20–25 MINS

Ingredients

FOR THE PASTRY DOUGH

75g (2½oz) unsalted butter

175g (6oz) plain flour

2 egg yolks

1½ tbsp caster sugar

salt

FOR THE FILLING

14–16 apples, total weight about 2.4kg (5lb 6oz)

1 lemon

125g (4½oz) unsalted butter

200g (7oz) caster sugar

crème fraîche, to serve

MAKE THE PASTRY DOUGH

1 **Using a rolling pin,** pound the butter to soften it slightly. Sift the flour on to a work surface, and make a well in the centre. Put the egg yolks, sugar, and a pinch of salt in the centre of the well, then add the softened butter and 1 tbsp water. Using your fingertips, work the ingredients in the well until thoroughly mixed.

2 **Work the flour** into the other ingredients until coarse crumbs form. If they seem dry, add a little more water. Press the dough into a ball. Lightly flour the work surface, then knead the dough for 1–2 minutes, until it is very smooth, and peels away from the work surface in 1 piece. Shape into a ball, wrap it tightly, and chill for about 30 minutes, until firm.

PREPARE THE APPLES

3 **With a vegetable peeler,** carefully peel the apples, then halve and core them. Cut the lemon in half, and rub the apples all over with the cut lemon to prevent discolouration.

CARAMELIZE THE APPLES AND BAKE THE TART

4 **Melt the butter** in a heavy-based ovenproof frying pan. Add the sugar. Cook over medium heat, stirring occasionally, for 3-5 minutes, until caramelized to a deep golden brown. Remove from the heat, and let cool to tepid. Arrange the apple halves over in concentric circles to fill the pan. They will shrink during cooking, so pack them tightly.

5 **Cook the apples** over high heat for 15–25 minutes, until caramelized. Turn once to caramelize on both sides. Take the pan from the heat, and let cool for 10-15 minutes. Meanwhile, preheat the oven to 190°C (375°F/Gas 5).

6 **Roll out the pastry** to a round, about 2.5cm (1in) larger than the pan. Roll up the dough around the rolling pin, then drape it over the pan. Tuck the edges around the apples. Bake for 20–25 minutes, until golden brown. Cool to tepid, then set a plate on top, hold firmly together, and invert. If any apples stick to the pan, replace on the tart. Spoon some caramel over the apples. Serve with crème fraîche.

 VARIATION: Pear tarte tatin

Pears are just as delicious in this recipe.

1 Peel, halve, and core 12–14 pears (total weight about 2.4kg/5lb 6oz). Make sure they are well-flavoured but firm examples, so they will hold up to the caramelization and baking processes without disintegrating. Be careful to keep the attractive teardrop-shape of the fruits while preparing them. Rub each all over with a cut lemon, as directed in the main recipe, to prevent discolouration.

2 Caramelize the pears as directed for the apples in the main recipe, arranging them on their sides in the pan with the tapered ends towards the centre, so that they resemble the petals of a flower. Pears may produce more liquid than apples, and so could take longer to cook in the caramel until all the liquid has completely evaporated. Do not rush this step, as you need to be sure that the fruit is dry before you place on the pastry, or your tart will become soggy during baking. This is because the fruit will steam in the oven beneath its pastry lid.

3 Cover with the pastry dough, tucking it well down around the pears. Bake the tart, and unmould as directed in the main recipe. Serve with crème fraîche, and offer lemon wedges as well, because this tart will taste even sweeter than the apple version.

Cherry strudel

DON'T BE INTIMIDATED by making the ultra-thin strudel pastry; the trick is to knead the dough thoroughly so it is elastic. You will, however, need a large work table and an old, but scrupulously clean, sheet to cover it. Because strudel dough dries out easily, the strudel should be assembled and cooked at once. It is at its best eaten slightly warm on the day of baking, but can be warmed through in the oven 1 day later to mimic the just-baked taste.

SERVES	PREP	COOK
SERVES 6-8	45-50 MINS PLUS RESTING	30-40 MINS

Ingredients

FOR THE STRUDEL DOUGH

250g (9oz) plain flour

1 egg

½ tsp lemon juice

salt

125g (4½oz) unsalted butter

FOR THE FILLING

500g (1lb 2oz) cherries

1 lemon

75g (2½oz) walnuts

100g (3½oz) light soft brown sugar

1 tsp ground cinnamon

icing sugar, to sprinkle

MAKE THE STRUDEL DOUGH

1 Sift the flour on to a work surface and make a well in the centre. In a bowl, beat the egg to mix with 125ml (4½fl oz) water, the lemon juice, and a pinch of salt, and pour into the well. Work the ingredients in the well, drawing in a little of the flour with your fingertips.

2 Gradually draw in the remaining flour. Gently knead in just enough flour so that the dough forms a ball; it should be quite soft. Work the dough in an electric mixer with dough hook for 5–7 minutes, or place on a floured work surface and knead by hand, picking it up and throwing it down, until shiny and smooth. Shape into a ball, cover with a bowl, and let rest for 30 minutes.

PREPARE THE FILLING

3 Stone all the cherries. Grate the zest from the lemon on to a plate. Coarsely chop the walnuts; nuts are best chopped by hand to control the finished texture, although this will always be uneven.

ROLL THE DOUGH AND BAKE THE STRUDEL

4 Cover the work table with a bed sheet and lightly flour it. Roll out the dough to as large a square as possible. Cover it with the damp tea towel and let rest about 15 minutes. Preheat the oven to 190°C (375°F/Gas 5) and butter a baking sheet. Melt the butter in a small saucepan.

5 Flour your hands and place them under the dough. Starting at the centre and working outwards, carefully stretch the dough with both hands. Continue to work outwards until the dough is as thin as possible. At once, brush the dough with about three-quarters of the melted butter.

6 Sprinkle the buttered strudel dough with the stoned cherries, chopped walnuts, brown sugar, lemon zest, and cinnamon. Trim the thick edge of the dough, pulling it out and pinching it off with your fingers.

7 **Roll up the strudel** with the help of the sheet. Transfer the roll to the baking sheet and shape it into a crescent. Brush with the remaining melted butter and bake for 30–40 minutes, until crisp and golden brown. Sprinkle with icing sugar and serve hot or cold, with cream or crème fraîche.

 VARIATION: Dried fruit strudel

Try this when fresh cherries are out of season.

1 Coarsely chop 500g (1lb 2oz) mixed dried fruit (apricots, prunes, dates, raisins, figs), discarding any stones you might find in the fruits. Put them into a small pan, cover with 125ml (4½fl oz) dark rum and 125ml (4½fl oz) water – or use all water if you like – and heat gently, stirring occasionally, for about 5 minutes. Remove from the heat and leave until completely cool and all the fruit has plumped up.

2 Drain the fruit thoroughly, discarding any remaining soaking liquid. Prepare and stretch the strudel dough as directed in the main recipe, brushing with the melted butter.

3 Sprinkle the dough evenly with the dried fruit, chopped walnuts, brown sugar, and cinnamon; omit the lemon zest, though orange zest can be substituted, if liked. Roll and bake the strudel as directed in the main recipe. Serve with plenty of cream.

Three-nut pie

INSPIRED BY THE TRADITIONAL AMERICAN PECAN PIE, this combines walnuts, hazelnuts, and almonds in a light filling. Choose your own combination of nuts, or just select one favourite. Serve with double cream for a real treat.

SERVES	PREP	COOK
SERVES 6-8	35-40 MINS PLUS CHILLING	60-65 MINS

Ingredients

FOR THE PASTRY DOUGH

330g (11oz) plain flour

½ tsp salt

150g (5½oz) butter

FOR THE FILLING

60g (2oz) walnut halves

60g (2oz) whole blanched almonds

30g (1oz) hazelnuts

60g (2oz) unsalted butter

4 eggs

300g (10oz) light soft brown sugar

1 tsp vanilla essence

¼ tsp salt

1 tbsp milk, to glaze

MAKE THE PASTRY DOUGH

1 Sift the flour and salt into a bowl. Cut in the fat with 2 round-bladed table knives. With your fingertips, rub the fat into the flour until the mixture forms coarse crumbs, lifting and crumbling the mixture to help aerate it. Sprinkle 6-7 tbsp cold water over the mixture, 1 tbsp at a time, and mix lightly with a fork.

2 When the crumbs are moist enough to start sticking together, press the dough lightly into a ball, wrap it tightly, and chill for about 30 minutes until firm. Brush a 23cm (9in) round tin or a 20cm (8in) square tin with melted butter and preheat the oven to 200°C (400°F/Gas 6). Put a baking sheet in the oven to heat.

LINE THE TIN AND BAKE BLIND

3 Lightly flour a work surface. Roll out the dough and trim it either to a 25cm (10in) round or square, depending on the shape of the tin you have chosen. Wrap the dough around the rolling pin and drape it over the tin. Press it well into the bottom edges and up the sides of the tin with your fingertips. It need not reach the rim.

4 Using a round-bladed table knife, trim the dough inside the tin, so that the shell is 4cm (1½in) deep. Prick the bottom of the pastry shell with a fork to prevent air bubbles during cooking. Chill until firm, about 15 minutes.

5 Line the shell with a double thickness of foil, pressing it well into the corners. Half-fill the foil with rice. Bake the shell on the baking sheet for about 10 minutes, until set. Remove the foil and rice and continue baking for about 5 minutes longer. Let the shell cool slightly in the tin on a wire rack. Reduce the oven temperature to 180°C (350°F/Gas 4).

PREPARE THE NUT FILLING

6 Set aside a third of the walnuts and almonds for decoration. Spread the remainder on a baking sheet and toast in the oven, stirring occasionally, for 8-10 minutes, until lightly browned. Remove. Toast the hazelnuts as for the walnuts and almonds, allowing 12-15 minutes. Leave the oven on. While the hazelnuts are still hot, rub them in a rough tea towel to remove the skins. Let cool.

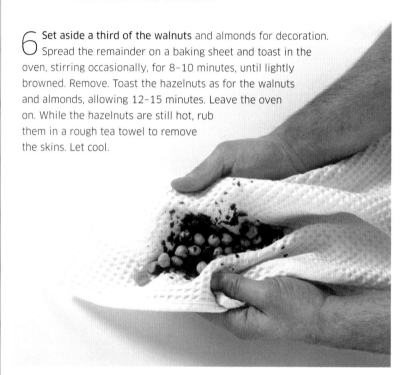

7 Roughly chop the toasted walnuts, almonds, and hazelnuts. Melt the butter in a small saucepan. Let cool. Put the eggs in a bowl. Add the brown sugar and whisk the eggs and sugar together until evenly mixed. Add the vanilla essence, salt, and cooled melted butter and stir until well combined.

8 Add the toasted chopped walnuts, almonds, and hazelnuts to the filling mixture. With a wooden spoon, stir the nuts into the filling mixture to distribute them evenly. Carefully pour the filling into the pastry shell.

BAKE THE PIE

9 Bake the pie on the baking sheet in the heated oven just until it starts to set. It should only take 8–10 minutes. Remove from the oven and, working quickly, brush any exposed pastry edges with the milk to glaze. Arrange the reserved nuts on top. Continue baking the pie until a metal skewer inserted in the centre comes out clean. It will probably take 35–40 minutes longer. Watch it very carefully, and cover with a sheet of foil if it threatens to scorch, as burned nuts have a bitter and very unpleasant flavour and will spoil the dish.

10 Transfer the pie to a wire rack. Let it cool to room temperature. When cool, transfer the wire rack to the top of the tin, turn both over together, then carefully lift off the tin. Make none of your motions too rapid or forceful, as this might dislodge some of the delicious, moist nutty filling from the rest of the pie. Set a second wire rack on the pie base and turn both over so the pie is right-side up once more. Slide the pie on to a serving platter. Serve just slightly warm, or at room temperature, with double cream, if desired.

Mincemeat tart with whisky butter

FRESH FRUIT IS ADDED to the traditional dried fruit for this fresh mincemeat, and the whisky butter makes this a really festive and indulgent treat for Christmas time.

SERVES	PREP	COOK
SERVES 8	40-45 MINS PLUS CHILLING	40-45 MINS

Ingredients

FOR THE SHORTCRUST PASTRY DOUGH

345g (12oz) plain flour

1½ tbsp caster sugar

½ tsp salt

60g (2oz) vegetable fat

90g (3oz) unsalted butter

1 egg, plus ½ tsp salt, to glaze

FOR THE MINCEMEAT

1 tart eating apple

1 lemon

200g (7oz) seedless grapes

1 tbsp chopped candied orange peel

20g (¾oz) slivered almonds

¼ tsp each ground cinnamon, nutmeg, and allspice

90g (3oz) each raisins and sultanas

100g (3½oz) light, soft brown sugar

3 tbsp whisky

FOR THE WHISKY BUTTER

125g (4½oz) unsalted butter

100g (3½oz) caster sugar

60ml (2fl oz) whisky

MAKE THE PASTRY AND **LINE** THE TIN

1 **Make the pastry** as for Blackberry and Apple Pie (p418). Brush a 25cm (10in) springform tin with melted butter. Lightly flour a work surface, and roll out two-thirds of the dough into a 30cm (12in) round. Wrap the rolled dough around the rolling pin, and drape it over the tin.

2 **Gently press the dough** into the tin, then roll the pin over the top to cut off excess. Press the dough up the side of the tin, to increase the height of the rim. Chill for about 15 minutes.

MAKE THE MINCEMEAT AND **FILL** THE TART

3 **Peel, core, and dice** the apple. Grate the lemon zest; squeeze the juice. Halve the grapes. Mix the apple, grapes, lemon zest and juice, candied peel, almonds, spices, dried fruit, sugar, and whisky. Spoon it into the pastry.

MAKE THE PASTRY LATTICE TOP

4 **Roll out the remaining dough** and cut into 14x2cm (¾in) strips. Form into a lattice over the pie (p427), brushing the ends with water to seal them to the shell. Lightly beat the egg and salt, and brush this on the lattice.

5 **Chill the tart** for 15 minutes. Preheat the oven to 180°C (350°F/Gas 4). Put a baking sheet in the oven to heat. Bake for 40–45 minutes, until lightly browned. Let cool slightly, remove the tin and slide on to a plate.

MAKE THE WHISKY BUTTER

6 **With an electric mixer,** beat the butter until creamy. Add the sugar, and beat for 2-3 minutes, until light and fluffy. Beat in the whisky, 1 spoon at a time. Chill for 1-2 hours, until firm. Serve with the tart.

Flaky pear tartlets

THESE ARE A PARTY FAVOURITE, a spectacular contrast of hot and cold, and need very little last-minute preparation. They are very easy to make, through they manage seriously to impress any guest. It's worth fanning out the pears on this occasion, as they look beautiful.

SERVES	PREP	COOK
SERVES 8	35-40 MINS PLUS CHILLING	30-40 MINS

Ingredients

FOR THE TARTLETS

450g (1lb) bought all-butter puff pastry

1 egg beaten with ½ tsp salt, to glaze

4 pears

juice of 1 lemon

50g (1¾oz) sugar

FOR THE CARAMEL SAUCE

150g (5½oz) caster sugar

125ml (4½fl oz) double cream

FOR THE CHANTILLY CREAM

125ml (4½fl oz) double cream

1-2 tsp icing sugar

½ tsp vanilla essence

MAKE AND BAKE THE PASTRY CASES

1 Sprinkle 2 baking sheets with cold water. Roll out the puff pastry dough, cut in half lengthways, then cut diagonally at 10cm (4in) intervals along the length of each piece, to make 8 diamond shapes. Transfer to the baking sheets, and brush with the glaze. With the tip of a knife, score a border around each. Chill for 15 minutes.

2 Preheat the oven to 220°C (425°F/Gas 7). Bake the cases for about 15 minutes, until they start to brown, then reduce the temperature to 190°C (375°F/Gas 5) and bake for 20-25 minutes more, until golden and crisp. Transfer to wire racks to cool, then cut out the lid from each case, and scoop out any under-cooked pastry from inside.

MAKE THE CARAMEL SAUCE AND CHANTILLY CREAM

3 Put 125ml (4fl oz) water in a saucepan, and dissolve the sugar. Boil, without stirring, until golden. Reduce the heat. Remove from the heat, stand back, and add the cream. Heat gently until the caramel dissolves. Cool.

4 Pour the cream for the Chantilly cream into a bowl, and whip until soft peaks form. Add the icing sugar and vanilla, and continue whipping until stiff peaks form. Chill.

PREPARE AND GRILL THE PEAR FANS

5 Butter a baking sheet. Heat the grill. Peel and core the pears. Thinly slice, keeping attached at the stalk end. With your fingers, flatten, transfer to the sheet, brush with lemon and sprinkle with sugar. Grill until caramelized.

ASSEMBLE THE TARTLETS

6 Transfer the pastry cases to plates, and place Chantilly cream and a pear fan in each. Pour a little cold caramel sauce over each fan, and partially cover with the pastry lids.

Mississippi mud pie

IN THIS POPULAR AMERICAN DESSERT, a chocolate crumb crust is filled with homemade coffee ice cream swirled with chocolate, and served with hot fudge sauce. You can use a tub of good-quality bought coffee ice cream if time is short.

SERVES	**PREP**	**COOK**
SERVES 6-8	45-50 MINS PLUS FREEZING	25-30 MINS

Ingredients

FOR THE COFFEE ICE CREAM

600ml (1 pint) milk

3 tbsp instant coffee granules

135g (5oz) caster sugar

8 egg yolks

2 tbsp cornflour

250ml (9fl oz) double cream

FOR THE CHOCOLATE CRUMB CRUST

125g (4½oz) unsalted butter

250g (9oz) plain dark crisp chocolate biscuits

3 tbsp caster sugar

FOR THE FUDGE SAUCE

60g (2oz) whole blanched almonds

150ml (5fl oz) double cream

60g (2oz) unsalted butter

100g (3½oz) caster sugar

135g (5oz) light soft brown sugar

90g (3oz) cocoa powder

salt

1 tbsp dark rum, or to taste

double cream, to serve

PREPARE THE COFFEE CUSTARD, **MAKE**, AND **BAKE** THE CRUST

1 **Put the milk** and coffee in a saucepan and heat, stirring, until the coffee dissolves. Set aside a quarter of this. Stir the sugar into the rest. In a bowl, whisk the yolks and cornflour. Whisk in the sweetened hot milk.

2 **Pour the custard back** into the saucepan and cook over medium heat, stirring constantly, just until it comes to a boil and thickens enough to coat the back of a spoon. Your finger will leave a clear trail across the spoon. It may curdle if cooked longer.

3 **Off the heat,** stir in the reserved milk until thoroughly combined. Strain into a cold bowl and cover tightly to prevent a skin forming. Let cool. Preheat the oven to 180°C (350°F/Gas 4). Put a baking sheet in to heat.

4 **Melt the butter.** Brush a 23cm (9in) pie dish with melted butter. Grind the biscuits to coarse crumbs in a food processor, using the pulse button. Transfer to a bowl and stir in the melted butter and sugar.

5 **Press the crumbs** evenly over the bottom and up the side of the pie dish. Chill until firm, about 15 minutes. Bake the crumb crust on the baking sheet in the heated oven for 15 minutes. Let cool on a wire rack. The crust will harden as it cools.

TOAST THE ALMONDS; **MAKE** THE FUDGE SAUCE

6 **Coarsely chop the almonds.** Spread them on the baking sheet and toast in the heated oven, stirring occasionally, for 10-12 minutes, until lightly browned. Watch carefully, as they burn easily.

7 **In a saucepan,** heat the double cream and butter, stirring occasionally, until the butter melts and the mixture comes just to a boil. Add the sugars and stir them in until dissolved. Sift the cocoa. Whisk it, with a pinch of salt, into the cream and sugar mixture, and bring back to a boil.

8 Gently simmer the fudge sauce, whisking constantly, until the cocoa powder has dissolved. Stir in the rum. Transfer 125ml (4½fl oz) of the fudge sauce to a bowl and combine with half the almonds. Let cool. Set the remaining sauce and almonds aside.

FREEZE THE ICE CREAM AND PIE

9 If the custard has formed a skin, whisk to dissolve it. Pour the coffee custard into an ice cream maker and freeze until slushy, following the manufacturer's directions. Meanwhile, chill 2 large bowls in the freezer.

10 Pour the cream into one of the chilled bowls and whisk to soft peaks. Add to the half-set custard and finish freezing in the ice cream maker. Transfer to the second chilled bowl. Add the cooled almond fudge mixture.

11 Spread the coffee ice cream and almond fudge mixture over the bottom of the crumb crust. Swirl the top with the back of a metal spoon and freeze for at least 1–2 hours, or up to 3 days.

FINISH THE PIE

12 If the pie has been frozen for more than 12 hours, let it soften in the refrigerator for 1 hour. Whip the double cream to stiff peaks. Sprinkle the reserved almonds over the pie. Reheat the fudge sauce.

13 Transfer the pie dish to a serving platter. Serve the pie directly from the dish, cut into wedges. Drizzle hot fudge sauce over the top of each serving, and serve at once, with double cream on the side.

Apple jalousie

IN FRANCE, A JALOUSIE IS A LOUVRED SHUTTER – perfect for the observation of wives by jealous husbands. In this pastry, the top layer of dough is slashed before baking to look like a shutter, revealing glimpses of the apple compote inside. The flavour of this dessert is best when made with tart eating apples, which hold their shape well. The puff pastry must be kept cold, so a marble slab is the ideal preparation surface.

SERVES
SERVES 6–8

PREP
1¼–1½ HRS
PLUS CHILLING

COOK
30–40 MINS

Ingredients

FOR THE PUFF PASTRY DOUGH

250g (9oz) plain flour

250g (9oz) unsalted butter

1 tsp salt

1 tsp lemon juice

FOR THE FILLING

1kg (2¼lb) tart eating apples

2.5cm (1in) piece of fresh root ginger

15g (½oz) unsalted butter

100g (3½oz) caster sugar

1 egg white

MAKE THE PUFF PASTRY

1 **Sift the flour** on to a work surface, and make a well in the centre. Cut 30g (1oz) of the butter into pieces, and add to the well with the salt, lemon juice, and 125ml (4fl oz) water. Gradually draw in the flour, working to form coarse crumbs. If the crumbs seem dry, add a little more water to form a dough.

2 **Cut and turn the dough** several times, until it forms a rough, slightly moist ball. At this stage, try to handle it as little as possible. Score the dough to prevent shrinkage, then wrap and chill for 15 minutes. Lightly flour the remaining butter. Pound the butter with a rolling pin, folding and pounding it until it is softened and pliable. It should be the same consistency as the dough.

3 **Shape the piece of butter** into a 12.5cm (5in) square. Roll out the chilled dough on a lightly floured work surface, to a 25cm (10in) square, slightly thicker in the centre. Set the butter diagonally in the centre, and pull the corners of the dough around to wrap it like an envelope. Pinch the edges to seal. Lightly flour the work surface again, and turn the dough package on to it, seam side down. Tap with the rolling pin to flatten.

4 **Roll out the dough** to 15x45cm (6x18in). Fold the dough into 3, bringing the top third down, and the bottom third up, like a letter. Turn it 90° to bring the seam to your right. Gently press the layered ends to seal. This is the first turn. Repeat this step to complete a second turn. Wrap and chill for 15 minutes. Repeat twice more, to make a total of 6 turns.

PREPARE THE FILLING

5 **Peel, core, and dice** the apples. Peel and finely chop the fresh root ginger. Melt the butter in a large frying pan. Add the apples, ginger, and all but 2 tbsp of the sugar. Sauté, stirring often, for 15–20 minutes, until the apples are tender and caramelized. Cook them briskly, so they do not dissolve into purée. Taste, adding more sugar if needed. Let cool.

ASSEMBLE AND BAKE THE JALOUSIE

6 **Sprinkle a baking sheet** evenly with cold water. Lightly flour a work surface, then roll out the puff pastry dough and trim it into a neat 28x32cm (11x 13in) rectangle. Cut the rectangle lengthways in half. Fold 1 half lengthways, and cut across the fold at 5mm (¼in) intervals to form the shutter effect, leaving an uncut border at the edges. Use a very sharp knife so you do not have to press down too hard, or the folded piece of pastry will be hard to unfold.

7 **Transfer the uncut rectangle** of dough to the prepared baking sheet and press it down lightly. Spoon the apple filling evenly down the centre, leaving a 2cm (¾in) border. With a pastry brush, moisten the border with cold water. Top with the slashed dough rectangle.

8 **Press the edges** together with your fingertips. With a sharp knife, trim the edges to neaten them. Holding the dough in place with a fingertip, scallop the edges at close intervals with the back of a small knife. Chill the jalousie for 15 minutes. Meanwhile, preheat the oven to 220°C (425°F/Gas 7). Bake for 20-25 minutes, until puffed and light brown. Meanwhile, whisk the egg white just until frothy.

9 **Brush the hot jalousie** with the egg white, and sprinkle the remaining sugar evenly over the top. Return to the oven and continue baking for 10-15 minutes, until the sugar glaze is crisp, and the pastry is deep golden. Transfer to a wire rack, and let cool. Cut the jalousie across into 6-8 slices. Serve warm or at room temperature.

Eggnog tart

THE AMERICAN EGGNOG, a rich drink, is transformed here into a creamy, rum-flavoured tart. The crust is made from almond-flavoured amaretti biscuits, but other crisp biscuits can also be used. This is a great tart to make around Christmas time.

SERVES
SERVES 6-8

PREP
40-45 MINS
PLUS SETTING

COOK
10-15 MINS

Ingredients

FOR THE CRUST

125g (4½oz) unsalted butter

250g (9oz) amaretti biscuits

FOR THE FILLING

500ml (16fl oz) milk

1 vanilla pod or 1 tsp vanilla essence

50g (1¾oz) caster sugar

2 tbsp cornflour

4 egg yolks

125ml (4½fl oz) double cream

7g (¼oz) powdered gelatine

60ml (2fl oz) dark rum, more to taste

whole nutmeg

MAKE AND BAKE THE AMARETTI CRUST

1 **Preheat the oven** to 180°C (350°F/Gas 4). Melt the butter in a saucepan. Brush a 23cm (9in) springform tin with melted butter. Crush the biscuits to fine crumbs and stir in the melted butter. Press over the bottom and 2.5cm (1in) up the side of the tin. Chill until firm. Put a baking sheet in the oven to heat. Bake the crust on the heated baking sheet for 10-15 minutes. Let cool on a wire rack.

MAKE THE CUSTARD

2 **Put the milk** in a heavy-based saucepan. Split the vanilla pod, if using, lengthways in half and add it to the milk. Bring just to a boil, then remove from the heat, cover and let stand in a warm place, 10-15 minutes. Remove the vanilla pod, rinse it, and store to use again.

3 **Set aside** a quarter of the milk. Add the sugar to the remaining hot milk in the saucepan; stir until dissolved.

4 **Put the cornflour** and egg yolks in a medium bowl and whisk them together until smooth. Whisk the sweetened hot milk into the cornflour mixture until smooth. Pour the mixture back into the saucepan, and cook over medium heat. Stir constantly with the wooden spoon, just until it comes to a boil, and is thick enough to coat the back of the spoon. Your finger will leave a trail across the back of the spoon.

5 **Do not continue** to boil the custard or it may curdle. Off the heat, stir the reserved milk into the custard and strain it into a cold bowl. Stir in the vanilla essence, if using. Cover tightly to prevent a skin forming on the surface of the custard, and let cool to tepid.

FINISH THE FILLING

6 **Pour the cream** into a bowl and whisk until soft peaks form; chill. Sprinkle the gelatine over the rum in a small saucepan. Let soak for 5 minutes. Set over low heat and melt. Do not stir.

7 **Stir the gelatine** mixture into the tepid custard. Taste the custard, adding more rum, if you like. Set the bowl of custard in a larger bowl, half-filled with iced water, and stir gently until it starts to thicken and set.

ASSEMBLE THE TART

8 **Remove the bowl** of setting custard immediately from the bowl of iced water and whisk briskly to lighten it. Add the whipped cream to the custard and fold together gently.

9 **Pour the filling** into the crust, smooth with a palette knife, then chill until set, 2–3 hours. Run a knife around the tin; loosen and remove the side. Grate nutmeg over the top. Serve chilled, in wedges.

Pistachio and ricotta filo pie

FILO PASTRY can be used to make many different shapes. Here, sheets of filo dough are filled with layers of ricotta cheese and ground pistachios, and finished with filo rosettes. The baked pie can be kept in the refrigerator for up to 2 days. Allow it to come to room temperature before serving. Filo pastry is very easy to work with, so don't be alarmed by its apparent fragility.

SERVES	PREP	COOK
SERVES 6–8	35–40 MINS	45–50 MINS

Ingredients

FOR THE FILLING

1 tbsp unsalted butter

90g (3oz) shelled pistachio nuts

3 tbsp caster sugar

3 tbsp light soft brown sugar

2 lemons

1 egg

175g (6oz) ricotta cheese

75ml (2½fl oz) soured cream

1 tsp vanilla essence

2 tbsp honey

2 tsp plain flour

salt

45g (1½oz) raisins

FOR THE FILO PASTRY CASE

500g (1lb 2oz) filo sheets

125g (4½oz) unsalted butter

FOR THE TOPPING

1 tsp ground cinnamon

1 tbsp caster sugar

MAKE THE FILLING

1 **Melt the butter** in a saucepan. In a food processor, coarsely chop the pistachio nuts. Add the sugars and work the nuts until finely chopped. While the blade is turning, add the melted butter and work until coarse crumbs form.

2 **Finely grate the zest** from each of the lemons, using a small brush to remove any zest remaining on the grater. Set aside. In a medium bowl, stir the egg. Add the ricotta cheese.

3 **Beat the egg** and ricotta cheese with an electric mixer, or with a hand whisk, until smooth. Make sure it is completely blended, so the final filling will be easy to work with.

4 **Add the soured cream,** lemon zest, vanilla essence, honey, flour, and a pinch of salt to the egg and ricotta mixture. Continue beating for 2–3 minutes, until light and fluffy. Stir in the raisins.

ASSEMBLE AND BAKE THE PIE

5 Preheat the oven to 180°C (350°F/Gas 4). Put a baking sheet in the oven to heat. Brush a 20cm (8in) square cake tin with melted butter; line with a strip of double thickness foil, draping the excess over the edges. Roll up the excess to form handles. Brush with melted butter.

6 Lay a tea towel on the work surface and sprinkle it lightly with water. Unroll the filo sheets on to it. Trim the sheets to 20x40cm (8x16in) rectangles. Cover the sheets and trimmings with a second dampened tea towel to stop them becoming brittle.

7 Put 1 of the sheets of dough on top of a third dampened tea towel and brush with melted butter. Lay it in the bottom of the tin so that part of the sheet drapes over one edge of the tin.

8 Butter a second sheet. Lay it in the bottom of the tin so that part drapes over the edge at right angles to the first sheet. Butter the third and fourth sheets, laying and pressing them into the tin so the excess drapes over the remaining 2 sides. Cut the remaining sheets in half to make 20cm (8in) squares; cover with the dampened tea towel.

9 Spread half of the ricotta cheese filling evenly over the dough in the tin. Butter 3 of the squares of filo dough and lay each one, butter-side up, over the filling. Evenly distribute half the nut mixture on top of the buttered dough, reserving 2 tbsp.

10 Butter and layer 3 more squares of pastry on top of the nut mixture. Layer the remaining cheese and nut fillings with the buttered filo, finishing the layering with 3 squares of buttered pastry. Fold the 4 overhanging pieces of pastry over the pie and brush the top with butter. Cut the reserved trimmings into 5cm (2in) wide strips.

11 Curl the strips to form loose rosettes and arrange on top of the pie. Combine the cinnamon and sugar in a small bowl. Brush the pie and rosettes with the remaining melted butter and sprinkle the cinnamon, sugar, and reserved pistachios over the top. Bake on the baking sheet until golden brown and flaky, 45–50 minutes. Let cool slightly in the tin. Transfer to a wire rack; let cool to room temperature and discard the foil. Drizzle with honey to serve.

Cherry clafoutis

THIS PUDDING COMES FROM LIMOUSIN in central France. Cherries are baked in batter that puffs up, and turns golden. Tart cherries give the most flavour, and contrast beautifully with the sweet batter. The cherry stones can be removed before cooking if you prefer, though this is not traditional, and the stones will lend the dessert a surprising, subtle taste reminiscent of bitter almonds. Crème fraîche is a really delicious accompaniment to this pudding. This is a dish for the early summer, when cherries are at the peak of their season.

SERVES	PREP	COOK
SERVES 6-8	20-25 MINS	30-35 MINS

Ingredients

100g (3½oz) caster sugar, plus more for the dish

625g (1lb 6oz) cherries

45g (1½oz) plain flour

salt

150ml (5fl oz) milk

75ml (2½fl oz) double cream

4 eggs, plus 2 egg yolks

3 tbsp kirsch

2 tbsp icing sugar

PREPARE THE DISH AND CHERRIES

1 **Brush a 2 litre (3½ pint) baking dish** with melted butter. Sprinkle some caster sugar into the dish. Turn the dish around and shake it, to coat the bottom and side evenly. Turn the dish upside-down and tap the base with your knuckles to remove any excess sugar.

2 **Stone the fresh cherries**, either with a cherry stoner or the tip of a vegetable peeler, or leave the stones in if you like. Spread the cherries in an even layer over the bottom of the prepared baking dish.

MAKE THE BATTER

3 **Sift the flour** and a pinch of salt into a bowl, holding the sieve up high to aerate the flour. Make a well in the centre with your fingers to take the wet ingredients.

4 **Pour the milk** and cream into the well at the same time, and stir with a whisk, gradually drawing in the flour and whisking constantly, to make a smooth paste and work out any lumps.

5 **Add the eggs**, egg yolks to add richness, and caster sugar, and continue whisking to make a smooth batter.

ASSEMBLE AND BAKE THE CLAFOUTIS

6 Preheat the oven to 180°C (350°F/Gas 4). Just before baking, ladle the batter evenly over the cherries – it should partially cover them – then sprinkle over the kirsch.

7 Bake the clafoutis in the heated oven for 30–35 minutes, until beautifully puffed up, and beginning to turn golden brown. If it threatens to scorch before it is cooked, cover with foil. When cooked, the clafoutis will begin slightly to pull away from the side of the baking dish. Just before serving, sift icing sugar over the top. Serve warm or at room temperature, with a pile of crème fraîche or whipped cream, if you like.

 VARIATION: Plum clafoutis

With cherries, clafoutis is a dish of early summer. This variation is for autumn or winter.

1 Omit the cherries. Prepare the baking dish and make the batter as directed.

2 Cut 625g (1lb 6oz) small plums in half around the stone. Using both hands, give a quick, sharp twist to each half to loosen it from the stone. Scoop out the stone with the tip of a small knife and discard it.

3 Arrange the plums, cut-side up, in the bottom of the prepared baking dish. Assemble, bake, and decorate the clafoutis as directed.

Hazelnut, chocolate, and orange tart

THE ITALIAN SWEET PASTRY pasta frolla acts as a container for a rich filling flavoured with ground hazelnuts, plain chocolate, and candied orange zest, all topped with a chocolate glaze. A most delicious recipe for a special occasion.

SERVES	PREP	COOK
SERVES 6-8	45-50 MINS PLUS CHILLING	35-40 MINS

Ingredients

FOR THE PASTA FROLLA DOUGH

1 orange

150g (5½oz) plain flour, plus more if needed

75g (2½oz) unsalted butter, plus more for the tin

50g (1¾oz) caster sugar

¼ tsp salt

1 egg

FOR THE FILLING

2 oranges

125g (4½oz) hazelnuts

150g (5½oz) caster sugar

60g (2oz) plain chocolate

150g (5½oz) unsalted butter

2 tsp plain flour

2 egg yolks, plus 1 egg

FOR THE CHOCOLATE GLAZE

125g (4½oz) plain chocolate

75g (2½oz) unsalted butter

2 tsp Grand Marnier

MAKE THE PASTA FROLLA DOUGH

1 **Grate the zest** from the orange. Sift the flour on to a work surface and make a well in the centre. Pound the butter with a rolling pin to soften. Put the softened butter, sugar, salt, orange zest, and egg into the well.

2 **With your fingertips,** work the ingredients in the well until thoroughly mixed. Work the flour in with your fingertips until coarse crumbs form. Press the dough into a ball. If it is sticky, work in a little more flour.

3 **Lightly flour the work surface.** Knead the dough for 1-2 minutes, until it is very smooth and peels away from the work surface in one piece. Shape into a ball, wrap it tightly and chill until firm, about 30 minutes.

LINE THE TIN

4 **Brush a 23cm (9in) springform tin** with melted butter. Lightly flour a work surface, and roll the dough into a 28cm (11in) round. Wrap it around the rolling pin and gently press into the tin, sealing any cracks.

5 **Roll the rolling pin** over the top of the tin, pressing down to cut off excess. With your thumbs, press the dough evenly up the side of the tin, to increase the height of the rim. Prick the bottom of the shell with a fork to prevent air bubbles forming. Chill for 15 minutes, until firm.

MAKE THE FILLING

6 **With a vegetable peeler,** pare the zest from the oranges; cut it into very fine julienne strips. Bring a small saucepan of water to a boil, add the zest and simmer for 2 minutes. Drain in a sieve and set aside.

7 **Preheat the oven** to 180°C (350°F/Gas 4). Spread out the nuts on a baking sheet, and toast in the heated oven until they are lightly browned, 6-15 minutes, depending on whether they are whole or chopped. Stir occasionally, so they colour evenly. To remove their skins, rub in a tea towel while still hot. Discard the skins. Let cool. Leave the oven on.

8 **Put a third of the sugar** into a pan, add 60ml (2fl oz) water and heat gently until dissolved, shaking the pan once or twice. Add the zest and simmer for 8-10 minutes, until all the water has evaporated and the strips are transparent and tender. With a fork, transfer the candied zest to a piece of baking parchment and let cool slightly. Coarsely chop two-thirds of it.

9 **Put a baking sheet** in the oven to heat. Cut the chocolate into chunks, then finely chop (or chop it in a food processor). Put the remaining sugar in a food processor, add the hazelnuts and finely grind.

10 **Beat the butter** until creamy. Add the flour and the hazelnut mixture and continue beating for 2-3 minutes, until light and fluffy. Add the yolks and egg, one at a time, beating after each addition. Mix in the chocolate and chopped candied orange zest. Spread the filling over the pastry shell and smooth the top. Bake the tart on the baking sheet in the heated oven until a metal skewer inserted in the centre comes out clean; it should take 35-40 minutes. Let cool on a wire rack.

MAKE THE CHOCOLATE GLAZE AND **FINISH** THE TART

11 **While the tart** is cooling, cut the chocolate into chunks. Heat the chocolate in a bowl set over a saucepan of hot water (make sure the base of the bowl does not touch the water), stirring occasionally, just until melted.

12 Cut the butter into small pieces and gently stir it into the warm melted chocolate in 2–3 batches. Work quickly, but do not beat, or the butter may turn oily.

13 Add the Grand Marnier. Let cool to tepid. Set the tart tin on a bowl to loosen and remove the side. Pour the glaze on to the tart and spread it smoothly over the top. Slide the tart from the tin base on to a plate. Decorate with the remaining candied orange zest.

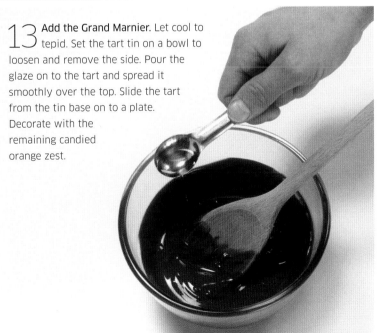

Amelia Simmons' pumpkin pie

BASED ON a recipe from the first American cook book, written in 1796. Miss Simmons suggested sweetening the filling with blackstrap molasses, but a little sugar – as well as some treacle – is more suited to our tastes today. You can use a 400g (14oz) can of pumpkin purée instead of fresh if you prefer, though the flavour will not be as good. This pie is best eaten on the day it is baked, though the dough can be made and the pumpkin cooked up to 2 days ahead and stored in the refrigerator.

SERVES	PREP	COOK
SERVES 6	45–50 MINS PLUS CHILLING	60–75 MINS

Ingredients

FOR THE SHORTCRUST PASTRY

215g (7½oz) plain flour

¼ tsp salt

1½ tbsp caster sugar (optional)

45g (1½oz) white vegetable fat

60g (2oz) unsalted butter

FOR THE FILLING

1.15–1.4kg (2½–3lb) piece of pumpkin

2 eggs

175ml (6fl oz) double cream

50g (1¾oz) caster sugar

½ tsp ground ginger

½ tsp ground nutmeg

¼ tsp ground mace

60ml (2fl oz) black treacle

MAKE THE PASTRY DOUGH

1 **Put the flour** into a food processor. Add the salt and sugar, if using, and blend for about 5 seconds only. Cut the fat and butter into small, even pieces and add it to the flour. (Use all butter instead of the white vegetable fat, if you prefer a richer flavour.) Pulse-blend until the mixture resembles coarse crumbs; it should take only 10–15 seconds.

2 **Sprinkle 3–4 tbsp cold water** over the mixture, 1 tbsp at a time, pulse-blending all the while, just until the crumbs start sticking together in larger clumps. Don't try to add too much water at once, as it is impossible to remove excess water from a dry dough, but easy to add a drop more. Transfer the dough to a work surface and press lightly into a ball. Do not handle the dough too much at this stage, or the pastry will be tough. Wrap tightly in clingfilm and chill until firm, about 30 minutes, or for up to 2 days.

COOK THE PUMPKIN

3 **Scoop out and discard** the seeds and fibres from the pumpkin. Cut the skin and flesh into wedges, then into large chunks and put into a large pan. Pour in enough water to come a quarter of the way up the pumpkin. Cover and simmer for 25–30 minutes, until tender.

4 **With a slotted spoon,** transfer to a colander and discard the cooking water. With a metal spoon, scrape the pumpkin flesh into a bowl and discard the skin.

5 **Put the pumpkin into a food processor** or blender and purée until smooth. Work it through a sieve to remove any fibres. There should be about 375g (13oz) of pumpkin purée.

MAKE THE PIE BASE

6 Brush a 23cm (9in) pie dish with melted butter. Lightly flour a work surface and roll out the dough into a round 5cm (2in) larger than the dish. Wrap the dough around the rolling pin and drape it over the dish.

7 Gently press the dough into the dish, then trim off excess with a knife. Chill the trimmings. Pinch the dough edge between thumb and finger to make it stand up. With scissors, make 1cm (½in) diagonal cuts around the rim at 1cm (½in) intervals.

8 With your fingertips, push one point towards the centre and the next point towards the edge. Continue around the edge. Prick the bottom of the shell with a fork. Chill for about 15 minutes, until firm. Meanwhile, preheat the oven to 200°C (400°F/Gas 6) and put in a baking sheet.

9 Line the prepared shell with a double thickness of foil, then half-fill it with dried beans or rice. Roll out the pastry trimmings and cut out 3 maple leaf shapes, if you like, scoring them with the back of a knife to resemble veins. Set the pie on a plate and chill.

10 Bake on the baking sheet for 10 minutes, or until the rim just starts to brown. Remove the foil and beans and reduce the oven temperature to 180°C (350°F/Gas 4). Bake for 5 minutes longer, until lightly browned.

PREPARE THE FILLING AND BAKE THE PIE

11 Beat the eggs lightly. Add the cream and eggs to the pumpkin. Beat with an electric mixer or hand whisk until thoroughly mixed. Add the sugar, ginger, nutmeg, and mace. Pour in the treacle and beat to combine. Pour into the shell and bake on the baking sheet for 20 minutes.

12 Add the leaves to the baking sheet, if using, and continue baking for 25–30 minutes, until the filling is firm and a metal skewer inserted into the centre comes out clean. Transfer the pie (and leaves) to a wire rack and let cool. Set the leaves on the filling, if liked, and serve at room temperature, with lightly whipped cream.

Apple cake

A FIRM DESSERT APPLE is best for this moist and dense Italian cake, which is perfect for picnics. Any flavourful apple that holds its shape during cooking is suitable. The cake is best eaten warm from the oven, but it can be stored for up to 2 days in an airtight container. Try to buy unwaxed lemons or, if not available, scrub lemons before using their zest.

SERVES	PREP	COOK
SERVES 8	20-25 MINS	1¼-1½ HRS

Ingredients

175g (6oz) unsalted butter

175g (6oz) plain flour

½ tsp salt

1 tsp baking powder

1 lemon

625g (1lb 6oz) apples

200g (7oz) sugar, plus 60g (2oz) to glaze

2 eggs

4 tbsp milk

PREPARE THE INGREDIENTS

1 **Preheat the oven** to 180°C (350°F/Gas 4). Brush a 23-25cm (9-10in) springform tin with melted butter, and sprinkle with a little flour, discarding the excess. Sift the measured flour with the salt and baking powder. Grate the zest from the lemon.

2 **Peel, core, and thinly slice the apples** lengthways. Squeeze the lemon juice over the apple slices and toss well, ensuring they are all covered to prevent discolouration.

MAKE AND BAKE THE CAKE

3 **With an electric mixer,** beat the butter in a large bowl until soft and creamy. Add the sugar and zest, and beat until light and crumbly. Add the eggs one by one, beating well after each addition. Gradually beat in the milk until the batter is very smooth.

4 **Sift in the flour mixture** and stir gently until evenly mixed. Stir in half the apple slices. Spoon the batter into the prepared tin and smooth the top. Arrange the remaining apple slices in concentric circles on top. Bake the cake in the heated oven for 1¼-1½ hours.

MAKE THE GLAZE AND FINISH THE CAKE

5 **Meanwhile,** make the glaze: heat 4 tbsp water, and the sugar to glaze, in a small saucepan over low heat, until the sugar has dissolved. Bring to a boil and simmer for 2 minutes, without stirring, then let cool.

6 **The cake is done** when it shrinks slightly from the side of the tin, and a skewer inserted in the centre comes out clean. It will still be moist. Brush the sugar syrup glaze on top of the cake as soon as it comes out of the oven. Let the cake cool in the tin. Remove the side of the tin, then transfer the cake to a serving plate.

Walnut cake with caramel topping

ANOTHER SIMPLE ITALIAN CAKE, this time with a crisp layer of caramel topping. This rich cake is flavoured with grappa or rum, so is great for a celebration. This recipe is perfect for entertaining, as it actually benefits from being made up to 2 days ahead, and stored in an airtight container; the flavours will mellow beautifully. Add the caramel topping just before serving.

SERVES	PREP	COOK
SERVES 8	25–30 MINS	1–1¼ HRS

Ingredients

1 lemon

2 slices of white bread

175g (6oz) walnut halves

4 eggs

125g (4½oz) unsalted butter

135g (5oz) caster sugar, plus 100g (3½oz) more for the caramel

2 tbsp grappa or rum

PREPARE AND BAKE THE CAKE

1 **Preheat the oven** to 180°C (350°F/Gas 4). Brush a 23cm (9in) cake tin with melted butter and line the base with baking parchment. Brush the paper with more butter. Grate the zest from the lemon. Toast the bread in the oven for 5–7 minutes, or until very dry; don't let it brown.

2 **Break the bread** into pieces and put them in a food processor. Work until finely ground. Separately grind 8 walnut halves for garnish. Add the remaining walnuts to the food processor and grind until quite fine.

3 **Separate the eggs.** Cream the butter in an electric mixer. Add two-thirds of the sugar and beat until light and fluffy. Add the egg yolks, beating well. Beat in the zest and grappa. Add the breadcrumb mixture and stir well.

4 **Whisk the** egg whites until stiff. Sprinkle with the remaining sugar and whisk until glossy. Gently fold a spoonful into the batter. Now fold the walnut mixture into the remaining whites. Spoon into the tin and smooth the top. Bake for 1–1¼ hours, until a skewer inserted in the centre comes out clean. Let cool slightly, invert on to a wire rack and leave until cold.

MAKE THE CARAMEL TOPPING

5 **Heat 4 tbsp water** and the sugar for caramel in a saucepan over low heat until the sugar has dissolved. Boil, without stirring, until the syrup starts to turn golden. Do not stir, or it may crystallize. Reduce the heat and continue cooking, swirling the syrup in the pan once or twice so it colours evenly.

6 **Cook** until the caramel is deep golden for best flavour. Do not overcook or the caramel may burn. Quickly plunge the base of the pan into a bowl of cold water to stop the cooking. As soon as the caramel has stopped bubbling, pour it over the cake. Using a palette knife, spread it quickly in a thin layer. Immediately arrange the reserved walnuts on top.

Lemon-blueberry muffins

FEATHERLIGHT MUFFINS glazed with lemon juice and sugar for an extra burst of lemon flavour. Absolutely delicious. These are best freshly baked and glazed to serve warm. The most important thing to remember when making muffins is to stir the batter as little as possible, only just to combine.

SERVES	PREP	COOK
MAKES 12	20-25 MINS	15-20 MINS

Ingredients

60g (2oz) unsalted butter

280g (10oz) unbleached strong white flour

1 tbsp baking powder

½ tsp salt

100g (3½oz) caster sugar

1 egg

juice and zest, finely grated, of 1 lemon

1 tsp vanilla essence

250ml (8fl oz) milk

225g (8oz) blueberries

MAKE THE BATTER

1 Preheat the oven to 220°C (425°F/Gas 7). Melt the butter in a saucepan. Sift the flour, baking powder, and salt into a large bowl. Set 2 tbsp sugar aside and stir the rest into the flour. Make a well in the centre.

2 In a bowl, beat the egg just until mixed. Add the melted butter, lemon zest, vanilla, and milk and beat until foamy. In a slow, steady stream, pour the egg mixture into the well in the flour.

3 Stir with a rubber spatula, gradually drawing in the dry ingredients to make a smooth batter. Gently fold in the blueberries, taking care not to bruise them. Do not overmix, or the muffins will be tough.

BAKE AND GLAZE THE MUFFINS

4 Place 12 muffin cases in a medium-sized muffin tin. Spoon the batter evenly between the cases and bake until a metal skewer inserted in the centre of a muffin comes out clean. It may take up to 15–20 minutes, but start checking after 12, as some ovens can be faster than others. (Be sure, though, not to check too often, or you will let out the heat and prevent even baking.) Let the muffins cool slightly on a wire rack.

5 In a small bowl, stir the reserved sugar with the lemon juice. While the muffins are still warm, dip the crown of each into the sugar and lemon mixture and set upright on a wire rack to continue cooling. The fact that the muffins are warm will mean they absorb the maximum amount of the wonderful lemony glaze. Serve the glazed muffins while still warm.

 VARIATION: Lemon poppy-seed muffins

The poppy seeds add a pleasing crunch.

1 Omit the blueberries. Heat the oven to 220°C (425°F/Gas 7), and place 9 muffin cases in a muffin tin. Melt the butter for the batter as directed. Grate the zest from the lemon and squeeze the juice.

2 Sift the flour, baking powder, and salt into a large bowl. Stir in all the sugar. In a medium bowl, beat the egg just until mixed. Add the melted butter, vanilla, and milk, and whisk as directed. Stir in 2 tbsp poppy seeds, then add the lemon zest and lemon juice.

3 Combine the ingredients as directed and spoon the mixture into the muffin cases. Sprinkle the muffins with 2 tsp sugar and bake as directed. Makes 9.

Rich chocolate cake

THIS TRIPLE-LAYER CHOCOLATE CAKE has got everything the chocolate and cake lover could wish for: moist sponge, fluffy vanilla cream, and unctuous, shiny chocolate icing. It's a surefire hit for any special occasion. Best of all, it is very simple to make: even a novice baker will be able to produce their own masterpiece. Because of the fresh cream, eat this in one sitting (that shouldn't prove difficult); any leftovers should be refrigerated.

SERVES
SERVES 12

PREP
15 MINS
PLUS COOLING

COOK
30-35 MINS

Ingredients

FOR THE CAKE

300g (10oz) self-raising flour

4 tbsp cocoa powder

1 heaped tsp bicarbonate of soda

300g (10oz) unsalted butter, softened

300g (10oz) golden caster sugar

5 large eggs

1 tsp vanilla essence

4 tbsp milk

FOR THE CHOCOLATE CURLS, FILLING, AND ICING

175g (6oz) plain chocolate

450ml (15fl oz) double cream

a knob of unsalted butter

1 tbsp caster sugar

a few drops of vanilla essence

PREPARE THE TINS

1 Preheat the oven to 180°C (350°F/Gas 4). Lightly butter 3 x 20cm (8in) sandwich tins and line the bases with baking parchment.

MAKE AND BAKE THE CAKES

2 Sift the flour, cocoa, and bicarbonate of soda together into a bowl. Place the butter and sugar in another bowl together, then use an electric whisk to beat them until pale and fluffy.

3 Add the sifted flour, eggs, vanilla, and milk, then whisk for 1 minute, until the mixture is uniform and fluffy. Divide the mixture evenly between the 3 cake tins and use the back of a spoon to level the surface. Bake in the hot oven for 30-35 minutes, or until the centre of the sponge springs back when lightly pressed with your finger. Leave the cakes to cool in the tins for 5 minutes. Remove from the tins, transfer to a wire rack, and leave until cold.

MELT THE CHOCOLATE FOR THE CURLS

4 Break 50g (2oz) of the chocolate into pieces and place in a heatproof bowl. Put it over a pan of gently simmering water, making sure the base of the bowl does not touch the water, and stir until the chocolate is melted and smooth. Pour on to a baking sheet – or a marble slab if you have one – and leave to set in a cool place.

DECORATE THE CAKE

5 When the chocolate has set, (or just use a bar of chocolate if you're short on time), push a sharp knife or vegetable peeler across the surface at a 45° angle, so that curls of chocolate form. Set aside in a cool place.

6 Measure 150ml (5fl oz) of the cream into a heatproof bowl. Break the remaining chocolate into squares and add to the bowl. Place over a pan of gently simmering water, making sure the base of the bowl does not touch the water, and stir until the chocolate melts and a smooth shiny icing forms. Remove from the heat, stir in the butter, and leave to cool.

7 **Pour the remaining cream** into a large bowl, add the sugar and vanilla and whisk until the cream forms soft peaks. Divide the cream between 2 of the cakes, stack them on top of each other, then cover with the third cake.

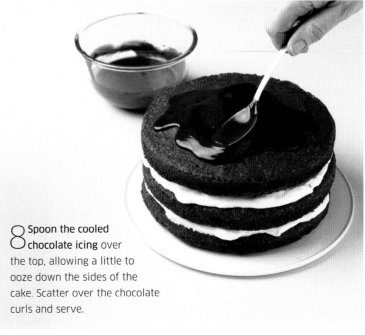

8 **Spoon the cooled chocolate icing** over the top, allowing a little to ooze down the sides of the cake. Scatter over the chocolate curls and serve.

Chocolate orange pound cake

FOR A TREAT, candy your own peel. To save time, you can substitute 125g (4½oz) of bought peel; if it seems dry, soak in boiling water for 5-10 minutes to plump it up, then drain and dry very well before chopping. The cake can be stored for up to 1 week in an airtight container; it will become moist and sticky the longer it is kept.

SERVES SERVES 6-8	**PREP** 2 HRS PLUS CANDIED PEEL	**COOK** 50-60 MINS

Ingredients

FOR THE CANDIED PEEL	1 tsp baking powder
2 oranges	salt
200g (7oz) caster sugar	175g (6oz) unsalted butter
	200g (7oz) caster sugar
FOR THE CAKE	3 eggs
125g (4½oz) plain flour	
3 tbsp cocoa powder	**FOR THE ORANGE ICING**
	60g (2oz) icing sugar
	2-3 tsp orange juice (reserved from orange for peel)

MAKE THE CANDIED PEEL

1 **Roll each orange** gently on a work surface to loosen the peel. Score the orange peel lengthways into quarters with a small knife, then strip away the peel and pith with your fingers.

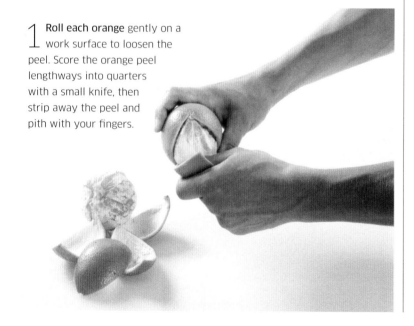

2 **Cut the peel** into 5mm (¼in) strips with a sharp knife. Cut one orange in half and squeeze the juice; reserve it for the icing.

3 **Heat the sugar** with 250ml (9fl oz) water in a saucepan until dissolved, then bring just to a boil, and tip in the peel. Press a circle of baking parchment on top, and weigh it down with a plate. Heat slowly to a simmer, then poach for about 1 hour, until tender. Allow it to soak at room temperature for 24 hours, then drain on a rack placed over a tray for 3-5 hours longer.

MAKE THE CAKE

4 **Reserve several pieces of peel** for decoration, and finely chop the rest. Preheat the oven to 180°C (350°F/Gas 4). Butter, line, and flour a 21x11x7.5cm (8½x4½x3in) loaf tin. Sift the flour into a bowl with the cocoa powder, baking powder, and a pinch of salt.

5 **With an electric mixer,** cream the butter. Add the sugar and continue beating for 2-3 minutes, until light and fluffy. Add the eggs one by one, beating thoroughly with the electric mixer after each addition. Stir the finely chopped candied orange peel evenly into the mixture.

6 **Stir in the flour** and cocoa powder mixture until just mixed. Transfer the mixture to the prepared loaf tin. Tap the tin on a work surface to level the surface, and knock out large air bubbles. Bake in the heated oven for 50-60 minutes, until it shrinks slightly from the sides of the tin, and a skewer inserted in the centre comes out clean.

MAKE THE ICING AND FINISH THE CAKE

7 Remove the cake from the oven. Run a small knife round the sides of the loaf tin to loosen the cake, then invert the tin and transfer the cake to a wire rack, keeping a baking sheet below the rack to catch any drips from the icing later. Carefully remove the baking parchment. Leave the cake to cool completely.

8 Sift the icing sugar into a small bowl, and stir in enough of the orange juice to make a soft paste. Adjust the consistency by adding more icing sugar if it seems too thin, or more orange juice if it's a little too thick, adding just a very little of either at a time as it's a finely balanced process to get the consistency just right. Place the bowl in a saucepan of hot (not simmering) water, and heat until the icing is warm, and will pour easily from the spoon. Drizzle the icing evenly over the cake, then top with the reserved candied peel. Leave to stand for about 1 hour, until the icing has set. Serve the cake in generous slices, with afternoon tea.

 VARIATION: Chocolate orange marble pound cake

An attractive cake with a swirl of plain orange mixture.

1 Make the candied orange peel as directed, then chop all of it. Sift the flour with the baking powder, and salt, and divide evenly between 2 bowls. Sift 3 tbsp cocoa powder into 1 of the bowls.

2 Continue making the cake mixture as directed until the end of step 5, then divide it in half. Stir the cocoa mixture into 1 portion, and the plain flour mixture into the other. Pour the plain mixture into the prepared loaf tin.

3 Pour the chocolate mixture over the plain mixture in the tin. Using the tip of a knife, swirl the mixtures together in a marbled pattern, taking care not to overmix them or the marbled effect will be lost. Bake and ice the cake as directed.

Marbled chocolate cheesecake

THIS ALL-AMERICAN FAVOURITE has swirls of plain and chocolate cheesecake fillings flavoured with vanilla, in a crumbled biscuit base. The marbled filling is dense and rich, making it an indulgent finishing touch to a dinner party. Even better, the cheesecake can be made up to 3 days ahead and kept, tightly wrapped, in the refrigerator, so you have far less to prepare on the day. The filling has very few ingredients, so you must use the very best quality chocolate you can afford.

SERVES	PREP	COOK
SERVES 8-10	35-40 MINS PLUS COOLING AND CHILLING	50-60 MINS

Ingredients

FOR THE BISCUIT BASE

75g (2½oz) unsalted butter, plus more, melted, for the tin

150g (5½oz) digestive biscuits

FOR THE CHEESECAKE FILLING

150g (5½oz) good-quality plain chocolate

500g (1lb 2oz) cream cheese, softened

150g (5½oz) caster sugar

1 tsp vanilla essence

2 eggs

MAKE THE BISCUIT BASE

1 **Generously brush** the inside of a 20cm (8in) springform tin with melted butter, and chill it. Work the digestive biscuits to fine crumbs in a food processor (or crush with a rolling pin); transfer to a bowl. Melt the butter in a small saucepan; add to the crumbs.

2 **Stir with a wooden spoon** until all the crumbs are moistened with melted butter. Press the crumb mixture evenly over the bottom and up the side of the prepared tin. Chill for 30-60 minutes, until firm.

MAKE THE CHEESECAKE FILLING

3 **Preheat the oven** to 180°C (350°F/Gas 4). Cut the chocolate into large chunks with a sharp knife, or in a food processor using the pulse button. Melt the chocolate in a bowl suspended over – but not touching the surface of – a pan of simmering water, stirring as little as possible until smooth, then allow to cool.

4 **Beat the cream cheese** with an electric mixer or wooden spoon for 2-3 minutes, until smooth. Add the sugar and vanilla essence, and beat just until smooth once more. Add the eggs one by one, beating very well after each addition.

ASSEMBLE AND MARBLE THE CHEESECAKE

5 **Pour half of the filling** into the biscuit base. It will be nowhere near full, as the chocolate mixture is still to come. It is fine if the surface is not level, as you will be marbling the fillings later.

6 **Mix the cooled, melted chocolate** into the remaining filling. It is important to have waited long enough for the melted chocolate to become cool, otherwise there is a risk that the eggs in the mixture may begin to scramble.

7 **Slowly spoon** a ring of the chocolate filling over the plain filling. Don't worry about neatness here; as long as you make a rough, even band of chocolate filling, the cheesecake will look great.

8 **Using a table knife,** swirl the fillings together to make a marbled pattern. Don't over-mix, or the marbled effect will be lost. Bake in the oven for 50–60 minutes, until the side is set but the centre remains soft. Turn off the oven and leave the cheesecake there until completely cool, or it may crack. Refrigerate for at least 4 hours. Run a knife round the side of the cheesecake to loosen it, remove the tin and transfer to a serving plate.

VARIATION: All-chocolate cheescake

You have 2 options here: either use all plain, or all white chocolate, depending on which you would prefer.

1 Make the base as directed. Chop and melt 300g (10oz) plain chocolate, or 250g (9oz) white chocolate, as directed, making sure that the base of the bowl containing the chocolate does not touch the simmering water, or there is a risk the chocolate may "seize" and be spoiled.

2 Prepare the filling as directed, using only 100g (3½oz) sugar and stirring in all the cooled, melted plain or white chocolate after the eggs, without dividing the mixture into 2 portions.

3 Pour all the filling into the prepared base, level the surface, and bake as directed. Let cool, then serve with fresh raspberries.

Spectacular desserts

Impressive, indulgent,
and delicious puddings

Chocolate orange truffle cake

A LAYER OF CHOCOLATE SPONGE CAKE, crowned with chocolate ganache, and flavoured with Grand Marnier. Orange segments steeped in Grand Marnier provide the perfect accompaniment. Make sure you leave yourself at least 6 hours' chilling time.

SERVES SERVES 10-12	**PREP** 35-40 MINS PLUS CHILLING	**COOK** 40 MINS

Ingredients

FOR THE CHOCOLATE CAKE

60g (2oz) butter

100g (3½oz) plain flour

30g (1oz) cocoa powder

salt

4 eggs

135g (5oz) caster sugar

4-5 tbsp Grand Marnier

FOR THE CHOCOLATE GANACHE

375g (13oz) plain chocolate

375ml (13fl oz) double cream

3 tbsp Grand Marnier

TO DECORATE AND FINISH

6 oranges

3 tbsp Grand Marnier

3 tbsp cocoa powder

MAKE THE CAKE

1 **Preheat the oven** to 220°C (425°F/Gas 7). Butter a 25cm (10in) round cake tin, and line the bottom with baking parchment. Butter the parchment. Sprinkle in 2-3 tbsp flour, and turn the tin to coat the bottom and side; tap the tin upside down to remove excess flour. Melt the butter and allow to cool.

2 **Sift together** the flour, cocoa powder, and a pinch of salt. Put the eggs in a large bowl, and beat with an electric mixer for a few seconds. Add the sugar and continue beating at high speed for about 5 minutes, until the mixture leaves a ribbon trail when the beaters are lifted.

3 **Sift about a third of the flour** and cocoa mixture over the egg mixture, and fold together as lightly as possible. Add another third of the flour and cocoa mixture, and fold together in the same way. Add the remaining flour and cocoa mixture, and the cooled, melted butter, and fold them in gently but quickly.

4 **Pour the mixture** into the prepared tin, then gently tap the tin on the work surface to level the mixture, and knock out any large air bubbles. Bake in the heated oven for about 40 minutes, until the cake is risen and just firm to the touch. Turn the cake out on to a wire rack. Peel off the paper. Leave the cake to cool.

PREPARE THE BASE

5 **Trim the cooled cake** to fit a 23cm (9in) springform tin, using the base of the tin as a guide. Lightly butter the bottom and side. Carefully transfer the trimmed cake to the tin. Sprinkle 4-5 tbsp Grand Marnier evenly over the top of the cake. Cover and set aside while making the chocolate ganache.

MAKE THE CHOCOLATE GANACHE

6 **Cut the chocolate** into large chunks with a sharp knife, or in a food processor. Put the chocolate in a large bowl. Heat the cream until almost boiling, then pour it over the chopped chocolate. Stir until the chocolate has melted. Allow to cool, stirring occasionally.

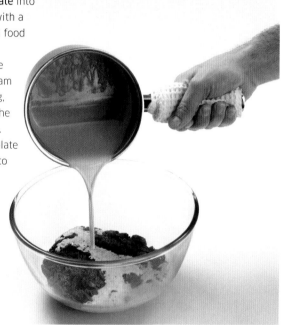

7 **Add the 3 tbsp Grand Marnier** to the cream and chocolate mixture, and stir until blended. Do not stir too vigorously, as melted chocolate should always be treated gently and with care. Using the electric mixer, beat the chocolate ganache for 5-10 minutes, until fluffy. Do not overbeat the mixture, or it will be very stiff and hard to spread. You just want to incorporate a little air.

8 With a rubber spatula, or a wooden spoon, turn out the chocolate ganache on top of the cake, and smooth the surface. Cover with cling film and chill for at least 6 hours, until firm.

PREPARE THE DECORATION AND FINISH THE CAKE

9 Using a citrus zester, remove the zest from 3 of the oranges, working over a sheet of baking parchment to catch all the essential oils. Be careful not to include any of the white pith. Set aside on a plate in the refrigerator until needed.

10 Trim both ends of each orange, set the fruits upright on a chopping board, and cut away all the remaining peel and the white pith, following the curve of the oranges. Working over a bowl, cut down between each side of the orange segments to separate them from the thin membranes. Put the segments in a bowl and squeeze each empty orange shell over, to extract all the remaining juice and flavour. Sprinkle with the Grand Marnier.

11 Just before serving, take the cake from the refrigerator. Stand it on top of a bowl, then release the side of the tin. Carefully remove the base of the tin, using a palette knife. Place the cake on a wire rack with a baking sheet beneath. Sift cocoa powder over the top, using a stencil if you like, then transfer to a serving plate, and sprinkle with the reserved orange zest. Serve the orange segments and liquid in small bowls alongside.

Strawberry shortcakes

REAL STRAWBERRY SHORTCAKE, MADE WITH A SCONE-LIKE DOUGH. This is a rich version of the dish, but a tangy strawberry coulis mingles well with the shortcakes and cream, and cuts through the richness. These are best eaten fresh from the oven.

SERVES	PREP	COOK
SERVES 6	15-20 MINS	12-15 MINS

Ingredients

FOR THE SHORTCAKES

250g (9oz) plain flour

1 tbsp baking powder

½ tsp salt

45g (1½oz) caster sugar

60g (2oz) unsalted butter, cut into pieces

175ml (6fl oz) double cream, plus more if needed

FOR THE STRAWBERRY COULIS

500g (1lb 2oz) strawberries

2-3 tbsp icing sugar

2 tbsp kirsch (optional)

FOR THE STRAWBERRIES

500g (1lb 2oz) strawberries

45g (1½oz) caster sugar

FOR THE CHANTILLY CREAM (optional)

250ml (9fl oz) double cream

2-3 tbsp caster sugar

1 tsp vanilla essence

PREPARE THE SHORTCAKES

1 **Preheat the oven** to 220°C (425°F/Gas 7). Butter a baking sheet. Sift the flour into a bowl with the baking powder, salt, and caster sugar.

2 **Cut the butter** into the flour mixture using 2 round-bladed knives. Rub with your fingertips to form fine crumbs. Add the cream, and toss quickly to form crumbs. Add a little more cream if it seems dry.

BAKE THE SHORTCAKES

3 **Press all the crumbs** together with your hands, to form a rough ball of dough. It doesn't matter at this stage if it seems a little crumbly, as that will disappear once you work the dough. Remember to handle it lightly at all times.

4 **Turn the dough** on to a floured surface and knead lightly for a few seconds; the dough should remain quite rough, but all the ingredients should be evenly mixed, without any big lumps. Pat the dough out to a round 1cm (½in) thick.

5 **Cut out rounds** with an 8cm (3in) pastry cutter, or a glass of the same diameter. Pat out the trimmings, and cut additional rounds, for a total of 6 rounds. Transfer to the prepared baking sheet, spacing them out evenly.

6 **Bake until very lightly browned:** it should take 12-15 minutes. Transfer them to a wire rack to cool.

MAKE THE COULIS

7 Hull and pick over the strawberries, washing them only if dirty. Purée them in a food processor. Transfer to a bowl and stir in the icing sugar and kirsch, if using. It should be thick enough to coat the back of a spoon.

PREPARE THE STRAWBERRIES AND CHANTILLY CREAM

8 Hull the strawberries and cut into slices, reserving 6 small whole berries. Sprinkle the sliced strawberries with the caster sugar and let stand to soften for 5–10 minutes. Slice the reserved strawberries and set aside.

9 Pour the cream into a chilled bowl. Set the bowl over iced water, if your kitchen is hot. Whip until soft peaks form. Add the sugar and vanilla and whip until it forms stiff peaks.

ASSEMBLE THE SHORTCAKES

10 Cut the cooled shortcakes in half, with a serrated knife. Spoon the strawberries on the bottom halves. Pile on the cream, and top each with its lid and the reserved sliced strawberries. Spoon the coulis around.

 VARIATION: Lemon shortcakes with blueberries

The lemon here accents the blueberry filling.

1 Make the shortcakes as directed in the main recipe, adding the grated zest and juice of 1 unwaxed lemon along with the unsalted butter. Remember to handle the shortcake dough as lightly and gently as possible at all times during the making and cutting out process, or they will be tough. Use the trimmings to make miniature shortcakes.

2 Pick over 500g (1lb 2oz) firm and plump blueberries, discarding any that are very soft; they do not need to be sprinkled with sugar unless they are very tart. Taste a berry to check how sweet yours are, and take a view on whether you would like to sweeten them or not; you know your palate better than anyone else.

3 Assemble the shortcakes as directed in the main recipe, piling the Chantilly cream on top of the blueberries, then decorate the top of each shortcake with an edible flower or a herb sprig. Lemon verbena, if you can get hold of it, or you grow it in the garden, would be a good choice of herb to use here. Otherwise sprinkle with the leaves stripped from a sprig of lemon thyme.

Orange and cinnamon crème brûlée

IN THIS DESSERT, translated as "burnt cream", a rich custard is sprinkled with sugar just before serving, and then grilled. The top will crack when tapped with a spoon, while the cinnamon and orange give complexity to the satin-smooth baked cream. Fresh berries or a peach compote would make a perfect accompaniment. It can be made up to the end of step 5 and refrigerated for up to 8 hours.

SERVES	PREP	COOK
SERVES 8	15-20 MINS PLUS CHILLING	30-35 MINS

1 litre (1¾ pints) whipping cream	
8 egg yolks	
200g (7oz) granulated sugar	

Ingredients

1 orange

1 cinnamon stick

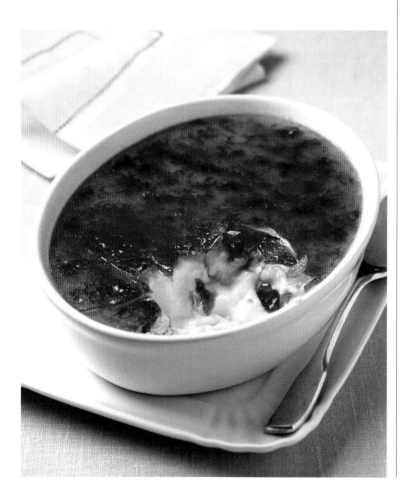

MAKE THE ORANGE-CINNAMON CUSTARD

1 **Preheat the oven** to 190°C (375°F/Gas 5). Grate the zest from the orange. Snap the cinnamon stick in half and place in a saucepan. Warm over low heat for 40-60 seconds, until you can smell the spice. Let cool slightly, then add the cream and grated orange zest. Bring just to a boil. Remove from the heat, cover, and let the cream infuse for 10-15 minutes.

2 **Put the yolks** and a third of the sugar in a large bowl. Whisk just until mixed, using an electric mixer or a hand whisk. Slowly pour the cream mixture into the egg yolks, whisking constantly until evenly mixed. You must continue to whisk all the time, or there is a risk that the egg yolks will start to scramble, splitting the custard base.

BAKE THE CUSTARD

3 **Ladle the cream mixture** through a large sieve into a 1.5 litre (2¾pint) gratin dish. Fold an old, clean tea towel, and put it on the bottom of a roasting tin. Then set the gratin dish on the towel.

4 **Pour enough hot water** into the roasting tin to come about halfway up the sides of the gratin dish. Bring the water bath to a boil on top of the stove, then carefully transfer to the heated oven.

5 **Bake for 30-35 minutes, until a thin skin forms** on top and the cream underneath is almost firm when the dish is gently moved from side to side. Remove from the roasting tin. Let cool to room temperature. Chill for 3-8 hours.

CARAMELIZE THE CREAM

6 **Heat the grill** to its highest setting. Sprinkle the remaining sugar over the surface of the cream in an even layer. Half-fill a roasting tin with cold water, and set the gratin dish in it. Add some ice cubes to the water to keep the custard cool. Grill for 3 minutes, until the sugar melts and caramelizes on top. Let cool a few minutes so the caramel becomes crisp, then serve.

Tiramisu

THIS RICH ITALIAN DESSERT has many versions. The name means "pick me up". To be truly authentic, use espresso coffee. This can be assembled 2 days ahead and kept, covered, in the refrigerator. Add the cocoa and coffee decoration just before serving.

SERVES	PREP	COOK
SERVES 8-10	35-40 MINS PLUS CHILLING	30-40 MINS

Ingredients

FOR THE MASCARPONE MIXTURE

6 egg yolks

60g (2oz) caster sugar

500g (1lb 2oz) mascarpone cheese

1 tsp vanilla essence

TO SOAK AND TOP THE TIRAMISU

150ml (5fl oz) espresso coffee

4 tbsp Tia Maria or Kahlúa (coffee liqueur)

4 tbsp brandy

32 sponge fingers (preferably Savoiarde)

1 tbsp cocoa powder

1 tbsp coffee powder

icing sugar, to serve (optional)

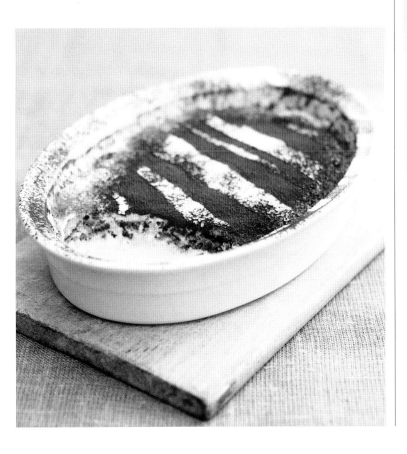

PREPARE THE MASCARPONE MIXTURE

1 **Put the egg yolks** and sugar in a large heatproof bowl and beat them with an electric mixer. Set the bowl over a saucepan of hot, but not simmering, water. Make sure the base of the bowl does not touch the water. Whisk for 3-5 minutes, until pale and thick enough to leave a "ribbon" trail when the whisk is lifted.

2 **Take the bowl** from the pan of hot water, and continue beating for 1-2 minutes, until the mixture has cooled slightly. Let cool completely. Combine the mascarpone and vanilla essence in another bowl, and stir with a rubber spatula until smooth and creamy. Add the egg yolk and sugar mixture to the mascarpone, and fold them together.

ASSEMBLE THE TIRAMISU

3 **Combine the espresso,** Tia Maria, and brandy in a shallow dish. Dip each of the sponge fingers, cut-side down, in the coffee, then place in the bottom of a large serving dish.

4 **Continue to moisten** a third of the sponge fingers, to make a single layer. Sprinkle them with 2 tbsp of the remaining coffee mixture.

5 **Spoon one-third of the mascarpone mixture** over the sponge fingers to cover them completely. Continue layering the moistened cake fingers and mascarpone mixture, ending with a layer of mascarpone.

6 **Smooth the surface** with a large metal spoon. Cover and chill for at least 6 hours. Mix together the cocoa and coffee powders. Sift them over the top of the tiramisu, then sift over a little icing sugar, if using, and serve.

Pavlova with tropical fruit

A GIANT MERINGUE PUFF, with a crisp outside and a soft, chewy interior, filled with whipped cream and fruit. This luscious dessert was created for the famous ballerina Anna Pavlova, and originates from Australia and New Zealand. This recipe makes a huge meringue, but you will find it disappears very rapidly! The meringue can be baked up to the end of step 3 and kept for up to 1 week in a large airtight container. It can also be frozen. Assemble the pavlova just before serving.

SERVES	PREP	COOK
SERVES 6-8	25-30 MINS	2-2½ HRS

Ingredients

FOR THE MERINGUE

6 egg whites

350g (12oz) caster sugar

1 tbsp cornflour

1 tsp distilled malt vinegar

2 tbsp chopped pistachios, to serve

FOR THE FRUIT

3 mangoes, total weight about 1kg (2¼lb)

5 kiwi fruit

1 pineapple, weighing about 750g (1lb 10oz)

45g (1½oz) caster sugar

2 tbsp kirsch

FOR THE CREAM

375ml (13fl oz) double cream

45-60g (1½-2oz) caster or icing sugar

1 tsp vanilla essence

MAKE THE MERINGUE

1 Line a baking sheet with baking parchment. Using a 20cm (8in) cake tin as a guide, draw a circle on the paper. Preheat the oven to 130°C (250°F/ Gas ½). Whisk the egg whites until stiff. Sprinkle in 75g (2½oz) of the sugar, and continue whisking for about 20 seconds until glossy. Sift the cornflour and remaining sugar over, and add the vinegar.

2 Fold the mixture together until thoroughly mixed. Pile the meringue in the centre of the circle drawn on the paper, making sure it keeps within the line. With the back of a large metal spoon, spread out the meringue to an even round, making a deep hollow in the centre. Bake in the oven for 2-2½ hours, until firm and very lightly coloured. If it starts to brown during cooking, reduce the heat and cover loosely with foil.

3 Let the pavlova cool to lukewarm, then lift it off the baking sheet with two large palette knives, and set it on a wire rack to cool completely. When cold, peel off the paper. The exterior of the baked meringue will become crisp as it cools, while the interior stays moist and chewy.

PREPARE THE MANGO

4 Removing the flat, central stone and cubing mango flesh is easy, if you use this method. Cut each mango into two pieces lengthways, slightly off-centre, to just miss the stone. Cut the flesh away from the other side of the stone. Discard the stone.

5 Slash one piece - or "cheek" - in a lattice, cutting through the flesh but not the skin. Repeat with the other mango cheeks. Try to keep the lattice as even as possible.

6 Holding a mango cheek flesh side upwards, push the centre of the skin with your fingers to turn it inside out, opening the cuts of the flesh to reveal cubes. It will look a little like a hedgehog. Cut the cubes away from the skin.

PREPARE THE REMAINING FILLING

7 Pour the cream into a chilled bowl, and whip until soft peaks form. Add the sugar and vanilla essence, and continue whipping until stiff peaks form. Set aside.

8 With a small knife, trim the ends of the kiwi fruit. Set the fruit upright and trim off the skin in strips, working from top to bottom. Cut the kiwi fruit into neat slices.

9 Cut off the plume and base of the pineapple, then peel it, working from top to bottom following the curve of the fruit. Cut the pineapple lengthways in half, then into quarters. Cut out the core from each quarter. Cut the quarters lengthways into strips, then across into neat chunks.

10 Put all the fruit in a large bowl. Sprinkle the fruit with the sugar and kirsch. Stir very gently with a scrupulously clean wooden spoon (now is not the time for a scent of garlic!) to distribute the flavourings evenly, taking care not to break up any of the fruit pieces.

ASSEMBLE THE PAVLOVA

11 Put the cooled pavlova on a serving plate and spoon in the sweetened vanilla cream to form an even layer. Arrange the mixed fruit neatly over the top, sprinkle with the chopped pistachios, and serve immediately. Do not leave it to stand, or the cream will seep into the meringue, and make it soggy.

Cold lemon soufflé

A FAVOURITE ENDING to a grand dinner, this dessert is cool, light, and fluffy, with just the right balance of tart and sweet. Choose unwaxed lemons that feel heavy for their size, indicating they are full of juice. If unwaxed lemons are unavailable, scrub the fruits very well with a small, stiff brush before cooking with the zest.

SERVES	**PREP**	**COOK**
SERVES 8	35-40 MINS PLUS CHILLING	15-20 MINS

Ingredients

FOR THE SOUFFLÉ

10g (¼oz) powdered gelatine

4 large lemons

4 eggs, and 2 egg whites

250g (9oz) caster sugar

250ml (9fl oz) double cream

FOR THE CANDIED ZEST

2 tbsp caster sugar

FOR THE CHANTILLY CREAM

125ml (4½fl oz) double cream

1-2 tbsp caster sugar

½ tsp vanilla essence

PREPARE THE SOUFFLÉ DISH

1 **Cut a piece of foil,** 5cm (2in) longer than the circumference of a 1 litre (1¾ pint) soufflé dish. Fold the foil lengthways in half. Wrap the foil around the dish. It should stand well above the rim, so the soufflé will appear to have "risen". Secure with tape.

MAKE THE SOUFFLÉ BASE

2 **Put 75ml (2½fl oz) water** in a small saucepan, sprinkle the gelatine on top, and set aside for about 5 minutes, to soften until spongy. Make sure every crystal is soaked in water, or there will be crystals in the final soufflé.

3 **Grate the zest** from 3 of the lemons. Pare strips of zest from the remaining lemon, and reserve it to candy. Squeeze the juice from all 4 lemons – there should be 150ml (5fl oz). Separate the whole eggs. In a saucepan, mix together the egg yolks, grated lemon zest, lemon juice, and two-thirds of the sugar until blended.

4 **Cook, stirring,** just until the mixture boils. Pour into a large bowl, and beat with an electric mixer for 5-7 minutes, until light and thick enough to leave a "ribbon" trail when the whisk is lifted.

5 **Warm the gelatine** over low heat, shaking the pan, for 1-2 minutes, until the gelatine is melted and pourable; do not stir, or you risk inhibiting the setting qualities of the gelatine. Whisk into the lemon mixture, and continue whisking until cool.

FINISH AND CHILL THE SOUFFLÉ

6 Pour the cream into a bowl, and whip until soft peaks form; chill. Heat the remaining sugar with 125ml (4fl oz) water, until dissolved. Boil without stirring until it reaches the hard-ball stage: to test, remove a teaspoon of syrup. Take it between finger and thumb; it should form a firm, pliable ball. (Or it should register 120°C (248°F) on a sugar thermometer.)

7 While the syrup is boiling, put the 6 egg whites in a bowl and whisk. until stiff peaks form when the whisk is lifted. Gradually pour the hot sugar syrup into the egg whites, whisking constantly.

8 Continue whisking for about 5 minutes, until the meringue is cool and stiff. Set the bowl of lemon mixture in a larger bowl of iced water, and stir the mixture gently until it starts to thicken. Remove the bowl from the ice bath. Gently fold in the chilled whipped cream, then fold in the meringue in 2 batches.

9 Pour the soufflé mixture into the prepared dish; it should come at least 5cm (2in) above the rim of the dish, but below the edge of the foil collar. Chill the soufflé for at least 2 hours, until firmly set.

CANDY THE LEMON ZEST

10 Cut the pared lemon zest into very fine strips. Bring a small pan of water to the boil, add the zest and simmer for 2 minutes, then drain. In the same pan, gently heat the sugar with 2 tbsp water until dissolved. Add the zest and simmer for 8–10 minutes, until the moisture has evaporated. Remove with a fork, gently separate, and set on baking parchment to cool.

MAKE THE CHANTILLY CREAM

11 To make the Chantilly cream, pour the cream into a chilled bowl, and whip until soft peaks form. Add the sugar and vanilla, and continue whipping until the cream forms stiff peaks.

12 Transfer the Chantilly cream into a serving bowl. Remove the soufflé from the refrigerator, and allow to stand at room temperature for 30 minutes to lose its chilled stiffness, Sprinkle with the candied lemon zest, carefully remove the foil collar, being gentle so as not to spoil the appearance of the "risen" sides, and serve with the Chantilly cream.

Chocolate ice cream

HOME-MADE ICE CREAM still beats them all. Serve with langues de chats biscuits, or even a colourful assortment of seasonal fruit, if you like. Strawberries and peaches are especially good. The ice cream can be made 2 weeks ahead and kept in a covered container in the freezer. It will become very hard, so soften it in the refrigerator before serving.

SERVES SERVES 6-8	**PREP** 15-20 MINS PLUS FREEZING	**COOK** 10-15 MINS

Ingredients

250g (9oz) good-quality plain chocolate

600ml (1 pint) milk

125g (4½oz) caster sugar

8 egg yolks

2 tbsp cornflour

250ml (9fl oz) double cream

1 bar plain chocolate for chocolate curls (optional)

MAKE THE CHOCOLATE CUSTARD

1 **With a sharp knife,** cut the chocolate into large chunks, then chop finely with a knife or in a food processor using the pulse button. Put the milk in a saucepan, add the chocolate and heat, stirring, until smooth. Make sure you stir constantly, so the chocolate does not stick and burn on the pan.

2 **Add the sugar** to the chocolate milk, and stir until it has completely dissolved. In a bowl, whisk the egg yolks with the cornflour until smooth. Gradually whisk three-quarters of the chocolate milk into the egg yolk mixture, until smooth. Reserve the remainder in a measuring jug. Do not overwhisk, or the custard will be frothy instead of smooth.

COOK THE CHOCOLATE CUSTARD

3 **Return the mixture** to the saucepan, and cook over medium heat, stirring constantly, until the custard thickens enough to coat the back of the spoon. Stir in the reserved chocolate milk. Strain the chocolate custard sauce into a cold bowl, and leave to cool. If the custard forms a skin, whisk to dissolve it back into the mixture.

FREEZE THE ICE CREAM

4 **Pour the custard** into an ice-cream maker, and churn, according to the manufacturer's instructions. Meanwhile, chill 2 large bowls in the freezer. Whip the cream in 1 chilled bowl until it forms peaks, and holds its shape.

5 **Add the whipped cream** to the partially-set chocolate custard, and continue freezing until firm. Transfer the ice cream to the second chilled bowl, cover, and freeze for at least 4 hours.

6 **Make the chocolate curls,** if wanted: the chocolate bar should be at room temperature. With a vegetable peeler, shave curls on to a sheet of baking parchment. Scoop out the ice cream, and sprinkle with chocolate curls.

Blackberry fool

THE NAME "FOOL" dates back at least to 16th-century England, and probably comes from the French "fouler", meaning to purée. Fools are traditionally made with a tart fruit. There are simpler versions, but this is a delicious recipe.

SERVES	PREP	COOK
SERVES 8	20-25 MINS PLUS CHILLING	15-20 MINS

Ingredients

FOR THE BLACKBERRIES

500g (1lb 2oz) blackberries

60-75g (2-2½oz) caster sugar, plus more if needed

250ml (9fl oz) double cream

fresh mint sprigs, to decorate

FOR THE PASTRY CREAM

375ml (13fl oz) milk

1 vanilla pod, or 2 tsp vanilla essence

5 egg yolks

60g (2oz) caster sugar

30g (1oz) plain flour

knob of unsalted butter

MAKE THE BLACKBERRY PURÉE

1 Pick over the blackberries, and set aside 8 for decoration. Put the berries in a saucepan with 4 tbsp water. Simmer over medium heat, stirring, for 8-10 minutes, until soft but thick. Transfer to a food processor, and purée to a fairly coarse texture.

2 Press the purée through a sieve to remove the pips. There should be 375ml (13fl oz). Stir in sugar to taste, and set the purée aside to cool. The flavours will blend and develop.

MAKE THE PASTRY CREAM

3 Put the milk in a small saucepan and add the split vanilla pod, if using. Bring to a boil, then remove from the heat, cover, and let stand for 10-15 minutes. In a large bowl, whisk the yolks, sugar, and flour just to mix. Whisk the hot milk into the egg yolk mixture until thoroughly combined.

4 Return the mixture to the pan, and cook over low heat, whisking constantly, for 2-3 minutes, until the flour has cooked and the pastry cream has thickened. Simmer over low heat for 2 minutes longer. Transfer to a bowl and remove the vanilla pod, if using, or stir in the vanilla essence. Using the fork, rub the butter over the surface to prevent a skin from forming. Set aside to cool.

FINISH THE FOOL

5 Pour the cream into a chilled bowl. Whip until stiff peaks form, and the whisk leaves clear marks in the cream. Set aside. Add the blackberry purée to the cooled pastry cream, and stir to mix thoroughly.

6 Fold in the whipped cream gently. Taste; add more sugar if necessary. Spoon into stemmed glasses. Cover and chill for at least 2 hours. Decorate each fool with a blackberry and a mint sprig, and serve chilled.

Caramelized mango tartlets

THE FAME OF TARTE TATIN (p442) has spread worldwide, but this modern version, using mangoes, is equally good. The tartlets are turned out to serve upside-down, and are best eaten warm.

SERVES	PREP	COOK
SERVES 6	40-45 MINS	20-25 MINS

Ingredients

FOR THE PÂTE SUCRÉE DOUGH

90g (3oz) unsalted butter

3 egg yolks

½ tsp vanilla essence

215g (7½oz) plain flour, plus more if needed

60g (2oz) caster sugar

¼ tsp salt

FOR THE FILLING

200g (7oz) caster sugar

4 mangoes, total weight about 1.5kg (3lb 3oz)

juice of ½ lime, or to taste

1-2 tbsp icing sugar (optional)

MAKE THE DOUGH

1 **Cut the butter** into pieces. In a small bowl, mix the egg yolks with the vanilla. Put the flour in a food processor with the sugar and salt, and blend for about 5 seconds. Add the butter and pulse-blend to coarse crumbs,.

2 **Add the egg yolks**, and work until the mixture resembles small peas. If it is dry, work in 1-2 tbsp water. Transfer to a floured work surface. Work with the heel of your hand until smooth. Chill for 30 minutes, until firm.

MAKE THE CARAMEL SYRUP

3 **Put the sugar** and 125ml (4fl oz) water in a saucepan, and heat gently until dissolved, stirring occasionally. Boil, without stirring, until the mixture starts to turn golden around the edge. Do not stir the sugar syrup during boiling, or it may crystallize.

4 **Lower the heat** and continue cooking, swirling the saucepan once or twice so the syrup colours evenly, until the caramel is golden. Cook the caramel only until medium gold; if it gets too dark, it will become bitter in the oven.

5 **Remove the saucepan** from the heat, and immediately plunge the base of the saucepan into a bowl of cold water, until cooking stops. Stand back in case of splashes: there are few things hotter than caramel.

6 **Pour about one-sixth of the caramel** into the bottom of a 10cm (4in) baking dish. Working quickly, tilt the dish so the bottom is coated with a thin, even layer. Repeat with 5 more dishes. Let cool.

PREPARE THE MANGOES

7 Peel each of the mangoes with a small knife, taking care to remove the minimum amount of mango flesh with the skin. Cut each lengthwise on both sides of the stone, so the knife just misses the stone. Cut the remaining flesh away from each stone in 2 long slices, and set aside for the coulis. Discard the stones.

8 Cut each of the large pieces of mango into 3 diagonal slices. Arrange 3 slices, cut-side up, on top of the caramel in 1 dish. Repeat until all the dishes are filled. Add the remaining slices to the mango for the coulis.

ASSEMBLE AND BAKE THE TARTLETS

9 Preheat the oven to 200°C (400°F/Gas 6). Lightly flour a work surface. With your hands, shape the dough into a cylinder about 30cm (12in) long. Cut it into 6 equal pieces. Shape each piece into a ball.

10 Roll out each ball into a 12cm (5in) round. Drape one of the rounds over a baking dish, and tuck the edge down around the mango slices. Repeat for the remaining tartlets. Chill for 15 minutes, until the dough is firm. Bake for 20-25 minutes.

MAKE THE MANGO COULIS

11 Put the reserved mango flesh into a food processor or a blender, and purée it until smooth. Transfer to a bowl; add the lime juice, and stir it in. Taste and add icing sugar, if necessary, or even more lime juice if you prefer. Chill the coulis.

12 Remove the tartlets from the oven when golden brown. Let cool in the dishes for 2-3 minutes. To unmould, set a small plate on top and invert. If any mango slices stick to the dish, remove with a palette knife and replace on the tartlet. Repeat for the remaining tartlets. Serve at once with lime wedges, if you like. Pass the coulis separately.

Ricotta cheesecake

THIS IS PERFECTION: a classic Italian dish of ricotta, flavoured with candied orange peel and almonds, baked in a sweet, lemon pastry. The fresher the cheese, the better the cake.

SERVES	PREP	COOK
SERVES 8-10	35-40 MINS PLUS CHILLING	1-1¼ HRS

Ingredients

FOR THE SWEET PASTRY DOUGH

175g (6oz) unsalted butter

250g (9oz) plain flour, plus more if needed

1 lemon

50g (1¾oz) caster sugar

4 egg yolks

1 whole egg, to glaze

FOR THE FILLING

1 orange

2 tbsp chopped candied orange peel

1.25kg (2¾lb) ricotta cheese

100g (3½oz) caster sugar

1 tbsp plain flour

salt

1 tsp vanilla essence

45g (1½oz) sultanas

30g (1oz) slivered almonds

4 egg yolks

MAKE THE SWEET PASTRY DOUGH

1 **With a rolling pin,** pound the butter between 2 sheets of baking parchment to soften it slightly. Sift the flour on to a work surface, and make a large well in the centre. Grate the zest from the lemon. Put the butter, grated lemon zest, sugar, egg yolks, and a pinch of salt in the well.

2 **Using your fingertips,** work together all the ingredients in the well, until they are thoroughly mixed. Gradually draw the flour into the other ingredients. Press the dough into a ball. Lightly flour the work surface, then knead the dough for 1-2 minutes, until it is very smooth, and peels away from the work surface in one piece. Shape into a ball, wrap, and refrigerate for about 30 minutes, until firm.

ROLL OUT THE DOUGH AND LINE THE TIN

3 **Brush the bottom** and side of a 23-25cm (9-10in) springform tin with melted butter. Lightly flour the work surface, and roll out three-quarters of the dough, to make a 35-37cm (14-15in) round. Roll up the dough around the rolling pin, then unroll it loosely so that it drapes over the tin.

4 **Press the dough** gently into the bottom of the tin, then press it gently up the side of the tin with your fingers. Using a table knife, trim excess dough even with the outer edge of the tin. Chill the shell, together with the remaining dough and trimmings, for 15 minutes. Meanwhile, make the filling.

MAKE THE FILLING

5 **Grate the zest** from the orange on to a small plate. Finely chop the candied orange peel.

6 **Place the ricotta** in a large bowl and beat in the sugar, flour, and ½ tsp salt. Make sure all the ingredients are well mixed into the ricotta, so you have a smooth base for the cheesecake filling, without any lumps.

7 **Add the grated orange zest,** candied peel, vanilla essence, sultanas, slivered almonds, and egg yolks to the ricotta. Beat the mixture together thoroughly to combine, again being very sure that everything is very well blended.

8 Spoon the filling into the chilled pastry shell. Tap the tin on the work surface, to eliminate any air pockets that might remain through the ricotta mixture. Smooth the top of the filling, using the back of a wooden spoon.

MAKE THE LATTICE TOP AND BAKE THE CHEESECAKE

9 Press any dough trimmings into the remaining dough, and roll it into a 25cm (10in) round on a lightly floured surface. Using a sharp knife, cut into strips about 1cm (½in) wide. Use them to make a lattice on top of the cheesecake.

10 Make an egg glaze: lightly beat the whole egg with ½ tsp salt. Moisten the ends of each of the strips with the glaze, then seal them firmly to the pastry rim. Brush the lattice with the glaze, and chill the cheesecake for 15–30 minutes, or until firm. Meanwhile, preheat the oven to 180°C (350°F/Gas 4), and put in a baking sheet near the bottom.

11 Bake the cheesecake on the heated baking sheet, until the top is firm and golden brown. It will take 1–1¼ hours. Let cool in the tin until just warm, then remove the side of the tin and let the cake cool completely. Serve at room temperature.

 VARIATION: Chocolate ricotta pie

Discovered in a pastry shop in Assisi.

1 Make the pastry as directed in the main recipe, with 175g (6oz) flour, 3 egg yolks, 45g (1½oz) sugar, and 125g (4½oz) butter; omit the lemon zest. Roll out to line a 33x23x5cm (13x9x2in) buttered baking dish.

2 Finely chop 125g (4½oz) plain chocolate in a food processor. Make the filling as directed, adding the chocolate and grated orange zest in place of the candied fruit, sultanas, and almonds. Fill the pastry shell, chill, and bake as directed for 35–40 minutes. Let cool completely in the baking dish.

3 Chop 30g (1oz) more chocolate. Melt it in a bowl in a saucepan of hot water, until smooth. Stir in ½ tsp vegetable oil. Dip a fork in the chocolate and flick over the top.

Creamy rice pudding with peaches

THE LENGTHY COOKING FOR THIS RICE PUDDING results in a golden dessert. In summer, serve it just warm, with the chilled peaches macerated in red wine. Both the rice and the peaches can be prepared 1 day ahead and kept, covered, in the refrigerator. Let the rice come to room temperature, or warm it in a low oven, before serving.

SERVES	PREP	COOK
SERVES 4-6	15-20 MINUTES PLUS MACERATING AND STANDING	3 HOURS

Ingredients

FOR THE PEACHES

4 ripe peaches

60g (2oz) caster sugar, plus more if needed

250ml (9fl oz) dry red wine, plus more if needed

FOR THE RICE PUDDING

65g (2¼oz) short-grain rice

1 litre (1¾pints) milk, plus more if needed

5cm (2in) cinnamon stick

50g (1¾oz) caster sugar

salt

PREPARE THE PEACHES

1 **Peel and stone** the peaches: bring a saucepan of water to a boil. Immerse the peaches in the water for 10 seconds, then transfer them to a bowl of cold water to stop the cooking. If the peaches are very ripe, you may not need to blanch them in boiling water before peeling.

2 **Using a small knife,** cut each peach in half, using the indentation on 1 side as a guide. With both hands, give a sharp twist to each half, then lift out the stones. Carefully peel the skin from the peaches; it should come away easily. The skinned peaches will absorb more wine during macerating.

MACERATE THE PEACHES IN RED WINE

3 **Cut each peach half** into 2 wedges, and put them into a non-metallic bowl. Sprinkle the peaches with sugar; they may need more or less sugar than specified, depending on their sweetness.

4 **Pour over the red wine,** to cover the fruit completely. Set a plate on top. Leave to macerate in the refrigerator for at least 2 and up to 24 hours. Strain the liquid into a saucepan, bring to a boil, and simmer for 2 minutes, until syrupy. Stir it back into the peaches.

MAKE THE RICE PUDDING AND SERVE

5 **Preheat the oven** to 150°C (300°F/Gas 2). In the ovenproof bowl, stir the rice, milk, cinnamon, sugar, and a pinch of salt. Bake, stirring gently every 30 minutes, for 3 hours.

6 **Remove the pudding** from the oven. Carefully slip a spoon down the side, and stir from the bottom. Let stand for 1 hour. Discard the cinnamon. Serve with the peaches and wine syrup.

Ginger cheesecake

CLASSIC CHEESECAKE LENDS ITSELF to an assortment of delicious flavourings. Chopped stem ginger adds sparkle to the rich, smooth filling, baked in a crumbly biscuit crust. During baking, the ginger sinks to make a delicate layer in the creamy filling.

SERVES SERVES 8-10	**PREP** 40-45 MINS PLUS CHILLING	**COOK** 50-60 MINS

Ingredients

FOR THE CRUST

150g (5½oz) digestive biscuits

75g (2½oz) unsalted butter

FOR THE FILLING

500g (1lb 2oz) cream cheese, at room temperature

125g (4½oz) pieces of preserved stem ginger in syrup, plus 3 tbsp syrup

1 lemon

250ml (9fl oz) soured cream

150g (5½oz) granulated sugar

1 tsp vanilla essence

4 eggs

FOR THE TOPPING (optional)

150ml (5fl oz) double cream

MAKE THE CRUMB CRUST

1 Generously butter the bottom and side of a 20cm (8in) springform tin, then chill, to set the butter. Work the biscuits in a food processor to form crumbs (or crush with a rolling pin in a plastic bag). Put them in a bowl.

2 Melt the butter in a saucepan, and add it to the crumbs. Stir with a wooden spoon until all the crumbs are moistened. Press the crumb mixture evenly over the bottom, and 4cm (1½in) up the side of the tin. Chill for 30-60 minutes, until firm. Meanwhile, make the filling.

MAKE THE FILLING

3 Using a wooden spoon, beat the cream cheese in a bowl until soft and smooth. Chop the stem ginger. Reserve 2 tbsp ginger for the topping. Finely grate the lemon zest and squeeze out 2 tsp of juice.

4 Add the chopped ginger, ginger syrup, lemon zest and juice, soured cream, sugar, and vanilla essence to the cream cheese, and beat just until smooth. Add the eggs, one at a time, to the cream cheese and ginger mixture, beating well after each addition.

BAKE AND FINISH THE CHEESECAKE

5 Preheat the oven to 180°C (350°F/Gas 4). Pour the filling into the crust, and gently shake to level the surface. Place the tin on a baking sheet.

6 Bake the cheesecake for 50-60 minutes. Turn off the oven; leave the cheesecake in for 1½ hours to prevent cracks, then chill for 4 hours.

7 Whip the double cream, if using, to soft peaks. Run a knife round the cheesecake, then remove the tin. Swirl the cream on top, if liked. Scatter with the reserved chopped stem ginger.

Chocolate walnut torte

IN THE TRUE TRADITION of flourless cakes, this is based on ground walnuts and chocolate, lightened with meringue. The mixture is baked slowly in a low oven so the edges of the cake do not dry, and the result is beautifully moist.

SERVES SERVES 8	**PREP** 20-25 MINS PLUS CHILLING	**COOK** 60-70 MINS

Ingredients

FOR THE CAKE

125g (4½oz) unsalted butter

30g (1oz) plain flour, for the tin

375g (13oz) plain chocolate

250g (9oz) walnut pieces

4 eggs

200g (7oz) caster sugar

FOR THE CHANTILLY CREAM (optional)

250ml (9fl oz) double cream

1 tbsp caster sugar

½ tsp vanilla essence

LINE THE TIN

1 **Melt 30g (1oz) of the butter,** and use to brush the base and sides of a 23cm (9in) springform tin. Line the base with a circle of baking parchment, and butter that too. Sprinkle in 30g (1oz) plain flour, then turn and shake the tin to evenly coat. Shake out the excess. Set aside.

MAKE THE TORTE MIXTURE

2 **Preheat the oven** to 150°C (300°F/Gas 2). Chop 110g (3¾oz) of the chocolate and set a few walnuts aside. Grind the chocolate with half the remaining walnuts in a food processor. Repeat with another 110g (3¾oz) chocolate and the remaining nuts. Separate the eggs. With a wooden spoon, cream the butter. Add three-quarters of the sugar, and beat for 2-3 minutes, until light and fluffy.

3 **Add the egg yolks** one by one, beating thoroughly after each addition to avoid the risk of the mixture curdling. Stir in both batches of the ground chocolate and walnut mixture.

4 **Whisk the egg whites** until stiff. Sprinkle in the remaining sugar, and continue whisking until glossy. Add the meringue to the chocolate mixture, and fold them together.

BAKE THE TORTE

5 **Transfer the torte mixture** to the prepared tin and smooth the top. Bake until a skewer inserted in the centre of the torte comes out clean. It should take 60-70 minutes.

6 **Allow the torte** to cool completely in the tin. When completely cold, release the hinge on the side of the cake tin, and lift it gently away from the cake. The torte is so delicate, it is best served still on the base of the cake tin.

7 **You can choose** to serve the torte now, as it is, or dusted with icing sugar, or cocoa powder. Serve crème fraiche or lightly whipped cream on the side. If you wish to make it more spectacular, however, follow the next steps to finish the decoration.

FINISH THE TORTE

8 **Make the Chantilly cream,** if wanted: whip the cream in a bowl set within a larger bowl of iced water, until soft peaks form. Add the sugar and vanilla, and whip until soft peaks form again. Taste, to see if it is sweet enough; you may want to add more sugar.

9 **With a palette knife,** spread the cream evenly over the top of the cake. Place the cake on a serving plate and chill for about 1 hour. For the topping, chop the remaining chocolate, and melt it in a bowl placed in a saucepan of hot water (make sure the base of the bowl does not touch the water). Meanwhile, chop the reserved walnuts. Make a baking parchment piping cone and fill with the chocolate. Pipe the chocolate lightly over the cake, and sprinkle with the walnuts.

 VARIATION: Chocolate almond torte

Almonds add crunch to this variation.

1 Replace the walnuts with the same quantity of whole blanched almonds. Toast the almonds before grinding, and make the cake as directed.

2 Omit the Chantilly cream and chocolate topping, and decorate the cake as follows: cut 4–5 x 2cm (¾in) wide strips of thin card, and lay them on top of the cake. Sprinkle with icing sugar. Carefully lift off the strips and discard the excess sugar.

3 Lay the strips back on the cake to make a diagonal lattice on the sugar bands. Sift cocoa powder generously over the top, and carefully lift off the card strips, discarding the excess cocoa powder.

Oeufs à la neige

A TIME-HONOURED FRENCH DESSERT, where simple meringues are poached, then served on a pool of vanilla custard, decorated with flaked almonds and trails of caramel. If you don't have a vanilla pod, use 1 tsp vanilla extract instead for this recipe. Never buy anything labelled 'vanilla essence'; it is synthetic and tastes nothing like the real thing. The custard can be made 1 day ahead and kept, covered, in the refrigerator.

SERVES	PREP	COOK
SERVES 8	35-40 MINS	45-50 MINS

Ingredients

FOR THE VANILLA CUSTARD

750ml (1¼ pints) milk

1 vanilla pod, or 1 tsp vanilla extract

100g (3½oz) caster sugar

8 egg yolks

2 tbsp cornflour

FOR THE MERINGUE

8 egg whites

salt

400g (14oz) caster sugar

FOR THE DECORATION

45g (1½oz) flaked almonds

200g (7oz) caster sugar

MAKE THE CUSTARD AND TOAST THE ALMONDS

1 **Pour the milk** into a saucepan. Cut the vanilla pod, if using, lengthways, and add to the milk. Bring the milk just to a boil, then remove the pan from the heat. Cover, and let stand in a warm place for 10-15 minutes.

2 **Set aside one-quarter** of the milk. Add the sugar to the remaining hot milk, and stir until dissolved. Beat the egg yolks with the cornflour in a bowl. Whisk in the sweetened hot milk just until the mixture is smooth.

3 **Pour the custard** back into the saucepan and cook over medium heat, stirring constantly, until it comes just to a boil and is thick enough to coat the back of the spoon; the custard will curdle if boiled further.

4 **Remove the pan** from the heat, stir in the reserved milk, then strain into a bowl. Rinse the vanilla pod, dry, and store to use again. Stir in the vanilla extract, if using. Cover tightly with clingfilm to prevent a skin from forming on the surface of the custard, and let cool. Finally, chill the custard sauce.

5 **Preheat the oven** to 180°C (350°F/Gas 4). Spread the almonds on a baking sheet, and toast in the oven for 10-12 minutes, until lightly browned, stirring occasionally so that they colour evenly. Set aside.

MAKE AND POACH THE MERINGUES

6 **Put the egg whites** into a metal bowl with a pinch of salt, and whisk until stiff. Sprinkle in 60-75g (2-2½oz) of the sugar, and continue whisking for about 30 seconds, until glossy, to make a light meringue. Fold in the remaining sugar gradually and thoroughly.

7 **Bring a large, wide pan** of water to a simmer. Dip a dessert spoon into the water, then use it to scoop out a large spoonful of meringue. Use a second spoon to shape the meringue into a neat oval, turning the spoons one against the other.

8 **Drop the meringue** into the simmering water. Quickly continue shaping 6-7 more, dipping the spoons into the water so that they do not stick. Poach for 5-7 minutes, until firm and puffed.

9 **Lift the meringues** out of the water with a slotted spoon; drain on kitchen paper. Shape and cook the remaining meringue in the same way. The meringues will deflate slightly as they cool.

MAKE THE CARAMEL AND FINISH THE DISH

10 **Pour the chilled custard** into a wide, shallow serving dish. Using a slotted spoon, arrange the meringues over the custard. Make the caramel: put the sugar and 125ml (4fl oz) water into a small frying pan, and heat gently until the sugar is dissolved, stirring occasionally. Bring to a boil, and boil without stirring, until the syrup starts to turn golden around the edge; it should take 8-10 minutes, but watch it like a hawk as it can easily burn.

11 **Reduce the heat,** and continue cooking until the caramel is a deep golden brown, swirling the pan once or twice so it colours evenly. Remove from the heat, and immediately plunge the base of the pan into a bowl of cold water to stop the caramel cooking. Delicately drizzle the caramel over the meringues. Sprinkle with the toasted almonds and serve immediately.

Baked peaches with amaretti

A CLASSIC FROM NORTHERN ITALY, as delicious as it is easy to prepare, this can be served hot or cold. Amaretti biscuits, with their hint of bitter almonds, pick up the sweetness of the peaches. Choose fruits that feel heavy for their size, showing they contain lots of juice.

SERVES	PREP	COOK
SERVES 6	15–20 MINS	1–1¼ HRS

Ingredients

FOR THE PEACHES

7 large peaches, total weight about 1kg (2¼lb)

8–10 amaretti biscuits

60g (2oz) caster sugar

1 egg yolk

unsalted butter, for the dish

FOR THE FLAVOURED CREAM

125ml (4fl oz) double cream

1–2 tbsp caster sugar

1–2 tbsp amaretto liqueur

SCALD, STONE, AND PEEL 1 PEACH

1 **Bring a small saucepan** of water to a boil. Immerse 1 peach in the water for 10 seconds. Remove and plunge into iced water. With a small knife, cut the peach in half, using the indentation on one side of the peach, as a guide.

2 **Using both hands,** give a quick, sharp twist to each half to loosen it from the stone. Scoop out the stone with a small knife. Peel the skin from the peach halves. Discard the stone and skin.

PREPARE THE FILLING

3 **Preheat the oven** to 180°C (350°F/Gas 4). Crush the amaretti in a plastic bag with a rolling pin and pour them into a bowl. Put the 2 peeled peach halves in the food processor. Process to a thick, smooth purée.

4 **Transfer the peach purée** to a large bowl, scraping it from the food processor with a spatula. Add the sugar, egg yolk, and amaretti crumbs to the peach, and mix well.

PREPARE, FILL, AND BAKE THE PEACHES

5 **Butter a baking dish.** Halve and remove the stone from the remaining peaches, without peeling them. If necessary, spoon out a little of the flesh from the centre of each, so the cavity is large enough for the filling.

6 **Set the peach halves,** cut-side up, in the baking dish. Spoon some filling into each. Bake for 1–1¼ hours, until tender. Meanwhile, whip together the cream, sugar, and liqueur until stiff peaks form. Transfer the hot peaches to individual serving plates, and spoon any juices over. Serve the flavoured cream in a separate bowl.

Profiteroles with ice cream

LIGHT AND AIRY CHOUX PASTRY PUFFS are filled with chocolate ice cream for extra decadence, and topped with a hot chocolate sauce. The choux puffs can be kept in an airtight container for up to 3 days. Assemble the profiteroles just before serving.

SERVES	PREP	COOK
SERVES 8	25–30 MINS	25–30 MINS

Ingredients

FOR THE ICE CREAM

¾ quantity chocolate ice cream (p486), or 750ml (1¼ pints) bought good-quality chocolate ice cream

FOR THE CHOUX PASTRY

75g (2½oz) unsalted butter

½ tsp salt

100g (3½oz) plain flour, sifted

4 eggs

FOR THE EGG GLAZE

1 egg

½ tsp salt

FOR THE CHOCOLATE SAUCE

375g (13oz) good-quality plain chocolate

250ml (9fl oz) double cream

2 tbsp Cognac (optional)

PREPARE THE CHOUX PASTRY

1 **Preheat the oven** to 200°C (400°F/Gas 6). Brush a baking sheet with butter. Cut the butter into pieces. Put them into a saucepan, with 175ml (6fl oz) water and the salt. Heat until melted. Bring just to a boil. Add the flour all at once and beat vigorously, until smooth. Return to low heat and beat to dry out the dough, then remove from the heat.

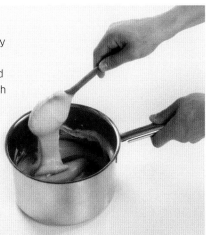

2 **Mix in** and beat 3 of the eggs, 1 at a time, beating thoroughly after each addition. Beat the remaining egg in a small bowl, and add it little by little until the dough is shiny and soft. You may not need it all. Fit a piping bag with a plain nozzle, and add the choux dough. Squeeze out the dough in 30–35 x 2.5cm (1in) mounds on the baking sheet, spaced well apart.

MAKE THE GLAZE; BAKE THE PROFITEROLES

3 **Beat the egg** with the salt; leave for 2–3 minutes until smooth. Brush some on each profiterole. Press down lightly on each round with the tines of a fork, in one direction and then in the other, for a criss-cross pattern.

4 **Bake in the heated oven** for 25–30 minutes, until firm and brown. Transfer to a wire rack. With a sharp knife, make a slit in each to release steam. Let cool. Meanwhile, allow the ice cream to soften in the refrigerator.

MAKE THE CHOCOLATE SAUCE AND FINISH THE PROFITEROLES

5 **Chop the chocolate** and put in a medium heavy-based saucepan with the cream. Heat gently, stirring with a wooden spoon, until the chocolate has melted and the mixture is smooth and thick.

6 **If using Cognac,** stir it into the chocolate-and-cream mixture. Keep the sauce warm. Fill each profiterole with a ball of ice cream. Pile in a shallow dish, pour the warm chocolate sauce over and serve immediately.

Apricot and hazelnut ice cream

VANILLA ICE CREAM IS TRANSFORMED by hazelnuts and dried apricots in this Burgundian recipe. A hazelnut liqueur, such as Frangelico, adds sparkle to the recipe. Use apricot brandy instead, if you prefer. The ice cream can be made up to 2 weeks ahead; but if it has been frozen for more than 12 hours, let it soften for about 30 minutes in the refrigerator before serving.

SERVES	PREP	COOK
SERVES 6	2½–3 HRS PLUS FREEZING	25–30 MINS

Ingredients

90g (3oz) dried apricots

175ml (6fl oz) hazelnut liqueur

125g (4½oz) hazelnuts

600ml (1 pint) milk

1 vanilla pod

135g (5oz) caster sugar

8 egg yolks

2 tbsp cornflour

250ml (8fl oz) double cream

1tsp vanilla essence (optional)

PREPARE THE APRICOTS AND HAZELNUTS

1 **Put the apricots** into a bowl, and pour over enough boiling water to cover them. Let soak for 10–15 minutes. Drain and put into a small jar. Pour over the liqueur and cover tightly. Let soak for at least 2 hours, and up to 2 days. Strain, reserving the liqueur. Purée the apricots in a food processor and set aside.

2 **Toasting nuts** intensifies their flavour, and adds crunch to their texture. It also loosens the skin for easy removal. Preheat the oven to 180°C (350°F/Gas 4). Toast the nuts on a baking sheet for 12–15 minutes, until lightly browned, stirring occasionally. While the nuts are still hot, rub them in an old, clean tea towel to remove the skins, then let cool. The skins will slip off easily while you rub; discard the skins. Place the nuts on a chopping board.

3 **With a sharp knife,** coarsely chop the hazelnuts. Reserve half the nuts for serving. If you are making the ice cream well ahead of time, store both the reserved hazelnuts and the liqueur in airtight containers.

MAKE THE VANILLA CUSTARD

4 **Pour the milk** into a heavy saucepan. Cut the vanilla pod lengthways, if using. Add to the pan. Bring the milk just to a boil. Remove from the heat. Cover, and let stand in a warm place for 10–15 minutes. Set aside one-quarter of the milk. Add the sugar to the remaining hot milk, and stir until dissolved.

5 **Beat the egg yolks** with the cornflour in a bowl. Add the sweetened hot milk, and whisk just until smooth. Pour the custard back into the saucepan and cook over medium heat, stirring constantly with a wooden spoon, until it comes just to a boil and thickens enough to coat the back of the spoon. Your finger will leave a clear trail across the spoon.

6 **Remove the pan** from the heat, stir in the reserved milk, then strain into a bowl. Stir in the vanilla essence, if using. Cover tightly with clingfilm to prevent a skin forming on the surface of the custard, and let cool. The vanilla pod can be rinsed and dried to use again.

FREEZE THE ICE CREAM

7 **If the custard has formed a skin,** whisk to dissolve it back into the mixture. Pour the custard into an ice-cream maker and churn it until slushy, following the manufacturer's directions. Meanwhile, chill 2 bowls in the freezer. Pour the cream into 1 of the chilled bowls, and whip until soft peaks form. Do not over-whip until it is too stiff, or the cream may separate; you are aiming for a floppy consistency.

8 **Add half the hazelnuts** and the apricot purée to the slushy vanilla ice cream, and stir until evenly mixed. Add the whipped cream, stir lightly, and continue freezing in the ice-cream maker until firm. Transfer the ice cream to the second chilled bowl. Cover tightly and store in the freezer until needed. If necessary, bring it from the freezer and allow to soften in the refrigerator before serving. Scoop the ice cream into chilled glasses or bowls, spoon over the reserved apricot soaking liqueur, top with the reserved hazelnuts, and serve at once.

 ## VARIATION: Prune and Armagnac ice cream

A combination of 2 Gascon favourites, prunes and Armagnac, makes this a fine end to a festive meal.

1 Omit the apricots, hazelnut liqueur, and hazelnuts. Put 150g (5½oz) pitted prunes into a small bowl. Pour over 175ml (6fl oz) Armagnac, and let the prunes soak as directed for the apricots. Strain the prunes, reserving the liqueur. Purée the prunes.

2 Make and chill the vanilla custard as directed. Make and freeze the ice cream as directed, substituting the prunes and Armagnac for the apricots and hazelnut liqueur.

3 Serve the ice cream with the reserved liqueur as directed, topped with more pitted prunes, if you like.

Strawberry-raspberry hazelnut tart

TRADITIONALLY, ITALIAN FRUIT TARTS ARE SIMPLE, often nothing more than fresh fruit on a pastry base. This *crostata* is packed with delicious Marsala-flavoured whipped cream. The hazelnut pastry dough can be made up to 2 days ahead and refrigerated, or it can be frozen.

SERVES
SERVES 6-8

PREP
35-40 MINS

COOK
30-35 MINS

Ingredients

FOR THE HAZELNUT PASTRY DOUGH

125g (4½oz) hazelnuts

75g (2½oz) granulated sugar

125g (4½oz) plain flour, plus more if needed

125g (4½oz) unsalted butter

1 egg

FOR THE FILLING

250ml (9fl oz) double cream

3-4 tbsp icing sugar, plus more to dust

2 tbsp Marsala wine

125g (4½oz) raspberries

300g (10oz) strawberries

MAKE THE HAZELNUT PASTRY DOUGH

1 **Toast and skin the hazelnuts** (p500). Reserve a few for decoration. In a food processor, grind the remaining hazelnuts, with the sugar, to a fine powder. Do not overwork or the oil from the nuts will create a paste. Sift the flour on to a work surface, add the ground nut mixture, and make a large well in the centre.

2 **Cut the butter** into pieces, and add to the well with the egg. Using your fingertips, work the ingredients in the well until soft and thoroughly mixed, then draw in the hazelnut powder and the flour. Work with your fingers until you form coarse crumbs that start sticking together. Lightly press the crumbs together to form a ball of dough.

3 **Lightly flour** the work surface, then blend the dough by pushing it away from you with the heel of your hand. Gather it up and continue to blend, until it peels easily from the work surface. Shape into a ball, wrap, and chill for at least 30 minutes, until firm.

BAKE THE PASTRY SHELL

4 **Preheat the oven** to 180°C (350°F/Gas 4). Brush a 23-25cm (9-10in) springform tart tin with melted butter. With the back of a spoon, or the heel of your hand, press the dough into the tin to make an even shell. Chill for at least 15 minutes, until firm. Bake for 30-35 minute until golden brown and shrinking slightly from the tin. Cool, then remove the sides of the tin.

ASSEMBLE THE TART

5 **Make the Marsala whipped cream:** using a whisk, whip the double cream in a chilled bowl until it forms soft peaks. Add the icing sugar and Marsala. Continue whipping until the cream forms stiff peaks.

6 **Pick over the raspberries.** Hull the strawberries, and wash them only if they are dirty (washing softens strawberries). With a small knife, cut the strawberries in half, or into quarters if they are large.

7 **Using a palette knife,** spread two-thirds of the Marsala whipped cream evenly over the cooled hazelnut pastry, just to the edge. Ensure your pastry is completely cold before you start.

8 **Arrange most of the strawberries** and raspberries evely over the Marsala whipped cream. Top with the remaining Marsala cream, then scatter with the remaining fruits and the reserved hazelnuts. Chill, then sift over a little icing sugar to serve.

Raspberry soufflés, kirsch custard

A HOT, BAKED SOUFFLÉ need not be intimidating. What could be simpler than puréed fruit folded into meringue and baked? Given the few ingredients of this recipe, it is important that the raspberries be as sweet, juicy, and highly flavoured as possible.

SERVES	PREP	COOK
SERVES 6	20–25 MINS	10–12 MINS

Ingredients

FOR THE KIRSCH CUSTARD

375ml (13fl oz) milk

50g (1¾oz) caster sugar

5 egg yolks

1 tbsp cornflour

2–3 tbsp kirsch

FOR THE SOUFFLÉS

100g (3½oz) caster sugar

500g (1lb 2oz) raspberries

5 egg whites

2–3 tbsp icing sugar, to serve

MAKE THE CUSTARD

1 **Pour the milk** into a heavy-based saucepan and bring just to a boil over medium heat. Set aside a quarter of the milk. Add the sugar to the remaining milk, and stir until dissolved. Put the yolks and cornflour into a bowl. Whisk together lightly, until the mixture is smooth. Add the sweetened milk to the egg yolks, whisking until just smooth.

2 **Cook the custard** over medium heat, stirring constantly, until it comes just to a boil and thickens enough to coat the back of a spoon. (Your finger will leave a clear trail across the spoon.) Remove from the heat. Stir the reserved milk into the custard, then strain into a cold bowl and let cool. If it forms a skin, whisk to dissolve. Stir in the kirsch. Cover tightly and refrigerate.

PREPARE AND BAKE THE PUDDINGS

3 **Brush 6 ramekins** with butter. Sprinkle with sugar, tilting to coat evenly. Preheat the oven to 190°C (375°F/Gas 5). Purée the raspberries with half the sugar in a food processor. Taste; add more sugar if the purée is tart.

4 **Using a small ladle,** work the purée through a sieve into a large bowl to remove the pips. Whisk the egg whites until stiff. Sprinkle in the remaining caster sugar and continue whisking for about 20 seconds, until glossy, to form a light meringue.

5 **Add about one-quarter** of the meringue to the raspberry purée, and stir. Add this mixture to the remaining meringue and fold together, until the mixture is an even colour.

6 **Spoon the mixture** into the prepared ramekins. Set them on a baking sheet for easy handling. Bake in the oven for 10–12 minutes, until puffed and lightly browned on top. Sift over the icing sugar, and serve immediately, with the kirsch custard on the side.

Gratin of fresh berries with sabayon

FLUFFY SABAYON SAUCE HERE IS FLAVOURED with lemon zest and Grand Marnier or Marsala, and is grilled to an attractive golden brown. Use a blow torch instead of a grill, if you have one. Be sure to choose berries that are plump, and full of flavour.

SERVES	PREP	COOK
SERVES 4	15-20 MINS	1-2 MINS

3 egg yolks
50g (1¾oz) caster sugar
90ml (3fl oz) Grand Marnier or Marsala

Ingredients

375g (13oz) mixed berries, such as raspberries, strawberries, blackberries, or blueberries

1 lemon

PREPARE THE BERRIES

1 **Pick over the berries,** washing them only if they are dirty. Hull the strawberries. Cut any large berries into halves or quarters. Divide the berries evenly among 4 individual gratin dishes or heatproof dessert plates, and chill in the refrigerator.

MAKE THE SABAYON

2 **Heat the grill.** Grate the zest from half the lemon. Put the egg yolks, sugar, and Grand Marnier in a large heatproof bowl, and whisk them to mix. Set the bowl over a saucepan half-filled with hot but not simmering water (the base of the bowl must not touch the water), and start to whisk.

3 **Continue whisking** for 5-8 minutes, until the mixture is frothy and thick enough to leave a ribbon trail. Take the sauce from the pan of hot water, whisk in the zest, and continue whisking for 1-2 minutes until slightly cooled.

BROWN THE GRATIN

4 **Arrange the gratin dishes** on a baking sheet, and spoon the sabayon over and around the berries. Grill about 15cm (6in) from the heat for 1-2 minutes, until the sabayon is golden brown and the fruit is warm.

5 **Put each of the hot dishes** on to plates to prevent burning you or your guests' hands. Serve immediately while the berries are juicy, and the dishes still crackling from the heat of the grill.

Chocolate decadence

RICH AND DENSE, this cake relies wholly on melted chocolate, butter, and eggs, with only 2 spoons of sugar and 1 of flour, so your ingredients – most especially the chocolate – must be of the very best quality you can afford to make this dessert a show-stopper. A tart raspberry coulis cuts through the richness of the dish. This cake can be stored for up to 1 week in an airtight container (it will become even more moist), and it also freezes well.

SERVES	PREP	COOK
SERVES 8	30–40 MINS PLUS CHILLING	20 MINS

Ingredients

FOR THE CAKE

500g (1lb 2oz) plain chocolate

150g (5½oz) unsalted butter

6 eggs

2 tbsp caster sugar

1 tbsp plain flour, plus more for the tin

FOR THE RASPBERRY COULIS

750g (1lb 10oz) raspberries, plus more to serve

2–3 tbsp icing sugar

TO SERVE

crème fraîche or whipped double cream

MAKE THE CHOCOLATE CAKE

1 **Preheat the oven** to 200°C (400°F/Gas 6). Butter and base line a 23cm (9in) springform tin. Sprinkle in 2–3 tbsp flour, turn and shake to coat, then tap to remove excess. Coarsely pulse-chop the chocolate in a food processor. Cut the butter into pieces, and put them in a large heatproof bowl with the chocolate. Set over a pan of hot, but not simmering, water. Stir until melted and smooth. Let cool, stirring occasionally.

2 **Separate the eggs.** Beat the egg yolks into the chocolate mixture with the wooden spoon, until evenly mixed. It is vital that the chocolate should be cool before you attempt this, or the eggs will cook and split the mixture.

3 **Put the egg whites** in a scrupulously clean metal bowl, and beat with a hand whisk or electric mixer, until stiff. Add the sugar; continue whisking for about 20 seconds, until glossy, to make a light meringue.

4 **Stir the flour** into the chocolate mixture, then fold in one-third of the egg whites to lighten it. Fold in the remaining whisked egg whites in 2 batches. Transfer to the cake tin. Tap on the work surface to knock out any air bubbles. Bake for about 20 minutes, until crusty on top but soft in the centre. Let cool completely in the tin, set on a wire rack. When cold, chill for 2 hours. Unmould and peel off the paper.

PREPARE THE RASPBERRY COULIS

5 Pick over the raspberries, washing them only if they are dirty. Put the raspberries in a food processor or blender. Work the raspberries in the machine until they are puréed. Add icing sugar to taste. Purée again until the sugar is evenly blended.

6 Work the puréed raspberries through a sieve into a bowl to remove the seeds. Discard the seeds. If making in advance, wrap tightly and store in the refrigerator, being sure to bring the coulis to room temperature before serving.

FINISH THE CAKE

7 Using a serrated knife, cut the cake into 8 wedges. Set 1 wedge in the centre of each plate. Dipping the knife in hot water between slices makes it easy to cut neat wedges. Ladle a small pool of raspberry coulis on to each plate, near the tip of the wedge of cake.

8 If you like, dip the tip of a small knife into some double cream, and drizzle a curved line on the coulis. Pull the tip of the knife across the cream to make a feathered design. Decorate each plate with a few whole raspberries, and serve with crème fraîche or whipped cream.

VARIATION: Chocolate decadence with passion fruit sauce

If passion fruit are not available, substitute 2 ripe mangoes.

1 Omit the raspberries and the raspberry coulis. Make and bake the cake exactly as directed in the main recipe.

2 Make a passion fruit sauce: halve 18-20 passion fruit, and scrape the orange pulp and black seeds into a fine sieve set over a bowl. (When buying passion fruit, be sure to buy those with wrinkled skins. This may seem counterintuitive, but the wrinkled fruits are the ripest, and contain the maximum delicious juice and pulp.) Now you can choose how you would prefer your sauce: either rub the pulp through a sieve, with a wooden spoon, then discard the seeds, or don't sieve the pulp and keep in the crunchy seeds. Some people love their crunch; others find them too hard to eat. Beat 30-37g (1-1¼oz) icing sugar into the passion fruit pulp and taste, adding more sugar if you would prefer to have a sweeter sauce. Chill, tightly covered, until ready to serve.

3 Serve the cake as directed, on a pool of the orange passion fruit sauce. Serve whipped cream or crème fraîche in a pile next to each slice of cake, if you like.

Crêpes Suzette

IN THIS MOST CLASSIC OF FRENCH DESSERTS, thin crêpes are spread with orange butter, sautéed to caramelize, then flamed just before serving. A sure way to create culinary drama, as well as a nostalgic treat. The crêpes can be made up to 3 days ahead; they won't suffer if you layer them up with a sheet of baking parchment between each one and store in a plastic bag in the refrigerator.

SERVES	PREP	COOK
SERVES 6-8	40-50 MINS PLUS STANDING	45-60 MINS

Ingredients

FOR THE CRÊPES

90g (3oz) unsalted butter, plus more if needed

175g (6oz) plain flour

1 tbsp caster sugar

½ tsp salt

4 eggs

375ml (13fl oz) milk, plus more if needed

FOR THE ORANGE BUTTER

175g (6oz) unsalted butter, at room temperature

30g (1oz) icing sugar

3 large oranges

1 tbsp Grand Marnier (optional)

FOR FLAMING

75ml (2½fl oz) brandy

75ml (2½fl oz) Grand Marnier

MAKE THE CRÊPE BATTER

1 **Melt the butter** in a small saucepan, and set aside to cool; do not skip this step, as the butter needs to be cool when it is added to the rest of the batter ingredients, or it could begin to cook the eggs. Sift the flour into a large bowl, holding the sieve up high to aerate the flour as it falls down. Add the caster sugar and the salt, and stir so everything is evenly mixed. Make a well in the centre of the flour, and break the eggs into the well. Whisk the eggs together in the well just until mixed.

2 **Pour half the milk** into the eggs in a slow, steady stream, whisking constantly and gradually drawing in the flour from the sides of the well, to make a smooth batter. Gradually whisk in half the cooled, melted butter, still drawing in the flour, until all has been incorporated. Whisk the mixture well, until it is completely smooth. Now add enough of the remaining milk to give a batter that is about the consistency of single cream (you may not need all the milk). Cover and let the batter stand at room temperature for at least 30 minutes.

MAKE THE ORANGE BUTTER AND ORANGE JULIENNE

3 **Put the butter** and icing sugar in a bowl, and cream them together with a wooden spoon. This may take up to 5 minutes, as you must make sure the mixture is smooth, light, and airy.

4 **Finely grate the zest** from 2 of the oranges. With a vegetable peeler, pare the zest from the remaining orange; set aside. Cut the pith and skin from all 3 oranges. Slide the knife down both sides of each segment to cut it free. Reserve the segments and their juice. Add the zest, and 2 tbsp of juice, to the butter with the Grand Marnier, if using. Beat until smooth. Cover, and keep at room temperature.

5 **Make the orange julienne:** cut the pared orange zest lengthways into the thinnest possible julienne strips. Bring a small pan of cold water to a boil, add the strips, and simmer for 2 minutes. Drain, rinse, and drain again. Reserve the strips for decoration.

FRY THE CRÊPES

6 **If necessary,** stir a little more milk into the batter to make it the consistency of single cream again (it may have thickened on standing). Add the remaining melted butter to the crêpe pan and heat gently, then pour any excess butter into a small bowl, leaving a thin film in the pan.

7 **Reheat the pan,** then add a drop of batter to test the temperature: when it splatters briskly, it is hot enough for frying. Stir the batter in the bowl briefly, then quickly ladle a little (2–3 tbsp) into the pan. Do not add too much, or the crêpe will be thick. If too little is added, it will have holes.

8 **Immediately tilt the pan** with a twist of the wrist, shaking so the base is evenly covered with batter. Fry over medium-high heat for about 1 minutes, until set on top, and brown underneath. Gently loosen the edge of the crêpe with a palette knife.

9 **Turn the crêpe** quickly: either slide the palette knife underneath and flip it over, or use the fingertips of both hands. You can also toss the crêpe, if you are feeling brave. Continue frying over medium-high heat for 30–60 seconds, until brown on the other side. Slide on to a plate, with the side cooked first facing up. Continue frying the crêpes, buttering the pan sparingly again only when the crêpes start to stick, until all the batter has been used up.

ASSEMBLE AND FLAME THE CRÊPES

10 **Spread the orange butter** over the side of each crêpe that was cooked first, stacking the buttered crêpes up again on another plate. Heat the frying pan over medium heat. Add 1 crêpe, orange-butter-side down. Cook briskly for about 1 minute, until very hot.

11 **Using a palette knife,** fold the crêpe in half and then into quarters to make a triangle. Transfer the folded crêpe to a plate, and add another crêpe to the pan, again orange-butter-side down. Continue to fry and fold the crêpes in this way, overlapping them around the side of the plate.

12 **Arrange the caramelized crêpes** in the hot frying pan, distributing them evenly. If the pan becomes too full, you may have to flame them in 2 batches (keep the first batch warm while you flame the remaining crêpes). Heat the brandy and Grand Marnier in a small saucepan, then pour them over the crêpes.

13 **Hold a lighted match** to the side of the pan, to set the alcohol alight. Baste the crêpes with the alcohol until the flames die; it should only take 2–3 minutes. (Stand back and keep your hair and face away from the pan). Divide the flamed crêpes among warmed plates, and spoon the sauce from the pan over them. Decorate with the orange segments and orange julienne, and serve immediately.

Apple and almond galettes

THIS ELEGANT DESSERT IS DECEPTIVELY SIMPLE to make. A delicate layer of marzipan adds richness to the thin, crisp pastry bases, and the galettes are caramelized halfway through baking by a sprinkling of sugar, forming the only decoration necessary. A scoop of ice-cold Apple and Calvados Sorbet (p515) would make the perfect finishing touch. The galettes must be baked just before serving.

SERVES	PREP	COOK
SERVES 8	25–30 MINS	20–30 MINS

1 lemon
8 small, tart, green eating apples
50g (1¾oz) granulated sugar

Ingredients

500g (1lb 2oz) puff pastry
215g (7½oz) marzipan

PREPARE THE PUFF PASTRY ROUNDS

1 **Lightly flour** a work surface. Roll out half the pastry to a 35cm (14in) square, about 3mm (⅛in) thick. Using a 15cm (6in) plate as a guide, cut out 4 rounds. Sprinkle 2 baking sheets with water. Set the rounds on 1 baking sheet, and prick each with a fork, avoiding the edge. Repeat with the remaining dough. Chill for 15 minutes. Divide the marzipan into 8, and roll each portion into a ball.

2 **Spread a sheet** of baking parchment on the work surface. Set 1 ball of marzipan on the parchment, and cover with another sheet. Roll out the marzipan to a 12.5cm (5in) round between the sheets. Set on top of a pastry dough round, leaving a 1cm (½in) border. Repeat with the remaining marzipan and pastry bases. Chill, until ready to bake.

PREPARE THE APPLES

3 **Cut the lemon** in half, and squeeze the juice from 1 half into a small bowl. Peel the apples, then halve and core them. Rub them with the remaining lemon half, to prevent them from turning brown. Cut into thin slices, brushing with lemon juice as you work.

FINISH AND BAKE THE GALETTES

4 **Preheat the oven** to 220°C (425°F/Gas 7). Arrange the apple slices, overlapping them slightly, in a ring on the marzipan rounds, covering them completely. Leave a thin border of puff pastry dough around the edge.

5 **Bake the apple** and almond galettes for 15–20 minutes, until the pastry edges have risen around the marzipan, and are light golden. Sprinkle the apples evenly with the sugar.

6 **Return to the oven,** and continue baking for 5–10 minutes, or until the apples are golden brown, caramelized around the edges and just tender when tested with the tip of a small knife. Transfer to warmed individual serving plates, and serve at once.

Grapefruit granita, almond biscuits

A REFRESHING END to a rich dinner. Unlike a smooth sorbet, the texture should resemble coarse snow. This effect is achieved by whisking during the freezing process. The almond All Souls' Day biscuits are a lovely accompaniment.

SERVES	PREP	COOK
SERVES 4	15-20 MINS PLUS FREEZING	35-40 MINS

Ingredients

FOR THE GRANITA

3 grapefruit

½ lemon

50g (1¾oz) sugar, plus more to taste

FOR THE ALL SOULS' DAY BISCUITS

90g (3oz) plain flour

15g (½oz) butter

1 lemon

150g (5½oz) ground almonds

125g (4½oz) caster sugar

1 tbsp brandy

1 egg

12-15 whole, blanched almonds

MAKE AND FREEZE THE GRANITA

1 **Thinly pare the zest** from half a grapefruit, leaving behind the white pith. Reserve the pared zest. Squeeze the juice from all the grapefruits. Strain the juice into a non-metallic bowl, along with the lemon juice. Add half the sugar and stir until dissolved. Taste, adding more sugar if you like.

2 **Freeze the liquid** for 45-60 minutes, until ice starts to form on top. Whisk to break the ice. Continue freezing, whisking the mixture to break the ice about once an hour, until the granita is slushy and slightly granular. Allow 4-5 hours.

MAKE THE BISCUITS

3 **Preheat the oven** to 180°C (350°F/Gas 4). Butter a baking sheet and sprinkle with flour. Sift the flour into a bowl. Add butter, grated lemon zest, ground almonds, sugar, and brandy. Whisk the egg and stir into the flour mixture to form a dough.

4 **Wet your hands** and roll the dough into 2.5cm (1in) balls. Place on the baking sheet, leaving 2.5cm (1in) between the biscuits. Press an almond into each. Bake for 15-20 minutes, until light brown. Let cool on a wire rack.

PREPARE THE ZEST

5 **With a very sharp knife,** cut the pared grapefruit zest into fine julienne. In a small pan, dissolve the remaining 2 tbsp sugar in 2 tbsp water. Add the zest. Simmer for 12-15 minutes, until the water has evaporated and the zest is translucent. Spread on baking parchment. Let cool.

6 **Spoon the grapefruit granita** into 4 chilled glasses or bowls. Pile the candied zest on top, and serve at once, with the biscuits on the side.

Hazelnut meringue gâteau

THIS CLASSIC CAKE IS A SPECIALITY of Dax, a town in the foothills of the Pyrenees, and is known as a Dacquoise. Crisp rounds of hazelnut meringue are sandwiched with buttercream, flavoured with kirsch, in delicate tones of ivory and white. Use apricot brandy if you don't have any kirsch; it will be equally delicious.

SERVES	PREP	COOK
SERVES 6–8	50–60 MINS PLUS CHILLING	40–50 MINS

Ingredients

FOR THE HAZELNUT MERINGUE

250g (9oz) hazelnuts

300g (10oz) caster sugar

2 tbsp cornflour

6 egg whites

icing sugar, to dust

FOR THE BUTTERCREAM

100g (3½oz) caster sugar

4 egg yolks

250g (9oz) unsalted butter, at room temperature

2 tbsp kirsch, plus more if needed

MAKE THE HAZELNUT MERINGUE

1 **Brush 3 baking sheets** with melted butter, and line with baking parchment. Butter the paper and sprinkle with flour, discarding the excess. Trace 1 circle on each baking sheet, using a 20cm (8in) round cake tin as a guide. Toast the hazelnuts in the oven for 12–15 minutes, then skin (p500). Reserve a third for decoration. Put half the sugar and the remaining nuts in a food processor.

2 **Process, until the mixture is quite fine.** Do not overwork the nuts or they will release their oil, creating a paste. (Grinding with sugar helps prevent this.) Transfer the ground hazelnuts and sugar to a bowl, and stir in the cornflour.

3 **Put the egg whites** in a metal bowl. Beat with a whisk or electric mixer until stiff peaks form. Sprinkle in the remaining caster sugar and continue whisking, until glossy, to make a light meringue. Add a third of the hazelnut mixture, and fold together as lightly as possible. Fold in the remaining hazelnut mixture, in 2 batches.

BAKE THE MERINGUES

4 **Preheat the oven** to 130°C (250°F/Gas ½). Divide the hazelnut meringue evenly among the traced circles on the baking parchment, and spread it out with a palette knife to make 3 even, flat discs. Bake them in the oven, rotating the baking sheets occasionally for even cooking, for 40–50 minutes, or until the rounds are all lightly browned, and feel dry to the touch. Remove the baking sheets from the oven. Carefully peel the paper from the meringue rounds while they are still warm, transfer the meringues to a wire rack, and let cool completely.

MAKE THE BUTTERCREAM

5 **Put 150ml (5fl oz) water** and the caster sugar in a saucepan, and heat until dissolved. Boil the syrup without stirring, until it reaches the soft ball stage. To test, take the pan from the heat, dip a teaspoon in the hot syrup, remove, and let cool a few seconds. Take a little syrup between your finger and thumb; it should form a soft ball. (A sugar thermometer should register 115°C/239°F.)

6 **While the syrup is boiling,** beat the egg yolks with an electric mixer or whisk, just until mixed. Gradually pour the hot sugar syrup into the egg yolks in a steady stream, beating constantly. Continue beating at high speed for about 5 minutes, until the mixture is cool, and forms a thick mousse.

7 **Put the butter** in a bowl and beat it with an electric mixer or wooden spoon, until it is smooth and creamy. Gradually add the butter to the cool egg mousse, and beat to combine. (Be sure the egg mousse has cooled, or it will melt the butter). Beat in the kirsch, adding more to taste, if necessary.

ASSEMBLE THE GÂTEAU

8 **Cut a round of cardboard** to fit the gâteau. Add a dab of buttercream, set 1 meringue round (choose the ugliest) on the cardboard, and press down lightly so it sticks. Place the cardboard on an upturned cake tin, to raise it a little off the work surface, if you like.

9 **Spoon about a half** the buttercream on to the meringue round, and spread it out with a palette knife to cover the meringue evenly. Place a second meringue round on top, and spread it with all the remaining buttercream. Cover with the third, most attractive, of the meringue rounds, making sure all 3 rounds are stacked neatly.

DECORATE THE GÂTEAU

10 **With a small sieve,** cover the top of the gâteau thickly with a layer of sifted icing sugar. Finely chop the reserved hazelnuts. Sprinkle them on top of the gâteau. Chill for at least 1 hour, until firm. Transfer to a cake stand or serving plate.

 VARIATION: Almond meringue gâteau

Armagnac-flavoured butter cream and almond meringue combine in a punchy version of the classic Dacquoise.

1 Make the meringue mixture as directed in the main recipe, substituting 150g (5½oz) ground, toasted almonds for the hazelnuts. Shape and bake the meringue rounds as directed.

2 Make the buttercream as directed, substituting Armagnac or cognac for the kirsch. Alternatively, flavour the buttercream with coffee: dissolve 2 tbsp instant coffee granules in 2 tbsp hot water, cool it slightly, and beat into the buttercream.

3 Toast 90g (3oz) flaked almonds in the oven, watching carefully so that they do not catch and burn. Assemble the cake as directed. Decorate with the toasted almonds instead of the hazelnuts, and sprinkle with a few chocolate-coated coffee beans, if you like (these are especially appropriate if you chose to make a coffee-flavoured buttercream).

Trio of sorbets

WHAT BETTER WAY TO ENJOY the essence of fresh fruit? This trio makes a pretty picture in a bowl, complete with fresh fruit and berries. If you prefer, choose your favourite fruit, and increase the quantities to make just 1 sorbet. The sorbets can be kept for up to 1 week in the freezer. If they have been frozen for more than 1 day, remember to let them soften for 30 minutes in the refrigerator before serving, both to improve the texture and release the full flavour of the fruits.

SERVES	PREP	COOK
SERVES 8	40–50 MINS PLUS FREEZING	15–20 MINS

Ingredients

FOR THE SUGAR SYRUP

300g (10oz) granulated sugar, plus more if needed

FOR THE SORBETS

400g (14oz) raspberries, plus more if needed

3 lemons, plus more if needed

750g (1lb 10oz) ripe pears

2 tbsp Poire Williams liqueur, or to taste

625g (1lb 6oz) ripe peaches

PREPARE THE SUGAR SYRUP

1 **Combine the sugar** and 375ml (13fl oz) water in a saucepan, and heat until the sugar has dissolved. Bring to a boil, and boil without stirring for 2–3 minutes, until the syrup is clear. Pour the sugar syrup into a measuring jug, and let cool completely.

MAKE THE RASPBERRY SORBET

2 **Pick over the raspberries,** washing them only if they are dirty. Purée them in a food processor. Work the purée through a sieve held over a bowl, to remove the seeds. There should be 175ml (6fl oz) purée. If necessary, purée a few more berries.

3 **Squeeze the lemons;** there should be just over 125ml (4fl oz) juice. Keep the lemon halves. Add 4 tbsp water, 2 tbsp of the lemon juice, and one-third of the sugar syrup, to the raspberry purée. Taste, and stir in more lemon or sugar if needed. Chill, then taste again. Remember, flavours are blunted by the cold, so be sure they are concentrated.

4 **Pour the raspberry mixture** into an ice-cream maker, and churn until firm, following the manufacturer's directions. Meanwhile, chill a bowl in the freezer. Transfer the sorbet to the chilled bowl. Cover and freeze for at least 4 hours, to allow the flavour to mellow.

MAKE THE PEAR SORBET

5 **Pour half the remaining sugar syrup** into a small saucepan. Add 2 tbsp of the lemon juice. Peel the pears, then cut out the flower and stalk ends with a small knife. Cut each pear in half, then into quarters, and cut out the core. Rub all over with the reserved, squeezed lemon halves.

6 **Cut the pear quarters** into chunks, and drop them immediately into the saucepan of syrup. Bring to a boil, then simmer the pears for 5–10 minutes, until soft and translucent, depending on ripeness. Purée the pears with their syrup in a food processor, or purée them in 2 batches, in a blender. Always remember not to fill a blender jug too full; it could cause splashes and burns.

7 **Work the purée** through a sieve held over a bowl. There should be nearly 500ml (16fl oz) pear purée. Stir in the liqueur, and taste, adding more liqueur, lemon juice, or sugar if needed. Freeze the pear sorbet, as for the raspberry sorbet.

PREPARE THE PEACH SORBET

8 Immerse the peaches in a pan of boiling water for 10-20 seconds, depending on ripeness. Transfer them immediately to a bowl of cold water with a slotted spoon. Cut each in half. Using both hands, give a quick twist to each half, to loosen it from the stone. Discard the stone. With a small knife, peel off the skin; it should come off easily.

9 Cut the skinned peach halves into chunks, put them into a food processor, and add the remaining sugar syrup and lemon juice. Purée until smooth. There should be nearly 500ml (16fl oz) purée. Taste, and add more lemon juice, or sugar, if needed. Freeze as for the raspberry sorbet.

10 Soften all the sorbets in the refrigerator for 30 minutes before serving, so the texture is pleasing, and the true flavours emerge. Scoop the sorbets into bowls, and serve with fresh fruit, if liked.

 VARIATION: Apple and Calvados sorbet

A rich and indulgent scoopful.

1 Omit the raspberries, pears, Poire Williams liqueur, peaches, and all but ½ lemon. Make the sugar syrup as directed in the main recipe, using 200g (7oz) sugar and 250ml (9fl oz) water.

2 Peel 1.4kg (3lb) tart apples (they should be quite tart for the maximum flavour), quarter, and core. Rub each quarter with the lemon half so they do not discolour. Continue as directed for the pear sorbet, adding 2 tbsp Calvados in place of the Poire Williams liqueur.

3 Scoop small balls of the sorbet into shallow glasses or bowls. If you like, add a spoonful of Calvados to each glass, and serve with a crisp biscuit. This amount of sorbet will serve 6 people.

Chocolate mousse with hazelnuts

TOASTED HAZELNUTS CREATE TEXTURE, and whisky gives zip, to this version of classic dark chocolate mousse. If you prefer, you can substitute almost any spirit or liqueur for the whisky used in the recipe. Rum, brandy, or Grand Marnier taste particularly good with chocolate, but you may well have your own favourite.

SERVES SERVES 6	**PREP** 20-25 MINS	**COOK** 20-25 MINS

Ingredients

FOR THE MOUSSE

60g (2oz) hazelnuts
250g (9oz) plain chocolate
15g (½oz) unsalted butter

3 eggs
2 tbsp whisky
50g (1¾oz) caster sugar

FOR THE WHISKY CREAM (optional)

125ml (4fl oz) double cream
1 tbsp caster sugar
2 tsp whisky

TOAST AND GRIND THE NUTS

1 **Preheat the oven** to 180°C (350°F/Gas 4). Spread the nuts on a baking sheet and bake until lightly browned. Rub in a rough towel while hot, to remove the skins. Grind in a food processor, reserving a few for decoration.

MAKE THE CHOCOLATE MIX

2 **Cut the chocolate** into large chunks. Chop with a sharp knife, or in a food processor, then place in a heavy-based saucepan and add 65ml (2¼fl oz) water. Heat gently, stirring, for 3-5 minutes, until melted and the consistency of double cream.

3 **Remove the chocolate** from the heat, and stir in the butter, cut in pieces. Separate the eggs. Whisk the yolks into the chocolate one by one. Whisk over low heat for 4 minutes to ensure the yolks are cooked. Remove from the heat, and whisk in the hazelnuts and whisky. Allow to cool to tepid.

FINISH THE MOUSSE

4 **Meanwhile,** put 60ml (2fl oz) water in a small pan, add the sugar and heat until dissolved. Boil without stirring until syrup is 120°C (248°F) on a sugar thermometer, or a teaspoon of it forms a firm, pliable ball.

5 **Whisk the egg whites** until stiff. Gradually whisk in the syrup, until the meringue is cool and stiff. Stir a quarter into the tepid chocolate, then fold in the remaining meringue. Spoon into glasses, and chill for 1 hour.

MAKE THE WHISKY CREAM, IF LIKED

6 **Whisk the cream** until soft peaks form, adding the sugar and whisky. Top each mousse with the reserved hazelnuts and serve with the cream.

Poires belle Hélène

THIS DESSERT OF POACHED PEARS, vanilla ice cream, and hot chocolate sauce dates from the 19th century when it was created for the star of Offenbach's opera, *La Belle Hélène*. If you're pressed for time, just use good-quality bought vanilla ice cream.

SERVES
SERVES 6

PREP
30–35 MINS
PLUS FREEZING

COOK
25–35 MINS

Ingredients

FOR THE VANILLA ICE CREAM

600ml (1 pint) milk

1 vanilla pod

150g (5½oz) caster sugar

8 egg yolks

2 tbsp cornflour

250ml (9fl oz) double cream

FOR THE PEARS

2 lemons

6 firm pears

1 vanilla pod (optional)

150g (5½oz) caster sugar

FOR THE CHOCOLATE SAUCE

250g (9oz) good-quality plain chocolate, chopped

1 tbsp brandy

MAKE THE ICE CREAM

1 **Put the milk** in a saucepan. Split and add the vanilla pod. Bring to a boil. Remove from the heat, and let stand for 10–15 minutes. Set aside a quarter of it. Add the sugar to the remaining milk and stir until dissolved.

2 **Put the egg yolks** and cornflour in a bowl. Whisk in the milk. Stir over medium heat, until thick enough to coat the back of a spoon. Stir in the reserved milk. Cool, pour into an ice-cream maker, and churn. Whip the cream to soft peaks. Add to the custard, and freeze for at least 4 hours.

PREPARE THE PEARS

3 **Cut 1 lemon** in half. Peel the pears, leaving the stalks intact. Rub the lemon all over the pears. From the bottom, scoop out the pips and core.

POACH THE PEARS

4 **Make the poaching syrup:** combine 750ml (1¼ pints) water, the vanilla pod, if using, the zest and juice from the remaining lemon, and sugar in a shallow pan, wide enough to take all 6 pears in a single layer. Heat until the sugar has dissolved, then bring to a boil. Remove from the heat. Carefully add the pears. If necessary, add more water to cover them.

5 **Cut a disk** of baking parchment the same diameter as the pan. Dampen it, then place it on top of the pears to keep them submerged. Simmer gently for 25–35 minutes, depending on ripeness, until tender when pierced with a small knife. Let cool in the liquid.

MAKE THE CHOCOLATE SAUCE

6 **Mix the chocolate** with 125ml (4fl oz) water in a pan. Melt over gentle heat. Add the brandy. Serve warm with the pears and ice cream.

Grand Marnier soufflé

RISEN TO LOFTY HEIGHTS, this impressive dessert will make a truly grand ending to a special meal. As with all soufflés, it should be baked only until soft in the centre, forming a fluffy accompaniment to the crisper outside. It's served here with a refreshing compote of orange segments, to help cut through the richness. If you would prefer to make a non-alcoholic version of the soufflé, simply substitute the same amount of fresh orange juice for the Grand Marnier in the recipe.

SERVES	PREP	COOK
SERVES 6	30–35 MINS	20–25 MINS

Ingredients

FOR THE SOUFFLÉ

375ml (13fl oz) milk

4 egg yolks

150g (5½oz) caster sugar

45g (1½oz) plain flour

75ml (2½fl oz) Grand Marnier

6 egg whites

icing sugar, to serve

FOR THE ORANGE COMPOTE

4 oranges

2 tbsp orange marmalade

1 tbsp Grand Marnier

MAKE THE ORANGE COMPOTE

1 **With a vegetable peeler,** pare the zest from 1 of the oranges, taking care not to include any bitter white pith. Cut the zest lengthways into the finest possible julienne strips. Bring a small saucepan of water to a boil. Add the julienne strips and simmer for 2 minutes. Drain, rinse under cold running water, and drain again. Transfer the strips to a bowl. Finely grate the zest from a second orange into a dish, and reserve for the soufflé.

2 **Segment all 4 oranges,** working over a bowl to catch the juice: with a sharp knife, cut away both ends of the oranges, set upright on a chopping board and, working from top to bottom, cut away the zest and pith, following the curve of the fruit. Slide the knife down both sides of a segment, cutting it from the membrane, and let it slide into the bowl.

3 **Add the orange segments** to the julienned zest. Put the juice from segmenting the oranges, and the marmalade, into a small saucepan. Heat gently until the marmalade has melted, stirring occasionally. Remove from the heat and let cool slightly. Add the marmalade mixture to the orange segments and julienne, and stir to mix. Stir in the Grand Marnier. Cover, and chill until ready to serve.

MAKE THE PASTRY CREAM BASE

4 **Scald the milk,** bringing it just to a boil in a saucepan. Meanwhile, whisk the egg yolks with three-quarters of the caster sugar for 2–3 minutes, until thick and light coloured. Make sure the mixture is really airy and foamy.

5 **Stir in the flour** with a whisk. Then gradually stir in the hot milk until the mixture is smooth. Make sure you are constantly beating the mixture, as otherwise there is a risk that the egg yolks may cook and scramble.

6 **Pour the pastry cream** back into the saucepan. Bring to a boil over medium heat, whisking constantly until it thickens. If lumps form, remove from the heat at once and whisk until the cream is smooth again. Reduce the heat to low and cook the pastry cream, still whisking constantly, for about 2 minutes, until it softens slightly. Remove the pan from the heat. Add the reserved grated orange zest and the Grand Marnier, and stir in with the whisk.

FINISH AND BAKE THE SOUFFLÉ

7 Preheat the oven to 200°C (400°F/Gas 6). Generously butter a 1.5 litre (2¾ pint) soufflé dish. If necessary, reheat the pastry cream until hot to the touch. Whisk the egg whites in a metal bowl until stiff. Sprinkle in the remaining caster sugar, and continue whisking for about 20 seconds to form a glossy light meringue. Fold the meringue and pastry cream base together.

8 Gently pour into the prepared dish. Tap on the table to eliminate any pockets of air. The mixture should fill the dish to within 1cm (½in) of the rim. Smooth the top, then run your thumb around the edge to make a shallow indentation. Place in the oven and bake for 20-25 minutes, until puffed and golden brown. When gently shaken, the soufflé should be firm outside but still slightly soft and wobbly in the centre.

9 Sift icing sugar over the top of the soufflé, working quickly, as the soufflé will lose volume within minutes as it cools. Serve at once, with the fresh orange compote in a separate bowl.

 VARIATION: Hot coffee soufflé

This classic soufflé takes an innovative turn with a flavouring of cardamom, echoing true Turkish coffee.

1 Omit the orange compote. Put 375ml (13fl oz) single cream in a saucepan; add 2 lightly crushed cardamom pods. Bring just to a boil. Remove from the heat and infuse for 10-15 minutes. When cool, strain and chill, covered.

2 For the pastry cream base, add 30g (1oz) coarsely ground coffee to the milk before heating, then cover, and set aside to infuse for 10-15 minutes. Whisk the egg yolks, sugar, and flour, then strain in the milk. Continue as directed, omitting the zest and replacing the Grand Marnier with Tia Maria.

3 Butter the soufflé dish. Finish and bake the soufflé as directed. Quickly sift cocoa powder over the top of the soufflé and serve immediately, with the spiced cardamom cream as an accompanying sauce.

Tri-chocolate terrine

MAURICE FERRE WAS THE PASTRY CHEF at Maxim's in Paris. This is his frozen terrine, with three sumptuously flavoured chocolate layers, served with a pool of delicate mint custard. Use very good-quality chocolate and be extra careful to buy only white chocolate containing cocoa butter, not other tropical fats, whenever you are intending to use it for cooking.

SERVES MAKES 12-16 SLICES	**PREP** 35-40 MINS PLUS FREEZING	**COOK** 20-25 MINS

Ingredients

FOR THE CHOCOLATE TERRINE

vegetable oil

125g (4½oz) good-quality plain chocolate

9 tbsp double cream

6 eggs

135g (5oz) unsalted butter

6 egg whites

3 tbsp caster sugar

150g (5½oz) good-quality white chocolate

150g (5½oz) good-quality milk chocolate

FOR THE MINT CUSTARD

1 bunch of mint

500ml (16fl oz) milk

60g (2oz) caster sugar

6 egg yolks

1½ tbsp cornflour

MAKE THE DARK CHOCOLATE LAYER

1 **Lightly brush the sides** and bottom of a 30x7.5x7.5cm (12x3x3in) terrine with oil. Using the base of the terrine as a guide, draw and then cut out 2 strips of baking parchment. Use one to line the bottom of the terrine, and reserve the other.

2 **Cut the plain chocolate** into large chunks. Chop them with a sharp knife, or in a food processor using the pulse button. Melt the chocolate in a large bowl placed in a saucepan half-filled with hot water (make sure the base of the bowl does not touch the water).

3 **In a small saucepan,** bring 3 tbsp of the double cream to boiling point, then whisk it into the chocolate. Separate 2 of the eggs. Whisk the egg yolks into the chocolate one at a time, stirring well between each addition.

4 **Cut 45g (1½oz)** of the butter into small pieces, and add a few pieces at a time, whisking so the butter melts smoothly into the warm mixture. In another large bowl, whisk 2 of the egg whites until stiff.

5 **Sprinkle in 1 tbsp** of the sugar and whisk until glossy, to make a light meringue. Fold the meringue into the chocolate mixture as lightly as possible. This can be done in 2 batches, if you like.

ASSEMBLE AND FREEZE THE TERRINE

6 **Pour the dark chocolate** mixture into the terrine. Spread the chocolate mixture in the terrine, pushing it into the corners and smoothing the top evenly. Freeze for 30-40 minutes while preparing the remaining layers.

7 **Follow the instructions** for making the dark chocolate layer, using white instead of plain chocolate. Pour the white chocolate mixture into the terrine. Spread over the dark chocolate layer and freeze for 30-40 minutes.

8 **Make the milk chocolate layer,** using the same process as for the preceding layers, and pour it into the terrine on top of the white chocolate layer. Smooth the top layer, using a rubber spatula.

9 **Lightly press** the reserved piece of baking parchment on top of the milk chocolate layer, making sure it comes into contact with the whole surface of the terrine. Chill the terrine in the freezer for at least 6 hours, until firm.

MAKE THE MINT CUSTARD

10 **Rinse the mint** and trim the ends of the stalks. Reserve 12–16 sprigs for decoration, and lightly crush the remainder with a rolling pin. Put the milk in a heavy-based saucepan, and bring just to a boil. Add the crushed mint, cover and leave to infuse in a warm place for 10–15 minutes.

11 **Strain the milk** into a measuring jug or bowl, and discard the crushed mint. Stir in the sugar until dissolved. Whisk the egg yolks with the cornflour in a bowl. Add the infused milk, reserving about 125ml (4fl oz). Whisk until just smooth, then return the custard to the saucepan.

12 **Cook over moderate heat**, stirring constantly with a wooden spoon, until the custard just comes to a boil and thickens enough to coat the back of the spoon. (Your finger will leave a clear trail across the spoon.) Stir in the reserved milk. Strain the custard into a chilled bowl, and leave to cool.

TURN OUT THE TERRINE

13 **Fill a roasting tin** with hot water. Dip the base of the terrine into the hot water for 10–15 seconds, then lift it out. Peel off the baking parchment. Set a dish on top of the terrine, and turn them over together. Remove the terrine. Serve sliced, with the custard and mint sprigs.

Mango sorbet

THE KEY TO GOOD SORBET is smoothness: the ice crystals that form naturally during freezing must be removed by stirring the mixture constantly, usually by machine. As freezing any food will diminish its flavour, be sure the fruit is at its peak of ripeness. The citrus juices in this recipe heighten the taste and balance the mango's sweetness.

SERVES	**PREP**	**COOK**
SERVES 6	25-30 MINS PLUS FREEZING	2-3 MINS

Ingredients

100g (3½oz) caster sugar, plus more if needed

3 mangoes, total weight 1.25-1.4kg (2¾-3lb)

juice of 1 lemon

juice of 1 orange

lime zest, to serve

MAKE THE SUGAR SYRUP

1 **Combine the sugar** and 125ml (4fl oz) water in a small saucepan. Heat until the sugar has dissolved, then boil the syrup for 2-3 minutes, until it is clear. Set aside to cool.

MAKE THE SORBET MIXTURE

2 **Peel the mangoes.** Cut each mango lengthwise into 2 pieces, slightly off-centre just to miss the stone (p482). Cut the flesh away from the other side of the stone.

3 **Cut the remaining thin layer** of flesh from the stone. Cut all the mango into cubes. Purée it in batches, in a food processor. It must be very smooth for the best results.

4 **With all the pureé** in the food processor, and the blade turning, pour in the cooled syrup and citrus juices. Taste, adding more sugar if it is tart, remembering the flavours will be dulled by freezing.

FREEZE THE SORBET

5 **Pour the sorbet mixture** into an ice-cream maker and freeze until firm, following the manufacturer's directions. Meanwhile, chill a bowl in the freezer.

6 **Transfer the sorbet** to the chilled bowl. Cover it and freeze for at least 4 hours to allow the flavour to mellow. If necessary, transfer the sorbet to the refrigerator to soften slightly. Scoop the sorbet into chilled glasses and serve immediately, sprinkled with lime zest.

Chocolate soufflés

THE CHOCOLATE IS SO THICK AND RICH that it holds the whisked egg white without any flour. Be careful not to overcook the soufflés; the best part is the soft, creamy centre that forms a sauce for the crisp outside layer. Serve them with crisp biscuits for extra texture, if you like. Never open the oven while cooking a soufflé, or it may deflate.

SERVES	PREP	COOK
SERVES 4	20–25 MINS	15–18 MINS

Ingredients

125g (4½oz) plain chocolate

125ml (4fl oz) double cream

3 eggs, plus 2 egg whites

2 tbsp brandy

½ tsp vanilla essence

3 tbsp caster sugar

2–3 tbsp icing sugar, to dust (optional)

START THE CHOCOLATE MIXTURE

1 **Brush 4 ramekins** with melted butter. Preheat the oven to 220°C (425°F/Gas 7). Cut the chocolate into large chunks. Chop them with a knife, or in a food processor using the pulse button. Put the chocolate in the saucepan, add the cream, stir to mix, then heat gently, stirring, for about 5 minutes, until melted and smooth.

2 **If the mixture is a little thin**, simmer it until it is the consistency of double cream. Remove the pan from the heat. Separate the eggs. Whisk the yolks into the hot mixture 1 at a time, stirring well after each addition.

FINISH THE CHOCOLATE MIXTURE

3 **Whisk the chocolate mixture** over low heat for about 4 minutes to ensure that the egg yolks are cooked. Remove from the heat and whisk in the brandy and vanilla essence. If necessary, reheat the chocolate mixture until it's hot to the touch.

4 **Whisk the 5 egg whites** until stiff. Sprinkle in the sugar and continue whisking for about 20 seconds until glossy, to form a light meringue. Fold the meringue and chocolate mixtures together.

BAKE THE CHOCOLATE SOUFFLÉS

5 **Gently pour the soufflé mixture** into the ramekins. Carefully place the soufflés in the heated oven and bake for about 10 minutes, until puffed.

6 **Remove the soufflés** from the oven and sift over icing sugar, if you like. Take to the table immediately, before the soufflés have a chance to deflate, and serve with crisp biscuits, if you like.

Amaretti and chocolate bombe

AN ICE CREAM BOMBE, with its attractive shape and contrasting centre, is always festive. Here, amaretto ice cream surrounds an amaretti biscuit and chocolate filling. This is a great dessert for entertaining, as it can be prepared ahead and frozen, with only the chocolate sauce to be made before serving. There's no need to invest in a special bombe mould, as a Pyrex dish will serve the purpose just as well.

SERVES	PREP	COOK
SERVES 8-10	40-60 MINS PLUS FREEZING	20-25 MINS

Ingredients

FOR THE AMARETTO ICE CREAM

600ml (1 pint) milk

125g (4½oz) caster sugar

8 egg yolks

2 tbsp cornflour

3 tbsp amaretto liqueur

250ml (8fl oz) double cream

FOR THE CHOCOLATE FILLING

100g (3½oz) caster sugar

4 egg yolks

125ml (4fl oz) double cream

125g (4½oz) plain chocolate

100g (3½oz) small amaretti biscuits, plus more to serve

FOR THE CHOCOLATE SAUCE

250g (9oz) plain chocolate

MAKE THE AMARETTO ICE CREAM

1 Put the milk in a saucepan and bring just to a boil. Remove from the heat, set aside one-quarter of the milk, and add the sugar to the remainder. Stir until the sugar has completely dissolved into the milk. Put the egg yolks and cornflour in another bowl. Whisk together very well, until smooth and evenly combined, with no lumps.

2 Pour the sweetened milk into the egg yolk mixture, whisking just until evenly blended. Be sure to whisk constantly, so the hot milk does not begin to cook the egg. Return the mixture to the pan and cook over medium heat, stirring constantly, until the custard comes just to a boil and thickens enough to coat the back of a spoon; your finger, when drawn across the spoon, should leave a clear trail. Remove the saucepan from the heat.

3 Stir the reserved milk into the custard. Strain into a bowl and let cool completely. If a skin has formed, whisk to dissolve it, then whisk in the amaretto liqueur. Pour the cooled custard into an ice-cream maker and churn it until slushy, following the manufacturer's directions.

CONSTRUCT THE BOMBE SHELL

4 Chill a 2 litre (3½ pint) bombe mould or Pyrex bowl in the freezer. Pour the cream into a chilled bowl, and whip until it forms soft peaks and just holds a shape. Add the whipped cream to the half-frozen custard, and continue freezing until the ice cream is firm but still soft enough to spread. The cream will soften the texture.

5 Line the bombe mould or bowl with cling film, then spoon the ice cream into the mould, and spread it over the bottom and side in an even layer about 4cm (1½in) thick.

6 Make a neat, even hollow in the centre of the ice cream. Make sure it is well centred, so each serving of bombe will have an even amount of amaretto ice cream and chocolate filling. Cover and freeze for 30-60 minutes, until firm. Meanwhile, make the bombe filling.

MAKE THE CHOCOLATE FILLING AND FREEZE THE BOMBE

7 Put the sugar and 125ml (4fl oz) water in a small saucepan, and heat until dissolved, stirring occasionally. Boil without stirring until the syrup reaches the soft-ball stage. To test, dip a teaspoon in the hot syrup. Let the syrup cool a few seconds, then take a little between finger and thumb; it should form a soft ball. If using a sugar thermometer, it should register 115°C (239°F).

8 While the syrup is boiling, lightly beat the egg yolks in a large bowl. Gradually pour the hot sugar syrup into the egg yolks, beating constantly with an electric mixer or hand whisk for about 5 minutes, until the mixture is cool, very thick, and pale. Pour the cream into a chilled bowl, and whip until it forms soft peaks and just holds a shape.

9 Add the whipped cream to the egg yolk mousse, and fold the mixtures together. Make sure the mousse is completely cool before adding the cream. Grate the chocolate. Put 7–8 amaretti biscuits in a plastic bag, and crumble them coarsely by pounding with a rolling pin. Reserve the remaining biscuits for decoration.

10 Add the grated chocolate and crumbled biscuits to the filling mixture, and fold in. Remove the ice-cream-lined mould from the freezer, and spoon in the bombe filling. Smooth the top with the palette knife. Cover with baking parchment and the lid, or a piece of foil, and freeze for at least 8 hours, until very firm.

MAKE THE CHOCOLATE SAUCE

11 Cut the chocolate into large chunks. Chop them in a food processor using the pulse button, or with a sharp knife. Combine the chocolate and 175ml (6fl oz) water in a small saucepan, and stir over gentle heat until the sauce is smooth, making sure that the chocolate does not catch on the bottom of the pan. Simmer until thickened slightly to the consistency of single cream; it should only take 2–3 minutes to reach this stage. Remove from the heat, and keep warm.

UNMOULD AND SERVE

12 Remove the lid or foil from the bombe, and dip the mould in a bowl of cool water for 30–60 seconds; this should help loosen the bombe from its mould. Lift the mould out and wipe it dry. Run the small knife around the inside edge of the mould. Peel off the baking parchment. Set a chilled serving plate on top of the bombe then, holding both firmly, invert. Wrap a damp cloth around the mould for a few moments, then lift it off. The bombe should fall out on to the plate. Keep the bombe chilled in the freezer until ready to serve.

13 Serve the bombe immediately with the warm chocolate sauce and reserved amaretti biscuits. Sprinkle with chocolate shavings as well, if you like. Cut the bombe into wedges at the table.

Chocolate and pear tartlets

THESE TARTLETS ARE SUPERBLY FLAVOURED.
The pastry can be made up to 2 days in advance,
tightly wrapped, and kept in the refrigerator, or it
can be frozen. The tartlets can be kept for 6-8
hours, but are best eaten the day they are baked.
Make sure your pears are fully ripe and juicy.

SERVES	PREP	COOK
MAKES 8	30-35 MINS PLUS CHILLING	25-30 MINS

Ingredients

FOR THE PASTRY

175g (6oz) plain flour

90g (3oz) unsalted butter

60g (2oz) caster sugar

½ tsp salt

½ tsp vanilla essence

3 egg yolks

FOR THE FILLING

150g (5½oz) plain chocolate

2 large, ripe pears

1-2 tbsp caster sugar, to sprinkle

FOR THE CUSTARD

1 egg

125ml (4½fl oz) single cream

1 tbsp kirsch (optional)

MAKE THE PASTRY

1 **Sift the flour** on to a work surface, tapping
the side of the sieve. Put the butter
between 2 sheets of baking parchment and
pound with a rolling pin to soften it slightly.
Make a well in the centre of the flour
with your hand. Put the sugar, salt,
and vanilla essence in the well.
Add the butter to the
ingredients in the well.
With your fingertips,
work the ingredients
in the well
together until
thoroughly mixed.

2 **Add the egg yolks** and work into
the ingredients in the well. Draw
in the flour with a palette knife. With
your fingers, work the flour into the
other ingredients until coarse
crumbs form. Press the dough
into a ball. Sprinkle the
work surface lightly
with flour, then
blend the dough
by pushing the
ball away from
you with the heel
of your hand.

3 **Gather up the dough** and continue to
blend for 1-2 minutes, until it is very
smooth and peels away from the work
surface in 1 piece. Shape the dough into
a ball again, wrap in cling film, and
chill for about 30 minutes, until
firm. Pastry doughs made with
sugar are particularly
delicate. Be sure to chill
the dough well before
rolling out.

LINE THE TARTLET TINS

4 **Brush the insides of 8 x 10cm (4in) tartlet tins** with melted butter. Group
4 of the tartlet tins together, with their edges nearly touching. Sprinkle
the work surface lightly with flour. Divide the ball of dough in half, and roll
1 piece out to 3mm (⅛in) thick. Roll the dough loosely round the rolling pin,
and drape it over the 4 tins to cover them completely.

5 **Tear off a small piece of dough** from the edge, form it into a ball, dip it in
flour, and use it to push the dough into the tins. Roll the rolling pin over
the tops of the tins to cut off excess dough (it can be rolled out again and
used to line the remaining tartlet tins). Repeat with the 4 remaining tins and
the second piece of dough.

FILL AND BAKE THE TARTLETS

6 **Preheat the oven** to 200°C (400°F/Gas 6). Heat a baking sheet on an
oven shelf near the bottom of the oven. Cut the chocolate into large
chunks. Finely chop them with a sharp knife, or in a food processor using the
pulse button. Sprinkle into each tartlet shell.

7 **To make the custard,** whisk the egg, cream, and kirsch, if using, together until thoroughly mixed. For an extra-smooth custard, rub the mixture through a sieve. Spoon 2–3 tbsp of the kirsch custard over the chocolate in each tartlet shell.

8 **Peel the pears,** cut them in half, and remove the cores. With a small knife, cut each pear half across into very thin slices. Arrange the slices on the custard so that they overlap. Press them down very lightly into the custard, so it will bake up around the fruit, then sprinkle each tartlet evenly with the sugar.

9 **Place the tartlet tins** on the heated baking sheet. Bake them for 10 minutes, then reduce the heat to 180°C (350°F/Gas 4) and continue baking until the pastry is golden and the custard has set. It should take 15–20 minutes longer.

10 **Leave the tartlets** to cool slightly. Once cool enough to handle, unmould them carefully, and place the tartlets on to individual plates to serve.

 VARIATION: Chocolate and apple tartlets

A touch of cinnamon adds spice to this version.

1 Prepare the pastry dough and carefully line the tartlet tins as directed in the main recipe. Peel and core 3 apples, total weight about 500g (1lb 2oz). Cut them into small chunks. Each time you prepare apples for cooking, do so at the last minute, to prevent discolouration.

2 Heat about 2 tbsp unsalted butter in a large saucepan. Tip in all the apple chunks and sprinkle them with 1–2 tbsp sugar and 2 tsp ground cinnamon. Sauté briskly for 3–5 minutes, until slightly softened and caramelized, stirring occasionally. Make sure you get some good colour on the apples, for a deeper flavour.

3 Sprinkle the chopped chocolate evenly into the tartlet shells and spoon the custard over the top. Spread the apples on the custard, pressing them down lightly. Bake as directed, on a hot baking sheet. (The hot baking sheet will conduct heat immediately to the base of the tarts and cook the pastry.)

Almond milk curd with exotic fruit

MADE FROM SWEETENED MILK AND ALMOND ESSENCE, this dish resembles a Chinese bean curd dessert in appearance, but its delicate texture and flavour make it far friendlier to Western palates, and a perfect light finish to a meal. A heavy-based saucepan is essential, so the milk does not scorch.

SERVES	PREP	COOK
SERVES 8	40 MINS PLUS CHILLING	15 MINS

Ingredients

FOR THE ALMOND MILK CURD

600ml (1 pint) milk

60g (2oz) caster sugar

2 tbsp powdered gelatine

1 tsp almond essence

FOR THE SUGAR SYRUP

60g (2oz) caster sugar

FOR THE FRUIT

4 ripe, crinkly passion fruits

500g (1lb 2oz) lychees

1 small mango

PREPARE THE ALMOND MILK CURD

1 **Combine the milk and sugar** in a heavy-based saucepan, and slowly bring to a boil over medium heat, stirring occasionally until the sugar has completely dissolved. Sprinkle the gelatine over 2 tbsp water in a small saucepan and let stand for about 5 minutes, until spongy. Warm the pan over very low heat, shaking it occasionally, but not stirring, until the gelatine is melted.

2 **Off the heat, stir the gelatine** into the milk mixture, then stir in the almond essence. Pour the almond-flavoured mixture into a 20cm (8in) square cake tin. Let cool to room temperature, then cover tightly, and refrigerate for 3–4 hours, until the almond milk curd has set.

MAKE THE SYRUP

3 **For the syrup,** combine 125ml (4fl oz) and the sugar in a small saucepan and heat, stirring occasionally, until the sugar has dissolved. Bring to a boil and simmer the syrup for 1 minute. Remove from the heat and let cool.

PREPARE THE FRUIT

4 **Cut the passion fruits** in half and scrape the seeds and pulp into a bowl. Peel the lychees, slit them on one side and remove the stone. Add to the bowl. Peel and slice the mango (p482), and add to the bowl. Pour the sugar syrup over the fruits. Toss gently, cover and chill for at least 1 hour.

FINISH THE DISH

5 **With a small, sharp knife,** cut the almond curd in the tin into 4cm (1½in) diamonds or squares, as you prefer. Run a knife around the inside edge of the tin. Spoon the chilled fruit in to serving bowls. Loosen the almond curd and carefully lift out the pieces with a palette knife. Arrange them beside the fruit salad.

Chocolate mocha sorbet

THIS HAS A SURPRISINGLY CREAMY TEXTURE.
You can leave the sorbet plain, or decorate it with a sprinkling of chocolate-covered coffee beans. Though the sorbet can be stored in the freezer for up to 1 week, the texture may coarsen, so do not make it too far in advance of serving. As there are so few ingredients in this recipe, the chocolate has to be of the best quality you can afford.

SERVES	PREP	COOK
SERVES 6–8	25–30 MINS PLUS FREEZING	15–20 MINS

Ingredients

90g (3oz) good-quality plain chocolate

2–3 tbsp instant coffee powder

300g (10oz) caster sugar

MAKE THE SORBET BASE

1 **Cut the chocolate** into large chunks, then finely chop in a food processor using the pulse button. Put 375ml (13fl oz) water in a medium heavy-based saucepan, add the chocolate and the coffee, and heat, stirring, until melted and smooth.

2 **Add the sugar** and 375ml (13fl oz) more water and heat, stirring, until the sugar has dissolved. Bring to a boil and simmer for 8–10 minutes, stirring; the mixture should thicken very slightly. Remove from the heat, and allow to cool completely.

FREEZE THE SORBET

3 **Pour the sorbet mixture** into an ice-cream maker and churn until slushy, following the manufacturer's instructions. Meanwhile, chill a large bowl in the freezer to store your sorbet.

4 **Transfer the sorbet** to the chilled bowl, cover it, and freeze for at least 4 hours to allow the flavour to mellow. Freezing time varies greatly depending on the machine you use.

5 **If the sorbet has been frozen** for more than 12 hours, it will need to soften for 15–20 minutes in the refrigerator before serving. This will allow the flavours to come out, and the texture to mellow and smoothen.

6 **Serve in chilled glasses,** in scoops or quenelles. To make a quenelle, dip 2 metal spoons in cold water. Use one spoon to scoop out a generous spoonful of sorbet, then use the other to shape the mixture into a neat oval, turning each spoon against the other.

Hazelnut torte with strawberries

AN IMPRESSIVE THREE-LAYER CASTLE of hazelnut pastry, sandwiched with strawberries and whipped cream. A tart raspberry coulis makes the ideal accompaniment. The pastry can be baked up to 2 days ahead and kept in an airtight container, or can be frozen. The torte should be assembled no more than 4 hours ahead of serving, and should be kept refrigerated.

SERVES	PREP	COOK
SERVES 8	40-45 MINS PLUS CHILLING	15-18 MINS

Ingredients

FOR THE HAZELNUT PASTRY

250g (9oz) hazelnuts

135g (5oz) caster sugar

125g (4½oz) plain flour, plus more to dust

½ tsp salt

150g (5½oz) unsalted butter

1 egg yolk

FOR THE RASPBERRY COULIS

500g (1lb 2oz) raspberries

2-3 tbsp icing sugar, or to taste

1-2 tbsp kirsch (optional)

FOR THE CHANTILLY CREAM

375ml (13fl oz) double cream

1½ tbsp caster sugar

1 tsp vanilla essence

FOR THE STRAWBERRIES AND DECORATION

750g (1lb 10oz) strawberries

mint sprigs, to decorate

MAKE THE HAZELNUT PASTRY DOUGH

1 **Preheat the oven** to 180°C (350°F/Gas 4). Spread the hazelnuts on a baking sheet. Toast for 8-10 minutes, until lightly browned, stirring occasionally so the nuts colour evenly. While still hot, rub the nuts in a clean tea towel to remove the skins, then leave to cool.

2 **In a food processor,** grind the hazelnuts with the caster sugar to a fine powder. Put the ground nut mixture on a work surface and sift the flour and salt on top. Make a well in the centre of the ingredients and add the butter and egg yolk.

3 **Using your fingertips,** work the butter and egg yolk together in the well, drawing in a little of the ground nut and flour mixtures, until soft and thoroughly mixed. Press the dough into a ball. Sprinkle the work surface lightly with flour; place the dough on the work surface and knead the dough gently until very smooth.

4 **Shape the dough** into a ball, wrap it tightly, and chill for at least 30 minutes, until firm. Pastry doughs made with nuts are particularly delicate, so be sure to give the dough enough time to chill.

SHAPE AND BAKE THE PASTRY LAYERS

5 **Preheat the oven** to 200°C (400°F/Gas 6). Divide the chilled dough into 3 equal pieces. With the heel of your hand or the back of a spoon, press each piece into a 20cm (8in) round on a baking sheet. (Use a pan lid or an upturned cake tin as a guide.) You can cook 2 pastry layers on 1 sheet, but space the rounds about 2.5cm (1in) apart, as they expand during baking.

6 **Bake the pastry** in the heated oven for 15-18 minutes, until the edges begin to brown. While they are still warm, trim them with a very sharp knife into neat rounds, using a pan lid or cake tin as a guide. Do not let the pastry cool before trimming, or the rounds may break.

7 **Using a sharp knife,** cut 1 of the layers across into 8 equal wedges. Let all the layers and wedges cool to tepid on the baking sheets. Carefully transfer to wire racks to cool completely.

MAKE THE COULIS, CREAM AND DECORATION

8 **To make the raspberry** coulis, pick over the berries, then purée them in a food processor. Stir in icing sugar to taste, and the kirsch, if you like. Work the purée through a sieve to remove the pips.

9 **Hull the strawberries,** washing them only if they are dirty. Set aside 8 small berries for decoration. Halve the remaining strawberries, or quarter them if they are large.

10 **To make the Chantilly** cream, pour the cream into a chilled bowl and whip until soft peaks form. Add the sugar and vanilla and whip until the cream forms stiff peaks and the whisk leaves clear marks in the cream.

ASSEMBLE THE TORTE

11 **Set a round of pastry** on a serving plate. Cover with about one-quarter of the Chantilly cream, and arrange half the strawberries on top. Work neatly, as the final look of this torte is important.

12 **Cover the strawberries** with more Chantilly cream, spreading lightly with a rubber spatula. Try not to dislodge any of the strawberries on the bottom layer, and do not press, or they will begin to leak their juices.

13 **Set the second round of pastry** on top, and spread with half the remaining Chantilly cream. Slide the pastry round directly from the wire rack to avoid breaking it. Remember it is quite fragile.

14 **Cover with the remaining strawberries,** and spread the rest of the Chantilly cream on top. Top with the wedges of pastry, setting them at an angle. Put the whole strawberries on top. To serve, cut into wedges, and drizzle each individual serving with the coulis.

Chocolate chestnut roll

A WINTER FAVOURITE, especially over the Christmas period, this is filled with a rich chestnut purée mixed with whipped cream. Be as elaborate or simple as you like with the decoration. Once assembled, it will keep for up to 2 days in the refrigerator; add decorations just before serving.

SERVES	**PREP**	**COOK**
SERVES 8-10	50-55 MINS	5-7 MINS

Ingredients

FOR THE CHOCOLATE SPONGE ROLL

35g (1¼oz) cocoa powder

1 tbsp plain flour

salt

5 eggs

150g (5½oz) caster sugar

FOR THE FILLING

175ml (6fl oz) double cream

125g (4½oz) chestnut purée

2 tbsp dark rum

30g (1oz) plain chocolate

caster sugar, to taste (optional)

TO FINISH AND DECORATE (optional)

25g (1oz) caster sugar

2 tbsp dark rum

8-10 marrons glacés

90g (3oz) plain chocolate

MAKE THE CHOCOLATE CAKE MIXTURE

1 Preheat the oven to 220°C (425°F/Gas 7). Brush a 30x37cm (12x15in) baking sheet with melted butter, line with baking parchment, and butter the parchment. Sift the cocoa powder, flour, and a pinch of salt into a bowl.

2 Separate the eggs. Beat the egg yolks with two-thirds of the sugar until light, and the mixture leaves a ribbon trail when the whisk is lifted; it will take 3-5 minutes.

3 Whisk the egg whites until stiff. Your bowl and whisk must be completely free of any trace of water, grease, or egg yolk, or the egg whites will not whisk to full volume. Sprinkle in the remaining sugar and whisk for about 20 seconds, until glossy, to make a light meringue.

4 Sift about one-third of the cocoa mixture over the egg-yolk mixture. Add one-third of the meringue. Fold the mixtures together as lightly as possible. Add the remaining cocoa mixture and meringue in the same way in 2 batches.

BAKE AND ROLL THE SPONGE

5 Pour the chocolate mixture, all at once, on to the prepared baking sheet. Use a spatula to scrape out the bowl. Spread the mixture evenly on the baking sheet almost to the edges. Put in the heated oven, near the bottom, and bake for 5-7 minutes. The cake is done when it is risen, and just firm to the touch. Do not overbake or it will be difficult to roll.

6 Dampen a tea towel. Remove the cake from the oven, and immediately cover with the tea towel. Take a second baking sheet and set it on top of the cake. Quickly invert the cake so the original baking sheet is on top. Place the cake on the work surface, and carefully remove the uppermost baking sheet.

7 Holding the baking parchment by its edges, carefully peel it off the cake. Be very careful about this, as the cake is quite fragile and you don't want to tear the sponge. It will be easier if you work as quickly as you can. Starting at the short end nearest you, tightly roll up the cake and towel lengthways. Be very careful and work quickly, as it will be easier when hot. Set aside to cool

MAKE THE FILLING

8 Pour the cream into a chilled bowl, and whip until it forms soft peaks and just holds a shape. Put the chestnut purée in another bowl, and add the rum. Cut the chocolate into large chunks, then chop in a food processor.

9 Melt the chocolate in a bowl placed in a saucepan half-filled with hot water (make sure the base of the bowl does not touch the water). Add the melted chocolate to the chestnut purée, and stir well with a wooden spoon to remove any lumps.

FINISH AND DECORATE THE CAKE

10 Leave the chocolate to cool slightly; if it is too hot when added to the cream, the cream may become oily. Stir about 2 tbsp of the whipped cream into the chocolate mixture to soften it, then fold the remaining chocolate and chestnut mixture into the whipped cream. If necessary, add sugar to taste.

11 Make a rum syrup: in a small saucepan, over low heat, heat the sugar in 60ml (2fl oz) of water until it dissolves. Simmer the syrup for 1 minute. Allow to cool, then stir in the rum.

12 Unroll the cake, then roll it up again without the towel. Place the cake on a sheet of baking parchment and unroll it. The smooth top will be on the outside. Brush the cake with the cooled rum syrup. Using a palette knife, spread the chestnut filling evenly over. Using the paper underneath, carefully roll up the filled cake as tightly as possible.

13 Bring the paper up over the cake; fold it in tightly. Insert the edge of the baking sheet against the fold, and push away from you to tighten the roll. With a serrated knife, trim each end of the cake neatly. Transfer the cake to a serving plate.

14 Chop the marrons glacés. Arrange them on top of the roll, sprinkling them randomly or placing in a neat line, as you prefer. Melt the chocolate in the same way as in step 9, cool it slightly, then place into a small piping bag. Pipe the melted chocolate back and forth over the roll, being as freeform as you like.

Sticky rice with mangoes

A WELL-KNOWN THAI DESSERT, this is simply a coconut-flavoured rice pudding, with slices of ripe, juicy mango. You should use pudding rice – or even glutinous or sticky rice if you can get hold of it from Asian stores – all are starchy varieties ideal for making creamy desserts. If you like, reserve about 4 tbsp of the thick "cream" that rises to the top of the coconut milk in its tin, then spoon it over the rice to finish the dish.

SERVES	PREP	COOK
SERVES 6	40 MINS PLUS SOAKING	40–50 MINS

Ingredients

400g (14oz) pudding rice

100g (3½oz) caster sugar

½ tsp salt

300ml (10fl oz) canned coconut milk

3 large, ripe mangoes, total weight about 1kg (2¼lb)

lime zest, to serve

PREPARE THE RICE

1 **Put the rice** in a bowl, and pour cold water over. Cover, and let soak for at least 3 hours or overnight. Pour the rice into a sieve to drain off the liquid. Rinse thoroughly with cold water, to remove excess starch.

COOK THE RICE

2 **Pour enough water** into a wok so it almost touches the bottom of a bamboo steamer basket, when the basket is placed inside the wok. Cover the wok with its lid, and bring the water to a boil. Line the bottom and side of the basket with a double thickness of damp muslin.

3 **Tip the rice** into the basket, and spread it evenly. Uncover the wok, and place the basket of rice over the boiling water. Cover the basket with its lid. Reduce the heat to medium. Steam the rice for 40–50 minutes, until tender. The longer it has been soaked, the faster it will cook.

MAKE THE STICKY RICE

4 **In a saucepan, combine the sugar** and salt with the coconut milk. Bring slowly to a boil, stirring, until the sugar dissolves. Remove from the heat. Stir in the rice. Cool to room temperature.

PREPARE THE MANGOES AND FINISH THE DISH

5 **Peel the mangoes** with a small knife. Carefully cut the mangoes lengthways on both sides of the stone, so the knife just misses the stone. Slice them into 5mm (¼in) slices.

6 **Mound the rice** in a serving dish, and arrange the mango around it. Decorate with curls of lime zest, and a few more mango slices, and serve at room temperature.

Chocolate charlotte

A DREAM COME TRUE for chocolate lovers. Half fudge, half cake, this is a wonderful recipe to have in your repertoire. Decorate with chocolate curls (p486), or crystallized violets, if you like. The charlotte can be prepared as much as 1 week ahead and kept, covered, in the refrigerator; it can also be frozen very successfully.

SERVES	PREP	COOK
SERVES 6-8	40-45 MINS PLUS CHILLING	70 MINS

Ingredients

FOR THE CHARLOTTE

250g (9oz) good-quality plain chocolate

175ml (6fl oz) strong black coffee

250g (9oz) unsalted butter

200g (7oz) caster sugar

4 eggs

cocoa powder, to dust

FOR THE CHANTILLY CREAM (optional)

375ml (13fl oz) double cream

1½ tbsp caster sugar

¾ tsp vanilla extract

MAKE THE CHOCOLATE CHARLOTTE

1 Brush a 1 litre (1¾ pint) mould or Pyrex bowl with melted butter. Line the bottom with baking parchment, and butter the paper. Chill. Preheat the oven to 180°C (350°F/Gas 4). Pulse-chop the chocolate in a food processor. Put into a heavy saucepan, add the coffee, and heat, stirring, until smooth. Add the butter and sugar, and melt. Bring almost to a boil, stirring well.

2 Remove the saucepan from the heat and whisk in the eggs, one by one, whisking well after each addition. The eggs will cook and thicken in the heat of the mixture. Strain into the prepared mould or bowl.

BAKE THE CHARLOTTE

3 Bake for 70 minutes, until a thick crust forms on top, watching so it does not scorch. Allow to cool, cover, and refrigerate for at least 24 hours. The charlotte will shrink slightly. Under the crust, it will still be quite soft.

TURN OUT THE CHARLOTTE

4 Run a thin-bladed knife between the charlotte and the mould, to loosen it. Dip the mould briefly in warm water, then dry the mould.

5 Hold a serving plate over the mould, invert, then lift off the mould. Peel off the paper. Chill the charlotte, tightly wrapped, until ready to serve.

MAKE THE CHANTILLY CREAM (OPTIONAL)

6 Pour the cream into a chilled bowl and whip to soft peaks. Add the sugar and vanilla, and whip to stiff peaks. Serve the charlotte, dusted with cocoa, with the Chantilly cream, or with crème fraîche.

Baked Alaska

THIS STRIKING DESSERT IS A FESTIVE WAY to conclude a celebration. The surprise of still-frozen ice cream hidden beneath hot, lightly browned meringue never fails to excite. The secret is the cake base, which insulates the ice cream from the oven's heat. Assemble the Alaska carefully, and seal it properly, to achieve the best results after baking. Make this recipe when you have a large crowd to feed, as it needs to be eaten straight from the oven.

SERVES	PREP	COOK
SERVES 8-10	45-50 MINS	30-40 MINS

Ingredients

FOR THE CAKE

60g (2oz) unsalted butter

125g (4½oz) plain flour

pinch of salt

4 eggs135g (5oz) caster sugar

1 tsp vanilla extract

FOR THE FILLING

300g (10oz) strawberries

2-3 tbsp icing sugar, to taste

1.5 litres (2¾ pints) vanilla ice cream

FOR THE MERINGUE

450g (1lb) caster sugar, plus more to sprinkle

9 egg whites

MAKE THE CAKE

1 **Preheat the oven** to 180°C (350°F/Gas 4). Butter a 20cm (8in) square cake tin, and line the bottom with baking parchment. Butter the paper. Sprinkle in 2 tbsp flour and turn the tin to coat the bottom and sides; turn the tin upside down, and tap to remove excess flour.

2 **Sift the flour** with the salt. Melt the butter in a small saucepan, and let cool. Put the eggs in a large bowl, and beat with an electric mixer for a few seconds, to mix. Add the sugar, and beat at high speed for about 5 minutes, or until the mixture is pale and thick, and leaves a ribbon trail when the beaters are lifted. Beat in the vanilla extract.

3 **Sift about a third of the flour** over the egg mixture, and fold them together as lightly as possible. Add another third of the flour and fold it in. Fold in the remaining flour and the cooled, melted butter. Pour into the tin, then tap on the work surface to level the mixture and knock out any air bubbles.

4 **Bake in the heated** oven for 30-40 minutes, until the cake has risen, and is just firm to the touch. Run a knife around the edge of the cake, and unmould it on to a wire rack. Peel off the paper, and allow to cool.

MAKE THE STRAWBERRY COULIS

5 **Hull the strawberries** with a small knife, washing them only if dirty. Purée in a food processor or blender, then pour into a bowl. Stir in icing sugar, to taste. You should have about 375ml (13fl oz) strawberry coulis.

PREPARE THE MERINGUE

6 **Heat the sugar** with 250ml (9fl oz) water in a saucepan, until dissolved. Boil without stirring until the syrup reaches the hard ball stage. To test, dip a teaspoon in the syrup. Take a little between finger and thumb; it should form a pliable ball. On a sugar thermometer, it should register 120°C (248°F).

7 **Meanwhile,** put the egg whites in a bowl and beat with an electric mixer for 3-5 minutes, until stiff peaks form. Gradually pour in the hot syrup, beating constantly for about 5 minutes, until the meringue is cool and stiff.

PREPARE THE BASE

8 **Lightly butter** a large heatproof serving plate. Remove the ice cream from the freezer, and leave until soft enough to scoop. Trim a 2.5cm (1in) strip from each side of the cake, leaving a 15cm (6in) square. Using a serrated knife, split the cake horizontally into 2 layers. Set the 2 squares of cake, cut side up and end to end, on the serving plate, to make a rectangle.

9 **Work the cake trimmings** in a food processor to form even crumbs. Add 250ml (9fl oz) of the strawberry coulis to the cake crumbs, and blend briefly to mix together.

ASSEMBLE AND BAKE THE DESSERT

10 **Spread the remaining coulis** over the cake. Scoop the ice cream into balls, and arrange them in a layer on the cake. Scoop and arrange a second layer of ice-cream balls. (Dip the scoop in warm water to prevent sticking).

11 **Quickly smooth the ice cream** layers with the palette knife, to even the surface and edges. Without delay, cover the top of the ice cream layer with the prepared strawberry cake crumbs.

12 **Using a large metal spoon,** spoon the meringue on top of the cake. Work quickly now, as the ice cream must stay as firm as possible at this point before baking.

13 **Spread the meringue** over the top and sides to cover completely, and seal it to the plate to insulate the ice cream. Keep in the freezer for up to 2 hours. Preheat the oven to 220°C (425°F/Gas 7). Take the dessert from the freezer, sprinkle with sugar, and let stand for 1 minute. Bake for just 3–5 minutes, until lightly browned. Serve at once.

INDEX

*Index entries in italics
refer to techniques*

A

aioli platter 126-7
almonds: almond and
raspberry tart 426-7
almond biscuits 511
almond meringue
gâteau 513
almond milk curd 528
apple and almond
galettes 510
chocolate almond torte
495
chocolate pie with
crunchy crust 432
Normandy pear tart
436-7
toasting 496
Amaretti and chocolate
bombe 524-5
Amelia Simmons' pumpkin
pie 462-3
apples: apple and almond
galettes 510
apple and Calvados
sorbet 515
apple cake 464
apple jalousie 452-3
blackberry and apple pie
418-19
chicken liver and apple
pâté 51
chocolate and apple
tartlets 527
rustic apple tart 433
tarte Tatin 442-3
Waldorf chicken salad
111
apricots: apricot and
hazelnut ice cream
500-501
duck with turnips and
apricots 196-7
filo apricot turnovers
440-41
pork loaf with apricots
355
artichokes *see* globe
artichokes
Asian noodle salad 112-13
asparagus: spring rice salad
102-3
aubergines: aubergine
cannelloni 144-5
aubergine feuilles 145
aubergine Parmigiana
166-7

Aunt Sally's meat loaf 354-5
avocados: avocado,
grapefruit, and Parma
ham 97
guacamole 72-3

B

bacon: Aunt Sally's meat
loaf 354-5
bacon-fried chicken 249
Brunswick stew 204-5
country omelette 55
quiche lorraine 372-3
red cabbage and bacon
salad 100
salade Lyonnaise 110
spicy tomato-bacon
pasta 346
tuna and bacon kebabs
265
walnut, bacon and herb
kugelhopf 408-9
baguette 390-91
baked Alaska 536-7
baking blind 372
barley: beef with mushrooms
and barley 212
Basque hot pepper omelette
54-5
Bavarian blueberry tart 429
Bavarian plum tart 428-9
beans *see* cannellini beans, red
kidney beans etc
beef: Aunt Sally's meat loaf
354-5
baked rigatoni with
meatballs 352-3
beef carpaccio 77
beef noodle soup (pho)
38-9
beef rendang 312
beef with barley and
mushrooms 212
boeuf à la Bourguignonne
220-21
chilli con carne 330
fillet of beef with
mushrooms 290-91
French beef and herb
potato pie 224-5
Hungarian beef goulash
187
Italian beef braised in
red wine 200
Korean grilled beef
314-15
minute steak Dijonnaise
269
minute steak marchand
du vin 268-9

peppery Tuscan beef
216-17
Provencal daube of beef
210-11
rib of beef pebronata 329
rib of beef with Yorkshire
pudding 328-9
Russian beef sauté 246
steak and wild
mushroom pie 368-9
steak au poivre 238-9
steak salad with red
onions 114
testing 328
beetroot:
borscht 63
bird's nest salad 99
biscuits, almond 511
blackberries: blackberry and
apple pie 418-19
blackberry fool 487
blinis 66-7
blueberries: Bavarian
blueberry tart 429
lemon-blueberry muffins
466-7
lemon shortcakes with
blueberries 479
boeuf à la Bourguignonne
220-21
bombe, Amaretti and
chocolate 524-5
borscht 63
bouillabaisse 318-19
bread: baguette 390-91
brioches 168, 410-11,
428
chocolate and orange
rolls 415
chocolate bread 414-15
cinnamon swirl bread
381
cornbread 386
crostini 32
dinner rolls 396-7
double wheat bread 383
focaccia 392-3
horseshoe rye bread 395
Irish soda bread 402
kneading dough 380
multi-grain breakfast
bread 388-9
onion and walnut crown
398-9
pesto garland bread
400-401
pitta bread 404-5
potato-chive monkey
bread 406-7
sage fettunta 217
seeded rye bread 394-5

sesame grisini 387
small brioches 410-11
sourdough bread 384-5
soured cream and dill
potato bread 407
split-top white bread
380-81
sun-dried tomato spiral
401
walnut, bacon and herb
kugelhopf 408-9
wholemeal bread 382-3
Yule bread 412-13
brioches *168*, 410-11, 428
broccoli: broccoli and
mushroom quiche
158-9
oriental stir-fried
chicken 242-3
Brunswick stew 204-5
Buddha's delight 134-5
bulghur wheat: double
wheat bread 383
stuffed veggies with
walnut sauce 156-7
tabbouleh with cacik 108
bulgogi (Korean grilled beef)
314-15
butterflied leg of lamb 288-9
butterflied loin of pork 289
buttermilk scones 403

C

cabbage: creamy coleslaw 86
pickled vegetables 314
poussins with plums and
cabbage 192-3
with chestnut and pork
350-51
see also red cabbage
Caesar salad 87
cakes: apple cake 464
chocolate almond torte
495
chocolate chestnut roll
532-3
chocolate decadence
506-7
chocolate orange pound
cake 470-71
chocolate orange truffle
cake 476-7
chocolate walnut torte
494-5
rich chocolate cake
468-9
walnut cake 465
see also muffins
calf's liver:
sautéed liver and onions
264

calzone, three-pepper 171
candied lemon 430
candied peel 470
cannellini beans:
Genoese minestrone 46-7
cannelloni, aubergine 144-5
caramel: caramelized mango
tartlets 488-9
oeufs à la neige 496-7
orange and cinnamon
crème brûlée 480
tarte Tatin 442-3
walnut cake with
caramel topping 465
carrots: celeriac rémoulade
with carrot salad 101
creamy coleslaw 86
cassoulet 198-9
caviar, blini with 67
celeriac: celeriac rémoulade
101
pumpkin stew 150-51
chard: three-cheese Swiss
chard crêpes 130-31
charlotte, chocolate 535
Cheddar and courgette
soufflés 60-61
cheese: aubergine
cannelloni 144-5
aubergine feuilles 145
aubergine Parmigiana
166-7
baked polenta with wild
mushrooms 152
baked ziti with mozzarella
and olives 353
beef carpaccio 77
Cheddar and courgette
soufflés 60-61
cheese gougères with
salmon 64-5
cheese wafers 88-9
Chicago deep-dish pizza
358-9
chicken and cheese
quesadillas 72-3
chicken en cocotte with
Parmesan 344-5
Greek salad 90
Mexican cheese-stuffed
peppers 138-9
onion and Roquefort
quiche 164-5
onion confit and
gorgonzola pizzas
338-9
Parma ham pizzas 74-5
pear, fennel, and walnut
salad 109
perfect pasta and cheese
153

pinwheel chicken Italienne 231

potato and blue cheese filo pie 162

quiche lorraine 372-3

roast pepper lasagne 143

three-cheese Swiss chard crêpes 130-31

three-pepper calzone 171

three-pepper pizza 170-71

see also goat's cheese; ricotta

cheesecakes: all-chocolate 473

ginger 493

marbled chocolate 472-3

ricotta 490-91

cherries: cherry clafoutis 458-9

cherry pie 435

cherry strudel 444-5

sweet-sour duck with cherries 284-5

chestnuts: cabbage with pork and chestnuts 350-51

chocolate chestnut roll 532-3

Chicago deep-dish pizza 358-9

chicken: bacon-fried chicken 249

Brunswick stew 204-5

chicken and beer stew 184-5

chicken and cheese quesadillas 72-3

chicken and prawn laksa 194-5

chicken dhansak 203

chicken en cocotte 344-5

chicken mousse 42-3

chicken paprika 182-3

chicken Pojarski 300

chicken pot pies 214-15

chicken with Cognac 185

chicken with kidney beans and garlic sausage 205

chicken with tarragon dressing and rice 263

Cobb salad 119

cold chicken and ham pie 340-41

cold chicken mousse 43

coq au vin 278-9

curried chicken 262-3

devilled drumsticks 241

grilled chicken thighs in yogurt 270

herbed roast chicken 331

Hindle Wakes chicken 298-9

hunter's chicken 175

Indonesian chicken satay 247

Indonesian fried rice 334-5

Japanese one-pot yosenabe 218-19

jointing 184

lacquered chicken salad 105

lemongrass chicken 76

Moroccan chicken tagine 275

oriental stir-fried chicken 242-3

paella 178-9

pinwheel chicken with goat's cheese 230-31

poaching 194

poule au pot 188-9

sauté of chicken with mussels 286

sauté of chicken with prawns 287

southern fried chicken 248-9

sweet and sour stir-fried chicken 243

Szechuan pepper chicken 282-3

Tex-Mex chicken 259

Thai skewered chicken 62

very garlicky sautéed chicken 324

Waldorf chicken salad 111

see also poussins

chicken liver and apple pâté 51

chicory: gratin of chicory and ham 48-9

herb and flower garden salad 82

Chilean pork and beans 207

chillies: Basque hot pepper omelette 54-5

chicken and cheese quesadillas 72-3

chilli con carne 330

cucumber-chilli salad 95

Malaysian fried rice noodles 256-7

roast monkfish with two sauces 294-5

spicy tomato-bacon pasta 346

Chinese roast duck 296-7

Chinese stir-fried vegetables 141

chips 238-9, 336-7

chocolate: all-chocolate cheesecake 473

Amaretti and chocolate bombe 524-5

chocolate almond torte 495

chocolate and apple tartlets 527

chocolate and orange rolls 415

chocolate and pear tartlets 526-7

chocolate bread 414-15

chocolate charlotte 535

chocolate chestnut roll 532-3

chocolate decadence 506-7

chocolate ganache 476-7

chocolate ice cream 486

chocolate mocha sorbet 529

chocolate mousse 516

chocolate orange pound cake 470-71

chocolate orange truffle cake 476-7

chocolate pie with crunchy crust 432

chocolate ricotta pie 491

chocolate soufflés 523

chocolate walnut torte 494-5

curls 468

hazelnut, chocolate, and orange tart 460-61

marbled chocolate cheesecake 472-3

melting 468

Mississippi mud pie 450-51

poires belle Hélène 517

profiteroles with ice cream 499

rich chocolate cake 468-9

tri-chocolate terrine 520-21

turkey mole 190-91

choux pastry 64-5, 499

chowder 44-5, 174

cinnamon swirl bread 381

clafoutis 458-9

clams: Portuguese pork and clams 206-7

preparation 218

Cobb salad 119

cod: cod and mussel chowder 44-5

grilled cod steaks 323

perfect fish and chips 336-7

coffee: chocolate charlotte 535

chocolate mocha sorbet 529

coffee ice cream 450-51

hot coffee soufflé 519

tiramisu 481

coleslaw, creamy 86

coq au vin 278-9

cornbread 386

country omelette 55

country terrine 366-7

courgettes: Cheddar and courgette soufflés 60-61

courgette tian 146-7

prawn, courgette, and saffron salad 92-3

couscous, vegetable 154-5

crab: Maryland crab cakes 71

preparation 180

seafood and tomato cioppino 180-81

crème brûlée, orange and cinnamon 480

crêpes 130-31, 508-9

flaming 509

crostini 32

crudités 33

crumbles, individual fish 349

cucumber: cucumber-chilli salad 95

Greek salad 90

nori-maki sushi 78-9

tabbouleh with cacik 108

Turkish lamb kebabs 234

curries: beef rendang 312

chicken dhansak 203

curried chicken 262-3

lamb dhansak 202-3

lamb korma 274

mixed vegetable curry 148-9

winter vegetable curry 149

D

devilled drumsticks 241

dinner rolls 396-7

dolmades 68-9

dough: brioche 168

kneading 74

dried fruit strudel 445

duck: Chinese roast duck 296-7

duck with turnips and apricots 196-7

jointing 196

quick duck confit 198

sweet-sour duck 284-5

trussing 284

dumplings 182-3, 187

E

eggnog tart 454-5

eggs: herbed aioli platter 126-7

summer frittata with ratatouille 133

see also omelettes

escarole: hunter's chicken 175

F

fennel: Greek-style vegetables 122

griddled swordfish with 251

lamb chops in paper with 332-3

pear, fennel, and walnut salad 109

fettuccine, making 374-5

fig and mulled wine tart 438-9

filo pastry:filo apricot turnovers 440-41

filo berry turnovers 441

pistachio and ricotta filo pie 456-7

potato and blue cheese filo pie 162

fish: bouillabaisse 318-19

fisherman's pie 348-9

panache of steamed fish 245

seafood and tomato cioppino 180-81

see also cod, salmon etc

flaming crêpes 509

Flemish vegetable tart 168-9

focaccia 392-3

fool, blackberry 487

French beef and herb potato pie 224-5

frittata with ratatouille 133

fritters: tempura 128-9

fruit: almond milk curd with exotic fruit 528

gratin of fresh berries 505

pavlova with tropical
    fruit 482-3
    see also apples,
        raspberries etc
fusilli: fusilli with pesto 132
    pasta and mussel salad
        116-17

G

Gado-gado 98-9
game terrine 367
gâteaux, meringue 512-13
Genoese minestrone 46-7
German potato salad 115
ginger cheesecake 493
globe artichokes: artichokes
    stuffed with olives 136-7
    preparation 52, 126-7,
        136
    roast pepper and
        artichoke salad 88-9
    Roman herb and garlic
        artichokes 52-3
    tomato tagliatelle with
        artichokes 124-5
gnocchi, spinach 356-7
goat's cheese: marinated
    goat's cheese salad 83
    pinwheel chicken with
        230-31
    three-cheese Swiss
        chard crêpes 130-31
gougères, cheese with
    salmon 64-5
goulash, Hungarian beef
    187
Grand Marnier soufflé
    518-19
granita, grapefruit 511
grapefruit: avocado,
    grapefruit, and Parma
        ham 97
    grapefruit granita 511
gratins 48-9, 142
Greek salad 90
Greek-style vegetables 122
grisini, sesame 387
guacamole 72-3
guinea fowl, very garlicky
    sautéed 325

H

hddock: fisherman's pie
    348-9
    individual fish crumbles
        349
    spicy fish with mixed
        peppers 267
halibut en papillote 236-7
ham: avocado, grapefruit,
    and Parma ham 97

cold chicken and ham
    pie 340-41
country terrine 366-7
German potato salad
    115
gratin of chicory and
    ham 48-9
ham with prunes in a
    wine sauce 364-5
Parma ham pizzas 74-5
pinwheel chicken
    Italienne 231
straw and hay pasta
    374-5
veal saltimbocca 253
haricot beans, roast lamb
    with 342-3
hazelnuts: apricot and
    hazelnut ice cream
        500-501
    chocolate mousse with
        hazelnuts 516
    hazelnut, chocolate, and
        orange tart 460-61
    hazelnut meringue
        gâteau 512-13
    hazelnut pastry 530
    hazelnut torte with
        strawberries 530-31
    sautéed trout with
        hazelnuts 271
    strawberry-raspberry
        hazelnut tart 502-3
herb and flower garden
    salad 82
Hindle Wakes chicken with
    prunes 298-9
horseshoe rye bread 395
Hungarian beef goulash 187
hunter's chicken 175

I

ice cream: Amaretti and
    chocolate bombe 524-5
    apricot and hazelnut ice
        cream 500-501
    baked Alaska 536-7
    chocolate ice cream 486
    coffee ice cream 450-51
    profiteroles with ice
        cream 499
    prune and Armagnac ice
        cream 501
    vanilla ice cream 517
Indonesian chicken satay
    247
Indonesian fried rice 334-5
Irish soda bread 402
Italian beef braised in red
    wine 200

J

Japanese one-pot yosenabe
    218-19
Jerusalem artichokes,
    tomato tagliatelle with
        walnuts and 125
jointing: duck 196
    chicken 184

K

kebabs: Indonesian chicken
satay 247
    Thai skewered chicken
        62
    tropical prawn kebabs
        58-9
    tuna and bacon kebabs
        265
    Turkish lamb kebabs 234
    vegetable couscous
        154-5
kneading dough 74, 380
Korean grilled beef 314-15
kugelhopf, walnut, bacon
    and herb 408-9

L

lamb: butterflied leg of lamb
    288-9
    cassoulet 198-9
    lamb and rice stuffed
        vine leaves 69
    lamb chops champvallon
        201
    lamb chops in paper
        cases with leeks 333
    lamb chops in paper
        with fennel 332-3
    lamb dhansak 202-3
    lamb korma 274
    lamb ratatouille 209
    lamb shanks in red wine
        222-3
    leg of lamb with
        potatoes 309
    leg of lamb with roasted
        garlic 308-9
    navarin of lamb 208-9
    Old Emily's shepherd's
        pie 225
    Provencal lamb stew
        with green olives 211
    rack of lamb coated with
        parsley 280-81
    roast lamb with haricot
        beans 342-3
    spiced lamb pies 360-61
    Turkish lamb kebabs 234
lasagne, roast pepper 143
leeks: lamb chops in paper
    cases with leeks 333

leeks vinaigrette 50
    poule au pot 188-9
    salmon fillets with
        mushroom and leek
        julienne 255
lemon: candied slices 430
    cold lemon soufflé 484-5
    lemon-blueberry muffins
        466-7
    lemon meringue pie
        420-21
    lemon poppy seed
        muffins 467
    lemon shortcakes with
        blueberries 479
    lemon tart 430-31
lemongrass chicken 76
lime and cardamom tart
    431
liver: chicken liver and
    apple pâté 51
    sautéed liver and onions
        264
Loire sea bass 277
lotus root: Buddha's delight
    134-5

M

macaroni: Genoese
    minestrone with red
        pesto 46-7
mackerel: fish plaits with
    warm vinaigrette 244-5
    pan-fried mackerel in
        rolled oats 258
Madeira sauce, chicken
    mousse with 42-3
Malaysian fried rice noodles
    256-7
mangetout: Buddha's delight
    134-5
mangoes: caramelized mango
    tartlets 488-9
    mango relish 202-3
    mango sorbet 522
    preparation 482
    sticky rice with mangoes
        534
Manhattan chowder 45
marble pound cake,
    chocolate orange 471
marbled chocolate
    cheesecake 472-3
Maryland crab cakes 71
marzipan: apple and almond
    galettes 510
mascarpone cheese:
    tiramisu 481
meat loaf, Aunt Sally's 354-5
meatballs, baked rigatoni
    with 352-3

melon and mint salad 96
melting chocolate 468
meringue: almond meringue
    gâteau 513
    baked Alaska 536-7
    hazelnut meringue
        gâteau 512-13
    lemon meringue pie
        420-21
    oeufs à la neige 496-7
    pavlova with tropical
        fruit, 482-3
Mexican barbecued pork
    with salsa 240
Mexican cheese-stuffed
    peppers 138-9
Milanese veal escalopes
    232-3
mincemeat tart with whisky
    butter 448
minestrone with red pesto
    46-7
mint: tabbouleh with cacik
    108
minute steak Dijonnaise
    269
minute steak marchand du
    vin 268-9
Mississippi mud pie 450-51
mocha sorbet 529
monkey bread, potato-chive
    406-7
monkfish: grilled monkfish
    escalopes with garlic and
        chilli sauces 295
    monkfish and red wine
        stew 177
    monkfish and white
        wine stew 176-7
    monkfish Americaine
        302-3
    roast monkfish with two
        sauces 294-5
    spicy, saucy fish 266-7
Moroccan chicken tagine
    275
mousses: chicken mousse
    with Madeira sauce
        42-3
    chocolate mousse with
        hazelnuts 516
    cold chicken mousse 43
    smoked trout mousse 37
    spinach mousse 307
    unmoulding 37
    wild mushroom mousse
        306-7
muffins: lemon-blueberry
    muffins 466-7
    lemon poppy seed
        muffins 467

multi-grain breakfast bread 388-9

mushrooms: artichokes stuffed with olives 136-7
baked polenta with wild mushrooms 152
beef with barley and mushrooms 212
boeuf à la Bourguignonne 220-21
broccoli and mushroom quiche 158-9
coq au vin 278-9
crêpes with wild mushrooms and herbs 131
fillet of beef with mushrooms 290-91
fillets of sole with mushrooms and tomatoes 377
Flemish vegetable tart 168-9
Greek-style vegetables 122
marinated prawn and mushroom salad 93
perfect pasta and cheese 53
poussins with mushroom sauce 320-21
roast pepper lasagne 143
Russian beef sauté 246
salmon fillets with mushroom and leek julienne 255
sole bonne femme 376-7
sole turbans with wild mushrooms 306-7
spicy tomato-bacon pasta 346
spinach and mushroom tian 147
steak and wild mushroom pie 368-9
stuffed mushrooms with herbs 36
vegetarian spring rolls 57
warm salad of wild mushrooms 91
mussels: cod and mussel chowder 44-5
grilled pepper-stuffed mussels 229
mussels with saffron-cream sauce 41
paella 178-9
pasta and mussel salad 116-17

preparation 41, 116
sauté of chicken with mussels 286

N
nasi goreng 334-5
navarin of lamb 208-9
Niçoise salad 84-5
noodles: Asian noodle salad 112-13
beef noodle soup (pho) 38-9
chicken and prawn laksa 194-5
Japanese one-pot yosenabe 218-19
Malaysian fried rice noodles 256-7
Thai noodle salad 113
nori-maki sushi 78-9
Normandy pear tart 436-7
nuts: three-nut pie 446-7
see also almonds, walnuts etc

O
oats: individual fish crumbles 349
pan-fried mackerel in rolled oats 258
oeufs à la neige 496-7
Old Emily's shepherd's pie 225
olives: artichokes stuffed with olives 136-7
baked ziti with mozzarella and olives 353
crostini 32
Provençal lamb stew with green olives 211
tapenade 33
omelettes: Basque hot pepper omelette 54-5
country omelette 55
onions: chopping 282
country omelette 55
Greek-style vegetables 122
lamb chops champvallon 201
minute steak Dijonnaise 269
onion and Roquefort quiche 164-5
onion and sage soufflé 61
onion and walnut crown 398-9
onion confit and gorgonzola pizzas 338-9

sautéed liver and onions 264
steak salad with red onions 114
oranges: candied peel 470
chocolate and orange rolls 415
chocolate orange pound cake 470-71
chocolate orange truffle cake 476-7
crêpes Suzette 508-9
hazelnut, chocolate, and orange tart 460-61
julienne 104
orange and cinnamon crème brûlée 480
orange compote 518
roast leg of pork with orange 301
warm salmon and orange salad 118
oriental halibut 236-7
oriental stir-fried chicken 242-3
osso bucco 313
oysters, preparation 218-19

P
paella 178-9
pancakes: blinis 66-7
crêpes 130-31, 508-9
yellow flower pork 304-5
Parma ham: avocado, grapefruit, and Parma ham 97
Parma ham pizzas 74-5
pinwheel chicken Italienne 231
veal saltimbocca 253
parsley: rack of lamb coated with parsley 280-81
tabbouleh with cacik 108
passion fruit sauce, chocolate decadence with 507
pasta: making 124, 374-5
pasta and mussel salad 116-17
pasta and scallop salad 117
spicy tomato-bacon pasta 346
straw and hay pasta 374-5
see also cannelloni, fusilli etc
pastries: apple jalousie 452-3
cheese gougères with salmon 64-5
cherry strudel 444-5

dried fruit strudel 445
profiteroles with ice cream 499
see also pies, quiches tarts
pastry: baking blind 159, 372
choux pastry 499
hazelnut pastry 502, 530
pasta frolla 460
pâte brisée 372
pâte sucrée 430-31, 433, 488
polenta pastry 438
puff pastry 452-3
quick puff pastry 368
shortcrust pastry 448, 462-3
sweet pastry 436, 490
walnut pastry 424-5
pâté, chicken liver and apple 51
pavlova with tropical fruit 482-3
peaches: baked peaches with Amaretti 498
creamy rice pudding with peaches 492
peach pie 434-5
peach sorbet 514-15
stoning and peeling 498
peanuts: Gado-gado 98-9
Indonesian chicken satay 247
peanut sauce 58-9
pears: chocolate and pear tartlets 526-7
flaky pear tartlets 449
Normandy pear tart 436-7
pear, fennel, and walnut salad 109
pear pie with walnut pastry 424-5
pear sorbet 514
pear tarte Tatin 443
poires belle Hélène 517
venison stew with pears 223
peas: rice salad with smoked trout and peas 102
straw and hay pasta 374-5
peel, candied 470
penne: perfect pasta and cheese 153
peppercorns: steak au poivre 238-9
peppers: Basque hot pepper omelette 54-5

grilled pepper-stuffed mussels 229
Hungarian beef goulash 187
Mexican cheese-stuffed peppers 138-9
red peppers stuffed with sweetcorn 139
rib of beef pebronata 329
roast pepper and artichoke salad 88-9
roast pepper lasagne 143
sautéed peppers 232-3
spicy fish with mixed peppers 267
three-pepper pizza with cheese 170-71
tortilla bean salad 106-7
peppery Tuscan beef 216-17
pesto: crisp salmon with coriander pesto 235
fusilli with pesto 132
pesto garland bread 400-401
tomato pesto 46-7
pho (beef noodle soup) 38-9
pickles: mixed pickled vegetables 123
pickled vegetables 314
pies: Amelia Simmons' pumpkin pie 462-3
blackberry and apple pie 418-19
cherry pie 435
chicken pot pies 214-15
cold chicken and ham pie 340-41
filo apricot turnovers 440-41
filo berry turnovers 441
fisherman's pie 348-9
French beef and herb potato pie 224-5
lemon meringue pie 420-21
Mississippi mud pie 450-51
Old Emily's shepherd's pie 225
peach pie 434-5
pear pie with walnut pastry 424-5
pistachio and ricotta filo pie 456-7
potato and blue cheese filo pie 162
rhubarb and strawberry pie 422-3
spiced lamb pies 360-61
steak and wild mushroom pie 368-9

three-nut pie 446-7
  see also pastries,
    quiches, tarts
pilaf 302-3
pineapple: sweet and sour
    stir-fried chicken 243
pinwheel chicken 230-31
pistachio and ricotta filo pie
    456-7
pistou 47
pitta bread 404-5
pizza: Chicago deep-dish
    pizza 358-9
  onion confit and
    gorgonzola pizzas
    338-9
  Parma ham pizzas 74-5
  three-pepper pizza with
    cheese 170-71
plaice: turbans of plaice
    with spinach mousse 307
plums: Bavarian plum tart
    428-9
  plum clafoutis 459
  poussins with plums and
    cabbage 192-3
poires belle Hélène 517
polenta: baked polenta with
    wild mushrooms 152
  polenta pastry 438
  polenta with vegetable
    stew 160-61
poppy seed muffins 467
pork: butterflied loin of
    pork 289
  cabbage with chestnut
    and pork 350-51
  Chilean pork and beans
    207
  cold chicken and ham
    pie 340-41
  country terrine 366-7
  Mexican barbecued pork
    with salsa 240
  pork and ginger sukiyaki
    252
  pork chops with mustard
    sauce 347
  pork loaf with apricots
    355
  pork loin with garlic and
    rosemary 316-17
  pork mole 191
  pork quesadillas 73
  Portuguese pork and
    clams 206-7
  roast leg of pork with
    orange 301
  Szechuan sweet and sour
    spare ribs 40
  Thai noodle salad 113

Vietnamese spring rolls
    56-7
yellow flower pork 304-5
Portuguese pork and
    clams 206-7
pot roasts: boeuf à la
    Bourguignonne
    220-21
  Italian beef braised in
    red wine 200
potatoes: chips 238-9, 336-7
  country omelette 55
  fisherman's pie 348-9
  French beef and herb
    potato pie 224-5
  German potato salad 115
  gratin dauphinois 142
  lamb chops champvallon
    201
  leg of lamb with
    potatoes 309
  mashed potatoes 264
  Old Emily's shepherd's
    pie 225
  potato and blue cheese
    filo pie 162
  potato-chive monkey
    bread 406-7
  potato salad 241
  scallops with lemon-herb
    potatoes 370-71
  soured cream and dill
    potato bread 407
  spinach gnocchi in
    tomato cream 356-7
  tuna Niçoise salad 84-5
poule au pot 188-9
poussins: poussins in vine
    leaves 292-3
  trussing 192
  with mushroom sauce
    320-21
  with plums and cabbage
    192-3
prawns: Asian noodle salad
    112-13
  chicken and prawn laksa
    194-5
  Indonesian fried rice 334-5
  Malaysian fried rice
    noodles 256-7
  marinated prawn and
    mushroom salad 93
  paella 178-9
  prawn, courgette, and
    saffron salad 92-3
  prawn risotto 363
  sauté of chicken with
    prawns 287
  tropical prawn kebabs
    58-9

Vietnamese spring rolls
    56-7
profiteroles with ice cream
    499
Provencal daube of beef
    210-11
Provencal lamb stew with
    green olives 211
prunes: ham with prunes in
    a wine sauce 364-5
  Hindle Wakes chicken
    with prunes 298-9
  prune and Armagnac ice
    cream 501
puff pastry 368, 452-3
pumpkin: Amelia Simmons'
    pumpkin pie 462-3
  pumpkin stew 150-51

Q

quesadillas 72-3
quiches: broccoli and
    mushroom 158-9
  onion and Roquefort
    164-5
  quiche lorraine 372-3
  see also tarts

R

rabbit Provençal 186
raspberries: almond and
    raspberry tart 426-7
  filo berry turnovers 441
  raspberry coulis 506-7,
    530
  raspberry sorbet 514
  raspberry soufflés 504
  strawberry-raspberry
    hazelnut tart 502-3
ratatouille: lamb ratatouille
    209
  summer frittata with 133
red cabbage: bird's nest
    salad 99
  red cabbage and bacon
    salad 100
red kidney beans: chicken
    with garlic sausage
    and 205
  Chilean pork and beans
    207
  Genoese minestrone
    with red pesto 46-7
  red bean, sweetcorn, and
    onion salad 107
  tortilla bean salad 106-7
red snapper: fish plaits with
    warm vinaigrette 244-5
relishes: mango relish
    202-3

sweetcorn relish 70-71
rhubarb and strawberry pie
    422-3
rice: chicken with tarragon
    dressing and rice 263
  courgette tian 146-7
  creamy rice pudding
    with peaches 492
  curried chicken with
    saffron rice 262-3
  Indonesian fried rice
    334-5
  mixed vegetable curry,
    148-9
  nori-maki sushi 78-9
  paella 178-9
  pilaf 302-3
  prawn risotto 363
  rice salad with smoked
    trout and peas 102
  spring rice salad 102-3
  sticky rice with mangoes
    534
  stir-fried Thai vegetables
    140-41
  stuffed vine leaves 68-9
  vegetable trio with
    carrot-rice stuffing
    157
ricotta: chocolate ricotta pie
    491
  pistachio and ricotta filo
    pie 456-7
  ricotta cheesecake
    490-91
  roast pepper lasagne 143
rigatoni with meatballs 352-3
risotto, prawn 363
rolls: chocolate and orange
    rolls 415
  dinner rolls 396-7
Roman herb and garlic
    artichokes 52-3
rum: eggnogg tart 454-5
Russian beef sauté 246
rye bread 394-5

S

salads: Asian noodle salad
    112-13
  avocado, grapefruit, and
    Parma ham 97
  bird's nest salad 99
  Caesar salad 87
  celeriac rémoulade with
    carrot salad 101
  Cobb salad 119
  creamy coleslaw 86
  cucumber-chilli salad 95
  festive wild rice salad
    104

Gado-gado 98-9
German potato salad 115
Greek salad 90
herb and flower garden
    salad 82
lacquered chicken salad
    105
lemongrass chicken 76
marinated goat's cheese
    salad 83
marinated prawn and
    mushroom salad 93
melon and mint salad 96
pasta and mussel salad
    116-17
pasta and scallop salad
    117
pear, fennel, and walnut
    salad 109
potato salad 241
prawn, courgette, and
    saffron salad 92-3
red bean, sweetcorn, and
    onion salad 107
red cabbage and bacon
    salad 100
rice salad with smoked
    trout and peas 102
roast pepper and
    artichoke salad 88-9
salade Lyonnaise 110
spiced seafood salad 94
spring rice salad 102-3
steak salad with red
    onions 114
tabbouleh with cacik 108
Tex-Mex chicken 259
Thai noodle salad 113
tortilla bean salad 106-7
tuna Niçoise salad 84-5
Waldorf chicken salad
    111
warm salad of wild
    mushrooms 91
warm salmon and orange
    salad 118
salmon: cheese gougères
    with salmon 64-5
  crisp salmon with
    coriander pesto 235
  five-spice fillet of
    salmon 254-5
  herbed salmon cakes
    70-71
  poached salmon,
    watercress sauce
    310-11
  salmon fillets with
    mushroom and leek
    julienne 255

saltimbocca of salmon 260-61

warm salmon and orange salad 118

see also smoked salmon

satay, Indonesian chicken 247

sausages: cassoulet 198-9

Chicago deep-dish pizza 358-9

scallops: pasta and scallop salad 117

poached scallops in cider sauce 371

scallop and sweetcorn chowder 174

scallops with lemon-herb potatoes 370-71

scones: buttermilk scones 403

chicken pot pies with herb crust 214-15

sea bass: clear soup with sea bass 34-5

Loire sea bass 277

roast sea bass with herb butter 276-7

seafood: seafood and tomato cioppino 180-81

seafood paella 179

spiced seafood salad 94

see also mussels, prawns etc

seeded rye bread 394-5

sesame grisini 387

shepherd's pie, Old Emily's 225

shortcakes: lemon shortcakes with blueberries 479

strawberry shortcakes 478-9

shortcrust pastry 448, 462-3

smoked salmon: blini with smoked salmon 66-7

saltimbocca of salmon 260-61

spring rice salad 102-3

smoked trout: rice salad with peas and 102

smoked trout mousse 37

soda bread, Irish 402

sole: fillets of sole with mushrooms and tomatoes 377

fish plaits with warm vinaigrette 244-5

sole bonne femme 376-7

sole fillets in wine vinegar 228

sole turbans with wild mushrooms 306-7

sorbets: apple and Calvados sorbet 515

chocolate mocha sorbet 529

mango sorbet 522

peach sorbet 514-15

pear sorbet 514

raspberry sorbet 514

soufflés: Cheddar and courgette soufflés 60-61

chocolate soufflés 523

cold lemon soufflé 484-5

Grand Marnier soufflé 518-19

hot coffee soufflé 519

onion and sage soufflé 61

raspberry soufflés 504

soups: beef noodle soup (pho) 38-9

borscht 63

bouillabaisse 318-19

clear soup with sea bass 34-5

cod and mussel chowder 44-5

Genoese minestrone with red pesto 46-7

Manhattan chowder 45

scallop and sweetcorn chowder 174

soupe au pistou 47

sourdough bread 384-5

soured cream and dill potato bread 407

southern fried chicken 248-9

spaghetti primavera 163

spare ribs, Szechuan sweet and sour 40

spinach: Aunt Sally's meat loaf 354-5

cheese gougères with salmon 64-5

salade Lyonnaise 110

spinach and mushroom tian 147

spinach gnocchi in tomato cream 356-7

spinach-stuffed veal 362

turbans of plaice with spinach mousse 307

spinach pasta: pasta and scallop salad 117

straw and hay pasta 374-5

split-top white bread 380-81

spring rice salad 102-3

spring rolls 56-7

spring veal blanquette 213

squid: seafood paella 179

steak and wild mushroom pie 368-9

steak au poivre 238-9

steak salad with red onions 114

stews: beef with barley and mushrooms 212

Brunswick stew 204-5

cassoulet 198-9

chicken and beer stew 184-5

chicken paprika 182-3

chicken with Cognac 185

Chilean pork and beans 207

coq au vin 278-9

duck with turnips and apricots 196-7

Hungarian beef goulash 187

lamb shanks in red wine 222-3

monkfish and red wine stew 177

monkfish and white wine stew 176-7

navarin of lamb 208-9

osso bucco 313

peppery Tuscan beef 216-17

polenta with vegetable stew 160-61

pork mole 191

Portuguese pork and clams 206-7

Provencal daube of beef 210-11

Provencal lamb stew with green olives 211

pumpkin stew 150-51

spicy, saucy fish 266-7

spring veal blanquette 213

turkey mole 190-91

venison stew with pears 223

see also curries

sticky rice with mangoes 534

stoning peaches 498

straw and hay pasta 374-5

strawberries: baked Alaska 536-7

filo berry turnovers 441

hazelnut torte with strawberries 530-31

rhubarb and strawberry pie 422-3

strawberry-raspberry hazelnut tart 502-3

strawberry shortcakes 478-9

strudels: cherry strudel 444-5

dried fruit strudel 445

sugar syrup 514

sultanas: Yule bread 412-13

summer frittata with ratatouille 133

sun-dried tomato spiral 401

sushi, nori-maki 78-9

sweet and sour stir-fried chicken 243

sweet-sour duck with cherries 284-5

sweetcorn: Buddha's delight 134-5

cornbread 386

red peppers stuffed with sweetcorn 139

scallop and sweetcorn chowder 174

tortilla bean salad 106-7

Swiss chard: three-cheese Swiss chard crêpes 130-31

swordfish with fennel and sun-dried tomatoes 251

Szechuan pepper chicken 282-3

Szechuan sweet and sour spare ribs 40

T

tabbouleh with cacik 108

tagine, Moroccan chicken 275

tagliatelle: tomato tagliatelle with artichokes 124-5

tomato tagliatelle with Jerusalem artichokes and walnuts 125

tapenade 33

tarts: almond and raspberry tart 426-7

apple and almond galettes 510

Bavarian blueberry tart 429

Bavarian plum tart 428-9

caramelized mango tartlets 488-9

chocolate and apple tartlets 527

chocolate and pear tartlets 526-7

chocolate pie with crunchy crust 432

chocolate ricotta pie 491

eggnogg tart 454-5

fig and mulled wine tart 438-9

flaky pear tartlets 449

Flemish vegetable tart 168-9

hazelnut, chocolate, and orange tart 460-61

lemon tart 430-31

lime and cardamom tart 431

mincemeat tart with whisky butter 448

Normandy pear tart 436-7

pear tarte Tatin 443

rustic apple tart 433

strawberry-raspberry hazelnut tart 502-3

tarte Tatin 442-3

see also quiches

tempura 128-9

terrines: country terrine 366-7

game terrine 367

tri-chocolate terrine 520-21

Tex-Mex chicken 259

Thai noodle salad 113

Thai skewered chicken 62

Thai-style halibut en papillote 237

thermometers, meat 328

tians 146-7, 167

tiramisu 481

toasting almonds 496

tofu: Buddha's delight 134-5

Gado-gado 98-9

Japanese one-pot yosenabe 218-19

tomatoes: aubergine cannelloni 144-5

aubergine Parmigiana 166-7

baked rigatoni with meatballs 352-3

barbecue sauce 240

borscht 63

cassoulet 198-9

Chicago deep-dish pizza 358-9

chicken and cheese quesadillas 72-3

chicken Pojarski 300

chilli con carne 330

cold chicken mousse with tomato and mint coulis 43

crostini 32

fillets of sole with mushrooms and tomatoes 377
Greek salad 90
Greek-style vegetables 122
Manhattan chowder 45
osso bucco 313
Parma ham pizzas 74-5
peppery Tuscan beef 216-17
Provencal daube of beef 210-11
rabbit Provençal 186
rib of beef pebronata 329
rice salad with smoked trout and peas 102
roast pepper lasagne 143
sauté of chicken with prawns 287
seafood and tomato cioppino 180-81
skinning 84
spicy, saucy fish 266-7
spicy tomato-bacon pasta 346
spinach gnocchi in tomato cream 356-7
sun-dried tomato spiral 401
tabbouleh with cacik 108
tomato pesto 46-7
tomato tagliatelle with artichokes 124-5
tomato tagliatelle with Jerusalem artichokes and walnuts 125
tortes 494-5, 530-31
tortillas: chicken and cheese quesadillas 72-3
    tortilla bean salad 106-7
tropical prawn kebabs 58-9
trout: sautéed trout with hazelnuts 271
    trout with orange-mustard glaze 322-3
    see also smoked trout
trussing: duck 284
    poussins 192
tuna: griddled tuna steaks with salsa 250-51
    nori-maki sushi 78-9
    tuna and bacon kebabs 265
    tuna Niçoise salad 84-5
turkey: festive wild rice salad 104
    turkey mole 190-91
Turkish lamb kebabs 234
turnips, duck with apricots and 196-7
turnovers 440-41

V
vanilla ice cream 517
veal: Milanese veal escalopes 232-3
    osso bucco 313
    spinach-stuffed veal 362
    spring veal blanquette 213
    veal saltimbocca 253
vegetables: Chinese stir-fried vegetables 141

crudités 33
five-spice fillet of salmon 254-5
Flemish vegetable tart 168-9
Genoese minestrone with red pesto 46-7
herbed aioli platter 126-7
julienne 254
lamb ratatouille 209
mixed pickled vegetables 123
mixed vegetable curry, 148-9
navarin of lamb 208-9
polenta with vegetable stew 160-61
ratatouille 133
spaghetti primavera 163
stir-fried Thai vegetables 140-41
stuffed veggies with walnut sauce 156-7
tempura 128-9
tian of Mediterranean vegetables 167
vegetable couscous 154-5
vegetable trio with carrot-rice stuffing 157
winter vegetable curry 149
    see also aubergines, peppers etc
vegetarian spring rolls 57
venison stew with pears 223
Vietnamese spring rolls 56-7

vine leaves: poussins in 292-3
    stuffed vine leaves 68-9

W
Waldorf chicken salad 111
walnuts: chocolate walnut torte 494-5
    onion and walnut crown 398-9
    pear, fennel, and walnut salad 109
    pear pie with walnut pastry 424-5
    stuffed mushrooms with herbs 36
    stuffed veggies with walnut sauce 156-7
    Waldorf chicken salad 111
    walnut, bacon and herb kugelhopf 408-9
    walnut cake with caramel topping 465
watercress: poached salmon, watercress sauce 310-11
white beans: cassoulet 198-9
wholemeal bread 382-3
wild rice salad, festive 104
wine: coq au vin 278-9
    creamy rice pudding with peaches 492
    fig and mulled wine tart 438-9
    ham with prunes in a wine sauce 364-5

Italian beef braised in red wine 200
lamb shanks in red wine 222-3
winter vegetable curry 149

Y
yeast: brioche dough 168
yellow flower pork 304-5
Yorkshire puddings 328-9
Yule bread 412-13

Z
ziti with mozzarella and olives 353

Dorling Kindersley would like to thank:

Photographers: David Murray, William Reavell, William Shaw, Jon Whitaker

Prop stylist: Liz Belton

Food stylists: Lizzie Harris, Sal Henley, Cara Hobday, Jane Lawrie, Phil Mundy, Jenny White

Art directors: Nicky Collings, Anne Fisher, Luis Peral

Indexer: Hilary Bird

Proofreader: Irene Lyford

Useful information

Refrigerator and freezer storage guidelines

FOOD	REFRIGERATOR	FREEZER
Raw poultry, fish, and meat (small pieces)	2–3 days	3 months
Raw minced beef and poultry	1–3 days	3 months
Cooked whole roasts or whole poultry	2–3 days	9 months
Cooked poultry pieces	2–3 days	3 months
Soups and stocks	2–3 days	3–6 months
Stews	2–3 days	3 months
Pies	2–3 days	3–6 months

Oven temperature equivalents

CELSIUS	FAHRENHEIT	GAS	DESCRIPTION
110°C	225°F	¼	Cool
130°C	250°F	½	Cool
140°C	275°F	1	Very low
150°C	300°F	2	Very low
160°C	325°F	3	Low
180°C	350°F	4	Moderate
190°C	375°F	5	Moderately hot
200°C	400°F	6	Hot
220°C	425°F	7	Hot
230°C	450°F	8	Very hot
240°C	475°F	9	Very hot